The Work of the Holy Spirit

The Work of the Holy Spirit

By
Abraham Kuyper, D.D., LL.D.

Translated from the Dutch with Explanatory Notes

by

Rev. Henri De Vries

AMG
PUBLISHERS
Chattanooga, TN 37422

The Work of the Holy Spirit
by Abraham Kuyper

Originally published by
Funk & Wagnalls Company, 1900
in New York.

ISBN 0-89957-180-8

Printed in the United States of America
06 05 04 03 02 01 –R– 6 5 4 3 2 1

Contents

Foreword

The Work of the Holy Spirit is a systematic and explicitly detailed approach to the study of the Holy Spirit by one of the Reformed faith's most brilliant thinkers. Working from the basis of Scripture, Dutch theologian Abraham Kuyper describes the manifestations of the Holy Spirit in the church and in our individual lives. He addresses various interpretations of the Person and Godhead of the Holy Spirit from a Reformed perspective, and clearly explicates all dimensions of the Spirit's work.

In creating this new edition of *The Work of the Holy Spirit,* which was originally published by Funk and Wagnalls Company in 1900, we at AMG Publshers have made a few minor changes to the original text to help make its content more clear for modern readers. We have updated spelling in accordance with how our language has changed over the years, and in some cases unusual forms of punctuation have been simplified. Readers should also be aware that points of current history mentioned by Kuyper are from the Netherlands of the late nineteenth century.

Our desire is that this volume may help readers deepen their knowledge and love of Scripture and feel the Holy Spirit's presence more closely in their lives.

Preface of the Author

Special treatises on the Person of the Holy Spirit are comparatively few, and systematic treatment of His Work is still more uncommon. In dogmatics, it is true, this subject is introduced, developed, and explained, but special treatment is exceptional.

As much as there is written on Christ, so little is there written on the Holy Spirit. The work of John Owen on this subject is most widely known and still unsurpassed. In fact, John Owen wrote three works on the Holy Spirit, published in 1674, 1682, and 1693. He was naturally a prolific writer and theologian. Born in 1616, he died at the good old age of seventy-five years, in 1691. From 1642, when he published his first book, he continued writing books until his death.

In 1826 Richard Baynes reissued the works of John Owen, D.D., edited by Thomas Russell, A.M., with memoirs of his life and writings (twenty-one volumes). This edition is still in the market, and offers a treasury of sound and thorough theology.

Besides Owen's works I mention the following:

David Rungius, "Proof of the Eternity and Eternal Godhead of the Holy Spirit," Wittenberg, 1599.

Seb. Nieman, "On the Holy Spirit," Jena, 1655.

Joannes Ernest Gerhard, "On the Person of the Holy Spirit," Jena, 1660.

Theod. Hackspann, "Dissertation on the Holy Spirit," Jena, 1655.

J. G. Dorsche, "On the Person of the Holy Spirit," Köningsberg, 1690.

Fr. Deutsch, "On the Personality of the Holy Spirit," Leipsic, 1711.

Gottfr. Olearius (John F. Burgius), "On the Adoration and Worship of the Holy Spirit," Jena, 1727.

J. F. Buddeuss, "On the Godhead of the Holy Spirit," Jena, 1727.

J. C. Pfeiffer, "On the Godhead of the Holy Spirit," Jena, 1740.

G. F. Gude, "On the Martyrs as Witnesses for the Godhead of the Holy Spirit," Leipsic, 1741.

J. C. Danhauer, "On the Procession of the Holy Spirit from the Father and the Son," Strasburg, 1663. J. Senstius, Rostock, 1718, and J. A. Butstett, Wolfenbüttel, 1749. John Schmid, John Meisner, P. Havercorn, G. Wegner, and C. M. Pfaff.

The Work of the Holy Spirit has been discussed separately by the following: Anton, "The Holy Spirit Indispensable." Carsov, "On the Holy Spirit in Conviction." Wensdorf, "On the Holy Spirit as a Teacher." Boerner, "The Anointing of the Holy Spirit." Neuman, "The Anointing which Teaches All Things." Fries, "The Office of the Holy Spirit in General." Weiss, "The Holy Spirit Bringing into Remembrance." Foertsch, "On the Holy Spirit's Leading of the Children of God." Hoepfner, "On the Intercession of the Holy Spirit." Beltheim, Arnold, Gunther, Wendler, and Dummerick, "On the Groaning of the Holy Spirit." Meen, "On the Adoration of the Holy Spirit." Henning and Crusius, "On the Earnest of the Holy Spirit."

The following Dutch theologians have written on the same subject: Gysbrecht Voetius in his "Select-Disput.," I., p. 466. Sam. Maresius, "Theological Treatise on the Personality and Godhead of the Holy Spirit," in his "Sylloge-Disput.," I., p. 364. Jac. Fruytier, "The Ancient Doctrine Concerning God the Holy Spirit, True, Proven, and Divine"; exposition of John 15:26, 27. Camp. Vitringa, Jr., "Duae Disputationes Academicae de Notione Spiritus Sancti," in his Opuscula.

Works on the same subject during the present century can scarcely be compared with the studies of John Owen. We notice the following: Herder, "Vom Paraclet." Kachel, "Von der Lästerung wider den Heiligen Geist," Nürnberg, 1875. E. Guers, "Le Saint-Esprit, Étude doctrinale et pratique sur Sa Personne et Son OEuvre," Toulouse, 1865. A. J. Gordon, "Dispensation of the Spirit."

This meager bibliography shows what scant systematic treatment is accorded to the Person of the Holy Spirit. Studies of the Work of the Holy Spirit are still more scanty. It is true there are several dissertations on separate parts of this Work, but it has never been treated in its organic unity. Not even by Guers, who acknowledges that his little book is not entitled to a place among dogmatics.

In fact, Owen is still unsurpassed, and is therefore much sought after by good theologians, both lay and clerical. And yet Owen's masterpiece does not seem to make a closer study of this subject superfluous. Although invincible as a champion against the Arminians and Semi-Arminians of the latter part of the seventeenth century, his armor is too light to meet the doctrinal errors of the present time. For this reason the author has undertaken to offer the thinking Christian public an exposition of the second part of this great subject, in a form adapted to the claims of the age and the errors of the day. He has not treated the first part, the Person of the Holy Spirit. This is not a subject for controversy. The Godhead of the Holy Spirit is indeed being confessed or denied, but the principles of which confession or denial is the necessary result are so divergent that a discussion between confessor and denier is impossible. If they ever enter the arena they should cross lances on the point of first principles, and discuss the Source of Truth. And when this is settled they might come to discuss a special subject like that of the Holy Spirit. But until then such a discussion with them that deny the Revelation would almost be sacrilegious.

But with the Work of the Holy Spirit it is different. For although professing Christians acknowledge this Work, and all that it includes, and all that flows from it, yet the various groups into which they divide represent it in very divergent ways. What differences on this point between Calvinists and Ethicals, Reformed, Kohlbruggians, and Perfectionists! The representations of the practical Supernaturalists, Mystics, and Antinomians can scarcely be recognized.

It seemed to me impracticable and confusing to attack these deviating opinions on subordinate points. These differences should never be discussed but systematically. He that has not first staked off the entire domain in which the Holy Spirit works cannot successfully measure any part of it, to the winning of a brother and to the glory of God.

Hence leaving out polemics almost entirely, I have made an effort to represent the Work of the Holy Spirit in its organic relations, so that the reader may be enabled to survey the entire domain. And in surveying, who is not surprised at the ever-increasing dimensions of the Work of the Holy Spirit in all the things that pertain to God and man?

Even though we honor the Father and believe on the Son, how little do we live in the Holy Spirit! It even seems to us sometimes that for our sanctification only, the Holy Spirit is added accidentally to the great redemptive work.

This is the reason why our thoughts are so little occupied with the Holy Spirit; why in the ministry of the Word He is so little honored; why the people of God, when bowed in supplication before the Throne of Grace, make Him so little the object of their adoration. You feel involuntarily that of our piety, which is already small enough, He receives a too scanty portion.

And since this is the result of an inexcusable lack of knowledge and appreciation of His glorious Work in the entire creation, holy enthusiasm constrained me, in the power of God, to offer my fellow champions for the faith once delivered by the fathers, some assistance in this respect.

May the Holy Spirit, whose divine Work I have uttered in human words and with stammering tongue, crown this labor with such blessing that you may feel His unseen Presence more closely, and that He may bring to your disquieted heart more abundant consolation.

Amsterdam, April 10, 1888.

Postscript for American readers, I add one more observation.

This work contains occasional polemics against Methodism which to the many ministers and members of the churches called "Methodist" may appear unfair and uncalled for. Be it, therefore, clearly stated that my controversy with Methodism is never with these particular churches. The Methodism that I contend with prevailed until recently in nearly all the Protestant churches as an unhealthy fruit of the *Reveil* in the beginning of this century. Methodism as here intended is identical with what Mr. Heath, in *The Contemporary Review* (May, 1898), criticized as woefully inadequate to place Protestantism again at the head of the spiritual movement.

Methodism was born out of the spiritual decline of the Episcopal Church of England and Wales. It arose as the reaction of the individual and of the spiritual subjective against the destructive power of the objective in the community as manifested in the Church of England. As such the reaction was precious and undoubtedly a gift of God, and in its workings it would have continued just as salutary if it had retained its character of a predominant reaction.

It should have supposed the Church as a community as an objective power, and in this objective domain it should have vindicated the significance of the individual spiritual life and of the subjective confessing.

But it failed to do this. From vindicating the subjective rights of the individual it soon passed into antagonism against the objective rights of the community. This resulted dogmatically in the controversy about the objective work of God, viz., in His decree and His election, and ecclesiastically in antagonism against the objective work of the office through the confession. It gave supremacy to the subjective element in man's free will and to the individual element in the deciding of unchurchly conflicts in the Church. And so it retained no other aim than the conversion of individual sinners; and for this work it abandoned the organic, and retained only the mechanical method.

As such it celebrated in the so-called Reveil its most glorious triumph, and penetrated nearly all the Protestant churches, and even the Episcopal Church under the name of Evangelicalism or Low Churchism. As a second reaction against the second decline of the Protestant churches of that time this triumph undoubtedly brought a great blessing.

But when the necessity arose to reduce this new spiritual life to a definite principle, upon this to construct a Protestant-Christian life and world-view in opposition to the unchristian philosophies and to the essentially pantheistic life and world-view, and to give these position and to maintain it, then it pitiably failed. It lacked conscious, sharply defined principles; with its individualism and subjectivity it could not reach the social questions, and by reason of its complete lack of organic unity it could not formulate an independent life and world-view; yea, it stood everywhere as an obstacle to such formations.

For this reason it is absolutely necessary to teach the Protestant churches clearly to see this dark shadow of Methodism, while at the same time they should continue to study its precious significance as a spiritual reaction.

Hence my contending with Methodism and my persistent pointing to the imperative necessity of vindicating over against and alongside of the purely mechanical subjectivity the rights of the organic social in all human life, and of satisfying the need of the power of objectivity in presence of the extravagant statements of subjectivity. This presses all the more since in the Methodist theology of America the modern tendency is gaining ground.

The Work of the Holy Spirit may not be displaced by the activity of the human spirit.

KUYPER.

AMSTERDAM, April 21, 1899.

Explanatory Notes to the American Edition

Dr. Kuyper's work on the Holy Spirit first appeared in the *Heraut* in the weekly installments, after which it was published in book form, Amsterdam, 1888.

This explains the object of the author in writing the book, viz., the instruction of the people of the Netherlands. Written in the ordinary language of the people, it meets the need of both laity and clergy.

However, depth of thought was not sacrificed to simplicity of speech. On the contrary, the latter was only the instrument to make the former lucid and transparent.

The *Heraut* is a religious weekly of which Dr. Kuyper has been the editor-in-chief for more than twenty years. It is published on Friday, and forms the Sunday reading of a large constituency. Through its columns Dr. Kuyper has taught again the people of the Netherlands, in city and country, the principles of the Reformed faith, and how to give these principles a new development in accordance with the modern conscience of our time.

Dr. Kuyper is not an apologist, but an earnest and conscientious reconstructionist. He has made the people acquainted with the symbols of the Reformed faith, and by expounding the Scriptures to them he has maintained and defended the positions of those symbols. His success in this respect appears conspicuously in the reformation of the Reformed Churches in 1886, and in the subsequent development of marvelous energy and activity in Church and State which are products of revived and reconstructed Calvinism. Without the patient toil and labor of this quarter of a century, that reformation would have been impossible.

In his religious and political reformations, Dr. Kuyper proceeded from the personal conviction that the salvation of Church and State could be found only in a return to the deserted foundations of the national Reformed theology, but not to reconstruct it in its worn-out form. "His fresh, brave spirit is entirely free from all conservatism" (Dr. W. Geesink). He is a man *of* his time as well as *for* his time. The new superstructure which he has been rearing upon the carefully reuncovered foundations of the Reformed theology he seeks to adapt to all the needs, demands, and distresses of the present. In how far he has succeeded time only can tell.

Since 1871 he has published in the columns of the *Heraut* and afterward in book form the following: *Out of the Word,* Bible studies, four volumes; *The Incarnate Word, The Work of the Holy Spirit,* three volumes, and *E Voto Dordraceno,* an explanation of the Heidelberg Catechism, four volumes. This last work is a rich treasury of sound and thorough theology, dogmatic and practical. He has published several other treatises which have not yet appeared in book form. Among these we notice especially *On Common Grace,* which, still in process of publication, is full of most excellent reading. The number of his works amounts already to over one hundred and fifty, a partial list of which is to be found following this introduction.

The following works have been translated into English*: Encyclopedia of Sacred Theology* (Charles Scribner's Sons, 1898); *Calvinism and Art; Calvinism and Our Constitutional Liberties; Pantheism and Destruction of the Boundaries; The Stone Lectures.*

For the better understanding of the work, the translator begs to offer the following explanations:

"Ethical Irenical," or simply "Ethical," is the name of a movement in the Netherlands that seeks to mediate between modern Rationalism and the orthodox confession of the old Reformed Church. It seeks to restore peace and tranquillity not by a return to the original church order, nor by the maintenance of the old Confession and the removal of deviating ministers through trial and deposition (Judicial Treatment), but by making efforts to find a common ground for both parties. It proceeds from the idea that that which is diseased in the Church can and will return to health partly by letting the disease alone to run its course (*Doorzieken*)—forgetting that corruption in the Church is not a disease, but a sin;* partly by a liberal diffusion of Bible knowledge among the people (Medical Treatment).

Dr. Chantepie de la Saussaye, a disciple of Schleiermacher, was the spiritual father of this Ethical theology. Born in 1818, Dr. De la Saussaye entered the University of Leyden in 1836. Dissatisfied with the rational supernaturalism of a former generation, unable to adapt himself to the vagueness and ambiguousness of the so-called Groninger school, or to find a basis for the development of his theological science in the treasures of the Calvinistic theology, he felt himself strongly attracted to the school of Schelling, and through him he came under the influence of Pantheism. During the years of his pastorate in Leeuwarden (1842–48) and in Leyden to 1872, he modified and developed the ideas of Schleiermacher in an independent way. The Ethical theology was the result. Its basic thought may be comprehended as follows:

"Transcendent above nature, God is also immanent in nature. This immanence is not merely physical, but also, on the ground of this, ethical. This ethical immanence manifests itself in the religious moral life, which is the real and true life of man. It originates in the heathen world, and through Israel ascends to Christ, in whom it attains completion. Among the heathen it manifests itself especially in the conscience with its two elements of fear and hope; among Israel in Law and Prophecy; and in Christ in His perfect union with God and humanity. For this reason He is the Word *par excellence,* the Central Man, in whom all that is human is realized. However, while until Christ it proceeded from circumference to center, after Christ it proceeds in ever-widening circles from center to circumference. Life flows from Christ into the Church, which, having temporarily become an institution for the education of the nations, became through the Reformation and the French Revolution what it should be, a confessing Church. Its power lies no more in ecclesiastical organization, neither in authoritative creed and confession, but in moral activity and influence. The divine Word in the conscience begins to work and to govern; Christianity is being transferred into the moral domain. However, the perfect ethical immanence of God is not attained in this dispensation; being always possible, it may be realized in the succeeding eons."†

---

* Dr. W. Geesink † Dr. Bavink

It is not surprising that this theology, obliterating with its pantheistic current the boundary-lines between the Creator and the creature, should have come in hostile contact with the Reformed theology, which most zealously guards these boundary-lines. In fact, instead of uniting the two existing parties on one common ground, the Ethical movement added a third, which in the subsequent conflict was much more bitter, arbitrary, and tyrannical than the moderns, and which has already abandoned the Holy Scriptures in the manner of Wellhausen and Kuenen.

In 1872 Dr. Chantepie de la Saussaye was appointed professor of theology in the University of Groningen, succeeding Hofstede de Groot. He filled this position but thirteen months. He fell asleep February 13, 1874.

His most excellent disciple is the highly gifted Dr. J. H. Gunning, till 1899 professor of theology at the University of Leyden.

The name of Dr. Kohlbrugge is frequently found in the following pages. Born a Lutheran, a graduate of the seminary of Amsterdam, a candidate for the Lutheran ministry, Dr. Kohlbrugge became acquainted with the Reformed theology through the study of its earlier exponents. Known and feared as an ardent admirer of the doctrine of predestination, the authorities first of the Lutheran then of the State Church refused him admission to the ministry. He left Holland for Germany, where for the same reason he was debarred from the pulpits of the German Reformed churches. At last he was called to the pulpit of a Free Reformed church at Elberfeld, established by himself.

He was a profound theologian, a prolific writer, and one zealous for the honor of his Master. His numerous writings, half Lutheran, half Reformed, were spread over Holland, the Rhenish provinces, the cantons of Switzerland, and even among some Reformed churches of Bohemia.

Some of his disciples fell into Antinomianism, and occupy pulpits in the State Church at the present time. They are called Neo-Kohlbruggians. Professor Böhl, of Vienna, is the learned representative of the Old Kohlbruggians. Both the old and the new school are strongly opposed to Calvinism.

The translation of "The Work of the Holy Spirit" was undertaken by appointment of the author, to whom the proof-sheets of almost all the first volume were submitted for correction. Being "overwhelmed" with work, and being fully satisfied with the translation so far as he had seen it, the author decided not to delay the work for the reading of the remaining volumes, but to leave that to the discretion of the translator. A question of the omission of matter referring to local conditions and to current theological discussions was also left to the translator's judgment.

Grateful thanks are due to Rev. Thomas Chalmers Straus, A.M., of Peekskill, N. Y., for valuable assistance in preparing this work for the press.

TRANSLATOR.

PEEKSKILL, N. Y., January 27, 1900.

Introductory Note

By Prof. Benjamin B. Warfield, D.D., LL.D.,
of Princeton Theological Seminary

It is fortunately no longer necessary formally to introduce Dr. Kuyper to the American religious public. Quite a number of his remarkable essays have appeared of late years in our periodicals. These have borne such titles as "Calvinism in Art," "Calvinism the Source and Pledge of Our Constitutional Liberties," "Calvinism and Confessional Revision," "The Obliteration of Boundaries," "The Antithesis between Symbolism and Revelation"; and have appeared in the pages of such publications as *Christian Thought, Bibliotheca Sacra, The Presbyterian and Reformed Review*—not, we may be sure, without delighting their readers with the breadth of their treatment and the high and penetrating quality of their thought. The columns of *The Christian Intelligencer* have from time to time during the last year been adorned with examples of Dr. Kuyper's practical expositions of Scriptural truth; and now and again a brief but illuminating discussion of a topic of present interest has appeared in the columns of *The Independent.* The appetite whetted by this taste of good things has been partially gratified by the publication in English of two extended treatises from his hand —one discussing in a singularly profound way the principles of "The Encyclopedia of Sacred Theology" (Charles Scribner's Sons, 1898), and the other expounding with the utmost breadth and forcefulness the fundamental principles of "Calvinism" (The Fleming H. Revell Company, 1899). The latter volume consists of lectures delivered on "The L. P. Stone Foundation," at Princeton Theological Seminary in the autumn of 1898, and Dr. Kuyper's visit to America on this occasion brought him into contact with many lovers of high ideas in America, and has left a sense of personal acquaintance with him on the minds of multitudes who had the good fortune to meet him or to hear his voice at that time. It is impossible for us to look longer upon Dr. Kuyper as a stranger, needing an introduction to our favorable notice, when he appears again before us; he seems rather now to be one of our own prophets to whose message we have a certain right, and a new book from whose hands we welcome as we would a new gift from our near friend charged in a sense with care for our welfare. The book that is at present offered to the American public does not indeed come fresh from his hands. It has already been within the reach of his Dutch audience for more than a decade (it was published in 1888). It is only recently, however, that Dr. Kuyper has come to belong to us also, and the publication of this book in English, we may hope, is only another step in the process which will gradually make all his message ours.

Certainly no one will turn over the pages of this volume—much less will he, as our Jewish friends would say, "sink himself into the book"—without perceiving that it is a very valuable gift which comes to us in it from our newly found teacher. It is, as will be at once observed, a comprehensive treatise on the Work of the Holy Ghost—a theme higher than which none can occupy the attention of the Christian man, and yet one on which really comprehensive treatises are comparatively rare. It is easy, to be sure, to exaggerate the significance of the latter fact. There never was a time, of course, when Christians did not confess their faith in the Holy Ghost; and there never was a time when they did not speak to one another of the work of the Blessed Spirit, the Executor of the Godhead not only in the creation and upholding of the worlds and in the inspiration of the prophets and apostles, but also in the regenerating and sanctifying of the soul. Nor has there ever been a time when, in the prosecution of its task of realizing mentally the treasures of truth put in its charge in the Scriptural revelation, the Church has not busied itself also with the investigation of the mysteries of the person and work of the Spirit; and especially has there never been a time since that tremendous revival of religion which we call the Reformation when the whole work of the Spirit in the application of the redemption wrought out by Christ has not been a topic of the most thorough and loving study of Christian men. Indeed, it partly arises out of the very intensity of the study given to the saving activities of the Spirit that so few comprehensive treatises on the work of the Spirit have been written. The subject has seemed so vast, the ramifications of it have appeared so far-reaching, that few have had the courage to undertake it as a whole. Dogmaticians have, to be sure, been compelled to present the entire range of the matter in its appropriate place in their completed systems. But when monographs came to be written, they have tended to confine themselves to a single segment of the great circle; and thus we have had treatises rather on, say, Regeneration, or Justification, or Sanctification, on the Anointing of the Spirit, or the Intercession of the Spirit, or the Sealing of the Spirit, than on the work of the Spirit as a whole. It would be a great mistake to think of the doctrine of the Holy Spirit as neglected, merely because it has been preferably presented under its several rubrics or parts, rather than in its entirety. How easily one may fall into such an error is fairly illustrated by certain criticisms that have been recently passed upon the Westminster Confession of Faith—which is (as a Puritan document was sure to be) very much a treatise on the work of the Spirit—as if it were deficient, in not having a chapter specifically devoted to "the Holy Spirit and His Work." The sole reason why it does not give *a* chapter to this subject, however, is because it prefers to give *nine* chapters to it; and when an attempt was made to supply the fancied omission, it was found that pretty much all that could be done was to present in the proposed new chapter a meager summary of the contents of these nine chapters. It would have been more plausible, indeed, to say that the Westminster Confession comparatively neglected the work of Christ, or even the work of God the Father. Similarly the lack in our literature of a large number of comprehensive treatises on the work of the Holy Spirit is in part due to the richness of our literature in treatises on the separate portions of that work severally. The significance of Dr. Kuyper's book is, therefore, in part due only to the fact that he has had the courage to attack and the gifts successfully to accomplish a task which few have possessed the breadth either of outlook or of powers to undertake. And it is no small gain to be able to survey the whole field of the work of the Holy Spirit in its organic unity under the guidance of so fertile, so systematic, and so practical a mind. If we cannot look upon it as breaking entirely new ground, or even say that it is the only work of its kind since Owen, we can at least say that it brings together the material belonging to this great topic with a systematizing genius that is very rare, and presents it with a penetrating appreciation of its meaning and a richness of apprehension of its relations that is exceedingly illuminating.

It is to be observed that we have not said without qualification that the comparative rarity of such comprehensive treatises on the work of the Holy Spirit as Dr. Kuyper's is due simply to the greatness and difficulty of the task. We have been careful to say that it is only in part due to this cause. It is only in the circles to which this English translation is presented, to say the truth, that this remark is applicable at all. It is the happiness of the Reformed Christians of English speech that they are the heirs of what must in all fairness be spoken of as an immense literature upon this great topic; it may even be said with some justice that the peculiarity of their theological labor turns just on the diligence and depth of their study of this *locus*. It is, it will be remembered, to John Owen's great "Discourse Concerning the Holy Spirit" that Dr. Kuyper points as hitherto the normative treatise on the subject. But John Owen's book did not stand alone in his day and generation, but was rather merely symptomatic of the engrossment of the theological thought of the circle of which he was so great an ornament in the investigation of this subject. Thomas Goodwin's treatise on "The Work of the Holy Ghost in Our Salvation" is well worthy of a place by its side; and it is only the truth to say that Puritan thought was almost entirely occupied with loving study of the work of the Holy Spirit, and found its highest expression in dogmatico-practical expositions of the several aspects of it—of which such treatises as those of Charnock and Swinnerton on Regeneration are only the best-known examples among a multitude which have fallen out of memory in the lapse of years. For a century and a half afterward, indeed, this topic continued to form the hinge of the theologizing of the English Nonconformists. Nor has it lost its central position even yet in the minds of those who have the best right to be looked upon as the successors of the Puritans. There has been in some quarters some decay, to be sure, in sureness of grasp and theological precision in the presentation of the subject, but it is possible that a larger number of practical treatises on some element or other of the doctrine of the Spirit continue to appear from the English press annually than on any other branch of divinity. Among these, such books as Dr. A. J. Gordon's *The Ministry of the Spirit,* Dr. J. E.

Cumming's *Through the Eternal Spirit,* Principal H. C. G. Moule's *Veni Creator,* Dr. Redford's *Vox Dei,* Dr. Robson's *The Holy Spirit, the Paraclete,* Dr. Vaughan's *The Gifts of the Holy Spirit*—to name only a few of the most recent books—attain a high level of theological clarity and spiritual power; while, if we may be permitted to go back only a few years, we may find in Dr. James Buchanan's "The Office and Work of the Holy Spirit," and in Dr. George Smeaton's "The Doctrine of the Holy Spirit," two treatises covering the whole ground—the one in a more practical, the other in a more didactic spirit—in a manner worthy of the best traditions of our Puritan fathers. There has always been a copious stream of literature on the work of the Holy Spirit, therefore, among the English-speaking churches; and Dr. Kuyper's book comes to us not as something of a novelty, but as a specially finely conceived and executed presentation of a topic on which we are all thinking.

But the case is not the same in all parts of Christendom. If we lift our eyes from our own special condition and view the Church at large, it is a very different spectacle that greets them. As we sweep them down the history of the Church, we discover that the topic of the work of the Holy Spirit was one which only at a late date really emerged as the explicit study of Christian men. As we sweep them over the whole extent of the modern Church, we discover that it is a topic which appeals even yet with little force to very large sections of the Church. The poverty of Continental theology in this *locus* is, indeed, after all is said and done, depressing. Note one or two little French books, by E. Guers and G. Tophel,* and a couple of formal studies of the New Testament doctrine of the Spirit by the Dutch writers Stemler and Thoden Van Velzen, called out by The Hague Society—and we have before us almost the whole list of the older books of our century which pretend in any way to cover the ground. Nor has very much been done more recently to remedy the deficiency. The amazing theological activity of latter-day Germany has, to be sure, not been able to pass so fruitful a theme entirely by; and her scholars have given us a few scientific studies of sections of the Biblical material. The two most significant of

* Guers' "Le Saint-Esprit: Étude Doctrinale et Practique" (1865); G. Tophel's "The Work of the Holy Spirit in Man" (E. T., 1882), and also more recently "Le Saint-Esprit; Cinq Nouvelles Études Bibliques" (1899).

these appeared, indeed, in the same year with Dr. Kuyper's book—Gloel's *Der heilige Geist in des Heilsverkündigung des Paulus,* and Gunkel's *Die Wirkungen des heiligen Geistes nach d. populär. Anschauung der apostolischen Zeit und der Lehre d. A. Paulus* (2d ed., 1899); these have been followed in the same spirit by Weienel in a work called *Die Wirkungen des Geistes und der Geister im nachapostolischen Zeitalter* (1899); while a little earlier the Dutch theologian Beversluis issued a more comprehensive study, *De Heilige Geest en zijne werkingen volgens de Schriften des Nieuwen Verbonds* (1896). Their investigation of the Biblical material, however, is not only very formal, but it is also dominated by such imperfect theological presuppositions that it can carry the student scarcely a step forward. Very recently something better in this respect has appeared in such books as Th. Meinhold's *Der heilige Geist und sein Wirken am einzelnen Menschen, mit besonderer Beziehung auf Luther* (1890, 12mo, pp. 228);* W. Kölling's *Pneumatologie, oder die Lehre von der Person des heiligen Geistes* (1894, 8vo, pp. 368); Karl von *Lechler's Die biblische Lehre vom heiligen Geiste* (1899, 8vo, pp. 307); and K. F. *Nösgen's Geschichte von der Lehre vom heiligen Geiste* (1899, 8vo, pp. 376); which it is to be hoped are the beginnings of a varied body of scholarly works from the Lutheran side, out of which may, after a while, grow some such comprehensive and many-sided treatment of the whole subject as that which Dr. Kuyper has given our Dutch brethren, and now us in this English translation. But none of them provides the desired treatise itself, and it is significant that no one even professes to do so. Even where, as in the case of the books of Meinhold and von Lechler, the treatment is really topical, the author is careful to disclaim the purpose to provide a well-compacted, systematic view of the subject, by putting on his title-page a hint of a historical or exegetical point of view.

In fact, only in a single instance in the whole history of German theological literature—or, we may say, prior to Dr. Kuyper in the entire history of continental theological literature—has anyone had the courage or found the impulse to face the task Dr. Kuyper has so admirably exe-

---

* Meinhold's book is mainly a Lutheran polemic in behalf of fundamental principles, against the Ritschlian rationalism on this subject. As such its obverse is provided in the recent treatise of Rudolf Otto, "Die Anschauung vom heiligen Geiste bei Luther" (1898).

cuted. We are referring, of course, to the great work *on Die Lehre vom heiligen Geiste,* which was projected by that theological giant, K. A. Kahnis, but the first part of which only was published—in a thin volume of three hundred and fifty-six pages, in 1847. It was doubtless symptomatic of the state of feeling in Germany on the subject that Kahnis never found time or encouragement in a long life of theological pursuits to complete his book. And, indeed, it was greeted in theological circles at the time with something like amused amazement that anyone could devote so much time and labor to this theme, or expect others to find time and energy to read such a treatise. We are told that a well-known theologian remarked caustically of it that if things were to be carried out on that scale, no one could expect to live long enough to read the literature of his subject; and the similar remark made by C. Hase in the preface to the fifth edition of his "Dogmatic," though it names no names, is said to have had Kahnis's book in view.* The significance of Kahnis's unique and unsuccessful attempt to provide for German Protestantism some worthy treatment of the doctrine of the Holy Spirit is so great that it will repay us to fix the facts concerning it well in our minds. And to this end we extract the following account of it from the introduction of the work of von Lechler which we have just mentioned (p. 22 *sqq.*):

> We have to indicate, in conclusion, another circumstance in the history of our doctrine, which is in its way just as significant for the attitude of present-day science toward this topic as was the silence of the first Ecumenical Council concerning it for the end of the first theological age. It is the extraordinary poverty of monographs on the Holy Spirit. Although there do exist some, and in some instances important, studies dealing with the subject, yet their number is out of all proportion to the greatness and the extent of the problems. We doubtless should not err in assuming that vital interest in a scientific question will express itself not merely in comprehensive handbooks and encyclopedic compendiums, the latter of which are especially forced to see to the completeness of the list of subjects treated, but of necessity also in those separate investigations in which especially the fresh vigor of youth is accustomed to make proof of its fitness for higher studies. What lacunae we should have to regret in other branches of theological science if a rich development of monographic literature did not range itself by the side of the compendiums, breaking out here and there new paths, laying deeper foun-

* See Holtzmann in the *Theolog. Literaturzeitung* of 1896, 25, p. 646.

dations, supplying valuable material for the constructive or decorative completion of the scientific structure! All this, in the present instance, however, has scarcely made a beginning. The sole separate treatise which has been projected on a really profound and broad basis of investigation—the Lehre vom heiligen Geiste of K. A. Kahnis (then at Breslau), 1847—came to a standstill with its first part. This celebrated theologian, who had certainly in his possession in surprising measure the qualities and acquisitions that fitted him to come forward as a preparer of the way in this uncertain and little worthily studied subject, had set before himself the purpose of investigating this, as he himself called it, 'extraordinarily neglected' topic, at once on its Biblical ecclesiastical, historical, and dogmatic sides. The history of his book is exceedingly instructive and suggestive with respect to the topic itself. He found the subject, as he approached it more closely, in a very special degree a difficult one, chiefly on account of the manifoldness of the conception. At first his results became ever more and more negative. A controversy with the 'friends of light' of the time helped him forward. Testium nubes magis juvant, quam luciferorum virorum importuna lumina. But God, he says, led him to greater clearness: the doctrine of the Church approved itself to him. Nevertheless it was not his purpose to establish the Scriptural doctrine in all its points, but only to exhibit the place which the Holy Spirit occupies in the development of the Word of God in the Old and New Testaments. There was a feeling that came to him that we were standing upon the eve of a new outpouring of the Spirit. But the wished-for dawn, he says, still held back. His wide survey, beyond his special subject, of the whole domain of science in the corporate life of the Church, is characteristic no less of the subject than of the man. It was not given to him, however, to see the longed-for flood poured over the parched fields. His exegetical 'foundation' (chaps. 1–3) moves in the old tracks. Since he shared essentially the subjective point of view of Schleiermacher and committed the final decision in the determining conceptions to philosophy, in spite of many remarkable flashes of insight into the Scriptures he remained fixed in the intellectualistic and ethical mode of conceiving the Holy Ghost, though this was accompanied by many attempts to transcend Schleiermacher, but without the attaining of any unitary conception and without any effort to bring to a Scriptural solution the burning question of the personality or impersonality of the Spirit. The fourth chapter institutes a comparison between the Spirit of Christianity and that of heathenism. The second book deals first with the relation of the Church to the Holy Spirit in general, and then enters upon a history of the doctrine, which is carried, however, only through the earliest fathers, and breaks off with a survey of the scanty harvest which the first age supplied to the succeeding epochs, in which the richest development of the doctrine took place. Here the book closes. . . .*

* Compare the remarks of Dr. Smeaton, op. cit., ed. 2, p. 396.

Thus the only worthy attempt German theology has made to produce a comprehensive treatise on the work of the Holy Ghost remains a neglected *torso* till today.

If we will gather up the facts to which we have thus somewhat desultorily called attention into a propositional statement, we shall find ourselves compelled to recognize that the doctrine of the Holy Spirit was only slowly brought to the explicit consciousness of the Church, and has even yet taken a firm hold on the mind and consciousness of only a small section of the Church. To be more specific, we shall need to note that the early Church busied itself with the investigation within the limits of this *locus* of only the doctrine of the person of the Holy Ghost—His deity and personality—and of His one function of inspirer of the prophets and apostles, while the whole doctrine of the work of the Spirit at large is a gift to the Church from the Reformation;* and we shall need to note further that since its formulation by the Reformers this doctrine has taken deep root and borne its full fruits only in the Reformed churches, and among them in exact proportion to the loyalty of their adherence to, and the richness of their development of, the fundamental principles of the Reformed theology. Stated in its sharpest form this is as much as to say that the developed doctrine of the work of the Holy Spirit is an exclusively Reformation doctrine, and more particularly a Reformed doctrine, and more particularly still a Puritan doctrine. Wherever the fundamental principles of the Reformation have gone, it has gone, but it has come to its full rights only among the Reformed churches, and among them only where what we have been accustomed to call "the Second Reformation" has deepened the spiritual life of the churches and cast back the Christian with special poignancy of feeling upon the grace of God alone as his sole dependence for salvation and all the goods of this life and the life to come. Indeed, it is

* For the epoch-making character of the Reformation in the history of this doctrine *cf.* also Nösgen, op. cit., p. 2. "For its development, a division-line is provided simply and solely by the Reformation, and this merely because at that time only was attention intensely directed to the right mode of the application of salvation. Thus were the problems of the specially saving operation of the Holy Spirit, of the manner of His working in the congregation of believers cast into the foreground, and the theological treatment of this doctrine made of ever-increasing importance to the Church of Christ," etc.

possible to be more precise still. The doctrine of the work of the Holy spirit is a gift from John Calvin to the Church of Christ. He did not, of course, invent it. The whole of it lay spread out on the pages of Scripture with a clearness and fullness of utterance which one would think would secure that even he who ran should read it; and doubtless he who ran did read it, and it has fed the soul of the true believer in all ages. Accordingly hints of its apprehension are found widely scattered in all Christian literature, and in particular the germs of the doctrine are spread broadcast over the pages of Augustine. Luther did not fail to lay hold upon them; Zwingli shows time and again that he had them richly in his mind; they constituted, in very fact, one of the foundations of the Reformation movement, or rather they provided its vital breath. But it was Calvin who first gave them anything like systematic or adequate expression; and it is through him and from him that they have come to be the assured possession of the Church of Christ. There is no phenomenon in doctrinal history more astonishing than the commonly entertained view as to the contribution made by John Calvin to the development of Christian doctrine. He is thought of currently as the father of doctrines, such as that of predestination and reprobation, of which he was the mere heir, taking them as wholes over from the hands of his great master Augustine. Meanwhile his real personal contributions to Christian doctrine are utterly forgotten. These are of the richest kind and cannot be enumerated here. But it is germane to our present topic to note that at their head stand three gifts of the first value to the Church's thought and life, which we should by no means allow to pass from our grateful memory. It is to John Calvin that we owe that broad conception of the work of Christ which is expressed in the doctrine of His threefold office of Prophet, Priest, and King; he was the first who presented the work of Christ under this *schema,* and from him it was that it has passed into a Christian commonplace. It is to John Calvin that we owe the whole conception of a science of "Christian Ethics"; he was the first to outline its idea and develop its principles and contents, and it remained a *peculium* of his followers for a century. And it is to John Calvin that we owe the first formulation of the doctrine of the work of the Holy Ghost; he himself gave it a very rich statement, developing it especially in the broad departments of "Common Grace" "Regeneration," and "the Witness of the Spirit"; and it is, as we have seen, among his spiritual descendants only that it has to this day received any adequate attention in the churches. We must guard ourselves, of course, from exaggeration in such a matter; the bare facts, when put forth without pausing to allow for the unimportant shadings, sound of themselves sufficiently like an exaggeration.* But it is simply true that these great topics received their first formulation at the hands of John Calvin; and it is from him that the Church has derived them, and to him that it owes its thanks for them.

And if we pause to ask why the formulation of the doctrine of the work of the Spirit waited for the Reformation and for Calvin, and why the further working out of the details of this doctrine and its enrichment by the profound study of Christian minds and meditation of Christian hearts has come down from Calvin only to the Puritans, and from the Puritans to their spiritual descendants like the Free Church teachers of the Disruption era and the Dutch contestants for the treasures of the Reformed religion of our own day, the reasons are not far to seek. There is, in the first place, a regular order in the acquisition of doctrinal truth, inherent in the nature of the case, which therefore the Church was bound to follow in its gradual realization of the deposit of truth given it in the Scriptures; and by virtue of this the Church could not successfully attack the task of assimilating and formulating the doctrine of the work of the Spirit until the foundations had been laid firmly in a clear grasp on yet more fundamental doctrines. And there are, in the next place, certain forms of doctrinal construction which leave no or only a meager place for the work of the personal Holy Spirit in the heart; and in the presence of these constructions this doctrine, even where in part apprehended and acknowledged, languishes and falls out of the interest of men. The operation of the former cause postponed the development of the doctrine of the work of the Spirit until the way was prepared for it; and this preparation was complete only at the Reformation. The operation of the second cause has retarded where it has not stifled the proper assimilation of the doctrine in many parts of the Church until today.

---

* So, for example, a careless reading of pp. 65–67 of Pannier's "Le Témoignage du Saint-Esprit" gives the impression of exaggeration, whereas it is merely the suppression of all minor matters to emphasize the salient facts that is responsible for this effect.

To be more specific, the development of the doctrinal system of Christianity in the apprehension of the Church has actually run through —as it theoretically should have run through—a regular and logical course. First, attention was absorbed in the contemplation of the objective elements of the Christian deposit, and only afterward were the subjective elements taken into fuller consideration. First of all it was the Christian doctrine of God that forced itself on the attention of men, and it was not until the doctrine of the Trinity had been thoroughly assimilated that attention was vigorously attracted to the Christian doctrine of the God-man; and again, it was not until the doctrine of the Person of Christ was thoroughly assimilated that attention was poignantly attracted to the Christian doctrine of sin—man's need and helplessness; and only after that had been wrought fully out again could attention turn to the objective provision to meet man's needs in the work of Christ; and again, only after that to the subjective provision to meet his needs in the work of the Spirit. This is the logical order of development, and it is the actual order in which the Church has slowly and amid the throes of all sorts of conflicts—with the world and with its own slowness to believe all that the prophets have written—worked its way into the whole truth revealed to it in the Word. The order is, it will be observed, Theology, Christology, Anthropology (Hamartialogy), Impetration of Redemption, Application of Redemption; and in the nature of the case the topics that fall under the rubric of the application of redemption could not be solidly investigated until the basis had been laid for them in the assimilation of the preceding topics. We have connected the great names of Athanasius and his worthy successors who fought out the Christological disputes, of Augustine and of Anselm, with the precedent stages of this development. It was the leaders of the Reformation who were called on to add the capstone to the structure by working out the facts as to the application of redemption to the soul of man through the Holy Spirit. Some elements of the doctrine of the Spirit are indeed implicated in earlier discussions. For example, the deity and personality of the Spirit—the whole doctrine of His person—was a part of the doctrine of the Trinity, and this accordingly became a topic for early debate, and patristic literature is rich in discussions of it. The authority of Scripture was fundamental to the whole doctrinal discussion, and the doctrine of the inspiration of the prophets and apostles by the Spirit was therefore asserted from the beginning with great emphasis. In the determination of man's need in the Pelagian controversy much was necessarily determined about "Grace"—its necessity, its prevenience, its efficacy, its indefectibility—and in this much was anticipated of what was afterward to be more orderly developed in the doctrine of the interior work of the Spirit; and accordingly there is much in Augustine which adumbrates the determination of later times. But even in Augustine there is a vagueness and tentativeness in the treatment of these topics which advises us that while the facts relative to man and his needs and the methods of God's working upon him to salvation are firmly grasped, these same facts relative to the personal activities of the Spirit as yet await their full assimilation. Another step had to be taken: the Church needed to wait yet for Anselm to set on foot the final determination of the doctrine of a vicarious atonement; and only when time had been given for its assimilation, at length men's minds were able to take the final step. Then Luther rose to proclaim justification by faith, and Calvin to set forth with his marvelous balance the whole doctrine of the work of the Spirit in applying salvation to the soul. In this matter, too, the fullness of the times needed to be waited for; and when the fullness of the times came the men were ready for their task and the Church was ready for their work. And in this collocation we find a portion of the secret of the immense upheaval of the Reformation.

Unfortunately, however, the Church was not ready in all its parts alike for the new step in doctrinal development. This was, of course, in the nature of the case: for the development of doctrine takes place naturally in a matrix of old and hardened partial conceptions, and can make its way only by means of a conflict of opinion. All Arians did not disappear immediately after the Council of Nice; on the contrary, for an age they seemed destined to rule the Church. The decree of Chalcedon did not at once quiet all Christological debate, or do away with all Christological error. There were remainders of Pelagianism that outlived Augustine; and indeed that after the Synod of Orange began to make headway against the truth. Anselm's construction of the atonement only slowly worked its way into the hearts of men. And so, when Calvin had for the first time formulated the fuller and more precise doctrine of the work of the Spirit, there were antagonistic forces in the world which crowded upon it and curtailed its influence and clogged its advance in the apprehension of men. In general, these may be said to be two: the sacerdotal tendency on the one hand and the libertarian tendency on the other. The sacerdotal tendency was entrenched in the old Church; from which the Reformers were extruded indeed by the very force of the new leaven of their individualism of spiritual life. That Church was therefore impervious to the newly formulated doctrine of the work of the Spirit. To it the Church was the depository of grace, the sacraments were its indispensable vehicle, and the administration of it lay in the hands of human agents. Wherever this sacramentarianism went, in however small a measure, it tended so far to distract men's attention from the Spirit of God and to focus it on the *media* of His working; and wherever it has entrenched itself, there the study of the work of the Spirit has accordingly more or less languished. It is easy indeed to say that the Spirit stands behind the sacraments and is operative in the sacraments; as a matter of fact, the sacraments tend, in all such cases, to absorb the attention, and the theoretical explanations of their efficacy as vested in the Spirit's energy tend to pass out of the vivid interest of men. The libertarian tendency, on the other hand, was the nerve of the old semi-Pelagianism which in Thomism and Tridentinism became in a modified form the formal doctrine of the Church of Rome; and in various forms it soon began to seep also into and to trouble the churches of the Reformation—first the Lutheran and after that also the Reformed. To it, the will of man was in greater or less measure the decisive factor in the subjective reception of salvation; and in proportion as it was more or less developed or more or less fully applied, interest in the doctrine of the subjective work of the Spirit languished, and in these circles too men's minds were to that degree distracted from the study of the doctrine of the work of the Spirit, and tend to focus themselves on the autocracy of the human will and its native or renewed ability to obey God and seek and find communion with Him. No doubt here too it is easy to point to the function which is still allowed the Spirit, in most at least of the theological constructions on this basis. But the practical effect has been that just in proportion as the autocracy of the human will in salvation has been emphasized, the interest in the internal work of the Spirit has declined. When we take into consideration the widespread influence that has been attained even in the Protestant world by these two antagonistic tendencies, we shall cease to wonder at the widespread neglect that has befallen the doctrine of the work of the Spirit. And we shall have prosecuted our inquiry but a little way before we become aware how entirely these facts account for the phenomena before us: how completely it is true that interest in the doctrine of the work of the Spirit has failed just in those regions and just in those epochs in which either sacramentarian or libertarian opinions have ruled; and how true it is that engagement with this doctrine has been intense only along the banks of that narrow stream of religious life and thought the keynote of which has been the *soli Deo gloria* in all its fullness of meaning. With this key in hand the mysteries of the history of this doctrine in the Church are at once solved for us.

One of the chief claims to our attention which Dr. Kuyper's book makes, therefore, is rooted in the fact that it is a product of a great religious movement in the Dutch churches. This is not the place to give a history of that movement. We have all watched it with the intensest interest, from the rise of the Free Churches to the union with them of the new element from the *Doleantie.* We have lacked no proof that it was a movement of exceptional spiritual depth, but had there lacked any such proof, it would be supplied by the appearance of this book out of its heart. Wherever men are busying themselves with holy and happy meditations on the Holy Ghost and His work, it is safe to say the foundations of a true spiritual life are laid, and the structure of a rich spiritual life is rising. The mere fact that a book of this character offers itself as one of the products of this movement attracts us to it; and the nature of the work itself—its solidity of thought and its depth of spiritual apprehension—brightens our hopes for the future of the churches in which it has had its birth. Only a spiritually minded Church provides a soil in which a literature of the Spirit can grow. There are some who will miss in the book what they are accustomed to call "scientific" character;* it has no lack certainly of scientific exactitude of conception, and if it seems to any to lack "scientific" form, it

* Thus Beversluis, op. cit., speaks of it as Dr. Kuyper's bulky book, which "has no scientific value," though it is full of fine passages and treats the subject in a many-sided way.

assuredly has a quality which is better than anything that even a "scientific" form could give it—it is a religious book. It is the product of a religious heart, and it leads the reader to a religious contemplation of the great facts of the Spirit's working. May it bring to all, into whose hands it finds its way in this fresh vehicle of a new language, an abiding and happy sense of rest on and in God the Holy Ghost, the Author and Lord of all life, to whom in our heart of hearts we may pray:

Veni, Creator Spiritus
Spiritus recreator,
Tu deus, tu datus coelitus,
Tu donum, tu donator.

Princeton Theological Seminary
April 23, 1900.

Volume One

The Work of the Holy Spirit in the Church as a Whole

First Chapter
Introduction

1

Careful Treatment Required

Who hath also given unto us His Holy Spirit—1 Thessalonians 4:8.

The need of divine guidance is never more deeply felt than when one undertakes to give instruction in the work of the Holy Spirit—so unspeakably tender is the subject, touching the inmost secrets of God and the soul's deepest mysteries.

We shield instinctively the intimacies of kindred and friends from intrusive observation, and nothing hurts the sensitive heart more than the rude exposure of that which should not be unveiled, being beautiful only in the retirement of the home circle. Greater delicacy befits our approach to the holy mystery of our soul's intimacy with the *living God.* Indeed, we can scarcely find words to express it, for it touches a domain far below the social life where language is formed and usage determines the meaning of words.

Glimpses of this life have been revealed, but the greater part has been withheld. It is like the life of Him who did not cry, nor lift up nor cause His voice to be heard in the street. And that which was heard was whispered rather than spoken—a soul-breath, soft but voiceless, or rather a radiating of the soul's own blessed warmth. Sometimes the stillness has been broken by a cry or a raptured shout, but there has been mainly a silent working, a ministering of stern rebuke or of sweet comfort by that wonderful Being in the Holy Trinity whom with stammering tongue we adore as the Holy Spirit.

Spiritual experience can furnish no basis for instruction; for such experience rests on that which took place in our own soul. Certainly this has value, influence, voice in the matter. But what guarantees correctness and fidelity in interpreting such experience? And again, how can we distinguish its various sources—from ourselves, from without, or from the Holy Spirit? The twofold question will ever hold: Is our experience shared by others, and may it not be vitiated by what is in us sinful and spiritually abnormal?

Although there is no subject in whose treatment the soul inclines more to draw upon its own experience, there is none that demands more that our sole source of knowledge be the Word given us by the Holy Spirit. After that, human experience may be heard, attesting what the lips have confessed; even affording glimpses into the Spirit's blessed mysteries, which are unspeakable and of which the Scripture therefore does not speak. But this cannot be the ground of instruction to others.

The Church of Christ assuredly presents abundant spiritual utterance in hymn and spiritual song; in homilies hortatory and consoling; in sober confession or outbursts of souls wellnigh overwhelmed by the floods of persecution and martyrdom. But even this cannot be the foundation of knowledge concerning the work of the Holy Spirit.

The following reasons will make this apparent:

First, the difficulty of discriminating between the men and women whose experience we consider pure and healthy, and those whose testimony we put aside as strained and unhealthful. Luther frequently spoke of his experience, and so did Caspar Schwenkfeld, the dangerous fanatic. But what is our warrant for approving the utterances of the great Reformer and warning against those of the Silesian nobleman? For evidently the testimony of the two men cannot be equally true. Luther condemned as a lie what Schwenkfeld commended as a highly spiritual attainment.

Second, the testimony of believers presents only the dim outlines of the work of the Holy Spirit. Their voices are faint as coming from an unknown realm, and their broken speech is intelligible only when we, initiated by the Holy Spirit, can interpret it from our own experience.

Otherwise we hear, but fail to understand; we listen, but receive no information. Only he that hath ears can hear what the Spirit has spoken secretly to these children of God.

Third, among those Christian heroes whose testimony we receive, some speak clearly, truthfully, forcibly, others confusedly as though they were groping in the dark. Whence the difference? Closer examination shows that the former have borrowed all their speech from the Word of God, while the others tried to add to it something novel that promised to be great, but proved only bubbles, quickly dissolved, leaving no trace.

Last, when, on the other hand, in this treasury of Christian testimony we find some truth better developed, more clearly expressed, more aptly illustrated than in Scripture; or, in other words, when the ore of the Sacred Scripture has been melted in the crucible of the mortal anguish of the Church of God, and cast into more permanent forms, then we always discover in such forms certain *fixed types.* Spiritual life expresses itself otherwise among the earnest-souled Lapps and Finns than among the light-hearted French. The rugged Scotchman pours out his overflowing heart in a different way from that of the emotional German.

Yea, more striking still, some preacher has obtained a marked influence upon the souls of men of a certain locality; an exhorter has got hold of the hearts of the people; or some mother in Israel has sent forth her word among her neighbors; and what do we discover? That in that whole region we meet no other expressions of spiritual life than those coined by that preacher, that exhorter, that mother in Israel. This shows that the language, the very words and forms in which the soul expresses itself, are largely borrowed, and spring but rarely from one's own spiritual consciousness; and so do not insure the correctness of their interpretation of the soul's experience.

And when such heroes as Augustine, Thomas, Luther, Calvin, and others present us something strikingly original, then we encounter difficulty in understanding their strong and vigorous testimony. For the individuality of these choice vessels is so marked that, unless sifted and tested, we cannot fully comprehend them.

All this shows that the supply of knowledge concerning the work of the Holy Spirit, which, judging superficially, was to gush forth from the deep wells of Christian experience, yields but a few drops.

Hence for the knowledge of the subject we must return to that wondrous Word of God which as a mystery of mysteries lies still uncomprehended in the Church, seemingly dead as a stone, but a stone that strikes fire. Who has not seen its scintillating sparks? Where is the child of God whose heart has not been kindled by the fire of that Word?

But Scripture sheds scant light on the work of the Holy Spirit. For proof, see how much the Old Testament says of the Messiah and how comparatively little of the Holy Spirit. The little circle of saints, Mary, Simeon, Anna, John, who, standing in the vestibule of the New Testament, could scan the horizon of the Old Testament revelation with a glance—how much they knew of the Person of the Promised Deliverer, and how little of the Holy Spirit! Even including all the New Testament teachings, how scanty is the light upon the work of the Holy Spirit compared with that upon the work of Christ!

And this is quite natural, and could not be otherwise, for Christ is the Word made Flesh, having visible, well-defined form, in which we recognize our own, that of a man, whose outlines follow the direction of our own being. Christ can be seen and heard; once men's hands could even handle the Word of Life. But the Holy Spirit is entirely different. Of Him nothing appears in visible form; He never steps out from the intangible void. Hovering, undefined, incomprehensible, He remains a mystery. He is as the wind! We hear its sound, but cannot tell whence it cometh and whither it goeth. Eye cannot see Him, ear cannot hear Him, much less the hand handle Him. There are, indeed, symbolic signs and appearances: a dove, tongues of fire, the sound of a rushing, mighty wind, a breathing from the holy lips of Jesus, a laying on of hands, a speaking with foreign tongues. But of all this nothing remains; nothing lingers behind, not even the trace of a footprint. And after the signs have disappeared, His being remains just as puzzling, mysterious, and distant as ever. So almost all the divine instruction concerning the Holy Spirit is likewise obscure, intelligible only so far as He makes it clear to the eye of the favored soul.

We know that the same may be said of Christ's work, whose real import is apprehended solely by the spiritually enlightened, who behold the eternal wonders of the Cross. And yet what wonderful fascination is there even for a little child in the story of the manger in Bethlehem, of the Transfiguration, of Gabbatha and Golgotha. How easily can we interest him by telling of the heavenly Father who numbereth the hairs of his head, arrayeth the lilies of the field, feedeth the sparrows on the house-top. But is it possible so to engage his attention for the Person of the Holy Spirit? The same is true of the unregenerate: they are not unwilling to speak of the heavenly Father; many speak feelingly of the Manger and of the Cross. But do they ever speak of the Holy Spirit? They cannot; the subject has no hold upon them. The Spirit of God is so holily sensitive that naturally He withdraws from the irreverent gaze of the uninitiated.

Christ has fully revealed Himself. It was the love and divine compassion of the Son. But the Holy Spirit has not done so. It is His saving faithfulness to meet us only in the secret place of His love.

This causes another difficulty. Because of His unrevealed character the Church has taught and studied the Spirit's work much less than Christ's, and has attained much less clearness in its theological discussion. We might say, since He gave the Word and illuminated the Church, He spoke much more of the Father and the Son than of Himself; not as though it had been selfish to speak more of Himself—for sinful selfishness is inconceivable in regard to Him—but He must reveal the Father and the Son before He could lead us into the more intimate fellowship with Himself.

This is the reason that there is so little preaching on the subject; that text-books on Systematic Theology rarely treat it separately; that Pentecost (the feast of the Holy Spirit) appeals to the churches and animates them much less than Christmas or Easter; that unhappily many ministers, otherwise faithful, advance many erroneous views upon this subject—a fact of which they and the churches seem unconscious.

Hence special discussion of the theme deserves attention.

That it requires great caution and delicate treatment need not be said. It is our prayer that the discussion may evince such great care and caution as is required, and that our Christian readers may receive our feeble efforts with that love which suffereth long.

2

Two Standpoints

By the word of the Lord were the heavens made; and all the host of them by the breath of His mouth—Psalm 33:6.

The work of the Holy Spirit that most concerns us is the *renewing of the elect after the image of God.* And this is not all. It even savors of selfishness and irreverence to make this so prominent, as though it were His only work.

The redeemed are not sanctified without Christ, who is made to them sanctification; hence the work of the Spirit must embrace the Incarnation of the Word and the *work of the Messiah.* But the work of the Messiah involves preparatory working in the Patriarchs and Prophets of Israel, and later activity in the Apostles, that is, the foreshadowing of the Eternal Word in Scripture. Likewise this revelation involves the conditions of man's nature and the historical development of the race; hence the Holy Spirit is concerned in the formation of the human mind and the unfolding of the spirit of humanity. Lastly, man's condition depends on that of the earth; the influences of sun, moon, and stars; the elemental motions; and no less on the actions of spirits, be they angels or demons from other spheres. Wherefore the Spirit's work must touch the entire *host of heaven and earth.*

To avoid a mechanical idea of His work as though it began and ended at random, like piece-work in a factory, it must not be determined nor limited till it extends to all the influences that affect the sanctification of the Church. The Holy Spirit is God, therefore sovereign; hence He cannot depend on these influences, but completely controls them. For this He must be able to operate them; so His work must be honored *in all the host of heaven, in man and in his history, in the preparation of Scripture, in the Incarnation of the Word, in the salvation of the elect.*

But this is not all. The final salvation of the elect is not the last link in the chain of events. The hour that completes their redemption will be the hour of reckoning for all creation. The Biblical revelation of Christ's return is not a mere pageant closing this preliminary dispensation, but the great and notable event, the consummation of all before, the catastrophe whereby *all that is shall receive its due.*

In that great and notable day the elements with commotion and awful change shall be combined into a new heaven and earth, that is, out of these burning elements shall emerge the real beauty and glory of God's original purpose. Then all ill, misery, plague, every thing unholy, every demon, every spirit turned against God shall become truly hellish; that is, everything ungodly shall receive its due, that is, a world in which sin has absolute sway. For what is hell other than a realm in which unholiness works without restraint in body and soul? Then man's personality will recover the unity destroyed by death, and God will grant His redeemed the fruition of that blest hope confessed on earth amid conflict and affliction in the words: "I believe in the resurrection of the body." Then shall Christ triumph over every power of Satan, sin, and death, and thus receive His due as the Christ. Then wheat and tares shall be separated; the mingling shall cease, and the hope of God's people become sight; the martyr shall be in rapture and his executioner in torment. Then, too, shall the veil be drawn from the Jerusalem that is above. The clouds shall be dispelled that kept us from seeing that God was righteous in all His judgments; then the wisdom and glory of all His counsels shall be vindicated both by Satan and his own in the pit, and by Christ and His redeemed in the city of our God, and the Lord be glorious in all His works.

Thus radiating from the sanctification of the redeemed, we see the work of the Spirit embracing in past ages the Incarnation, the preparation of Scripture, the forming of man and the universe; and, extending into the ages, the Lord's return, the final judgment, and that last cataclysm that shall separate heaven from hell forever.

This standpoint precludes our viewing the work of the Spirit from that of the salvation of the redeemed. Our spiritual horizon widens; for the chief thing is not that the elect be fully saved, but *that God be justified in all His works* and glorified through *judgment.* To all who acknowledge that "He that believeth not on the Son shall not see life, but the wrath of God abiding on him," this must be the only true standpoint.

If we subscribe this awful statement, not having lost our way in the labyrinth of a so-called *conditional immortality,* which actually annihilates man, then how can we dream of a state of perfect bliss for the elect as long as the lost ones are being tormented by the worm that dieth not? Is there no more love or compassion in our hearts? Can we fancy ourselves for a single moment enjoying heaven's bliss while the fire is not quenched and no lighted torch is carried into the outer darkness?

To make the bliss of the elect the final end of all things while Satan still roars in the bottomless pit is to annihilate the very thought of such bliss. Love suffers not only when a human being is in pain, but even when an animal is in distress; how much more when an angel gnashes his teeth in torture, and that angel beautiful and glorious as Satan was before his fall. And yet the very mention of Satan unconsciously lifts from our hearts the burden of fellow pain, suffering, and compassion; for we feel immediately that the knowledge of Satan's suffering in the pit does not in the least appeal to our compassion. On the contrary, to believe that Satan exists but *not* in utter misery were a wound to our profound sense of justice.

And this is the point: to conceive of the blessedness of a soul not in absolute union with Christ is unholy madness. No one but Christ is blessed, and no man can be blessed but he who is vitally one with Christ—Christ in him and he in Christ. Equally it is unholy madness to conceive of man or angel lost in hell unless he has identified himself with Satan, having become morally one with him. The conception of a soul in hell not morally one with Satan is the most appalling cruelty from which every noble heart recoils with horror.

Every child of God is furious at Satan. Satan is simply unbearable to him. In his inward man (however unfaithful his nature may be) there is bitter enmity, implacable hatred against Satan. Hence it satisfies our holiest conscience to know that Satan is in the bottomless pit. To encourage a plea for him in the heart were treason against God. Sharp agony may pierce his soul like a dagger for the unspeakable depth of his fall, yet as Satan, author of all that is demoniac and fiendish, who has bruised the heel of the Son of God, he can never move our hearts.

Why? What is the sole, deep reason why in regard to Satan compassion is dead, hatred is right, and love would be blameworthy? Is it not that we never can look upon Satan without remembering that he is the adversary of our God, the mortal enemy of our Christ? Were it not for that we might weep for him. But now our allegiance to God tells us that such weeping would be treason against our King.

Only by measuring the end of things by what belongs to God can we stand right in this matter. We can view the matter of the redeemed and the lost from the right standpoint only when we subordinate both to that which is highest, that is, the glory of God. Measured by Him, we can conceive of the redeemed in a state of bliss, enthroned, yet not in danger of pride; since it was and is and ever shall be by His *sovereign grace* alone. But also measured by Him, we can think of those identified with Satan, joyless and miserable, without once hurting the sense of justice in the heart of the upright; for to be mercifully inclined toward Satan is impossible to him who loves God with love deep and everlasting. And such is the love of the redeemed.

Considered from this far superior standpoint, the work of the Holy Spirit necessarily assumes a different aspect. Now we can no more say that His work is the sanctification of the elect, with all that precedes and follows, but we confess that it is the *vindication of the counsel of God* with all that pertains thereto, from the creation and throughout the ages, unto the coming of the Lord Jesus Christ, and onward throughout eternity, both in heaven and in hell.

The difference between these two viewpoints can easily be appreciated. According to the first, the work of the Holy Spirit is only *subordinate.* Unfortunately man is fallen; hence he is diseased. Since he is impure and unholy, even subject to death itself, the Holy Spirit must purify and sanctify him. This implies, first, that had man not sinned the Holy Spirit would have had no work. Second, that when the work of sanctification is finished, His activity will cease. According to the correct viewpoint, the work of the Spirit is continuous and perpetual, beginning with the creation, continuing throughout eternity, begun even before sin first appeared.

It may be objected that some time ago the author emphatically opposed the idea that Christ would have come into the work even if sin had not entered in; and that now he affirms with equal emphasis that the Holy Spirit would have wrought in the world and in man if the latter had remained sinless.

The answer is very simple. If Christ had not appeared in His capacity of Messiah, He would have had, as the Son, the Second Person in the Godhead, His own divine sphere of action, seeing that all things consist through Him. On the contrary, if the work of the Holy Spirit were confined to the sanctification of the redeemed, He would be absolutely inactive if sin had not entered into the world. And since this would be equal to a denial of His Godhead, it cannot for a moment be tolerated.

By occupying this superior viewpoint, we apply to the work of the Holy Spirit the fundamental principle of the Reformed churches: "That all things must be measured by the glory of God."

3

The Indwelling and Outgoing Works of God

And all the host of them by the breath of His mouth—
Psalm 33:6.

The thorough and clear-headed theologians of the most flourishing periods of the Church used to distinguish between the *indwelling* and *outgoing* works of God.

The same distinction exists to some extent in nature. The lion watching his prey differs widely from the lion resting among his whelps. See the blazing eye, the lifted head, the strained muscles and panting breath. One can see that the crouching lion is laboring intensely. Yet the act is now only in contemplation. The heat and the ferment, the nerve-tension are all within. A terrible deed is about to be done, but it is still under restraint, until he pounces with thundering roar upon his unsuspecting victim, burying his fangs deep into the quivering flesh.

We find the same distinction in finer form among men. When a storm has raged at sea, and the fate of the absent fishing-smacks that are expected to return with the tide is uncertain, a fisherman's awe-stricken wife sits on the brow of the sand-hill watching and waiting in speechless suspense. As she waits, her heart and soul labor in prayer; the nerves are tense, the blood runs fast, and breathing is almost suspended. Yet there is no outward act; only labor within. But on the safe return of the smacks, when she sees her own, her burdened heart finds relief in a cry of joy.

Or, taking examples from the more ordinary walks of life, compare the student, the scholar, the inventor thinking out his new invention, the architect forming his plans, the general studying his opportunities, the sturdy sailor nimbly climbing the mast of his ship, or yonder blacksmith raising the sledge to strike the glowing iron upon the anvil with concentrated muscular force. Judging superficially, one would say the blacksmith and sailor work, but the men of learning are idle. Yet he that looks beneath the surface knows better than this. For if those men perform no apparent manual labor, they work with brain, nerve, and blood; yet since those organs are more delicate than hand or foot, their invisible, indwelling work is much more exhausting. With all their labor the blacksmith and sailor are pictures of health, while the men of mental force, apparently idle among their folios, are pale from exhaustion, their vitality being almost consumed by their intense application.

Applying this distinction without its human limitations to the works of the Lord, we find that the outgoing works of God had their beginning when God created the heavens and the earth; and that before that moment which marks the birth of time, nothing existed but God working within Himself. Hence this twofold operation: The *first,* externally manifest, known to us in the acts of creating, upholding, and directing all things—acts that, compared to those of eternity, seem to have begun but yesterday; for what are thousands of years in the presence of the eternal ages? The *second,* behind and underneath the first—an operation not begun nor ended, but eternal like Himself; deeper, richer, fuller, yet not manifested, hidden within Him, which we therefore designate *indwelling.*

Although these two operations can scarcely be separated—for there never was one manifest *without* which was not first completed *within*—yet the difference is strongly marked and easily recognized. The indwelling works of God are from *eternity,* the outgoing belong to *time.* The former *precede,* the latter *follow.* The foundation of that which becomes visible lies in that which remains *invisible.* The *light* itself is hidden, it is the *radiation* only that appears.

The Scripture, speaking of the indwelling works of God, says: "The counsel of the Lord standeth forever, and the thoughts of His heart to all generations" (Ps. 33:11). Since in God heart and thought have no separate existence, but His undivided Essence thinks, feels, and wills, we learn from this significant passage that the Being of God works in Himself from all eternity. This answers the oft-repeated and foolish question, "What did God do before He created the universe?" which is as unreasoning as to ask what the thinker did before he expressed his thoughts, or the architect before he built the house!

God's indwelling works, which are from everlasting to everlasting, are not insignificant, but surpass His outgoing works in depth and strength as the student's thinking and the sufferer's anguish surpass their strongest utterances in intensity. "Could I but weep," says the afflicted one, "how much more easily could I bear my sorrow!" And what are tears but the outward expression of grief, relieving the pain and strain of the heart? Or think of the child-*bearing* of the mother before delivery. It is said of the decree that it hath *"brought forth"* (Zeph. 2:2), which signifies that the phenomenon is only the result of preparation hidden from the eye, but more real than the production, and without which there would be nothing to bring forth.

Thus the expression of our earlier theologians is justified, and the difference between the indwelling and the outgoing works is patent.

Accordingly the indwelling works of God are the activities of His *Being,* without the distinction of Persons; while His outgoing works admit and to some extent demand this distinction: *e.g.,* the common and well-known distinguishing of the Father's work as that of creation, the Son's as that of redemption, and the Holy Spirit's as that of sanctification relates only to God's outgoing works. While these operations —creation, redemption, and sanctification—are hidden in the thoughts of His heart, His counsel, and His Being, it is Father, Son, and Holy Ghost who creates, Father, Son, and Holy Ghost who redeems, Father, Son, and Holy Ghost who sanctifies, without any division or distinction of activities. The rays of light hidden in the sun are indivisible and indistinguishable until they radiate; so in the Being of God the indwelling working is one and undivided; His personal glories remain invisible until revealed in His outgoing works. A stream is one until it falls over the precipice and divides into many drops. So is the life of God one and undivided while hidden within Himself, but when it is poured out into created things its colors stand revealed. As, therefore, the indwelling works of the Holy Spirit are common to the three Persons of the Godhead, we do not discuss them, but treat only those operations that bear the personal marks of His outgoing works.

But we do not mean to teach that the distinction of the personal attributes of Father, Son, and Holy Ghost did not exist in the divine *Being,* but originated only in His outward *activities.*

The distinction of Father, Son, and Holy Spirit is the divine characteristic of the Eternal Being, His mode of subsistence, His deepest foundation; to think of Him without that distinction would be absurd. Indeed, in the divine and eternal economy of Father, Son, and Holy Spirit, each of the divine Persons lives and loves and lauds according to His own personal characteristics, so that the Father remains Father toward the Son, and the Son remains Son toward the Father, and the Holy Spirit proceeds from both.

It is right to ask how this agrees with the statement made above, that the indwelling works of God belong, without distinction of Persons, to Father, Son, and Holy Ghost, and are therefore the works of the divine Being. The answer is found in the careful distinction of the twofold nature of the indwelling works of God.

Some operations in the divine Being are destined *to be revealed in time;* others will remain *forever unrevealed.* The former concern the creation; the latter, only the relations of Father, Son, and Holy Spirit. Take, for instance, election and eternal generation. Both are indwelling operations of God, but with marked difference. The Father's eternal generation of the Son can never be revealed, but must ever be the mystery of the Godhead; while election belongs as decree to the indwelling works of God, yet is destined in the fullness of time to become manifest in the call of the elect.

Regarding the *permanently* indwelling works of God that do not relate to the creature, but flow from the mutual relation of the Father, the Son, and the Holy Spirit, the distinctive characteristics of the three Persons must be kept in view. But with those that are to become manifest, relating to the creature, this distinction disappears. Here the rule applies that all indwelling works are activities of the divine Being without distinction of Persons. To illustrate: In the home there are two kinds of activities, one flowing from the mutual relation of parents and children, another pertaining to the social life. In the former the distinction between parents and children is never ignored; in the latter, if the relation be normal, neither the father nor the children act alone, *but the family as a whole.* Even so in the holy, mysterious economy of the divine Being, every operation of the Father upon the Son and of both upon the Holy Spirit is distinct, but in every outgoing act it is always the one divine Being, the thoughts of whose heart are for all His creatures. On that account the natural man knows no more than that he has to do with a God.

The Unitarians, denying the Holy Trinity, have never reached anything higher than that which can be seen by the light of the darkened human understanding. We often discover that many baptized with water but *not* with the Holy Spirit speak of the Triune God because others do. For themselves they know only that He is God. This is why the discriminating knowledge of the Triune God cannot illuminate the soul until the light of redemption shines within, and the Day-star arises in man's heart. Our Confession correctly expresses this, saying: "All this we know as well from the testimony of Holy Writ as from their operations, and chiefly by those we feel in ourselves" (art. 9).

4

The Work of the Holy Spirit Distinguished

*And the Spirit of God moved upon the face of the waters—
Genesis 1:2.*

What, in general, is the work of the Holy Spirit as distinguished from that of the Father and of the Son?

Not that every believer needs to know these distinctions in all particulars. The existence of faith does not depend upon intellectual distinctions. The main question is not whether we can distinguish the work of the Father from that of the Son and of the Holy Spirit, but whether we have experienced their gracious operations. The *root* of the matter, not the *name,* decides.

Must we then slightly value a clear understanding of sacred things? Shall we deem it superfluous and call its great matters hair-splitting questions? By no means. The human mind searches every department of life. Scientists deem it an honor to spend their lives in analyzing the minutest plants and insects, describing every particular, naming every member of the dissected organism. Their work is never called "hair-splittings," but is distinguished as "scientific research." And rightly so, for without differentiation there can be no insight, and without insight there can be no thorough acquaintance with the subject. Why, then, call this same desire *unprofitable* when it directs the attention not to the creature, but to the Lord God our Creator?

Can there be any worthier object of mental application than the eternal God? Is it right and proper to insist upon correct discrimination in every other sphere of knowledge, and yet regarding the knowledge of God to be satisfied with generalities and confused views? Has God not invited us to share the intellectual knowledge of His Being? Has He not given us His Word? And does not the Word illumine the mysteries of His Being, His attributes, His perfections, His virtues, and the mode of His subsistence? If we aspired to penetrate into things too high for us, or to unveil the unrevealed, reverence would require us to resist such audacity. But since we aim in godly fear to listen to Scripture, and to receive the proffered knowledge of the deep things of God, there can be no room for objection. We would say rather to those who frown upon such effort: "Ye can discern the face of the sky, but ye cannot discern the face of your Father in heaven."

Hence the question concerning the work of the Holy Spirit as distinguished from that of the Father and of the Son is quite legitimate and necessary.

It is deplorable that many of God's children have confused conceptions in this respect. They cannot distinguish the works of the Father and of the Son and of the Holy Spirit. Even in prayer they use the divine names indiscriminately. Although the Holy Spirit is explicitly called the Comforter, yet they seek comfort mostly from the Father or the Son, unable to say why and what in sense the Holy Spirit is especially called Comforter.

The early Church already felt the need of clear and exact distinctions in this matter; and the great thinkers and Christian philosophers whom God gave to the Church, especially the Eastern Fathers, expended their best powers largely upon this subject. They saw very clearly that unless the Church learned to distinguish the works of the Father, Son, and Holy Ghost, its confession of the Holy Trinity could be but a dead sound. Compelled not by love of subtleties, but by the necessity of the Church, they undertook to study these distinctions. And God let heretics vex His Church so as to arouse the mind by conflict, and to lead it to search God's Word.

So we are not pioneers exploring a new field. The writing of these articles can so impress those alone who are ignorant of the historical treasures of the Church. We propose simply to cause the light, which for so many ages shed its clear and comforting rays upon the Church, to reenter the windows, and thus by deeper knowledge to increase its inward strength.

We begin with the general distinction: That in every work effected by Father, Son, and Holy Ghost in common, the power *to bring forth* proceeds from the Father; the power *to arrange* from the Son; the power *to perfect* from the Holy Spirit.

In 1 Corinthians 8:6, St. Paul teaches that: "There is but one God the Father, *of whom* are all things, and one Lord Jesus Christ *by whom* are all things." Here we have two prepositions: *of* whom and *by* whom. But in Romans 11:38 he adds another: "For of Him and through Him and *to* Him are all things."

The operation here spoken of is threefold: first, that by which all things are originated (*of* Him); second, that by which all things consist (*through* Him); third, that by which all things attain their final destiny (*to* Him). In connection with this clear, apostolic distinction the great teachers of the Church, after the fifth century, used to distinguish the operations of the Persons of the Trinity by saying that the operation whereby all things originated proceeds from the Father; that whereby they received consistency from the Son; and that whereby they were led to their destiny from the Holy Spirit.

These clear thinkers taught that this distinction was in line with that of the Persons. Thus the Father is *father.* He generates the Son. And the Holy Spirit proceeds from the Father and the Son. Hence the peculiar feature of the First Person is evidently that He is the Source and Fountain not only of the material creation, but of its very conception; of all that was and is and ever shall be. The peculiarity of the Second Person lies evidently not in generating, but in being generated. One is a son by being generated. Hence since all things proceed from the Father, nothing can proceed from the *Son.* The source of all things is not in the Son. Yet He adds a work of creation to that which is coming into existence; for the Holy Spirit proceeds also from Him, but not from Him alone, but from the Father and the Son, and that in such a way that the procession of the Son is due to His sameness of essence with the Father.

The Scripture agrees with this in teaching that the Father created all things by the Son, and that without Him was nothing made that was made. For the difference between "created by" and "created from," we refer to Colossians 1:17: "By Him all things consist," that is, by Him they hold together. Hebrews 1:3 is even clearer, saying that the Son upholds all things by the *Word of His power.* This shows that as the essentials of the creature's existence proceed from the Father as Fountain of all, so the forming, putting together, and arranging of its constituents are the proper work of the Son.

If we were reverently to compare God's work to that of man we would say: A king proposes to build a palace. This requires not only material, labor, and plans, but also putting together and arranging of the materials according to the plans. The king furnishes the materials and plans, the builder constructs the palace. Who, then, built it? Neither the king nor the builder alone, but the builder erects it out of the royal treasure.

This expresses the relation between Father and Son in this respect as far as human relations can illustrate the divine. In the construction of the universe two operations appear: first, the *causative,* which produces the materials, forces, and plans; second, the *constructive,* which with these forces forms and orders the materials according to the plan. And as the first proceeds from the Father, so does the second from the Son. The Father is the Royal Source of the necessary materials and powers; and the Son as the Builder constructs all things with them according to the counsel of God. If the Father and the Son existed independently, such cooperation would be impossible. But since the Father generates the Son, and by virtue of that generation the Son contains the entire Being of the Father, there can be no division of *Being,* and only the distinction of *Persons* remains. For the entire wisdom and power whereby the Son gives consistency to all is generated in Him by the Father; while the counsel which designed all is a determination by the Father of that divine wisdom which He as Father generates in the Son. For the Son is forever the effulgence of the Father's glory, and the express image of His Person—Hebrews 1:3.

This does not complete the work of creation. The creature is made not simply to exist, or to adorn some niche in the universe like a statue. Rather was everything created with a purpose and a destiny; and our creation will be complete only when we have become what God designed. Hence Genesis 2:3 says: "God rested from all His work which

He had created *to make it perfect"* (Dutch translation). Thus to lead the creature to its destiny, to cause it to develop according to its nature, to make it perfect, is the proper work of the Holy Spirit.

Second Chapter
The Creation

5

The Principle of Life in the Creature

By His Spirit He hath garnished the heavens; His hand hath formed the crooked serpent—Job 26:13.

We have seen that the work of the Holy Spirit consists in leading all creation *to its destiny,* the final purpose of which is the glory of God. However, God's glory in creation appears in various degrees and ways. An insect and a star, the mildew on the wall and the cedar on Lebanon, a common laborer and a man like Augustine, are all the creatures of God; yet how dissimilar they are, and how varied their ways and degrees of glorifying God.

Let us therefore illustrate the statement that the glory of God is the ultimate end of every creature. Comparing the glory of God to that of an earthly king, it is evident that nothing can be indifferent to that glory. The building material of his palace, its furniture, even the pavement before its gate, either enhance or diminish the royal splendor. Much more, however, is the king honored by the persons of his household, each in his degree, from the master of ceremonies to his prime minister. Yet his highest glory is his family of sons and daughters, begotten of his own blood, trained by his wisdom, animated by his ideals, one with him in the plans, purposed, and spirit of his life. Applying this in all reverence to the court of the King of heaven, it is evident that while every flower and star enhance His glory, the lives of angels and men are of much greater significance to His Kingdom; and again, while among the latter they are most closely related to His glory whom He has placed in positions of authority, nearest of all are the children begotten by His Spirit, and admitted to the secret of His pavilion. We conclude, then, that God's glory is reflected most in His children; and since no man can be His child unless he is begotten of Him, we confess that His glory is most apparent in His elect or in His Church.

His glory is not, however, confined to these; for they are related to the whole race, and live among all nations and peoples with whom they share the common lot. We neither may nor can separate their spiritual life from their national, social, and domestic life. And since all differences of national, social, and domestic life are caused by climate and atmosphere, meat and drink, rain and drought, plant and insect—in a word, by the whole economy of this material world, including comet and meteor, it is evident that all these affect the outcome of things and are related to the glory of God. Hence as connected with the task of leading creation to its destiny, the whole universe confronts the mind as a mighty unit organically related to the Church as the shell to the kernel.

In the accomplishment of this task the question arises in what way the *fairest, noblest,* and *holiest* part of the creation is to attain its destiny; for to this all other parts must be made subservient.

Hence the question, How are the multitude of the elect to attain their final perfection? The answer to this will indicate what is the Holy Spirit's action upon all other creatures.

The answer cannot be doubtful. God's children can never accomplish their glorious end unless God dwell in them as in His temple. It is the love of God that constrains Him to live in His children, by their love for Him to love Himself, and to see the reflection of His glory in the consciousness of His own handiwork. This glorious purpose will be realized only when the elect know as they are known, behold their God face to face, and enjoy the felicity of closest communion with the Lord.

Since all this can be wrought in them only by His indwelling in their hearts, and since it is the Third Person in the Holy Trinity who enters the spirits of men and of angels, it is evident that God's highest purposes are realized when the Holy Spirit makes man's heart His dwelling-place. Who or what ever we are by education or position, we cannot attain our highest destiny unless the Holy Spirit dwell in us and operate upon the inward organism of our being.

If this His highest work had no bearing upon anything else, we might say that it consists merely in finishing the perfection of the creature. But this is not so. Every believer knows that there is a most intimate connection between his life *before* and *after* conversion; not as though the former determined the latter, but in such a way that the life in sin and the life in the beauty of holiness are both *conditioned* by the same *character* and *disposition,* by similar *circumstances* and *influences.* Wherefore, to bring about our final perfection the Holy Spirit must influence the previous development, the formation of character, and the disposition of the whole person. And this operation, although less marked in the natural life, must also be traced. However, since our personal life is only a manifestation of human life in general, it follows that the Holy Spirit must have been active also in the creation of man, although in a less marked degree. And finally, as the disposition of man as such is connected with the host of heaven and earth, His work must touch the formation of this also, though to a much less extent. Hence the Spirit's work reaches as far as the influences that affect man in the attaining of his destiny or in the failure to attain it. And the measure of the influence is the degree in which they affect his perfecting. In the departure of the redeemed soul everyone acknowledges a work of the Holy Spirit, but who can trace His work in the star-movements? Yet the Scripture teaches not only that we are born again by the power of the Spirit of God, but that "by the Word of the Lord were the heavens made, and all the host of them *by the breath* [Spirit] *of His mouth.*"

Wherefore the Spirit's work leading the creature to its destiny includes an influence upon all creation from the beginning. And, if sin had not come in, we might say that this work is done in *three* successive steps: first, *impregnating* inanimate matter; second, *animating* the rational soul; third, *taking up His abode* in the elect child of God.

But *sin* entered in, that is, a power appeared to keep man and nature *from their destiny.* Hence the Holy Spirit must *antagonize* sin; His calling is to annihilate it, and despite its opposition to cause the elect children of God and the entire creation to reach their end. Redemption is therefore not a *new* work *added* to that of the Holy Spirit, but it is *identical* with it. He undertook to bring all things to their destiny either *without* the disturbance of sin or *in spite of it;* first, by saving the elect, and then by restoring all things in heaven and on earth at the return of the Lord Jesus Christ.

Things incidental to this, such as the inspiration of *Scripture,* the preparation of the *Body of Christ,* the extraordinary *ministration of grace to the Church,* are only connecting-links, connecting the beginning with its own predetermined end; that in spite of sin's disturbance the destiny of the universe to glorify God might be secured.

Condensing all into one statement, we might say: Sin having once entered, a factor which *must* be taken into account, the Holy Spirit's work shines most gloriously in gathering and saving the elect; prior to which are His operations in the work of *redemption* and in the economy of the *natural* life. The same Spirit who in the beginning moved upon the waters has in the dispensation of grace given us the *Holy Scripture,* the *Person of Christ,* and the Christian *Church;* and it is He who, in connection with the original creation and by these means of grace, now regenerates and sanctifies us as the children of God.

Regarding these mighty and comprehensive operations, it is of first importance to keep in view the fact that in each He effects only that which is *invisible* and *imperceptible.* This marks all the Holy Spirit's operations. Behind the visible world lies one invisible and spiritual, with outer courts and inner recesses; and underneath the latter are the unfathomable depths of the soul, which the Holy Spirit chooses as the scene of His labors—His temple wherein He sets up His altar.

Christ's redemptive work also has visible and invisible parts. Reconciliation in His blood was visible. The sanctification of His Body and the adorning of His human nature with manifold graces were invisible. Whenever this hidden and inward work is specified the Scripture always connects it with the Holy Spirit. Gabriel says to Mary: "The Holy Ghost shall come upon thee." It is said of Christ: "That He had the Spirit without measure."

We observe also in the host of heaven a life material, outward, tangible which in thought we never associate with the Holy Spirit. But, however weak and impalpable, the visible and tangible has an invisible background. How intangible are the forces of nature, how full of majesty the forces of magnetism! But life underlies all. Even through the apparently dead trunk sighs an imperceptible breath. From the unfathomable depths of all an inward, hidden principle works upward and outward. It shows in nature, much more in man and angel. And what is this quickening and animating principle but the Holy Spirit? "Thou sendest forth Thy Spirit, they are created; Thou takest away Thy breath, they die."

This inward, invisible something is God's direct touch. There is in us and in every creature a point where the living God touches us to uphold us; for nothing exists without being *upheld* by Almighty God from moment to moment. In the elect this point is their spiritual life; in the rational creature his rational consciousness; and in all creatures, whether rational or not, their life-principle. And as the Holy Spirit is the Person in the Holy Trinity whose office it is to effect this direct touch fellowship with the creature in his inmost being, it is He who *dwells* in the hearts of the elect; who *animates* every rational being; who sustains the *principle of life* in every creature.

6

The Host of Heaven and of Earth

The Spirit of God hath made me—Job 33:4.

Understanding somewhat the characteristic note of the work of the Holy Spirit, let us see what this work was and is and shall be. The Father brings forth, the Son disposes and arranges, the Holy Spirit perfects. There is one God and Father of whom are all things, and one Lord Jesus Christ through whom are all things, but what does the Scripture say of the special work the Holy Spirit did in creation and is still doing?

For the sake of order we examine first the account of the creation. God says in Genesis 1:2: "The earth was without form and void, and darkness was upon the face of the deep. And the Spirit of God moved upon the waters." See also Job 26:13: "By His Spirit He hath garnished the heavens; His hand hath formed the crooked serpent [the constellation of the Dragon, or, according to others, the Milky Way]." And also Job 33:4: "The Spirit of God hath made me; and the breath of the Almighty hath given me life." And again Psalm 33:6: "By the Word of the Lord were the heavens made, and all the host of them by the breath of His mouth." So also Psalm 104:30: "Thou sendest forth Thy Spirit, they are created, and Thou renewest the face of the earth." And with different import, in Isaiah 40:13: "Who hath directed the Spirit of the Lord [in creation], or being His counselor hath taught Him?"

These statements show that the Holy Spirit did a work of His own in creation. They show, too, that His activities are closely connected with those of the Father and the Son. Psalm 33:6 presents them as almost identical. The first clause reads: "By the Word of the Lord were the heavens made"; the second: "And all the host of them by the breath [Spirit] of His mouth." It is well known that in Hebrew poetry parallel clauses express the same thought in different ways; so that from this passage it appears that the work of the *Word* and that of the *Spirit* are the same, the latter adding only that which is peculiarly His own.

It should be noticed that hardly any of these passages mention the Holy Spirit by *His own name.* It is not the *Holy* Spirit, but the "Spirit of His mouth," "His Spirit," "the Spirit of the Lord." On account of this, many hold that these passages do not refer to the Holy Spirit as the Third Person in the Holy Trinity, but speak of God as One, without personal distinction; and that the representation of God as creating anything by His hand, fingers, word, breath, or Spirit is merely a human way of speaking, signifying only that God was thus engaged.

The Church has always opposed this interpretation, and rightly so, on the ground that even the Old Testament, not merely in a few places but throughout its entire economy, bears undoubted testimony to the three divine Persons, coequal yet of one essence. It is true that this too has been denied, but by a wrong interpretation. And to the reply, "But our interpretation is as good as yours," we answer that Jesus and the apostles are our authorities; the Church received its confession from their lips.

Secondly, we deny that "His Spirit" does not refer to the Holy Ghost, for the reason that in the New Testament similar expressions occur that undoubtedly do refer to Him, for example, God hath sent forth the Spirit of His Son" (Gal. 4:6); "Whom the Lord shall consume by the Spirit of His mouth" (2 Thess. 2:8); etc.

Thirdly, judging from the following passages—"By the *Word* of the Lord were the heavens made" (Ps. 33:6); "And God *said,* Let there be light" (Gen. 1:3); and "All things were made by Him, and without Him was not anything made that was made" (John 1:3)—there can be no doubt that Psalm 33:6 refers to the Second Person in the Godhead. Hence also the second clause of the same verse, "And all their host by the Spirit of His mouth," must refer to the Third Person.

Finally, to speak of a Spirit of God that is not the Holy Spirit is to transfer to the Holy Scripture a purely Western and human idea. We *as men* often speak of a wrong spirit which controls a nation, an army, or a school, meaning a certain tendency, inclination, or persuasion—a spirit that proceeds from a man *distinct* from his person and being. But this may not and cannot apply to God. Speaking of Christ in His humiliation, one may rightly say, "To have the mind of Christ," or "to have the spirit of Jesus," which indicates His disposition. But to distinguish the divine *Being* from a *spirit* of that Being is to conceive of the Godhead in a human way. The divine consciousness differs wholly from the human. While in us there is a difference between our persons and our consciousness, with reference to God such distinctions disappear, and the distinction of Father, Son, and Holy Spirit takes their place.

Even in those passages where "the breath of His mouth" is added to explain "His Spirit," the same interpretation must be maintained. For all languages show that our breathing, even as the "breathing of the elements" in the wind which blows before God's face, corresponds to the being of spirit. Nearly all express the ideas of spirit, breath, and wind by cognate terms. Blowing or breathing is in all the Scripture the symbol of spirit-communication. Jesus breathed on them and said: "Receive ye the Holy Ghost" (John 20:22). Thus the breath of His mouth must signify the Holy Spirit.

The ancient interpretation of the Scripture should not be hastily abandoned. Accept the dictum of modern theology that the distinction of the three divine Persons is not found in the Old Testament, and allusions to the work of the Holy Spirit in Genesis, Job, Psalms, or Isaiah are out of the question. Consequently nothing is more natural for the supporters of this modern theology than to deny the Holy Spirit altogether in the passages referred to.

But if from inward conviction we still confess that the distinction of Father, Son, and Holy Spirit is clearly seen in the Old Testament, then let us examine these passages concerning the Spirit of the Lord with discrimination, and gratefully maintain the traditional interpretation, which finds at least in many of these statements references to the work of the Holy Spirit.

These passages show that His peculiar work in creation was: first, hovering over chaos; second, creation of the host of heaven and of earth; third, establishing the heavens; fourth, animating the brute creation, and calling man into existence; and last, the operation whereby every creature is made to exist according to God's counsel concerning it.

Hence the material forces of the universe do not proceed from the Holy Spirit, nor did He deposit in matter the dormant seeds and germs of life. His special task begins only *after* the creation of matter with the germs of life in it.

The Hebrew text shows that the work of the Holy Spirit moving upon the face of the waters was similar to that of the parent bird which with outspread wings hovers over its young to cherish and cover them. The figure implies that not only the earth existed, but also the germs of life within it; and that the Holy Spirit impregnating these germs caused the life to come forth in order to lead it to its destiny.

Not by the Holy Spirit, but by the *Word* were the heavens created. And when the created heavens were to receive their host, then only did the moment come for the exercise of the Holy Spirit's peculiar functions. What "the host of heaven" means is not easily decided. It may refer to sun, moon, and stars, or to the host of angels. Perhaps the passage means not the *creation* of the heavenly bodies, but their reception of heavenly glory and celestial fire. But Psalm 33:6 refers certainly not to the creation of the matter of which the heavenly host are composed, but to the production of their glory.

Genesis 1:2 reveals first the creation of matter and its germs, then their quickening; so Psalm 33:6 teaches first the preparation of the being and nature of the heavens, then the bringing forth of their host by the Holy Spirit. Job 26:13 leads to a similar conclusion. Here is the same distinction between the heavens and their ordaining, the latter being represented as the special work of the Holy Spirit. This ordaining is the same as the brooding in Genesis 1:2, by which the formless took form, the hidden life emerged, and the things created were led to their destiny. Psalm 104:30 and Job 33:4 illustrate the work of the Holy Spirit in creation still more clearly. Job informs us that the Holy Spirit had a special part in the making of man; and Psalm 104 that He performed a similar work in the creation of the animals, of the fowls and the fishes; for the two preceding verses imply that verse 27—"Thou sendest forth Thy Spirit, they are created"—refers not to man, but to the monsters that play in the deep.

Grant that the matter out of which God made man was already present in the dust of the earth, that the type of his body was largely present in the animal, and that the idea of man and the image after which he was to be created existed already; yet from Job 33:4 it is evident that he did not come to be without a special work of the Holy Spirit. So Psalm 104:30 proves that, although the matter existed out of which whale and unicorn were to be made, and the plan or model was in the divine counsel, yet a special act of the Holy Spirit was needed to cause them to be. This is still plainer in view of the fact that neither passage refers to the *first* creation, but to a man and animals formed *later.* For Job speaks not of Adam and Eve, but of himself. He says: "The spirit of God hath made *me,* and the breath of the Almighty hath given me life." In Psalm 104 David means not the monsters of the deep created in the beginning, but those that were walking the paths of the sea while he was singing this psalm. If, therefore, the bodies of existing man and of mammals are not immediate creations, but are taken from the flesh and blood, the nature and kind of existent beings, then it is more evident that the hovering of the Holy Spirit over the unformed is a present act; and that therefore His creative work was to bring out the life already hidden in chaos, that is, in the germs of life.

This agrees with what was said at first of the general character of His work. "To lead to its destiny" is to bring forth the hidden life, to cause the hidden beauty to reveal itself, to rouse into activity the slumbering energies.

Only let us not represent it as a work performed in successive stages —first by the Father, whose finished work was taken up by the Son, after which the Holy Spirit completed the work thus prepared. Such representations are unworthy of God. There is *distribution,* no *division,* in the divine activities; wherefore Isaiah declares that the Spirit of the Lord, that is, the Holy Spirit, throughout the entire work of creation, from the beginning—yea, from *before* the beginning—directed all that was to come.

7

The Creaturely Man

The Spirit of God hath made me, and the breath of the Almighty hath given me life—Job 33:4.

The Eternal and Ever-blessed God comes into vital touch with the creature by an act proceeding not from the Father nor from the Son, but from the Holy Spirit.

Translated by sovereign grace from death unto life, God's children are conscious of this divine fellowship; they know that it consists not in inward agreement of disposition or inclination, but in the mysterious touch of God upon their spiritual being. But they also know that neither the Father nor the Son, but the Holy Spirit, has made their hearts His temple. It is true Christ comes to us through the Holy Spirit, and through the Son we have fellowship with the Father, according to His word, "I and the Father will come unto you, and make Our abode with you"; yet every intelligent Bible student knows that it is more especially the Holy Spirit who enters into his person and touches his innermost being.

That the Son incarnate came into closer contact with us proves nothing to the contrary. Christ never entered into a human *person.* He took upon Himself our human *nature,* with which He united Himself much more closely than the Holy Spirit does, but He did not touch the *inward man* and his hidden *personality.* On the contrary, He said that it was expedient for the disciples that He should go away; "for if I go not away, the Comforter will not come unto you, but if I depart I will send Him unto you." Moreover, the Incarnation was not accomplished without the Holy Spirit, who overshadowed Mary; and the blessings that Christ imparted to all around Him were largely owing to the gift of the Holy Spirit, which was given Him without measure.

Hence the principal thought remains intact: When God comes into direct contact with the creature it is the work of the Holy Spirit to effect such contact. In the visible world this action consists in the kindling and fanning of the spark of life; hence it is quite natural and in full harmony with the general tenor of the teaching of Scripture that the Spirit of God moves upon the face of the waters, that He brings forth the host of heaven and earth, ordered, animated, and resplendent.

Besides this visible creation there is also an invisible, which, so far as our world is concerned, concentrates itself *in the heart of man;* hence, in the second place, we must see how far the work of the Holy Spirit may be traced in man's creation.

Of the animal world we do not speak. Not as though the Holy Spirit had nothing to do with their creation. From Psalm 104:30 we have proven the contrary. Moreover, no one can deny the admirable traits of cunning, love, fidelity, and thankfulness in many of the animals. Not that we would be foolish on that ground to call the dog *half human;* for these higher animal properties are evidently but instinctive preformations, sketches of the Holy Spirit, carried to their proper destiny in man alone. And yet, however striking these traits may be, it is not a *person* that meets us in the animal. The animal proceeds from the world of matter, and returns to it; in *man* alone appears that which is new, invisible, and spiritual, justifying us in looking for a special work of the Holy Spirit in *his* creation.

Of himself, that is, of a *man,* Job declares: "The Spirit of God hath made me, and the breath of the Almighty hath given me life." The Spirit of God hath made *me.* That which I am as a *human personality* is the work of the Holy Spirit. To Him I owe the human and personal that constitute me the being that I am. He adds: "The breath of the Almighty hath given me life"; which evidently echoes the words: "The Lord God breathed into His nostrils the breath of life."

Like Job, we ought to feel and to acknowledge that in Adam you and I are created; when God created Adam He created *us;* in Adam's nature He called forth the nature wherein we now live. Genesis 1 and 2 is not the record of *aliens,* but of *ourselves*—concerning the flesh and blood which we carry with us, the human nature in which we sit down to read the Word of God.

He that reads his Bible without this personal application reads amiss. It leaves him cold and indifferent. It may charm him in the days of his childhood, when one is fond of tales and stories, but has no hold of him in the days of conflict, when he meets the stern facts and realities of life. But if we accustom ourselves to see in this record the history of our own flesh and blood, of our own human nature and life, and acknowledge that by human generation we spring from Adam, and therefore were in Adam when he was created—then we shall also know that when God formed Adam out of the dust He also formed us; that we also were in Paradise; that Adam's fall was also ours. In a word, the first page of Genesis relates the history not of an alien, but of our own real selves. The breath of the Almighty gave *us* life, when the Lord formed man of the dust, and breathed into his nostrils and made him a living soul. The root of our life lies in our parents, but through and beyond them the tender fiber of that root goes back through the long line of generations, and received its earliest beginning when Adam first breathed God's pure air in Paradise.

And yet, though in Paradise we received the first inception of our being, there is also a *second* beginning of our life, viz., when from the race, by conception and birth, each of us was called into being *individually.* And of this also Job testifies: "The Spirit of the Lord hath given me life."

And again, in the life of sinful man there comes a *third* beginning, when it pleases God to convert the wicked; and of this also the soul testifies within us: "The Spirit of the Lord hath given me life."

Leaving this new birth out of the question, the testimony of Job shows us that he was conscious of the fact that he owed his existence as a man, as a person, as an ego, hence his creation *in Adam* as well as his *personal being,* to God.

And what does the Scripture teach us concerning the creation of man? This: that the dust of the ground out of which Adam was formed was so wrought upon that it became a living soul, which indicates the *human being.* The result was not merely a moving, creeping, eating, drinking, and sleeping creature, but a *living soul* that came into existence at the moment when the breath of life was breathed into the dust. It was not first the dust, and then human life within the dust, and after that the soul with all its higher faculties in that human life; nay, as soon as life went forth into Adam, he was a *man,* and all his precious gifts were *natural* endowments.

Sinful man being born from above receives gifts that are *above* nature. For this reason the Holy Spirit merely *dwells* in the quickened sinner. But in heaven this will not be so; for in death the human nature is so completely changed that the impulse to sin disappears entirely; wherefore in heaven the Holy Spirit will work in the human *nature itself* forever and ever. In the present state of humiliation the nature of the regenerate is still the Adam-nature. The great mystery of the work of the Holy Spirit in him is this: that *in* and *by* that *broken* and *corrupt nature* He works the *holy works of God.* It is as light shining through our window-panes, but in no wise identical with the glass.

In Paradise, however, man's nature was whole, intact; everything about him was holy. We must avoid the dangerous error that the newly created man had an *inferior* degree of holiness. God made man *upright,* with nothing crooked in or about him. All his inclinations and powers with all their workings were pure and holy. God delighted in Adam, saw that he was good, surely nothing more can be desired. In this respect Adam differed from the child of God by grace in *not* having eternal life; he was to attain this as the reward for holy works. On the other hand, Abraham, the father of the faithful, begins with eternal life, from which holy works were to proceed.

Hence a perfect contrast. Adam must attain eternal life by works. Abraham has eternal life through which he obtains holy works. Hence for Adam there can be no indwelling of the Holy Spirit. There was no antagonism between him and the Spirit. So the Spirit could *pervade* him, not merely *dwell* in him. The nature of sinful man repels the Holy Spirit, but Adam's nature attracted Him, freely received Him, and let Him inspire his being.

Our faculties and inclinations are impaired, our powers are enervated, the passions of our hearts corrupt; hence the Holy Spirit must come to us from *without.* But since Adam's faculties were all intact, and the whole expression of his inward life undisturbed, therefore could the Holy Spirit work through the *common* powers and operations of his *nature.* To Adam spiritual things were not a *super*natural, but a natural good—except eternal life, which he must earn by fulfilling the law. Scripture expresses this unity between Adam's natural life and spiritual powers by identifying the two expressions—"To breathe into the breath of life," and "to become a living soul."

Other passages show that this divine "inbreathing" indicates especially the Spirit's work. Jesus breathed upon His disciples and said: "Receive ye the Holy Ghost." He compares the Holy Spirit to the wind. In both the Biblical languages, Hebrew and Greek, the word spirit means wind, breathing or blowing. And as the Church confesses that the Son is eternally generated by the Father, so it confesses that the Holy Spirit proceedeth from the Father and the Son as by *breathing.* Hence we conclude that the passage, "And breathed into his nostrils the breath of life"—in connection with, "The Spirit of God moved on the face of the waters," and the word of Job, "The Spirit of God hath given me life"—points to a special work of the Holy Spirit.

Before God breathed the breath of life in the lifeless dust, there was a conference in the economy of the divine Being: "Let Us make man in Our image, after Our likeness." This shows—

First, that each divine Person had a distinct work in the creation of man—"Let *Us* make man." Before this the singular is used of God—"He spake," "He saw," but now the plural is used, "Let Us make man," which implies that, here specially and more clearly than in any preceding passage, the activities of the Persons are to be distinguished.

Secondly, that man was not created *empty,* afterward to be endowed with higher spiritual faculties and powers, but that the very act of creation made him after God's image, without any subsequent addition to his being. For we read: "Let Us *create* man in Our *image* and after Our *likeness.*" This assures us that by *immediate* creation man received the impress of the divine image; that in the creation the divine Persons each performed a distinct work; and, lastly, that man's creation with reference to his higher destiny was effected by a going forth of the breath of God.

This is the basis of our statement that the Spirit's creative work was making all man's powers and gifts instruments for His own use, connecting them vitally and immediately with the powers of God. This agrees with Biblical teachings regarding the Holy Spirit's regenerating work, which also, though differently, brings the power and holiness of God in immediate contact with human powers.

We deny, therefore, the frequent assertion of ethical theologians, that the Holy Spirit created the *personality* of man, since this opposes the entire economy of Scripture. For what is our personality but the realization of God's plan concerning us? Such as God from eternity has thought each of us, as distinct from other men, with our own stamp, life-history, calling, and destiny—as such each must develop and show himself to become a person. Thus alone each obtains character; anything else so called is pride and arbitrariness.

If our personality result directly from God's plan, then it and what we have in common with all other creatures cannot be from the Holy Spirit, but from the Father; like all other things, it receives its disposition from the Son; and the Holy Spirit acts upon it as upon every other creature, by kindling the spark, imparting the glow of life.

8

Gifts and Talents

And the Spirit of the Lord came upon him—Judges 3:10.

We now consider the Holy Spirit's work in bestowing gifts, talents, and abilities upon artisans and professional men. Scripture declares that the special animation and qualification of persons for work assigned to them by God proceed from the Holy Spirit.

The construction of the tabernacle required capable workmen, skillful carpenters, goldsmiths, and silversmiths, and masters in the arts of weaving and embroidering. Who will furnish Moses with them? The Holy Spirit. For we read in Exodus 31:2, 3: "I have called by name Bezaleel, the son of Uri, . . . and I have filled him with the Spirit of God, in wisdom, and in understanding, and in knowledge, and in all manner of workmanship, to devise cunning works, to work in gold, and in silver, and in brass, and in cutting of stones, to set them, and in carving of timber, to work in all manner of workmanship." Verse 6 shows that this activity of the Holy Spirit included others: "In the hearts of all that are wisehearted I have put wisdom, that they may make all that I have commanded them." And to give clearest light on this subject, Scripture says also: "Then hath He filled with wisdom of heart, to work all manner of work of the engraver and of the cunning workman, and of the embroiderer in blue and in purple and in scarlet and in fine linen of the weaver, even of them that do any work and of these that devise cunning work."

The Spirit's working shows not only in ordinary skilled labor, but also in the higher spheres of human knowledge and mental activity; for military genius, legal acumen, statesmanship, and power to inspire the masses with enthusiasm are equally ascribed to it. This is generally expressed in the words, "And the Spirit of the Lord came upon" such a hero, judge, statesman, or tribune of the people, especially in the days of the Judges, when it is said of Joshua, Othniel, Barak, Gideon, Samson, Samuel, and others that the Spirit of the Lord came upon them. Also of Zerubbabel rebuilding the temple, it is said: "Not by might nor by power, but by My Spirit, saith the Lord." Even of the heathen king, Cyrus, we read that Jehovah had called him to His work and anointed him with the Spirit of the Lord—Isaiah 45.

This last instance introduces another aspect of the case, viz., the operation of the Holy Spirit in qualifying men for *official functions.* For although this operation upon and through the office receives its fullest significance only in the dispensation of grace, yet the case of Cyrus shows that the Holy Spirit has originally a work to perform in this respect which is not only a result of grace, but belongs essentially to the nature of the work, even though it is obvious only in the history of God's special dealings with His own people.

It is especially noticeable in the struggle between Saul and David. There is no reason to consider Saul one of God's elect. After his anointing the Holy Spirit comes upon him, abides with him, and works upon him as long as he remains the Lord's chosen king over His people. But as soon as by willful disobedience he forfeits that favor, the Holy Spirit departs from him and an evil spirit from the Lord troubles him. Evidently this work of the Holy Spirit has nothing to do with regeneration. For a time it may operate upon a man and then forever depart from him; while the Spirit's saving operation, even though suspended for a time, can never be wholly lost. David's touching prayer, "Take not Thy Holy Spirit from me," must therefore refer to gifts qualifying him for the kingly office. David had the terrible example of Saul before him. He had seen what becomes of a man whom the Holy Spirit leaves to himself, and his heart trembled at the possibility of an evil spirit coming upon him, and an end as sad as Saul's. Like Judas, Saul dies a suicide.

From the whole Scripture teaching we therefore conclude that the Holy Spirit has a work in connection with mechanical arts and official functions—in every special talent whereby some men excel in such art or office. This teaching is not simply that such gifts and talents are not of man but from God like all other blessings, but that they are not the work of the Father, nor of the Son, but of the Holy Spirit.

The distinction discovered in creation may be observed here: gifts and talents come from the Father; are disposed for each personality by the Son; and kindled in each by the Holy Spirit as by a spark from above.

Let us distinguish *art itself, personal talent to practice it,* and the *vocation thereto.*

Art is not man's invention, but God's creation. In all nations and ages men have pursued the arts of weaving, embroidering, skillful dressmaking, casting and chasing noble metals, cutting and polishing diamonds, molding iron and brass; and in all these countries and ages, without knowing of each other's efforts, have applied the same arts to all these materials. Of course there is a difference. Oriental work bears a stamp quite different from that of the West. Even French and German work differ. But under the differences, the endeavor, the art applied, the material, the ideal pursued are the same. So, too, art did not attain perfection all at once; among the nations, forms at first crude and awkward gradually developed into forms chaste, refined, and beautiful. Successive generations improved upon previous achievements, until among the various nations comparative perfection of art and skill was attained. Hence art is not the result of man's thought and purpose, but God has placed in various materials certain possibilities of workmanship, and by applying this workmanship man must make out of each what there is in it, and not whatever he chooses.

Two things must cooperate to effect this. In the creation of gold, silver, wood, iron, God must have placed in them certain possibilities, and have created inventive power in man's mind, perseverance in his will, strength in his muscle, accurate vision in his eye, delicacy of touch and action in his fingers, thus qualifying him to evolve what is latent in the materials. Sin this labor has the same nature among all nations, the perpetual progress of the same great work being accomplished according to the same majestic plan, through successive generations, all artistic skill and executive ability must be wrought in man by a higher power and according to a higher command. Viewing the treasures of an industrial exposition in the light of the revealed Word, we shall see in their gradual development and genetic unity the downfall of human pride, and exclaim: "What is all this art and skill but the manifestation of the possibilities which God has placed in these materials, and of the powers of mind and eye and finger which He has given the children of men!"

Consider, now, *personal talent* as utterly distinct from *art.*

The goldsmith in his craft and the judge in his office enter upon a work of God. Each labors in his divine vocation, and all the skill and judgment that he may develop therein come from the treasures of the Lord.

Still, workman differs from workman, general from general. The one copies the product of the generation before him and bequeaths it without increasing the artistic skill. He began as an apprentice, and imparts this skill to other apprentices, but the artistic proficiency is the same. The other manifests something akin to genius. He quickly surpasses his master; sees, touches, discovers something new. In his hand art is enriched. It is given him to transfer from the treasures of divine artistic skill new beauties into human skill.

So also of men in office and profession. Thousands of officers trained in our military schools become good teachers of the science of tactics as practiced heretofore, but add nothing to it; while among these thousands there may be two or three possessed of military genius who in the event of war will astonish the world by their brilliant exploits.

This talent, this individual genius so intimately connected with man's personality, is a *gift.* No power in the world can create it in the man that possesses it not. The child is born with or without it; if without it, no education nor severity—not even ambition—can call it forth. But as the gift of grace is freely bestowed by the sovereign God, so is also the gift of genius. When the people pray, let them not forget to ask the Lord to raise up among them men of talent, heroes of art and of office.

When in 1870 Germany had victory only, and France defeat only, it was God's sovereignty that gave the former talented generals, and in displeasure denied them to the latter.

Consider the *vocation.* Official and mechanical men have a high call. All have not the same ability. One is adapted for the sea, another for the plow. One is a bungler in the foundry, but a master at woodcarving, while another is the reverse. This depends upon the personality, nature, and inclination. And since the Holy Spirit lights the personality, He also determines every man's calling to trade or profession. The same applies to the life of nations. The French excel in taste as well as in artistic workmanship; while the English seem created for the sea, our masters in all the markets of the world. The Holy Spirit even bestows artistic skill and talent upon a nation at one time and withdraws it at another. Three centuries ago Holland surpassed all Europe in weaving, making porcelain, printing, painting, and engraving. But how great the subsequent decline in this respect—although now progress again appears.

What we find in Israel is related to this. This very thirst and capacity for knowledge had caused man to fall. The first impetus was given to artistic skill among Cain's descendants; the Jubals and the Jabals and the Tubal-Cains were the first artists. And yet this whole development, although feeding upon the treasures of God, departed more and more from Him, while His own people utterly lacked it. In the days of Samuel there was no smith found in all the land of Canaan. Hence the Spirit's coming upon Bezaleel and Aholiab, upon Othniel and Samson, upon Saul and David, signifies something more than a mere imparting of artistic skill and talent; namely, the restoration of what sin had corrupted and defiled. And thus the illumination of a Bezaleel links the Holy Spirit's work in the material creation and that in the dispensation of grace.

Third Chapter
Re-Creation

9

Creation and Re-Creation

Behold I will pour out My Spirit unto you—Proverbs 1:23.

We approach the special work of the Holy Spirit in Re-creation. We have seen that the Holy Spirit had a part in the creation *of all things,* particularly in creating *man,* and most particularly in endowing him with *gifts and talents;* also that His creative work affects the upholding of "things," of "man," and of "talents," through the providence of God; and that in this double series of threefold activity the Spirit's work is intimately connected with that of the Father and that of the Son, so that every thing, every man, every talent springs from the Father, is given disposition in their respective natures and being through the Son, and receives the spark of life by the Holy Spirit.

The old church hymn, "Veni, Creator Spiritus," and the ancient confession of the Holy Spirit as the "Vivificans" agree with this perfectly. For the latter signifies that Person in the Trinity who imparts the spark of life; and the former means, "Seeing that the things which are to live and shall live are ready, come Holy Spirit and quicken them."

There is always the same deep thought: the Father remains outside of the creature; the Son touches him outwardly; by the Holy Spirit the divine life touches him directly in his inward being.

However, let us not be understood to say that God comes into contact with the creature only in the regeneration of His children, which would be untrue. To the Gentiles at Athens, St. Paul says: "In Him we live and move and have our being." And again: "For of His offspring we are." To say nothing of plant or animal, there is on earth no life, energy, law, atom, or element but the Almighty and Omnipresent God quickens and supports that life from moment to moment, causes that energy to work, and enforces that law. Suppose that for an instant God should cease to sustain and animate this life, these forces, and that law; in that same instant they would cease to be. The energy that proceeds from God must therefore touch the creature in the very center of its being, whence, its whole existence must spring. Hence there is no sun, moon, nor star, no material, plant, or animal, and, in much higher sense, no man, skill, gift, or talent unless God touch and support them all.

It is this act of coming into immediate contact with every creature, animate or inanimate, organic or inorganic, rational or irrational, that, according to the profound conception of the Word of God, is performed not by the Father, nor by the Son, but by the Holy Spirit.

And this puts the work of the Holy Spirit in a light quite different from that in which for many years the Church has looked upon it. The general impression is that His work refers to the life of grace only, and is confined to regeneration and sanctification. This is due more or less to the well-known division of the Apostolic Creed by the Heidelberg Catechism, question 29, "How are these articles divided?" which is answered: "Into three parts—of God the Father and our creation, of God the Son and our redemption, and of God the Holy Spirit and our sanctification." And this, too, although Ursinus, one of the authors of this catechism, had already declared, in his "Thesaurus," that: "All the three Persons create and redeem and sanctify. But in these operations they observe this order—that the Father creates of Himself by means of the Son; the Son creates by means of the Father; and the Holy Spirit by means of both."

But since the deeper insight into the mystery of the adorable Trinity was gradually lost, and the pulpit's touch upon it became both rare and superficial, the Sabellian error naturally crept into the Church again, viz., that there were three successive periods in the activities of the divine Persons: First, that of the Father alone creating the world and upholding the natural life of all things. This was followed by a period of activity for the Son, when nature had become unnatural and fallen man a subject for redemption. Lastly, came that of the Holy Spirit regenerating and sanctifying the redeemed on the ground of the work of Christ.

According to this view, in childhood, when eating, drinking, and playing occupied all our time, we had to do with the Father. Later, when the conviction of sin dawned upon us, we felt the need of the Son. And not until the life of sanctification had begun in us did the Holy Spirit begin to take notice of us. Hence while the Father wrought, the Son and the Holy Spirit were inactive; when the Son undertook His work, the Father and the Holy Spirit were inactive; and now since the Holy Spirit alone performs the work, the Father and the Son are idle. But since this view of God is wholly untenable, Sabellius, who elaborated it philosophically, came to the conclusion that Father, Son, and Holy Ghost were after all but one Person; who first wrought in creation as Father, then having become the Son wrought out our redemption, and now as the Holy Spirit perfects our sanctification.

And yet, inadmissible as this view may be, it is more reverent and God-fearing than the crude superficialities of the current views that confine the Spirit's operations entirely to the elect, beginning only at their regeneration.

True, sermons on creation referred, in passing, to the moving of the Holy Spirit on the face of the waters, and His coming upon Bezaleel and Aholiab is treated in the catechetical class, but the two are not connected, and the hearer is never made to understand what the Author of our regeneration had to do with the moving upon the waters; they were merely isolated facts. Regeneration was the principal work of the Holy Spirit.

Our Reformed theologians have always warned against such representations, which are only the result of making man the starting-point in the contemplation of divine things. They always made *God Himself* the starting-point, and were not satisfied until the work of the Holy Spirit was clearly seen in all its stages, throughout the ages, and in the heart of every creature. Without this the Holy Spirit could not be God, the object of their adoration. They felt that such superficial treatment would lead to a denial of His personality, reducing Him to a mere *force.*

Hence we have spared no pain, and omitted no detail, in order, by the grace of God, to place before the Church two distinct thoughts, viz.:

First, *The work of the Holy Spirit is not confined to the elect, and does not begin with their regeneration, but it touches every creature, animate and inanimate, and begins its operations in the elect at the very moment of their origin.*

Second, *The proper work of the Holy Spirit in every creature consists in the quickening and sustaining of life with reference to his being and talents, and, in its highest sense, with reference to eternal life, which is his salvation.*

Thus we have regained the true standpoint requisite for considering the work of the Holy Spirit in the re-creation. For thus it appears:

First, that this work of re-creation is not performed in fallen man independently of his original creation, but that the Holy Spirit, who in regeneration kindles the spark of *eternal* life, has already kindled and sustained the spark of natural life. And, again, that the Holy Spirit, who imparts unto man born from above gifts necessary to sanctification and to his calling in the new sphere of life, has in the first creation endowed him with natural gifts and talents.

From this follows that fruitful confession of the unity of man's life before and after the new birth which nips every form of Methodism* in its very root, and which characterizes the doctrine of the Reformed churches.

Second, it is evident that the work of the Holy Spirit bears the same character in creation and re-creation. If we admit that He quickens life in that which is created by the Father and by the Son, what does He do in the re-creation but once more quicken life in him that is called of the Father and redeemed by the Son? Again, if the Spirit's work is God's touching the creature's being by Him, what is re-creation but the Spirit entering man's heart, making it His temple, comforting, animating, and sanctifying it?

Thus following the Sacred Scripture and the superior theologians, we reach a confession that maintains the unity of the Spirit's work, and makes it unite organically the natural and the spiritual life, the realm of nature and that of grace.

---

* For the sense in which the author takes Methodism, see section 5 in the Preface.

Of course His work in the latter surpasses that in the former:

First, since it is His work to touch the inward being of the creature, the more tender and natural the contact the more glorious the work. Hence it appears more beautiful in man than in the animal; and more lustrous in the spiritual man than in the natural, since the contact with the former is more intimate, the fellowship sweeter, the union complete.

Secondly, since creation lies so far behind us and re-creation touches us personally and daily, the Word of God directs more attention to the latter, claiming for it more prominence in our confession. But, however different the measures of operation and of energy, the Holy Spirit remains in creation and re-creation the one omnipotent Worker of all life and quickening, and is therefore worthy of all praise and adoration.

10

Organic and Individual

Where is He that put His Holy Spirit among them?—Isaiah 63:2

The subsequent activity of the Holy Spirit lies in the realm of grace. In nature the Spirit of God appears as creating, in grace as re-creating. We call it *re*-creation, because God's grace creates not something inherently new, but a new life in an old and degraded nature.

But this must not be understood as though grace restored only what sin had *destroyed.* For then the child of God, born anew and sanctified, must be as Adam was in Paradise before the fall. Many understand it so, and present it as follows: In Paradise Adam became diseased; the poison of eternal corruption entered his soul and penetrated his whole being. Now comes the Holy Spirit as the physician, carrying the remedy of grace to heal him. He pours the balm into his wounds, He heals his bruises and renews his youth; and thus man, born again, healed, and renewed, is, according to their view, precisely what the first man was in the state of rectitude. Once more the provisions of the covenant of works are laid upon him. By his good works he is again to inherit eternal life. Again he may fall like Adam and become a prey of eternal death.

But this whole view is wrong. Grace does not place the ungodly in a state of *rectitude,* but *justifies* him—two very different things. He that stands in a state of rectitude has certainly an original righteousness, but this he may lose; he may be tried and fail as Adam failed. He must vindicate his righteousness. Its inward consistency must discover itself. He who is righteous today may be unrighteous tomorrow.

But when God justifies a sinner, He puts Him in a totally different state. The righteousness of Christ becomes his. And what is this righteousness? Was Jesus in a state of rectitude only? In no wise. His righteousness was tested, tried, and sifted; it was even tested by the consuming fire of God's wrath. And this righteousness converted from *"original rectitude"* into *"righteousness vindicated"* was imputed to the ungodly.

Therefore the ungodly, when justified by grace, has nothing to do with Adam's state *before the fall,* but occupies the position of Jesus *after the resurrection.* He possesses a good that cannot be lost. He works no more for wages, but the inheritance is his own. His works, zeal, love, and praise flow not from his own poverty, but from the overflowing fullness of the life that was obtained for him. As it is often expressed: For Adam in Paradise there was first work and then the Sabbath of rest, but for the ungodly justified by grace the Sabbath rest comes first, and then the labor which flows from energies of that Sabbath. In the beginning the week closed with the Sabbath; for us the day of the resurrection of Christ opens the week which feeds upon the powers of that resurrection.

Hence the great and glorious work of re-creation has two parts:

First, the removing of corruption, the healing of the breach, the death to sin, the atonement for guilt.

Second, the reversing of the first order, the changing of the entire state, the bringing in and establishing of a new order.

The last is of greatest importance. For many teach differently. Although they grant that a new-born child of God is not precisely what Adam was before the fall, yet they see the difference only in the reception of a higher nature. The state is the same, differing only in degree. This is the current theory. This nature of higher degree is called the *"divine-human,"* which Christ bears in His Person, which being consolidated by His Passion and Resurrection is now imparted to the newborn soul, raising the lower and degraded nature to this higher life.

This theory directly conflicts with the Scripture, which never speaks of conditions similar yet differing in degree and power, but of a condition sometimes far inferior in power and degree to that of Adam, but transferred into an entirely different order.

For this reason the Scripture and the Confession of our fathers emphasize the doctrine of the Covenants; for the difference between the Covenant of Works and of Grace shows the difference between the two orders of spiritual things. They who teach that the new birth merely imparts a higher nature remain under the Covenant of Works. Theirs is the wearisome toil of rolling the Sisyphus stone up the mountain, even though it be with the greater energy of the higher life. The Scriptural doctrine of Grace ends this impossible Sisyphus task; it transfers the Covenant of Works from our shoulders to Christ's, and opens unto us a new order in the Covenant of Grace in which there can be no more uncertainty or fear, loss or forfeit of the benefits of Christ, but of which Wisdom doth cry, "and Understanding putteth forth her voice, standing in the top of high places," saying that all things are now ready.

The work of re-creation has this peculiarity, that it places the elect at once at the end of the road. They are not like the traveler still half way from home, but like one who has finished his journey; the long, dreary, and dangerous road is entirely behind him. Of course, he did not run that road; he could never have reached the goal. His Mediator and Daysman traveled it for him and in his stead. And by mystic union with his Savior it is as though he had traveled the whole distance; not as we reckon, but as God reckons.

This will show why the work of the Holy Spirit appears more powerful in re-creation than in creation. For what is the road spoken of, but that which leads from the center of our degenerate hearts to the center of the loving heart of God? All godliness aims to bring man into communion with God; hence to make him travel the road between him and God. Man is the only being on earth in whom contact with God means conscious *fellowship*. Since this fellowship is broken by the alienation of sin, at the end of the road the contact and fellowship must be perfect, so far as concerns man's state and principle. If fellowship is the terminus and God's grace puts His child there at once, at least so far as his state is concerned, there is an obvious difference between him and the unregenerate; for the latter is infinitely distant from God, while the former has sweetest fellowship with Him. Since it is the inward operation of the Holy Spirit that accomplishes this, His hand must appear more powerful and glorious in re-creation than in creation.

If we could see His work in re-creation all at once as an accomplished fact, we should understand it more thoroughly, and escape the difficulties that we now meet in comparing the Old Testament with the New regarding it.

Re-creation brings to us that which is eternal, finished, perfected, completed; far above the succession of moments, the course of years, and the development of circumstances. Here lies the difficulty. This *eternal* work must be brought to a *temporal* world, to a race which is in process of development; hence that work must *make* history, increasing like a plant, growing, blossoming, and bearing fruit. And this history must include a time of *preparation, revelation,* and lastly of filling the earth with the streams of grace, salvation, and blessing.

If it did not relate to man but to irrational beings, there would be no difficulty, but when it began its course man was already in the world, and as the ages passed the stream of humanity broadened. Hence the important question: Whether the generations that lived during the long period of preparation before Christ, in whom the work of re-creation was finally revealed, were partakers of its blessings?

The Scripture answers affirmatively. In the ages before Christ God's elect shared the blessings of the work of re-creation. Abel and Enoch, Noah and Abraham, Moses and David, Isaiah and Daniel were saved by the same faith as Peter, Paul, Luther, and Calvin. The Covenant of Grace, although made with Abraham and for a time connected with the national life of Israel, existed already in Paradise. The theologians of the Reformed churches have clearly unfolded the truth, that God's elect of both Dispensations entered the same gate of righteousness and walked the same way of salvation which they still walk to the marriage-supper of the Lamb.

But how could Abraham, living so many years before Christ, in whom alone grace and truth have been revealed, have his faith accounted unto him for righteousness, so that he saw the day of Jesus and was glad?

This difficulty has confused many minds regarding the Old and New Dispensations, and causes many vainly to ask: How could there be any saving operation of the Holy Spirit in the Old Testament if He were poured out only on Pentecost? The answer is found in the almost unsearchable work of the Holy Spirit, whereby, on the one hand, He brought into the history of our race that eternal salvation already finished and complete which must run through the periods of preparation, revelation, and fruit-bearing; and whereby, on the other hand, during the preparatory period, this very preparation was made the means, through wondrous grace, of saving souls even before the Incarnation of the Word.

11

The Church before and after Christ

All these having obtained a good report through faith, received not the promise—Hebrews 11:39.

Clearness requires to distinguish two operations of the Holy Spirit in the work of re-creation before the Advent, viz., (1) preparing redemption for the whole Church, and (2) regenerating and sanctifying the saints then living.

If there had been no elect before Christ, so that He had no church until Pentecost; and if, like Balaam and Saul, the bearers of the Old Testament revelation had been without personal interest in Messiah, then it is self-evident that, before the Advent, the Holy Spirit could have had but one work of re-creation, viz., the preparation of the coming salvation. But since God had a church from the beginning of the world, and nearly all the bearers of the revelation were partakers of His salvation, the Spirit's re-creative work must consist of two parts: first, of the preparation of redemption for the whole Church; and, secondly, of the sanctification and consolation of the Old Testament saints.

However, these two operations are not independent, like two separate water-courses, but are like drops of rain falling in the same stream of revelation. They are not even like two streams of different colors mingling in the same river-bed; for neither did the one contain anything for the Church of the future which had not meaning also for the saints of the Old Covenant; nor did the latter receive any revelation or commandment without significance also for the Church of the New Covenant. The Holy Spirit so interwove and interlaced this twofold work that what was the preparing of redemption for us, was at the same time revelation and exercise of faith for the Old Testament saints; while, on the other hand, He used their personal life, conflict, suffering, and hope as the canvas upon which He embroidered the revelation of redemption for us.

Not that the revelation of old did not contain a large element that had a different sense and purpose for them from what it has for us. Before Christ, the entire service of types and shadows had significance which it lost immediately after the Advent. To continue it after the Advent would be equivalent to a denial and repudiation of His coming. One's shadow goes before him; when he steps into the light the shadow disappears. Hence the Holy Spirit performed a special work for the saints of God by giving them a temporary service of types and shadows.

That this service overshadowed *all* their life made its impression all the stronger. This shadow lay upon Israel's entire history; was outlined in all their men from Abraham to John the Baptist; fell upon the judicial and political systems, and more heavily upon the social and domestic life; and in purest images lay upon the service of worship. Hence the *Old Testament* passages which refer to this service have not the meaning for us which they had for them. Every feature of it had a binding force for them. On the contrary, we do not circumcise our boys, but baptize our children; we do not eat the Passover, nor observe the Feast of Tabernacles, nor sacrifice the blood of bulls or heifers, as every discriminating reader of the Old Testament understands. And they who in the New Testament Dispensation seek to reintroduce tithing, or to restore the kingdom and the judiciary of the days of the *Old Testament,* undertake, according to past experience, a hopeless task: their efforts show poor success, and their whole attitude proves that they do not enjoy the full measure of the liberty of the children of God. *Actually* all Christians agree in this, acknowledging that the relation which we sustain toward the law of Moses is altogether different from that of ancient Israel.

The Decalogue alone is occasionally cause of contention, especially the Fourth Commandment. There are still Christians who allow no difference between that which has a passing, ceremonial character and that which is perpetually ethical, and who seek to substitute the last day of the week for the Day of the Lord.

However, leaving these serious differences alone, we repeat that the Holy Spirit had a special work in the days before Christ, which was intended for the saints of those days, but which has lost for us all its former significance.

Not, however, that we may therefore discard this work of the Holy Spirit, and that the books containing these things may be left unread. This view has obtained currency especially in Germany, where the Old Testament is less read than even the books of the Apocrypha, with the exception of the Psalms and a few selected pericopes. On the contrary, this service of shadows has even in the smallest details a special significance to the *New Testament* Church; only the significance is different.

This service in the *history* of the Old Covenant witnesses to us the wonderful deeds of God, whereby of infinite mercy He has delivered us from the power of death and hell. In the *personalities* of the Old Covenant it reveals the wonderful work of God in implanting and preserving faith in spite of human depravity and Satanic opposition. The service of *ceremonies* in the *sanctuary* shows us the image of Christ and of His glorious redemption in the minutest details. And finally, the service of shadows in *Israel's political, social,* and *domestic life* reveals to us those divine, eternal, and unchangeable principles that, set free from their transient and temporal forms, ought to govern the political and social life of the Christian nations throughout all ages.

And yet this does not exhaust the significance that this service always had, and still has, for the Christian Church.

Not only does it reveal to us the outlines of the spiritual house of God, but it actually operated in our salvation:

First, it prepared and preserved amid heathen idolatry a people which, as bearers of the divine oracles, offered the Christ at His coming a place for the sole of His foot and a *base of operations.** He could no more have come to Athens or Rome than to China or India. No one

---

* In Dutch, "*life-center.*"

there could have understood Him, or have furnished instrument or material to build the Church of the New Covenant. The salvation which was cast like a ripe fruit into the lap of the Christian Church had grown upon a tree deeply rooted in this service of shadows. Hence the history of that period is part of our own, as the life of our childhood and youth remains ours, even though as men we have put away childish things.

Secondly, the knowledge of this service and history, being parts of the Word of God, were instrumental in translating God's children from nature's darkness into His marvelous light.

However, as the Holy Spirit performed special work for the saints of those days that has a different though not less important significance for us, so also He performed a work in those days that was intended more directly for the Church of the New Testament, which also had a different but not less important significance for the saints of the Old Covenant. This was the work of *Prophecy.*

As Christ declares, the purpose of prophecy is to predict future things so that, the events predicted having come to pass, the Church may believe and confess that it was the Lord's work. The Old Testament often states this, and the Lord Jesus declared it to His disciples, saying: "And now I have told you, before it come to pass that, when it is come to pass, ye might believe" (John 14:29). And again: "Now I tell you before it come to pass, that when it is come to pass ye may believe that I am He" (John 13:19). And still more clearly: "But these things have I told you, that when the time shall come, ye may remember that I told you of them." These statements, compared with the words of Isaiah 41:23, 42:9, and 43:19, leave no doubt as to the design of prophecy.

Not that this exhausts prophecy, or that it has no other aims, but its chief and final end is reached only when, on the ground of its fulfillment, the Church believes its God and Savior and magnifies Him in His mighty acts.

But while its center of gravity is the fulfillment, that is, in the Church of the New Testament, it was equally intended for contemporary saints. For, apart from the prophetic activities that referred solely to the people of Israel living at that time, and the prophecies fulfilled in Israel's national life, prophecy even as boldly outlining Christ yielded precious fruit for the Old Testament saints. Connected with theophanies it produced in their minds such a fixed and tangible form of the Messiah that fellowship with Him, which alone is essential to salvation, was made possible to them by *anticipation,* as to us by *memory.* Not only did this fellowship become possible at the end of the Dispensation, in Isaiah and Zacharias; Christ testifies that Abraham desired to see His day, saw it, and was glad.

Fourth Chapter
The Holy Scripture of the Old Testament

12

The Holy Scripture

All Scripture is given by inspiration of God, and is profitable for doctrine, for reproof, for correction, for instruction in righteousness; that the man of God may be perfect, thoroughly furnished unto all good works—2 Timothy 3:16, 17.

Among the divine works of art produced by the Holy Spirit, the Sacred Scripture stands first. It may seem incredible that the printed pages of a book should excel His spiritual work in human hearts, yet we assign to the Sacred Scripture the most conspicuous place without hesitation.

Objectors can never have considered what this holy Book is, or any other book, writing, or language is, or what the putting down of a world of thought in a collection of Sacred Scripture means. We deny that a book, especially such as the Sacred Scripture, opposes a world of divine thought, the current of life, and spiritual experience. A book is not merely paper printed in ink, but is like a portrait—a collection of lines and features in which we see the likeness of a person. *Standing* near, we see not the person, but spots and lines of paint, but at the right distance these disappear and we see the likeness of a person. Even now it does not speak to us, for it is the face of a stranger; we may be able to judge the man's character, yet he fails to interest us. But let his children look, and instantly the image which left us cold appeals to him with warmth and life, which were invisible to us because our hearts lacked the essentials. What appeals to the child is not in the picture, but in his memory and imagination; the cooperation of the features in the painting and the father's image in his heart makes the likeness speak.

This comparison will explain the mysterious effect of the Scripture. Guido de Brès spoke of it in his debates with the Baptists: "That which we call Holy Scripture is not paper with black impressions, but that which addresses our spirits by means of those impressions." Those letters are but tokens of recognition; those words are only the clicks of the telegraph-key signaling thoughts to our spirits along the lines of our visual and auditory nerves. And the thoughts so signaled are not isolated and incoherent, but parts of a complete system that is directly antagonistic to man's thoughts, yet enters their sphere.

Reading the Scripture brings to our minds the sphere of divine thoughts so far as needful for us as sinners, in order to glorify God, love our neighbor, and save the soul. This is not a mere collection of beautiful and glittering ideas, but the reflection of the divine life. In God life and thought are united: there can be no life without thought, no thought not the product of life. Not so with us. Falsehood entered us, that is, we can sever thought from life. Or rather, they are always severed, unless we have voluntarily established the former unity. Hence our cold abstractions; our speaking without doing; our words without power; our thoughts without working; our books that, like plants cut off from their roots, wither before they can blossom, much less bear fruit.

The difference between divine and human life gives Scripture its uniqueness and precludes antagonism between its letter and its spirit, such as a false exegesis of 2 Corinthians 3:6 might suggest. If the Word of God were dominated by the falsehood that has crept into our hearts, and in the midst of our misery continues to place word and life in opposition as well as separation, then we would take refuge in the standpoint of our dissenting brethren, with their exaltation of the life above the Word. But we need not do so, for the opposition and separation are not in the Scripture. For this reason it is the *Holy* Scripture; for it was not lost in the unholy tearing asunder of thought and life, and is therefore distinct from writings in which yawns the gulf between the words and the reality of life. What other writings lack is in this Book; perfect agreement between the life reflected in the divine thought and the thoughts which the Word begets in our minds.

The Holy Scripture is like a diamond: in the dark it is like a piece of glass, but as soon as the light strikes it the water begins to sparkle, and the scintillation of life greets us. So the Word of God apart from the divine life is valueless, unworthy even of the name of Sacred Scripture. It exists only in connection with this divine life, from which it imparts life-giving thoughts to our minds. It is like the fragrance of a flower-bed that refreshes us only when the flowers and our organs of smell correspond. Hence the illustration of the child and his father's picture is exact.

While the Bible always flashes thoughts born of the divine life, yet the effects are not the same in all. As a whole, it is the portrait of Him who is the brightness of God's glory and the express image of His Person, aiming either to show us His likeness or to serve as its background.

Notice the difference when a child of God and an alien face that image. Not as though it has nothing to say to the unregenerate—this is a mistake of Methodism which should be corrected.* It addresses itself to all men as the King's Word, and everyone must receive its impress in his own way. But while the alien sees only a strange face, which annoys him, contradicts his world, and so repels him, the child of God understands and recognizes it. He is in holiest sympathy with the life of the world from which that image greets him. Thus reading what the stranger could not read, he feels that God is speaking to him, whispering peace to his soul.

Not as though the Scripture were only a system of signals to flash thought into the soul; rather it is the instrument of God to awaken and increase spiritual life, not as by magic, giving a sort of attestation of the genuineness of our experience—a fanatical view always opposed and rejected by the Church—but by the Holy Spirit through the use of the Word of God.

He regenerates us by the Word. The mode of this operation will be discussed later on; let it suffice here to say that the operations of the

---

* For the author's sense of Methodism, see section 5 in the Preface.

Word and the Holy Spirit never oppose each other, but, as St. Paul declares emphatically, that the Holy Scripture is prepared by the Spirit of God and given to the Church *as an instrument* to perfect God's work in man; as he expresses it: *"That the man of God may be perfect,"* that is, a man formerly of the world, made a man of God by divine act, to be perfected by the Holy Spirit; wherefore he is already perfect in Christ through the Word. To this end, as St. Paul declares, the Scripture was inspired of God. Hence this work of art was prepared by the Holy Spirit to lead the new-born man to this high ideal. And to emphasize the thought he adds: "That he may be thoroughly furnished unto all good works."

Hence Scripture serves this twofold purpose:

First, as an instrument of the Holy Spirit in His work upon man's heart.

Secondly, to qualify man perfectly and to equip him for every good work.

Consequently the working of Scripture embraces not only the *quickening* of the faith, but also the *exercise* of faith. Therefore instead of being a dead-letter, unspiritual, mechanically opposing the spiritual life, it is the very fountain of living water, which, being opened, springs up to eternal life.

Hence the Spirit's preparation and preservation of Scripture is not subordinate, but prominent with reference to the life of the entire Church. Or to put it more clearly: if prophecy, for example, aims first to benefit contemporary generations, and secondly to be part of the Holy Scripture that is to minister comfort to the Church of all ages, the latter is of infinitely higher importance. Hence the chief aim of prophecy was not to benefit the people living at that time, and through Scripture to yield fruit for us only indirectly, but through Scripture to yield fruit for the Church of all ages, and indirectly to benefit the Church of old.

13

The Scripture a Necessity

For whatsoever things were written aforetime were written for our learning, that we through patience and comfort of the Scriptures might have hope—Romans 15:4.

That the Bible is the product of the Chief Artist, the Holy Spirit; that He gave it to the Church and that in the Church He uses it as His instrument, cannot be over-emphasized.

Not as though He had lived in the Church of all ages, and given us in Scripture the record of that life, its origin and history, so that the life was the real substance and the Scripture the accident; rather the Scripture was the end of all that preceded and the instrument of all that followed.

With the dawn of the Day of days the Sacred Volume will undoubtedly disappear. As the New Jerusalem will need no sun, moon, or temple, but the Lord God will be its light, so will there be no need of Scripture, for the revelation of God shall reach His elect directly through the unveiled Word. But so long as the Church is on earth, face-to-face communion withheld, and our hearts accessible only by the avenues of this imperfect existence, Scripture must remain the indispensable instrument by which the Triune God prepares men's souls for higher glory.

The cause of this lies in our personality. We think, we are self conscious, and the threefold world *about* and *above* and *within* us is reflected in our thoughts. The man of confused or unformed consciousness or one insane cannot act as a man. True, there are depths in our hearts which the plummet of our thinking has not sounded, but the influence that is to affect us deeply, clearly, with outlasting effect upon our personality, must be wrought through our self-consciousness.

The history of sin proves it. How did sin enter the world? Did Satan infuse its poison into man's soul while he slept? By no means. While Eve was fully herself, Satan began to discuss the matter with her. He wrought upon her consciousness with words and representations, and she, allowing this, drank the poison, fell, and dragged her husband with her. Had not God thus foretold it? Man's fall was to be known neither by his recognized nor by his unrecognized emotions, but by the *tree of knowledge of good and evil.* The knowledge that caused his fall was not merely abstract, intellectual, but *vital.* Of course the operating cause was external, but it wrought upon his consciousness and bore the form of *knowledge.*

And as his fall, so also must be his *restoration.* Redemption must come from *without,* act upon our *consciousness,* and bear the form of *knowledge.* To affect and win us in our personality we must be touched in the very spot where sin first wounded us, viz., in our proud and haughty self-consciousness. And since our consciousness mirrors itself in a world of thought—thoughts expressed in words so intimately connected as to form, as it were, but *one word*—therefore it was of the highest necessity that a new, divine world of thought should speak to our consciousness in a *Word,* that is, in a *Scripture.* And this is the work of Holy Scripture.

Our thought-world is full of falsehood, and so is the outer world. But one thought-world is absolutely true, and that is the world of God's thoughts. Into this world we must be brought, and it into us with the life that belongs to it, as brightness to light. Therefore redemption depends upon faith. To believe is to acknowledge that the entire world of thought within and around us is false, and that only God's world of thought is true and abiding, and as such to accept and confess it. So it is still the Tree of knowledge. But the fruit now taken and enjoyed grows upon the inward plant of self-emptying and self-denial, whereby we renounce our own entire world of thought, no longer judging between good and evil, but faithfully repeating what God teaches, as ever little children in His school.

But this would not avail us if God's thoughts came in unintelligible words, which would have been the case if the Holy Spirit had used mere words. We know how hopeless it is to try to describe the felicities of heaven. Every effort has been so far a failure. That bliss passes our imagination. And the Scripture revelation concerning it is couched in earthly imagery—as a Paradise, a Jerusalem, or a wedding-feast—which, beautiful as it may be, leaves no clear impressions. We know heaven must be beautiful and entrancing, but a concrete conception of it is out of the question. Nor can we have clear ideas of the relation of the glorified Son of man to the Trinity, His sitting at the right hand of God, the life of the redeemed, and their condition when, passing from the chambers of death, they enter the palace of the great King.

Hence if the Holy Spirit had presented the world of divine thoughts concerning our salvation in writing directly from heaven, a clear conception of the subject would have been impossible. Our conception would have been vague and figurative as that concerning heaven. Hence these thoughts were not directly written, but *translated into the life of this world,* which gave them *form* and *shape;* and thus they came down to us in *human language,* in the pages of a book. Without this there could not even be a language to embody such sacred and glorious realities. St. Paul had visions, that is, he was freed from the limitations of consciousness and enabled to contemplate heavenly things, but having returned to his limitations, could not speak of what he had seen, as he said: "They are unspeakable."

And that the equally unspeakable things of salvation may be rendered *expressible* in *human* words, it pleased God to bring to this world the life which originated them; to accustom our human consciousness to them, from it to draw words for them, and thus to exhibit them to every man.

God's thoughts are inseparable from His life; hence His life must enter the world before His thoughts, at least at first; afterward the thoughts became the vehicle of the life.

This appears in the creation of Adam. The first man is *created;* after him men are *born.* At first human life appeared at once in full stature; from that life once introduced, new life will be born. First, new life originated by forming Eve from Adam's rib; then, by the union of man and woman. So also here. At first God introduced spiritual life into the world, finished, perfect, by a miracle; afterward differently, since the thought introduced as life into this world is *pictured* to our view. Henceforth the Holy Spirit will use the product of this life to awaken new life.

So redemption cannot begin with the gift of Holy Scripture to the Church of the Old Covenant. Such Scripture could not be produced until its content is wrought out in life, and redemption is objectively accomplished.

But the two should not be separated. Redemption was not first completed and then recorded in Scripture. Such conception would be mechanical and unspiritual, directly contradicted by the nature of Scripture, which is living and life-giving. Scripture was produced spontaneously and gradually by and from redemption. The promise in Paradise already foreshadowed it. For though redemption precedes Scripture, yet in the regeneration of the first men the Word was not idle; the Holy Spirit began with speaking to man, acting upon his consciousness. Even in Paradise, and subsequently when the stream of revelation proceeds, a divine Word always precedes the life and is life's instrument, and a divine thought introduces redemptive work. And when redemption is fulfilled in Christ He appears first as the Speaker, then as the Worker. The Word that was from the beginning reveals Himself to Israel as the Seal of Prophecy, saying: "This day is this Scripture fulfilled in your ears."

Hence the work of the Holy Spirit is never purely magical nor mechanical. Even in the preparatory period He always acted through the Word in translating a soul from death unto life. However, between then and now there is a decided difference:

First, *then,* the Word came to the soul directly by inspiration or by a prophet's address. *Now,* both these have ceased, and in their stead comes the Word sealed in the Sacred Scripture, interpreted by the Holy Spirit in preaching in the Church.

Secondly, *then,* the bringing in of life was confined to Israel, expressed itself in words and originated relations that strictly separated the servants of the only true God from the life of the world. *Now,* this extraordinary, preparatory dispensation is closed; the Israel of God are no more the natural descendants of Abraham, but the spiritual; the stream of the Church flows through all nations and peoples; it stands no more outside the world's life and development, but rather governs them.

Thirdly, although in the Old Dispensation redemption existed partly already in Scripture, and the Psalmist shows everywhere his devotion thereto, yet Scripture could be used so to a small extent only, and needed constant supplementing by direct revelations and prophecies. But *now,* Scripture reveals the whole counsel of God, and nothing can be added to it. Woe to him who dares diminish or increase this Book of Life which discloses the world of divine thought!

But notwithstanding difference, the fact remains that the Holy Spirit mastered the problem of bringing to man lost in sin, by human language intelligible to all nations and ages, the world of divine thoughts, so as to use them as the instrument of man's quickening.

It does not alter the case that the Holy Scripture shows so many seams and uneven places, and looks different from what we should expect. The chief virtue of this masterpiece was so to enfold God's thoughts in our sinful life that out of our language they could form a speech in which to proclaim through the ages, to all nations, the mighty words of God. This masterpiece is finished and lies before us in the Holy Scripture. And instead of losing itself in criticizing these apparent defects, the Church of all ages has received it with adoration and thanksgiving; has preserved it, tasted it, enjoyed it, and always believed to find eternal life in it.

Not as though critical and historical examination were prohibited. Such endeavor for the glory of God is highly commendable. But as the physiologist's search for the genesis of human life becomes sinful if immodest or dangerous to unborn life, so does every criticism of Holy Scripture become sinful and culpable if irreverent or seeking to destroy the life of God's Word in the consciousness of the Church.

14

The Revelation to Which the Scripture of the Old Testament Owes Its Existence

O Lord, . . . Thou art stronger than I, and hast prevailed—Jeremiah 20:7.

The understanding of the Holy Spirit's work in Scripture requires us to distinguish the *preparation,* and the *formation* that was the outcome of the preparation. We will discuss these two separately.

The Holy Spirit prepared for Scripture by the operations which from Paradise to Patmos supernaturally apprehended the sinful life of this world, and thus raised up believing men who formed the developing Church.

This will seem very foolish if we consider the Scripture a mere paper-book, a lifeless object, but not if we hear God speaking therein directly to the soul. Severed from the divine life, the Scripture is unprofitable, a letter that killeth. But when we realize that it radiates God's love and mercy in such form as to transform our life and address our consciousness, we see that the supernatural revelation of the life of God must precede the radiation. The revelation of God's tender mercies must precede their scintillation in the human consciousness.

First, the revelation of the mystery of Godliness; then, its radiation in the Sacred Scripture, and *thence* into the heart of God's Church, is the natural and ordained way.

For this purpose the Holy Spirit first chose individuals, then a few families, and lastly a whole nation, to be the sphere of His activities; and in each stage He began His work with the Word, always following the *Word of Salvation* with the *Facts of Salvation.*

He began this work in Paradise. After the fall, death and condemnation reigned over the first pair, and in them entombed the race. Had the Spirit left them to themselves, with the germ of death ever developing in them, no star of hope would ever have arisen for the human race.

Therefore the Holy Spirit introduces His work at the very beginning of the development of the race. The first germ of the mystery of Godliness was already implanted in Adam, and the first mother-word of which the Holy Scripture was to be born was whispered into his ear.

This word was followed by the deed. God's word does not return void; it is not a sound, but a power. It is a plowshare subsoiling the soul. Behind the word stands the propelling power of the Holy Spirit, and thus it becomes effectual, and changes the whole condition of things. We see it in Adam and Eve; especially in Enoch; and "By faith Abel obtained witness that he was righteous."

After these operations in individuals the Spirit's work in the family begins, partly in Noah, more especially in Abraham.

The judgment of the flood had completely changed former relations, had caused a new generation to arise, and perhaps had changed the physical relations between the earth and its atmosphere. And then, for the first time, the Holy Spirit begins to work in the family. Our Ritual of Baptism points emphatically to Noah and his eight, which has often been a stumblingblock to a thoughtless unspirituality. And yet needlessly, for by pointing to Noah our fathers meant to indicate, in that sacramental prayer, that it is not the baptism of *individuals,* but of the *people* of God, that is, of the Church and *its seed.* And since the salvation of families emerges first in the history of Noah and his family after the flood, it was perfectly correct to point to the salvation of Noah and his family as God's first revelation of salvation for us *and our seed.*

But the work of the Holy Spirit in Noah's family is only preliminary. Noah and his sons still belong to the old world. They formed a transition. After Noah the holy line disappears, and from Shem to Terah the Holy Spirit's work remains invisible. But with Terah it appears in clearest light; for now Abraham goes out, not with sons, but alone. The promised son was still resting in the hand of God. And he could not beget him but *by faith;* so that God could truly say, "I am the Almighty God," that is, a God "who quickeneth the dead and calleth the things that are not as though they were." Hence Abraham's family is almost in literal sense the product of the Holy Spirit's work in that there is nothing in his life without faith. The product of art in Abraham's history is not the image of a pious shepherd-king or virtuous patriarch, but the wonderful work of the Holy Spirit operating in an old man—who again and again "kicks against the pricks," who brings forth out of his own heart nothing but unbelief—working in him a steadfast and immovable faith, *bringing that faith into direct connection with his family life.* Abraham is called "the Father of the Faithful," not in the superficial sense of a spiritual connection between our faith and Abraham's history, but because the faith of Abraham was interwoven with the fact of Isaac's birth, whom he obtained by faith, and of whom there was given him a seed as the stars of the heaven and as the sand of the seashore.

From the individual the Holy Spirit's work passes into the family, and thence into the nation. Thus Israel receives his being.

It was Israel, that is, not one of the nations, but a people newly created, added to the nations, received among their number, perpetually distinct from all other nations in origin and significance. And this people is also born of faith. To this end God casts it into death: on Moriah; in Jacob's flight; in the distresses of Joseph, and in the fears of Moses; alongside the fiery furnaces of Pithon and Ramses; when the infants of the Hebrews floated on the Nile. And from this death it is again and again faith that saves and delivers, and therefore the Holy Spirit who continues His glorious work in the generation and regeneration of this coming people. After this people is born it is again thrown into death: first, in the wilderness; then, during the time of the Judges; finally, in the Exile. Yet it cannot die, for it carries in its bosom the hope of the promise. However maimed, plagued, and decimated, it multiplies again and again; for the Lord's promise fails not, and in spite of shameful backslidings and apostasy, Israel manifests the glory of a people born, living, and dying by faith.

Thus the work of the Holy Spirit passes through these three stages: Abel, Abraham, Moses; the individual, the family, the nation. In each of these three the work of the Holy Spirit is visible, inasmuch as everything is wrought by faith. Is faith not wrought by the Holy Spirit? Very well; by faith Abel obtained witness; by faith Abraham received the son of the promise; and by faith Israel passed through the Red Sea.

And what is the relation between *life* and the *word of life* during these three stages? Is it, as according to current representations, first life, and then the word springing therefrom as token of the conscious life?

Evidently history proves the very opposite. In Paradise the word *precedes* and the life *follows.* To Abraham in Ur of the Chaldees, first the word. "Get thee out from thy country, and I will bless thee, and in thee shall all the families of the earth be blessed." In the case of Moses it is first the word in the burning bush and then the passage through the Red Sea. This is the Lord's appointed way. He first speaks, then works. Or more correctly, He speaks, and by speaking He quickens. These two stand in closest connection. Not as though the word *causes* life; for the Eternal and Triune God is the only Cause, Source, and Fountain of life. But the word is the instrument with which He wills to complete His work in our hearts.

We cannot stop here to consider the work of the Father and the Son, which either preceded or followed that of the Holy Spirit, and which is interwoven with it. Of the miracles we speak only because we discover in them a special twofold work of the Holy Spirit. The *working* of the miracle is of the Father and of the Son, and not so much of the Holy Spirit. But often as it pleased God to use men as instruments in the performance of miracles, it is the Spirit's special work to qualify them by working faith in their hearts. Moses smiting the rock believed not, but he imagined that by smiting he himself could produce water from the rock; which God alone can do. To him that believes it is the same whether he speaks or smites the rock. Stick nor tongue can in the least affect it. The power proceeds from God alone. Hence the greatness of the sin of Moses. He thought that he was to be the worker, and not God. And this is the very work of sin in God's people.

Hence we see that when Moses cast down his rod, when he cursed the Nile, when Elias and other men of God wrought miracles, they did nothing, they only *believed.* And by virtue of their faith they became to the bystanders and interpreters of God's testimony, showing them the works of God and not their own. This is what St. Peter exclaimed: "Why look ye so earnestly on us as though by our own power or holiness we had made this man to walk?"

To work this faith in the hearts of men who were to perform these miracles was the Holy Spirit's first task. His second was to quicken faith in the hearts of those upon whom the miracle was to be wrought. Of Christ it is written, that in Capernaum He could not do many powerful works because of their unbelief; and we read repeatedly: "Thy faith hath made thee whole."

But the miracle alone has no convincing power. The unbeliever begins with denying it. He explains it from natural causes. He neither will nor can see God's hand in it. And when it is so convincing that he cannot deny it, he says: "It is of the devil." But he will not acknowledge that it is the power of God. Therefore to make the miracle effectual, the Holy Spirit must also open the eyes of them that witness it to see the power of God therein. All our reading of the miracles in our Bible is unprofitable unless the Holy Spirit opens our eyes, and then we see them live, hear their testimony, experience their power, and glorify God for His mighty works.

15

The Revelation of the Old Testament in Writing

Then I said, I will not speak any more in His Name. But His word was in my heart as a burning fire, shut up in my bones: and I was weary with forbearing, but I could not—Jeremiah 20:9.

Although the miracles performed for and in the midst of Israel created a glorious life-center in the midst of the heathen world, yet they did not constitute a Holy Scripture; for this cannot be created except God *speak* to man, even to His people Israel. "God, who at sundry times and in diverse manners *spake* in times past unto the fathers by the prophets, hath in these days *spoken* unto us by His Son."

This divine speaking is not limited to prophecy. God spoke also to others than prophets, *e.g.,* to Eve, Cain, Hagar, etc. To receive a revelation or a vision does not make one a prophet, unless it be accompanied by the command to communicate the revelation to others. The word *nabi,* the Scriptural term for prophet, does not indicate a person who receives something of God, but one who brings something to the people. Hence it is a mistake to confine the divine revelation to the prophetic office. In fact, it extends to the whole race in general; prophecy is only one of its special features. As to the divine revelation in its widest scope, it is evident from the Scripture that God spoke to men from Adam to the last of the apostles. From Paradise to Patmos revelation runs like a golden thread through every part of Sacred History.

As a rule, the Scripture does not treat this divine speaking metaphorically. There are exceptions, *e.g.*, "God spake to the fish" (Jonah 2:10); "The heavens declare the glory of God, and day unto day uttereth speech" (Ps. 19:2, 3). However, it can be proven, from a thousand passages against one to the contrary, that the ordinary speaking of the Lord may not be taken in other than the literal sense. This is evident from the call of God to Samuel, which the child mistook for that of Eli. It is evident also from the names, numbers, and localities that are mentioned in this divine speaking; especially from the dialogues between God and man, as in the history of Abraham in the conflict of his faith concerning the promised seed, and in his intercession for Sodom.

And therefore we cannot agree with those who would persuade us that the Lord did not really speak; that if it reads so, it must not be so understood; and that a clearer insight shows that "a certain influence from God affected the inner life of the person addressed. In connection with the person's peculiar character and the influences of his past and present this working gave special clearness to his consciousness, and wrought in him such a conviction that, without hesitation, he declared: 'Since I will as God wills, I know that the Lord has thus spoken to me.' " This representation we reject as exceedingly pernicious and hurtful to the life of the Church. We call it false, since it dishonors the truth of God; and we refuse to tolerate a theology that starts from such premises. It annihilates the authority of the Scripture. Although commended by the Ethical wing it is exceedingly *un*-ethical, inasmuch as it directly opposes the clearly expressed truth of the Word of God. Nay, this divine speaking, whose record the Scripture offers, must be understood as real speaking.

And what is *speaking?* Speaking presupposes a person who has a thought that he wishes to transfer directly to the consciousness of another, without the intervention of a third person or of writing or of gesture. Hence when God speaks to man three things are implied:

First, that God has a thought which He wills to communicate to man.

Second, that He executes His design in a direct way.

Third, that the person addressed now possesses the divine thought with this result, that he is conscious of the same idea which a moment ago existed only in God.

With every explanation doing full justice to these three points we will agree; every other we reject.

As to the question whether speech is possible without sound, we answer: "No, not among men." Surely the Lord can speak and has spoken at times by means of *air-vibrations, but* He can speak to man without the use of either sound or ear. As men we have access to each other's consciousness only by means of the organs of sense. We cannot communicate with our neighbor except he hear or see or feel our touch. The unfortunate who is devoid of these senses cannot receive the slightest information from without. But the Lord our God is not thus limited. He has access to man's heart and consciousness from within. He can impart to our consciousness whatever He will in a direct way, without the use of eardrum, auditory nerve, and vibration of air. Though a man be stone-deaf, God can make him hear, inwardly speaking to his soul.

However, to accomplish this God must condescend to our limitations. For the consciousness is subject to the mental conditions of the world in which it lives. A foreigner, for example, can have no other consciousness than that developed by his own environment and acquired by his native language. Speaking to a foreigner unacquainted with our tongue, we must adapt ourselves to his limitations and address him in his own language. Hence in order to make Himself intelligible to man, God must clothe His thoughts in human language and thus convey them to the human consciousness.

To the person thus addressed it must seem therefore as though he had been spoken to in the ordinary way. He received the impression that he heard words of human language conveying to him divine thoughts. Hence the divine speaking is always adapted to the capacities of the person addressed. Because in condescension the Lord adapts Himself to every man's consciousness, His speaking assumes the form peculiar to every man's condition. What a difference, for instance, between God's word to Cain and that to Ezekiel! This explains how God could mention names, dates, and various other details; how He could make use of the dialect of a certain period; of derivation of words, as in the changing of names, as in the case of Abraham and Sarah.

This also shows that God's speaking is not limited to godly and susceptible persons prepared to receive a revelation. Adam was wholly unprepared, hiding himself from the presence of God. And so were Cain and Balaam. Even Jeremiah said: "I will not speak any more in His Name. But His word was in my heart as a burning fire, shut up in my bones: and I was weary with forbearing, but I could not" (chap. 20:9). Hence the divine omnipotence is unlimited. The Lord can impart the knowledge of His will to whomsoever He pleases. The question why He has not spoken for eighteen centuries must not be answered, "Because He has lost the power," but, "Because it seemeth not good to Him." Having once spoken and in the Scripture brought His word to our souls, He is silent now that we may honor the Scripture.

However, it should be noticed that in this divine speaking from Paradise to Patmos there is a certain order, unity, and regularity; wherefore we add:

First, the divine speaking was not confined to individuals, but, having a message for all the people, God spoke through His chosen prophets. That God can speak to a whole nation at once is proven by the events of Sinai. But it pleased Him not always to do this. On the contrary, He never spoke to them in that way afterward, but introduced prophetism instead. Hence the peculiar mission of prophetism is to receive the words of God and immediately to communicate them to the people. God speaks to Abraham what is for Abraham alone, but to Joel, Amos, etc., a message not for themselves, but for others to whom it must be conveyed. In connection with this we notice the fact that the prophet stands not alone, but in relation with a class of men among whom his mind was gradually prepared to *speak to the people,* and to receive the divine Oracle. For the peculiar feature of prophecy was the condition of ecstasy, which differed greatly from the way by which God spoke to Moses.

Secondly, these divine revelations are mutually related and, taken together, constitute a whole. There is first the foundation, then the superstructure, until finally the illustrious palace of the divine truth and knowledge is completed. Revelation as a whole shows therefore a glorious plan, into which are dovetailed the special revelations to individuals.

Thirdly, the speaking of the Lord, especially of the *inward* word, is peculiarly the work of the Holy Spirit, which, as we have found before, appears most strikingly when God comes into closest contact with the creature. And the consciousness is the most intimate part of man's being. Wherefore, as often as the Lord our God enters human consciousness to communicate His thoughts, clothed in human thoughts and speech, the Scripture and the believer honor and adore therein the comforting operation of the Holy Spirit.

16

Inspiration

And unto the angel of the church in Sardis write, These things saith He that hath the seven Spirits of God—Revelation 3:1.

We do not speak here of the New Testament. Nothing has contributed more to falsify and undermine faith in the Scripture and the orthodox view concerning it than the unhistoric and unnatural practice of considering the Scripture of the Old and the New Testament at the same time.

The Old Testament appears first; then came the Word in the flesh; and only after that the Scripture of the New Testament. In the study of the work of the Holy Spirit the same order ought to be observed. Before we speak of His work in the Incarnation, the inspiration of the New Testament may not even be mentioned. And until the Incarnation, there existed no other Scripture than the Old Testament.

The question is now: How is the work of the Holy Spirit to be traced in the *construction* of that Scripture?

We have considered the question how it was prepared. By wonderful *works* God created a new life in this world; and, in order to make men believe in these works, He *spoke* to man either directly or indirectly, that is, by the prophets. But this did not create a Sacred Scripture. If nothing more had been done there would never have been such a Scripture; for events take place and belong to the past; the word once spoken passes away with the emotion in the consciousness.

Human writing is the wonderful gift which God bestowed on man to perpetuate what otherwise would have been forgotten and utterly lost. Tradition falsifies the report. Among holy men this would not be so. But we are sinful men. By sin a lie can be told. Sin is also the cause of our lack of earnestness, and the root of all forgetfulness, carelessness, and thoughtlessness. These are the two factors, lying and carelessness, that rob tradition of its value. For this reason God gave our race the gift of writing. Whether on wax, on metal, on the face of the rock, on parchment, on papyrus, or on paper, is of no importance, but that God enabled man to find the art of committing to posterity a thought, a promise, an event, independent from his person, attaching it to something material, so that it could endure and be read by others even after his death—this is of greatest importance.

For us, men, reading and writing are means of *fellowship.* It begins with speaking, which is essential to fellowship. But mere speaking confines it to narrow limits, while reading and writing give it wider scope, extending it to persons far away and to generations yet unborn. Through writing past generations actually live together. Even now we can meet with Moses and David, Isaiah and John, Plato and Cicero; we can hear them speak and receive their mental utterances. Writing is therefore no contemptible thing as some, who are overspiritual and sneer at the written Word, consider it. On the contrary, it is great and glorious—one of the mighty factors whereby God keeps men and generations in living communication and exercise of love. Its discovery was a wonderful grace, God's gift to man, more than doubling his treasures.

The gift has often been abused; yet even in its rightful use there is ascending glory. How much more glorious appears the art of writing when Dante, Shakespeare, and Schiller write their poetry, than when the pedagogue compiles his spelling-books or the notary public scribbles the lease of a house!

Since writing may be used or abused, may serve low or high purposes, the question arises: "What is its highest end?" And without the least hesitation we answer: "The writing of the Holy Scripture." As human speech and language are of the Holy Spirit, so is writing also taught us of Him. But while man uses the art to record human thoughts, the Holy Spirit employs it to give fixed and lasting form to the thoughts of God. Hence there is a human employment of it and a divine. The highest and wholly unique is that in the Holy Scripture.

Actually there is no other book which sustains communication among men and generations as does the Sacred Scripture. To honor His own work the Holy Spirit has caused the universal distribution of this book alone, thereby putting men of all stations and classes into communication with the oldest generations of the race.

From this standpoint the Holy Scripture must be considered, being in fact "the Scripture *par excellence.*" Hence the divine and oft-repeated command: "Write." God did not only speak and act, leaving it to man whether His deeds and the tenor of His words were to be forgotten or remembered, but He also commanded that they should be recorded in writing. And when just before the announcement and close of the divine revelation to John on Patmos, the Lord commanded him, "Write to the church" of Ephesus, Pergamos, etc., He repeated in a summary what was the design of all preceding revelations, viz., that they should be written and in the form of a Scripture, a gift of the Holy Spirit, and be deposited in the Church, which for that reason is called the "pillar and ground of the truth." Not, according to a later interpretation, as though the truth were *concealed* in the Church, but, according to the ancient rendering, that Holy Scripture was entrusted to the Church for preservation.

However, we do not mean to say that with reference to every verse and chapter the Holy Spirit commanded, "Write," as though the Scripture as we possess it had come into existence page after page. Assuredly the Scripture is divinely inspired: a statement distorted and perverted beyond recognition by our Ethical theologians, if they understand by it that "prophets and apostles were personally animated by the Holy Spirit." This confounds *illumination* with *revelation,* and revelation with *inspiration.* "Illumination" is the clearing up of the spiritual consciousness which in His own time the Holy Spirit gives more or less to every child of God. "Revelation" is a communication of the thoughts of God given in extraordinary manner, by a miracle, to prophets and apostles. But "inspiration," wholly distinct from these, is that special and unique operation of the Holy Spirit whereby He directed the minds of the writers of the Scripture in the *act of writing.* "All Scripture is given by *inspiration* of God"; and this has no reference to ordinary *illumination,* nor extraordinary *revelation,* but to an operation that stands entirely alone and which the Church has always confessed under the name of Inspiration. Hence inspiration is the name of that all-comprehensive operation of the Holy Spirit whereby He has bestowed on the Church a complete and infallible Scripture. We call this operation all-comprehensive, for it was organic, not mechanical.

The practice of writing dates back to remote antiquity; preceded, however, by the preservation of the verbal tradition by the Holy Spirit. This is evident from the narrative of the Creation. Noted physicists like Agassiz, Dana, Guyot, and others have openly declared that the narrative of the Creation recorded many centuries ago what so far no man could know of himself, and what at the present time is only partly revealed by the study of geology. Hence the narrative of the Creation is not *myth,* but *history.* The events took place as recorded in the opening chapters of Genesis. The Creator Himself must have communicated them to man. From Adam to the time when writing was invented the remembrance of this communication must have been preserved correctly. That there are two narratives of the Creation proves nothing to the contrary. Creation is considered from the natural and from the spiritual points of view; hence it is perfectly proper that the image of Creation should be completed in a twofold sketch.

If Adam did not receive the special charge, yet from the revelation itself he obtained the powerful impression that such information was not designed for himself alone, but for all men. Realizing its importance and the obligation it imposed, succeeding generations have perpetuated the remembrance of God's wonderful words and deeds, first *orally,* afterward by *writing.* In this way there gradually arose a collection of documents which through Egyptian influence were put in book form by the great men of Israel. These documents being collected, sifted, compiled, and expanded by Moses, formed in his day the beginning of a Holy Scripture properly so called.

Whether Moses and those earlier writers were conscious of their inspiration is immaterial; the Holy Spirit directed them, brought to their knowledge what they were to know, sharpened their judgment in the choice of documents and records, so that they should decide aright, and gave them a superior maturity of mind that enabled them always to choose the right word.

Although the Holy Spirit spoke directly to men, human speech and language being no human inventions, yet in writing He employed human agencies. But whether He dictates directly, as in the Revelation of St. John, or governs the writing indirectly, as with historians and evangelists, the result is the same: the product is such in form and content as the Holy Spirit designed, an infallible document for the Church of God.

Hence the confession of inspiration does not exclude ordinary numbering, collecting of documents, sifting, recording, etc. It recognizes all these matters which are plainly discernible in Scripture. Style, diction, repetitions, all retain their value. But it must be insisted that the Scripture as a whole, as finally presented to the Church, as to content, selection, and arrangement of documents, structure, and even words, owes its existence to the Holy Spirit, that is, that the men employed in this work were consciously or unconsciously so controlled and directed by the Spirit, in all their thinking, selecting, sifting, choice of words, and writing, that their final product, delivered to posterity, possessed a perfect warrant of divine and absolute authority.

That the Scriptures themselves present a number of objections and in many aspects do not make the impression of absolute inspiration does not militate against the other fact that all this spiritual labor was controlled and directed by the Holy Spirit. For the Scripture had to be constructed so as to leave room for the exercise of *faith.* It was not intended to be approved by the critical judgment and accepted on this ground. This would eliminate faith. Faith takes hold directly with the fullness of our personality. To have faith in the Word, Scripture must not grasp us in our *critical thought,* but in the life of the *soul.* To believe in the Scripture is an act of life of which thou, O lifeless man, art not capable, except the Quickener, the Holy Ghost, enable thee. He that caused Holy Scripture to be written is the same that must teach thee to read it. Without Him this product of divine art cannot affect thee. Hence we believe:

First, that the Holy Spirit chose this human construction of the Scripture purposely, that we as men might more readily live in it.

Secondly, that these stumblingblocks were introduced that it might be impossible for us to lay hold of its content with mere intellectual grasp, without the exercise of faith.

Fifth Chapter
*The Incarnation of the Word**

17

Like One of Us

But a body Thou hast prepared Me—Hebrews 10:5.

The completion of the Old Testament did not finish the work that the Holy Spirit undertook for the whole Church. The Scripture may be the instrument whereby to act upon the consciousness of the sinner and to open his eyes to the beauty of the divine life, but it cannot impart that life to the Church. Hence it is followed by another work of the Holy Spirit, viz., the *preparation of the body of Christ.*

The well-known words of Psalm 40:6, 7: "Sacrifice and offering Thou didst not desire; *mine ears Thou hast pierced;* burnt-offering and sin-offering hast Thou not required. Then said I, Lo, I come: in the volume of the book it is written of me,"—are rendered by St. Paul: "Sacrifice and offering Thou wouldst not, *but a body Thou hast prepared me;* in burnt-offerings and sin-offerings Thou hast no pleasure: lo, I come, in the volume of the book it is written of me." We do not discuss how the words, "Mine ears hast Thou pierced," can mean also, "A body Thou hast prepared me." For our present purpose it is immaterial whether one says with Junius: "The ear is a member of the body;

* Owing to the publication of the author's work, *The Incarnation of the Word,* this subject is presented here in an abbreviated form.

by the piercing of the ear hearing becomes possible; and only by the hearing does the body become an instrument of obedience"; or with another: "As the body of the slave became an instrument of obedience by the piercing of the ear, so did the body of Christ become an instrument of obedience by the conception of the Holy Spirit"; or finally: "As the Israelite became a servant by having his ear pierced, so has the Eternal Son adopted the form of a servant by becoming partaker of our flesh and blood." St. Paul's infallible exposition of Psalm 40:7 does not raise any serious objection to any of these renderings. It suffices our present purpose if it be only acknowledged that, according to Hebrews 10:5, the Church must confess *that there was a preparation of the body of Christ.*

This being conceded and taken in connection with what the Gospel relates concerning the conception, it cannot be denied that in the preparing of the body of the Lord there is a peculiar work of the Holy Spirit. For the angel said to Mary: "The Holy Ghost shall come upon thee and the power of the Highest shall overshadow thee; therefore also that holy thing which shall be born of thee shall be called the Son of God" (Luke 1:35). And again: "Joseph, thou son of David, fear not to take unto thee Mary thy wife, for that which is conceived in her is of the Holy Ghost" (Matt. 1:20). Both passages, apart from their proper meanings, evidently seek to produce the impression that the conception and birth of Jesus are extraordinary; that they did not occur after the will of man, but result from an operation of the Holy Spirit.

Like all other outgoing works of God, the preparation of the body of Christ is a divine work common to the three Persons.

It is erroneous to say that the Holy Spirit is the Creator of the body of Jesus, or, as some have expressed it, "That the Holy Spirit was the Father of Christ, according to His human nature." Such representations must be rejected, since they destroy the confession of the Holy Trinity. This confession cannot be maintained when any of the outgoing works of God are represented as not common to the three Persons.

We wish to emphasize, therefore, that not the Holy Spirit alone, but the Triune God, prepared the body of the Mediator. The Father and even the Son cooperated in this divine act.

However, as we have seen in Creation and Providence, in this cooperation the work of each Person bears its own distinctive mark. From the Father, of whom are all things, proceeded the material of the body of Christ, the creation of the human soul, and of all His gifts and powers, together with the whole plan of the Incarnation. From the Son, who is the wisdom of the Father, disposing and arranging all things in Creation, proceeded the holy disposition and arrangement with reference to the Incarnation. And as the correlated acts of the Father and the Son in Creation and Providence receive animation and perfection through the Holy Spirit, so there is in the Incarnation a peculiar act of the Holy Spirit through which the acts of Father and Son in this mystery receive completion and manifestation. Therefore it is said in Hebrews 10:7 of the Triune God: "A body Thou hast prepared Me"; while it is also declared that that which is conceived in Mary is of the Holy Ghost.

This, however, may not be explained in the ordinary sense. It might be said that there is nothing wonderful in this, for Job declares (chap. 33:4), "The Spirit of the Lord hath given me life," and of Christ we read that He was born of Mary, being conceived by the Holy Ghost. These two cover the same ground. Both instances connect the birth of a child with an act of the Holy Spirit. While, as regards the birth of Christ, we do not deny this ordinary act of the Holy Spirit, which is essential to the quickening of all life, especially that of a human being, yet we do deny that the conception by the Holy Spirit was the ordinary act. The ancient confession, "I believe in Jesus Christ, His Only-Begotten Son our Lord, who *was conceived by the Holy Ghost,"* refers to a divine miracle and a deep mystery, in which the work of the Holy Spirit must be glorified.

Accordingly a complete analysis of this work is impossible. If not, it would cease to be a miracle. Wherefore let us look into this matter only with deepest reverence, and not advance theories contrary to the Word of God. What God has been pleased to reveal we know; what His Word only hints we can know only in faint outlines; and what is advanced outside of the Word is only the effort of a meddlesome spirit or unhallowed curiosity.

In this work of the Holy Spirit two things must be distinguished: First, the creation of the human nature of Jesus. Secondly, His separation from sinners.

On the first point, the Scripture teaches that no man ever could claim paternal connection with Jesus. Joseph appears and acts as the stepfather of Christ, but of a fellowship of life and origin between him and Jesus the Scripture never speaks. Indeed, Joseph's neighbors regarded Jesus as the Son of the carpenter, but the Scripture always treats this as an error. St. John, declaring that the children of God are born not of the will of man, nor of the will of the flesh, but of God, undoubtedly borrowed this glorious description of our higher birth from the extraordinary act of God which scintillates in the conception and birth of Christ. The fact that Mary was called a virgin; that Joseph was troubled at the discovery of his bride's condition; that he intended secretly to leave her, and that an angel appeared to him in a dream—in a word, the whole Gospel narrative, as well as the unbroken tradition of the Church, allows no other confession than that the conception and birth of Christ were of Mary the virgin, but not of Joseph her betrothed husband.

Excluding the man, the Scripture thrice puts the Holy Spirit in the foreground as the Author of the conception. St. Matthew says (chap. 1:18): "When Mary had been betrothed to Joseph, before they came together, she was found with child by the Holy Ghost." And again, in verse 20: "For that which is conceived in her is of the Holy Ghost." Lastly, Luke says (chap. 1:35): "The Holy Ghost shall come upon thee and the power of the Highest shall overshadow thee; therefore also that holy thing which shall be born of thee shall be called the Son of God." These clear statements do not receive full recognition unless it be plainly confessed that the conception of the germ of a human nature in the womb of the virgin was an act of the Holy Spirit.

It is not expedient nor lawful to enter more deeply into this matter. How human life originates after conception, whether the embryo immediately contains a human person or whether he is created therein afterward, and other similar questions, must remain unanswered, perhaps forever. We may advance theories, but the Omnipotent God allows no man to discover His workings in the hidden laboratories of His creative power. Wherefore all that may be said according to Scripture is contained in the following four particulars:

First, in the conception of Christ not a new being was called into life as in all other cases, but One who had existed from eternity, and who then entered into vital relation with the human nature. The Scripture clearly reveals this. Christ existed from before the foundation of the world. His goings forth were of old, from the days of *eternity.* He took upon Himself the form of a servant. Even though the biologist should discover the mystery of the human birth, it could not reveal anything regarding the conception of the Mediator.

Second, it is not the conception of a human *person,* but of a human nature. Where a new being is conceived, a human person comes into existence. But when the Person of the Son, who was with the Father from eternity, partakes of our flesh and blood, He adopts our human nature in the unity of His Person, thus becoming a true man, but it is not the creation of a *new* person. The Scripture clearly shows this. In Christ appears but one *ego,* being in the same Person at once the Son of God and the Son of man.

Third, from this it follows not that a *new* flesh was created in Mary as the Mennonites used to teach, but that the fruit in Mary's womb, from which Jesus was born, was taken from and nourished with her own blood—the very blood which through her parents she had received from *fallen Adam.*

Last, the Mediator born of Mary not only partook of our flesh and blood, such as it existed in Adam and as we have inherited it from Adam, but He was born a true man, thinking, willing, and feeling like other men, susceptible to all the human emotions and sensations that cause the countless thrills and throbs of human life.

And yet He was separate from sinners. Of this we speak in the next article.

Let this suffice for the fact of the conception, from which fact we derive the precious comfort: *"That it covers in the sight of God my sin and guilt wherein I was conceived and brought forth"* (Heidelberg Catechism, q. 36).

18

Guiltless and without Sin

For such a high Priest became us, who is holy, harmless, undefiled, separate from sinners, and made higher than the heavens—Hebrews 7:26.

Throughout the ages the Church has confessed that Christ took upon Himself real human nature from the virgin Mary, not as it was before the fall, but such as it had become *by* and *after* the fall. This is clearly stated in Hebrews 2:14, 17: "Forasmuch as the children are partakers of flesh and blood, He also Himself took part of the same. . . . Wherefore in all things it behooved Him to be made like unto His brethren, to make reconciliation for the sins of the people." It was even such a partaking of our nature as would make Him feel Satan's goad, for there follows: "In that He Himself hath suffered, *being tempted,* He is able to succor them that are tempted." Upon the authority of the divine Word we cannot doubt then that the Son of God became man in our fallen nature. It is our misery, by virtue of the inherited guilt of Adam, that we cannot live and act but as partakers of the flesh and blood corrupted by the fall. And since we as children are partakers of flesh and blood, so is He also become partaker of the same. Hence it cannot be too strongly emphasized that the Son of God, walking among men, bore the same origin as our flesh; that the blood which ran through His veins is the same as our blood, and came to Him as well as to us from the same fountain in Adam. We must feel, and dare confess, that in Gethsemane our Savior agonized in our flesh and blood; that it was our flesh and blood that were nailed to the cross. The "blood of reconciliation" is taken from the very blood which thirsts after reconciliation.

With equal assurance, however, bowing to the authority of the Scripture, we confess that this intimate union of the Son of God with the fallen human nature does not imply the least participation of our sin and guilt. In the same epistle in which the apostle sets forth distinctly the fellowship of Jesus with the human flesh and blood, he bears equally clear testimony to the fact of His sinlessness, so that every misunderstanding may be obviated. As by virtue of our conception and birth we are *unholy, guilty,* and *defiled, one with sinners,* and therefore burdened with the *condemnation of hell,* so is the Mediator conceived and born *holy, harmless, undefiled, separate from sinners, made higher than the heavens.* And with equal emphasis the apostle declares that sin did not enter into His temptations, for, although tempted in all things, like as we are, yet He was ever without sin.

Therefore the mystery of the Incarnation lies in the apparent contradiction of Christ's union with our fallen nature, which on the one hand is so intimate as to make Him susceptible to its temptations, while on the other hand He is completely cut off from all fellowship with its sin. The confession which weakens or eliminates either of these factors must, when logically developed, degenerate into serious heresy. By saying, "The Mediator is conceived and born in our nature, as it was before the fall," we sever the fellowship between Him and *us;* and by allowing that He had the least personal part of our guilt and sin, we sever His fellowship with the *divine nature.*

Does the Scripture not teach then that the Mediator was made sin and bore the curse for us, and "as a worm and no man" suffered deepest distress?

We answer: Yea, verily, without this we could have no redemption. But in all this He acted as our Substitute. His own personality was not in the least affected by it. His burdening Himself with our sins was a High-Priestly act, performed vicariously. He was made *sin,* but never a *sinner.* Sinner means one who is *personally* affected by sin; Christ's person never was. He never had any fellowship with sin other than that of love and compassion, to bear it as our High Priest and Substitute. Yet, though He was exceedingly sorrowful even unto death, though He was sorely tempted so that He cried out, “Let this cup pass from Me,” in the center of His personal being He remained absolutely free from the least contact with sin.

A close examination of the way by which we become partakers of sin will shed more light on this subject.

Every individual sin is not of our own begetting only, but a participation in the common sin, the one mighty sin of the whole race against which the anger of God is kindled. Not only do we partake of this sin by an act of the will as we grow up; it was ours already in the cradle, in our mother’s womb—yea, even in our conception. “Conceived and born in sin” is the awful confession which the Church of God’s redeemed can never deny.

For this reason the Church has always laid such stress upon the doctrine of inherited guilt, as declared by St. Paul in Romans 5. Our inherited guilt does not spring from inherited *sin;* on the contrary, we are conceived and born in sin *because* we stand in *inherited guilt.* Adam’s guilt is imputed to all that were in his loins. Adam lived and fell as our natural and federal head. Our moral life stands in root-relation to his moral life. We were *in* him. He carried us in himself. His state determined our state. Hence by the righteous judgment of God his guilt was imputed to all his posterity, for as much as, by the will of man, they should successively be born of his loins. By virtue of this inherited guilt we are conceived in sin and born in the participation of sin.

God is our Creator, and from His hands we came forth pure and undefiled. To teach otherwise is to make Him the Author of individual sin, and to destroy the sense of guilt in the soul. Hence sin, especially original sin, does not originate in our *creation* by the hand of God, but by our *vital relation* with the sinful race. Our person does not proceed from our parents. This is in direct conflict with the indivisibility of spirit, with the Word of God, and its confession that God is *our* Creator, “who has also made *me.*”

However, all creation is not the same. There is mediate and immediate creation. God created light by immediate creation, but grass and herbs mediately, for they spring from the ground. The same difference exists between the creation of Adam and that of his posterity. The creation of Adam was immediate: not of his body, which was taken from the dust, but of his person, the human being called Adam. His posterity, however, is a mediate creation for every conception is made to depend upon the will of man. Hence while we come from the hand of God pure and undefiled, we become at the same time partakers of the inherited and imputed guilt of Adam; and by virtue of this inherited guilt, through our conception and birth, God brings us into fellowship with the sin of the race. How this is brought about is an unfathomable mystery, but this is a fact, that we become partakers of the sin of the race by generation, which begins with conception and ends with birth.

And now, with reference to the Person of Christ, everything depends upon the question whether the original guilt of Adam was imputed also to the man Jesus Christ.

If so, then, like all other men, Christ was conceived and born in sin *by virtue of this original guilt.* Where imputed original guilt is, there must be sinful defilement. But, on the other hand, where it is not, sinful defilement cannot be; hence He that is called holy and harmless must be undefiled. Adam's guilt was not imputed to the man Jesus Christ. If it were, then He was also conceived and born in sin; then He did not suffer vicariously, but for Himself personally; then there can be no blood of reconciliation. If the original guilt of Adam was imputed to the man Jesus Christ, then by virtue of His sinful conception and birth He was also subject to death and condemnation, and He could not have received life but by *regeneration.* Then it also follows that either this Man is Himself in need of a Mediator, or that we, like Him, can enter into life without a Go-between.

But this whole representation is without foundation, and is to be rejected without qualification. The whole Scripture opposes it. Adam's guilt is imputed to his posterity. But Christ is not a descendant of Adam. He existed before Adam. He was not born passively as we, but Himself took upon Him the human flesh. He does not stand under Adam as His head, but is Himself a new Head, having others under Him, of whom He saith: "Behold Me and the children whom Thou hast given Me" (Heb. 2:13). True, Luke 3:23, 28 contains the genealogy of Joseph, which closes with the words, "The son of Adam, the son of God," but the Evangelist adds emphatically, "as was supposed";

hence Jesus was not the son of Joseph. And in Matthew His genealogy stops at Abraham. Although on Pentecost St. Peter says that David knew that God would raise up Christ out of the fruit of his loins, yet he adds this limitation, "according to the flesh." Moreover, realizing that the Son did not assume a human person, but the human nature, so that His Ego is that of the Person of the Son of God, it necessarily follows that Jesus cannot be a descendant of Adam; hence the imputation of Adam's guilt to Christ would annihilate the divine Person. Such imputation is utterly out of the question. To Him nothing is imputed. The sins He bore He took upon Himself voluntarily, vicariously, as our High Priest and Mediator.

19

The Holy Spirit in the Mystery of the Incarnation

The Word was made flesh and dwelt among us, and we beheld His glory—John 1:14.

There is one more question in the treatment of this subject: What was the extraordinary operation of the Holy Spirit that enabled the Son of God to assume our fallen nature without being defiled by sin?

Although we concede it to be unlawful to pry into that behind the veil which God does not freely open to us, yet we may seek the meaning of the words that embody the mystery; and this we intend to do in the discussion of this question.

The Incarnation of Christ, with reference to His sinlessness, is connected with the being of sin, the character of original sin, the relation between body and soul, regeneration, and the working of the Holy Spirit in believers. Hence it is necessary for a clear understanding to have a correct view of the relation of Christ's human nature to these important matters.

Sin is not a spiritual bacillus hiding in the blood of the mother and received into the veins of the child. Sin is not material and tangible; its nature is moral and spiritual, belonging to the invisible things whose results we can perceive but whose real being escapes detection. Wherefore in opposition to Manicheism and kindred heresies, the Church has always confessed that sin is not a material substance in our flesh and blood, but that it consists in the loss of the original righteousness in which Adam and Eve bloomed and prospered in Paradise. Nor do believers differ on this point, for all acknowledge that sin is the loss of original righteousness.

However, tracing the next step in the course of sin, we meet a serious difference between the Church of Rome and our own. The former teaches that Adam came forth perfect from the hand of his Maker, even before he was endowed with original righteousness. This implies that the human nature is finished without original righteousness, which is put on him like a robe or ornament. As our present nature is complete without dress or ornament, which are needed only to appear respectable in the world, so was the human nature, according to Rome, complete and perfect in itself without righteousness, which serves only as dress and jewel. But the Reformed churches have always opposed this view, maintaining that original righteousness is an essential part of the human nature; hence that the human nature in Adam was not complete without it; that it was not merely added to Adam's nature, but that Adam was created in the possession of it as the direct manifestation of his life.

If Adam's nature was perfect before he possessed original righteousness, it follows that it remains perfect after the loss of it; in which case we describe sin simply as "carentia justitiae originalis," that is, the want of original righteousness. This used to be expressed thus: Is original righteousness a natural or supernatural good? If natural, then its loss caused the human nature to be wholly corrupt; if supernatural, then its loss might take away the glory and honor of that nature, but as a human nature it retained nearly all of its original power.

Bellarminus said that desire, disease, conflict, etc., naturally belong to human nature; and original righteousness was a golden bridle laid upon this nature, to check and control this desire, disease, conflict, etc. Hence when the golden bridle was lost, disease, desire, conflict, and death broke loose from restraint (tom. 4, chap. 5, col. 15, 17, 18). Thomas Aquinas, to whom Calvin was greatly indebted, and whom the present Pope has earnestly commended to his priests, had a more correct view. This is evident from his definition of sin. If disease, desire, etc., existed in man when he came from the hand of God, and only supernatural grace can restrain them, then sin is merely the loss of original righteousness, hence purely negative. But if original righteousness belongs to human nature and was not simply added to it supernaturally, then sin is twofold: first, the loss of original righteousness; second, the ruin and corruption of *human nature* itself, disorganizing and disjointing it. Thomas Aquinas acknowledges this last aspect, for he teaches (*Summa Theologiae,* prima secundae, 9, sect. 2, art. 1) that sin is not only *deprivation* and loss, but also a state of corruption, wherein must be distinguished the lack of what ought to be present, that is, original righteousness, and the presence of what ought to be absent, viz., an abnormal derangement of the parts and powers of the soul.

Our fathers held almost the same view. They judged that sin is not material, but the loss of original righteousness. But since original righteousness belongs to the sound human nature, the loss did not leave that nature intact, but damaged, disjointed, and corrupted it.

To illustrate: A beautiful geranium that adorned the window was killed by the frost. Leaves and flowers withered, leaving only a mass of mildew and decay. What was the cause? Merely the loss of the sun's light and heat. But that was enough; for these belong to the nature of the plant, and are essential to its life and beauty. Deprived of them it remains not what it is, but its nature loses its soundness, and this causes decay, mildew, and poisonous gases, which soon destroy it. So of human nature: In Paradise Adam was like the blooming plant, flourishing in the warmth and brightness of the Lord's presence. By sin he fled from that presence. The result was not merely the loss of light and heat, but since these were essential to his nature, that nature languished, drooped, and withered. The mildew of corruption formed upon it; and the positive process of dissolution was begun, to end only in eternal death.

Facts and history prove even now that the human body has weakened since the days of the Reformation; that bad habits of a certain character sometimes pass from father to child even where the early death of the former precludes propagation by education and example. Hence the difference between Adam, body and soul, before the fall and his descendants after the fall is not merely the loss of the Sun of Righteousness, which by nature shines no longer upon them, but the damage caused by this loss to the human nature, in body and soul, which thereby are weakened, diseased, corrupted, and thrown out of balance.

This corrupt nature passes from the father to the child, as the Confession of Faith expresses it in article 15: "That original sin is a corruption of the whole nature, and a hereditary disease, wherewith infants themselves are infected in their mother's womb, and which produces in man all sorts of sin, being in him as a root thereof."

However, the relation between a person and his ego must be taken into account. The disordered condition of our flesh and blood inclines and incites to sin, a fact that has been observed in the victims of certain terrible diseases as their effect. But this could not result in sin if there were no personal ego to allow itself to be excited. Again, though the unbalanced powers of the soul which cause the darkening of the understanding, the blunting of the sensibilities, and the weakening of the will arouse the passions, yet even this could not result in sin if no personal ego were affected by this working. Hence sin puts its own mark upon this corruption only when the personal ego turns away from God, and in that disordered soul and diseased body stands condemned before Him.

If according to established law the unclean brings forth the unclean, and if God has made our birth to depend upon generation by sinful men, it must follow that by nature we are born—first, without original righteousness; secondly, with an impaired body; thirdly, with a soul out of harmony with itself, lastly, with a personal ego which is turned away from God.

All of which would apply to the Person of the Mediator if, like one of us, He had been born a human person by the will of man and not of God. But since He was not born a human person, but took our human nature upon Himself, and was conceived not by the will of man, but by an operation of the Holy Spirit, there could not be in Him an ego turned away from God, nor could the weakness of His human nature for a moment be a sinful weakness. Or to put it in the concrete: Although there was in that fallen nature something to incite Him to desire, yet it never became desire. There is a difference between the temptations and conflicts of Jesus and those of ourselves; while our ego and nature desire against God, His holy Ego opposed the incitement of His adopted nature and was never overcome.

Hence the proper work of the Holy Spirit consisted in this:

First, the creation not of a new person, but of a human nature, which the Son assumed into union with His divine nature in one Person.

Second, that the divine-human Ego of the Mediator, who according to His human nature, also possessed spiritual life, was kept from the inward defilement which by virtue of our birth affected our ego and personality.

Hence regeneration, which affects not our nature but our person, is out of the question with reference to Christ. But what Christ needed was the gifts of the Holy Ghost to enable His weakened nature, in increasing measure, to be His instrument in the working out of His holy design; and finally to transform His weakened nature not by regeneration, but by resurrection into a glorious nature, divested of the last trace of weakness and prepared to unfold its highest glory.

Sixth Chapter
The Mediator

20

The Holy Spirit in the Mediator

Who through the Eternal Spirit offered Himself without spot to God—Hebrews 9:14.

The work of the Holy Spirit in the Person of Christ is not exhausted in the Incarnation, but appears conspicuously in the *work* of the Mediator. We consider this work in the *development of His human nature;* in the *consecration to His office;* in *His humiliation unto death;* in *His resurrection, exaltation, and return in glory.*

First—The work of the Holy Spirit in the *development of the human nature in Jesus.* We have said before, and now repeat, that we consider the effort to write the "Life of Jesus" either *unlawful* or its title a *misnomer:* a *misnomer* when, pretending to write a biography of Jesus, the writer simply omits to explain the psychological facts of His life; *unlawful* when he explains these facts from the human nature of Jesus.

There never was a life of Jesus in the sense of a human, personal existence; and the tendency to substitute the various biographies of Jesus of Nazareth for the simple Gospel narratives aims really at nothing else than to place the unique Person of the God-man on the same level with the geniuses and great men of the world, to humanize Him, and thus to annihilate the Messiah in Him—in other words, to *secularize Him.* And against this we solemnly protest with all the power that is in us.

The God-human Person of the Lord Jesus did not live a life, but rendered one mighty act of obedience by humbling Himself unto death; and out of that humbling He ascended not by powers developed from His human nature, but by a mighty and extraordinary act of the power of God. Anyone who successfully undertook to write the life of Christ could do no more than draw the picture of His human nature. For the divine nature has no history, does not run through a process of time, but remains the same forevermore.

However, this does not prevent us from inquiring, according to the need of our limitations, in what manner the human nature of Christ was developed. And then the Scripture teaches us that there was indeed growth in His human nature. St. Luke relates that Jesus increased in wisdom and stature and in favor with God and men. Hence there was in His human nature a growth and development from the less unto the greater. This would have been impossible if in the Messiah the divine nature had taken the place of the human ego; for then the majesty of the Godhead would always and completely have filled the human nature. But this was not the case. The human nature in the Mediator was real, that is, in body and soul it existed as it exists in us, and all inworking of divine life, light, and power could manifest itself only by adapting itself to the peculiarities and limitations of the human nature.

When maintaining the mistaken view that the development of sinless Adam would have been accomplished without the aid of the Holy Spirit, it is natural to suppose that the sinless nature of Christ did equally develop itself without the assistance of the Spirit of God. But knowing from the Scripture that not only man's gifts, powers, and faculties, but also their working and exercise are a result of the work of the Holy Spirit, we see the development of the human nature of Jesus in a different light and understand the meaning of the words that He received the *Holy Spirit without measure.* For this indicates that His human nature also received the Holy Ghost; and not this only after He had lived for years without Him, but every moment of His existence according to the measure of His capacities. Even in His conception and birth the Holy Spirit effected not only a separation from sin, but He also endowed His human nature with the glorious gifts, powers, and faculties of which that nature is susceptible. Hence His human nature received these gifts, powers, and faculties not *from the Son* by communication from the divine nature, but from the *Holy Ghost* by communication to the human nature; and this should be thoroughly understood.

However, His human nature did not receive these gifts, powers, and faculties in full operation, but wholly inoperative. As there are in every infant powers and faculties that will remain dormant, some of them for many years, so there were in the human nature of Christ powers and faculties which for a time remained slumbering. The Holy Spirit imparted these endowments to His human nature without measure—John 3:34. This has reference to a contrast between *others,* whom the Holy Spirit endowed not *without measure,* but in limited degree according to their individual calling or destiny; and *Christ,* in whom there is no such distinction or individuality—to whom, therefore, gifts, powers, and faculties are imparted in such a measure that He never could feel the lack of any gift of the Holy Spirit. He lacked nothing, possessed all; not by virtue of His divine nature, which cannot receive anything, being the eternal fullness itself, but by virtue of His human nature, which was endowed with such glorious gifts by the Holy Spirit.

However, this was not all. Not only did the Holy Spirit adorn the human nature of Christ with these endowments, but He also caused them to be exercised, gradually to enter into full activity.

This depended upon the succession of the days and years of the time of His humiliation. Although His heart contained the germ of all wisdom, yet as a child of one year, for example, He could not know the Scripture by means of His human understanding. As the Eternal Son He knew it, for He Himself had given it to His Church. But His human knowledge had no free access to His divine knowledge. On the contrary, while the latter never increased, knowing all things from eternity, the former was to learn everything; it had nothing of itself. This is the increase in wisdom of which St. Luke speaks—an increase not of the faculty, but of its exercise. And this affords us a glimpse into the extent of His humiliation. He that knew all things by virtue of His divine nature began as man with knowing nothing; and that which He knew as a man He acquired by learning it under the influence of the Holy Spirit.

And the same applies to His increase in stature and in favor with God and men. Stature refers to His physical growth, including all that in the human nature depends upon it. Not created an adult like Adam, but born a child like each of us, Jesus had to grow and develop physically; not by magic, but in reality. When He lay in Mary's lap, or as a boy looked around in his stepfather's shop, He was a child not only in appearance with the wisdom of a venerable, hoary head, but a real child, whose impressions, feelings, sensations, and thoughts kept step with His years. No doubt His development was quick and beautiful, surpassing anything ever seen in other children, so that the aged rabbis in the Temple were astonished when they looked upon the Boy only twelve years old; yet it always remained the development of a child that first lay upon His mother's lap, then learned to walk, gradually became a boy and youth, until He attained the fullness of man's stature.

And as the Holy Spirit with every increase of His human nature enlarged the exercise of its powers and faculties, so He did also with reference to the relation of the human nature to God and men, for He increased in favor with God and men. Favor has reference to the unfolding and development of the inward life, and may manifest itself in a twofold way, either pleasing or displeasing to God and men. Of Jesus it is said that in His development such gifts and faculties, dispositions and attributes, powers and qualifications manifested themselves from the inward life of His human nature that God's favor rested upon them, while they affected those around Him in a refreshing and helpful way.

Even apart from His Messiahship Jesus stood, with reference to His human nature, during all the days of His humiliation, under the constant and penetrating operation of the Holy Spirit. The Son, who lacked nothing, but as God in union with the Father and the Holy Spirit possessed all things, compassionately adopted our human nature. And inasmuch as it is the peculiarity of that nature to derive its gifts, powers, and faculties not from itself, but from the Holy Spirit, by whose constant operation alone they can be exercised, so did the Son not violate this peculiarity, but although He was the Son, He did not take its preparation, enriching, and operation into His own hand, but was willing to receive them from the hand of the Holy Spirit.

The fact that the Holy Spirit descended upon Jesus at His Baptism, although He had received Him without measure at His conception, can only be explained by keeping in view the difference between the *personal* and *official* life of Jesus.

21

Not Like unto Us

Then was Jesus led up of the Spirit into the wilderness—Matthew 4:1.

The representation that Christ's human nature received animating and qualifying influences and impulses directly from His divine nature, although on the whole incorrect, contains also some truth.

We often distinguish between our ego and nature. We say: "I have my nature against me," or "My nature is in my favor"; hence it follows that our person animates and actuates our nature. Applying this to the Person of the Mediator, we must distinguish between His human nature and His Person. The latter existed from eternity, the former He adopted in time. And since in the Son the divine Person and the divine nature are nearly one, it must be acknowledged that the Godhead of our Lord directly controlled His human nature. This is the meaning of the confession of God's children that His Godhead supported His human nature.

But it is wrong to suppose that the divine Person accomplished in His human nature what in us is effected by the Holy Spirit. This would endanger His true and real humanity. The Scripture positively denies it.

Second—The work of the Holy Spirit in the *consecration of Jesus to His office* (see "First," in previous chapter, p. 101).

This ought to be carefully noticed, especially since the Church has never sufficiently confessed the influence of the Holy Spirit exerted upon the work of Christ. The general impression is that the work of the Holy Spirit begins when the work of the Mediator on earth is finished, as though until that time the Holy Spirit celebrated His divine day of rest. Yet the Scripture teaches us again and again that Christ performed His mediatorial work controlled and impelled by the Holy Spirit. We consider this influence now with reference to His *consecration to His office.*

By the spirit of the prophets already Christ testified of this saying by the mouth of Isaiah: "The Spirit of the Lord Jehovah is upon me, because the Lord hath anointed me to preach good tidings unto the meek." But the great fact which could not be learned from prophecy is that of the descent of the Holy Spirit at Jordan. Surely Isaiah referred partly to this event, but principally to the anointing in the counsel of peace. However, when Jesus went up out of Jordan, and the Holy Spirit descended upon Him like a dove, and a voice was heard from heaven saying, "This is My beloved Son," then only the anointing became actual.

In regard to the event itself, only a few words. That Christ's Baptism was not a mere form, but the fulfilling of all righteousness proves that He descended into the water burdened with our sins. Hence St. John makes the words, "Behold the Lamb of God," precede the account of His Baptism. Wherefore it is incorrect to say that Christ was installed into His Messianic office only at His Baptism. On the contrary, He was anointed from eternity. Wherefore He may not be represented as being for a moment unconscious, according to the measure of His development, of the Messiah task that rested upon Him. This lay in His holy Person; it was not added to Him at a later period, but was His before Adam fell. And as in His human consciousness His Person gradually attained stature, it was always the stature of the Messiah. This is evident from His answer when, at the age of twelve, He spoke of the things of His Father which were to occupy Him; and still more clearly from His words to John the Baptist commandingly saying: "Suffer it to be so now, for thus it becometh us to fulfill all righteousness."

And yet it is only at His Baptism that Jesus receives the actual consecration to His office. This is proven from the fact that immediately after this He entered publicly upon His office as a Teacher; and also from the event itself, and the voice from heaven pointing to Him as the Messiah; and especially from the descent of the Holy Spirit, which cannot be interpreted in any other way than as His consecration to His holy office.

What we have said with reference to the communication of the Holy Spirit qualifying one for office, as in the case of Saul, David, and others, is of direct application here. Although in His human nature Jesus was personally in constant fellowship with the Holy Spirit, yet the official communication was established only at the time of His Baptism. Yet with this difference, that while in others the person and his office are separated at death, in the Messiah the two remain united even in and after death, to continue so until the moment that He shall deliver the Kingdom unto God the Father, that God may be all in all. Hence the descriptive remark of John: "I saw the Spirit descending from heaven, *and it abode on Him*" (John 1:32).

And finally, to the question why the Person of the Mediator needed this remarkable event and the three signs that accompany it, we answer:

First, Christ must be a true man even in His office, wherefore He must be installed according to the human custom. He enters upon His public ministry at thirty; He is publicly installed; and He is anointed with the Holy Spirit.

Second, for His human consciousness this striking revelation from heaven was of the utmost necessity. The conflict of the temptation was to be absolute, that is, *indescribable;* hence the impression of His consecration must be *indestructible.*

Third, for the apostles and the Church it was necessary to distinguish unmistakably the true Messiah from all the pseudo-messiahs and antichrists. This is the reason of St. John's strong appeal to this event.

If the work of the Holy Spirit with reference to the consecration is conspicuous and clearly indicated, the fact that the official influences of the Holy Spirit accompanied the Mediator throughout the entire administration of His office is not less clearly set forth in the Holy Scripture. This appears from the events immediately following the Baptism. St. Luke relates that Jesus being full of the Holy Spirit, was led by the Spirit into the wilderness. St. Matthew adds: "To be tempted of the devil." Of Elias, Ezekiel, and others it is said that the Spirit took them up and transferred them to some other place. This stands in evident connection with what we read here concerning Jesus. With this difference, however, that while the propelling power came to them from without, Jesus, being full of the Holy Spirit, felt its pressure in the very depths of His soul. And yet, although operating in His soul, this action of the Holy Spirit was not identical with the impulses of Christ's human nature. Of Himself Jesus would not have gone into the desert; His going there was the result of the Holy Spirit's leading. Only in this way this passage receives its full explanation.

That this leading of the Holy Spirit was not limited to this one act appears from St. Luke, who relates (chap. 4:14) that after the temptation He returned in the power of the Holy Spirit into Galilee, thus entering upon the public ministry of His prophetic office.

It is evidently the purpose of the Scripture to emphasize the fact of the inability of the human nature which Christ had adopted to accomplish the work of the Messiah without the constant operation and powerful leading of the Holy Spirit, whereby it was so strengthened that it could be the instrument of the Son of God for the performance of His wonderful work.

Jesus was conscious of this, and at the beginning of His ministry expressly indicated it. In their synagogue He turned to Isaiah 61:1, and read to them: "The Spirit of the Lord is upon me, because the Lord hath anointed me"; then added: "This day is this Scripture fulfilled in your ears."

The Holy Spirit did not support His human nature in the temptation and in the opening ministry only, but in all His mighty deeds, as Christ Himself testified: "If I cast out devils by the Spirit of God, then the Kingdom of God is come unto you" (Matt. 12:28). Moreover, St. Paul teaches that the gifts of healing and miracles proceed from the Holy Spirit, and this, in connection with the statement that these powers worked in Jesus (Mark 6:14), convinces us that these were the very powers of the Holy Spirit. Again, it is frequently said He rejoiced in the Spirit or was troubled in the Spirit, which may be interpreted as a rejoicing or being troubled in His own spirit, but this is not a complete explanation. When it refers to His own spirit it reads: "And He sighed deeply in His spirit" (Mark 8:12). But in the other cases we interpret the expressions as pointing to those deeper and more glorious emotions of which our human nature is susceptible only when abiding in the Holy Spirit. For although St. John states that Jesus groaned in Himself (chap. 11:38), this is not contradictory, especially with reference to Jesus. If the Holy Spirit always abode in Him, the same emotion may be attributed both to Him and to the Holy Spirit.

Apart, however, from these passages and their interpretations, we have said enough to prove that that part of Christ's work of mediation, beginning with His Baptism and closing in the upper chamber, was marked by the operation, influence, and support of the Holy Spirit.

According to the divine counsel, human nature is adapted in creation to the inworking of the Holy Spirit, without which it cannot unfold itself any more than the rosebud without the light and influence of the sun. As the ear cannot hear without sound, and the eye cannot see without light, so is our human nature incomplete without the light and indwelling of the Holy Spirit. Wherefore, when the Son assumed human nature He took it just as it is, that is, incapable of any holy action without the power of the Holy Spirit. Hence He was conceived by the Holy Spirit, that from the beginning His human nature should be richly endowed with powers. The Holy Spirit developed these powers; and He was consecrated to His office by the communication to His human nature of the Messianic gifts by which He still intercedes for us as our High Priest, and rules us as our King. And for this reason He was guided, impelled, animated, and supported by the Holy Spirit at every step of His Messianic ministry.

There are three differences between this communication of the Holy Spirit to the human nature of Jesus and that in us:

First, the Holy Spirit always meets with the resistance of evil in our hearts. Jesus' heart was without sin and unrighteousness. Hence in His human nature the Holy Spirit met no resistance.

Secondly, the Holy Spirit's operation, influence, support, and guidance in our human nature is always individual, that is, in part, imperfect; in the human nature of Jesus it was central, perfect, leaving no void.

Thirdly, in our nature the Holy Spirit meets with an ego which in union with that nature opposes God; while the Person which He met in the human nature of Christ, partaking of the divine nature, was absolutely holy. For the Son having adopted the human nature in union with His Person, was cooperating with the Holy Spirit.

22

The Holy Spirit in the Passion of Christ

Who through the Eternal Spirit offered Himself—Hebrews 9:14.

Thirdly—Let us now trace the work of the Holy Spirit in the *suffering, death, resurrection, and exaltation of Christ* (see "First" and "Second," pp. 101 and 105).

In the Epistle to the Hebrews the apostle asks: "If the blood of goats and calves and the ashes of the heifer sprinkling the unclean, sanctifieth to the purification of the flesh, how much more shall the blood of Christ purge your conscience from dead works?" adding the words: "Who through the Eternal Spirit offered Himself without spot to God." The meaning of these words has been much disputed. Beza and Gomarus understood the Eternal Spirit to signify Christ's *divine nature.* Calvin and the majority of reformers made it to refer to the Holy Spirit. Expositors of the present day, especially those of rationalistic tendencies, understand by it merely the tension of Christ's human nature.

With the majority of orthodox expositors we adopt the view of Calvin. The difference between Beza and Calvin is that already referred to. The question is, whether as regards His human nature Christ substituted the inworking of the Son for that of the Holy Spirit; or did He have the ordinary operation of the Holy Spirit?

At the present time many have adopted the former view without clearly understanding the difference. They reason thus: "Are the two natures not united in the Person of Jesus? Why, then, should the Holy Spirit be added to qualify the human nature? Could the Son Himself not do this?" And so they reach the conclusion that since the Mediator is God, there could be no need of a work of the Holy Spirit in the human nature of Christ. And yet this view must be rejected, for—

First, God has so created human nature that without the Holy Spirit it cannot have any virtue or holiness. Adam's original righteousness was the work and fruit of the Holy Spirit as truly as the new life in the regenerate is today. The shining-in of the Holy Spirit is as essential to holiness as the shining of light into the eye is essential to seeing.

Second, the work of the Son according to the distinction of three divine Persons is other than the work of the Holy Spirit with reference to the human nature. The Holy Spirit could not become flesh; this the Son alone could do. The Father has not delivered all things to the Holy Spirit. The Holy Spirit works from the Son, but the Son depends upon the Holy Spirit for the application of redemption to individuals. The Son adopts our nature, thus relating Himself with the whole race, but the Holy Spirit alone can so enter into individual souls as to glorify the Son in the children of God.

Applying these two principles to the Person of Christ, we see that His human nature could not dispense with the constant in-shining of the Holy Spirit. For which reason Scripture declares: "He gave Him the Spirit without measure." Nor could the Son according to His own nature take the place of the Holy Spirit, but in the divine economy, by virtue of His union with the human nature, ever depended upon the Holy Spirit.

As to the question, whether the Godhead of Christ did not support His humanity, we answer: Undoubtedly, but never independently of the Holy Spirit. We *faint* because we resist, grieve, and repel the Holy Spirit. Christ was always victorious because His divinity never relaxed His hold upon the Holy Spirit in His humanity, but embraced Him and cleaved unto Him with all the love and energy of the Son of God.

Human nature is limited. It is susceptible of receiving the Holy Spirit so as to be His temple. But that susceptibility has its limits. Opposed by eternal death, it loses its tension and falls away from the fellowship of the Holy Spirit. Hence we have no unlosable good in ourselves, but only as members of the body of Christ. Apart from Him, eternal death would have power over us, would separate us from the Holy Spirit and destroy us. Wherefore all our salvation lies in Christ. He is our anchor cast within the veil. As to the human nature of Christ, it encountered and passed through eternal death. This could not be otherwise. If He had passed only through temporal death, eternal death would still be unvanquished.

To the question how His human nature could pass through eternal death and not perish, having no Mediator to support it, we answer: The human nature of Christ would have been overwhelmed by it, the in-shining of the Holy Spirit would have ceased if His divine nature, that is, the infinite might of His Godhead, had not been underneath it. Hence the apostle declares: "Who through the *Eternal* Spirit offered Himself"; not through the *Holy* Spirit. The two expressions are not identical. There is a difference between the Holy Spirit, the third Person in the Godhead, *apart from* me, and the Holy Spirit *working within* me.

The word of Scripture, "He was full of the Holy Ghost," refers not only to the Person of the Holy Spirit, but also to His work in man's soul. So with reference to Christ, there is a difference between: "He was conceived by the Holy Ghost," "The Holy Ghost descended upon Him," "Being full of the Holy Spirit," "Who offered Himself by the Eternal Spirit." The last two passages indicate the fact that the spirit of Jesus had *taken in* the Holy Spirit and *identified* itself with Him, in almost the same sense as Acts 15:28: "It seemed good to the Holy Ghost *and to us.*" The term "Eternal Spirit" was chosen to indicate that the divine-human Person of Christ entered into such indissoluble fellowship with the Holy Spirit as even eternal death could not break.

A closer examination of the sufferings of Christ will make this clear.

Christ did not redeem us by His sufferings alone, being spit upon, scourged, crowned with thorns, crucified, and slain, but this passion was made effectual to our redemption by His *love* and *voluntary* obedience. These are generally called His *passive* and *active* satisfaction. By the first we understand His actual bearing of pain, anguish, and death; by the second, His zeal for the honor of God, the love, faithfulness, and divine pity by which He became obedient even unto death—yea, the death of the cross. And these two are essentially distinct. Satan, for example, bears punishment also and shall bear it forever, but he lacks the willingness. This, however, does not affect the validity of the punishment. A murderer on the gallows may curse God and men to the end, but this does not invalidate his punishment. Whether he curses or prays, it is equally valid.

Hence there was in Christ's sufferings much more than mere passive, penal satisfaction. Nobody compelled Jesus. He, partaker of the divine nature, could not be compelled, but offered Himself quite voluntarily: "Lo, I come to do Thy will, O God; in the volume of the book it is written of Me." To render that voluntary sacrifice He had with equal willingness adopted the prepared body: "Who being in the form of God thought it no robbery to be equal with God, but made Himself of no reputation; and being found in fashion as a man, He humbled Himself and became obedient unto death, even the death of the cross"; "Who, though He were a Son, yet learned He obedience." And to give highest proof of this obedience unto death, He inwardly consecrated Himself to death, as He Himself testified: "I sanctify Myself for them."

This leads to the important question, whether Jesus rendered this obedience and consecration outside of His human nature, or in it, so that it manifested itself in His human nature. Undoubtedly the latter. The divine nature cannot learn, or be tempted; the Son could not love the Father with other than eternal love. In the divine nature there is no *more* or *less.* To suppose this is to annihilate the divine nature. The statement that, "though He were the Son, yet learned He obedience," does not mean that as *God* He learned obedience; for God cannot obey. God rules, governs, commands, but never obeys. As King He can serve us only in the form of a slave, hiding His princely majesty, having emptied Himself, standing before us as one despised among me. "Though He were the Son" means, therefore: although in His inward Being He is God the Son, yet He stood before us in such lowliness that nothing betrayed His divinity; yea, so lowly that He even learned obedience.

Wherefore if the Mediator as man showed in His human nature such zeal for God and such pity for sinners that He willingly gave Himself in self-sacrifice unto death, then it is evident that His human nature could not exercise such consecration without the inworking of the Holy Spirit; and again that the Holy Spirit could not have effected such inworking unless the Son willed and desired it. The cry of the Messiah is heard in the words of the psalmist: "I delight to do Thy will, O God." The Son was willing so to empty Himself that it would be possible for His human nature to pass through eternal death; and to this end He let it be filled with all the mightiness of the Spirit of God. Thus the Son offered Himself "through the Eternal Spirit that we might serve the living God."

Hence the work of the Holy Spirit in the work of redemption did not begin only at Pentecost, but the same Holy Spirit who in creation animates all life, upholds and qualifies our human nature, and in Israel and the prophets wrought the work of revelation, also prepared the body of Christ, adorned His human nature with gracious gifts, put these gifts into operation, installed Him into His office, led Him into temptation, qualified Him to cast out devils, and finally enabled Him to finish that eternal work of satisfaction whereby our souls are redeemed.

This explains why Beza and Gomarus could not be fully satisfied with Calvin's exposition. Calvin said that it was the working of the Holy Spirit apart from the divinity of the Son. And they felt that there was something lacking. For the *Son* made Himself of no reputation and became obedient, but if all this is the work of the Holy Spirit, then nothing is left of the work of the Son. And to escape from this, they adopted the other extreme, and declared that the Eternal Spirit had reference only to the Son according to His divine nature—an exposition that cannot be accepted, for the divine nature is never designated as spirit.

Yet they were not altogether wrong. The reconciliation of these contrary views must be looked for in the difference between the *existence of the Holy Spirit without us,* and *His working within us as received by our nature and identified with its own working.* And inasmuch as the Son, by His Godhead, enabled His human nature, in the awful conflict with eternal death, to effect this union, therefore the apostle confesses that the sacrifice of the Mediator was rendered by the working of the Eternal Spirit.

23

The Holy Spirit in the Glorified Christ

Declared to be the Son of God with power, according to the Spirit of holiness, by the resurrection from the dead—Romans 1:4.

From the foregoing studies it appears that the Holy Spirit performed a work in the human nature of Christ as He descended the several steps of His humiliation to the death on the cross.

The question now arises, whether He had also a work in the several steps of Christ's exaltation to the excellent glory, that is, in *His resurrection, ascension, royal dignity, and second coming.*

Before we answer this question, let us first consider the nature of this work in the exaltation. For it is evident that it must greatly differ from that in His humiliation. In the latter His human nature suffered *violence.* His sufferings antagonized not only His divine nature, but also His human nature. To suffer pain, insult, and mockery, to be scourged and crucified, goes against human nature. The effort to resist such sufferings and to escape from them is perfectly natural. Christ's groaning in Gethsemane is the natural utterance of the human feeling. He was burdened with the curse and wrath of God against the sin of the race. Then human nature struggled against the burden, and the cry, "Father, let this cup pass from Me," was the sincere and natural cry of horror which human nature could not repress.

And not in Gethsemane alone; through His whole humiliation He experienced the same, though in less degree. His self-emptying was not a single loss or bereavement, but a growing poorer and poorer, until at last nothing was left Him but a piece of ground where He could weep and a cross whereon He could die. He renounced all that heart and flesh hold dear, until, without friend or brother, without one tone of love, amid the mocking laughter of His slanderers, He gave up the ghost. Surely He trod the winepress alone.

His humiliation being so deep and real, it is not surprising that the Holy Spirit succored and comforted His human nature so that it was not overwhelmed. For it is the proper work of the Holy Spirit by gifts of grace to enable human nature, tempted by sorrow to sin, to stand firm and overcome. He animated Adam before the fall; He comforts and supports all the children of God today; and He did the same in the human nature of Jesus. What air is to man's physical nature, the Holy Spirit is to his spiritual nature. Without air there is death in our bodies; without the Holy Spirit there is death in our souls. And as Jesus had to die, though He was the Son, when breath failed Him, so He could not live according to His human nature, though He was the Son, except the Holy Spirit dwelt in that nature. Since, according to the spiritual side of His human nature, He was not dead as we are, but was *born* possessed of the life of God, so it was impossible for His human nature for a single moment to be without the Holy Spirit.

But how different in the state of His exaltation! Honor and glory are *not* against human nature, but satisfy it. It covets them and longs for them with all its energy of desire. Hence this exaltation created no conflict in the soul of Jesus. His human nature needed no support to bear it. Hence the question: What, then, could the Holy Spirit do for the human nature in the state of glory?

Regarding the resurrection, the Scripture teaches more than once that it was connected with a work of the Holy Spirit. St. Paul says (Rom. 1:4) that Jesus was "declared to be the Son of God, by the *Spirit of holiness* with power, by the *resurrection* from the dead." And St. Peter says (1 Peter 3:18) that Christ "being put to death in the flesh, was quickened by the Spirit," which evidently refers to the resurrection, as the context shows: "For Christ once suffered for our sins, the just for the unjust, that He might bring us to God." His death points to the crucifixion, and His quickening, being the opposite of the latter, undoubtedly refers to His resurrection.

In Romans 8:2, speaking of our resurrection, St. Paul explains these more or less puzzling utterances, affirming that "if the Spirit of Him that raised up Jesus from the dead dwell in you, He that raised up Christ from the dead shall also quicken your mortal bodies by His Spirit that dwelleth in you." This passage tells three things concerning our resurrection:

First, that the Triune God shall raise us up.

Second, that this shall be wrought by a special work of the Holy Spirit.

Third, that it shall be effected by the Spirit that dwelleth in us.

St. Paul induces us to apply these three to Christ; for He compares our resurrection with His, not only as regards the fact, but also as regards the working whereby it was effected. Hence with reference to the latter it must be confessed:

First, that the Triune God raised Him from the dead. St. Peter stated this clearly on the day of Pentecost: "Whom God has raised up, having loosed the pains of death"; St. Paul repeated it in Ephesians 1:20, where he speaks of "His mighty power" which He wrought in Christ, when He raised Him from the dead.

Second, that God the Holy Spirit performed a peculiar work in the resurrection.

Third, that He wrought this work in Christ *from within,* dwelling in Him: "Which dwelleth in you."

The nature of this work is apparent from the Holy Spirit's part in Adam's *creation* and in *our birth.* If the Spirit kindles and brings forth all life, especially in man, then it was He who rekindled the spark quenched by sin and death. He did so in Jesus; He will do so in us.

The only remaining difficulty is on the third point: "Which dwelleth in you." The work of the Holy Spirit in our creation, and therefore in that of Christ's human nature, came *from without;* in the resurrection it works *from within.* Of course persons dying without being temples of the Holy Spirit are excluded. St. Paul speaks exclusively of men whose hearts are His temples. Hence representing Him as dwelling in them, he speaks of Him as the *Spirit of holiness,* and Peter as the *"Spirit,"* indicating that they do not refer to a work of the Holy Spirit in *opposition* to the spirit of Jesus, but in which His spirit agreed and cooperated. And this harmonizes with Christ's own words, that in the resurrection He would not be passive, but active: "I have power to lay down life and I have power to take it again. This commandment I have received of My Father." The apostles declare again and again not only that Jesus *was raised* from the dead, but that He has *risen.* He had thus foretold it, and the angels said: "Behold, He is risen."

Hence we reach this conclusion, that the work of the Holy Spirit in the resurrection was different from that in the humiliation; was similar to that in the creation; and was performed from *within* by the Spirit *who dwelt in Him* without measure, who continued with Him *through His death,* and in whose work His *own spirit* fully concurred.

The work of the Holy Spirit in the *exaltation* of Christ is not so easily defined. The Scripture never speaks of it in connection with His ascension, His sitting at the right hand of the Father, nor with the Lord's second coming. Its connection with the descent at Pentecost will be treated in its proper place. Light upon these points can be obtained only from the scattered statements concerning the work of the Holy Spirit upon human nature in general. According to Scripture, the Holy Spirit belongs to our nature as the light to the eye; not only in its sinful condition, but also in the sinless state. From this we infer that Adam before he fell was not without His inworking; hence that in the heavenly Jerusalem our human nature will possess Him in richer, fuller, more glorious measure. For our sanctified nature is a habitation of God through the Spirit—Ephesians 2:22.

If, therefore, our blessedness in heaven consists in the enjoyment of the pleasures of God, and it is the Holy Spirit who comes into contact with our innermost being, it follows that in heaven He cannot leave us. And upon this ground we confess, that not only the elect, but the glorified Christ also, who continues to be a true man in heaven, must therefore forever continue to be filled with the Holy Spirit. This our churches have always confessed in the Liturgy: "The same Spirit which dwelleth in Christ as the Head and in us as His members."

The same Holy Spirit who performed His work in the conception of our Lord, who attended the unfolding of His human nature, who brought into activity every gift and power in Him, who consecrated Him to His office as the Messiah, who qualified Him for every conflict and temptation, who enabled Him to cast out devils, and who supported Him in His humiliation, passion, and bitter death, was the same Spirit who performed His work in His resurrection, so that Jesus was justified in the Spirit (1 Tim. 3:16), and who dwells now in the glorified human nature of the Redeemer in the heavenly Jerusalem.

In this connection it should be noticed that Jesus said of His body: "Destroy this temple, and in three days I will raise it up." The Temple was God's habitation on Zion; hence it was a symbol of that habitation of God that was to be set up in our hearts. Hence this saying refers not to the indwelling of the Son in our flesh, but to that of the Holy Spirit in the human nature of Jesus. Wherefore St. Paul writes to the Corinthians: "Know ye not that your body is the temple of the Holy Ghost, which is in you?" If the apostle calls our bodies temples of the Holy Ghost, why should we take it in another sense with reference to Jesus?

If Christ dwelt in our *flesh,* that is, in our human nature, body and soul, and if the Holy Ghost dwells, on the contrary, in the temple of our *body,* we see that Jesus Himself considered His death and resurrection an awful process of suffering through which He must enter into glory, but without being for a single moment separated from the Holy Spirit.

Seventh Chapter
The Outpouring of the Holy Spirit

24

The Outpouring of the Holy Spirit

The Holy Spirit was not yet given because that Jesus was not yet glorified—John 7:39.

We have come to the most difficult part in the discussion of the work of the Holy Spirit, viz., the outpouring of the Holy Spirit on the tenth day after the ascension.

In the treatment of this subject it is not our aim to create a new interest in the celebration of Pentecost. We consider this almost impossible. Man's nature is too unspiritual for this. But we shall reverently endeavor to give a clearer insight into this event to those in whose hearts the Holy Spirit has already begun His work.

For, however simple the account of the second chapter of the Acts may seem, it is very intricate and hard to explain; and he who earnestly tries to understand and explain the event will meet more and more serious difficulties as he penetrates more deeply into the inward connection of the Holy Scripture. For this reason we claim not that our exposition will entirely solve this mystery. We shall endeavor only to fix the sanctified mind of the people of God more earnestly upon it, and convince them that on the whole this subject is treated too superficially.

Four difficulties meet us in the examination of this event:

First, How shall we explain the fact that while the Holy Spirit was poured out only on Pentecost, the saints of the Old Covenant were already partakers of His gifts?

Second, How shall we distinguish the outpouring of the Holy Spirit nineteen centuries ago from His entering into the soul of the unconverted today?

Third, How could the apostles—having already confessed the good confession, forsaking all, following Jesus, and upon whom He had breathed, saying, "Receive ye the Holy Ghost"—receive the Holy Spirit only on the tenth day after the ascension?

Fourth, How are we to explain the mysterious signs that accompany the outpouring? There are no angels praising God, but a sound is heard like that of a rushing, mighty wind, the glory of the Lord does not appear, but tongues of fire hover over their heads; there is no theophany, but a speaking in peculiar and uncommon sounds, understood, however, by those present.

With reference to the *first difficulty:* How to explain the fact that, while the Holy Spirit was poured out only on Pentecost, the saints of the Old Covenant were already partakers of His gifts. Let us put this in the concrete: How are the following passages to be reconciled?—"I am with you, saith the Lord of Hosts, and My Spirit remaineth among you, fear ye not" (Hag. 2:4, 5); and "This spake He of the Holy Spirit which they that believe should receive, for the Holy Spirit was not yet given, because that Jesus was not yet glorified" (John 7:39).

Scripture evidently seeks to impress us with the two facts, that the Holy Spirit came only on the day of Pentecost, and that the same Spirit had wrought already for centuries in the Church of the Old Covenant. Not only does St. John declare definitely that the Holy Spirit was not yet given, but the predictions of the prophets and of Jesus and the whole attitude of the apostles show that this fact may not in the least be weakened.

Let us first examine the prophecies. Isaiah, Ezekiel, and Joel bear undeniable witness to the fact that this was the expectation of the prophets.

Isaiah says: "The palaces shall be forsaken, the multitudes of the city shall be left—*until the Spirit shall be poured upon us from on high; then* the wilderness shall be a fruitful field, and the fruitful field shall be counted for a forest; *then* judgment shall dwell in the wilderness, and righteousness remain in the fruitful field." This prophecy evidently refers to an outpouring of the Holy Spirit that shall effect a work of salvation on a large scale, for it closes with the promise: "And the work of righteousness shall be peace, and the effect of righteousness, quietness, and assurance forever" (Is. 32:14–17).

In like manner did Ezekiel prophesy: "Then will I sprinkle clean water upon you, and ye shall be clean; a new heart also will I give you, and a new spirit will I put within you; and I will put My Spirit within you, and cause you to walk in My statutes; and ye shall keep My judgments, and do them; and I will save you from all your uncleanness. Not for yourselves will I do this, saith the Lord, be it known unto you" (36:25). Ezekiel 11:19 gives the prelude of this prophecy: "Thus saith the Lord God, I will give them one heart, and I will give a new Spirit within them; and I will take the stony heart out of their flesh, that they may walk in My statutes."

Joel uttered his well-known prophecy: "And it shall come to pass afterward that I will pour My Spirit upon all flesh, and your sons and your daughters shall prophesy, your old men shall dream dreams, your young men shall see visions; and also upon thy servants and upon thy handmaidens in those days will I pour out My Spirit" (Joel 2:30, 31); a prophecy which, according to the authoritative exposition of St. Peter, refers directly to the day of Pentecost.

Zechariah adds a beautiful prophecy (12:10): "I will pour out the Spirit of grace and of supplication."

It is true that these prophecies were given to Israel during its later period, when the vigorous spiritual life of the nation had already departed. But Moses expressed the same thought in his prophetic prayer: "Would God that all the Lord's people were prophets, and that the Lord would put His Spirit upon them" (Num. 11:29). But these prophecies are evidence of the Old Testament prophetic conviction that the dispensation of the Holy Spirit in those days was exceedingly imperfect; that the real dispensation of the Holy Spirit was still tarrying; and that only in the days of the Messiah was it to come in all its fullness and glory.

Regarding the *second difficulty,* our Lord repeatedly put the stamp of His divine authority upon this prophetic conviction, announcing to

His disciples the still future coming of the Holy Spirit: "I will pray the Father and He shall give you another Comforter, that He may abide with you forever; even the Spirit of truth, whom the world cannot receive, because it seeth Him not, neither knoweth Him, for He dwelleth with you *and shall be in you*" (John 14:16, 17); "When the Comforter is come whom I will send from the Father, even the Spirit of truth, which proceedeth from the Father, He shall testify of Me" (John 15:26); "Behold, I send the promise of the Father upon you, and ye shall be endued with power from on high" (Luke 24:49); "It is expedient for you that I go away; for if I go not away the Comforter will not come unto you, but if I depart, I will send Him unto you. And when He is come, He will reprove the world of sin, of righteousness, and of judgment" (John 16:7, 8). And lastly: He commanded them not to depart from Jerusalem, but to wait for the promise of the Father, "which, saith He, ye have heard of Me; for John truly baptized with water, but ye shall be baptized with the Holy Ghost not many days hence. And ye shall receive power after that the Holy Ghost is come upon you" (Acts 1:4, 5, 8).

The *third difficulty* is met by the fact that the communications of the apostles agree with the teaching of Scripture. They actually tarried in Jerusalem, without even attempting to preach during the days between the ascension and Pentecost. And they explain the Pentecost miracle as the fulfillment of the prophecies of Joel and Jesus. They see in it something new and extraordinary; and show us clearly that in their day it was considered that a man who stood outside the Pentecost miracle knew nothing of the Holy Ghost. For the disciples of Ephesus being asked, "Have ye received the Holy Ghost?" answered naively: "We have not so much as heard whether there be any Holy Ghost."

Wherefore it cannot be doubted that the Holy Scripture means to teach and convince us that the outpouring of the Holy Spirit on Pentecost was His first and real coming into the Church.

But how can this be reconciled with Old Testament passages such as these?—"Yet now be strong, O Zerubbabel, saith the Lord; and be strong, O Joshua, the High Priest; . . . for I am with you, . . . and My Spirit *remaineth among you: fear ye not*" (Hag. 2:4, 5); and again: "Then He remembered the days of old, Moses, and His people, saying, Where is He that brought them up out of the sea with the Shepherd of His flock? Where is He that put His Holy Spirit within them?" (Is. 63:2). David is conscious that he had received the Holy Spirit, for after his fall he prays: "Take not Thy Holy Spirit from me" (Ps. 51:13). There was a sending forth of the Spirit, for we read: "Thou sendest forth Thy Spirit, and they are created; and Thou renewest the face of the earth" (Ps. 104:30). There seems to have been an actual descending of the Holy Spirit, for Ezekiel says: "The Spirit of the Lord fell upon me" (chap. 11:5). Micah testified: "Truly I am full of the power by the Spirit of the Lord" (chap. 3:8). Of John the Baptist it is written, that he should be filled with the Holy Ghost from his mother's womb—Luke 1:15. Even the Lord Himself was filled with the Holy Spirit, whom He received without measure. That Spirit came upon Him at Jordan, how then could He be spoken of as still to come?—a question all the more puzzling since we read that in the evening of the resurrection Jesus breathed upon His disciples, saying: "Receive ye the Holy Ghost" (John 20:22).

It has been necessary to present this large series of testimonies to show our readers the difficulty of the problem which we will endeavor to solve in the next article.

25

The Holy Spirit in the New Testament Other than in the Old

By His Spirit which dwelleth in you—Romans 8:2.

In order to understand the change inaugurated on Pentecost we must distinguish between the various ways in which the Holy Ghost enters into relationship with the creature.

With the Christian Church we confess that the Holy Spirit is true and eternal God, and therefore omnipresent; hence no creature, stone or animal, man or angel, is excluded from His presence.

With reference to His omniscience and omnipresence, David sings: "Whither shall I go from Thy Spirit, or whither shall I flee from Thy presence? If I ascend up to heaven, Thou art there; if I make my bed in hell, behold, Thou art there. If I take the wings of the morning and dwell in the uttermost parts of the sea, even there shall Thy hand lead me and Thy right hand shall hold me." These words state positively that omnipresence belongs to the Holy Spirit; that neither in heaven nor in hell, in the east nor in the west, is there a spot or point from which He is excluded.

This simple consideration is, for the matter under discussion, of the greatest importance; for it follows that the Holy Spirit cannot be said ever to have moved from one place to another; to have been among Israel, but not among the nations; to have been present after the day of Pentecost where He was not before. All such representations directly oppose the confession of His omnipresence, eternity, and immutability. The Omnipresent One cannot go from one place to another, for He cannot come where He is already. And to suppose that He is omnipresent at one time and not at another is inconsistent with His eternal Godhead. The testimony of John the Baptist, "I saw the Spirit descending from heaven like a dove, and it abode on Him," and that of St. Luke, "The Holy Spirit fell on all them which heard the Word," may not therefore be understood as though the Holy Spirit came to a place where He was not before, which is impossible.

However—and this is the first distinction which will throw light upon the matter—David's description of omnipresence applies to *local presence in space,* but not to *the world of spirits.*

We know not what spirits are, nor what our own spirit is. In the body we can distinguish between nerves and blood, bones and muscles, and we know something of their functions in the organism, but how a spirit exists, moves, and works, we cannot tell. We only know that it exists, moves, and works in an entirely different way from that of the body. When a brother dies nobody opens a door or window for the exit of the soul; for we know that neither wall nor ceiling can hinder it in its heavenward flight. In prayer we whisper so as not to be overheard; yet we believe that the man Jesus Christ hears every word. The swiftness of a thought exceeds that of electricity. In a word, the limitations of the material world seem to disappear in the realm of spirits.

Even the working of spirit on matter is wonderful. The average weight of an adult is about once hundred and sixty pounds. It takes three or four men to carry a dead body of that weight to the top of a high building; yet when the man was alive his spirit had the power to carry this weight up and down those flights of stairs easily and quickly. But *where* the spirit takes hold of the body, *how* it moves it, and where it obtains that swiftness, is for us a perfect mystery. Yet this shows that spirit is subject to laws wholly different from those that govern matter.

We emphasize the word *law.* According to the analogy of faith, there must be laws that govern the spiritual world as there are in the natural; yet owing to our limitations we cannot know them. But in heaven we shall know them, and all the glories and particulars of the spiritual world, as our physicians know the nerves and tissues of the body.

This we know, however, that that which applies to matter does not therefore apply to spirit. God's omnipresence has reference to all space, but not to every spirit. Since God is omnipresent, it does not follow that He also dwells in the spirit of Satan. Hence it is clear that the Holy Spirit can be omnipresent without dwelling in every human soul; and that He can descend without changing place, and yet enter a soul hitherto unoccupied by Him; and that He was present among Israel and among the Gentiles, and yet manifested Himself among the former and not among the latter. From this it follows that in the spiritual world He can come where He was not; that He came among Israel, not having been among them before; and that then He manifested Himself among them less powerfully and in another way than on and before the day of Pentecost.

The Holy Spirit seems to act upon a human being in a twofold manner—from without, or from within. The difference is similar to that in the treatment of the human body by the physician and the surgeon: the former acts upon it by medicines taken inwardly; the latter by incisions and outward applications. A very defective comparison, indeed, but it may illustrate faintly the twofold operation of the Holy Spirit upon the souls of men.

In the beginning we discover only an outward imparting of certain gifts. On Samson He bestows great physical strength. Aholiab and Bezaleel are endowed with artistic talent to build the tabernacle. Joshua is enriched with military genius. These operations did not touch the center of the soul, and were not saving, but merely external. They become more enduring when they assume an official character as in Saul; although in him we find the best evidence of the fact that they are only outward and temporal. They assume a higher character when they receive the prophetic stamp; although Balaam's example shows us that even thus they penetrate not to the center of the soul, but affect man only outwardly.

But in the Old Testament there was also an inward operation in believers. Believing Israelites were saved. Hence they must have received saving grace. And since saving grace is out of the question without an inward working of the Holy Spirit, it follows that He was the Worker of faith in Abraham as well as in ourselves.

The difference between the two operations is apparent. A person outwardly wrought upon may become enriched with outward gifts, while spiritually he remains as poor as ever. Or having received the inward gift of regeneration, he may be devoid of every talent that adorns man outwardly.

Hence we have these three aspects:

First, there is the omnipresence of the Holy Spirit in space, the same in heaven and in hell, among Israel and among the nations.

Second, there is a spiritual operation of the Holy Spirit according to choice, which is not omnipresent; active in heaven, but not in hell; among Israel, but not among the nations.

Third, this spiritual operation works either from without, imparting losable gifts, or from within, imparting the unlosable gift of salvation.

We have spoken so far of the work of the Holy Spirit upon individual persons, which was sufficient to explain that work in the days of the Old Testament. But when we come to the day of Pentecost, this no longer suffices. For His particular operation, on and after that day, consists in the extending of His operation to a *company of men* organically united.

God did not create humanity as a string of isolated souls, but as a *race.* Hence in Adam the souls of all men are fallen and defiled. In like manner the new creation in the realm of grace has not wrought the generation of isolated individuals, but the resurrection of a *new race,* a peculiar people, a holy priesthood. And this favored race, this peculiar people, this holy priesthood is also organically one and partaking of the same spiritual blessing.

The Word of God expresses this by teaching that the elect constitute one *body,* of which all are members, one being a foot, another an eye, and another an ear, etc.—a representation that conveys the idea that the elect mutually sustain the relation of a vital, organic, and spiritual union. And this is not merely outwardly, by mutual love, but much more through a vital communion which is theirs by virtue of their spiritual origin. As our Liturgy beautifully expresses it: "For as out of many grains one meal is ground and one bread baked, and out of many berries, being pressed together, one wine floweth and mixeth itself together, so shall we all, who by a true faith are ingrafted into Christ, be altogether one body."

This spiritual union of the elect did not exist among Israel, nor could it exist during their time. There was a union of love, but not a spiritual and vital fellowship that sprang from the root of life. This spiritual union of the elect was made possible only by the incarnation of the Son of God. The elect are men consisting of body and soul; therefore it is partly at least a visible body. And only when in Christ the perfect man was given, who could be the temple of the Holy Spirit body and soul, did the inflowing and outpouring of the Holy Spirit become established in and through the body thus created.

However, this did not occur directly after the birth of Christ, but after His ascension; for His human nature did not unfold its fullest perfection until after He had ascended, when, as the glorified Son of God, He sat down at the right hand of the Father. Only then the perfect Man was given, who on the one hand could be the temple of the Holy Ghost without hindrance, and on the other unite the spirits of the elect into one body. And when, by His ascension and sitting down at the right hand of God, this had become a fact, when thus the elect had become one body, it was perfectly natural that from the Head the indwelling of the Holy Spirit was imparted to the whole body. And thus the Holy Spirit was poured out into the body of the Lord, His elect, the Church.

In this way everything becomes plain and clear: clear why the saints of the Old Testament did not receive the promise, that without us they should not be made perfect, waiting for that perfection until the formation of the body of Christ, into which they also were to be incorporated; clear that the tarrying of the outpouring of the Holy Spirit did not prevent saving grace from operating upon the individual souls of the saints of the Old Covenant; clear the word of John, that the Holy Spirit was not yet given because Jesus was not yet glorified; clear that the apostles were born again long before Pentecost and received official gifts on the evening of the day of the resurrection, although the outpouring of the Holy Spirit in the body thus formed did not take place until Pentecost. It becomes clear how Jesus could say, "If I go not away the Comforter will not come unto you," and again, "But if I go I will send Him unto you"; for the Holy Spirit was to flow into His body from Himself, who is the Head. It becomes clear also that He would not send Him from Himself, but from the Father; clear why this outpouring of the Spirit into the body of Christ is never repeated, and could occur but once; and lastly, clear that the Holy Spirit was indeed standing in the *midst* of Israel (Is. 63:12), working upon the saints from without, while in the New Testament He is said to be *within* them.

We arrive, therefore, at the following conclusions:

First, the elect must constitute one body.

Second, they were not so constituted during the days of the Old Covenant, of John the Baptist, and of Christ while on earth.

Third, this body did not exist until Christ ascended to heaven and, sitting at the right hand of God, bestowed upon this body its unity, in that God gave Him to be Head over all things to the Church—Ephesians 4:12.

Lastly, Christ as the glorified Head, having formed His spiritual body by the vital union of the elect, on the day of Pentecost poured out His Holy Spirit into *the whole body,* never more to let Him depart from it.

That these conclusions contain nothing but what the Church of all ages has confessed appears from the fact that the Reformed churches have always maintained:

First, that our communion with the Holy Spirit depends upon our mystic union with the body of which Christ is the Head, which is the underlying thought of the Lord's Supper.

Second, that the elect form one body under Christ their Head.

Third, that this body began to exist when it received its Head; and that, according to Ephesians 1:22, Christ was given to be the Head after His resurrection and ascension.

26

Israel and the Nations

Because that on the Gentiles also was poured out the gift of the Holy Ghost—Acts 10:45.

The question that arises with reference to Pentecost is: Since the Holy Spirit imparted saving grace to men before and after Pentecost, what is the difference caused by that descent of the Holy Spirit?

An illustration may explain the difference. The rain descends from heaven and man gathers it to quench his thirst. When house-holders collect it each in his own cistern, it comes down for every family separately, but when, as in modern city life, every house is supplied from the city reservoir, by means of mains and water-pipes, there is no more need of pumps and private cisterns. Suppose that a city whose citizens for ages have been drinking each from his own cistern proposes to construct a reservoir that will supply every home. When the work is completed the water is allowed to run through the system of mains and pipes into every house. It might then be said that on that day the water was poured out into the city. Hitherto it fell upon every man's roof; now it streams through the organized system into every man's house.

Apply this to the pouring out of the Holy Spirit, and the difference before and after Pentecost will be apparent. The mild showers of the Holy Spirit descended upon Israel of old in drops of saving grace, but in such a manner only that each gathered of the heavenly rain *for himself,* to quench the thirst of each heart *separately.* So it continued until the coming of Christ. Then there came a change; for He gathered the full stream of the Holy Spirit for us all, *in His own Person.* With Him all saints are connected by the channels of faith. And when, after His ascension, this connection with His saints was completed, and He had received the Holy Spirit from His Father, then the last obstacle was removed and the full stream of the Holy Spirit came rushing through the connecting channels into the heart of every believer.

Formerly isolation, every man for himself; now organic union of all the members under their one Head: this is the difference between the days before and after Pentecost. The essential fact of Pentecost consisted in this, that on that day the Holy Spirit entered for the first time into the organic body of the Church, and individuals came to drink, not each by himself, but all together in organic union.

To the question where that system of connecting channels uniting us in one body under our Head may be found, we can give no answer. This belongs to things invisible and spiritual which escape our observation, of which we can have no other representation than that by an image.

Yet this does not alter the fact that the organic union really exists. The Word of God is to us its undeniable witness. Organic life appears in nature in two forms: in the plant, and in the body of man and animal. These are the very types that Christ uses to illustrate the spiritual union between Himself and His people. He said: "I am the Vine, ye are the branches." And St. Paul speaks of having become one plant with Christ. And he frequently uses the image of the body and its members.

Hence there can be no doubt that there exists a mystic union between Christ and believers which works by means of an organic connection, uniting the Head and the members in a for us invisible and incomprehensible manner. By means of this organic union the Holy Spirit was poured out on Pentecost from Christ the Head into us, the members of His body.

If it were possible to construct the city's water-works in the air above the city, the chief engineer could properly say: "When I turn on the water for the first time I will baptize the city with water." In similar sense Christ may be said to have baptized His Church with the Holy Spirit. For the word of John the Baptist, "I indeed baptize you with water, but He that cometh after me is mightier than I; He shall baptize you with the Holy Ghost," is explained by Christ Himself as referring to the day of Pentecost (Acts 1:5): "And being assembled together with Him, He commanded them that they should not depart from Jerusalem, but wait for the promise of the Father, which, saith He, ye have heard of Me. For John truly baptized with water, but ye shall be baptized with the Holy Ghost not many days hence"; a promise that undoubtedly referred to the Pentecost miracle. This agrees with the fact that Jesus during His ministry allowed His disciples to continue the Baptism of John. And this shows that even before the crucifixion, John and Peter, Philip and Zaccheus, and many others received saving grace of the Holy Spirit, each for himself, but none of them was baptized with the Holy Spirit before the day of Pentecost.

With reference to the apostles, we must therefore distinguish a threefold giving of the Holy Spirit:

First, that of *saving grace* in regeneration and subsequent illumination—Matthew 16:17.

Secondly, *official gifts* qualifying them for the apostolic office—John 20:22.

Thirdly, the *Baptism with the Holy Ghost*—Acts 1:5 in connection with Acts 2:1ff.

One more difficulty remains. We often read of outpourings of the Holy Spirit after Pentecost. How can this be reconciled with our explanation? In Acts 10:44, 45 we read: "While Peter yet spake these words, the Holy Ghost fell on all who heard the word. And they of the circumcision which believed were astonished, as many as came with Peter, because on the Gentiles also was poured out the gift of the Holy Ghost." And Peter confirms this by saying: "Can any man forbid water that these should not be baptized, which have received the Holy Ghost *as well as we?"* From this it is evident that the outpouring on the house of Cornelius was of the same nature as that on Pentecost. Moreover, we hear of a descent of the Holy Ghost in Samaria (Acts 8), and of another in Ephesus (Acts 19:6). This descent took place in both instances after the laying on of hands by the apostles; and at Caesarea and Corinth it was followed by a speaking with foreign tongues as in Jerusalem.

It is evident, therefore, that the outpouring of the Holy Spirit was not limited to Pentecost in Jerusalem, but was afterward repeated in a weaker and modified form, but still extraordinarily, as on Pentecost.

And who would deny that there is an outpouring of the Holy Spirit today in the churches? Without it there can be no regeneration, no salvation. Yet the Pentecost signs are lacking, for example, there is no more speaking with tongues. Hence it is necessary to distinguish between the ordinary outpouring which occurs now, and the extraordinary at Corinth, Caesarea, Samaria, and Jerusalem.

Hence the question stands as follows: If on the day of Pentecost the Holy Spirit was poured out *once for all and forever,* how do we account for the ordinary and extraordinary outpourings?

Allow us once more to recur to our former illustration. Suppose that the city above referred to consisted of a lower and an upper part, both to be supplied from the same reservoir. Upon the completion of its system the lower city may receive the water first, and the upper part receive it only after the system shall have been extended. Here we notice two things: the distribution of the water took place but once, which was the *formal opening* of the water-works, and could take place but once; while the distribution of the water in the upper city, although extraordinary, was but an after-effect of the former event. This is a fair illustration of what took place in the outpouring of the Holy Spirit. The Church consisted of two parts sharply defined, viz., the Jewish and the Gentile world. Yet both are to constitute one body, one people, one Church; both are to live one life in the Holy Ghost. On Pentecost He is poured out into the body, but only to quench the thirst of one part, that is, the Jewish; the other part is still excluded. But now apostles and evangelists start from Jerusalem and come into contact with the Gentiles, and the hour has come for the stream of the Holy Ghost to pour forth into the Gentile part of the Church, and the *whole* body is refreshed by the same Holy Spirit. Hence there is an *original* outpouring in Jerusalem on the day of Pentecost, and a *supplementary* outpouring in Caesarea for the Gentile part of the Church; both of the same nature, but each bearing its own special character.

Besides these there are some isolated outpourings of the Holy Spirit, attended by the laying on of the apostles' hands, as in the case of Simon Magus. We explain this as follows: as from time to time new connections are made between individual houses and the city reservoir, so new parts of the body of Christ were added to the Church from without, into whom the Holy Spirit was poured forth from the body as into new members. It is perfectly natural that in these cases the apostles appear as instruments; and that, receiving into the Church persons that come from a part of the world not yet connected with the Church, they extend to them by the laying on of hands the fellowship of the Holy Ghost who dwells in the body.

This also explains why today newly converted persons receive the Holy Spirit only in the ordinary way. For they who are converted *among us* stand already in the *covenant,* belong already to the *seed of the Church* and to the *body of Christ.** Hence no new connection is formed, but a work of the Holy Spirit is wrought in a soul with which He was already related by means of the body.

And thus every objection is met and every detail is put in its own place, and the lines of the domain which had become vague and confused are once more clearly drawn.

It is evident also that the prayer for another outpouring or baptism of the Holy Spirit is incorrect and empty of real meaning. Such prayer actually denies the Pentecost miracle. For He that came and abides with us can no more come to us.

---

* The author refers either to persons baptized in infancy, instructed by the ministers of the Word in the doctrines of the Church and at suitable age received into the Church on confession of their faith, or to persons not so received into the Church, and then on the ground that Holland belongs to the baptized nations—Trans.

27

The Signs of Pentecost

Signs in the earth beneath—Acts 2:19.

Let us now consider the signs that accompanied the outpouring of the Holy Spirit—the sound of a rushing, mighty wind; tongues of fire; and the speaking with other tongues—which constitute the *fourth difficulty* that meets us in the investigation of the events of Pentecost (see p. 113). The first and second precede, the third follows the outpouring.

These signs are not merely symbolic. The speaking with other tongues, at least, appears as part of the narrative. Symbols are intended to represent or indicate something or to call the attention to it; hence it may be omitted without affecting the matter itself. A symbol is like a finger-post on the road; it may be removed without affecting the road. If the Pentecost signs were purely symbolic, the event would have been the same without them, but the absence of the sign of other tongues would have modified the character of the subsequent history completely.

This justifies the supposition that the two preceding signs were also *constituent* parts of the miracle. The fact that neither of them is an apt symbol strengthens the supposition; for a symbol must speak. The finger-post that leaves the traveler in doubt concerning the direction he is to take is no finger-post. Considering the fact that for eighteen centuries theologians have been unable to ascertain the significance of the so-called symbols with any degree of certainty, it must be acknowledged that it is difficult to believe that the apostles or the multitude understood their significance at once and in the same way. The issue proves the contrary. They did not understand the signs. The multitude, confounded and perplexed, said one to another: "What meaneth this?" And when Peter arose as an apostle, enlightened by the Holy Spirit, to interpret the miracle, he made no effort to attach any symbolic significance to the signs, but simply declared that an event had taken place by which the prophecy of Joel was fulfilled.

Did the event of Pentecost then exhaust the prophecy of Joel? By no means; for the sun was not turned into darkness, nor the moon into blood; and we hear nothing of the dreams of old men. Nor could it; the notable day that will exhaust this and so many other prophecies cannot come until the return of the Lord. But the holy apostle meant to say, that the day of the Lord's return was brought so much nearer by this event. The outpouring of the Holy Spirit is one of the great events which pledge the coming of that great and notable day. Without it that day cannot come. Looking back from heaven, the day of Pentecost will appear to us as the last great miracle immediately preceding the day of the Lord. And since that day shall be attended by awful signs, as was the preparatory day of Pentecost, the apostle puts them together and makes them appear as one, showing that in Joel's prophecy God points to both events.

If it be certain that the signs attending the Lord's return—blood, fire, and vapor of smoke—shall not be *symbolic,* but *constituent* elements of that last part of the world's history, viz., its last conflagration, then it is certain that Peter did not understand the signs of Pentecost to be symbolic.

Neither can the still more unsatisfactory explanation be entertained that these signs were intended to draw and fix the attention of the multitude.

The senses of sight and hearing are the most effectual means by which the outside world can act upon our consciousness. In order suddenly to arouse and excite a person, one need only startle him by an explosion or by the flash of a dazzling light. Acting upon this, some of the earlier Methodists used to fire pistols at their revival meetings, hoping that the report and flash would create the desired state of mind.

The subsequent excitement of the people would tend to make them more susceptible to the operation of the Holy Spirit. Similar experiments are those of the Salvation Army. According to this notion, the signs of Pentecost bore a similar character. It is supposed by some that the disciples, still unconverted men, were sitting together in the upper chamber on the day of Pentecost. To render them susceptible to the inflowing of the Holy Spirit they must be aroused by a noise and fire. It must seem as though a violent thunder-storm had burst upon the city; flashes of lightning and peals of thunder were seen and heard. And when the multitude were startled and terrified, then the desired condition for receiving the Holy Spirit prevailed and the outpouring took place. Such extravagances only hurt the tender sense of the children of God; while it is almost sacrilege to compare the signs of Pentecost to the report of a pistol.

Hence there remains only one other explanation, that is, to consider the Pentecost signs as actual and real *constituents* of the event; indispensable links in the chain of occurrences.

When a ship enters the harbor we see the foaming spray under the bow and hear the waters dashing against the sides. When a horse runs through the street we hear the noise of his hoofs against the pavement and see the clouds of dust. But who will say that these things seen and heard are symbolic? They necessarily belong to those actions and are parts of them, impossible without them. Therefore we do not believe that the Pentecost signs were symbolic, or intended to create a sensation, but that they belonged inseparably to the outpouring of the Holy Ghost, and were caused by it. The outpouring could not take place without creating these signs. When the mountain-stream dashes down the steep sides of the rocks we must hear the sound of rushing waters, we must see the flying spray; so when the Holy Spirit flows down from the mountains of God's holiness, the sound of a rushing, mighty wind must be heard, and glorious brightness must be seen, and a speaking with foreign tongues must follow.

This will sufficiently explain our meaning. Not that we deny that these signs had also a significance for the multitude. The noise of the horse's hoofs warns travelers on the road. And we concede that the purpose of the signs was realized in the perplexity and consternation the sound of a rushing, mighty wind would have been heard and the fiery tongues would have been seen. As the horse's hoofs cause the ground to vibrate though there be no traveler in sight, so the Holy Spirit could not come down without that sound and that brightness, even though not a single Jew were to be found in all Jerusalem.

The outpouring of the Holy Spirit was real, not apparent. Having found His temple in the glorified Head, He must necessarily flow down into the body and descend from heaven. And this descent from heaven and this flowing into the body could not take place without causing these signs.

To penetrate more deeply into this matter is not lawful. On Horeb Elijah *heard* the Lord pass by in a gentle breeze; Isaiah *heard* the moving of the door-posts in the Temple. This seems to indicate that the approach of the divine majesty causes a commotion in the elements perceptible to the auditory nerve. But how, we cannot tell. We observe, however:

First, that spirit can act upon matter is evident, for our spirits act upon the body every moment, and by that action are able to produce sounds. Speaking, crying, singing are nothing but our spirit acting upon the currents of air. And if our spirit is capable of such action, why not the Spirit of the Lord? Why, then, call it mysterious when the Holy Spirit in His descent so wrought upon the elements that the effects vibrated in the ears of those present?

Secondly, in making the covenant with Israel upon Sinai, the Lord God spoke in peals of thunder so terrible that even Moses said, "I am exceedingly fearful and quaking"; yet not with the intention of terrifying the people, but because a holy and angry God cannot speak otherwise to a sinful generation. It is not therefore surprising that the coming of God to His New Covenant people is attended by similar signs, not in order to draw men's attention, but because it could not be otherwise.

The same applies to the tongues of fire. Supernatural manifestations are always attended by light and brightness, especially when the Lord Jehovah or His angel appears. Recall, for example, God's covenant-making with Abraham, or the occurrences at the burning bush. Why, then, should it surprise us that the descent of the Holy Spirit was attended by phenomena such as those seen by Elijah on Horeb, Moses in the bush, St. Paul on the way to Damascus, and St.

John on Patmos? That the cloven tongues sat upon each of them proves nothing to the contrary; for He proceeded to each of them and entered their hearts, and in each going He left a trace of light behind.

The question, whether the fire seen by these men on those occasions belonged to a higher sphere, or was the effect of God's action upon the elements of the earth, cannot be answered.

Both views have much in their favor. There is no darkness in heaven; and the heavenly light must be of a higher nature than ours, even above the brightness of the sun, according to St. Paul's description of the light on the way to Damascus. It is very probable, therefore, that in these great events the boundary of heaven overlapped the earth, and a higher glory shone in upon our atmosphere.

But, on the other hand, it is possible that the Holy Spirit wrought this mysterious brightness directly by a miracle. And this seems to be confirmed by the fact that the signs attending the law-giving on Sinai, which event was parallel to this, were not from higher spheres, but wrought from earthly elements.

Finally, let it be noticed, that the outpouring of the Holy Spirit on the house of Cornelius and on the disciples of Apollos was attended by a speaking with other tongues, but not by the other signs. This confirms our theory; for it was not a *coming* to the house of Cornelius, but a conducting of the Holy Spirit into another part of the body of Christ. If symbolism had been intended, the signs would have been repeated; not being symbols, they did not appear.

28

The Miracle of Tongues

If any man speak in an (unknown) tongue, . . . let one interpret. But if there be no interpreter, let him speak to himself, and to God—1 Corinthians 14:27, 28.

The third sign following the outpouring of the Holy Spirit consisted in extraordinary sounds that proceeded from the lips of the apostles—sounds foreign to the Aramaic tongue, never before heard from their lips.

These sounds affected the multitude in different ways: some called them babblings of inebriated men; others heard in them the great works of God proclaimed. To the latter, it seemed as though they heard them speaking in their own tongues. To the Parthian it sounded like the Parthian, to the Arabian like the Arabic, etc.; elation, for it was the fulfillment of the prophecy of Joel that all the people should become partakers of the operation of the Holy Spirit.

The question how to interpret this wonderful sign has occupied the thinking minds of all times. Allow us to offer a solution, which we present in the following observations:

In the first place, this phenomena of spiritual speaking in extraordinary sounds is not confined to Pentecost nor to the second chapter of Acts.

On the contrary, the Lord told His disciples, even before the ascension, that they should speak with new tongues (Mark 16:17). And from the epistles of St. Paul it is evident that this prophecy did not refer to

Pentecost alone; for we read in 1 Corinthians 12:10 that in the apostolic Church, spiritual gifts included that of tongues; that some spoke in γένη γλωσσῶν, that is, in kinds of tongues or sounds. In verse 28 the apostle declares that God has set this spiritual phenomenon in the Church. It is noteworthy that in 1 Corinthians 14:1–33 the apostle gives special attention to this extraordinary sign, showing that then it was quite ordinary. That the gift of tongues mentioned by St. Paul and the sign of which St. Luke speaks in Acts 2 are substantially one and the same cannot be doubted. In the first place, Christ's prophecy is general: "They shall speak with new tongues." Secondly, both phenomena are said to have made irresistible impressions upon unbelievers. Thirdly, both are treated as spiritual gifts. And lastly, to both is applied the same name.

Yet there was a very *perceptible difference* between the two: the miracle of tongues on the day of Pentecost was intelligible to a large number of hearers of different nationalities; while in the apostolic churches it was understood only by a few who were called interpreters. Connected with this is the fact that the miracle on Pentecost made the impression of speaking at once to different hearers in different tongues so that they were edified. However, this is no fundamental difference. Although in the apostolic churches there were but few interpreters, yet there were some who understood the wonderful speech.

There was, moreover, a marked difference between the men thus endowed: some understood what they were saying; others did not. For St. Paul admonishes them, saying: "Let him that speaketh in an unknown tongue, pray that he may interpret" (1 Cor. 14:13). Yet even without this ability, the speaking with tongues had an edifying effect upon the speaker himself, but it was an edification not understood, the effect of an unknown operation in the soul.

From this we gather that the miracle of tongues consisted in the uttering of extraordinary sounds which from existing data could be explained neither by the speaker nor by the hearer; and to which another grace was sometimes added, viz., that of interpretation. Hence three things were possible: that the speaker *alone* understood what he said; or, that others understood it and *not* himself; or, that both speaker and hearers understood it. This understanding has reference to one or more persons.

On the ground of this we comprise these miracles of tongues in one class; with this distinction, however, that on the day of Pentecost the miracle appeared *perfect,* but later on *incomplete.* As there is in the miracles of Christ in raising the dead a perceptible increase of power: first, the raising up of one just dead (the daughter of Jairus), then, of one about to be buried (the young man of Nain), and lastly, of one already decomposing (Lazarus); so there is also in the miracle of tongues a difference of power—*not increasing,* but *decreasing.* The mightiest operation of the Holy Spirit is seen first, then those less powerful. It is precisely the same as in our own heart: first, the mighty fact of regeneration; after that, the less marked manifestations of spiritual power. Hence on Pentecost there was the miracle of tongues in its perfection; later on in the churches, in weaker measure.

Secondly, there is no evidence that the miracle of tongues consisted in the speaking of one of the known languages not previously acquired.

If this had been the case, St. Paul could not have said: "If I pray in an *unknown* tongue, my spirit prayeth, but my understanding is unfruitful" (1 Cor. 14:14). The word "unknown" appears in italics, not being found in the Greek. Moreover, he says that tongues are for a sign not to them that believe, but to them that believe not—verse 22. If it had been a question of foreign but ordinary languages, the matter of understanding them could not depend upon faith, but simply upon the fact whether the language was acquired by study or was one's native tongue.

Finally, the notion that these tongues refer to foreign languages not acquired by study is contradicted by St. Paul: "I thank my God that I speak with tongues more than ye all." By which he cannot mean that he had mastered more languages than others, but that he possessed the gift of tongues in greater degree than other men. The following verse is evidence: "Yet in the Church I had rather speak five words with my understanding, that I may teach others also, than ten thousand words in an (unknown) tongue." According to the other view, this ought to have been: "I wish to speak in one language, so that the Church may understand me, rather than in ten or twenty languages which the Church understands not." But the apostle does not say this. He speaks not of *many* languages in opposition to *one,* but of five *sounds* or *words* against ten thousand *words.* From this it follows that St. Paul's "I speak with *glottai* (languages or sounds) more than ye all," must refer to the miracle of sounds.

For although it is objected very naturally that on Pentecost the apostles spoke the Arabic, Hebrew, and Parthian tongues besides many others, yet the fact appealed to is not proven to be a fact. Surely we learn from Acts 2 that these Parthians, Elamites, etc., received the impression that they were addressed each in his own tongue; yet the narrative itself proves rather the contrary. Let the experiment be tried. Let fifteen men (the number of languages mentioned in Acts 2) speak in fifteen different languages at once and together, and the result will be not that everyone hears his own language, but that no one can hear anything. But the narrative of Acts 2 is fully explained in that the apostles uttered sounds intelligible to Parthians, Medes, Cretans, etc., because they understood them, receiving the impression that these sounds agreed with their own mother-tongues. As a Dutch child seeing a problem on the blackboard worked out by an English or German child naturally receives the impression that it was done by a Dutch child, simply because figures are signs not affected by the difference of language, so must the Elamite have received the impression that he heard the Elamitian, and the Egyptian that he was addressed in the Egyptian tongue, when on Pentecost they heard sounds uttered by a miracle, which, being independent from the difference of language, were intelligible to man as *man.*

We must not forget that speaking is nothing else than to produce impressions upon the soul of the hearer by means of vibrations in the air. But if the same impressions can be produced without the aid of air-vibrations, the effect upon the hearer must be the same. Try the experiment upon the eye. The sight of twinkling stars or dissolving figures excites the retina. The same effect can be produced by rubbing the eye with the finger when reclining on a couch in a dark room. And this applies here. The air-vibrations are not the principal thing, but the emotion produced in the mind by the speaking. The Pamphylian, accustomed to receive emotions by hearing his mother-tongue, and receiving the same impression in *another way,* must think that he is addressed in the Pamphylian tongue.

Thirdly—According to St. Paul's interesting information, the miracle of tongues consisted in this, that the vocal organs produced sounds not by a working of the mind, but by an operation of the Holy Spirit upon those organs.

St. Luke writes: "They began to speak with other tongues, as the Spirit gave them utterance" (Acts 2:4); and St. Paul proves exhaustively that the person speaking with tongues spoke not with his understanding, that is, as a result of his own thinking, but in consequence of an entirely different operation. That this is possible, we see, first, in delirious persons, who say things outside of their own personal thinking; second, in the insane, whose incoherent talk has no sense; third, in persons possessed, whose vocal organs are used by demons; fourth, in Balaam, whose vocal organs uttered words of blessing upon Israel against his will.

Hence it must be conceded that in man three things are possible: First, that for a time he may be deprived of the use of his vocal organs. Second, that the use of these organs may be appropriated by a spirit who has overcome him. Third, that the Holy Spirit, appropriating his vocal organs, can produce sounds from his lips which are "new," and "other" than the language which ordinarily he speaks.

Fourthly, in the Greek these sounds invariably are designated by the word γλῶτται, that is, tongues, hence language. In the Greek world, from which this word is taken, the word *glotta* always stands in strong opposition to the *lógos,* reason.

A man's thinking is the hidden, invisible, imperceptible process of his mind. Thought has a soul, but no body. But when the thought manifests itself and adopts a body, then there is a word. And the tongue being the movable organ of speech, it was said that the tongue gives a body to the thought. Hence the contrast between the logos, that is, that which he utters with the vocal organs.

Ordinarily the *glotta* comes only through and after the *lógos.* But in the miracle of tongues we discover the extraordinary phenomena that while the logos remained inactive, the glotta uttered sounds. And since it was a phenomenon of *sounds* which proceeded not from the thinking mind, but from the tongue, the Holy Scripture calls it very appropriately a gift of the *glottai,* that is, a gift of tongue—or sound-phenomena.

Lastly—In answer to the question, How must this be understood? we offer the following representation: Speech in man is the result of his thinking; and this thinking in a sinless state is an in-shining of the Holy Spirit. Speech in a sinless state is therefore the result of inspiration, in-breathing of the Holy Spirit.

Hence in a sinless state man's language would have been the pure and perfect product of an operation of the Holy Spirit. He is the Creator of human language; and without the injury and debasing influence of sin the connection between the Holy Ghost and our speech would have been complete. But sin has broken the connection. Human language is damaged: damaged by the weakening of the organs of speech; by the separation of tribes and nations; by the passions of the soul; by the darkening of the understanding; and principally by the lie which has entered in. Hence that infinite distance between this pure and genuine human language which, as the direct operation of the Holy Spirit upon the human mind, should have manifested itself, and the empirically existing languages that now separate the nations.

But the difference is not intended to remain. Sin will disappear. What sin destroyed will be restored. In the day of the Lord, at the wedding-feast of the Lamb, all the redeemed will understand one another. In what way? By the restoration of the pure and original language upon the lips of the redeemed, which is born from the operation of the Holy Spirit upon the human mind. And of that great, still-tarrying event the Pentecost miracle is the germ and the beginning; hence it bore its distinctive marks. In the midst of the Babeldom of the nations, on the day of Pentecost, the one pure and mighty human language was revealed which one day all will speak, and all the brethren and sisters from all nations and tongues will understand.

And this was wrought by the Holy Spirit. They spake as the Holy Spirit gave them utterance. They spoke a heavenly language to praise God—not of angels, but a language above the influence of sin.

Hence the understanding of this language was also a work of the Holy Spirit. At Jerusalem, only they understood it who were specially wrought upon by the Holy Spirit. The others understood it not. And at Corinth it was not comprehended by the masses, but by him alone to whom it was given of the Holy Ghost.

Eighth Chapter
The Apostolate

29

The Apostolate

That ye also may have fellowship with us: and truly our fellowship is with the Father, and with His Son Jesus Christ—1 John 1:3.

The apostolate bears the character of an extraordinary manifestation, not seen before or after it, in which we discover a proper work of the Holy Spirit. The apostles were ambassadors extraordinary—different from the prophets, different from the present ministers of the Word. In the history of the Church and the world they occupy a unique position and have a peculiar significance. Hence the apostolate is entitled to a special discussion.

Moreover, the apostolate belongs to the great things which the Holy Spirit has wrought. All that the Holy Scripture declares concerning the apostles compels us to look for an explanation of their persons and mission in a special work of the Holy Spirit. Before His ascension Jesus predicted repeatedly that they should be His witnesses only after they shall have received the Holy Spirit in an extraordinary manner. Until this promise is fulfilled they remain hiding in Jerusalem. And when they raise the banner of the cross in Jerusalem and in the ends of the earth, they appeal to the power of the Holy Spirit as the secret of their appearance.

The apostolate was *holy,* and we call them *holy* apostles, not because they had attained a higher degree of perfection, but "holy" in the Scriptural sense of being separated, set apart, like the Temple and its furniture, for the service of a holy God.

By sin many things have become unholy. Before sin entered into the world all things were holy. That part of creation which became unholy stands in opposition to that which remained holy. The latter is called Heaven; that which was made holy is called Church. And all that belongs to the Church, to its being and organism, is called holy.

Hence Jesus could say to the disciples who were about to deny Him: "Ye are clean through the word which I have spoken unto you." In like manner the members of the Church and their children are called "sanctified"; and in his epistles St. Paul addresses them as *holy* and *beloved:* not because they were sinless, but because God had set them as called saints in the realm of His holiness, which by His grace He had separated from the realm of sin. In like manner the Scripture is called holy: not to indicate that it is the record of holy things only, but that its origin is not in man's sinful life, but in the holy realm of the life of God.

We confess, therefore, that the apostles of Jesus were set apart for the service of God's holy Kingdom, and that they were qualified for their calling by the power of the Holy Spirit.

By omitting the word "holy," as many do, we make the apostles common; we consider them as ordinary preachers; in degree above us undoubtedly, being more richly developed, especially by their intercourse with Christ, and as His witnesses very dear to us, but still occupying the same level with other teachers and ministers of the Church of all ages. And so the conviction will be lost that the apostles are men different in *kind* from all other men; lost the realization that in them appeared a peculiar and unique ministry; lost also the grateful confession that the Lord our God gave us in these men extraordinary grace.

And this explains why some ministers, at the special occasion of installation, departure, or jubilee, apply to themselves apostolic utterances that are not applicable to their persons, but exclusively to the men who occupy a peculiar and unique position in the Church of all ages and all lands. For this reason we repeat purposely the title of honor, "holy apostles," in order that the peculiar significance of the apostolate may again receive honorable recognition in our churches.

This peculiar significance of the apostolate appears in the Holy Scripture in various ways.

We begin with referring to the prologue of the First Epistle of St. John, in which, from the fullness of the apostolic sense, the holy apostle solemnly addresses us. He opens his epistle by declaring that they, the apostles of the Lord, occupy an exceptional position regarding the miracle of the incarnation of the Word. He says: "The Word became flesh, and in that incarnate Word, Life was manifested; and that manifested Life was heard and seen and handled with hands." By whom? By everybody? No, by the apostles; for he adds emphatically: "That which we have seen and heard declare we unto you, and show you that eternal life which was with the Father and was manifested unto us."

And what was the aim of this declaration? To save souls? Surely this also, but not this in the first place. The purpose of this apostolic declaration is to bring the members of the Church into *connection with the apostolate.* For, clearly and emphatically, he adds: "This we declare unto you, that ye also may have fellowship with us." And only after this link is closed, and the fellowship with the apostolate an accomplished fact, he says: "And truly our fellowship is with the Father, and with His Son Jesus Christ."

The apostle's reasoning is as transparent as glass. Life was manifested in such a way that it could be seen and handled. They who saw and handled it were the apostles; and they were also to declare this life unto the elect. By this declaration the required fellowship between the elect and the apostolate is established. And in consequence of this, there is fellowship also for the elect with the Father and the Son.

This may not be understood as referring only to the people then living; and, regarding Rome, one's position, Bible in hand, is exceedingly weak if he maintain that this higher significance of the apostolate had reference only to the then living, and not in the same measure to us. Indeed, we, upon whom the end of the ages has come, must maintain the vital fellowship with the holy apostolate of our Lord Jesus Christ. Rome errs by making its bishops the successors of the apostles, teaching that fellowship with the apostolate depends upon fellowship with Rome: an error which is obvious from the fact that St. John expressly and emphatically connects the fellowship of the apostolate with men who have seen and heard and handled that which was manifested of the Word of Life—something to which no Roman bishop can appeal in the present day. Moreover, St. John says distinctly that this fellowship with the apostolate must be the result of the *declaration* of the Word of Life by the *apostles themselves.* And inasmuch as Rome established this fellowship not by the *preaching* of the Word, but by the sacramental sign, it is in direct opposition to the apostolic doctrine.

However, from this it follows not that Rome errs in the fundamental thought, viz., that every child of God must exercise communion with the Father and the Son *through the apostolate;* on the contrary, this is St. John's positive claim. The solution of this apparent conflict lies in the fact that they have not only *spoken,* but also *written:* that is, their declaration of the Word of Life was not limited to the little circle of the men that happened to hear them; on the contrary, by writing they have put their preaching into real and enduring forms; they have sent it out to all lands and nations; that, as the genuine, ecumenic apostles they might bring the testimony of the Life which was manifested to all the elect of God in all lands and throughout the ages.

Hence even now the apostles are preaching the living Christ in the churches. Their persons have departed, but their personal testimony remains. And that personal testimony, which as an apostolic document has come to every soul in every land and in every age, is the very testimony which even now is the instrument in the hand of the Holy Spirit to translate souls into the fellowship of the Life Eternal.

And if one says, "Surely in this sense their word is still effective; however, it results no longer in fellowship with the apostles, and by means of this fellowship with Christ, but it points us directly to the Savior of our souls, which is a more simple way," then we oppose this unscriptural notion most energetically.

Such reasoning ignores the body of Christ and overlooks the great fact of the outpouring of the Holy Spirit. There is not the saving of a few *individual* souls, but a bringing together of the *body* of Christ; and into that body everyone that is called must be incorporated. And inasmuch as the King of the Church gives His Spirit now not to separate persons, but exclusively to them that are incorporated, and the inflowing of the Holy Spirit into this body, and principally in the persons of the apostles, took place on Pentecost, therefore no one can receive at the present time any spiritual gift or influence of the Holy Spirit unless he stands in vital connection with the body of the Lord; and that body is unthinkable without the apostles.

In fact, the apostolic Word comes to the soul today as the testimony of what they have seen and heard and handled of the Word of Life. By virtue of this testimony souls are inwardly wrought upon, and by their being incorporated into the body of Christ they become manifest. And this fellowship becomes manifest as a fellowship with the very body of which the apostles are the leaders, in whose persons and in the persons of whose associates the Holy Spirit was poured out on the day of Pentecost.

We know that this view, or this confession rather, is in direct opposition to the view of Methodism,* which has pervaded all classes and conditions of men. And the deplorable results have become apparent in various ways. Methodism has killed the conscious appreciation of the sacrament; it is cold and indifferent toward church fellowship; it has cultivated an unlimited disregard for the truth in the confession.† And while the Lord our God has deemed it necessary to give us a voluminous Holy Scripture, consisting of six-and-sixty books, Methodism has boasted that it could write its Gospel upon a dime.

This error cannot be overcome except the Word of God become again our Teacher and we its docile scholars. And then we shall learn—

(1) Not that a few isolated persons are being rescued from the floods of iniquity, but that a body will be redeemed.

(2) That all that are to be saved will be incorporated into that body.

(3) That this body has Christ as its Head and the apostles as its permanent leaders.

(4) That on Pentecost the Holy Spirit was poured out into that body.

(5) That even now each of us experiences the gracious operations of the Holy Spirit only through fellowship with this body.

Only when these things are clear to the soul, the glorious word of Christ, "Father, I pray not for these alone, but from them also which

---

* See section 5 in the Preface—Trans.

† The truth of this is apparent in the Salvation Army, the latest exponent of Methodism. It denies the sacraments, stands isolated from the churches, and does not seem to care for truth in the confession, for it has no confession—Trans.

shall believe on Me *through their word,"* will be well understood. Taken in the current sense, this word has not the least comfort for us; for then the Lord has prayed only for these then living, who had the privilege of personally hearing the apostles, and who were converted by their verbal testimony. We are entirely excluded. But if this petition be taken in the sense indicated above, as though Christ would say, "I pray not for My apostles alone, but also for them who through their testimony shall believe on Me, now and in all ages and lands and nations," then it acquires widest scope, and contains a prayer for every child of God called even now and from our own households.

This unique significance of the apostolate is so deeply embedded in the heart of the Kingdom, that when in the Revelation of St. John we get a glimpse of the New Jerusalem, we see that the city has twelve *foundations,* and *on them* the *names* of the twelve apostles of the Lamb—Revelation 21:14. Hence their significance is not transient and temporary, but permanent and including the whole Church. And when its warfare shall be ended and the glory of the New Jerusalem shall be revealed, even then, in its heavenly bliss, the Church shall rest upon the very foundation on which it was built here, and therefore bear, engraved on its twelve foundations, the names of the holy apostles of the Lord.

The apostle Paul considers the apostolate so glorious and exalted that in his Epistle to the Hebrews he applies the name of Apostle to the Lord Jesus Christ. "Wherefore, holy brethren, partakers of the heavenly calling, consider the Apostle and High Priest of our profession, Christ Jesus." The meaning is perfectly clear. Properly speaking, it is Christ Himself calling and testifying in His Church. But as the white ray of light divides itself into many colors, so does Christ impart Himself to His twelve apostles, whom He has set as the instruments through whom He has fellowship with His Church. Hence the apostles stand not each by himself, but together they constitute the apostolate, the unity of which is found not in St. Peter nor in St. Paul, but in *Christ.* If we should wish to comprehend the whole apostolate in one, it must be He in whom is contained the fullness of the twelve—the Apostle and High Priest of our profession, Christ the Lord.

Not until we fully grasp these thoughts and live in them shall we be able to understand the epistles of St. Paul, and appreciate his spiritual conflict to maintain the honor of the apostolate for his divine mission. Especially in his epistles to the Corinthians and Galatians he sustains this conflict bravely and effectually, but in such a way that the Methodist cannot have eye or ear for it. He rather feels like deploring the apostle's zeal, saying: "If Paul had insisted less on his title and more humbly applied himself to the conversion of souls, his memory would have been much more precious." And from his standpoint he is quite right. If the apostolate has no higher significance than to be the first teachers and ministers of the Church, then there can be no reason why St. Paul should waste his strength contending for a meaningless title.

But the undeniable fact that St. Paul's energetic contending agrees not with the current opinions of the present time ought to make us oppose the notion that, since his contention does not comport with our opinions, he must be wrong, and acknowledge that the standpoint which we cannot occupy without condemning the apostle must be abandoned—the sooner the better. St. Paul must not conform himself to our opinions, but our opinions must be modified or altered according to St. Paul's.

30

The Apostolic Scriptures

And I think that I also have the Spirit of God—1 Corinthians 7:40.

We have seen that the apostolate has an extraordinary significance and occupies a unique position. This position is twofold, viz., temporary, with reference to the founding of the first churches, and permanent, with regard to the churches of all ages.

The first must necessarily be temporary, for what was then accomplished cannot be repeated. A tree can be planted only once; an organism can be born only once; the planting or founding of the Church could take place only once. However, this founding was not unprepared for. On the contrary, God has had a Church in the world from the beginning. That Church was even a *world*-Church. But it went down in idolatry; and only a small Church remained among an almost unknown people—the Church in Israel. When this particular Church was to become again a world-Church, two things were required:

First, that the Church in Israel lay aside its national dress. Secondly, that in the midst of the heathen world the Church of Christ appear, so that the two might become manifest as the on Christian Church.

By these two things the apostolic labor is almost exhausted. In St. Paul the two are united. No apostle labored more zealously to divest the Church of Israel of its Jewish attire, and no one was more abundant in the planting of new churches in all parts of the world.

The apostolate had, however, a much more extensive and higher calling, not only for those days, but also for the Church of the ages. It was the task of the apostles for which they were ordained: by giving to the churches fixed forms of government to determine their character; and by the written documentation of the revelation of Christ Jesus to secure to them purity and perpetuity.

This is evident from the character of their labors: for they not only founded churches, but also gave them ordinances. St. Paul writes to the Corinthians: "As I have given order to the churches of Galatia, even so do ye" (1 Cor. 16:1). Hence they were conscious of possessing power, of being clothed with authority. "And so ordain I in all the churches," says the same apostle (1 Cor. 7:17). This ordaining is not like that of our official church boards which have power to make rules; or as a minister in the name of the consistory announces from the pulpit certain regulations. Nay, the apostles exercised authority by virtue of a power they consciously possessed in themselves, independent of any church or church council. For St. Paul writes, after having given ordinances in the matter of marriages: "And I think that I also have the Spirit of God." Hence the power and authority to command, to ordain and to judge in the churches, they derived not from the Church, nor from church council, nor from the apostolate, but directly from the Holy Spirit. This is true even of the power to judge; for, concerning an incestuous person in the church of Corinth, St. Paul judged that he should be delivered to Satan; the execution of which sentence he left to the elders of that church, but upon which he had determined by virtue of his apostolic authority—1 Corinthians 5:3.

In this connection it is remarkable that St. Paul was conscious of a twofold current running through his word: (1) that of *tradition,* touching the things ordained by the Lord Jesus during His ministry; and (2) that of the *Holy Spirit,* touching the things to be decided by the apostolate. For he writes: "Now concerning virgins, I have no commandment of the Lord; yet I give my judgment as one that hath obtained mercy of the Lord to be faithful" (1 Cor. 7:25). And again he saith: "Unto the married I command, yet not I, but the Lord, Let not the wife depart from her husband" (v. 10). And in verse 12 he saith: "But to the rest speak I, not the Lord." Many have received the impression that St. Paul meant to say: "What the Lord commanded, you must keep, but the things by me enjoined are of less account and not binding"; a view destroying the authority of the apostolic word, and therefore to be rejected. The apostle has not the least intention of undermining his own authority; for having delivered the message, he adds expressly: "And I think that I also have the Spirit of God"; which, in connection with the commandment of the Lord, cannot mean anything else than this: "That which I have enjoined rests upon the same authority as the Lord's own words"; a declaration which was already contained in the word: "I have received mercy to be faithful," that is, in my work of regulating the churches.

By these ordinances and regulations the apostles not only gave to the churches of those days a fixed form of life, but they also prepared the channel that was to determine the future course of the life of the Church. They did this in two ways:

First, partly by the impressions they made upon the life of the churches, and which were never wholly obliterated.

Secondly, partly also and more particularly by leaving us in writing the image of that Church, and by sealing the principal features of these ordinances in their apostolic epistles.

Both these influences, that directly on the life of the churches, and that of the apostolic Scriptures, have taken care that the image of the Church should not be lost, and that, where it was in danger of such loss, by the grace of God it should be fully restored.

This leads us to consider the second activity of the apostles, whereby they operated upon the Church of all ages, viz., the inheritance of their writings.

Our writings are the richest and maturest products of the mind; and the mind of the Holy Spirit received its richest, fullest, and most perfect expression when His meaning was put into documental form. The literary labor of the apostles deserves, therefore, careful attention.

When the apostles Peter and Paul preached the Gospel, healed the sick, judged the unruly, and founded churches, giving them ordinances, they performed in each of these a great and glorious work. And yet the significance of St. Paul's labor when he wrote, for example, the Epistle to the Romans so far surpassed the value of preaching and healing that the two cannot be compared. When he wrote that one little book, which in ordinary pamphlet form would make no more than three sheets of printed matter, he performed the greatest work of his life. From this little book the most far-reaching influences have gone forth. By this one little book St. Paul became a historic person.

We know, indeed, that many of our present theologians reverse this order, and say: These apostles were profoundly spiritual men; they lived near the Lord and had entered deeply into the mind of Christ; they labored and preached and occasionally wrote a few letters, some of which have come down to us; yet this letter-writing was of little significance to their persons, but against this whole representation we protest with all our might. Nay, these men were not such excellent personalities that the few occasional letters from their hands could scarcely have any significance in their lives. On the contrary, their epistolary labor was the most important of all their lifework; small in compass, but rich in content; apparently of less, but by virtue of its comprehensive and far-reaching influence of much higher significance. And since the apostles may not be considered half-idiots, knowing scarcely anything of the future of the Church, and without any realization of what they were doing, we maintain that a man like St. Paul, having finished his Epistle to the Romans, was indeed conscious of the fact that this work would occupy a prominent place among his apostolic labors.

Even though it be granted that the apostle was unconscious of it, yet this alters not the fact. Today, when the churches founded eighteen centuries ago have all past away, and the church of Rome can scarcely be recognized; when the people who by his wonderful power were healed or saved have all crumbled to dust, and not a single memory remains of all his other toil; today his epistolary inheritance still governs the Church of Christ.

We cannot conceive what the condition of the Church would be without St. Paul's epistles; if we were to lose the inheritance of the great apostle that has come to us through our fathers. What is it that controls our confession, if not the truths developed by him; what is it that governs our lives, if not the ideals so highly exalted by him? We can safely say, with reference to our own Church, that without the Pauline epistles its whole form and appearance would be totally different.

This being so, we are also justified in saying that the objectifying of Christian truth in the apostolic epistles is the most important of all their labors. Instead of calling it a "dead-letter," we confess that in it their activity reached its very zenith.

However, the peculiar work of the Holy Spirit in the apostolate being the subject of our present inquiry, and not the apostolate itself, we will consider now the serious question: What is the *nature* of this work?

Our choice lies between the theory of the *mechanical,* and that of the *natural,* process.

The supporters of the first say: "Nothing can be more simple than the work of the Holy Spirit in the apostles. They had only to sit down, take pen and ink, and write at His dictation." The advocates of the natural process state its case as follows: "The apostles had entered more deeply into the mind of Christ; they were holier, purer, and more godly than others; hence they were better fitted to be the instruments of the Holy Spirit, who after all animates every child of God." These are the extreme views. On the one hand, the work of the Holy Spirit is considered as a foreign element introduced into the life of the Church and that of the apostles. Any schoolboy competent to write a dictation might have written the Epistle to the Romans just as well as St. Paul. The obvious difference of style and manner of presentation between his epistles and those of St. John does not spring from the difference of personalities, but from the fact that the Holy Spirit purposely adopted the style and way of speaking of His chosen scribe, be he St. Paul or St. John.

The other extreme considers that the persons of the apostles account for the whole matter; so that to speak of a work of the Holy Spirit is only to repeat a pious term. According to this view, the influence of Christ's personal intercourse had an educating effect upon His disciples, which left such impress of His life upon them that they could understand His Person and aims much better than others; hence being the best-developed minds of the Christian circle of those days, they adopted in their writings a certain apostolic authority.

Besides these two extremes, we must mention the view of certain friendly theologians who turn this natural into a supernatural, but still self-developed, process. They acknowledge, with us, that there is a work of the Holy Spirit which they also call regeneration, and allow that to this the gift of illumination is often added. And from this they argue: "Among the regenerated there are some in whom this divine work is only superficial, and others in whom He operates more deeply. In the former, the gift of illumination is undeveloped; in the latter, it attains great luster; and it is to this class that the apostles belonged, who were partakers of this gift in its highest degree. Owing to these two gifts, the work of the Holy Spirit attained in them such clearness and transparency that, in speaking or writing concerning the things of the Kingdom of God, they struck almost invariably the right note, chose the right word, and continued in the right direction. Hence the power of their writings, and the almost binding authority of their word."

Over against these three opponents we wish to present the view of the best theologians of the Christian Church, which, although fully appreciating the effects of regeneration and illumination in the apostles, still maintain that from these the infallible, apostolic authority cannot be explained; and that the authority of their word is recognized only by the unconditional confession that these operations of grace were but the means used by the Holy Spirit when, through the apostles, He cast His own testimony into documental forms for the Church of all ages.

31

Apostolic Inspiration

When He, the Spirit of truth, is come, He will guide you into all truth—John 16:13.

What is the nature of the work of the Holy Spirit in the inspiration of the apostles?

Apart from the mechanical and natural theories, which are vulgar and profane, there are two others, viz., the Ethical and the Reformed.

According to the former the inspiration of the apostles differs from the animation of believers only in degree, not in nature. They represent the matter as though, by the incarnation of the Word, a new sphere of life was created which they call the *"God-human."* They that have received the life of this higher sphere are called believers; others are unbelievers. In these believers the consciousness is gradually changed, illuminated, and sanctified. Hence they see things in a different light, that is, their eyes are opened so that they see much of the spiritual world of which unbelievers see nothing. However, this result is not the same in all believers. The more favored see more correctly and distinctly than the less favored. And the most excellent among them, who possess this God-human life most abundantly, and look into the things of the Kingdom with greatest clearness and distinctness, are the men called apostles. Hence the inspiration of the apostles and the illumination of believers are in principle the same; differing only in degree.

The Reformed churches cannot agree with this view. In their judgment the very effort to identify apostolic inspiration with the illumination of believers actually annihilates the former. They hold that the inspiration of the apostles was wholly *unique* in *nature* and *kind*, totally different from what the Scripture calls illumination of believers. The apostles possessed this latter gift even in its highest degree, and we heartily endorse all that the Ethical theologians say in this respect. But, when all is said, we hold that apostolic inspiration is not even touched upon; that it lies entirely outside of it; is not contained in, but added to, it; and that the Church must reverence it as an extraordinary, peculiar, and unique work of the Holy Spirit, which was wrought exclusively in the holy apostles.

Hence both sides concede that the apostles were born again, that they had received illumination in a peculiarly high degree. But while the Ethical theorists maintain that this extraordinary illumination includes inspiration, the Reformed hold that illumination in its highest degree has nothing to do with inspiration; which was unique in its kind, without equal, given to the apostles alone, never to other believers.

The difference between the two views is obvious.

According to the Ethical view, the epistles are the writings of very worthy, godly, and sanctified men; the thoughtful utterances of highly enlightened believers. And yet, having said all this, they are after all only fallible; they may contain ninety percent of truth, well expressed and accurately defined, but the possibility remains that the other ten percent is full of errors and mistakes. Even though there be one or more infallible epistles, how can this avail us, since we do not know it? In fact, we are without the least certainty in this matter. And for this reason it is actually conceded that the apostles have made mistakes.

Hence the Reformed churches cannot accept this fascinating representation; and the conscience of believers will always protest against it. What we expect in *"holy apostles"* is this very *certainty, reliability*, and *decision*. Reading their testimony, we want to rely upon it. This certainty alone has been the strength of the Church of all ages. This conviction alone has given her rest. And the Church of today feels as instinctively that the reliability of the Word that is its *Bible* is being taken away from it, inasmuch as these beautifully sounding theories strip the apostolic word of its infallibility.

The holy apostles appear in their writings as such, and not otherwise. St. John, the most beloved among the twelve, testifies that the Lord Jesus gave them as apostles a rare promise, saying, "He shall guide you into all truth," a word that may not be applied to others, but to the apostles exclusively. And again: "The Comforter which is the Holy Ghost shall teach you all things, and bring to your remembrance all things whatsoever I have said unto you" (John 14:26); which promise was not intended for all, but for the apostles only, securing them a gift evidently distinct from illumination. In fact, this promise was nothing else than the permanent endowment with the gift received only temporarily when they went forth on their first mission among Israel: "For it is not you that speak, but the Spirit of your Father which speaketh in you."

Moreover, the Lord Jesus did not only promise them that the word proceeding from their mouth would be a word of the Holy Spirit, but He granted them such personal power and authority that it would be as though God Himself spoke through them. St. Paul testified of this to the church of Thessalonica, saying: "For this cause we thank God that ye received it not as the word of men, but, *as it is in truth,* the Word of God" (1 Thess. 2:13). And St. John tells us that, both before and after the resurrection, the Lord Jesus gave His disciples power to bind on earth in the sense that their word would have binding power forever: "Whosoever sins ye remit, they are remitted unto them; and whosoever sins ye retain, they are retained"; words that are horrible and untenable except they be understood as implying perfect agreement between the minds of the apostles and the mind of God. Of similar import are the words of Christ to Peter: "Whatsoever thou shalt bind on earth shall be bound in heaven; and whatsoever thou shalt loose on earth shall be loosed in heaven."

However, reading and pondering these remarkable and weighty words, let us be careful not to fall into the error of Rome, or, in order to escape from this, make the Word of God of no effect, which is equally dangerous. For the Church of Rome applies these words of Jesus to His disciples, to the whole Church as an institution; especially the word to Peter, making it to refer to all Peter's successors (so-called) in the government of the Church of Rome. If that be indeed the meaning of these words, then Rome is perfectly right; then to the Pope is granted power to bind, and the priests of Rome have still the power to absolve. Our reason for denying that Rome has this power is not the impossibility for men to have it, for it was given to the apostles; Peter was infallible in his sentences *ex cathedra,* and the apostles could grant absolution. But we deny that Rome has the slightest authority to confer this power of Peter upon the Pope, or that of the apostles upon its priests. Neither Matthew 16:19 nor John 20:23 contains the least proof for such claim. And inasmuch as no man has the liberty to exercise such extraordinary power except he can show the credentials of his mission, so we deny Rome's qualifications to exercise it in pope or priest, not because this is impossible, but because Rome cannot substantiate its claims.

At the same time, let us, in our contending with Rome, not fall into the opposite error of disparaging the plain and clear meaning of the word. This is done by the Ethical theologians; for the words of Jesus referred to do not receive justice so long as we refuse to recognize in the apostles a working of the Holy Spirit entirely peculiar, unique, and extraordinary. We dilute the words of Jesus and violate their sense so long as we do not acknowledge that, if the apostles were still living, they would have the power to forgive us our sins; and that Peter, if he were still living, would have power and authority to issue ordinances binding upon the whole Church. The words are so plain, the qualification was granted in such definite terms, that it cannot be denied that John could forgive sin, and that Peter had power to issue an infallible decree. The Lord said to the disciples: "Whosoever sins ye remit, they are remitted unto them"; and to Peter: "Whatsoever thou shalt bind on earth shall be bound in heaven."

Thus acknowledging the unique position and extraordinary power of the apostles, we immediately add that this power was granted to them alone and to no one else.

We emphasize this in opposition to Rome and to those who apply the words of Christ, spoken to His disciples exclusively, to ministers and other believers. Neither Rome nor the Ethical theologians have the right to do this, unless they can show that the Lord Jesus gave them such right. But they never can. Care should be taken, therefore, in the choice of texts, proofs, and quotations from the Scripture, to ascertain not only *what* is said, but also *to whom* it was said. And thus the error concerning the apostolate will soon be overcome; and believers will see that the apostles occupy a different position from other Christians, that the promises quoted bear an exceptional character, and that the Word of the Lord is misunderstood when inspiration is confounded with illumination.

In opposition to these wrong views, which are Romish, clerical in principle, and at the same time strongly tending to rationalism, we maintain the ancient confession of the Christian Church which declares that, as the ambassadors extraordinary of Christ, the apostles occupied a unique position in the race, in the Church, and in the history of the world, and were clothed with extraordinary powers that required an extraordinary operation of the Holy Spirit.

But we do not deny that these men were born again and partakers of the heavenly illumination; so that the man of sin was driven back, and the new man was powerfully revealed in them. But their personal state and condition was the cause of their continued sinfulness until the hour of their death; hence their infallible authority could never spring from the fallible condition of their hearts. Even though they had been less sinful, such power could not be thus accounted for. And if they had fallen more deeply into sin, it would not have hindered the Holy Spirit's operation with reference to the exercise of this authority. It is remarkable that Peter, who was clothed with the highest power, fell again and again into great sin. They were *saints* because they were hid in Christ like other Christians, but they were *holy apostles* not on the ground of their spiritual state and condition, but only by virtue of their holy calling and the working of the Holy Spirit that was promised and given unto them.

Finally, the question arises, whether there was a difference between the operation of the Holy Spirit in the prophets and in the apostles. We answer in the affirmative. Ezekiel's oracles are different from St. John's Gospel. The Epistle to the Romans bears witness to a different inspiration from that of the prophecies of Zacharias. Undoubtedly the book of Revelation proves that the apostles were also susceptible to inspiration by visions; the book of the Acts is evidence that in those days there were also wonderful signs; and St. Paul speaks of visions and ecstasies. And yet the collective treasure that came down to us under the apostles' name bears evidence that the inspiration of the New Testament has another character than that of the Old. And the principal difference consists in the mighty fact of the outpouring of the Holy Spirit.

The prophets were inspired before Pentecost, and the apostles after it. This fact is so strongly marked in the history of their mission that before it the apostles sit still, while immediately after it they appear in their apostolic character before the world. And since in the outpouring the Holy Spirit came to dwell in the body of Christ, which before He had been preparing, it is obvious that the difference of inspiration in the Old and the New Testament consists in the fact that the former was wrought upon the prophets from *without,* while the latter wrought upon the apostles from *within,* proceeding from the body of Christ.

And this is the reason that the prophets give us more or less the impression of an inspiration independent of their personal, spiritual life, while the inspiration of the apostles acts almost always through the life of the soul. It is this very fact that offers to the error of the Ethical view its starting-point. Surely the person and his condition appear in the apostles much more in the foreground than in the prophets. And yet in both prophet and apostle inspiration is that wholly extraordinary operation of the Holy Spirit whereby, in a manner for us incomprehensible and to them not always conscious, they were kept from the possibility of error.

32

Apostles Today?

Am I not an apostle? am I not free? have I not seen Jesus Christ our Lord? are ye not my work in the Lord?
—1 Corinthians 9:1.

We may not take leave of the apostolate without a last look at the circle of its members. It is a *closed* circle; and every effort to reopen it tends to efface a characteristic of the New Covenant.

And yet the effort is being made again and again. We see it in Rome's apostolic succession; in the Ethical view gradually effacing the boundary-line between the apostles and believers; and in its boldest and most concrete form among the Irvingites.*

The latter assert not only that the Lord gave to His Church a college of apostles in the beginning, but that He has now called a body of apostles in His Church to prepare His people for the coming.

However, this position cannot be very successfully supported. Neither in the discourses of Christ, nor in the epistles of the apostles, nor in the Apocalypse, do we find the least intimation of such an event. The end of all things is repeatedly spoken of. The New Testament frequently rehearses the events and signs that must precede the Lord's return. They are recorded so minutely that some even say that the exact

* The Irvingites are known in England and America as the Catholic Apostolic Church —Trans.

date can be fixed. And yet, among all these prophecies, we fail to discover the slightest sign of a subsequent apostolate. In the panorama of the things to come there is literally no room for it.

Nor have the results realized the expectations of these brethren. Their apostolate has been a great disappointment. It has accomplished almost nothing. It has come and gone without leaving a trace. We do not deny that some of these men have done wonderful things, but be it noticed, in the first place, that the signs wrought were far below those performed by the apostles; second, that a man like Pastor Blumhardt has also wrought signs that greatly deserve to be noticed; third, that the Roman Catholic Church sometimes offers signs that are not pretended nor artificial; lastly, that the Lord has warned us in His Word that signs shall be wrought by men who are not His own.

Moreover, let us not forget that the apostles of the Irvingites completely lack the marks of the apostolate. These were: (1) a call directly from the King of the Church; (2) a peculiar qualification of the Holy Spirit making them infallible in the service of the Church. These men lack both marks. They tell us, indeed, of a call come to them by the mouth of prophets, but this is to little or no purpose, for a call from a prophet is not equal to one directly from Christ, and again the name "prophet" is exceedingly misleading. The word prophet has, on the sacred page, a wide application, and occurs in both a *limited* and a *general* sense. The former involves the revelation of a knowledge that mere illumination does not afford; while the latter applies to men speaking in holy ecstasy to the praise of God. We concede that prophesying, in the general sense, is an enduring charisma of the Church; for which reason the reformers of the sixteenth century attempted to revive this office. If the Irvingites, therefore, believe that in their circles the prophetic activity has been revived, we will not dispute it; although we cannot say that the reports of their prophesying have had a very overwhelming effect upon us. However, let it be granted that the gift has been restored, but even then we ask: What do you gain by it? For there is not the slightest proof that these prophets and prophetesses are like their predecessors in the Old Testament. The unrevealed will of God has not been revealed to them. If prophets at all, then their prophesying is merely a speaking to the praise of God in a state of spiritual ecstasy.

The uselessness of an appeal to such prophets for the support of this new apostolate is evident. It is merely the effort to support an unsupported apostolate by an equally unsupported prophetism.

Nor should it be forgotten that the labors of these so-called apostles have not carried our their own program. They have failed to exert any perceptible influence upon the course of events. The institutions founded by them have in no respect surpassed the many new church organizations witnessed by this century. They have established no new principle; their labors have manifested no new power. Whatever they have done lacks the stamp of a heavenly origin. And nearly all these new apostles have died not like the genuine twelve on cross or stake, but on their own beds surrounded by their friends and admirers.

However, this is not all. The name of apostle may be taken (1) in the sense of being called directly by Jesus as an ambassador for God, or (2) in a general sense, denoting every man sent by Jesus into His vineyard; for the word *apostle* means one that is sent. In Acts 14:14 Barnabas is called an apostle; not because he belonged to their number, but merely to indicate that he was sent out by the Lord as His missionary or ambassador. In Acts 13:1, 2 Barnabas is mentioned before Saul, who is not even called by his apostolic name; which shows that this call of the Holy Spirit bore only a temporary character, having in view only this special mission. For this reason the Lord Jesus Christ, as the One sent of the Father, the great Missionary come to this world, the Ambassador of God to His Church, is called Apostle: "Wherefore, holy brethren, . . . consider the Apostle and High Priest of our confession, Christ Jesus" (Heb. 3:1).

If the Irvingites had called the great reformers of the sixteenth century, or some prominent church leaders of the present time, apostles, there could have been no great objection. But they did not mean this. They claim that these new apostles shall stand before the Church in a peculiar character, on the same plane with the first apostles, although differently employed. And this cannot be conceded. It would be in direct opposition to the apostolic declaration of 1 Corinthians 4:9: "For I think that God hath set us forth as the *last* apostles, as it were appointed unto death" (see Dutch translation). How could St. Paul speak of the *last* apostles, if it were God's plan after eighteen centuries to send other twelve apostles into the world?

In view of this positive word of the Holy Spirit, we direct all those that come into contact with the Irvingites to what the Scripture says concerning them that call themselves apostles, and are not: "For such men are false apostles, deceitful workers, fashioning themselves into apostles of Christ." And the Lord Jesus testifies to the church at Ephesus: "I know that thou hast tried them which say they are apostles, and are not."

The notion that false apostles must be a sort of incarnate devils applies in no wise to the calm, respectable, and venerable men frequently seen in the circles of the Irvingites. But apart from this absurd notion, and considering that the false prophets of the Old Testament so closely resembled the true ones that at times even the people of God were deceived by them, we can understand that the false apostles of St. John's day could be detected only by a higher spiritual discernment; and that the pretended apostles of the nineteenth century, who by their similarity to the genuine twelve blinded the eyes of the superficial, could be detected only by the touchstone of the Word of God. And that Word declares that the twelve of St. Paul's day were the *last apostles,* which settles the matter of this pretended apostolate.

This error of the Irvingites is therefore not so very innocent. It is easy to explain how it originated. The wretched and deplorable state of the Church must necessarily give rise to a number of sects. And we heartily acknowledge that the Irvingites have sent forth many warnings and well-deserved rebukes to our superficial and divided Church. But these good offices by no means justify the doing of things condemned by the Word of God; and those who have allowed themselves to be carried away by their teachings will sooner or later experience their fatal result. It is already manifest that this movement, which started among us under the pretext of uniting a divided church by gathering together the Lord's people, has accomplished little more than to add another to the already large number of sects, thus robbing the Church of Christ of excellent powers that now are being wasted.

That the apostolate was a closed circle, and not a flexible theory, is evident from Acts 1:25: "Lord, show of these two, the one whom Thou hast chosen to take the place of this ministry and apostleship"; and again from St. Paul's word (Rom. 1:5): "By whom we have received grace and apostleship"; and again (1 Cor. 9:2): "For the seal of my apostleship are ye in the Lord"; and lastly from Galatians 2:8: "For He that wrought for Peter unto the apostleship of the circumcision, wrought for me also unto the Gentiles." And again it is evident from the fact that the apostles always appear as the twelve; and from their being specially appointed and installed by Jesus breathing upon them the official gift of the Holy Spirit; and from the exceptional power and gifts that were connected with the apostolate. And it is especially from its conspicuous place in the coming Kingdom of our Lord Jesus Christ that the apostolate obtains its definite character. For the Holy Scripture teaches that the apostles shall sit upon twelve thrones judging the twelve tribes of Israel; and also that the New Jerusalem has "twelve foundations upon which are written the twelve names of the apostles of the Lamb."

St. Paul offers us in his own person the most convincing proof that the apostolate was a closed college. If it had not been, the question whether he was an apostle or not could never have caused contention. Yet a large part of the Church refused to acknowledge his apostleship. He did not belong to the twelve; he had not walked with Jesus; how could he be a witness? It was against this seriously meant contention that St. Paul repeatedly lifted up his voice with such energy and animation. This fact is the key to the right understanding of his epistles to the Corinthians and Galatians. They glow with holy jealousy for the reality of his apostleship; for he was deeply convinced that he was an apostle as well as St. Peter and the others. Not by virtue of personal merit; in himself he was not worthy to be called an apostle—1 Corinthians 15:9, but no sooner is his office assailed than he arouses himself like a lion, for this touched the honor of his Master, who had appeared unto him in the way to Damascus; not, as is commonly said, to *convert* him—for this is not *Christ's* work, but that of the *Holy Spirit*—but to appoint him an apostle in that Church which he was persecuting.

As to the question, how the addition of St. Paul to the twelve is consistent with that number, we are convinced that not the name of Matthias, but that of St. Paul is written upon the foundations of the New Jerusalem with those of the others; and that not Matthias, but St. Paul shall sit down to judge the twelve tribes of Israel. As one of the tribes of Israel was replaced by two others, so in regard to the apostolate; for Simeon, who fell out, Manasseh and Ephraim were substituted, and Judas was replaced by Matthias and Paul.

We would not imply that the apostles erred in electing Matthias to fill the vacancy occasioned by the suicide of Judas. On the contrary, the completion of the apostolic number could not be delayed until the conversion of St. Paul. The vacancy had to be filled immediately. But it may be said that when the disciples chose Matthias they had too small a conception of the goodness of their Lord. They supposed that for Judas they would receive a Matthias, and, behold, Jesus gave them a Paul. As to the former, the Scripture mentions his election and no more. Yet even though to the Church of later times the apostolate without St. Paul is unthinkable, and though it allowed his person the first place among the apostles and his writings highest in authority among the Scriptures of the New Testament, to the person of Matthias the election to the apostolate must have brought highest honor. The apostolate stands so high that the fact of having been identified with it, even temporarily, imparts greater luster to a man's name than a royal crown.

Ninth Chapter
The Holy Scriptures in the New Testament

33

The Holy Scriptures in the New Testament

But these are written that ye might believe that Jesus is the Christ, the Son of God; and that believing ye might have life through His name—John 20:31.

Having considered the apostolate, we are now to discuss God's gift to the Church, viz., the New Testament Scripture. The apostolate placed a new power in the Church.

Surely all power is in heaven, but it has pleased God to let this power descend in the Church by means of organs and instruments, chief among which is the apostolate. This organ was a consolation of the Comforter, given to the Church after Jesus had ascended to heaven and was provisionally not to govern His Church in person. Hence it was a forsaken Church, not yet planted, and soon to be scattered, to which the Holy Spirit gave the apostolate as a *bond of union,* as an *organ for self-extension,* and as an instrument for its own *enrichment* with the full knowledge of the life of grace. Commissioned by the King of the Church, the apostles were animated by the Holy Spirit. As the King works for His Church only by the Spirit, so He caused the apostolate to work also by the higher powers of the Holy Spirit.

It was not the Lord's intention that His Church should set out in ignorance, to wander about in manifold error, finally, the long journey ended, to arrive at a clearer perception of the truth, but that from the beginning it should stand in the light of complete knowledge. Hence He gave it the apostolate, that from the cradle of its existence it should receive the full sunshine of grace, and that no subsequent development of Christendom should ever surpass that of the apostles.

This is a very significant fact.

Indeed, in the course of history there is development, especially in doctrine, which has not yet ceased, and which will continue until the end. The King has cast His Church into the midst of warfare and trouble; He has not permitted it to confess His name in an unmanly and indolent manner, but from age to age He has compelled it to defend that confession against error, misunderstanding, and hostility. It is only in this warfare that it has learned gradually to exhibit every part of its glorious inheritance of truth. God shall judge heretics, but, besides much mischief, they have rendered the Church this excellent service of compelling it to wake up from slumbering upon its gold-mines, to explore them, and to open the hidden treasure.

Hence our conscious insight into the truth is deeper than that of the preceding centuries. *Semper excelsior!* Ever higher! Research into holy things may never cease; even now the Lord fulfills His promise to every true theologian: "Ask, and it shall be given you; seek, and ye shall find." And in the development of the consciousness of the Church concerning its treasure of truth, the Holy Spirit has a special work, and he who denies it leaves the Church to petrify and is blind for the word of the Lord.

Yet, however great its present and future progress, it will never possess a grain of truth more than when the apostolate passed away. Afterward the gold-mine might be explored, but when the apostles died the mine itself existed already. Nothing can be added to it or ever will; it is complete in itself. For this reason the great men of God, who, in the course of ages, by brave words have animated the Church, have always pointed back to the treasures of the apostles, and without exception told the churches: "Your treasure lies not before, but behind you, and dates from the days of the apostles."

And herein was mercy; any other disposition would have been unmerciful. The people of one or eighteen centuries ago had the same spiritual needs as we have; nothing less than we have could suffice for them. Their wounds are ours; the balm of Gilead that has healed us, healed them also. Consequently the remedy for souls must be ready for immediate use. Delay would be cruel. Hence it is not strange and problematic, but perfectly in accord with God's mercy, that the whole treasure of saving truth was given to the Church directly in the first century.

To accomplish this was the mission of the apostolate. It is like medical science in this respect, which makes constant progress in the knowledge of herbs. But however great that progress, no *new* herb has been produced. Those that exist now, existed always, having the same medicinal properties. The only difference is, that we know better than our ancestors how to apply them. In like manner, since the days of the apostolate no new remedy for the healing of souls has been created or invented. Indeed, some of the powers then at work are lost to us, for example, the charisma of tongues. All the difference between Church then and now is, that we, according to this thinking and emotional age, understand more profoundly the connection between the effect of the remedy and the healing of our wounds.

This difference does not make us richer or poorer. For the simple peasant it is sufficient to receive the prescribed medicine, although he is ignorant of its ingredients and effects upon blood and nerves. In his world this need does not exist. But the man of thought, understanding the connection between cause and effect, has no confidence in any medicine unless he knows something of its working. To him, this knowledge is a positive need, and to the psychological effect it is even indispensable.

This is likewise true of the Church of Christ; it has not been always the same, neither have its needs. The development of our knowledge has been such that every age has received an insight adapted to satisfy its necessity. More than this: the very fermentation of the age has created the modified need, and has been used of God to give a clearer understanding of the truth.

And yet, whatever the increased clearness and maturity of the knowledge concerning the secret of the Lord during the ages, the secret itself has remained the same. Nothing has been added to it. And the mystery of the apostolate is, that by the labors of its members the whole secret of the Lord was made known to the Church, under the infallible authorship of the divine Inspirer, the Holy Spirit.

This is the great fact accomplished by the apostolate: the publication of the whole secret of the Lord, by which the revelation in the Old Testament, to John the Baptist and Christ was enlarged and worked out. For to complete a thing means to add that which before was lacking; after which nothing more can be added. And this is the *second point* that we emphasize.

Through the apostles the Church received something not possessed by Israel nor imparted by Christ. Christ Himself declares: "I have yet many things to say unto you, but ye cannot bear them now. Howbeit when He, the Spirit of truth, is come, He will guide you into all truth; for He shall not speak from Himself, but whatsoever He shall hear, that shall He speak; and He will show you things to come. He shall glorify Me; for He shall receive of Mine, and shall show it unto you" (John 16:12–14). St. Paul spoke not less clearly, saying: "That the mystery which was kept secret since the world began was now made manifest" (Rom. 16:25). And again: "To make men see what is the dispensation of the mystery which from all ages was hid in God." And again: "The mystery which has been hid from ages and from generations, but now is made manifest to his saints" (Col. 1:16). Finally, St. John declares that the apostles testify of what they had looked upon with their eyes, and their hands had handled of the Word of Life, which was with the Father, and which is manifested.

Although we do not deny that the germ of saving knowledge was given in Paradise, to the Patriarchs, and to Israel; yet the Scripture teaches distinctly that truth was revealed to the Patriarchs, unknown in Paradise; to Israel, of which the Patriarchs were ignorant; and by Jesus, truth that was hidden from Israel. In like manner, truth not declared by Jesus was revealed to the Church by the holy apostolate.

Against this last statement, however, objections are raised. Many unbelieving writers of the present century have frequently asserted that not Jesus, but Paul was the real founder of Christianity; while others have frequently exhorted us to abandon the orthodox theology of St. Paul, and to return to the simple teachings of Jesus; especially to His Sermon on the Mount.

And really, the more the Scripture is studied the more obvious the difference between the Sermon on the Mount and the Epistle to the Romans will appear. Not as though the two contradict each other, but in this way, that the latter contains elements of truth, new rays of light, not found in the former.

If one objects to the doctrines of the apostles, as does the Groninger School, it is natural to place the gospels above the epistles. Hence the fact that many half-believers still receive the Parables and the Sermon on the Mount, but reject the doctrine of justification as taught by St. Paul; while those who wish to break with Christianity entirely are inclined to consider the Pauline epistles as its real exponent, but only to reject them with the entire Pauline Christianity. For the Church of the living God, which receives both, there is in this unholy tendency an exhortation to have an open eye for the difference between the gospels and the epistles, and to acknowledge that our opponents are right when they call it a marked difference.

Yet while our opponents use the difference to attack either the authority of the apostolic doctrine or that of Christendom itself, the Church confesses that there is nothing surprising in this difference. Both are parts of the same doctrine of Jesus, with this distinction, that the first part was revealed directly by Christ, while the other He gave to His Church indirectly by the apostles.

Of course, so long as the apostles are considered as independent persons, teaching a new doctrine on their *own authority,* our solution does not solve the difficulty. But confessing that they are holy apostles, that is, organs of the Holy Spirit through whom Jesus Himself taught His people from heaven, then every objection is met, and there is not even a shadow of conflict.

For Jesus simply acted like an earthly father in the training of his children, who teaches them according to their comprehension; and in case of his death, his task still unfinished, he will leave them written instructions to be opened after his departure. But Jesus died to rise again, and even after His Ascension He continued to be in living contact with His Church through the apostolate. And what we would write before our decease, Jesus caused to be written by His apostles under the special direction of the Holy Spirit. Thus the Scriptures of the New Testament originate—a *New Testament* in a sense now easily understood.

The correctness of this representation is proven by Christ's own words, which teach us—

First, that there were things declared to the apostles before His departure, and there were things not declared, because they could not bear them then.

Secondly, that Jesus would declare the latter also, but by the Holy Spirit.

Thirdly, that the Holy Spirit would reveal these things to them, not apart from Jesus, but by taking them from Christ and declaring them unto them.

34

The Need of the New Testament Scripture

For I testify unto every man that heareth the words of the prophecy of this book, If any man shall add unto these things, God shall add unto him the plagues that are written in this book—Revelation 22:18.

If the Church after the Ascension of Christ had been destined to live only one lifetime, and had been confined only to the land of the Jews, the holy apostles could have accomplished their task by verbal teaching. But since it was to live at least for eighteen centuries, and to be extended over the whole world, the apostles were compelled to resort to the written communication of the revelation which they had received.

If they had not written, the churches of Africa and Gaul could never have received trustworthy information; and the tradition would have lost its reliable character ages ago. The written revelation has, therefore, been the indispensable means whereby the Church, during its long and ever-extending career, has been preserved from complete degeneration and falsification.

However, from their epistles it does not appear that the apostles clearly understood this. Surely, that the Church would sojourn in this world for eighteen centuries, they did not expect; and almost all their epistles bear a local character, as though not intended for the Church in general, but only for particular churches. And yet, although they understood it not, the Lord Jesus knew it; He had thus planned it; hence the epistle written exclusively for the church of Rome was intended and ordained by Him, and without Paul's knowledge, to edify the Church of all ages.

Hence two things had to be done for the Church of the future:

First, the image of Christ must be received from the lips of the apostles and be committed to writing.

Secondly, the things of which Jesus had said, "Ye cannot bear them now, but the Holy Spirit will declare them unto you," must be recorded. This is the postulate of the whole matter. The condition of the churches, their long duration in the future, and their world-wide extension demanded it.

And the facts show that the provision was made, but not immediately. So long as the Church was confined to a small circle, and the remembrance of Christ remained fresh and powerful, the apostles' spoken word was sufficient. The decree of the Synod of Jerusalem was probably the first written document that proceeded from them. But when the churches began to extend across the sea to Corinth and Rome, and northward to Ephesus and Galatia, then Paul began to substitute written for verbal instructions. Gradually this epistolary labor was extended and Paul's example followed. Perhaps each wrote in turn. And to these epistles were added the narratives of the life, death, and Resurrection of Christ and the Acts of the Apostles. At last the King commanded John from heaven to write in a book the extraordinary revelation given him on Patmos.

The result was a gradually increasing number of apostolic and non-apostolic writings, probably far exceeding that contained in the New Testament. At least Paul's epistles show that he wrote many more than we now possess. But even if he had not thus informed us, the fact would have been sufficiently well established; for it is improbable that such excellent writers as Paul and John should not have written more than a dozen letters during their long and eventful lives. Even in one year they must have written more than that. The controversy of former days over the assertion that no apostolic writings could have been lost was most foolish, and showed little reckoning with real life.

It is remarkable that from this great mass a small number of writings was gradually separated. A few were collected first, then more were added, and arranged in certain order. It took a long time before there was uniformity and agreement; indeed, some writings were not universally recognized until after three centuries. But in spite of time and controversy, the sifting took place, and the result was, that the Church distinguished in this great mass of literature two distinct parts: on the one hand, this arranged set of twenty-seven books; and on the other the remaining writings of early origin.

And when the process of sifting and separating was ended, and the Holy Spirit had borne witness in the churches that this set of writings constituted a whole, and was, indeed, the Testament of the Lord Jesus to His Church, then the Church became conscious that it possessed a second collection of sacred books of equal authority with the first collection given to Israel; then it put the Old and the New Testament together, which unitedly form the Holy Scripture, our Bible, the Word of God.

To the question, How did the New Testament Scripture originate? we answer without hesitation, By the Holy Spirit.

How? Did He say to Paul or John: "Sit down and write"?

The gospels and the epistles do not so impress us. It does indeed apply to the Revelation of St. John, but not to the other New Testament Scriptures. They rather impress us as being written without the slightest idea of being intended for the Church of all ages. Their authors impress us as writing to certain churches of their own definite time, and that after a hundred years perhaps not a single fragment of their writings would be in existence. They were indeed conscious of the Holy Spirit's aid in *writing* the truth even as they enjoyed it in *speaking, but* that they were writing parts of the Holy Scripture, they surely knew not.

When St. Paul had finished his Epistle to the Romans, it never occurred to him that in future ages his letter would possess for millions of God's children an authority equal to, or even higher than that of the prophecies of Isaiah and the Psalms of David. Nor could the first readers of his epistle, in the church of Rome, have imagined that after eighteen centuries the names of their principal men would still be household words in all parts of the Christian world.

But if St. Paul knew it not, surely the Holy Spirit did. As by education the Lord frequently prepares a maiden for her still unknown, future husband, so did the Holy Spirit prepare Paul, John, and Peter for their work. He directed their lives, circumstances, and conditions; He caused such thoughts, meditations, and even words to arise in their hearts as the writing of the New Testament Scripture required. And while they were writing these portions of the Holy Scripture, that one day would be the treasure of the universal Church in all ages, a fact not understood by them, but by the Holy Spirit, He so directed their thoughts as to guard them against mistakes and lead them into all truth. He foreknew what the complete New Testament Scripture ought to be, and what parts would belong to it. As an architect, by his mechanics, prepares the various parts of the building, afterward to fit them in their places, so did the Holy Spirit by different workers prepare the different parts of the New Testament, which afterward He united in a whole.

For the Lord, who by His Holy Spirit caused the preparation of these parts, is also King of the Church; He saw these parts scattered abroad; He led men to care for them, and believers to have faith in them. And, finally, by means of the men interested, He united these loose fragments, so that gradually, according to His royal decree, the New Testament originated.

Hence it was not necessary that the New Testament Scripture should contain only apostolic writings. Mark and Luke were no apostles; and the notion that these men must have written under the direction of Paul or Peter has no proof nor force. What is the benefit of writing under the direction of an apostle? That which gives divine authority to the writings of Luke is not the influence of an apostle, but that he wrote under the absolute inspiration of the Holy Spirit.

Believing in the authority of the New Testament, we must acknowledge the authority of the four evangelists to be perfectly equal. As to the *contents,* Matthew's gospel may surpass that of Luke, and John's may excel the gospel of Mark, but their authority is equally unquestionable. The Epistle to the Romans has higher value than that to Philemon, but their authority is the same. As to their *persons,* John stood above Mark, and Paul above Jude, but since we depend not upon the authority of their persons, but only upon that of the Holy Spirit, these personal differences are of no account.

Hence the question is not whether the New Testament writers were apostles, but whether they were inspired by the Holy Spirit.

Assuredly, it has pleased the King to connect His testimony with the apostolate; for He said: "Ye are My witnesses." Hence we know that Luke and Mark obtained their information concerning Christ from the apostles, but our guaranty for the accuracy and reliability of their statements is not the apostolic origin of the same, but the authority of the Holy Spirit. Hence the apostles are the channels through which the knowledge of these things flows to us from Christ, but whether this knowledge reaches us through their writings or through those of others makes no difference. The vital question is, whether the bearers of the apostolic tradition were infallibly inspired or not.

Even though a writing were endorsed by the twelve apostles, this would not be positive proof of its credibility or divine authority. For although they had the promise that the Holy Spirit would lead them into all truth, this does not exclude the possibility of their falling into mistakes or even untruths. The promise did not imply absolute infallibility, at all times, but merely when they should act as *the witnesses of Jesus.* Hence the information that a document comes from the hand of an apostle is insufficient. It requires the additional information that it belongs to the things which the apostle wrote as a *witness of Jesus.*

If, therefore, the divine authority of any writing does not depend upon its apostolic character, but solely upon the authority of the Holy Spirit, it follows, as a matter of course, that the Holy Spirit is entirely free to have the apostolic testimony recorded by the apostles themselves, or by anyone else; in both cases the authority of these writings is exactly the same. Personal preferences are out of the question. So far as form, content, wealth, and attractiveness are concerned, we may distinguish between John and Mark, Paul and Jude. But when it touches the question of the divine authority before which we must bow, then we no longer take account of any such distinctions, and we ask only: Is this or that gospel *inspired by the Holy Spirit?*

35

The Character of the New Testament Scripture

And these things write we unto you, that your joy may be full—1 John 1:4.

From the two preceding articles it is evident that the New Testament Scripture was not intended to bear the character of a notarial document. If this had been the Lord's intention we should have received something entirely different. It would have required a twofold legal evidence:

In the first place, the proof that the events narrated in the New Testament actually occurred as related.

Secondly, that the revelations received by the apostles are correctly communicated.

Both certifications should be furnished by witnesses, for example, to prove the miracle of the feeding of the five thousand would require:

1. A declaration of a number of persons, stating that they were eyewitnesses of the miracle.

2. An authentic declaration of the magistrates of the surrounding places certifying to their signatures.

3. A declaration of competent persons to prove that these witnesses were known as honest and trustworthy people, disinterested and competent to judge. Moreover, it would be necessary by proper testimony

to prove that, among the five thousand, there were only seven loaves and two fishes.

4. That the increase of bread took place while Jesus broke it.

In the presence of a number of such documents, each duly authenticated and sealed, persons not too skeptical might find it possible to believe that the event had occurred as narrated in the Gospel.

To prove this one miracle would require a number of documents voluminous as the whole of St. Matthew. If it were possible thus to prove all the events recorded in the gospels and the Acts of the Apostles, then the credibility of these narratives would be properly established.

And even this would be far from satisfactory. For the difficulty would remain to prove that the epistles contain correct communications of the revelations received by the apostles. Such proof would be impossible. It would require eye- and ear-witnesses to these revelations; and a number of stenographers to report them. If this had been possible, then, we concede, there would have been, if not mathematical certainty for every expression, yet sufficient ground for accepting the general tenor of the epistles.

But when the apostles wrote them there was no audible voice. And when a voice was heard, it could not be understood, as in the case of Paul's revelation on the way to Damascus. The same may be said of what occurred on Patmos: St. John actually heard a voice, but the hearing and the understanding of the words which it uttered required a peculiar, spiritual operation that was lacking in the people at the same time on the island.

The fact is, that the revelation of the Holy Spirit granted to the apostles was of such a nature that it could not be perceived by others. Hence the impossibility to prove its genuineness by notarial evidence. He that insists upon it ought to know that the Church cannot furnish it, either for the historical narratives of the gospels, or for the spiritual contents of the epistles.

Hence it is evident that every effort to prove the truth of the contents of the New Testament by external evidence only condemns itself, and must result in the absolute rejection of the authority of the Holy Scripture. If a judge of the present day should condemn or acquit an accused person on the ground of the insignificant evidence which satisfies many honest people with reference to the Scripture, what a storm of indignation would it raise! The whole list of the so-called evidences as to the credibility of the New Testament writers, that they were competent to judge, willing to testify, disinterested, etc., proves nothing indeed.

Such externals may suffice when it concerns ordinary events, of which one might say: "I believe that it has really happened, I have no reason to doubt it, but if tomorrow it should prove not to be so, I will lose nothing by it." But how can such superficial methods be applied when it concerns the extraordinary events related by the Holy Scripture, upon the positive certainty of which my own and my children's highest interests depend; so that, if they proved to be untrue, for example, the report of the resurrection of Christ, we should suffer the priceless and irreparable loss of an eternal salvation?

This cannot be; it is absolutely unthinkable. And experience proves that the efforts of foolish people to prop their faith by such proofs has always ended with the loss of all faith. Nay, such kind of proof is by its very insignificance either unworthy to be mentioned with reference to such serious matters, or, if it be worth anything, it cannot be furnished, nor ought it to be.

Notarial or mathematical proof neither can nor may be furnished, because the character and nature of the contents of Scripture are inconsistent with or repellent to such demonstration.

No man may demand legal proofs for the fact that the man whom he loves and honors as father is his father indeed, God has made such proof impossible by the very nature of the case. The delicacy which ennobles all family life cuts off the very appearance of such investigation; and, if it were possible, the son furnished with such proof, would *ipso facto* have lost his father and mother; they would be his parents no more; and beneath the pile of evidence his child-life would be buried.

The same principle applies to the Holy Scripture. The nature and character of the revelation has been so ordered that it allows no notarial demonstration. The revelation to the apostles is unthinkable, if other persons could have heard, recorded, and published it as well as they. It was an operation of holy energies, not intended to compel doubters to a mere outward faith, but simply to accomplish that for which God had sent it, without caring much for the contradiction of the skeptics. It concerns a work of God which legal or mathematical investigation cannot fathom; which manifests itself upon the spiritual domain where certainty obtains not by outward demonstration, but by personal faith of the one in the other.

As faith in father and mother springs not from mathematical demonstration, but from the contact of love, and fellowship of life, and personal trust in each other, even so here. A life of love unfolded itself. The mercies of God came bending down to us in tender compassion. And every man touched by this divine life was affected by its influence, taken up by it, lived in it, felt himself in sympathetic fellowship with it; and, in a way imperceptible and not understood, obtained a certainty, far above any other, that he was in the presence of *facts,* and that they were divinely revealed.

And such is the origin of faith; not supported by scientific proof, for then it would be no faith; which has mastered the reader of the Holy Scripture in an entirely different way. The existence of the Scripture is owing to an act of the unfathomable mercies of God; and for this reason man's acceptance must equally be an act of absolute self-denial and gratitude. It is only the broken and contrite heart, filled with thankfulness to God for His excellent mercy, that can cast itself into the Scripture as into its life-element, and feel that here is found real assurance, casting out all doubt.

Hence we must distinguish a threefold operation of the Holy Spirit with reference to faith in the New Testament Scripture:

First, a divine working giving a *revelation* to the apostles.

Second, a working called *inspiration.*

Third, a working, active today, creating *faith in the Scripture* in the heart at first unwilling to believe.

First comes *revelation* proper.

For example, when St. Paul wrote his treatise on the resurrection (1 Cor. 15), he did not develop that truth for the first time. Probably he had apprehended it previously, and in his sermons and private correspondence expounded it. Hence the revelation antedates the epistle. It belonged to the things of which Jesus had said. "When the Holy Spirit has come He shall guide you into all truth, and He will show you things to come." And he received that revelation in such a way that he had the positive conviction that thus the Holy Spirit had revealed it to him, and that thus he would see it in the Judgment day.

But the epistle was not yet written. This required a second act of the Holy Spirit—that of *inspiration.*

Without this the knowledge that St. Paul had received a revelation would be useless. What warrant should we have that he had correctly understood and faithfully recorded it? He might have made a mistake in the communication, adding to it or taking from it, thus making it an unreliable report. Hence *inspiration* was indispensable; for by it the apostle was kept from error while he recorded the revelation previously received.

Lastly, the spiritual bond must be created connecting the soul and the consciousness with the spiritual realities of the infallible Word of God—positive conviction of spiritual things.

The Holy Spirit accomplishes this by the implanting of faith, with the various preparations that ordinarily precede the breaking forth of the act of believing. The result is inward *conviction.* This is not wrought by referring us to Josephus or Tacitus, but in a spiritual way. The content of the Scripture is brought to the soul. The conflict between the Word and the soul is felt. The conviction thus wrought causes us to see not that the Scripture must make room for us, but we for the Scripture.

In the discussion of *regeneration* we shall refer to this point more largely. For the present we shall be satisfied if we have succeeded in showing that the existence of the New Testament Scripture and our faith in it are not the work of man, but a work in which the *Holy Spirit* alone must be honored.

Tenth Chapter
The Church of Christ

36

The Church of Christ

It is the Spirit that beareth witness, because the Spirit is truth—1 John 5:6.

We now proceed to discuss the work of the Holy Spirit wrought in the Church of Christ.

Although the Son of God has had a Church in the earth from the beginning, yet the Scripture distinguishes between its manifestation *before* and *after* Christ. As the acorn, planted in the ground, exists, although it passes through the two periods of germinating and rooting, and of growing upward and forming trunk and branches, even so the Church. At first hidden in the soil of Israel, wrapped in the swaddling-clothes of its national existence, it was only on the day of Pentecost that it was manifested in the world.

Not that the Church was founded only on Pentecost; this would be a denial of the Old Covenant revelation, a falsification of the idea of Church, and an annihilation of God's election. We only say that on that day it became the *Church for the world.*

And in it the Holy Spirit has wrought a very comprehensive work.

Not its formation, however, for that is the work of the Triune God in the divine decree; or, speaking more definitely, of Jesus the King when He bought His people with His own blood.

Indeed, the Spirit of God regenerates the elect, whom He does not find in the world, but already in the Church. Every representation as though the Holy Spirit gathers the elect out of a lost world, and so brings them into the Church, opposes the Scripture's representation of the Church as an organism. Christ's Church is a body, and as the members grow out of the body and are not added to it from without, so must the seed of the Church be looked for in the Church and not in the world. The Holy Spirit works that only which is already sanctified in Christ. Hence our form of Baptism reads: "Do you acknowledge that although our children are conceived and born in sin, and therefore are subject to all miseries, yea to condemnation itself; yet that they are sanctified in Christ?"

However, since regeneration belongs to His work in the *individual,* and we are considering now His work in the Church *as a whole,* as a community, we direct our attention, in the first place, to His work of imparting spiritual gifts, particularly those called *charismata.* Some New Testament passages speak of gifts like those offered to God (Matt. 5:23): "If thou bring thy gift to the altar"; or gifts communicated to others (2 Cor. 8:9 and Phil. 4:17); and the gift of salvation, but those we do not consider.

A gift offered to God is called in the Greek *doron;* imparted to others, it is commonly called *charis;* while the gift of grace is usually called *dorea.* Hence these gifts are distinct from those that now occupy our attention. And this distinction appears strongest when we compare the gift of the *Holy Spirit* with *spiritual gifts.* The Holy Spirit Himself is a gift of grace. But when He imparts *spiritual gifts* He adorns us with holy ornaments. The first refers to our *salvation;* the last to our *talents.*

Referring to our salvation, the Scripture calls it a free and gracious gift, generally *dorea* in the Greek, which, being derived from a root meaning *to give,* denotes that we were not entitled to it, having neither merited nor bought it, but that it is a *given good.* St. Paul exclaims: "Thanks unto God for His unspeakable gift," that is, of salvation (2 Cor. 9:15). And again: "Much more the grace of God and the gift of grace, which is by one man Jesus Christ, hath abounded unto many." "Much more they which receive abundance of grace and the gift of righteousness shall reign in life by one, Jesus Christ" (Rom. 5:15, 17).

And lastly: "But unto every one of us is given grace according to the measure of the gift of Christ" (Eph. 4:7).*

The same expression is used invariably for the imparting of the Holy Spirit: "Ye shall receive the gift of the Holy Ghost" (Acts 2:38). And: "Because that on the Gentiles also was poured out the gift of the Holy Ghost" (Acts 10:45). Hence it should be carefully noticed that this has nothing to do with the subject under consideration. When St. Paul speaks of faith as the gift of God, he refers to our *salvation* and God's saving work in the soul. But the gifts of which we now speak are wholly different. They are not unto salvation, but to the glory of God. They are lent to us as ornaments, that we should show their beauty as talents to gain other talents therewith. They are *additional* operations of grace, which cannot take the place of the proper work of the grace of salvation, nor confirm it, having an entirely different purpose. The work of grace is for our *own* salvation, joy, and upbuilding; the charismata are given us for *others.* The first implies that we have received the Holy Spirit; the latter that He imparts gifts unto us.

Properly speaking, the charismata are given to the *churches,* not to individual persons. When a ruler selects and trains men for officers in the army, it is evident that he does this not for their personal enjoyment, honor, and aggrandizement, but for the efficiency and honor of the army. He can search for men with talents for the military service, and train and instruct them, but he cannot create such talents. If this were possible, every king would endow his generals with the genius of a Von Moltke, and every admiral would be a De Ruyter.

But Jesus is not thus limited. He is independent; unto Him all power is given in heaven and on earth. He can create talents, and freely impart them to whomsoever He will. Hence, knowing what the Church requires for its protection and upbuilding, He can fully supply all its need. His purpose is not merely to please or enrich individuals, much less to give to some what He withholds from others, but with the persons thus endowed to adorn and favor *the whole Church.* We do not put a lamp

---

* It should be noticed that in Rom. 5:15, 16; 6:23; 11:29, the word "*charisma*" is found in the Greek text, referring to salvation. The reason is that these passages refer not to the graciousness of the gift, but to its scintillating brightness, in contrast with corruption and death. "The wages of sin is death, but the gift of God is eternal life."

upon the table to show it a special favor or because it is more excellent than chair or stove, but simply because thus it serves its purpose, and the whole room is lighted. To consider the charismata as intended merely to adorn and benefit the person endowed would be just as absurd as to say: "I light the fire to warm not the *room,* but the *stove";* and to be jealous of the charismata given to others in the Church would be just as foolish as for the table to be jealous of the stove because it gets all the fire.

The charismata must therefore be considered in an economical sense. The Church is a large household with many wants; an institution to be made efficient by the means of many things. They are to the Church what light and fuel are to the household; not existing for themselves, but for the family, and to be laid aside when the days are long and warm. This applies directly to the charismata, many of which, given to the apostolic Church, are not of service to the Church of the present day.

These charismata have undoubtedly more or less an official character. God has instituted offices in the Church; not in a mechanical way, or depending upon robe or gown, such unspiritual conception is foreign to the Scripture. But as there is division of labor in the army or in the human body, so there is in the Church.

Take, for example, the body. It must be protected against injury; blood must be carried to muscles and nerves; venous blood must be converted into arterial; the lungs must inhale fresh air, etc. All these activities are laid upon the various members of the body. Eye and ear keep watch; the heart propels the blood; the lungs supply the oxygen, etc. And this cannot be changed arbitrarily. The lungs cannot watch; the eye cannot supply oxygen; the skin cannot propel the blood. Hence this division of labor is neither arbitrary, by mutual consent, nor a matter of pleasure, but it is divinely ordained, and this ordinance must not be ignored. Hence the eye has the office and gift of watching over the body; the heart of circulating the blood; the lungs of supplying fresh air, etc.

And this applies to the Church in every respect. That great body requires the doing of many and various things for the common weal. There is need of guidance, of prophesying, of heroism; mercy must be exercised, the sick must be healed, etc. And this great, mutual task the Lord has divided among many members. He has given to His body, the Church, eyes, ears, hands, and feet; and to each of these organic members a peculiar task, calling, and office.

Hence to be called to an office simply means to be charged by Jesus, the King with a definite task. You have done some work. Very well, but how? From impulse, or in obedience to the charge of your Sender? This makes all the difference. The King may send us in the ordinary or in an extraordinary way. Zacharias was a priest of the course of Abijah, but his son John was the herald of Christ by extraordinary revelation. The Levite served by right of succession; the prophet because he was chosen of God. But this makes no difference; called in the one way or the other, the office remains the same, so long as we have the assurance that King Jesus has called and ordained us.

For this reason our fathers devoutly spoke of an *office of all believers.* In Christ's Church there are not merely a few officials and a mass of idle, unworthy subjects, but every believer has a calling, a task, a vital charge. And inasmuch as we are convinced that we perform the task because the King has laid it upon us not for ourselves, nor even from the motive of philanthropy, but to *serve the Church,* to this extent has our work an *official* character, although the world denies us the honor.

37

Spiritual Gifts

But desire earnestly the greater gifts. And a still more excellent way show I unto you—1 Corinthians 12:31 (R.V.).

The charismata or spiritual gifts are the divinely ordained means and powers whereby the King enables His Church to perform its task on the earth.

The Church has a calling in the world. It is being violently attacked not only by the powers of this world, but much more by the invisible powers of Satan. No rest is allowed. Denying that Christ has conquered, Satan believes that the time left him may yet bring him victories. Hence his restless rage and fury, his incessant attacks upon the ordinances of the Church, his constant endeavor to divide and corrupt it, and his ever-repeated denial of the authority and kingship of Jesus in His Church. Although he will never succeed entirely, he does succeed to some extent. The history of the Church in every country shows it, it proves that a satisfactory condition of the Church is highly exceptional and of short duration, and that for eight out of ten centuries its state is sad and deplorable, cause for shame and grief on the part of God's people.

And yet in all this warfare it has a calling to fulfill, an appointed task to accomplish. It may sometimes consist in being sifted like wheat, as in Job's case, to show that by virtue of Christ's prayer faith cannot be destroyed in its bosom. But whatever the form of the task, the Church always needs spiritual power to perform it; a power not in itself, but which the King must supply.

Every means afforded by the King for the doing of His work is a charisma, a gift of grace. Hence the internal connection between *work, office,* and *gift.*

Wherefore St. Paul says: "To each one is given the manifestation of the Spirit to profit withal," that is, for the general good (πρὸς τὸ συμφέρον) (1 Cor. 12:7). And, again, still more clearly: "Even so ye, forasmuch as ye are zealous of spiritual gifts, seek that ye may excel, to the *edifying of the Church"* (1 Cor. 14:12). Hence the petition, "Thy Kingdom come," which the Heidelberg Catechism interprets: "Rule us so by Thy Word and Spirit that we may submit ourselves more and more to Thee; preserve and increase Thy Church; destroy the works of the devil, and all violence which would exalt itself against Thee, and also all wicked counsels devised against Thy Holy Word, till the full perfection of the Kingdom takes place, wherein Thou shalt be all in all."

It is wrong, therefore, to consider the life of individual believers too much by itself, separating it from the life of the Church. They exist not but in connection with the body, and thus they become partakers of the spiritual gifts. In this sense the Heidelberg Catechism confesses the communion of saints: "First, that all and everyone who believes, being members of Christ, are in common partakers of Him and of all His riches and gifts; secondly, that everyone must know it to be his duty readily and cheerfully to employ his gifts for the advantage and salvation of other members." The parable of the talents has the same aim; for the servant who with his talent failed to benefit others receives a terrible judgment. Even the *hidden* gift must be stirred up, as St. Paul says; not to boast of it or to feed our pride, but because it is the Lord's and intended for the Church.

St. John writing, "Ye have an unction from the Holy One, and ye know all things" (1 John 2:20), and "Ye need not that any man teach you" (1 John 2:27), does not mean to say that every individual believer possesses the full anointing, and in virtue of this knoweth all things. For if this were so, who would not despair of salvation, nor dare say: "I have the faith"? Moreover, how could the statement, "Ye need not that any man teach you," be reconciled with the testimony of the same apostle, that the Holy Spirit qualifies teachers appointed by Jesus Himself?

Not the individual believer, but the whole Church *as a body* possesses the full anointing of the Holy One and knows all things. The Church as a body needs not that any come to teach it from without; for it possesses all the treasure of wisdom and knowledge, being united with the Head, who is the reflection of the glory of God, in whom dwelleth all wisdom.

And this applies not to the Church of one period, but of all ages. The Church of today is the same as in the day of the apostles. The life lived then is the life that animates it now. The gains of two centuries ago belong to its treasury, as well as those received today. The past is its capital. The wonderful and glorious revelation received by the Church of the first century was given, through it, to the Church of all ages, and is still effectual. And all the spiritual strength and insight, the inward grace, the clearer consciousness, received during the course of the ages are not lost, but form an accumulated treasure, increasing still by the ever-renewed additions of spiritual gifts.

He who realizes and acknowledges this fact feels himself rich and blessed indeed. For this apostolic view of the matter causes us to be thankful for our brother's gift, which otherwise we might envy; inasmuch as those gifts do not impoverish, but enrich us. In one city there may be twelve ministers of the Word, all gifted in various directions. According to the natural man, each will be jealous of his brother's gifts and fear that his talents will excel his own. But not so among the Lord's own servants. They feel that together they serve one Lord and one flock, and bless God for giving them *together* what the leading and feeding require. In an army the artillerist is not jealous of the cavalryman, for he knows that the latter is for his protection in the hour of danger.

Moreover, this apostolic standpoint excludes *isolation;* for it creates the longing for fellowship with distant brethren, even though they walk in more or less deviating paths. It is impossible, Bible in hand, to limit Christ's Church to one's own little community. It is everywhere, in all parts of the world; and whatever its external form, frequently changing, often impure, yet the gifts wherever received increase our riches.

This apostolic standpoint is also against the foolish notion that for eighteen centuries the Church has received no gifts whatever; and hence, that, like the early Church, each of us must take his Bible to formulate his own confession. That standpoint makes one so intensely conscious of the communion of spiritual gifts that he cannot but appreciate the Church's treasure accumulated during the centuries. In fact, Christ's Church has received greatest abundance of spiritual gifts; and today we have the disposition not only of the gifts of the churches in our own city, but of all those imparted to the churches elsewhere, and of the historic capital accumulated during eighteen centuries.

Hence the treasure of every particular church is threefold: First, the charismata *in its own circle;* secondly, those *given to other churches;* and lastly, those received since the *days of the apostles.*

According to their nature these spiritual gifts may be divided into three classes: the *official,* the *extraordinary,* and the *ordinary.*

St. Paul says: "To one is given through the Spirit the word of wisdom, and to another the word of knowledge, according to the same Spirit, and to another faith by the same Spirit; and to another gifts of healing in the one Spirit; and to another workings of miracles, and to another prophecy; and to another discerning of spirits; and to another diverse kinds of tongues; and to another the interpretation of tongues. But all these worketh the one and the same Spirit, dividing to each one severally even as He will" (1 Cor. 18:8–11). In like manner the apostle speaks to the Church of Rome: "Having then gifts differing according to the grace that is given to us, whether prophecy, let us prophesy according to the proportion of faith; or ministry, let us wait on our ministering; or he that teacheth, on teaching; or he that exhorteth, on exhortation; he that giveth let him do it with simplicity; he that ruleth, with diligence; he that showeth mercy, with cheerfulness" (Rom. 12:6–8).

From these passages it is evident that among these charismata St. Paul assigns the first place to the gifts pertaining to the ordinary service of the Church by its ministers, elders, and deacons. For by prophecy St. Paul designates animated preaching, wherein the preacher feels himself cheered and inspired by the Holy Spirit. By *"teaching"* he means ordinary catechizing. *"Ministry"* refers to the management of the temporalities of the Church. *"Giving"* has reference to the care for the poor and the miserable. *"He that ruleth"* refers to the officers in charge of the government of the Church. These are the ordinary offices embracing the care of the spiritual and temporal affairs of the Church.

Then follows a different series of charismata, viz., tongues, healing, discernment of spirits, etc. These non-official gifts divide themselves into two classes—those that *strengthen* the gifts of saving grace, and those *distinct from* the grace of salvation.

The former are, for example, *faith* and *love.* Without faith no one can be saved. It is therefore the portion of all God's children, and as such not a *"charisma,"* but a *"doron."* But while all have faith, God is free to let it *manifest itself* more strongly in the one than in another. Of one degree Scripture says: "Believe on the Lord Jesus Christ, and thou shalt be saved"; and of another: "If ye have faith as a grain of mustard-seed, ye shall say unto this mountain, Remove hence to yonder place, and it shall remove." The first works internally, the other externally. For this reason St. Paul speaks not only of *ministries* and *gifts,* but also of *"workings,"* which consist in a more vigorous exercise of the grace which the believer as such possesses already. Where the faith of many languishes, the Lord frequently grants extraordinary workings of faith to some, thus to refresh and comfort others. The same is true of *love,* which also is the portion of all, but not in the same effectual degree. And where the love of many waxes cold, the Lord sometimes quickens it in the few to such extent that others see it and are provoked to holy jealousy.

Besides these *ordinary* charismata, which are only more energetic manifestations of what every believer possesses in the germ, the Lord has also given to His church *extraordinary* gifts, working partly upon the spiritual and partly upon the physical domain. Of the latter are the charismata of self-restraint and healing of the sick. Of the former Christ speaks in Matthew 19:12, where he calls such persons "eunuchs for the sake of the Kingdom." St. Paul says that for the sake of the weak brother he will abstain from meat; and again, that he keeps under the body, bringing it into subjection, etc. The charisma of healing refers to the glorious gift of healing the sick: not only those who suffer from nervous diseases and psychological ailments, who are more susceptible to spiritual influences, but also those whose diseases are wholly outside the spiritual realm.

Of an entirely different nature are the *extraordinary,* purely *spiritual* charismata, of which St. Paul mentions five: wisdom, knowledge, discernment of spirits, tongues and their interpretation. These may also be divided in two classes, inasmuch as the first three mentioned are also found, although in a different form, *outside* of the Kingdom of God; and the last two, which present a wholly peculiar phenomenon, *within* the Kingdom. Wisdom, knowledge, and discernment of spirits exist even among the heathen, and are much admired by those who reject the Christ. But those natural gifts appear in the Church in a different way. The charisma of *wisdom* enables one without much investigation, with great tact and clearness, to understand *conditions* and to offer judicious advice. *Knowledge* is a charisma whereby the Holy Spirit enables one to acquire an unusually deep insight into the *mysteries of the Kingdom. Discernment of spirits* is a charisma whereby one can discern between the genuine spirits raised up of God and those that only pretend to be such. The charisma of tongues we have discussed at length in the twenty-eighth article.

The charismata now existing in the Church are those pertaining to the ministry of the Word; the ordinary charismata of increased exercise of faith and love; those of wisdom, knowledge, and discernment of spirits; that of self-restraint; and lastly, that of healing those suffering from nervous and psychological diseases. The others for the present are inactive.

38

The Ministry of the Word

He shall lead you into all truth—John 16:13.

Let us now consider the second activity of the Holy Spirit in the Church, which we prefer to designate as His *care-taking* of the Word. In this we distinguish three parts, viz.: the *Sealing*, the *Interpretation*, and the *Application* of the Word.

In the first place, it is the Holy Spirit who *seals* the Word. This has reference to the "testimonium Spiritus Sancti," of which our fathers used to speak and by which they understood the operation whereby He creates in the hearts of believers the firm and lasting convictions concerning the divine and absolute authority of the Word of God.

The Word is, if we may so express it, a child of the Holy Spirit. He has brought it forth. We owe it entirely to His peculiar activity. He is its *Auctor Primarius*, that is, its Principal Author. And thus it cannot seem strange that He should exercise that motherly care over the child of His own travail whereby He enables it to fulfill its destiny. And this destiny is, in the first place, to *be believed* in by the elect; secondly, to be *understood* by them; and lastly, to be *lived* by them; three operations that are successively effected in them by the sealing, the interpretation, and the application of the Word. The *sealing* of the Word quickens the "faith"; the *interpretation* imparts the "right understanding"; and *the application* effects the "living" of it.

We mention the *sealing* of the Word first, for without faith in its divine authority it cannot be God's Word to us.

The question is: How do we come in real contact and fellowship with the Holy Scripture, which, as a mere external object, lies before us?

We are told that it is the Word of God, but how can this become our own firm conviction? It can never be obtained by investigation. In fact, it ought to be acknowledged that the more one investigates the Word the more he loses his simple and childlike faith in it. It cannot even be said that the doubt created by superficial inquiry will be dispelled by deeper research; for even the profound scrutiny of earnest men has had but one result, viz., the increase of interrogation-points.

We cannot in this way examine the contents of the Scripture without destroying it for ourselves. If one wishes to examine the contents of an egg, he must not break it, for then he disturbs it and it is an egg no more, but he should ask them that know about it. In like manner we can learn the truth of the Scripture only by sealing and external communication.

For suppose that the final verdict of science will eventually confirm the divine authority of the Scripture, as we firmly believe it will, what would that avail us in our present spiritual need, since during our short life science will not reach that final verdict? And even if after thirty or forty years we should see it, would that avail my present distress? And if this difficulty could also be removed, we would still ask: Is it not cruel to give spiritual assurance only to Greek and Hebrew scholars? Do not men see and understand, then, that the evidence of the divine authority of the Scripture must come to us in such a manner that the simplest old woman in the poorhouse can see it just as well as I can?

Hence all learned investigation, as the basis for *spiritual conviction,* is out of the question. He who denies this maltreats souls and introduces an offensive clericalism. For what is the result? The notion that the unscholarly can have no assurance of themselves; that is what ministers are for; they have studied the matter; they ought to know, and the simple folk must believe upon their authority.

The absurdity of this notion if obvious. In the first place, the learned gentlemen are frequently the greatest doubters. Secondly, one minister almost always contradicts what another has laid down as the truth. And, thirdly, the congregation, treated as a *minor*, is delivered again into the power of men; a yoke is laid upon it which our fathers could not bear; and the mistake is made of trying to prove the testimony of God by that of men.

If we must bear a yoke, then give us that of *Rome* ten times rather than that of *the scholars;* for although Rome puts men between us and the Scripture, they speak at least with one mouth. They all repeat what the Pope has settled for them, and his authority rests not upon his scholarship, but upon his pretended *spiritual illumination.* Hence the Roman Catholic priests do not contradict one another. Neither is their teaching the fancy of a *defective* learning, but the result of a mental development that Rome attained in its most excellent men, and that in connection with the spiritual labor of many centuries.

Of all clericalism, that of the intellectual stamp is the most unbearable; for one is always silenced with the remark, "You don't know Greek," or, "You don't read Hebrew"; while the child of God feels *irresistibly* that in the matters that concern eternity, Greek and Hebrew cannot have the last word. And this apart from the fact that to a number of these scholars Professor Cobet might say in turn: "Dear sir, do you still know Greek yourself?" Of the shallow knowledge of Hebrew in the largest number of cases, it is better not to speak.

No, in that way we never get there. To make the divine authority of the Holy Scripture real to us, we need not a *human,* but a *divine* testimony, equally convincing to the simplest and to the most learned—a testimony that must not be cast as pearls before swine, but be limited to those who can gather from it noblest fruit, viz., to them that *are born again.*

And this testimony is not derived from the Pope and his priests, nor from the theological faculty with its ministers, but comes with the sealing from the Holy Spirit *alone.* Hence it is a divine testimony, and as such stops all contradiction and silences all doubt. It is a testimony the same to all, belonging to the peasant in the field and to the theologian in his study. Finally, it is a testimony which they alone receive who have open eyes, so that they can see *spiritually.*

However, this testimony does not work by magic. It does not cause the confused mind of unbelief suddenly to cry out: "Surely the Scripture is the Word of God!" If this were the case, the way of enthusiasts would be open, and our salvation would depend again upon a pretended spiritual insight. No, the testimony of the Holy Spirit works in an entirely different way. He begins to bring us into contact with the Word, either by our own reading or by the communication of others. Then He shows us the picture of the sinner according to the Scripture, and the salvation which mercifully saved him; and lastly, He makes us hear the song of praise upon his lips. And after we have seen this objectively, with the eye of the *understanding,* He then so works upon our *feeling* that we begin to see ourselves in that sinner, and to feel that the truth of the Scripture directly concerns *us.* Finally, He takes hold of the will, causing the very power seen in the Scripture to work in us. And when thus the whole man, mind, heart, and will, has experienced the power of the Word, then He adds to this the comprehensive operation of assurance, whereby the Holy Scripture in divine splendor commences to scintillate before our eyes.

Our experience is like that of a person who, from his brightly lighted room, looks out in the dusk. At first, owing to the brightness within, he sees nothing. But blowing out his light and looking out once more, he gradually distinguishes forms and figures, and after a while he enjoys the soft twilight. Let us apply this to the Word of God. So long as the light of our own insight flashes through the soul, we, looking through the window of eternity, fail to perceive anything. It is all wrapped in cloudy darkness. But when at last we prevail upon ourselves to extinguish that light, and look out again, then we see a divine world gradually coming up out of the gloom, and, to our surprise, where at first we saw nothing we now see a glorious realm bathed in divine light.

And thus God's elect obtain a firm assurance concerning the Word of God that nothing can shake, of which no learning can rob them. They stand firm as a wall. They are founded upon a rock. The winds may howl and the floods descend, but they fear not. They stay upon their indestructible faith, not only as a result of the Holy Spirit's first operation, but because He supports the conviction *continually.* Jesus said, "He abideth with you forever"; and this has primary reference to this testimony concerning the Word of God. In the believing heart He testifies continually: "Fear not, the Scripture is the Word of your God."

However, this is not all of the Holy Spirit's work in regard to the Word. It must also be *interpreted.*

And He, the Inspirer, alone can give the right interpretation. If among men each is the best interpreter of his own word, how much more here where no man shall ever have the boldness to say that he understands the Spirit's full and proper meaning as well as He Himself, if not better? Even if the authors of both Testaments should rise from the dead and tell us the meaning of their respective Scriptures—even that would not be the full and deep interpretation. For they wrote things the comprehensive meaning of which they did not understand. For example, when Moses wrote about the serpent's seed, it is obvious that he did not begin to see all that is contained in the "bruising of his heel."

Hence the Holy Spirit alone can interpret the Scripture. And how? After the manner of Rome, by means of an official translation as the Vulgate; an official interpretation of every word and sentences; and an official condemnation of every other explanation? By no means. This would be very easy, but also very unspiritual. Death would cleave to it. The full, boundless ocean of truth would be confined within the narrow limits of a formula. And the refreshing fragrance of life, which always meets us from the sacred page, would at once be lost.

Surely the churches may not be given over to an arbitrary, irresponsible translation of the Word; and we greatly appreciate the mutual care of the churches in providing a correct translation in the vernacular. We consider it even highly desirable that, under the seal of their approval, the churches should publish expository marginal readings. But neither the one nor the other should ever replace the Scripture itself. Scriptural research must ever be free. And when there is spiritual courage, then let the churches revise their translation and see whether their expository readings need modification. Not, however, to unsettle things every three years, but that in every period of vigorous, animated, spiritual life the light of the Holy Spirit may be shed in larger measure upon the things that always need more light.

Hence the work of the Holy Spirit with reference to interpretation is indirect, and the means employed are: (1) scientific study; (2) the ministry of the Word; and (3) the spiritual experience of the Church. And it is by the cooperation of these three factors that, in the course of ages, the Holy Spirit indicates which interpretation deviates from the truth, and which is the correct understanding of the Word.

This interpretation is followed by the *application.*

The Holy Scripture is a wonderful mystery, which is intended to meet the needs and conflicts of every age, nation, and saint. When preparing it He foreknew those ages, nations, and saints, and with an eye to their necessities He so planned and arranged it as it is now offered to us. And only then will the Holy Scripture attain the end in view, when to every age, nation, church, and individual it shall be applied in such a way that every saint shall receive at last whatever portion was reserved for him in the Scripture. Hence this work of application belongs to the Holy Spirit alone, for only He knows the relation which the Scripture must sustain at last to every one of God's elect.

As to the manner in which the work is performed, it is either *direct* or *indirect.*

The *indirect* application comes most generally through the ministry, which attains its highest end when standing before his congregation the minister can say: *"This is the message of the Word which at this time the Holy Spirit intends for you."* An awful claim, indeed, and only attainable when one lives as deeply in the Word as in the Church. Besides this there is also an application of the Word brought about by the spoken or written word of a brother, which sometimes is as effectual as a long sermon. The quiet perusal of some exposition of the truth has sometimes stirred the soul more effectually than a service in the house of prayer.

The *direct* application of the Word the Holy Spirit effects by the reading of the Scripture or by remembered passages. Then He brings to remembrance words deeply affecting us by their singular power. And, although the world smiles and even brethren profess ignorance concerning it, it is our conviction that the special application of that moment was for us and not for them, and that in our inward souls the Holy Spirit performed a work peculiar to Himself.

39

The Government of the Church

No man can say that Jesus is the Lord, but by the Holy Ghost—1 Corinthians 12:3.

The last work of the Holy Spirit in the Church has reference to *government.* The Church is a divine institution. It is the body of Christ, even though manifesting itself in a most defective way; for as the man whose speech is affected by a stroke of paralysis is the same friendly person as before, in spite of the defect, so is the Church, whose speech is impaired, still the same holy body of Christ. The visible and invisible Church are one.

We have written elsewhere: "The Church of Christ on earth is at once visible and invisible. Even as a man is at once a perceptible and imperceptible being without being therefore two beings, so does the distinction between the Church visible and invisible in no wise impair its unity. It is one and the same Church, which according to its *spiritual being* is hidden in the spiritual world, manifest only to the spiritual eye, and which according to its *visible form* manifests itself externally to believers and the world.

"According to its *spiritual* and *invisible being* the Church is one in all the earth, one also with the Church in heaven. In like manner it is also a holy Church, not only because it is skillfully wrought of God, dependent entirely upon His divine influences and workings, but also because the spiritual defilement and indwelling sin of believers belong not to it, but war against it. According to its *visible form,* however, it manifests itself only in fragments. Hence it is local, that is, widely distributed; and the national churches originate because these local churches form such connection as their own character and their national relations demand. More extensive combinations of churches can only be temporal or exceedingly loose and flexible. And these churches, as manifestations of the invisible church, are not *one,* neither are they *holy;* for they partake of the imperfections of all earthly life, and are constantly defiled by the power of sin which internally and externally undermines their well-being."

Hence the subject may not be presented as though the spiritual, invisible, and mystical Church were the object of Christ's care and government, while the affairs and oversight of the visible Church are left to the pleasure of men. This is in direct opposition to the Word of God. There is not one visible Church and another invisible, but one Church, invisible in the spiritual, and visible in the material world. And as God cares both for body and soul, so does Christ govern the external affairs of the Church just as certainly as with His grace He nourishes it internally.

Christ is the Lord; Lord not only of the soul, but before He can be that He must be Lord of the Church as a whole.

It should be noticed that the preaching of the Word and the administration of the sacraments belong not to the internal economy of the Church, but to the external; and that church government serves almost exclusively to keep the preaching pure and the sacraments from being profaned. Hence it is not expedient to say: "If the Word of God be only preached in its purity and the sacraments rightly administered, the church order is of minor importance"; eliminate these two from the church order and very little remains of it.

The question is, therefore, whether these means of grace are to be arranged according to *our pleasure,* or according to the *will of Jesus.* Does He allow us to trifle with them according to our own notions, or does He rebuke and abhor all self-willed religion? If the last, then also He must from heaven direct, govern, and care for His Church.

However, He does not compel us in this matter; He has left us the awful liberty of acting against His Word and of substituting our form of government for His own. And that is the very thing which misguided

Christendom has done again and again. Through unbelief, not seeing the King, it has frequently ignored, forgotten, deposed Him; it has established its own self-willed regime in His Church, until at last the very remembrance of the lawful Sovereign has been lost.

The individual church, still mindful of the kingship of Jesus professes to bow unconditionally to His kingly Word as contained in the Scripture. Therefore, we say that in the state church of the Netherlands, whose church order not only lacks such profession, but lays the supreme legislative power exclusively upon men, Christ's Kingship is mocked; that a pretender has usurped His place, who must be removed as surely as it is written: "Yet have I set My King upon My holy hill of Zion."

Hence it must be maintained firmly and fearlessly that Jesus is not only the King of souls, but also King in His Church; whose absolute prerogative it is to be the Lawgiver in His Church; and that the power which contests that right must be opposed for conscience's sake.

To the question, why the Church is so apt to forget the Kingship of Christ, so that many a godly minister has not the slightest feeling for it, often saying: "Surely Jesus is King in the realm of truth, but what does He care for the external church? I, at least, a spiritual man, never attend the meetings of the official board"; we answer: "If Jesus had an earthly throne and thence reigned personally over His Church, all men would bow before Him, but being enthroned in heaven at the right hand of the Father, the King is forgotten; out of sight, out of mind." Hence *ignorance concerning the work of the Holy Spirit* is the cause. Since Jesus governs His Church not directly, but by His Word and Spirit, there is no respect for the majesty of His sovereign government.

The spiritual eye of the believer must therefore be reopened for the work of the Holy Spirit in the churches. The unspiritual man has no eye for it. A consistory, classis, or synod is to him merely a body of men convened to transact business according to their own light, the same as a meeting of the directors of a board of trade, or some other secular organization. One is a shareholder and a committeeman, and as such assists in the administration of affairs to the best of his ability. But to the child of God, with an eye for the work of the Holy Spirit, these church assemblies assume an entirely different aspect. He acknowledges that this consistory is no consistory, this classis no classis, this synod only apparently so, except the Holy Spirit preside and decide matters together with the members.

The opening prayer of consistory, classis, or synod is therefore not the same as that of the Y.M.C.A., or of a missionary convention, simply a prayer for light and help, but an entirely different thing. It is the petition that the Holy Spirit stand in the midst of the assembly. For without Him no ecclesiastical meeting is complete. It cannot be held except He be present. Hence in the liturgical prayer at the opening of consistory, there is first a petition for the Holy Spirit's presence and leadership; secondly, the confession that the members can do nothing without His presence; and thirdly, a pleading of the promises to office-bearers.

The prayer reads: "Since we are at present assembled in Thy Holy Name, after the example of the apostolic churches, to consult, as our office requires, about those things which may come before us, for the welfare and edification of Thy churches, for which we acknowledge ourselves unfit and incapable, as we are by nature unable of ourselves to think any good, much less to put it into practice, therefore we beseech Thee, O Faithful God and Father, that Thou wilt be pleased to be present with Thy Spirit according to Thy promise, in the midst of our present assembly, to guide us in all truth."

In the prayer at the close of the consistory there follows the express giving of thanks that the Holy Spirit was present in the meeting:

"Moreover, we thank Thee that Thou now hast been present with Thy Holy Spirit in the midst of our assembly, directing our determinations according to Thy will, uniting our hearts in mutual peace and concord. We beseech Thee, O faithful God and Father, that Thou wilt graciously be pleased to bless our intended labor and effectually to execute Thy begun work; always gathering unto Thyself a true church and preserving the same in the pure doctrine and in the right use of Thy holy sacraments, and in a diligent exercise of discipline."

Hence church government signifies:

First, that King Jesus institutes the offices and appoints the incumbents.

Secondly, that the churches submit themselves unconditionally to the fundamental law of His Word.

Thirdly, that the Holy Spirit come in the assembly to direct the deliberations; as Walaeus expressed it: "That the Holy Spirit personally may stand behind the president to preside in every meeting." And this saying is so rich in meaning that we would seriously ask, whether it is not yet plain that a mere change of officers avails not, so long as the organization itself is not agreeable to the Word of God. The question is not whether *better men* come in power, but whether the *Holy Spirit preside* in the assembly; which He cannot do except the Word of God be the only rule and authority.

VOLUME TWO

The Work of the Holy Spirit in the Individual

First Chapter
Introduction

1

The Man to Be Wrought Upon

Behold, I will pour out My Spirit unto you, I will make known My words unto you—Proverbs 1:23.

The discussion so far has been confined to the Holy Spirit's work as a *whole.* We now consider His work in individual *persons.* There is a distinction between the Church as a whole and its individual members. There is a *Body* of Christ, and there are *members* which constitute a part of that Body. And the character of the Holy Spirit's work in the one is necessarily different from that in the other.

The Church, born of the divine pleasure, is complete in the eternal counsel, and sovereign choice has prepared all its course.

The same God who has numbered the hairs of our head has also numbered the members of Christ's Body. As every natural birth is foreordained, so is every Christian birth in the Church divinely predestinated.

The origin and awakening of eternal life are from above; not from the creature, but from the Creator, and are rooted in His free and sovereign choice. And it remains not merely a choice, but is followed by a divine *act* equally decisive that enforces and realizes that choice.

That is God's spiritual *omnipotence.* He is not as a man who experiments, but He is God who, never forsaking the work of His hands, is persistent and irresistible in the doing of all His pleasure. Hence His counsel becomes history; and the Church, whose form is outlined in that counsel, must in the course of ages be born, increase, and perfect itself according to that counsel; and since that counsel is indestructible the gates of hell shall not prevail against the Church. This is the ground of the security and consolation of the saints. They have no other ground of trust. From the fact that God is God, and that therefore His pleasure shall stand, they draw the sure conviction with which they prophesy against all that is visible and phenomenal.

In the work of grace there is no trace of chance or fatalism; God has determined not only the final issue, leaving the way by which it is to be attained undecided, but in His counsel He has prepared every means to realize His choice. And in that counsel ways disclose themselves which human eye cannot trace nor fathom. The divine omnipotence adapts itself to the nature of the creature. It causes the cedars of Lebanon to grow and the bulls of Bashan to increase, but it feeds and strengthens each according to its nature. The cedar eats no grass, and the ox does not burrow in the ground for food.

The divine ordinance requires that by its roots the tree shall absorb the juices from the ground, and that by the mouth the ox shall take his food and convert it into blood. And He honors His own ordinance by providing food in the soil for the one, and grass in the field for the other.

The same principle prevails in the Kingdom of Grace. To man as a subject of that Kingdom, and of the moral world belonging to it, God has given another organism than to the ox, cedar, wind, or stream. The movements of the latter are purely mechanical; from the steep mountain the stream *must* fall. In a different way He acts upon ox and tree; and in still another way upon man. In the human body chemical forces work mechanically, and other forces like those in the ox and cedar. And besides these there are in man *moral* forces which God operates also *according to their nature.*

Upon this ground our fathers rejected as unworthy of God the fanatical view that in the work of grace man is a stock or block; not because it attributes something to man, but because it represents God as denying His own work and ordinance. Creating an ox or a tree or stone each different from the other, giving each a nature of its own, it follows that He cannot violate this, but must adapt Himself to it. Hence all His spiritual operations are subject to the divinely ordained dispositions in man as a spiritual being; and this feature makes the work of grace exceedingly beautiful, glorious, and adorable.

For let us not deceive ourselves and speak any longer of a glorious work of grace if the omnipotent God treats man mechanically, as a stock or block. Then there is no mystery for angels to look into, but an immediate work of omnipotence breaking down and creating anew. To admire the work of grace we should take it as it is *revealed,* that is, as a complicated, unsearchable work by which, violating nothing, God adapts Himself to the delicate and manifold needs of man's spiritual being; and reveals His divine omnipotence in the victory over the endless and gigantic obstacles which human nature puts in His way.

Even the heart of God thirsts after love. His entire counsel may be reduced to one thought, viz., that in the end of the ages He may have a Church which shall understand His love and return it. But love cannot be ordered, neither can it be forced in an unspiritual way. It cannot be poured out in a man's heart mechanically. To be warm, refreshing, and satisfying, love must be quickened, cultivated, and cherished. Hence God does not instill an ounce of love into His people's hearts, in consequence of which they love Him, but He exhibits love to such an extent that He, who was from the beginning with God and was God, in unfathomable love dies for men on the cross.

This would have been superfluous if man were a stock or block. Then God would only have had to create love in his heart, and men would have loved Him from sheer necessity, as a stove emits heat when the fire is lighted. But the love so warmly portrayed in Scripture is not superfluous, when God deals with spiritual creatures spiritually. Then the cross of Christ is a manifestation of divine love far surpassing all human conceptions; hence exercising such irresistible power upon all God's elect.

And that which is preeminently true and apparent in *love* is equally true of every part of the work of grace in all its stages. In it God never denies Himself, nor the ordinance and plan after which man was created. Hence it is its glory that, while on the one hand God granted man the strongest means of resistance, on the other He overcame that resistance in a divine and kingly way by the omnipotence of redeeming grace.

When the apostle testifies, "We pray you in Christ's stead, *as though God did beseech you by us,* be ye reconciled to God," he reveals such a depth of the mystery of love that finally the relations are literally reversed, and the holy God beseeches His rebellious creature, who instead should cry to Him for mercy.

Tradition speaks of the fascination of mysterious beings exerted upon travelers and mariners so irresistibly that the latter cast themselves willingly and yet *against* their will into destruction. In love's revelation this tradition in a reversed and holy manner has become a reality. Here also is an almighty power of fascination, in the end irresistible to the condemned sinner, but allowing himself to be drawn unwillingly and yet willingly, eternal pity draws him not *into* destruction, but *out of it.*

However, the wonderful workings of love can scarcely be analyzed. Lovers never know who has attracted and who has been attracted, nor how in the struggle of the affections love performed its drawings. Love's being is too mysterious to reveal its various workings and how they succeed one another. And this applies in far greater measure to the love of God. Every saint knows by experience that at last it became irresistible, and prevailed. But how the victory was achieved cannot be told. This divine work comes to us from such infinite heights and depths, it affects us so mysteriously, and in the beginning there was such utter lack of spiritual light that one can scarcely more than stammer of these things. Who comprehends the mystery of the natural birth? Who had knowledge when he was being curiously embroidered in the lowest parts of the earth? And if this took place without our consciousness, how can we understand our spiritual birth? Indeed, subjectively, that is, depending upon our own experience, we know absolutely nothing of it; and all that ever was or can be said about it is taken exclusively from Scripture. It has pleased the Lord to lift only a corner of the veil covering this mystery—no more than the Holy Spirit deemed necessary for the support of our faith, for the glory of God and the benefit of others in the hour of their spiritual birth.

Wherefore in this series of articles we will try only to systematize and explain what God has revealed for the spiritual direction of His children.

Nothing is further from our minds than to exercise ourselves in things too high for us, or to penetrate into mysteries hid from our view.

Where Scripture stops we shall stop; to the difficulties left unexplained, we shall not add what must be only the result of human folly. But where Scripture proclaims unmistakably Jehovah's sovereign power in the work of grace, there neither the criticism nor the mockery of men will prevent us from demanding absolute submission to the divine sovereignty and giving glory to His Name.

2

The Work of Grace a Unit

Because the love of God is shed abroad in our hearts by the Holy Ghost, which is given unto us—Romans 5:5.

The final end of all God's ways is that He may be all in all. He cannot cease from working until He has entered the souls of individual men. He thirsts after the creature's love. In man's love for God He desires to see the virtues of His own love glorified. And love must spring from man's personal being, which has its seat in the heart.

The work of grace exhibited in the eternal counsel can never be sufficiently praised. From Paradise to Patmos, revealed to prophets and apostles, it is transcendently rich and glorious. Prepared in Immanuel, who ascended on high, who has received gifts for men, yea, for the rebellious also, that the Lord God might dwell among them, it exceeds the praise of men and angels. And ye its highest glory and majesty appear only when, overcoming the rebellious, operating in the soul, it causes its light so to shine that men, seeing it, glorify the Father which is in heaven.

Hence the outpouring of the Holy Spirit is the crowning event of all the great events of salvation, because it reveals *subjectively,* that is, in individual persons, the grace revealed hitherto objectively.

Assuredly in the days of the Old Covenant saving grace wrought in individuals, but it always bore a preliminary and special character.

Old-Covenant believers "received not the promise, that they without us should not be made perfect." And the dispensation of personal salvation, in its normal character, began only when, the work of reconciliation being finished, Immanuel risen, the other Comforter had come inwardly to enrich the members of the Body of Christ.

Hence the purpose of the Triune God steadily urges to this glorious consummation. The divine compassion cannot cease from working so long as the work of saving the individual soul is not begun. In all the preparatory work God aims persistently at His elect; not only after the fall, but even before creation, His wisdom rejoiced in His earthly world, and "His delights were with the sons of men." From eternity He foreknows all in whom His glorious light shall once be kindled. They are no strangers to Him, discovered only after the lapse of ages, upon examination either to be passed by as unprofitable, or to be wrought upon as proper and useful subjects, according to their respective merits; no, our faithful Covenant God never stands as a stranger before any of His creatures. He created them all and ordained how they should be create; they are not first created, then ordained, but ordained, then created. Even then the creature is not independent of the Lord, but *before* there is a word upon his tongue He knoweth it altogether; not by information of what already existed, but by divine knowledge of what was to come. Even the relations of cause and effect connecting the various parts of his life lie naked and open before Him; nothing is hid from Him; and much more intimately than man knows himself, God knows him.

The waters of salvation descending from the mountain-tops of God's holiness do not flow toward unknown fields, but their channel is prepared, and leaping over the mountain-sides they greet the acres below which they are to water.

Hence, although clearness demands divisions and subdivisions in the work of grace, yet they do not actually exist; the work of grace is a *unit,* it is one eternal, uninterrupted act, proceeding from the womb of eternity, unceasingly moving toward the consummation of the glory of the children of God which shall be revealed in the great and notable Day of the Lord. For instance, although in the moment of regeneration God calleth the things that are not, with all that they contain as in a germ, yet it should not be represented as though He had neglected that soul for twenty or thirty years. For even this apparent neglect is a divine work. Constrained by His love He would rather have turned to His chosen but lost creature immediately, to seek and save it. But He refrained Himself, if we may so express it; for this very neglect, this hiding of His countenance works together as a means of grace, in the hour of love, to make grace efficient in that soul.

Hence the salvation of a soul in its personal being is an eternal, uninterrupted, continuous act, whose starting-point lies in the decree whose end is in the glorification before the throne. It contains nothing formal or mechanical. There is not a period of eighteen centuries first, during which God is occupied with the preparation of objective grace, without a single gracious work in individual souls. Neither is there salvation prepared only for possible souls whose salvation was still uncertain. Nay, the love of God never works toward the *unknown.* He is perfect, and His way is perfect; hence His love always bears the high and holy mark of proceeding from heart to heart, from person to person, knowing and reading one with perfect knowledge. During all the day while Cain was being judged; while Noah and his eight were safe in the ark; while Abraham was called, and Moses talked with Jehovah face to face; while the seers were prophesying, the Baptist appeared in public, Jesus ascended Calvary, and St. John was seeing visions—throughout all those ages God foreknew us (if we are His own), the pressure of His love went out steadily toward us, He called us before we were, in order that we might come into being; and when we had come into being, He led us all our days. Even when we rebelled against Him and He turned His face from us, even then He led us as our true and faithful Shepherd. Surely all things *must* work together for good to them that love God, even the lives and characters of their ancestors—*for* they are the called according to His purpose.

Instead of being cold and formal, it is rather one act of love, energizing, pouring forth, shedding itself abroad. From its fountain-head on the highest mountains, traversing many highlands before it can reach you, divine love flows on, ever restless, until it pours itself forth into *your soul.* Hence the apostle boasts that at last love had attained this blessed end in his person and in Rome's beloved church. "Now we have peace with God, *because* the love of God (moving toward us from eternity) at last has reached us, and is now *shed abroad in our heart.*"

And this does not mean that now we possess a pure love of our own, but that *the love of God* for His elect, having descended from on high and overcome every obstacle, has poured itself into the deep bed of our regenerated hearts. And to this He adds the grace of making the soul understand, drink, and taste of that love. And when in contrition and shamefacedness the soul loses itself in love's delights and in the adorations of its eternal compassion, then His glory shines with greater brightness, and His rejoicings with the children of men are complete.

However, while the Triune God anticipates from before the foundation of the world the ingathering and glorification of the saints, Scripture clearly reveals that this ingathering and glorification is the adorable work of the Holy Spirit. God's love is shed abroad in our hearts by *the Holy Spirit* who is given unto us.

The Scriptures give this work of the Spirit a prominent place; not to the exclusion of the Father and the Son, yet so that this personal work is always effected by the Holy Spirit. And the Scripture puts this so strongly that the Catechism speaks, not incorrectly, of three things in our most holy faith: of God the Father and our Creation, of God the Son and our Redemption, and then only of God the Holy Ghost and our Sanctification. And this is not surprising. For—

First, as we have seen already, in the economy of the Triune God it is the Holy Spirit who comes in closest contact with the creature and fills him. Hence it is His peculiar work to enter man's heart, and in its recesses to proclaim God's grace until he believes.

Second, He brings every work of the Triune God to its consummation. Hence He perfects the work of objective grace by the saving of souls, thus realizing its final purpose.

Third, He quickens life. He hovers over the waters of chaos and breathes into man the breath of life. In perfect harmony with this, the sinner dead in trespasses and sin cannot live except he be quickened by the Spirit of all quickening, whom the Church has always invoked, saying: "Veni, Creator Spiritus."

Fourth, He takes the things of Christ and glorifies Him. The Son does not distribute His treasures, but the Holy Spirit. And since the entire salvation of the redeemed consists in the fact that their dead and withered hearts are joined to Christ, the Source of salvation, we must praise the Holy Spirit for doing it.

Hence in the constraining desire of divine love for the individual salvation of chosen but lost creatures, the work of the Holy Spirit evidently occupies the most conspicuous place. Our knowledge of God is not complete except we know Him as the Blessed Trinity, Father, Son, and Holy Ghost. But as "no man cometh to the Father but by Me," and "no man knoweth the Father save the Son, and he to whomsoever the Son will reveal Him," so no man can come to the Son but by the Holy Spirit, and no man can know the Son if the Holy Spirit does not reveal Him unto him.

But this does not imply any separation, even in thought, between the Persons of the Godhead. This would destroy the confession of the Trinity, substituting for it the false confession of tri-theism. Nay, it is eternally the same God subsisting in three Persons. The truth of our confession shines in the very acknowledgment of the unity in the Trinity. The Father is never without the Son, nor the Son without the Father. And the Holy Spirit can never come to us nor work in us except the Father and the Son cooperate with Him.

3

Analysis Necessary

Let us go on unto perfection; not laying again the foundation—Hebrews 6:1.

To systematize the work of the Holy Spirit in individuals, we must first consider their spiritual condition *before* conversion. Misunderstanding concerning this leads to error and confusion. It causes the various operations of the Holy Spirit to be confounded, so that the same terms are used to designate different things. And this confuses one's own thought, and leads others astray. This is most seriously apparent in ministers who discuss this subject in general terms, artlessly avoid definiteness, and consequently reiterate the same platitudes.

Such preaching makes little or no impression; its monotone is wearisome; it accustoms the ear to repetitions; it lacks stimulus for the inward ear. And the mind, which cannot remain inactive with impunity, seeks relief in its own way, often in unbelief, apart from the work of the Holy Spirit. The words "heart," "mind," "soul," "conscience," "inward man" are used indiscriminately. There are *frequent* calls for conversion, regeneration, renewing of life, justification, sanctification, and redemption; while the ear has not been accustomed to understand in each of these a special thing and a peculiar revelation of the work of the Holy Spirit. And in the end this chaotic preaching makes it impossible to discuss divine things intelligently, since one initiated and more thoroughly instructed cannot be understood.

We solemnly protest especially against the pious appearance that conceals the inward hollowness of this preaching by saying: "My simple Gospel has no room for these hair-splitting distinctions; they savor of the dry scholasticism with which quibbling minds terrify God's dear children, and bring them under the bondage of the letter. Nay, the Gospel of my Lord must remain to me full of life and spirit; therefore spare me these subtleties."

And no doubt there is some truth in this. By a dry analysis of soul-refreshing truth, abstract minds often rob simple souls of much comfort and joy. They discuss spiritual things in the mongrel terms of Anglicized Latin, as though souls could have no part with Christ unless they be experts in the use of these bastard words. Such terrifying of the weak betrays pride and self-exaltation. And a very foolish pride it is, for the boasted knowledge is readily acquired by mere effort of the memory. Such externalizing of the Christian faith is offensive. It substitutes glibness of tongue for genuine piety, and mental justification for that of faith. Thus piety of the heart moves to the head, and instead of the Lord Jesus Christ, Aristotle, the master teacher of dialectics, becomes the savior of souls.

To plead for such a caricature is far from our purpose. We believe that our salvation depends solely upon God's work in us, and not upon our testimony; and the little child with stammering lips, but wrought upon by the Holy Spirit, will precede these vain scribes into the Kingdom of Heaven. Let no one dare impose the yoke of his own thoughts upon others. Christ's yoke alone *fits* the souls of men.

And yet the Gospel does not condone shallowness, neither does it approve mere twaddle.

Of course there is a difference. We do not require our children to know the names of all the nerves and muscles of the human body, of the diseases to which it is subject, and of the contents of the pharmacopoeia. It would be a burden to the little fellows, who are happiest so long as they are unconscious of the curious organism they carry with them. But the physician who is not quite certain as to the locality of these vital organs; who, careless of details, is satisfied with the generalities of his profession; who, unable to diagnose the case correctly, fails to administer the proper remedies, is promptly dismissed and a more discriminating one is called in. And to some extent the same is required of all intelligent people. Well-informed men should not be ignorant of the vital organs of the human body and their principal functions; mothers and nurses should be still better informed.

The same applies to the life of the Church. The least gifted among the brethren cannot understand the distinctions of the spiritual life; unable to bear strong meat, they should be fed with milk alone. Neither should young children be wearied and blunted with phrases far above their comprehension. Both should be taught according to *"the tenor of their way."* A child talking on religious matters in discriminating terms unpleasantly affects the spiritual feeling. But not so the spiritual *physician,* that is, *the minister of the Word.* If the unskilled veterinarian be dismissed, how much more they who, pretending to treat and cure souls, betray their own ignorance of the conditions and activities of the spiritual life. Wherefore we insist that every minister of the Word be a specialist in this spiritual anatomy and physiology; familiar with the various forms of spiritual disease, and always able out of Christ's fullness to select the spiritual remedies required.

And the same knowledge we claim, if not in the same degree, of every intelligent man or woman. The physician or lawyer who smiles at our ignorance of the first principles of his profession ought to be equally ashamed when betraying his own lamentable ignorance of the condition of his soul. In the spiritual life each talent should bear interest. Every man ought to be symmetrically developed. According to his range of vision, strength of powers, and depth of penetration, he should be able to distinguish spiritual things and his own soul's need. And that this knowledge is largely found only among our plain, God-fearing people, and not among the higher classes, is a serious and deplorable sign of the times.

The knowledge which is power in the spiritual sphere, and able to heal, does not come in foreign terms, does not exhaust itself in the various criticism of Scripture, fond only of philosophic reasonings, starving souls by giving them stones for bread, but it searches the Word and work of God in the souls of men systematically, and proves that a man has *studied* the things in which he is to minister to the Church.

Our spiritual leaders, therefore, who at the university and in the catechetical class have replaced this spiritual knowledge by various criticism and apologetics, have much to answer for. For the last thirty years this knowledge has been neglected in both these institutions. And so knowledge was lost, the preaching became monotonous, and a great part of the Church perished. There was still eye and ear for the objective work of the Son, but the work of the Holy Spirit is slighted and neglected. Consequently spiritual life has sunk to such a degree that, while scarcely one third of the fullness of grace which is in Christ Jesus is being known and honored, men dare to assert that they preach Christ and Him crucified.

Hence the discussion of the Holy Spirit's work in individuals demands that, while risking the danger of being called "scholastic drivers," we leave the paths of shallowness and generalities and proceed to careful analysis. The Holy Spirit's operations upon the various parts of our being in their several conditions must be distinguished and treated separately; not only in the elect, but also in the non-elect, for they are not the same. It is true the Scripture teaches that God causes His sun to shine upon the good and the evil, and His rain to come down upon the just and the unjust, so that in nature every good gift coming down from the Father of lights is common to all, but in the kingdom of grace this is not so. The Sun of righteousness often shines upon one, leaving another in darkness; and the drops of grace often water one soul, while others remain utterly deprived of them.

Hence, although the Spirit's work in the elect is of primary importance, yet it does not exhaust His work in individuals. Christ was set also for a fall to many in Israel; and even this is wrought by the witness of the Holy Spirit. Not only the savor of life, but the savor of death also reaches the soul by Him; as the apostle declares regarding those who, having received the gift of the Holy Ghost, had fallen away. His activity in them, and their condition when He begins His saving or hardening operations, must be carefully noticed.

Of course, this is not the place to discuss the condition of fallen man exhaustively. This would require special inquiry. Many things which perhaps elsewhere will be explained more in detail can here receive but passing notice. But it will serve our purpose if we succeed in giving the reader such a clear view of the sinner's condition that he can understand us when we discuss the Holy Spirit's work upon the sinner.

By a sinner we understand man as he is, lives, and moves by nature, that is, without grace. And in that state he is dead in trespasses and sin; alienated from the life of God; wholly depraved and without strength; a sinner, and therefore guilty and condemned. And not only dead, but lying in the midst of death, ever sinking more deeply into death, which if not checked in its course opens underneath ever more widely, until eternal death stands revealed.

This is the fundamental thought, the mother-idea, the principal conception, of his state. "By one man sin entered into the world, and death by sin, and so death passed upon all men." And "the wages of sin is death." "Sin being finished bringeth forth death." To be translated into another state, one must pass from death into life.

But this general idea of death must be analyzed in its several relations, and to this end it must be determined what man was before, and what he has become after, this spiritual death.

4

Image and Likeness

Let Us make man in Our image, after Our likeness—Genesis 1:26.

Glorious is the divine utterance that introduces the origin and creation of man: "And God created man after His own image and after His own likeness; after the image of God created He him" (Dutch translation).

The significance of these important words was recently discussed by the well-known professor, Dr. Edward Böhl, of Vienna. According to him it should read: Man is created *"in"* not *"after"* God's image, that is, the image is not found in man's *nature* or *being,* but outside of him in *God.* Man was merely *set* in the *radiance* of that image. Hence, remaining in its light, he would live in that image. But stepping out of it, he would fall and retain but his own nature, which before and after the fall is the same.*

In the discussion of the corruption of the human nature we will consider this opinion of the highly esteemed professor of Vienna. Let

---

* In the Dutch the preposition "in" has not the meaning of "conformably to," as in the English, but denotes rest or motion within limits, whether of place, time, or circumstances. With nouns or adjectives the word governed by "in" indicates the sphere, the domain where a property manifests itself. Hence the Dutch expression, "Geschapen *in* het beeld God's" (created in the divine image), indicates the sphere in which Adam moved before he fell—Trans.

us state here simply that we reject this opinion, in which we see a return to Rome's errors. Dr. Böhl's negative character of sin, which is the basis of this representation, we cannot entertain. Moreover, it opposes the doctrine of the Incarnation, and of Sanctification as held by the Reformed Church. Hence we believe it to be safest, first to explain the confession of the fathers concerning this, and then to show that this representation is inconsistent with the Word.

Accepting the account of Creation as the Holy Spirit's direct revelation, we acknowledge its absolute credibility in every part. They who do not so accept it, or who, like many Ethical theologians, deny the literal interpretation, can have no voice in the discussion. If in the exposition of the account we are in earnest, and do not trifle with words, we must be thoroughly convinced that God actually said: "Let Us make men after Our image and after Our likeness." But denying this and holding that these words merely represent the form in which somebody, animated by the Holy Spirit, presented man's creation to himself, we can deduce nothing from them. Then we have no security that they are divine; we know only that a pious man *attributed* these thoughts to God and laid them upon His lips while they were but his own account of man's creation.

Hence the infallibility of Sacred Scripture is our starting-point. We see in Genesis 1:27 a direct testimony of the Holy Spirit; and with fullest assurance we believe that these are the words of the Almighty spoken before He created man. With this conviction, they have decisive authority; and bowing before it, we confess that man was created after God's likeness and after His image.

This statement, in connection with the whole account, shows that the Holy Spirit sharply distinguishes man's creation and that of all other creatures. They were all manifestations of God's glory, for He saw that they were good; an effect of His counsel, for they embodied a divine thought. But man's creation was special, more exalted, more glorious; for God said: "Let Us make men after Our image and after Our likeness."

Hence the general sense of these words is that man is totally different from all other beings; that his kind is nobler, richer, more glorious; and especially that this higher glory consists in the more *intimate bond* and *closer relation* to his Creator.

This appears from the words *image* and *likeness.* In all His other creative acts the Lord speaks, and it is done; He commanded, and it stood fast. There is a thought in His counsel, a will to execute it, and an omnipotent act to realize it, but no more; beings are created wholly *outside* and *apart* from Him. But man's creation is totally different. Of course, there is a divine thought proceeding from the eternal counsel, and by omnipotent power this thought is realized, but that new creature is connected with the image of God.

According to the universal significance of the word, a person's image is such a concentration of his essential features as to make it the very impress of his being. Whether it be in pencil, painting, or by photography, a symbol, an idea, or statue, it is always the concentration of the essential features of man or thing. An *idea* is an image which concentrates those features upon the field of the *mind;* a statue in marble or bronze, etc., but regardless of form or manner of expression, the essential image is such a concentration of the several features of the object that it represents the object to the mind. This fixed and definite significance of an image must not be lost sight of. The image may be imperfect, yet as long as the object is recognized in it, even though the memory must supply the possible lack, it remains an image.

And this leads to an important observation: The fact that we can recognize a person from a fragmentary picture proves the existence of a *soul-picture* of that person, that is, an image photographed through the eye upon the soul. This image, occupying the imagination, enables us mentally to see him even in his absence and without his picture.

How is such image obtained? We do not make it, but the person himself, who while we look at him draws it upon the retina, thus putting it into our soul. In photography it is not the artist, nor his apparatus, but the features of our own countenance which as by witchery draw our image upon the negative plate. In the same manner the person receiving our image is passive, while we putting it into his soul are active. Hence in deepest sense each of *us* carries his own image in or upon his face, and puts it into the human soul or upon the artist's plate. This image consists of features which, *concentrated,* form that peculiar expression which shows one's individuality. A man forms his own shadow upon a wall after his own image and likeness. As often as we cause the impress of our being to appear externally, we make it after our own image and likeness.

Returning, after these preliminary remarks, to Genesis 1:27, we notice the difference between (1) the divine image after which we are created, and (2) the image which consequently became visible in us. The image *after which* God made man is one, and that *fixed in us* quite another. The first is God's image after which we are created, the other the image created in us. To prevent confusion, the two must be kept distinct. The former existed before the latter, else how could God have created man after it?

It is not strange that many have thought that this image and likeness referred to Christ, who is said to be "the Image of the invisible God," and "the express Image of His Substance." Not a few have accepted this as settled. Yet, with our best ministers and teachers, we believe this incorrect. It conflicts with the words, "Let Us make men after Our image and after Our likeness," which must mean that the Father thus addressed the Son and the Holy Spirit. Some say that these words are addressed to the angels, but this cannot be so, since man is not created after the image of angels. Others maintain that God addressed Himself, arousing Himself to execute His design, using "We" as a plural of majesty. But this does not agree with the immediately following singular: "And God created man after His image." Hence we maintain the tried explanation of the Church's wisest and godliest ministers, that by these words the Father addressed the Son and the Holy Spirit. And then the unity of the Three Persons expresses itself in the words: "And God created man after *His* image." Hence this image cannot be the Son. How could the Father say to the Son and to the Holy Spirit: "Let Us make men after the image of the Son"?

That image must be, therefore, a concentration of the features of God's Being, by which He expresses Himself. And since God alone can represent His own Being to Himself, it follows that by the image of God we must understand the representation of His Being as it eternally exists in the divine consciousness.

"Image" and *"likeness"* we take to be synonyms; not because a difference could not be invented, but because in verse 27 the word *"likeness"* is not even mentioned. Hence we oppose the explanation that image refers to the soul, and likeness to the body. Allowing that by the indissoluble union of body and soul the features of the divine image must have an after-effect in the latter, which is His temple, yet there is

no reason nor suggestion why we should support such a precarious distinction between image and likeness. Hence the image after which we are created is the expression of God's Being as it exists in His own consciousness.

The next question is: What was or is there in man that caused him to be created after that image?

5

Original Righteousness

For in Him we live and move, and have our being: as certain also of your own poets have said, For we are also His offspring—*Acts 17:28.*

It is the peculiar characteristic of the Reformed Confession that more than any other it humbles the *sinner* and exalts the *sinless* man.

To disparage man is unscriptural. Being a sinner, fallen and no longer a real man, he must be humbled, rebuked, and inwardly broken. But the divinely created man, realizing the divine purpose or restored by omnipotent grace in the elect, is worthy of all praise, for God has made him after His own image.

Because he stood so high, he fell so low. He was such an excellent being, hence he became such a detestable sinner. The excellency of the former is the source of the damnableness of the latter.

It is said that while the present age properly appreciates and exalts man, our doctrine only disparages him, but with all its eulogy and praise this present age has never conceived a more exalted testimony than that of Scripture, saying: "God created man in His own image." We protest against the cry of the age, not because it makes of man *too much,* but too *little,* asserting that he is glorious even now in his *fallen state.*

What would you think of the man who, walking through your flower-garden, laid waste by a violent thunder-storm, called the stem-broken and mud-covered flowers, lying upon their disordered beds, *magnificent?* And this the present age is doing. Walking through the garden of this world, withered and disordered by sin's thunder-storms, it cries in proud ecstasy: "What glorious beings these men! How fair and excellent!" And as the botanist would say regarding his disordered garden: "Do you call this beautiful? You should have seen it before the storm destroyed it"; so say we to this age: "Do you call this fallen man glorious? Compared to what he ought to be he is utterly worthless. But he was glorious before sin ruined him, shining in all the beauty of the divine image."

Hence our doctrine exalts him to highest glory. Next to the glory of being *created after the image of God* comes the glory of *being God Himself.* As soon as man presumes to this he thrusts at once all his glory from him; it is his detestable sin that he aspires to be like God. If it be said that even in Paradise the law prevailed that God alone is great, and the creature nothing before Him; we answer, that he that is created after the divine image has no higher ambition than to be a *reflection* of God; excluding the idea of being above or against God. Hence it is certain that the original man was most glorious and excellent; wherefore fallen man is most despicable and miserable.

Has fallen man then lost the image of God?

This vital question controls our view of man in every respect, and hence requires closest examination; especially since the opinions of believers concerning this are diametrically opposed. Some maintain that after the fall man retained a few remains of it, and others that he has entirely lost it.

To avoid all misunderstanding, we must first decide whether to be created after the image of God (1) refers *only* to the *original righteousness,* or (2) included also man's *nature* which was clothed with this original righteousness. If the divine image consisted only in the original righteousness, then, of course, it was *completely and absolutely lost;* for by his fall man lost this original righteousness once for all. But if it was also impressed upon his *being,* his *nature,* and upon his *human existence,* then it cannot disappear entirely; for, however deeply sunk, fallen man remains *man.*

By this we do not imply that something spiritually good was left in man; among the finally lost even the deepest fallen will retain some evidence that he was created after the divine image. We do not even hesitate to subscribe to the opinion of the fathers, that if the angels, Satan included, were originally created after God's image (which Scripture does not teach positively), then even the devil in his deep fiendishness must show some features of that image.

We do not mean that after the fall man had any willingness, knowledge, or anything good; and they who in pulpit or writing infer this from "the few remains" of article 14 of the Confession of Faith pervert its plain teaching. Although it acknowledges that a few remains are retained, yet it follows that *"all* the light which is in us is changed into *darkness";* and it says before that "man is become wicked, perverse, and corrupt in all his ways," and "that he has corrupted his *whole* nature." Hence these "few remains" may never be understood to imply that there remained in man any strength, willingness, or desire for good. No, a sinner in his fallen nature is altogether condemnable. And there is, as the same article confesses, "no will nor understanding conformable to the divine will and understanding, but what Christ has wrought in man, which He teacheth us when He said, 'Without Me ye can do nothing.' "

And thus we disarm any suspicion that we look for something good in the sinner.

With Scripture we confess: "There is *none* righteousness, no not *one.* There is *none* that understandeth, there is *none* that seeketh after God. They are *all* gone out of the way, they are *together* become unprofitable; there is *none* that doeth good, no, not one."

But how is this to be reconciled? How can these two go together? On the one hand the sinner has nothing, absolutely nothing good or praiseworthy; and on the other, this same sinner always retains features of the image of God!

Let us illustrate. Two horses become mad; the one is a common truck horse, the other a noble Arabian stallion. Which is the more dangerous? The latter, of course. His noble blood will break loose into more uncontrollable rage and violence. Or, two clerks work in an office; the one a mere drudge of slow understanding, the other a youth with brains and piercing eye. Which could do his master the greater injury? The latter, of course, and all his schemes would show his superiority working in the wrong direction. This is always the case. There is no more dangerous enemy of the truth than an unbeliever religiously instructed. In all his impious rage he shows his superior training and knowledge. Satan is so mighty because before his fall he was so exceedingly glorious. Hence in his fall man did not put off the original nature, but he retained it. Only its action was reversed, corrupted, and turned against God.

When the captain of a man-of-war in a naval engagement betrays his king and raises the enemy's flag, he does not first damage or sink his ship, but he keeps it as efficient for service as possible, and with all its armament intact he does the very reverse of what he ought to do. *"Optimi coruptio pessima!"* says the proverb of the wise—that is, the greater the excellency of a thing, the more dangerous its defection. If the admiral of the fleet were to choose which of his ships should betray him, he would say: "Let it be the weakest, for defection of the strongest is the most dangerous." It is true in every sphere of life that the excellent qualities of a thing or being do not disappear in reversed action, but become most *excellently bad.*

In this way we understand man's fall. Before it he possessed the most exquisite organism which by holy impulse was directed toward the most exalted aim. Though reversed by the fall, this precious human instrument remained, but, directed by unholy impulse, it aims at a deeply unholy object.

Comparing man to a steamship, his fall did not remove the engine. But as before the fall he moved in righteousness, so he moves now in unrighteousness. In fact, as fast as he steamed then toward felicity, so fast he steams now toward perdition, that is, away from God. Hence the retaining of the engine made his fall all the more terrible and his destruction more certain. And thus we reconcile the two: that man retained his former features of excellency, and that his destruction is sure except he be born again.

But in the divine image we must carefully distinguish:

First, the wonderful and artistic organism called *human nature.*

Second, the *direction* in which it moved, that is, toward the holiest end, in that God created man in original righteousness.

That God created man good and after His own image does not mean that Adam was in a state of *innocence,* in that he had not sinned; nor that he was perfectly equipped to *become holy,* gradually to ascend to greater development, but that he was created in *true righteousness and holiness,* indicating not the degree of his development, but his *status.* This was his *original righteousness.* Hence all the inclinations and outgoings of his heart were perfect. He lacked nothing. Only in one respect his blessedness differed from that of God's children, viz., his good was *losable* and theirs not.

Of these two parts constituting the divine image—first, the inward, artistic organism of man's being, and, second, the original righteousness in which the organism moved naturally—the *latter* is completely lost, and the *former* is reversed, but the *being* of the instrument, though terribly marred, remained the same, to work in the wrong direction, that is, in unrighteousness. Hence the features or after-effects of the divine image are not found in the few good things that remain in the sinner, "but in *all that he does.*" Man could not sin so terribly *if God had not created him after His own image.*

Scripture teaches, therefore, that they are all gone aside, that they are altogether become filthy, and that all come short of the glory of God; while it also declares that even this fallen man is created after God's image—Genesis 9:6, and after His likeness—James 3:9.

6

Rome, Socinus, Arminius, Calvin

And that ye put on the new man, which after God is created in righteousness and true holiness—Ephesians 4:24.

It is not surprising that believers entertain different views concerning the significance of the image of God. It is a starting-point determining the direction of four different roads. The slightest deviation at starting must lead to a totally different representation of the truth. Hence every thinking believer must deliberately choose which road he will follow:

First, the path of Rome, represented by Bellarminus.

Second, that of Arminius and Socinus, walking arm-in-arm.

Third, that of the majority of the Lutherans, led by Melanchthon.

Lastly, the direction mapped out by Calvin, that is, that of the Reformed.

Rome teaches that the original righteousness does *not* belong to the divine image, but to the human nature as a superadded grace. Quoting Bellarminus, *first,* man is created consisting of two parts, flesh and spirit; *second,* the divine image is stamped partly on the flesh, but chiefly on the human spirit, the seat of the moral and rational consciousness; *third,* there is a conflict between flesh and spirit, the flesh lusting against the spirit; *fourth,* hence man has a natural inclination and desire for sin, which as desire alone is no sin as long as it is not yielded to; *fifth,* in His grace and compassion God gave man, independently of his nature, the original righteousness for a defense and safety-valve to control the flesh; *sixth,* by his fall man has willingly thrust this superadded righteousness from him: hence as sinner he stands again in his naked nature (*in puris naturalibus*), which, as a matter of course, is inclined to sin, inasmuch as his desires are sinful.

We believe that the Romish theologians will allow that this is the current view among them. According to Catechismus Romanus, question 38: "God gave to man from the dust of the earth a body, in such a way that he was partaker of immortality not by virtue of his nature, but by a superadded grace. As to his soul, God formed him in His image and after His likeness, and gave him a free will; *moreover* [*praeterea,* besides, hence not belonging to his nature], He so tempered his desires that they continually obey the dictates of reason. Besides this He has poured into him the original righteousness, and gave him dominion over all other creatures."

The view of Socinus, and of Arminius who followed him closely, is totally different. It is a well-known fact that the Socinians denied the Godhead of Christ, who, as they taught, was born a mere man. But (and by this they misled the Poles and Hungarians) they acknowledged that He had *become* God. Hence after His Resurrection He could be worshiped as God. But in what sense? That the divine nature was given Him? Not at all. In Scripture, magistrates, being clothed with the divine majesty which enabled them to exercise authority, are called *"gods."* This applies to Jesus, who, after His Resurrection, received of the Father power over all creatures in an eminent degree. Hence He is absolutely clothed with divine majesty. If a sinner, as a magistrate, is called god, how much more can we conceive of Christ as being called God, simply to express that He was clothed with divine authority?

In order to support this false view of Christ's Godhead, the Socinians falsified the doctrine of the image of God, and made it equivalent to man's dominion over the animals. This was in their opinion also a kind of higher majesty, containing something divine, which was the image of God. Hence the first Adam, being clothed with majesty and dominion over a portion of creation, was therefore of God's offspring and created in His image. And the second Adam, Christ, also clothed with majesty and dominion over creation, the Scripture therefore calls God.

That the Remonstrants also adopted this doubly false representation appears conclusively from what the moderate professor À Limborch wrote in the beginning of the eighteenth century: "This image consisted in the power and exalted position which God gave to man above all creation. By this dominion he shows most clearly the image of God in the earth." He adds: "That in order to exercise this power, he was endowed with glorious talents. But these are only means. Dominion over the animals is the principal thing." Hence we infer that the bravest and coarsest tamer of animals, playing with lions and tigers as if pet dogs, is the tenderest child of God. We say this in all seriousness and without a thought of mockery, to show the foolishness of the Socinian system.

The Lutheran view, as will be seen, occupies the middle ground between the Roman Catholic and the Reformed.

Its most prominent part (readily recognized in the representation of Dr. Böhl) is that the divine image is merely the original righteousness. They do not deny that man, as man, in his nature and being shows something beautiful and excellent, reminding one of the image of God, but the real image itself is not in man's nature, nor in his spiritual being, but only in the original wisdom and righteousness in which God created him. Gerhardt writes: "The real similarity with God lay in the soul of man, partly in his intelligence, partly in his moral and rational inclinations, which three excellencies together constitute his original righteousness." And Bauer: "Properly speaking, this image of God consists of some perfections of will, intellect, and feeling which God created together with man (*concreatas*), which is the original righteousness." Hence the Lutheran doctrine teaches that the proper image of God is now totally lost, and that the sinner is as helpless before the work of grace as a stock or block, as one fettered and unable even to rattle his chain.

The Reformed, on the contrary, have always denied this, and taught that the image of God, being one with His likeness, did not consist only in the original righteousness, but included also man's being and personality; not only his *state,* but also his *being.* Hence the original righteousness was not something additional, but his being, nature, and state were originally in the most beautiful harmony and causal relation. Ursinus says: "The image of God has reference: (1) to the immaterial substance of the soul with its gifts of knowledge and will; (2) to all in-created knowledge of God and of His will; (3) to the holy and righteous inclination of the will and moving of the heart, that is, the perfect righteousness; (4) to the bliss, holy peace, and abundance of all enjoyment; and (5) to the dominion over the creatures. In all these our moral nature reflects the image of God, though imperfectly. St. Paul explains the image of God from the true righteousness and holiness, without excluding, however, the wisdom and in-created knowledge of God. He rather presupposes them."

These four views concerning the divine image present four opposing opinions that are clearly drawn and sharply outlined. The Socinian conceives of the image of God as entirely outside of man and his moral being, and consisting in the exercise of something resembling *divine authority.* The Roman Catholic does indeed look for the divine image in man, but severs him from the divine ideal, that is, the original righteousness which is put upon him as a garment. The Lutheran, like the Socinian, puts the divine image outside of man, exclusively in the divine ideal, which he considers not as foreign to man, but calculated for him and originally created in his nature (however distinct from it). Lastly, the Reformed confesses that man's whole personality is the impress of God's image in his being and attributes; to which belongs naturally that ideal perfection expressed in the confession of original righteousness.

Undoubtedly the Reformed confession is the purest and most excellent expression of the Bible revelation; hence we maintain it from deepest conviction. It maintains that God created *man* in His image, and not his *nature* only, like Rome; nor his *authority* only, like the Socinians; nor his *righteousness* only, like the Lutherans.

His divine image does not belong merely to an attribute, state, or quality of man, but to the whole man; for He created *man* in His image; and the confession which subtracts from this detracts from the positive Scriptural statement, that is, from the Spirit's direct testimony: "Let Us *make* man in Our image and after Our likeness." and not: "Let Us *re-form* man in Our image."

Neither is the divine image only in man's *personality,* as the Vermittelungs (Mediation) theologians, following Fichte, hold. Man's personality certainly belongs to it, but it is not all, nor even the principal thing. Personality is *contrast* to our equals, and contrast cannot be after the image of God, for God is One. *Personality* is a very feeble feature of the divine image. True personality is no contrast, but glorious completeness, like that in God. One person is something defective; three persons in one being, completeness.

Wherefore we protest against these loud and emphatic assertions that the image is our imperfect personality, as leading the Church away from the Scripture. No; man himself is the image of God, his whole being as man—in his *spiritual* existence, in the being and nature of his soul, in the attributes and workings that adorn and express his being; not as though this human being were a locomotive without steam, posing as a model, but a living and active organism exerting influence and power.

As a being man is not defective, but perfect; not in a state of *becoming,* but of *being*—that is, he was not to *become* righteous, but *was* righteous. This is his original righteousness. Hence, that God created man in His image signifies:

1. That man's being is in *finite* form the impress of the *infinite* Being of God.
2. His attributes are in *finite* form the impress of God's attributes.
3. His state was the impress of the felicity of God.
4. The dominion which he exercised was image and impress of God's dominion and authority.

To which may be added that, since man's body is calculated for the spirit, it also must contain some shadows of that image.

This confession that Reformed churches must maintain in the pulpit, in the catechetical classes, and above all in the recitation-halls of theology.

7

The Neo-Kohlbruggians

And Adam lived a hundred and thirty years, and begat a son in his own likeness, and after his image; and called his name Seth—Genesis 5:3.

Many are the efforts made to alter the meaning of the word, "Let Us make man in Our image and after Our likeness," by a different translation; especially by making it to read *"in"* instead of *"after"* our likeness. This new reading is Dr. Böhl's main support. With this translation his system stands or falls.

According to him, man is not the bearer of the divine image, but by a divine act he was set *in* it, as a plant is set in the sun. As long as the plant stood in the dark, its shape and flowers are invisible; carried into the light its beauty becomes apparent. In like manner, man was without luster until God put him in the shining glory of His image, and then he appeared beautiful. Of course, this idea requires the translation: "Let Us create man *in* Our image."

Let us explain the difference: Genesis 1:26 in the Hebrew has two different prepositions. The one standing before "likeness" (כְּ) is invariably used in comparisons; while the other before "image" is mostly used to denote that one thing is found in another. Hence the translation, "in our image and after our likeness," has apparently much in its favor. This translation (although we believe it to be incorrect; for our reasons see the next article) does not alter the meaning, if rightly interpreted.

And what is that right interpretation? Not that of Dr. Böhl; for, according to him, the newly created man did not stand in the midst of that image, but only in its reflection and radiation. The plant is not set in the sun, but in the sun-rays. No; if Adam stood in the midst of God's image, then he was wholly encompassed by it.

Let us illustrate. There are wooden images covered with paper on which is printed a head or bust, colored to imitate marble or bronze. The wood may be said to be *in the image,* covered by it from all sides. Again, the sculptor actually chisels the image, in his mind, or posing as a model, *about the marble* until it encloses the whole block. In like manner it may be said that Adam, upon his first awakening to consciousness, was enclosed by God's image; not externally, and he only its reflection, but its ecotype penetrating his whole being.

The correctness of this exegesis appears from Genesis 5:1–3, the contents of which, though often overlooked, settle this matter. Here Scripture brings Adam's creation in direct connection with his own begetting a son after his own likeness. We read: "In the day that God created man, in the likeness of God made He him; male and female created He them; and blessed them, and called their name Adam, in the day when they were created. And Adam lived a hundred and thirty years, and begat a son in his own likeness, after his image; and called his name Seth."

In both instances the Hebrew word *zelem,* image, is used. Hence to obtain a clear and correct understanding of the statement, "to be created in the image and after the likeness of God," Scripture invites us to let the child's resemblance to the father assist us. And the father's likeness lies in the child's being, is part of it, and does not merely beam from the father upon the child externally. Even in his absence or after his death the resemblance of features continues.

Hence to beget a child in our image and after our likeness means to give existence to a being bearing our image and resemblance, although as a person distinct from us. From which it must follow that when Scripture says, regarding Adam, that God created him in His image and after His likeness, using the same words "image" (*zelem*) and "likeness" (*demoeth*), it cannot mean that the divine image shone upon him, so that he stood and walked in its light, but that God so created him that his whole being, person, and state reflected the divine image, *since he carried it in himself.*

It is remarkable that the prepositions used in Genesis 1:26 appear also in this passage, but *in a reversed order.* Rendering the preposition "ב" *"in,"* as in Genesis 1:26, it reads: "He begat a son *in* his likeness and after his image." And this is conclusive. It shows how utterly unfair it is to deduce a different meaning from the use of different prepositions. Even if we translate "כְּ" by *"in"—"in* the image of God"—the sense is the same; in both, the image is not a reflection falling upon man, indicating his state only, but also his form, both *state* and *being.*

However, before we proceed, let Dr. Böhl speak for himself. For we might possibly have wrongly understood him; it is therefore reasonable that his own words be laid before our readers.

We take these translated citations from his work, entitled, *Von der Incarnation des Gottlichen Wortes;* a dogmatic, highly important book, wherein he deals the Vermittellungs theologians blows that have filled our hearts with joy, partly because God is honored thereby, and also because of the consolation offered to broken hearts. Hence it does not enter our minds to belittle the labor of Dr. Böhl. We only contend that his presentation of the image of God is not the true one. We point, therefore, to the important and exceedingly clear sentences of pages 28 and 29:

> God ordered it so that immediately, from the beginning, man came to stand under the influence of that which is good, and consequently did that which is good. He created him in the image of God, after His likeness. The significance of this is made clear when we consider the restoration of fallen man (according to Eph. 4:24; Col. 3:9). Paul, speaking of the new man that we must put on, after having put off the old man, has reference to the original state. And now he describes this new man as one that is created after God in righteousness and holiness, as he truly is. These apostolic expressions contain a description of the same equipment that Moses characterizes with the words: 'In the image of God, after His likeness.' Regeneration is a new creation, which, however, is ordered after the model of the old, without taking anything from, or adding anything to it. *Hence man's standing in the image of God, wherein he was after the likeness of God, is something that can be taken away from man without removing God's creature itself.* Furthermore, the apostle describes the movements of the new man under the image of various garments which must be put on (Col. 3:12ff.). The ground and occasion of such being clothed upon is Christ,

> the Spirit whom Christ sends from the Father; or the standing in Christ, or in grace (*e.g.*, 2 Cor. 5:17; Gal. 5:16, 18, 25; Rom. 5:2). And in just the same way is the ground for likeness with God, the standing in the image of God, according to Genesis 1:26.

The words in italics dispel, alas! all doubt. It is possible to conceive of the image of God as having completely disappeared, and yet man remaining man.

Dr. Böhl repeats this clearly in the following words (p. 29): "If we now think of the creature to have left this standing, yet this creature remains intact."

This goes so far that Dr. Böhl himself felt how closely he thus returned to the boundaries of Rome, for which reason he continues, saying:

> With this understanding, however, that the creature has not retained enough strength, with the help of the gracious gift of Christ, to restore himself, as Rome teaches. But after the fall, man's ego, with the highest gifts received in his creation, has left his true standing and is delivered to Death as his ruler, and to the Law as his unmerciful driver.

But stronger still: Dr. Böhl is so firmly attached to this presentation that he says even of Christ, that He, before His Resurrection, lacked the divine image. See page 45: *"Our Lord and Savior stood outside the image of God."* "Ausserhalb des Bildes Gottes stand unser Herr." Which is all the more serious since in consequence of this presentation, the passions and desires toward the sinful are, considered by themselves, sinless, just as Rome teaches it.

So we read on page 73:

> The fact that man has desires, that he is led by passions, such as anger, fear, courage, jealousy, joy, love, hate, longing, pity, all this does not constitute sin; for the power to experience anger, displeasure, or pity, and the like passions, is created of God. Without these there would be no life nor stir in man. Hence desires and passions in general are no sin in themselves. They become and are sin in man's present condition, because, by an intervening law, and by that perverted tendency of life which Paul calls a law of sin, the human Ego is compelled to determine its relation to the passions and desires, that is, to adopt a good or bad attitude toward them.

Let each judge for himself whether we said too much when we spoke of the necessity of protesting, in the name of our Reformed Confession, against the creeping in of this Platonic presentation, which later on was defended partly by the Romish, partly by the Lutheran theologians.

Dr. Böhl is excellent when he shows that the original righteousness was not simply a germ, which had still to be developed, but that Adam's righteousness was complete, lacking nothing. Equally excellent is his proof against Rome, showing that man, in his naked nature, absolutely lacks the power to holiness. But he errs in representing the image of God as something without which man remains man. This places righteousness and holiness mechanically outside of us, while the organic connection between that image and our own being, which once existed and ought to exist, is the very thing that must be maintained.

And yet, it is not be thought that Dr. Böhl has any inclination toward Rome. If we see aright, his deviation, psychologically explained, springs from an entirely different motive.

It is a well-known fact that Dr. Kohlbrugge has contended, with a glorious ardor of faith, against the reestablishing of the Covenant of Works in the midst of the Covenant of Grace; and has reintroduced us with stress and emphasis to the completely finished work of our Savior, to which nothing can be added. Hence this preacher of righteousness was compelled to make the child of God remember *what he was outside of Christ.* Of course, outside of Christ, there is no difference between a child of God and a godless person. Then all lie in one heap; as the ritual of the Lord's Supper so beautifully confesses: "That we seek our life out of ourselves, in Jesus Christ, and thereby acknowledge that we lie in the midst of death"; as also the Heidelberg Catechism confesses: "That I have grossly transgressed all the commandments of God, and kept none of them, and am still inclined to all evil."

If we see aright, Dr. Böhl has tried to reduce this part of the truth to a dogmatic system. He has reasoned it out as follows: "If a child of God has his life outside of himself, then Adam, who was a child of God, must also have had his life outside of himself. Hence the image of God was not in, but outside of, man."

And what is the mistake of this reasoning? This, that the child of God remains a *sinner* until his death, and is only fully restored after his death. Then only complete redemption is his. While in Adam, before his fall, there was no sin; hence Adam could never say that in himself he lay in the midst of death.

With all the earnestness of our hearts we beseech all those who with us possess the treasure of Dr. Kohlbrugge's preaching carefully to notice this deviation. If the younger Kohlbruggians should be tempted to misunderstand their teacher in this respect, the loss would be incalculable, and the breach in the Reformed Confession would be lasting; since it touches a point which affects the whole confession of the truth.

8

After the Scripture

In the day that God created man, in the likeness of God created He him—Genesis 5:1.

In the preceding pages we have shown that the translation, *"in* Our image," actually means, *"after* Our image." To make anything *in* an image is no language; it is unthinkable, logically untrue. We now proceed to show how it should be translated, and give our reason for it.

We begin with citing some passages from the Old Testament in which occurs the preposition "B" which, in Genesis 1:27, stands before image, where it cannot be translated "in," but requires a preposition of comparison such as "like" or "after."

Isaiah 48:10 reads: "Behold I have refined thee, but not with silver; I have chosen thee in the furnace of affliction." Here the preposition "B" stands before silver, as in Genesis 1:27 before image. It is obvious that it cannot be translated "in silver," but "as silver." Surely the Lord would not cast the Jews in a pot of melted silver. The preposition is one of comparison; as in 1 Peter 1:17 the refining of Israel is compared to that of a noble metal. It may be translated: "I have refined thee, but not according to the nature of silver"; or simply: "as silver."

Psalm 102 reads: "My days are consumed like smoke, and my bones are burned as a hearth." In the Hebrew the same preposition "B" occurs before smoke, and almost all exegetes translate it, "as smoke."

Again, Psalm 35:2 reads: "Take hold of shield and buckler and stand up for mine help." "Stand up *in* my help" makes no sense. The thought allows no other translation than this: "Stand up so that Thou be my help"; or, "Stand up *as* my help"; or, as the Authorized Version has it: "Stand up *for* my help."

We find the same result in Leviticus 17:2: "The life of the flesh is in the blood, and I have given it to you upon the altar, to make an atonement for your souls; for it is the blood that maketh an atonement for the soul. Here the same preposition "B" occurs. In the Hebrew it reads. "Banefesh" (בַּנֶּפֶשׁ), which was translated *"for* the soul." It would be absurd to render it: *"in* the soul"; for the blood does not come *in* the soul, nor does the atonement take place in the soul, but on the altar. Here we have also a comparison (substitution). The blood is *as* the soul, *represents* the soul in the atonement, takes the place of the soul.

We notice the same in Proverbs 3:26, where the wisdom of Solomon wrote: "The Lord shall be thy confidence, and shall keep thy foot from being taken." The same preposition occurs here. The Hebrew text reads "Bkisleka" (בְּכִסְלֶךָ), literally, "For a loin to thee." And because the loins are a man's strength, it is used metaphorically to indicate the ground of confidence and hope in distress. The sense is therefore perfectly clear. Says Solomon: "The Lord shall be to thee as a ground of confidence, thy refuge, and thy hope," it might be inferred that, among other things, the Lord was also in the hope of the godly; which would be unscriptural and savor of Pelagianism. In the Scripture, the Lord alone is the hope of His people. Hence the preposition does not mean "in," but it indicates a comparison.

To add one more example, Exodus 18:4 reads: "The God of my father was my help, and delivered me from the sword of Pharaoh." Translate this, "The God of my father was *in* my help," and how unscriptural and illogical the thought!

From these passages, to which others might be added, it appears:

(1) That this preposition cannot always be translated by "in."

(2) That its use as a preposition of comparison, in the sense of "like," "for," "after," is far from being rare.

Armed with this information, let us now return to Genesis 1:26; and in our opinion, it does not offer us now any difficulty at all. As in Isaiah 48:10, the preposition and noun are translated "as silver"; in

Psalm 102:4, "as smoke"; in Psalm 35:2, "as" or "to my help"; in Leviticus 17:2, "as" or "in the place of my soul"; in Proverbs 3:16, "as," or "to my confidence," the German Version of the Vienna Hebrew Bible translates, "Let Us make men to, or as Our image," that is, let Us make men, who shall be Our image on the earth. Or more freely: "Let Us make a sort of being who will bear Our image on earth, who will be as Our image on earth, or be to Us on earth for an image."

Then it follows, in Genesis 1:27: "And God created man for His image, to be an image of God created He him." It is, of course, exactly the same whether I say, "God created man after His image," that is, so that man became bearer of His image, or "God created man for an image of Himself." In both instances, and in similar manner, it is expressed that man should exhibit an image of God. Thus far the image of God was lacking in the earth. When God had created man, the lack was supplied: for that image was man, upon whose being the Lord God had stamped His own image. Hence we see no difference in the two translations.

Speaking of the image stamped on sealing-wax by a seal, I can say, "I have stamped the wax after the image of the seal," referring to the *concave* image of the seal; or, "The image is stamped *on the wax,"* referring to the convex image on the wax.

We add three remarks: First, the word "man" in Genesis 1:26 does not refer to one person, but to the whole race. Adam was not merely a person, but our progenitor and federal head. The whole race was in his loins. Humanity consists at any given moment of the aggregate of those who live or will live in this world, whether many or few. Adam also was humanity; when Eve was given him he and she were humanity. "Let Us make man in Our image and after Our likeness," is equal to: "Let Us create humanity, which will bear Our image." But it refers also to the individual in that he is a member of the human family. Hence Adam begat children in his image and after his own likeness. Yet there is a difference. Men have different gifts, talents, and qualifications; the complete impress of the divine image could appear not in *individual* endowments, but in the full manifestation of the *race,* if it had remained sinless.

Hence the Dutch Version uses the plural, although the Hebrew has the singular "man": not Adam alone, but the genus man, humanity, was created in the divine image.

Hence when the original man fell, the second Adam came in Christ, who, as the second federal Head, contained in Himself the whole Church of God. In His mediatorial capacity Christ appeared as God's image in Adam's place. Wherefore every member of the Church must be transformed after His image—1 Corinthians 15:49; Romans 8:29. And the Church, representing regenerated humanity, is the *plḗrōma* of the Lord; for it is called "the fullness of Him that filleth all in all."

Secondly, since man is created to be God's image on earth, he must be willing to remain *image,* and never presume or imagine to be *being.* Being and image are opposites. God is God, and man is not God, but only the *image* of God. Hence it is the essence of sin when man refuses to remain image, reflection, shadow, exalting himself to be something real in himself. Conversion depends, therefore, solely upon his willingness to become image again, that is, to believe. He that becomes an image is nothing in himself, and exhibits all that he is in absolute dependence upon Him whose image he bears; and this is at once man's highest honor and completest dependence.

Lastly, God must have His image in the earth. For this purpose He created Adam. Having defiled it beyond recognition, man denies the existence of the divine image in the earth. And thus image-worship originated. Image-worship means that man says: "I will undertake to make an image of God." And this diametrically opposes God's work. It is His holy prerogative to make an image of Himself; and the creature should never dare undertake it. Hence it is presumption when, aspiring to be God, man refuses to remain his image, defiles it in himself, and undertakes to represent God in gold or silver.

Image-worship is an awful sin. God saith: "Thou shalt not make unto thee any graven image." This sin is from Satan. He always imitates God's work. He will not be less than God. When at last the Great Beast appears, the Dragon proclaims: "They that dwell in the earth should make *an image of the Beast!"* God has decreed to make His own image to be the object of His eternal pleasure. But Satan, opposing this, defiles that image and makes an image for himself; not of man, for he is defiled and ruined, but of *a beast.* And thus in his supreme manifestation he judges himself. God's Son became a *man,* Satan's creation is a *beast.*

When finally the Beast and its image are overthrown, by One who is like a son of man, it is the Lord's triumph over His enemies. Then the divine image is restored, nevermore to be defiled. And the Almighty God rejoices forever and ever in His own reflection.

9

The Image of God in Man

As we have borne the image of the earthy, we shall also bear the image of the heavenly—1 Corinthians. 15:49.

One more point remains to be discussed, viz., whether the divine image refers to the image of Christ.

This singular opinion has found many warm defenders in the Church from the beginning. It originated with Origen, who with his brilliant, fascinating, and seducing heresies has unsettled many things in the Church; and his heresy in this respect has found many defenders both East and West. Even Tertullian and Ambrose supported it, as well as Basil and Chrysostom; and it took no less a person than Augustine to uproot it.

Our Reformed theologians, closely following Augustine, have strongly opposed it. Junius, Zanchius and Calvin, Voetius and Coccejus condemned it as error. We can safely say that in our Reformed inheritance this error never had a place.

But in the last century it has crept again into the Church. The pantheistic philosophy occasioned it; and its after-effects have tempted our German and Dutch mediation theologians to return to this ancient error.

The great philosophers who enthralled the minds of men at the beginning of this century fell in love with the idea that God became man. They taught not that the Word became flesh, but God became man; and that in the fatal sense that God is ever *becoming*, and that

He becomes a better and a purer God as He becomes more purely man. This pernicious system, which subverts the foundations of the Christian faith, and under a Christian form annihilates essential Christianity, has led to the doctrine that in Christ Jesus this incarnation had become a fact; and from it was deduced that God would have become man even if man had *not* sinned.

We have often spoken of the danger of teaching this doctrine. The Scripture repudiates it, teaching that Christ is a Redeemer from and an atonement for sin. But a mere passing contradiction will not stop this evil; this poisonous thread, running through the warp and woof of the Ethical theology, will not be pulled from the preaching until the conviction prevails that it is philosophic and pantheistic, leading away from the simplicity of Scripture.

But for the present nothing can be done. Almost all the German manuals now used by our rising ministers feed this error; hence the widespread prevalence of the idea that the image in which man was created was *the Christ.*

And this is natural. So long as it is maintained that, even without sin, man was destined for Christ and Christ for man, it must follow that the original man was calculated for Christ, and hence was created after the image of Christ.

For evidence that this deviates from the truth, we refer theologians to the writings of Augustine, Calvin, and Voetius on this point, and to our lay-readers we offer a short explanation why we and all Reformed churches reject this interpretation.

We begin with referring to the many passages in Scripture, teaching that the redeemed sinner must be renewed and transformed after the image of Christ.

In 2 Corinthians 3:18 we read: "We all are changed into the same image from glory to glory, even as by the Spirit of the Lord"; and in Romans 8:29: "That we are predestinated to be conformed to the image of His Son"; and in 1 Corinthians 15:49: "As we have borne the image of the earthy, we shall also bear the image of the heavenly." To this category belong all such passages in which the Holy Spirit admonishes us to conform ourselves to the example of Jesus, which may not be understood as mere imitation, but which decidedly means a transformation into His image. And lastly, here belong those passages that teach that we must increase to a perfect man, "to the stature of the fullness of Christ"; and that "we shall be like Him, for we shall see Him as He is."

Hence believers are called to transform themselves after Christ's image, which is the final aim of their redemption. But this image is *not* the Eternal Word, the Second Person in the Trinity, but the Messiah, the *Incarnate* Word. 1 Corinthians 15:44 furnishes the undeniable proof. St. Paul declares there that the first man Adam was of the earth earthy, that is, not only after the fall, but by creation. Then he says that as believers have borne the image of the earthy, so they will also bear the image of the heavenly, that is, Christ. This shows clearly that in his original state man did not possess the image of Christ, but that afterward he will possess it. What Adam received in creation is clearly distinguished from what a redeemed sinner possesses in Christ; distinguished in this particular, that it was not according to his nature to be formed after Christ's image, which image he could receive only by grace after the fall.

This is evident also from what St. Paul teaches in 1 Corinthians 11. In the third verse, speaking of the various degrees of ascending glory, he says that the man is the head of the woman, and the head of every man is Christ, and the head of Christ is God. And yet, having spoken of these four, woman, man, Christ, God, he says emphatically, in verse 7, not as might be expected, "The woman is the glory of the man, the man the glory of Christ," but, omitting the link Christ, he writes: "For the man is the glory of God, and the woman the glory of the man." If this theory under consideration were correct, he should have said: "The man is the image of Christ."

Hence it is plain that according to Scripture the image after which we are to be *renewed* is not that after which we are *created;* the two must be distinguished. The latter is that of the Triune God whose image penetrated into the being of the *race.* The former is that of the holy and perfect Man Christ Jesus, our federal Head, and as such the Example [Dutch, *Voorbeeld;* literally, an image placed before one—Trans.], after which every child of God is to be renewed, and which at last he shall resemble.

Hence Scripture offers two different representations: first, the Son who is the image of the Father as the Second Person in the Trinity; second, the Mediator our Example [*Voorbeeld,* image put before one], hence our image after which we are to be renewed; and between the two there is almost no connection. The Scripture teaching that the Son of God is the express image of His Person and the image of the Invisible, refers to the relation between the Father and the Son in the hidden mystery of the Divine Being. But speaking of our calling to be renewed after the image of Christ, it refers to the Incarnate Word, our Savior, tempted like as we are in all things, yet without sin.

Mere similarity of sound should not lead us to make this mistake. Every effort to translate Genesis 1:26, "Let Us make man in or after the image of the Son," is confusing. Then "Let Us" must refer to the Father speaking to the Holy Spirit; and this cannot be. Scripture never places the Father and the Holy Spirit in such relation. Moreover, it would put the Son outside the greatest act of creation, viz., the creation of man. And Scripture says: "Without Him was not anything made that was made"; and again: "Through Him are created all things in heaven and on earth."

Hence this "Let Us" must be taken either as a plural of majesty, of which the Hebrew has not a single instance in the first person; or as spoken by the Triune God, the Three Persons mutually addressing each other; or the Father addressing the two other Persons. A third is impossible.

Supposing that the Three Persons address each other; the image cannot refer to the Son, because, speaking of His own, He cannot say, "Our image," without including the other Persons. Or suppose that the Father speaks to the Son and to the Holy Spirit; even then it cannot refer to the image of the Son, since He is the Father's image and not that of the Holy Spirit. In whatever sense it be taken, this view is untenable, outside the analogy of Scripture, and inconsistent with the correct interpretation of Genesis 1:26.

To put it comprehensively: If the divine image refers to the Christ, it must be that of the Eternal Son, or of the Mediator, or of Christ in the flesh. These three are equally impossible. First, the Son is Himself engaged in the creative work. Second, without sin there is no need of a Mediator. Third, Scripture teaches that the Son became flesh after our image, but never that in the creation we became flesh after His image.

The notion that the divine image refers to Christ's righteousness and holiness, implying that Adam was created in *extraneous* righteousness, confounds the righteousness of Christ which *we embrace by faith* and which did not exist when Adam was created, and the *original, eternal* righteousness *of God the Son.* It is true that David embraced the imputed righteousness, although it existed *not* in his day, but David was a *sinner* and Adam before the fall was *not.* He was created without sin; hence the divine image cannot refer to the righteousness of Christ, revealed only in relation *to sin.*

In our present sad condition, we confess unconditionally that even now we lie in the midst of death, and have our life outside of ourselves in Christ alone. But we add: Blessed be God, it shall not always be so. With our last *breath* we die wholly to sin, and in the resurrection morning *we shall be like Him;* hence in the eternal felicity our life shall be no more *without* us, but *in* us.

Wherefore, to put the separation which was caused only by sin, and which in the saint continues only on account of sin, in Adam before the fall, is nothing else than to carry something sinful into Creation itself, and to annihilate the divine statement *that man was created good.*

Wherefore we admonish preachers of the truth to return to the old, tried paths in this respect, and teach in recitation-hall, pulpit, and catechetical class that man was created *after the image of the Triune God.*

10

Adam Not Innocent, but Holy

Created in righteousness and true holiness—Ephesians 4:24.

It remains, therefore, as of old, that "God created man good and after His own image, that is, in true righteousness and holiness, that he might rightly know God his Creator, heartily love Him, and live with Him in eternal happiness, and glorify and praise Him." Or, as the Confession of Faith has it: "We believe that God created man, out of the dust of the earth, and made him and formed him after His own image and likeness, good and righteous and wholly capable in all things to will, agreeably to the will of God."

Every representation which depreciates in the least this original righteousness must be opposed.

Adam's righteousness lacked nothing. The idea that he was holy inasmuch as he had not sinned, and by constant development could increase his holiness, so that if he had not fallen he would have attained a still holier state, is incorrect, and betrays ignorance in this respect.

The difference between man in his original state and in the state of sin is similar to that between a healthy child and a sick man. Both must increase in strength. If the child remains what he is, he is not healthy. Health includes growth and increase of strength and development until maturity be attained. The same is true of the sick man; he cannot remain the same. He must recover or grow worse. If he is to recover, he must gain in strength. So far both are the same.

But here the similarity ceases. Increase the strength of the sick at once, and he will be well, and what he should be. But add the full strength of the man to the child, and he will be *unnatural* and *abnormal. For the present* the child needs no more than he has. He lacks nothing at *any given moment.* To be a normal child in perfect health, he must be just what he is. But the sick person needs a great deal. In order to be healthy and normal he must *not* be what he is. The child, so far as health and strength are concerned, is *perfect, but* the sick person is very *imperfect* as regards health and strength. The condition of the child is *good;* that of the sick man is *not* good. And the former's healthy growth is something entirely different from the latter's improvement in health and strength.

This shows how wrong it is to apply sanctification to Adam before the fall. Sanctification is inconceivable with reference to sinless man; foreign to the conception of a creature whom God calls *good.*

"Excellent," says one; hence Adam was born in childlike innocence gradually to attain a higher moral development without sin; hence sanctification after all!

Certainly not. A believer's sanctification ceases when he dies. In death he dies to all sin. Sanctification is merely the process which partly or wholly eliminates sin from man. Wholly freed from sin he is holy, and it is impossible to make him holier than holy. Even for this reason it is absurd to apply sanctification to holy Adam. What need of washing that which is clean? Sanctification presupposes unholiness, and Adam was not unholy. Sin being absolutely absent, holiness lacks nothing, but is complete. Adam possessed the same complete holiness now possessed by the child of God in which he stands by faith, and by and by in actuality when through death he has absolutely died unto sin.

Yet in heaven God's children will not stand still—their joy and glory will ever increase, but not their holiness, which lacks nothing. And to be more holy than perfectly holy is impossible. Their development will consist in drinking ever more copiously from the life of God.

The same is true of sinless Adam; he *could not* be sanctified. Sanctification is healing, and a healthy person cannot be healed. Sanctification is to rid one of poison, but poison cannot be drawn from the hand that is not bitten. The idea of holy, holier, holiest is absurd. That which is *broken* is not whole, and that which is *whole* is not broken. Sanctification is to make whole, and since in Adam *nothing* was broken, there was nothing to be made whole. More whole than whole is unthinkable.

Yet although holy, Adam did not remain what he was, he did not stand still without an aim in life. Take, for example, the difference between him and God's child. The latter possesses an unlosable treasure, but Adam's was losable, for he lost it. Not that he was less holy than the saint; for this has nothing to do with it.

Let us illustrate. Of two dishes, one is fine cut glass, hence breakable; the other coarse glass, but unbreakable. Is the latter now more whole than the former? Or can the former be made more whole? Of course not; its wholeness has nothing to do with its being breakable or not. Hence the fact that Adam's treasure was losable does not touch the question of holiness at all. Whether one is holy, or yet to be made holy, does not depend upon the losableness of the treasure, but upon its being lost or not.

How this holy development of Adam was to be effected we do not know. We may not inquire after things God has kept from us. As sinners we can no more conceive of such sinless development than of the unfolding of the heavenly glory of God's children.

Confining ourselves closely to Scripture, we know, *first,* that sinless man would not have died; *second,* that as a reward for his work he would have received eternal life, that is, being perfectly able from moment to moment to do God's will, he would always have desired and loved to do it; and for this he would have been rewarded continually with larger measures of the life and glory of God.

We compare the contrast between Adam's condition and ours to that between the royal child born possessor of vast treasures, and a child of poverty that must earn everything or have another to earn it for him. The former lacks nothing, although he has only toys to dispose of; for his father's whole estate is his. Growing up, he does not become richer, for his treasures remain the same, but he becomes more conscious of them. So Adam's treasures would never have increased, for all things were his; only as his life gradually unfolded would he have had more conscious enjoyment of his riches.

Hence original righteousness does not refer to Adam's *degree of development,* nor to his *condition,* but to his *state;* and that was *perfectly good.*

All those unscriptural notions of Adam's increase in holiness spring from the unscriptural ideas which men, tempted by pantheistic heresies, have formed of *holiness.*

"Be ye then perfect even as your Father which is in heaven is perfect," does not mean that you, boastful man, puffed up by philosophic madness, must become like *God.* A *creature* you will remain even in your highest glory. And in that glory the consciousness that you are *nothing* and God is *all* will be cause of your most fervent adoration and deepest delight. No, Christ's word simply means, *"Be whole,"* even as your Father in heaven is whole and complete. Saying that an earthen vessel must be as whole and sound as a porcelain vase does not mean it must become *like* that vase. The former costs but a few cents; the latter is paid for with gold. It only means that as the vase is whole *as a vase,* so must the earthen vessel be whole *as an earthen vessel.*

Hence Christ's word means: There are rents in your being; the edges are chipped; you are injured and damaged by sin. This must not be so. There may be no break in your being, nor should defect mar your completeness. Behold, as your Father in heaven is unbroken, so must you be wholly sound, unbroken, and perfect. That is, as God remained perfect as *God,* so must you remain whole and complete as *man,* a *creature* in the hand of you *Creator.*

But generally it is not so understood. The current view is as follows: The *first* step in holiness is conflict with sin. *Second,* sin becomes weak. *Third,* sin is almost overcome. *Fourth,* sin is *entirely* cast out. Then only, the *higher* sanctification sets in, and the whole ladder is being climbed; higher and higher, ever more holy, until holiness reaches the clouds.

Of course, those who accept these fancies cannot think of Adam otherwise than as created on a low plane of holiness and called to attain higher sanctification. But if there is but one sanctification, that is, *dying to sin* and *making* the broken nature *whole,* then higher sanctification regarding Adam is out of the question. To Adam's holiness nothing can be added. He would have known his Creator, heartily loved Him, and lived with Him in eternal happiness to glorify and praise Him, in ever-increasing consciousness, but all this would not have added anything to his righteousness and holiness. To suppose this would betray a lack of understanding concerning holiness. Thus love is confounded with holiness; righteousness with life; state with condition; word with being; and the very foundations are wrenched from their place.

Yea, worse. Souls are severed from Jesus. For he that fails to understand original righteousness cannot understand how Christ is given us of God for righteousness, sanctification, and redemption. He desires Jesus most assuredly. But how? "Jesus finds the sinner sick and perishing by the wayside. He puts him on His animal, and takes him to the inn, where He pays for him until he is restored." Hence always the same representation as though, after being redeemed, one must still seek for a righteousness and holiness which understand how Christ is given us of God for righteousness, sanctification, and redemption. He desires Jesus most assuredly. But how? "Jesus finds the sinner sick and perishing by the wayside. He puts him on His animal, and takes him to the inn, where He pays for him until he is restored." Hence always the same representation as though, after being redeemed, one must still seek for a righteousness and holiness which by constant progress will only gradually be attained.

If this is correct then Christ is not our righteousness, sanctification, nor redemption; at the most, He is a Friend supporting and strengthening us in our efforts to attain righteousness and holiness. No; if the Church is to glory once more in the comforting and blessed confession that in Christ it *possesses* now absolute righteousness, holiness, and redemption, it must first begin by understanding original righteousness, that is, that Adam cannot love, cannot live in blessed fellowship with God, except he be first *perfectly righteous* and *completely holy.*

Second Chapter
The Sinner to Be Wrought Upon

11

Sin Not Material

Sin is lawlessness—1 John 3:4 (R.V.).

What did sin blunt, corrupt, and destroy in God's image-bearer Adam? Although we can touch this question but lightly, yet it may not be slighted. It is evident that, for the right understanding of the Spirit's work regenerating and restoring the sinner, the knowledge of his condition is absolutely necessary. The mend must fit the rend. The wall must be rebuilt where the breach is made. The healing balm must suit the nature of the wound. As the disease is, so must also be the cure. Or stronger still, as is the death so must be the resurrection. The fall and the rising again are interdependent.

Generalities are useless in this respect. Ministers who seek to uncover and expose the man of sin by simply saying that men are wholly lost, dead in trespasses and sin, lack the cutting force which alone can lay open the putrefying sores of the heart. These serious matters have been treated too lightly. Hence by ignoring general and shallow statements we simply return to the tried and proven ways of the fathers.

We begin with pointing to one of the principal errors of the present time, viz., that of a resuscitated Manicheism.

It would be very interesting to present in a condensed form this sparkling and fascinating heresy to the Church of today. The immediate effect would be the discovery of the origin or the family likeness of much pernicious teaching that is brought into the Church under a Christian name, and by believing men. But this is impossible. We confine ourselves to a few features.

The mission of divine truth in this world is not to wanton with its wisdom, but to expose it as a lie. Divine Wisdom does not compromise with the speculations and delusions of worldly wisdom, but calls them folly and demands their surrender. In the Kingdom of truth, light and darkness are pronounced opposites. Hence the Church, in coming in contact with the learning and philosophy of the Gentile world, came into direct and open conflict with it.

Compared to Israel, the heathen world was wonderfully wise, learned, and scientific; and from her scientific standpoint, she looked down with deep contempt and infinite condescension upon the foolishness of Christianity. That foolish, ignorant, and unlettered Christianity was not only false, but beneath their notice, unworthy to be discussed. In Athens the good-natured people had for these unthinking men and their absurd babbling a Homeric smile, and the sinister ridiculed them with bitter satire. But neither the one nor the other ever *seriously* considered the matter, for it was unscientific.

And yet, after all, that stupid Christianity carried the day. It made progress. It obtained influence, even power. At last the great minds and geniuses of those days began to feel attracted to it; until, after a conflict of nearly a century, the hour came when the heathen world was *compelled* to come down from its proud self-conceit, and acknowledge that ignorant, unlettered, and unscientific Christianity. The lively preaching of these Nazarenes had drowned the disputations of those dry philosophers. Soon the stream of the world's life passed by their schools, and flowed into the channel of the wonderful and inexplicable Jesus. Even before the Church was two centuries old, proud heathendom discovered that, mortally wounded, its life was in jeopardy.

Then under the appearance of honoring Christianity, with cunning craftiness Satan vitally injured it, injecting poison into its heart. In the second century three learned and complicated systems, viz., Gnosticism, Manicheism, and Neo-Platonism, tried with one gigantic effort to smother it in the mortal embrace of their heathen philosophies.

When the cross was planted on Calvary, two empires existed in heathendom: one in the West, containing Rome and Greece, and the other in the East, with its centers in Babylon and Egypt. In each of these centers, Babylon and Athens, there were men of rare mental powers, comprehensive learning, and profound wisdom. Both centers were swayed by a worldly and heathen philosophy; although its character in both was different. And from these centers the effort proceeded to drown Christianity in the waters of their philosophy. Neo-Platonism tried to accomplish this in the West; Manicheism in the East; and Gnosticism in the center.

Manes was the man who conceived that magnificent, fascinating, and seducing system which bears his name. He was a profound thinker, and died about the year 270. He was a genial, pious, and seriously minded man; he confessed Christ. It was even the aim and object of his zeal to extend the Lord's Kingdom. But one thing annoyed him: the endless conflict between Christianity and his own science and philosophy. He thought there were points of agreement and contact between the two, and their reconciliation was not impossible. To bridge the chasm seemed beautiful to him. One might walk to the heathen world, and in its brilliant philosophies discover many elements of divine origin; and returning to Christianity lead some serious heathens to the cross of Christ. The profound glory of the Christian faith filled him with enthusiasm; yet he remained almost blind for the inherent falsehood of heathen philosophy. And as both lay mingled in his soul, so it was his aim to devise a system wherein both should be interwoven, and transformed into a brilliant whole.

It is impossible here to introduce his system, which shows that Manes had thought out every deep question of vital importance, and with comprehensive eye had measured all the dimensions of his cosmology. All that we can do is to show how this system led to false ideas of sin.

This was caused by his mistaken notion that the word "flesh" refers only to the *body;* while Scripture uses it as referring to *sin,* signifying the *whole human nature,* which does not love the things that are above, but the things of the flesh. Flesh in this sense refers more directly to the soul than to the body. The works of the flesh are twofold: one class, touching the body, are the sins related to fornication and lust; the other, touching the soul, consist of sins connected with pride, envy, and hatred. In the sphere of visible things it finishes its image with shameless fornication; in the realm of invisible things it ends with stiff-necked pride.

Scripture teaches that sin does not originate in the flesh, but in Satan, a being *without a body.* Coming from him it crept first into man's soul, then manifested itself in the body. Hence it is unscriptural to oppose "flesh" and "spirit" as "body" and "soul." This Manes did; and this is the object of his system in all its features. He taught that sin is inherent in *matter,* in the flesh, in all that is tangible and visible. The "soul," he says, "is your friend, but the body your enemy. The successful resistance of the excitement of the blood and the palate would free you from sin." In his own Eastern environment he saw much more carnal sin than spiritual; and deceived by this he closed his eyes for the latter, or accounted for it as caused by the excitement from evil matter.

And yet Manes was quite consistent, which, giant-thinker that he was, could not be otherwise. He arrived at this singular conclusion, essential to his system of inventions, that Satan was a fallen angel, not a spiritual, incorporeal being, but *matter itself.* Hid in matter was a power tempting the soul, and that power was Satan. This explains how Manes could offer the Church such a singular and anti-scriptural doctrine.

Manes's system bordered on materialism. The materialist says that our thinking is the burning of phosphorus in the brain; and that lust, envy, and hatred are the result of a discharge of certain glands in the body. Virtue and vice are only the result of chemical processes. In order to make a man better, freer, and nobler, we should send him to the laboratory of a chemist, rather than to school or church. And if it were possible for the chemist to lift the man's skull, and subject his cells and nerves to the necessary chemical process, then vice would be conquered, and virtue and higher wisdom would effectually sway him.

In a similar way Manes taught that as an inherent and inseparable power sin dwells in the blood and muscles, and is transmitted by them. He exhorted to eat certain herbs, as a means to overcome sin. There were, so he taught, animals, but chiefly plants, into which had penetrated a few redeeming and liberating particles of light from the kingdom of light which opposed evil; by eating these herbs the blood would absorb these saving particles of light, and thus the power of sin would be broken. In fact, the church of Manes was a chemical laboratory, in which sin was opposed by material agencies.

This shows the logical consistency of the system, and the weakness of the men who, having adopted the false notion of material sin, try to escape from its tight hold upon them. But they cannot, for, although discarding the draperies belonging to the system as unsuitable to our Western mode of thinking, they adopt his whole line of theories, and thus falsify not only the doctrine of sin, but almost every other part of the Christian doctrine.

And yet it is only in the doctrine of *inherited sin* that this error is so conspicuous that it cannot escape detection.

It is argued: By virtue of his birth man is a sinner. Hence every child must inherit sin from his parents. And since an infant in the cradle is ignorant of spiritual sin, and without spiritual development, the inherited sin must hide in his being, transmitted with the blood from the parents. And this is pure Manicheism, in that it makes sin to be transmitted as a power inherent in matter.

The Confession of the Reformed churches, speaking of inherited sin, says, in article 15:

> We believe that, through the disobedience of Adam, original sin is extended to all mankind; which is a corruption of the whole nature, and a hereditary disease, wherewith infants themselves are infected even in their mother's womb, and which produceth in man all sorts of sin, being in him as a root thereof; and therefore is so vile and abominable in the sight of God, that it is sufficient to condemn all mankind. Nor is it by any means abolished or done away by baptism; since sin always issues forth from this woeful source, as water from a fountain: notwithstanding it is not imputed to the children of God unto condemnation, but by His grace and mercy is forgiven them. Not that they should rest securely in sin, but that a sense of this corruption should make believers often to sigh, desiring to be delivered from the body of this death. Wherefore we reject the error of the Pelagians, who assert that sin only proceeds from imitation.

It is apparent, therefore that the Reformed churches positively acknowledge *inherited sin;* acknowledge also that the child *inherits sin* from the parents; even calls this sin an *infection,* which adheres even to the unborn child. But—and this is the principal thing—they never say that this inherited sin is something material, or is transmitted as something material. The word *infection* is used *metaphorically,* and therefore is not the proper expression for the thing which they wish to confess. Sin is not a drop of poison which, like a contagious disease, passes from father to child. No; the transmission of sin remains in our confession an unexplained mystery, only symbolically expressed.

But this does not satisfy the spirits of the present day. Hence the new school of Manicheists which has arisen among us.

Entangled in the meshes of this heresy are they who deny the doctrine of inherited guilt; who entertain false views of the sacraments, holding that in Baptism the poison of sin is at least partly removed from the soul, and that in the communion of the Holy Supper the sinful flesh absorbs a few particles of the glorified body; and lastly, who advocate the ridiculous efforts to banish demoniac influences from rooms and vacant lots. All this is foolish, unscriptural, and yet defended by believing men in our own land. O Church of Christ, whither art thou straying?

12

Sin Not a Mere Negation

I see another law in my members, warring against the law of my mind—Romans 7:23.

Dr. Böhl's theory, that sin is a mere *loss, default,* or *lack,* is an error almost as critical as Manicheism. This should not be misunderstood. This theory does not deny that the sinner is unholy, nor that he ought to be holy. It says two things: (1) that there is no holiness in the sinner, but—and this indicates the real character of sin—(2) that there ought to be holiness in him. A stone does not hear, nor a book see; yet the one is not deaf, nor the other blind. But the man who lost both hearing and seeing is both; for to his being as a man both are essential. A chair cannot walk; yet it is not lame, for it is not expected to walk. But the cripple is lame, for walking belongs to his being. A horse is not holy, neither is it a sinner. But man is a sinner, for he is unholy, and holiness belongs to his being; an unholy man is defective and unnatural. Sin, says St. John, "is unrighteousness," non-conformity to the law, or, literally, lawlessness, *anomie.* Hence sin appears only in beings subject to the *divine, moral law,* and consists in *non-conformity* to that law.

Thus far this view presents only clear, pure truth; and every effort to give sin positive, independent entity contradicts the Word and leads to Manicheism, as may be seen in the otherwise fervent and conscientious Moravian Brethren.

Scripture denies that sin has a positive character implying that it has independent being. Independent being is either created or uncreated. If uncreated, it must be eternal, and this is God alone. If created, God must be its Creator; which cannot be, for He is not sin's Author. Hence Scripture does not teach that the power of evil inheres in matter, but in Satan. And what is Satan? Not an evil substance, but a being intended for, and endued with holiness; who abandoned himself to unholiness, in which he entangled himself hopelessly, becoming absolutely unholy. The doctrine of Satan opposes the false notion that sin has entity. The idea that sin is a power, in the sense of a faculty exercised by an independent being, is inconsistent with Scripture.

So far we heartily agree with Dr. Böhl, and acknowledge that he has maintained the old and tried conviction of believers, and the positive confession of the Church.

But from this he infers that, before and after the fall, Adam remained the same, with this difference only, that after the fall he lost the splendor of righteousness in which he had walked hitherto. So far as his powers and being were concerned, he remained the same. And this we do not accept. It would make man like a lamp brightly burning but soon extinguished, when it became a dark body. Or like a fireplace radiant with the glow and heat of fire this moment, cold and dark the next. Or like a piece of iron magnetized by the electric current, which gives it power to attract, but the current withdrawn it ceases to be a magnet. When the light was blown out, the lamp remained uninjured. When the fire died, the hearth remained what it was before. And when the electric fluid left the iron, it was iron still.

And so says Dr. Böhl regarding man. As the current passes through the iron and magnetizes it, so did the divine righteousness pass through Adam and make him holy. As the lamp shines when lighted by the spark, so did Adam shine when touched by the spark of righteousness. And as the hearth is aglow with the fire, so was Adam radiant with the righteousness created in him. But now sin comes in. That is, the lamp goes out, the hearth becomes cold, the magnet is mere iron again. And man stands robbed of his splendor, dark and unable to attract. But for the rest he remained what he was. Dr. Böhl says distinctly that man remained the same before and after the fall.

And with this we do not agree. As a sinner he was still man, undoubtedly, but man as the fathers confessed at Dordt (3d and 4th, Head of Doctrine, art. 16): "That man by the fall did not cease to be a creature endowed with understanding and will, nor did sin, which pervaded the whole race of mankind, deprive him of the human nature, but brought upon him depravity and spiritual death." Dr. Böhl's statement, "Removed by sin from this state [of righteousness], man remains intact" directly contradicts this pure confession of the Reformed churches.

No, the creature did not remain intact, but sin so seriously injured him that he became corrupt even unto death. And though we acknowledge that sin has no real *being* in itself, yet with equal decision we confess, with our church, that its *workings* are by no means merely negative, nor exclusively privative, but most assuredly very *positive.*

Scripture and our best theologians (Rivet, Wallaeus, and Polyander by name, in their Synopsis) teach this so positively that it is almost unimaginable how Dr. Böhl could reach any other conclusion. Wherefore we are inclined to believe that on this point he agrees with the confession of the orthodox churches, but that he represents this matter in such a strange manner for the sake of something else and for an entirely different reason.

If we may be frank, we would represent Dr. Böhl's course of reasoning as follows: "My teacher, Dr. Kohlbrugge, used to oppose strenuously the men that proudly say to the unconverted: Touch me not, for I am holier than thou. He used to emphasize the fact that the child of God, considered for a moment out of Christ, lies in the midst of death, just as much as the unconverted. Hence regeneration does not change man in the least. Before and after regeneration he is exactly the same, with this difference only, that the converted man *believes* and by his *faith* walks in reflected righteousness. And if this be so, then regarding the fall the reverse is true; that is, before and after the fall man as such remained the same; the only change was that in the fall he left the righteousness in which he stood before."

Of course we may be mistaken, but we dare surmise that in this way Dr. Böhl was tempted to this strange representation, and even to declare, as Rome teaches, that desire in itself is no sin; something which the Reformed Church on the ground of the Tenth Commandment has always opposed.

In fact, the question regarding the fall and the restoration is the same. If the restoration does not affect our being, then neither can the fall have affected it. If redemption means only that a sinner is set in the light of Christ's righteousness, then the fall can mean no more than that man stepped out of that light. The two belong together. As it was in the fall, so it must be in the restoration. A man's confession regarding redemption will, if he be consistent, tell what his confession is regarding the fall.

Hence if Dr. Kohlbrugge had confessed that the restoration leaves our being unchanged and only translates us into a sphere of righteousness, then it should be conceded that he also represented the fall as leaving man and his nature intact. And this is the very thing which we cannot concede. Dr. Kohlbrugge has uncovered the actual corruption of our nature so forcibly and positively that we will never believe that according to his confession the fall left our being and nature intact. Neither can we concede that, according to his confession, in the restoration our being is left unchanged, even though he connected that change, very rightly, with the mystic union and with the dying to sin in death.

If he had actually intended to teach what many of his followers allege that he did teach, then we would call his tendency very definitely *erroneous.* But since we cannot interpret him without taking into account the misrepresentations which he so strongly opposed, and especially since his confession concerning the corruption of our nature was so complete, we maintain that he did not teach what many of his followers offer in his name.

Hence our way is the very opposite direction. Dr. Böhl says in other words: "Dr. Kohlbrugge, in his doctrine of redemption, starts from the idea that redemption leaves the sinner essentially unchanged; hence neither can sin have affected him essentially." While, on the contrary, we say: "The confession of Kohlbrugge regarding the corruption of our nature is so complete that he could not but confess that in the fall, and therefore in the restoration, our nature was changed."

But be that as it may, this is sure, that, according to the word and the constant doctrine of our Church, sin, although it is essentially and exclusively privative and lacking independent existence, is yet in its *consequences* positive and in its *workings* destructive.

Our nature did not remain *unchanged,* but it became *corrupt;* and *corruption* is the significant word which indicates the fatal, positive effects which resulted from this loss of life and light.

A plant needs light to flourish; light excluded, it not only languishes, but soon withers, decays, and at last mildews; and this is, corruption. Cancer and smallpox are not merely loss of health, but have a *positive* action, which destroys the tissues, creates morbid growth, and *corrupts* the body. A corpse is not merely a lifeless body, but the seat of dissolution and corruption. In like manner we are conscious that sin is not merely the *deprivation* of holiness, but we feel its fearful activity, corruption, and dissolution which destroy. Strongest proof is the fact that we do not joyfully welcome God's grace entering the heart, but with our whole nature oppose it. There is conflict which would be impossible if that deprivation and loss had not developed evil which opposes God.

This corruption does not stop until the body is dissolved into its original constituents. We do not know what became of the bodies of Moses, Enoch, and Elijah. The Scripture makes exceptions. Christ did not see corruption, and believers living at the Lord's return will escape bodily dissolution. But all others, millions upon millions, will sicken and die, and return to the dust. Physical disease and death are types of soul-corruption which mere words fail to express.

Scripture and experience show clearly that Satan is not merely bereaved, emptied, and lacking, but that he causes a positive, corrupting activity to proceed from him. And so, though in less degree, the soul has become corrupt; not only in the sense of being dark instead of light, chilled instead of warm, but that this deprivation has resulted in positive destruction and corruption. Cold is loss of heat, which on reaching the freezing-point causes positive injury to the body. And such is sin. As to its *being,* it is loss, deprivation, and nakedness. And these cause in body and soul a destructive working which affects man's whole nature, binding him with the fetters of corruption, although he ceases not to be man.

We reconcile sin's *privative being* with its *positive working* as follows: depriving the ceaseless activity of man's nature of correct guidance, it runs in the wrong direction, and wrests and destroys itself.

13

Sin a Power in Reversed Action

If ye live after the flesh ye shall die—Romans 8:13.

Although sin is originally and essentially a loss, a lack, and a deprivation, in its working it is a positive evil and a malignant power. This is shown by the apostolic injunction not only to put on the new man, but also to put off the old man with his works. The well-known theologian Maccovius, commenting on this, aptly remarks: "This could not be enjoined if sin were merely a loss of light and life; for a mere lack ceases as soon as it is supplied."

If sin were merely a loss of righteousness, nothing more would be needed than its restoration, and sin would disappear. The putting off of the old man, or the laying down of the yoke of sin, etc., would be out of the question. The light has only to dispel the soul's darkness, and its health will be restored. But experience shows that after we are enlightened, and the Holy Spirit has entered our heart, there is still a fearful power of evil in us; and this together with the oft-repeated command not only to accept the righteousness of God which is by faith, but also to put off, to lay aside, to be separate from all that is evil, proves sin's positive character and evil power in individuals and in society, in spite of its privative character.

Hence the Church confesses that our nature has become corrupt, which of course refers us back to the divine image. Our nature did not disappear, nor cease to be our nature, but in its original features and organs it remained the same; the divine image was not lost, not even partly lost, but remained stamped upon every man, and will remain even in the place of eternal destruction, simply because he cannot divest himself of his nature except by annihilation. But this being impossible, he must retain it *as man* and in *man's nature.* Wherefore Scripture teaches long after the fall that the sinner is created after the image of God. But concerning the *effects* of its features in the fallen human nature, the very *opposite* is true: these features have totally disappeared; the ruins which remain speak at the most only of the glory and beauty which have perished.

Hence the two meanings of the divine image should no longer be confounded. Forasmuch as it lies *in our nature* it will *remain evermore;* so far as its effects upon the quality, that is, the condition, of our nature are concerned, *it is lost.* The human nature can be corrupted, but not annihilated. It can exist *as nature,* even though its former attributes be lost, and replaced by opposite workings.

Our fathers discriminated between our nature's *being* and its *well-being.* In its *being* it remained uninjured and unharmed, that is, it is still the real, human nature. But in its *condition,* that is, in its attributes, workings, and influences, in its *well-being* it is wholly changed, and corrupt. Though a poisoned insect-sting destroys the sight, yet the eye remains. So is the human nature; deprived of its luster, checked in its normal activity, internally sore and foul, yet it is the human nature.

But it is corrupted by sin. It is true man has retained the power to think, will, and feel, besides many glorious talents and faculties, even genius sometimes, but this does not touch the corruption of his nature. Its corruption is this, that the life which should be devoted to God and animated by Him is devoted with downward tendencies to earthly things. And this reversed action has changed the whole organism of our being.

If the divine righteousness were essential to human life, this could not be so, but it is not. According to Scripture, death is not annihilation. The sinner is dead to God, but in this very death throbs and thrills his life to Satan, to sin, and to the world. If the sinner has no sinful life, Scripture could never say, "Mortify therefore your members which are upon the earth," for it is impossible to mortify that which is dead already.

Let not similarity of sound deceive us. Human life is indestructible. When the soul is active in conformity to the divine law, Scripture says that the soul lives, if not, it is dead. This death is the wages of sin. But for this reason man's nature does not cease to work, to use its organs, to exert its influence. This is the life of our members which are in the earth—our sinful life, the inward festering of evil in our corrupt nature; for this reason it must be mortified. Hence since sin does not stop our nature from breathing, working, feeding, but it causes these activities, which under the sway of the divine law did run well and were full of blessing, to go wrong and be corrupt.

The mainspring of a watch when detached from its pivot does not stop it immediately, but, being uncontrolled, it turns the wheels so rapidly as to ruin the mechanism. In some respects human nature resembles that watch. God has endowed it with power, life, and activity. Controlled by His law it worked well, and in harmony with His will. But sin deprived it of that control, and, while these powers and faculties remain, they run the wrong way, and destroy the delicate organism. If this condition lasted only for a moment, and the sinner were immediately restored to his original state, it could not lead to a positive evil. But sin lasts a *long* time; sixty centuries already. Its pernicious influence has its *effects;* a *secondary* disease after the *primary;* accumulations of sinful *dregs,* and increase of festering sores. The threads of our nature's woof pull awry. Everything wrenches itself out of joint. And, since this secondary *activity* continues unchecked, its pernicious working becomes more and more critical.

What causes a felon? A sliver in the finger slightly checks the circulation. But the blood continues to circulate, trying to overcome the obstacle. The additional pressure against the walls of the capillaries produces more friction, and raises the temperature. The surrounding tissue swells, the delicate blood-vessels contract, the friction increases, and the boil throbs. Although this is but the continued normal action of the circulation, yet it causes positive evil. There is a local congestion; poisonous matter inflames the healthy tissue, and the parts are thoroughly diseased.

And such is sin's course. The action of our powers continues, but in the wrong direction. This causes disorder and irregularities, which inflame our nature toward evil. This sinful inflammation creates unnatural and wicked deformations, which excite the tissues of the soul to a morbid growth, compared by Scripture to foul matter. And from this unholy marsh poisonous gases rise continually throughout our entire nature. Thus the whole economy is disordered. Having run away from the divine law without discipline, body and soul become unruly. Hence, incited by its own inherent action, it involves itself more deeply and runs farther away from God. As a train that is derailed destroys itself by its very speed, so does man, having left the *track of the divine law,* compass his own ruin by the inherent impetus and working. Nothing more is needed. Destruction results necessarily from the very life of our nature.

Hence the sinner is without knowledge, the feelings are perverted, the will is paralyzed, the imagination polluted, the desires are impure, and all his ways, tendencies, and outgoings are at once evil; not in our eyes, perhaps, but because everything fails to meet the demands of God, who wills that everything should meet Him at the terminus of the road, that is, to be with Him and in Him, making His glory the final end of all things.

And this makes many things sinful, unrighteous, and wicked that we consider fair and beautiful. Not our taste, but God's, decides what is right or wrong. He that wishes to know what that taste is, let him learn it from the law of God. That law is standard and plummet. But whatever the sinner seeks or desires to please God, he will not do this; for example, he may be perfectly willing to hang his coat on the wall and do it gracefully, but not on the nail that God has struck in the wall of our life; everywhere else, but not there. Thus everything in him becomes evil, his entire nature corrupt, incapable of any good, inclined to all evil, yea, prone to hate God and his neighbor. The deed may not be born, but the very inclination and desire are sin.

Like the Romish and some Lutheran theologians, Dr. Böhl denies this. He teaches that there was this desire in holy Adam and even in Christ; not indulged, but held in with bit and bridle—as though God had created man with this ravenous animal of desire in his heart, while He endowed him at the same time with the power to restrain it. To keep this desire in constant check would have been man's greatest excellence.

But this is not according to Scripture. Nothing shows that holy Adam had any desire for the things he saw. The possibility of desire was created only by the prohibition: "Of the tree of knowledge of good and evil thou shalt not eat." And even after that we do not discover a trace of desire in him. Such eager looking at the fruit was not witnessed until Satan had inwardly incited Eve *not to eat of the fruit,* but *through it to become like God.* This is the first desire awakened in man's heart, and that only after his eye was opened to see that the tree was good for food and pleasant to the eye.

In the righteous state Adam was filled with peace, harmony, and divine success; without a trace of the anxiety necessarily springing from the task of restraining a dangerous monster. And in the heavenly glory it will not be an endless desire to restrain desire, but a complete deliverance from desire; not the suction of a great deep in our bottomless heart, but all its depths filled with the love of God.

The commandment "Thou shalt not covet" is absolute. The Lord Jesus was a total stranger to covetousness. He never desired what God withheld. In Gethsemane's terrible denouement He desired, yet not to *receive* a gift, but to *retain* His own, that is, when under the curse not to be forsaken of His God.

14

Our Guilt*

Wherefore as by one man sin entered into the world, and death by sin; and so death passed upon all men, for that all have sinned—Romans 5:12.

Sin and guilt belong together, but may not be confounded or considered synonymous, any more than sanctification and righteousness. It is true guilt rests upon every sin, and in every sin there is guilt, yet the two must be kept distinct. There is a difference between the blaze and the blackened spot upon the wall caused by it; long after the blaze is out the spot remains. Even so with sin and guilt. Sin's red blaze blackens the soul, but long after sin is left behind, the black mark upon the soul continues.

Hence it is of the greatest importance that the difference between the two be clearly understood, especially since confounding sin and guilt must lead to confounding justification and sanctification, much to the injury of the earnestness of the Christian life.

If there were but one man on earth, he might sin against himself, but he could not be in debt to others. And if, in accordance with modern theology, there were no living God, but only an idea of good, he might sin against the idea of good, and be exceedingly bad, but he could not owe God anything.

* The Dutch word "*schuld,*" literally "debt," includes the ideas of *guilt* and of *indebtedness* in general—Trans.

Men owe God because He lives, exists, never departs, forever abides; and because from moment to moment they must transact business with Him. With men we open accounts at will, and the firms in town with which we do so we will owe, but those with which we do not deal we will never owe. Many apply this to God, under the mistaken notion that if they have no dealings with God they cannot owe Him anything and have nothing to do with Him. To them He is non-existing, how, then, could they be in debt to Him?

But He does exist. It is not left to our choice to have dealings with Him or not. No; in *all* our affairs, *at all times* and under *all* circumstances, we must deal and do deal with Him. There is no business transacted from which He is excluded. In all things whatever we do, He is the most interested. In all our dealings and enterprises He is the Preferred Creditor and Senior Partner, with whom we must settle the final account. We may bury ourselves in Sahara, or go down to the bottom of the ocean, but our account with Him never ceases. We can never get away from Him. Working with head, heart, or hand, we open an account with God; and while we can deceive other partners and withhold part of the accounts from them, He is omniscient, He knows the most secret items, He keeps account of the smallest fraction, charging it to us; and before we have begun our reckoning, He has already finished it and laid it before us.

Considering this, we realize what it is to be debtors to God; for while at every moment, under all circumstances, and in all transactions we are obliged to pay Him the whole profit, we never do it, at least not in full. Hence every act of head, heart, or hand creates an item of debt, which we withhold from Him through being either unwilling or unable to pay.

If God were not, or we were not related to Him, we would be *sinners,* but not *debtors.* If a few years ago the floods at Krakatoa had engulfed all Java, as was feared, would it not have canceled all our debts to Java firms? Or suppose that the Patriotic Party in China once more came into power, and the Emperor decreed to close the empire against all nations, so that during a whole lifetime it was impossible to settle business with Chinese firms. Would this not cancel all the debts owing to China? Hence if God should cease to be or dissolve every tie binding us to Him, all our debts would at once be obliterated. But this is impossible; the tie that binds us to Him cannot be broken. Our debt to

Him remains; we cannot cancel it; and our thinking that we can cancel it does not alter the fact.

God created us for Himself, and that creates our indebtedness to Him. If He had simply created us for the pleasure of creating us, as a boy blows soap bubbles for his entertainment, and for the rest did not care what became of us, there could be no debt. But He did create us for Himself, with the absolute charge, in all things, at every moment, and under all circumstances, to lay *life's gain* upon the alter of His name and glory. He does not allow us to live three days out of every ten for Him, and the rest for ourselves; in fact, He does not release us for a single day or moment. He demands the gain of our existence for His glory, unconditionally, *always* and *evermore.* He planned and created us for this. Thus He claims us. Hence, being our Lord and Ruler, He cannot forego the last farthing of life's gain; and since we *never* have rendered Him the tribute, we are *absolutely* His debtors.

What money is among men, *love* is to God. He says to you and me and every man: "As you thirst for gold, so do I thirst for love. I, your God, want your love, your whole heart's love. This is My due. This I claim. This debt I cannot cancel. Thou shalt love the Lord thy God with all thy heart, with all thy mind, and with all thy strength." The fact that we do not render Him this love, or render it unholily and fraudulently, makes us His debtors perpetually.

We know that this is called the *juridical* conception; and that in these effeminate days men desire to escape from the tension of the right; wherefore the ethical conception is lauded to the skies. But this whole sentiment springs directly from a lie. This opposition against the juridical conception sets God at naught or ignores Him. Even without believing in God, one can dream of an *ideal* of holiness, according to the ethical conception, and strive against sin with inward thirst after holiness. But with only an *ideal* to incite him, there can be no room for right, no debt to God; for one cannot owe an ideal, but only a *living person.* But when I acknowledge the living God, and that always and in all things I have to do with Him, then He has righteous claims upon me which I have *violated,* and which must be satisfied. Hence the juridical conception comes *first.*

The ethical idea is: "I am sick; how can I become well?" The juridical idea is: "How can God's violated right be restored?" The latter is therefore of primary importance. The Christian must not first consider *himself,* but *God.* It wounds the very heart of the Reformed confession when the pulpit aims at sanctification without zeal for justification. Dr. Kohlbrugge's chief merit lay in this, that for God's sake he grieved over this neglect, and with powerful hand stemmed the tide of despising God's right, saying to church and individual: "Brethren, justification first."

To say, "Oh, if I were only holy, my indebtedness to God would not much trouble me," sounds very nice, but is deeply sinful. God's children desire to be holy as the children of vanity desire riches, honor, and glory—that is, it is always a desire for ourselves, our own ego, in ourselves to be what we are not. And the Lord God is left out. It is the Pelagian regulating his relation to God according to his own satisfaction. In fact it is sin, though gilded, against the first and highest commandment.

Surely the soul's deep longing after holiness is good and right, but only after the question is settled: "How can I be restored to my right position before God, whose rights I have violated?" If this is our chief concern, then and then only do we love the Lord our God more than ourselves. Then the prayer for holiness will follow as a matter of course; not from the selfish desire to be spiritually enriched, but from the soul's deep longing nevermore to violate the divine right.

This is deep and far-reaching, and many will deem it harsh. Yet we may not hold it back. The unmanly and sickly Christianity now vaunted is not that of the fathers and of the godly of all ages and of the apostles and prophets. The Lord *must* be First and Highest; instead of being honored, His law is dishonored when, in the pursuit of holiness, God's *right* is forgotten. Even among men it is called dishonest when, with debts unpaid, a man goes to America only to make his fortune; and we would say to him: "Honestly to pay your debts is more honorable than merely to be successful." And this applies here. God's child does not enter the kingdom with a cry for *success,* but *to balance his accounts with God.*

And this explains the difference between *sin* and *guilt.* A burglar repents and returns the stolen treasure. Is he now entitled to freedom? Surely not, but if he fall into the hands of the law, he shall be tried, sentenced, and suffer in prison the penalty of the violated right. Let us apply this to sin. There is a *law* and God is its *Author.* Measured by it, transgressions of omission and commission are called *sin.* But that is not all. The law is not a fetish, nor the formula of a moral ideal, but *God's commandment;* "God spake all these words." God stands behind that law, maintains it, and lays it before us. Hence it is not enough to measure our act by the law and call it *sin,* but it must also be accounted for to the Lawgiver and acknowledged to be *guilt.*

Sin is non-conformity of an act, person, or condition to the divine *law; guilt,* encroachment by act, person, or condition upon the divine *right.* Sin creates guilt, because God has a claim upon all our acts. If it were possible to act independently of God, such acts, though deviating from the moral ideal, would not create guilt. But since every man's act in every condition stands in account with God, every sin creates guilt. Yet they are not identical. Sin always lies *in us* and leaves our relation to God untouched, but guilt does *not* lie in us, but always refers to our *relation* to God. Sin shows what we are in our antagonism to the moral ideal, but guilt refers to God's claim upon us and to our denial of that claim.

If God were like a man, this guilt would be compromised. But He is not. His claims are as pure gold, perfectly right; not arbitrary, but based invariably upon a firm and unchangeable foundation. Hence nothing can be deducted from that guilt. According to the strictest measure the whole remains forever charged to us.

Hence the *punishment.* For punishment is but God's act of resisting the encroachment upon His rights. Such encroachments rob God, and would, if persisted in, detract from His divinity. And this cannot be if He be God indeed. Hence His majesty operates directly against this encroachment. And this constitutes punishment. Sin, guilt, and punishment are inseparable. Only because guilt pursues sin, and punishment prosecutes guilt, can sin exist in God's universe.

15

Our Unrighteousness

My Spirit shall not always strive with man—Genesis 6:3.

Before discussing the work of the Holy Spirit in the sinner's restoration, let us consider the interesting but much-neglected question whether man stood in fellowship with the Holy Spirit *before the fall.*

If it is true that the original Adam returns in the regenerated man, it follows that the Holy Spirit must have dwelt in Adam as He now dwells in God's children. But this is not so. God's word teaches the following differences between the two:

1. Adam's treasure was *losable,* and that of God's children *un*losable.

2. The former was to obtain eternal life, while the latter already possess it.

3. Adam stood under the Covenant of *Works,* and the regenerated under the Covenant of *Grace.*

These differences are essential, and indicate a difference of *status.* Adam did not belong to the ungodly that are justified, but was sinlessly just. He did not live by an extraneous righteousness which is by faith, as the regenerated, but shone with an original righteousness truly his own. He lived under the law which says: "Do this and thou shalt live; if not, thou shalt die."

Hence Adam had no other faith than that which comes by "natural disposition." He did not live out of a righteousness which is *by faith,* but out of an *original* righteousness. The cloud of witnesses in Hebrews 11 does not begin with sinless Adam, but with Abel before he was slain.

If *every* right relation of the soul is one of faith, then original righteousness necessarily included faith. But this is not Scriptural. St. Paul teaches that faith is a temporary grace, which finally enters that higher and more intimate fellowship called "sight." Faith as a means of salvation is in Scripture always faith in Christ not as the Son of God, the Second Person in the Trinity, but as *Redeemer, Savior,* and *Surety*—in short, faith in Christ and *Him crucified.* And since "Christ and Him crucified" does not belong to unfallen man, it is incorrect to place Adam in line with the justified sinner as regards faith. Even in the state of righteousness Adam did not live in Christ; for Christ is only a *sinner's* Savior, and not a sphere or element in which man lives as *man.* In the absence of sin, Scripture knows no Christ; and St. Paul teaches that, when all the consequences of sin shall have ceased, Christ shall deliver the kingdom to the Father, that God may be all in all.

Hence Adam and the regenerate are not the same. The difference between their status is most obvious in the fact that out of Christ the latter lies in the midst of death, having no life in himself, as St. Paul says, "Yet not I, but Christ who liveth in me, who loved me and gave Himself for me"; while Adam had a natural righteousness *in himself.*

The fathers have always strongly emphasized this point. They taught that Adam's original righteousness was not accidental, supernatural, added to his nature, but inherent *in his nature;* not another's righteousness imputed to him and appropriated by faith, but a righteousness naturally his own. Wherefore Adam needed no substitute; he stood for himself in the nature of his own being. Hence his status was the opposite of that which constitutes for the child of God the glory of his faith.

Teachers of another doctrine are moved, consciously or unconsciously, by philosophic motives. The Ethical theory says: "Properly speaking, our salvation is not in the *cross,* but in Christ's *Person.* He was God and Man, hence divine-human; and this divine-human nature is communicable. This being imparted to us, our nature becomes superior in kind, and thus we become the children of God." This is a denial of the way of faith, and a rejection of the cross and of the whole doctrine of Scripture—a fearful error indeed. Its conclusion is: "First, even in sin's absence the Son of God would have become man; second, of course sinless Adam lived in the God-man."

Without assenting to these errors, others imprudently teach that sinless Adam lived by the righteousness of Christ. Let them be careful of the consequences. Scripture allows no theories which obliterate the difference between the Covenant of Works and that of Grace.

But maintaining the approved doctrine of Adam's original righteousness as *inherent in his nature,* and of the divine image as being *increated,* the important question arises: Was the fellowship of the Holy Spirit enjoyed by Adam the same as that now possessed by the newborn soul?

The answer depends upon one's opinion concerning the nature of the original righteousness. Adam's righteousness was intrinsic. He stood before God as man ought to stand. He lacked nothing but *debt.* He rendered the Lord all that he owed momentarily; for how long is unimportant. One second is long enough to lose one's soul forever, and equally long enough to get into the right position before God. Hence Adam possessed a perfect good; for righteousness implies holiness, and both are perfect. Even the least unholiness would have created an immediate deficiency in Adam's returns to God. And when that unholiness became a fact, that righteousness was immediately damaged, rent, and broken; the least unholiness causes all at once the loss of *all* righteousness. Righteousness has no degrees. That which is not perfectly straight is *crooked.* Right and perfectly right are exactly the same. Not perfectly right is *not* right.

The question *"How Adam was perfectly good"* received clearest light from the conflict of the Lutherans Flacius Illiricus and Victorinus Strigel. The former maintained that man was essentially righteous.

One's opinion of sin necessarily depends upon his view of *goodness,* and vice versa. A realistic nature is inclined to conceive of sin and goodness as material; sin in his opinion is a sort of invisible bacterium, almost perceptible by a powerful microscope. And virtue, goodness, and holiness have equally a tangible, independent existence, measurable and apportionable. This is not so. We may compare the spiritual to the material. What else is symbolism? The Scripture sets the example, comparing sin to a running sore, to a fire, etc.; and goodness to drops of water quenching thirst, becoming a fountain of living water in the soul. Let symbolism retain its honorable place in this respect. But symbolism is the comparison of things *dis*similar, hence their identity is *excluded.* Sin is *not* something substantial, hence virtue and goodness are not essentially independent.

And yet Flacius Illiricus felt that in this respect there was a difference between sin and virtue. Evil is unsubstantial, because it is the lack, the default of goodness. But goodness is not the lack, the default of evil. Loss indicates that which ought to be, but which is lacking. Evil never ought to be, hence never can be a lack. But regarding goodness the question is different, viz., whether goodness as an extraneous and independent element was added to the soul, so that it might be said, "Here is the soul, and there is goodness." And this cannot be. As a ray is unthinkable without light, so is goodness without a person from whom it proceeds.

And this tempted Flacius Illiricus to teach that originally man was *essentially* righteous. Of course he was wrong. What he wanted to attribute to man can be attributed to God alone. Goodness is goodness. God is goodness. Goodness is God. In God being and goodness are one. There is and can be no difference between the two, for God is perfectly good in all respects; hence the faintest separation between God and goodness is utterly unthinkable.

God alone is a simple Being; not as Professor Doedes interprets in his criticism on the Confession, as though in God there can be no distinction in *persons,* but that in God there can be no distinction of *essence,* as between Himself and His attributes. But this is not so in man. We are not simple, and cannot be, in the same sense. On the contrary, our being remains, though all our attributes are changed or modified. A man can be good and ought to be, but without goodness he remains a man; his nature becomes corrupt, but his being remains the same.

Man's being is either deceitful or truthful, not because his soul is inoculated with the matter of falsehood or of truth, but by a modification of *the quality* of his being. Inherent goodness has no reference to our *being,* but only to the *manner* of its existence. As a joyous or sorrowful expression of countenance is not the result of an external application, but of inward joy or sorrow, so is the soul either good or bad according to the manner of its standing before God.

And this goodness was Adam's direct inheritance from God. God alone is the overflowing Fountain of all grace; Adam never wrought a particle of good of himself on the ground of which he might have claimed a reward. Eternal life was promised him not as a prize or inherent element, but by virtue of the conditions of the covenant of works. Just as strongly as we oppose the application to sinless Adam of the conditions of the Covenant of Grace, as though he lived in Christ, so strongly do we oppose the representation that any virtue, holiness, or righteousness proceeded from Adam not wrought by God in him. To deny this would make sinless Adam a *little fountain of some good,* and oppose the confession that God alone is the Fountain of *all* good.

Hence we arrive at this conclusion, that in Adam all goodness was wrought by the *Holy Spirit,* according to the holy ordinance which assigns to the Third Person in the Trinity the inward operation of all rational beings.

However, this does not imply that before the fall the Holy Spirit *dwelt* in Adam as in His temple, as He does in the regenerated child of God. In the latter He can only *dwell,* since the human nature is corrupt and unfit to be His *vehicle.* But not so with Adam. His nature was created and calculated to be a *vehicle* of the Holy Spirit's operations. Hence Adam and the regenerated are similar in this respect, that in both there is no goodness not wrought by the Holy Spirit, but dissimilar, in that the latter can offer only his sinful heart for the Holy Spirit's *indwelling,* while Adam's being underwent His operations without His indwelling, organically and *naturally.*

16

Our Death

You who were dead in trespasses and sin—Ephesians 2:1.

Next in order comes the discussion of *death.* There is *sin,* which is deviation from and resistance against the *law.* There is *guilt,* which is withholding from God that which, as the Giver and Upholder of that law, is due to Him. But there is also *punishment,* which is the Lawgiver's act of upholding His law against the lawbreaker. The Sacred Scripture calls this punishment "death."

To understand what death is, we must first ask: *"What is life?"*

And the answer in its most general form is: "A thing lives if it moves from within." A man found in the street, leaning against a wall, perfectly motionless, is supposed to be dead, but if he turns his head, or moves his hand, we know that he is alive. The motion, though almost imperceptible and so feeble that it requires the practiced fingers of the physician to detect it, is always the sign of life. The muscles may be paralyzed, tendons and sinews rigid, yet so long as the pulse beats, the heart throbs, and the lungs inhale the air, life is not extinct. In the doubtful cases of drowning, trance, or paralysis, the doubt is not removed, if removed at all, until motion has been observed. Hence we may safely say a body lives if it moves from within.

This cannot be said of a clock, for its mechanism lacks inherent, self-moving power. By winding, energy may be stored in its mainspring, but when this is spent the clock stops. But life is not a force added to a prepared organism, mechanically and temporarily, but an energy that inheres in the organism as an organic principle.

Hence it is plain that the human body has no vital principle in itself, but receives it from the soul. The arm is motionless until moved by the soul. Even the functions of circulation, breathing, and digesting are animated by the soul; for when the soul leaves the body all these functions stop. A body without a soul is a corpse. As physical life depends upon the union of body and soul, so is physical death the result of the dissolution of that bond. As in the beginning God formed the human body out of the dust of the earth and breathed into its nostrils the breath of life, so that it became a living being, so is the dissolving of that bond, which is death to the body, an act of God. Death is therefore the removal of that wonderful gift, the bond of life. God withdraws the forfeited blessing, and the soul departs in separate disembodiment; while the body, freed as a corpse, is delivered unto corruption.

But this does not finish the process of death. Life and death are awful opposites, embracing body and soul. "Dying thou shalt die" is the divine sentence, which includes the entire person, and not the body only. That which possesses creaturely life can also die as a creature. Hence the soul, being a creature, can be dispossessed of its creaturely life.

We admit that in another aspect the soul is immortal, but to prevent confusion, we beg the reader to put this fact for a moment out of his mind. Presently we will return to it.

Applying our definition of life to the soul as a living creature, it follows that the soul lives only when it moves, when acts proceed from it, and energies work in it. But its vital principle is not inherent any more than in the body, but comes from without. Originally it was not self-existing, but God gave it an increated vital principle and moving power which He sustained and qualified for work from moment to moment. In this respect Adam differed from us. It is true that in the soul of the regenerated there is a vital principle, but the source of its energy is outside of ourselves in Christ. There is *indwelling*, but not *interpermeation*. The dweller and his house are distinct. Hence in the regenerated man life is extraneous, its seat is not in himself. But not so in Adam. Although the life-principle energizing the soul proceeded from God, yet it was deposited in Adam himself.

To obtain gas from the city's gas-works is one thing; to manufacture it at one's own cost, in one's own establishment, is quite another. The regenerated child of God receives life directly from Christ, who is outside of Him at the right hand of God, through the channels of faith, but Adam had the principle of life within him from the Fountain of all Good. The Holy Spirit had placed it in his soul, and kept it in active operation, not as something extraneous, but as inherent in and peculiar to his nature.

If Adam's life originated in the union which God had established between his soul and the life-principle of the Holy Spirit, it follows that Adam's death resulted from God's act of dissolving that union whereby his soul became a corpse.

But this is not all. When the body dies it does not disappear; the process of death does not stop there. As a unit it becomes incapable of organic action, but its constituent parts become capable of producing terrible and corrupting effects. Left unburied in a house, the poisonous gases of dissolution breed malignant fevers and cause death to the inhabitants and the community. After this dissolution of flesh and blood, which cannot inherit the kingdom of God, the body as such continues to exist, with the possibility of being reanimated and refashioned into a more glorious body, and of being reunited with the soul.

All this can almost literally be applied to the soul. When a soul dies, that is, is severed from its life-principle, which is the Holy Spirit, it becomes perfectly motionless and unable to perform any good work. Some things may remain, like loveliness upon the face of the dead; yet, however lovely, it is useless and unprofitable. And as a dead body is incapable of any act and inclined to all dissolution, so is a dead soul incapable of any good and inclined to all evil.

But this does not imply that a dead soul is devoid of all activity, any more than a dead body. As the latter contains blood, carbon, and lime, so does the former possess will, feeling, intelligence, and imagination. And these elements of a dead soul become equally active with still more terrible effects, which are sometimes fearful to behold. But as the dead body by all its activities can never produce anything to restore its organism, so can the dead soul by all its workings accomplish nothing to restore a harmonious utterance before God. All its utterances are sinful, even as the dead body emits only offensive odors.

Yea, the parallel goes still further. A corpse may be embalmed, stuffed with herbs, and encased as a mummy. Its corruption is invisible, all unsightliness carefully concealed. So do many men embalm the dead soul, fill it with fragrant herbs, and wrap it like a mummy in a shroud of self-righteousness, so that of the indwelling corruption scarcely anything appears. But as the Egyptians by their embalming never could restore life unto their dead, so can these soul-mummies with all their Egyptian arts never kindle one spark of life in their dead souls.

A dead soul is not annihilated, but continues to exist, and by divine grace can be reanimated to a new life. It continues to exist even more powerfully than the body. The latter is divisible, but the soul is not. Being a unit it cannot be divided. Hence soul-death is not followed by soul-dissolution. It is the poisonous working of the soul-elements after death that causes a terrible strain, creating in the indivisible soul a vehement desire for dissolution; friction and confusion of elements that cry for harmony and peace; violent excitement kindling unholy fires, but there is no *dissolution.* Therefore the soul is called *immortal,* that is, it cannot be divided nor annihilated. It becomes a corpse insusceptible of dissolution, in which the poisonous gases will continue their pestilential work in hell forever.

But the soul is also susceptible of new quickening and animation; dead in trespasses and sin, severed from the life-principle, its organism motionless, incapable, and unprofitable, corrupt and undone, but—still a human soul. And God, who is merciful and gracious, can reestablish the broken bond. The interrupted communion with the Holy Spirit can be restored, like the broken fellowship of body and soul.

And this quickening of the dead soul is regeneration.

We close this section with one more remark: The breaking of the bond which causes death is not always sudden. Death from paralysis is almost instantaneous, from consumption slow. When Adam had sinned, death came at once, but so far as the body was concerned, its complete severing from the soul required more than nine hundred years. But the soul died at once, died suddenly; the bond with the Holy Spirit was severed, and only its raveling threads remain active in the feelings of *shame.*

When we say that soul-death may be less pronounced in one case than in another, we do not mean to imply that while the one is dead the other is only dying. Nay, both are dead, the soul of each is a corpse, but the one is embalmed as a mummy, and the other is in the process of dissolution; or, the conflicting, poisonous, and destructive workings in the soul of the one have just commenced, while in the other they were stimulated and developed by education and other agencies. These differences among different persons depend upon the divine grace.

Dissolution in a body at the North Pole is checked; in a body under the Equator it is rapidly accomplished. In like manner dead souls are placed in different atmospheres. Hence the differences.

Third Chapter
Preparatory Grace

17

What Is It?

We know that we have passed from death unto life, because we love the brethren. He that loveth not his brother abideth in death—1 John 3:14.

It is unnecessary to say that the scope of these discussions does not include the redemptive work as a whole, which in its choicest sense is not of the Holy Spirit alone, but of the Triune God whose royal majesty shines and sparkles in it with excellent glory. It includes not only the work of the Holy Spirit, but even more that of the Father and of the Son. And in these three we see the triune activity of the tender mercies of the Triune God. These discussions treat only that part of the work which reveals the operation of the Holy Spirit.

The first question in order is that of the so-called "preparatory grace." This is a question of surpassing importance, since Methodism* neglects it and modern orthodoxy abuses it, in order to make the determining choice in the work of grace once more to depend upon man's free will.

Regarding the principal point, it must be conceded that there is a *"gratia praeparans,"* as our old theologians used to call it, that is, a preparatory

* See the author's explanation of Methodism, section 5 of the Preface.

grace; not a preparation of grace, but a grace which prepares, which is in its preparatory workings real grace, undoubted and unadulterated. The Church has always maintained this confession by its soundest interpreters and noblest confessors. It could not surrender it as long as God is indeed eternal, unchangeable, and omnipresent, but by it must forcibly protest against the untrue representation that God lets a man be born and live for years unnoticed and independent of Himself, suddenly to convert him at the moment of His pleasure, from that hour to make him the object of His care and keeping.

Though it cannot be denied that the sinner shared this delusion—because as he cared not for God, why then should God care for him?—yet the Church may not encourage him in this ungodly idea. For it belittles the divine virtues, glories, and attributes. Heretics of every name and origin have made the soul's salvation their chief study, but almost always have neglected the *knowledge of God.* And yet every creed begins with: "I believe in God the Father Almighty, Creator of heaven and earth"; and the value of all that follows concerning Christ and our redemption depends only upon the correct interpretation of that first article. Hence the Church has always insisted upon a pure and correct knowledge of God in every confession and in every part of the redemptive work; and has considered it its principal duty and privilege to guard the purity of this knowledge. Even a soul's salvation should not be desired at the expense of the slightest injury to the purity of that confession.

Regarding the work of preparatory grace, it was before all things necessary to examine whether the knowledge of God had been retained in its purity, or whether to favor the sinner it had been distorted and twisted. And tested by this, it cannot be denied that God's care for His elect does not begin at an arbitrary moment, but is interwoven with their whole existence, including their conception, and even before their conception, with the mysteries of that redeeming love which declares: "I have loved thee with an everlasting love." Hence it is unthinkable that God should have left a sinner to himself for years, to arrest him at a certain moment in the midst of his life.

Nay, if God is to remain *God* and His omnipresent power unlimited, a sinner's salvation must be an *eternal* work, embracing his entire existence—a work whose roots are hidden in the unseen foundations of the wondrous mercies which extend far beyond his conception. It cannot be denied that a man, converted at twenty-five, was during his godless life the subject of the divine labor, care, and protection; that in his conception and before his birth God's hand held him and brought him forth; yea, that even in the divine counsel the work must be traced which God has wrought for him long before his conversion.

The confession of election and foreordination is essentially the recognition of a grace active long before the hour of conversion. The idea that from eternity God had recorded a mere arbitrary name or figure, to quicken it only after many centuries, is truly ungodly. Nay, God's elect never stood before His eternal vision as mere names or figures, but every soul elect is also foreordained to stand before Him in his complete development, the object in Christ of God's *eternal* pleasure.

Christ's sacrifice on Calvary, which satisfies for the elect, justifying them by His Resurrection, was not accomplished independently of the elect, but included them all. The resurrection is a work of the divine omnipotence, in which God brings back from the dead not only Christ *without* His own, but Christ *with* His own. Hence every saint with clear spiritual vision confesses that His heavenly Father performs in him an eternal work, not begun only in his conversion, but wrought in the eternal counsel through the periods of old and new covenants; in his person all the days of his life, and which will work in him throughout eternity. Even in this general sense the Church may not neglect to confess preparatory grace.

However, the question is narrowed when, excluding what precedes our birth, we consider only our sinful life before conversion, or the years intervening between the age of discretion and the hour when the scales fell from our eyes.

During those years we departed from God, instead of coming more closely to Him. Sin broke out more violently in one than in another, but there was iniquity in us all. As often as the plummet was let down beside our souls, they appeared out of the perpendicular. And during this *sinful period,* many hold that *preparatory grace* is *out of the question.* They say, "Where sin is, there can be no grace"; hence during those years the Lord leaves the sinner to himself, to return to him when sin's bitter fruit shall be ripe enough to move him to faith and repentance. They deny not God's gracious election and foreordination, neither His care for His elect in their birth, but they do deny His preparatory grace during the years of alienation, and believe that His grace begins to operate only when it breaks forth in their conversion.

Of course there is some truth in this; there is such a thing as the abandoning of the sinner to iniquity, when God lets a man walk in his own ways, giving him up unto vile passions to do things that are unseemly. But instead of interrupting God's labor upon such a soul, the very words of Scripture, "to give them up," "to give them over" (Rom. 1:24, 28), show that this drifting away upon the current of sin is not without God's notice. Men have confessed that, if inward sin had not revealed itself, breaking forth in its fury, they would never have discovered the inward corruption nor have cried to God for mercy. The realization of their guilt and the remembrance of their fearful past have been to many saints powerful incitements to labor with strong hands and pitying hearts for the rescue of those hopelessly lost in the same deadly waters from which they had been saved. The remembrance of the deep corruption from which they are now delivered has been to many the most potent safeguard from fancied self-righteousness, proud bearing, and the conceit of being holier than others. Many depths of reconciliation and grace have been discovered and sounded only by hearts so deeply wounded that, for the covering of their guilt, a mere superficial confession of the atoning blood could not suffice. How deeply did David fall; and who ever shouted from mercy's depths more jubilantly than he? Who impressed the Church's pure confession more profoundly than Augustine, incomparable among the Church fathers, who from the abyss of his own guilt and inward brokenness had learned to gaze upon the firmament of God's eternal mercies. Even from this extreme view of man's sinful way it cannot be affirmed that in that way God's grace was suspended. Light and shadow are here necessarily blended.

And this is not all. Even though by sin we have forfeited all, and the sinful ego, however virtuous outwardly, has tinctured every action of life with sin, yet this is not all of life. In the midst of it all, life was shaped and developed. The sinner of five-and-twenty differs from the child of three, who by his ugly temper plainly showed his sinful nature. During all those years the child has become a man. That which slumbered in him has gradually manifested itself. Influences have wrought upon him. Knowledge has been mastered and increased. Talents have been awakened and developed. Memory and remembrance have accumulated treasures of experience. However sinful the form, the character has become settled and some of its traits have adopted definite lines. The child has become a man—a person, living, existing, and thinking differently from other persons. And in all this, so confesses the Church, was the hand of the Omnipresent and Almighty God. It is He who during all these years of resistance has guided and directed His creature according to His own purpose.

Sooner or later the Sun of Grace will rise upon him, and, since much depends upon the condition in which grace shall find him, it is the Lord God Himself who prepares that condition. He prepares it by graciously restraining his character from adopting traits which would prevent him later on from running his course in the kingdom of God, and, on the other hand, by graciously developing in him such character and such features as will appear after his conversion adapted to the task which God intended for him.

And so it is evident that even during the time of alienation God bestows grace upon His elect. Afterward he will perceive how evidently all things have worked together for good, not because he intended it so, but in spite of his sinful intentions, and only because the protecting grace of God was working in and by and through it all. His course might have been altogether different. That it is as it is, and not much worse, he owes not to himself, but to higher favor. Hence, reviewing his life's dark background, the saint thinks at first that it contains but a night of Satanic darkness; later on, being better instructed, he perceives through that darkness a faint glimmer of divine love.

In fact, in his life there are three distinct periods of thankfulness:

First, immediately after his conversion, when he can think of no other reason of thankfulness than the *newly found grace.*

Second, when he learns to render thanks also for the grace of his *eternal election,* extending far behind the first grace.

Lastly, when the darkness between election and conversion being dispelled, he thanks God for the *preparatory grace* which in the midst of that darkness watched over his soul.

18

What It Is Not

We are His workmanship—Ephesians 2:10.

In the preceding article we contended that there is preparatory grace. In opposition to the contemporary deism of the Methodists,* the Reformed churches ought to confess this excellent truth in all its length and breadth. But it should not be abused to reestablish the sinner's free will, as the Pelagians did, and the Arminians after them, and as the Ethicals do now, though differently.

The Methodist* errs in saying that God does not care for the sinner until He suddenly arrests him in his sinful way. Nor may we tolerate the opposite error, the denial of regeneration, the new starting-point in the life of the sinner, which would make the whole work of conversion but an *awakening* of *dormant* and suppressed energies. There is no gradual transition; conversion is not merely the healing of disease, or an uprising of what had been suppressed; least of all, the arousing of dormant energies.

As regards his first birth, the child of God was *dead,* and can be brought to life only by a second *birth* as real as the first. Generally the person so favored is not conscious of it. In the nature of the case, man is unconscious until the time of his conversion; and that may be ten or twenty years.

---

* See section 5 in Preface.

The grounds upon which the Church confesses that a large majority of men are born again *before* holy Baptism are *many* indeed; wherefore, in Baptism, it addresses the infants of believers as being regenerate.

And what do the Semi-Pelagians of all times and shades, and the Ethicals of the present time, teach concerning this? They lower the first act of God in the sinners to a sort of preparatory grace, imparted not only to the elect, but to all baptized persons. They represent it as follows:

First, all men are conceived and born in sin; and if God did not take the first step, all would perish.

Second, He imparts to the children born in the Christian Church a sort of assisting grace, relieving inability.

Third, hence every baptized person has the power to choose or reject the offered grace.

Fourth, wherefore, out of the many who received preparatory grace, some choose life and others perish.

And this is the confession not of Augustine, but of Pelagius; not of Calvin, but of Castellio; not of Gomarus, but of Arminius; not of the Reformed churches, but of the sects which they have condemned as heretical.

This impious lie, which pervades this whole representation, must be eradicated; and the Methodist brethren deserve our strongest support when with holy enthusiasm they oppose this false system. If this representation be true, then the counsel of God has lost its certainty and steadfastness; then the Mediator's redemptive work is uncertain in its application; then our passing from death unto life depends in the end upon our own will; and the child of God is robbed of all his comfort in life and death, since his new life may be lost.

It does not avail the Ethical theologians when under many beautiful forms they confess their belief in an eternal election, and that grace cannot be lost, and in the perseverance of saints. As long as they do not purge themselves of their principal error—viz., that in Baptism God relieves the inability of the sinner that he can choose life of himself—they do not stand on the basis of the Reformed churches, but are directly opposed to it. Nor will they be counted as children of the Reformed household of faith until, without any subterfuge, they confess definitely that preparatory grace does not operate at all, except upon persons who will surely come to life, and who will never be lost again.

To suppose that this grace can work in a man without saving him to the *uttermost* is to break with the doctrine of Scripture and to turn the back upon a vital feature of the Reformed churches. We do not deny that many persons are lost in whom many excellent powers have wrought. The apostle teaches this very clearly in Hebrews 6: "They may have tasted of the heavenly gift." But between God's work upon *them* and that in His *elect* is a great gulf. The workings in these non-elect have *nothing* in common with saving grace; hence preparatory grace, as well as saving grace, is altogether out of the question. Surely there is preparatory grace, but only for the elect who will certainly come to life, and who being once quickened will remain so. The fatal doctrine of three conditions—viz., that (1) of the spiritually *dead,* (2) of the spiritually *living,* and (3) of men hovering *between life and death*—must be abandoned. The spread of this doctrine in our churches will surely destroy their spiritual character, as it has done in the ancient Huguenot churches of France. Life and death are absolute opposites, and a third state between them is unthinkable. He that is scarcely alive belongs to the living; and he that has just died belongs to the dead. One apparently dead is living, and he that is apparently living is dead. The boundary-line is a hair's breadth, and a state between does not exist. This applies to the spiritual condition. One *lives,* although he has received no more than the vital germ, and still wanders unconverted in the ways of sin. And he is *dead,* though tasting the heavenly gift, so long as life is not rekindled in his soul. Every other representation is false.

Others advance the view that preparatory grace prepares not for the reception of life, but for *conversion.* And this is just as pernicious. For then the soul's salvation depends not upon regeneration, but upon conversion; and this makes the salvation of our deceased infants impossible. Nay, standing by the graves of our baptized young children, confident of their salvation through the one Name given under heaven, we reject the teaching that salvation depends upon conversion, but confess that it is effected by the divine act of creating in us a new life, which sooner or later manifests itself in conversion.

Preparatory grace always precedes the new life; hence it ceases even before holy Baptism, in infants quickened before being baptized. Hence in a more limited sense, preparatory grace operates only in persons quickened later on in life, shortly before conversion. For the sinner once quickened has received grace, that is, the germ of all grace; and that which exists cannot be prepared.

A third error, on this point, is the representation that certain moods and dispositions must be prepared in the sinner before God can quicken him; as though quickening grace were conditioned upon preparatory grace. The salvation of our deceased infants opposes this also. There were no moods or dispositions in them; yet no theologian will say that they are lost, or that they are saved by another name than the One in whom adults find salvation. No; the sinner needs nothing whatever to predispose him for the implanting of the new life; and, though he were the most hardened sinner, devoid of every predisposition, God is able at His own time to quicken him. The omnipotence of divine grace is unlimited.

The implanting of the new life is not a *moral,* but a *metaphysical* act of God—that is, He does not effect it by admonishing the sinner, but independently of his will and consciousness; yet despite his will, He plants something in him whereby his nature obtains another quality.

Even the representation, still maintained by some of our best theologians, that preparatory grace is like the drying of wet wood, so that the spark can more readily ignite it, we cannot adopt. Wet wood will not take the spark. It *must* be dried before it *can* be kindled. And this does not apply to the work of grace. The disposition of our souls is immaterial. Whatever it may be, omnipotent grace can kindle it. And, though we do not undervalue dispositions, yet we do not concede to them the potentiality of kindling.

For this reason the theologians of the flourishing period of our churches insisted that preparatory grace should not be treated loosely, but in the following order: "The grace of God first *precedes,* then *prepares,* and lastly *performs (praeveniens, praeparans, operans)—i.e.,* grace is always first, never waits for anything *in us,* but begins its work before there is anything *in us.* Second, the time before our quickening is not wasted, but during it grace prepares us for our lifework in the kingdom. Third, at the appointed time grace alone quickens us unaided;

hence, grace is the *operans,* the real worker. Hence preparatory grace must never be understood as a means to prepare for the impartation of life. Nothing prepares for such quickening. Life is enkindled, wholly unprepared, not from anything in us, but entirely by the working of God. All that preparatory grace accomplishes is this, that God by it so disposes our life, arranges its course, and directs our development that being quickened by His exclusive act, we shall possess the disposition required for the task assigned to us in the kingdom.

Our person is like the field wherein the sower is to scatter the seed. Suppose there are two fields in which the seed must be sown; the one has been plowed, fertilized, harrowed, and cleared of stones, while the other lies fallow, uncared for. What is the result? Does the former produce wheat of itself? By no means; though the furrows were never so deep and the ground never so rich and smooth, if it receives no seed-grain it will never yield a single ear. And the other, not cultivated, will surely germinate the seed scattered therein. The *origin* of the wheat sown has no connection with the cultivation of the field, since the seed-grain is conveyed thither from *elsewhere.* But to the growth of the wheat, cultivation is of greatest importance. And so it is in the spiritual kingdom. Whether great or small, preparatory grace contributes nothing to the origin of life, which springs from the "incorruptible seed" sown in the heart. But to its *development* it is of greatest importance.

This is why the Reformed churches so strongly insist upon the careful training of our children. For, although we confess that all our training cannot create the least spark of heavenly fire, yet we know that when God puts that spark into their hearts, kindling the new life, much will depend upon the condition in which it finds them.

Fourth Chapter
Regeneration

19

Old and New Terminology

That which is born of the flesh is flesh—John 3:6.

Before we examine the work of the Holy Spirit in this important matter, we must first *define the use of words.*

The word *"regeneration"* is used in a limited sense, and in a more extended sense.

It is used in the *limited* sense when it denotes exclusively God's act of *quickening,* which is the first divine act whereby God translates us from death into life, from the kingdom of darkness into the kingdom of His dear Son. In this sense regeneration is the *starting-point.* God comes to one born in iniquity and dead in trespasses and sins, and plants the principle of a new spiritual life in his soul. Hence he is born again.

But this is not the interpretation of the Confession of Faith, for article 24 reads: "We believe that this true faith, being wrought in man by the hearing of the Word of God and the operation of the Holy Ghost, doth regenerate and make him a new man, causing him to live a new life, and freeing him from the bondage of sin." Here the word *"regeneration,"* used in its *wider* sense, denotes the *entire* change by grace effected in our persons, ending in our dying to sin in death and our being born for heaven. While formerly this was the usual sense of the word, we are accustomed now to the limited sense, which we therefore adopt in this discussion. Respecting the difference between the two—formerly the work of grace was generally represented as the soul *consciously* observed it; while now the work itself is described *apart from the consciousness.*

Of course, a child knows nothing of the genesis of his own existence, nor of the first period of his life, *from his own observation.* If he were to tell his history from his own recollections, he would begin with the time that he sat in his high chair, and proceed until as a man he went out into the world. But, being informed by others of his antecedents, he goes back of his recollections and speaks of his parents, family, time, and place of birth, how he grew up, etc. Hence there is quite a difference between the two accounts.

The same difference we observe in the subject before us. Formerly it was customary, after the manner of Romish scholastics, to describe one's experience from one's *own recollections.* Being personally ignorant of the implanting of the new life, and remembering only the great spiritual disturbance, which led one to faith and repentance, it was natural to date the beginning of the work of grace not from regeneration, but from the conviction of sin and faith, thence proceeding to sanctification, and so on.

But this *subjective* representation, more or less incomplete, cannot satisfy us now. It was to be expected that the supporters of "free will" would abuse it, by inferring that the origin and first activities of the work of salvation spring from man himself. A sinner, hearing the Word, is deeply impressed; persuaded by its threats and promises, he repents, arises, and accepts the Savior. Hence there is nothing more than a mere moral persuasion, obscuring the glorious origin of the new life. To resist this repulsive deforming of the truth, Maccovius, already in the days of the Synod of Dort, abandoned this more or less critical method to make regeneration the starting-point. He followed this order: "Knowledge of sin, redemption in Christ, regeneration, and only then faith." And this was consistent with the development of the Reformed doctrine. For as soon as the subjective method was abandoned, it became necessary in answer to the question, "What had God wrought in the soul?" to return to the *first implanting of life.* And then it became evident that God did not begin by leading the sinner to repentance, for repentance must be preceded by conviction of sin; nor by bringing him under the hearing of the word, for this requires an opened ear. Hence the first *conscious* and comparatively cooperative act of man is always *preceded* by the original act of God, planting in him the first principle of a new life, under which act man is wholly *passive* and *unconscious.*

This led to the distinction of the *first* and *second* grace. The former denoted God's work in the *sinner,* creating a new life without his knowledge; while the latter denoted the work wrought in *regenerate* man with his full knowledge and consent.

The first grace was naturally called regeneration. And yet there was no perfect unanimity in this respect. Some Scottish theologians put it in this way: "God began the work of grace with the implanting of the *faith-faculty (fides potentialis),* followed by the new grace of the *faith-exercise (fides actualis),* and of the *faith-power (fides habitualis).* Yet it is only an apparent difference. Whether I call the first activity of grace, the implanting of the *"faith-faculty,"* or the *"new principle of life,"* in both instances it means that the work of grace does not begin with faith or with repentance or contrition, but that these are preceded by God's act of giving power to the powerless, hearing to the deaf, and life to the dead.

For a correct idea of the entire work of grace in its different phases let us notice the following successive stages or milestones:

1. *The implanting of the new life-principle,* commonly called *regeneration* in the limited sense, or the implanting of the faith-*faculty.* This divine act is wrought in man at different ages; when, no one can tell. We know from the instance of John the Baptist that it can be wrought even in the mother's womb. And the salvation of deceased infants constrains us, with Voetius and all profound theologians, to believe that this original act may occur very early in life.

2. *The keeping of the implanted principle of life,* while the sinner still continues in sin, so far as his consciousness is concerned. Persons who received the life-principle early in life are no more dead, but they live. Dying before actual conversion, they are not lost, but saved. In early life they often manifest holy inclinations, sometimes truly marvelous. However, they have no conscious faith, nor knowledge of the treasure

possessed. The new life is present, but dormant; kept not by the recipient, but by the Giver—like seed-grain in the ground in winter; like the spark glowing under the ashes, but not kindling the wood; like a subterranean stream coming at last to the surface.

3. The *call* by the Word and the Spirit, *internal and external.* Even this is a divine act, commonly performed through the service of the Church. It addresses itself not to the deaf but to the hearing, not to the dead but to the living, although still slumbering. It proceeds from the Word and the Spirit, because not only the faith-*faculty,* but faith itself—that is, the *power* and *exercise* of the faculty—are gifts of grace. The faith-faculty cannot exercise faith of itself. It avails us no more than the faculty of breathing when air and the power to breathe are withheld. Hence the preaching of the Word and the inward working of the Holy Spirit are divine, correspondent operations. Under the preaching of the Word the Spirit energizes the faith-*faculty,* and thus the call becomes effectual, for the sleeper arises.

4. This call of God produces *conviction of sin and justification,* two acts of the same exercise of faith. In this, God's work may be represented again either subjectively or objectively. Subjectively, it seems to the saint that conviction of sin and heart-brokenness came first, and that then he obtained the sense of being justified by faith. Objectively, this is not so. The realization of his lost condition was already a bold act of faith. And by every subsequent act of faith he becomes more deeply convinced of his misery and receives more abundantly from the fullness which is in Christ, his Surety.

Concerning the question, whether conviction of sin must not precede faith, there need be no difference. Both representations amount to the same thing. When a man can say for the first time in his life "I believe," he is at the same moment *completely lost* and *completely saved,* being justified in his Lord.

5. This exercise of faith results in *conversion;* at this stage in the way of grace the child of God becomes clearly *conscious* of the implanted life. When a man says and feels "I believe," and does not recall it, but God confirms it, faith is at once followed by conversion. The implanting of the new life *precedes* the first act of faith, but conversion *follows* it. Conversion does not become a fact so long as the sinner only *sees* his lost condition, but when he *acts* upon this principle; for then the old

man begins to die and the new man begins to rise, and these are the two parts of all real conversion.

In principle man *is* converted but *once,* viz., the moment of yielding himself to Immanuel. After that he converts *himself daily,* that is, as often as he discovers conflict between his will and that of the Holy Spirit. And even this is not man's work, but the work of God in him. "Turn Thou me, O Lord, and I shall be turned." There is this difference, however, that in regeneration and faith's first exercise he was *passive,* while in conversion grace enabled him to be *active.* One is converted and one converts himself; the one is incomplete without the other.

6. Hence conversion merges itself in *sanctification.* This is also a divine act, and not human; not a growing toward Christ, but an absorbing of His life through the roots of faith. In children of twelve or thirteen deceased soon after conversion, sanctification does not appear. Yet they partake of it just as much as adults. Sanctification has a twofold meaning: *first, sanctification* which as Christ's finished work is given and imputed to all the elect; and *second, sanctification* which from Christ is gradually wrought in the converted and manifested according to times and circumstances. These are not *two* sanctifications, but *one;* just as we speak sometimes of the rain that accumulates in the clouds *above* and then comes down in drops on the thirsty fields *below.*

7. Sanctification is finished and closed in the *complete redemption* at the time of death. In the severing of body and soul divine grace completes the dying to sin. Hence in death a work of grace is performed which imparts to the work of regeneration its fullest unfolding. If until then, considering ourselves out of Christ, we are still lost in ourselves and lying in the midst of death, the article of death ends all this. Then faith is *turned into sight,* sin's excitement is disarmed, and we are forever beyond its reach.

Lastly, our *glorification* in the last day, when the inward bliss will be manifest in outward glory, and by an act of omnipotent grace the soul will be reunited with its glorified body, and be placed in such heavenly glory as becomes the state of perfect felicity.

This shows how the operations of grace are riveted together as the links of a chain. The work of grace must begin with *quickening* the *dead.* Once implanted, the still slumbering life must be awakened by the *call.* Thus awakened, man finds himself in a new life, that is, he knows himself *justified.* Being justified, he lets the new life result in *conversion.* Conversion flows into *sanctification.* Sanctification receives its keystone through the *severing of sin* in death. And in the last day, *glorification* completes the work of divine grace in our entire person.

Hence it follows that that which succeeds is contained in that which precedes. A regenerate deceased infant died to sin in death just as surely as the man with hoary head and fourscore years. There can be no first without including the second and last. Hence the entire work of grace might be represented as one *birth* for heaven, one continued *regeneration* to be completed in the last day.

Wherefore there may be persons ignorant of these stages, which are as indispensable as milestones to the surveyor, but they may never be made to oppress the souls of the simple. He who breathes deeply unconscious of his lungs is often the healthiest.

Touching the question whether the Scripture gives reference to this arrangement over the old, we refer to the word of Jesus: "Except a man be born of water and the Spirit he cannot *see* the kingdom of God"; from which we infer that Jesus dates every operation of grace from regeneration. First life, and then the activity of life.

20

Its Course

No man can come unto Me, except the Father draw him—*John 6:44.*

From the preceding it is evident that preparatory grace is different in different persons; and that distinction must be made between the many regenerated in the *first days of life,* and the few born again at a more *advanced age.*

Of course, we refer only to the elect. In the non-elect saving grace does not operate; hence preparatory grace is altogether out of the question. The former are born, with few exceptions, *in the Church.* They do not enter the covenant of grace later on in life, but they belong to it from the first moment of their existence. They spring from the seed of the Church, and in turn contain in themselves the seed of the future Church. And for this reason, the first germ of the new life is imparted to the seed of the Church (which is, alas! always mixed with much chaff) oftenest either before or soon after birth.

The Reformed Church was so firmly settled in this doctrine that she dared establish it as the prevailing rule, believing that the seed of the Church (not the chaff of course) received the germ of life even before Baptism; wherefore it is actually sanctified in Christ already; and receives in Baptism the seal not upon something that is yet *to come,* but upon that which is *already present.* Hence the liturgical question to the parents: "Do you acknowledge that, although your children are conceived and born in sin, and therefore are subject to condemnation itself, yet that they are sanctified in Christ, and therefore as members of His Church ought to be baptized?"

In subsequent periods, less steadfast in the faith, men have shunned this doctrine, not knowing what to make of the words "are sanctified." This they interpreted to mean that as children of members of the covenant they were *counted* as belonging to the covenant, and as such were entitled to baptism. But the earnest and sound common sense of our people has always felt that this mere "counting in" did not do justice to the full and rich meaning of the liturgy.

And if you should inquire into the meaning of these words of the office of Baptism, "are sanctified," not of the weaker epigones, but of the energetic generation of heroes who have victoriously fought the Lord's battles against Arminius and his followers, then you would discover that those godly and learned theologians, such as Gysbrecht Voetius for instance, never for a moment hesitated to break with these half-way explanations, but spoke out plainly, saying: "They are entitled to Baptism not because they are *counted* as members of the covenant, but because as a rule they actually already *possess* the first grace; and for this reason, and this reason alone, it reads: 'That *our* children *are sanctified* in Christ, and therefore *as members of His body* ought to be baptized.' "

By this confession the Reformed Church proved to be in accord with God's Word and not less with the actual facts. With few exceptions, persons who afterward prove to belong to the regenerate do not begin life with riotous outbreaks of sin. It is rather the rule that children of Christian parents manifest from early childhood a desire and taste for holy things, warm zeal for the name of God, and inward emotions that cannot be attributed to an evil nature.

Moreover, this glorious confession gave the right direction to the education of children in our Reformed families, largely retained to the present time. Our people did not see in their children offshoots of the wild vine, to be grafted perhaps later on, with whom little could be done until converted after the manner of Methodism;* but they lived in

* For the sense in which the author takes Methodism, see section 5 in the Preface.

the quiet expectation and holy confidence that the child to be trained was already grafted, and therefore worthy to be nursed with tenderest care. We admit that, latterly, since the Reformed character of our churches has been impaired by the National Church as a church for the masses, this gold has been sadly dimmed, but its original, vital thought was beautiful and animating. It made God's work of regeneration precede man's work; to Baptism it gave its rich development; and it made the work of education, not dependent on chance, cooperate with God.

Hence we recognize among the rising generation in the Church four classes:

1. All elect persons regenerated before Baptism, in whom the implanted life remains hidden until they are converted at a later age.
2. Elect persons, not only regenerated in infancy, but in whom the implanted life was early manifested and ripened imperceptibly into conversion.
3. Elect persons born again, and converted in later life.
4. The non-elect, or the chaff.

Examining each of these four, with special reference to preparatory grace, we arrive at the following conclusions:

Regarding the elect of the *first class,* from the very nature of the case preparatory grace has scarcely room here, in its limited sense. In its direct form, it is unthinkable with reference to an unborn or new-born child. In such it is only indirect—that is, frequently it pleases God to give such child parents whose persons and natures practice a form of sin less outspoken in its war upon grace than other forms of sin. Not as though such parents had anything from which the child could be grafted, for that which is born of the flesh is flesh; nothing clean from the unclean; it is always the wild vine waiting for the grafting of the Lord. Nay, the preparatory grace in this case appears from the fact that the child receives from its parents a form of life adapted to its heavenly calling.

The same applies to the elect of the *second class.* Although we concede that the divine call works upon such during their tender years, yet, while it prepares for conversion, it does not prepare for regeneration, which it follows. The call is ineffectual unless the faculty of hearing be first implanted. Only he that has an ear can hear what the Spirit saith unto the churches and to his own soul. Hence, in this case, preparatory grace is scarcely perceptible. Surely there are many agencies that imperceptibly prepare for his conversion, but this is different from a preparing for regeneration, and we speak now only of the latter.

Properly speaking, preparatory grace in its limited sense is applied only to the *third class* of elect persons. It comprehends their whole life with all its turns and changes, relations and connections, heights and depths, events and adversities. Not as though all these could produce the slightest germ of life or possibility of quickening. No; the germ of life can never spring from preparatory grace, any more than the preparation of ten cradles, of a dozen of clothes-baskets, and of closets full of expensive infant-garments can ever juggle a single infant into any of those cradles. The vital spark is produced only by an act of the mighty God, independent of all preparation. But, from its birth, God guards that wild vine and controls the growth of its wild shoots, so that in the hour of His pleasure, when He shall graft upon it the true vine, it may be all that it ought to be.

And this ends the discussion, for regarding the *fourth class,* by and by they will be separated from the wheat and blown away by the fan which is in His hand; hence preparatory grace is out of the question.

And from this it is evident that the proper work of the Holy Spirit regarding preparatory grace is scarcely perceptible.

Every feature of this work, so far presented, points directly not to the operation of the Holy Spirit, nor to that of the Son, but almost exclusively to that of the Father. For the circumstances of the child's birth—that is, the hereditary character of his family and more especially of his parents, and the future course of his life until the moment of his conversion—belong to the realm of the divine Providence. The appointed place of our habitation, our generation and family, the formation of our immediate environment, the influences previously determined to affect us—all belong to the leadings of God's providence, ascribed by Scripture to the work of the *Father.* The Lord Jesus said: "No man can come unto Me, except the Father draw him." And although this drawing of the Father has a higher aim and must be spiritually understood, yet it indicates generally that the determining of those things, which afterward regulates their direction and course, is attributed particularly to the First Person.

We notice a work of the Holy Spirit in this matter only as far as He animates all personal life, since He is the Spirit of Life; and as He cooperates with the Father in that special providence which refers to the elect. For, although in our mind we can analyze the work of grace, yet we may never forget that the eternal reality does not fully correspond to this part of our analysis.

Hence, in the elect, the work of providence and that of grace often flow together, being one and the same. Our Church has tried to express this, in her confession of a *general* providence which includes all things and all persons, and a *special* providence which works only in the lives of God's elect. When thus the operations of Providence adopt a special character regarding the elect but not yet regenerate persons, the Holy Spirit cooperates with the Father and the Son to carry out the counsels of God's will concerning them.

And this closes the discussion of preparatory grace, and we now proceed to discuss regeneration proper. We might speak of the grace that flows from regeneration and prepares the way for conversion, but this would *improperly* be called preparatory grace. All that which aims at the awakening of the life still slumbering in the regenerate soul is not preparatory grace, but belongs to the "call." And although we would not absolutely condemn the use of the word in that sense, yet neither would we encourage it by our own example.

Let us recapitulate. Physical life is the result of the union of body and soul; the dissolution of this union is physical death, which will be abolished only when body and soul are reunited. The same applies to things spiritual. Spiritual life results from a union between the soul and the life-principle of the Holy Spirit. Hence sin which annihilates this union causes death. This death cannot be overcome until it please the Lord to reunite the soul with the Spirit's life-principle.

Everything that precedes this reunion is *preparatory grace.* That which effects it is the *first grace—i.e., working grace, saving grace,* but no longer *preparatory* grace. When the Holy Spirit begins His work of effecting this union, preparatory grace ceases; hence it does not belong to the proper work of the Holy Spirit.

21

Regeneration the Work of God

The hearing ear, and the seeing eye, the Lord hath even made both of them—Proverbs 20:12.

The hearing ear, and the seeing eye, the Lord hath even made both of them." This testimony of the Holy Spirit contains the whole mystery of *regeneration.*

An unregenerate person is deaf and blind; not only as a stock or block, but *worse.* For neither stock nor block is corrupt or ruined, but an unregenerate person is wholly dead and a prey to the most fearful dissolution.

This rigid, uncompromising, and absolute confession must be our starting-point in this discussion, else we shall fail to understand the claims of regeneration. This is the reason why every heresy that has conceded in one way or other that man has a share, most generally a lion's share, in the work of redemption, has always begun by calling in question the nature of sin. "Undoubtedly," they said, "sin is very bad—a terrible and abominable evil, but there is surely some remnant of good in man. That noble, virtuous, and amiable being, man, cannot be dead in trespasses and sin. That may be true of some scoundrel or knave behind the bars, or of robbers and unscrupulous murderers, but really, it cannot be applied to our honorable ladies and gentlemen, to our lovely girls, roguish boys, and attractive children. These are not prone to hate God and their neighbors, but disposed, with all their heart, to love all men, and render unto God the reverence due unto Him."

Therefore away with all ambiguity in this matter! This method of smoothing over unpalatable truths, now so much in vogue among the affable people, we cannot endorse. Our confession is, and ever shall be, that by nature man is dead in trespasses and sin, lying under the curse, ripe for the just judgment of God, and still ripening for an eternal condemnation. Surely his *being,* as man, is unimpaired; wherefore we protest against the presentation that the sinner is in this respect as a stock or block. No; as man he is unimpaired, his being is intact, but his *nature* is corrupt, and in that corrupt nature he is dead.

We compare him to the body of a person who has died of an ordinary disease. Such a body retains all the members of the human organism *intact.* There is the eye with its muscles, and the ear with its organs of hearing; in the post-mortem examination heart, spleen, liver, and kidneys appear to be perfectly normal. A dead body may sometimes appear so natural that one is tempted to say: "He is *not* dead, but sleeping." And yet, however perfect and natural, its *nature* is corrupt with the corruption of death. And the same is true of the sinner. His *being* remains intact and whole, containing all that which constitutes a man, but his *nature* is corrupt, yea, so corrupt that he is dead; not only apparently, but actually dead; dead in all the variations which can be played upon the term "dead."

Hence without regeneration the sinner is utterly unprofitable. What is the use of an ear except it hear, or of an eye except it see? Therefore the Holy Ghost testifies: "The hearing ear and the seeing eye, the Lord has made even both of them." And since in the world of spiritual things deaf ears and blind eyes do not avail anything, the Church of Christ confesses that every operation of saving grace must be preceded by a quickening of the sinner, by an opening of blind eyes, an unstopping of deaf ears—in short, by the implanting of the faculty of faith.

And as the man that sat in darkness can see as soon as his eyes are opened, so we, without moving a hair's breadth, are translated from the kingdom of darkness into the kingdom of light. "Translated" does not denote here an actual going, nor does "to be translated" denote an actual change of place, but simply life entering into the dead, so that he that was blind can now see.

This wonderful act of regeneration may be examined in two classes of persons: in the *infant* and in the *adult.*

It is the safest way to examine it in the infant: not because this work of grace is different in an infant from what it is in an adult, for it is the same in all persons thus favored, but to the conscious observation of an adult the workings of regeneration are so mingled with those of conversion that it is difficult to distinguish the two.

But this difficulty does not exist in the case of an unconscious child, as, for example, in John the son of Zacharias and Elizabeth. Such infant has no consciousness to create confusion. The matter appears in a pure and unmixed form. And thus we are enabled to distinguish between regeneration and conversion in an adult. It is evident that in the case of an infant which, like John, is still unborn, there can be nothing but mere passivity—that is, the child underwent something, but himself did *nothing;* something was done *to* him, and *in* him, but not *by* him; and every idea of cooperation is absolutely excluded.

Hence, in regeneration, man is neither *worker* nor *coworker;* he is merely wrought upon; and the only Worker in this matter is God. And, for this very reason, because God is the sole Worker in regeneration, it must be thoroughly understood that His work does not begin only with regeneration.

No; while the sinner is still dead in trespasses and sins, before the work of God has begun in him, he is already chosen and ordained, justified and sanctified, adopted as God's child and glorified. This is what filled St. Paul with such ecstasy of joy when he said: "For whom He did foreknow, He also did predestinate; and whom He did predestinate, them He also called; and whom He called, them He also justified; and whom He justified, them He also glorified" (Rom. 8:29, 30). And this is not the recital of what took place in the regenerate, but the glad summing up of the things which God accomplished for us *before we existed.* Hence our election, foreordination, justification, and glorification precede the new birth. It is true that, in the hour of love when regeneration was to be effected in us, the things accomplished outside of our consciousness were to be revealed to the consciousness of faith, but so far as God was concerned all things were ready and prepared. The dead sinner whom God regenerates is to the divine consciousness a beloved, elect, justified, and adopted child already. God quickens only His dear children.

Of course, God justifies the ungodly and not the righteous; He calls *sinners* to repentance and not just persons, but it should be remembered that this is spoken from the point of view of *our own consciousness of sin.* The still unregenerate does not feel himself God's child, nor that he is justified; does not believe his own election, yea, often gainsays it; yet he cannot alter the things divinely wrought in his behalf, viz., that before the supreme bar of justice God declared him just and free, long before he was so declared before the bar of his own conscience. Long before he believed, he was justified before God's tribunal, by and by to be justified *by faith* before his own *consciousness.*

But, however wonderful and unfathomable the mystery of election may be—and none of us shall ever be able to answer the question why one was chosen to be a vessel of honor, and another was left as a vessel of wrath—in the matter of regeneration we do not face that mystery at all. That God regenerates one and not another is according to a fixed and unalterable rule. He comes with regeneration to all the elect; and the non-elect He passes by. Hence this act of God is *irresistible.* No man has the power to say, "I will *not* be born again," or to prevent God's work or to put obstacles in His way, or to make it so difficult that it cannot be performed.

God effects this gracious work in His own way, that is, He so royally perseveres that all creatures together could not rob Him of one of His elect. If all men and devils should conspire to pluck a brutal man, belonging to the elect, from His saving power, all their efforts would be mere vanity. As we brush away a spider's web, so would God laugh at all their commotion. The powerful steam borer pierces the iron plate not more noiselessly and with less effort than silently and majestically God penetrates the heart of whomsoever He will, and changes the nature of His chosen. Isaiah's word concerning the starry heavens—"Lift up your eyes on high, and behold who hath created these things, that bringeth out their hosts by number; He calleth them all by name, by the greatness of His might, for that He is strong in power; *not one faileth*"—may be applied to the firmament in which God's elect shine as stars: "Because of the greatness of His might, and that He is strong in power, not one faileth." All that are ordained to eternal life are quickened at the divinely appointed hour.

And this implies that the work of regeneration is not a moral work; that is, it is not accomplished by means of advice or exhortation. Even taken in its wider sense, including conversion, as, for example, the canons of Dort use it now and then, regeneration is not a *moral* working in the soul.

It is not simply a case of misunderstanding, the sinner's will being still uncorrupt, so that it requires only instruction and advice to induce it to choose rightly. No; such advice and admonition are wholly out of the question regarding the unborn son of Zacharias; and the thousands of infants of believing parents, of whom at Dort it was correctly confessed that they may be supposed to have died in the Lord, that is, being born again; and regarding those regenerated before Baptism but converted later in life.

For this reason it is so necessary to examine regeneration (in its limited sense) in an infant, and not in an adult, in whom it necessarily includes conversion.

The following reasoning cannot be disputed:

1. All men, infants included, are born dead in trespasses and sins.

2. Of these infants many die before they come to self-consciousness.

3. Of these gathered flowers the Church confesses that many are saved.

4. Being dead in sin, they cannot be saved without being born again.

5. Hence regeneration does actually take place in persons that are not self-conscious.

These statements being indisputable, it is evident, therefore, that the nature and character of regeneration can be determined most correctly by examining it in these still unconscious persons.

Such an unborn infant is totally ignorant of human language; it has no ideas, has never heard the Gospel preached, cannot receive instruction, warning, or exhortation. Hence moral influence is out of the question; and this convinces us that regeneration is not a moral, but a metaphysical act of God, just as much as the creation of the soul of an unborn child, which is effected independently of the mother. God regenerates a man wholly without his foreknowledge.

What it is that constitutes the act of regeneration cannot be told. Jesus Himself tells us so, for He says: "The wind bloweth where it listeth, and thou hearest the sound thereof, but canst not tell whence it cometh and whither it goeth; so is everyone that is born of the Spirit." And, therefore, it is befitting to investigate this mystery with the utmost discretion. Even in the natural kingdom the mystery of life and its origin is almost entirely beyond our knowledge. The most learned physician is entirely ignorant concerning the manner in which a human life comes into existence. Once existing, he can explain its development, but of the inception that precedes all else he knows absolutely nothing. In this respect he is just as ignorant as the most innocent peasant boy. The mystery cannot be penetrated, simply because it lies beyond our observation; it is perceptible only that life exists.

And this applies in stronger sense to the mystery of our second birth. Post-mortem examination can detect the embryo and its locality, but spiritually even this is impossible. Subsequent manifestations are instructive to a certain extent, but even then much is uncertain and unsettled. By what infallible standard can it be determined how much of the old nature enters into the expressions of the new life? Is there no hypocrisy? Are there no conditions unexplained? Are there no obstacles to spiritual development? Hence experience in this respect cannot avail; though pure and simple, it can reveal only the development of that which is, and not the origin of life unborn.

The only source of truth on this subject is the Word of God; and in that Word the mystery remains not only unrevealed, but veiled. And for good reasons. If we were to effect regeneration, if we could add to or take from it, if we could advance or hinder it, then Scripture would surely have sufficiently instructed us concerning it. But since God has reserved this work altogether to Himself, man need not solve this mystery any more than that of his first creation, or that of the creation of his soul.

22

The Work of Regeneration

Therefore if any man be in Christ, he is a new creature; old things are passed away; behold all things are become new—2 Corinthians 5:17.

In our former article we contended that regeneration is a real act of God in which man is absolutely passive and unable, according to the ancient confession of the Church. Let us now reverently examine this matter more closely; not to penetrate into things too high for us, but to cut off error and to clear the consciousness.

Regeneration is not sacramentally effected by holy Baptism, relieving the sinner's inability, offering him another opportunity to choose for or against God, as the Ethicals maintain.

Nor is it a mere rectifying of the understanding; nor a simple change of disposition and inclination, making the unwilling willing to conform to the holy will of God.

Neither is it a change of ego; nor, as many maintain, a leaving the ego undisturbed, the personality unchanged, simply putting the evil ego in the light and reflection of the righteousness of Christ. The last two errors must be refuted and rejected as positively as the first two.

In regeneration a man does not receive another ego; that is, our *being as man* is not changed nor modified, but before and after regeneration it is the same ego, the same person, the same human being. Although sin has terribly corrupted man, his *being* remained intact.

Nothing is lacking. All its constituent parts, that distinguish it from all other beings, are present in the sinner. Not his being, but his *nature* became totally corrupt.

Nature and being are not the same. Applied to a steam-engine, *being* is the engine itself, with its cylinders, pipes, wheels, and screws, but its *nature* is the *action* manifest as soon as steam enters the cylinder. Applied to man, being is that which makes him man, and nature that which manifests the character of his being and working.

If sin had ruined man's being, he would be no more man, and regeneration would be impossible. But since his being, his ego, his person remained intact and the deep corruption affected only his nature, regeneration, that is, restoration of his nature, is possible; and this restoration is effected by the new birth. Let this be firmly maintained. In regeneration we do not receive a new being, ego, or person, but our *nature* is reborn.

The best and most satisfactory illustration of the manner of regeneration is furnished by the curious art of grafting. The successful grafting of a budding shoot of the cultivated grape upon the wild vine results in a good tree growing upon the wild trunk. This applies to all fruit-trees and flowering plants. The cultivated can be grafted upon the wild. Left to itself, the wild will never yield anything good. The wild pear and the wild rose remain stunted and chary of fruit and blossom. But let the gardener graft a finely flavored pear upon the wild pear, or a beautiful double tea-rose upon the wild rose, and the former will yield luscious fruit and the latter magnificent flowers.

This miracle of grafting has always been a wonder to thinking men. And it is a wonder. The trunk to be grafted is absolutely wild; with its wild roots it sucks the saps and forces them into its wild cells. But that little graft has the wonderful power of converting the sap and vital forces into something good, causing that wild trunk to bear noble fruit and rich flowers. It is true the wild trunk vigorously resists the reformation of its nature by its wild shoots below the graft, and if successful its wild nature will forcibly assert itself and prevent the sap from passing through the bud. But by keeping down those wild shoots the sap can be forced to the bud with excellent results. Forcing down the wild trunk, the graft will gradually reach almost to the roots, and we nearly forget that the tree was ever wild.

This clearly represents regeneration so far as this divine mystery can be represented objectively. For in regeneration something is planted in man which by nature he lacks. The fall did not merely remove him from the sphere of divine righteousness, into which regeneration brings him back, but regeneration effects a radical modification in man as man, creating a difference between him and the unregenerate so great that finally it leads to direct opposites.

To say that between the regenerate and the unregenerate there is no difference is equivalent to a denial of the work of the Holy Spirit. Generally, however, no difference is noticed at first, no more than in the grafted tree. Twins lie in the same cradle, one regenerated, the other not, but we cannot see the slightest difference between the two. The former may even have a worse temper than the latter. They are exactly alike. Both spring from the same wild trunk. Dissecting knife nor microscope could detect the least difference; for that which God has wrought in the favored child is wholly spiritual and invisible, discernible to God alone.

This fact must be confessed definitely and emphatically, in opposition to those who say that the seed of regeneration is material. This error occupies the same ground as the Manichean heresy in the matter of sin. The latter makes sin a microbe, and this makes the seed of regeneration a sort of perceptible germ of life and holiness. And this falsifies the truth against which, among others, Dr. Böhl has earnestly protested.

The seed of regeneration is intangible, invisible, purely spiritual. It does not create *two* men in one being, but before and after regeneration there is but one being, one ego, one personality. Not an old and a new man, but one man—viz., the old man *before* regeneration, and the new man *after* it—who is created after God in perfect righteousness and holiness. For that which is born of God cannot sin. His seed remaineth in him. "Old things *are passed away,* behold, *all things are become new.*"

Yet the nature of the ego or personality is truly changed, and in such a way that, putting on the new nature in principle, he still continues to *work* through the *old* nature. The grafted tree is not two trees, but one. Before the grafting it was a wild rose, after it a cultivated one. Still the new nature must draw its saps through the *old* nature; apart from the graft, the trunk remains wild.

Hence before as well as after regeneration we lie in the midst of death, as soon as we consider ourselves outside of the divine seed. Wherefore, trying to avoid one false position, we must be careful not to run into another; trying to escape the Siamese twinship of the old and the new man, and maintaining the unity of the ego before and after regeneration, we should not begin to teach that regeneration leaves our person unchanged, that it does not affect the sinner himself, but merely translates him into the sphere of an extraneous righteousness. No; the Scripture speaks of a *new creature,* another *birth,* a being *changed* and *renewed.* And this cannot be reconciled with the notion that the sinner should remain *unchanged.*

Regarding the question, what it is in the bud that has the potency to regenerate the wild trunk, the best-informed botanist cannot discover the fiber or liquid that might have this power. He only knows that every bud has its own nature, and possesses the potency to produce another branch or tree of the same nature by its own formative power.

And this applies to the work of regeneration. In the center of our being, ego, personality rules our nature, disposition, form of being, and existence, imparting its impress, form, character, and spiritual quality to what we are and work and speak. That all-controlling center is by nature sinful and wicked. Under its fairest forms it is but unrighteous. Hence, willingly or unwillingly, we press upon our being, working, and speaking the stamp of unrighteousness. According to age and development this nature of the ego chisels out of the marble of our being an *evil* and *sinful* man, corresponding to the image contained in our nature from which it proceeds. In regeneration God performs in this controlling center of our being a wonderful act, converting this nature, this formative force into something entirely different. Consequently our being, working, and speaking are henceforth controlled by another commandment, law of life, and government; and this new formative force chisels another man in us, new and holy, a child of God, created in righteousness.

But this change is not completed at once. The tree grafted in March may remain inactive during that entire month, because there is as yet no working in its nature. But this is sure: as soon as there is any action it will be according to the new, engrafted nature.

And so it is here. The new, engrafted life may lie dormant for a season, like a grain of wheat in the earth, but when it begins to work it will be according to the nature of the new life. Hence regeneration implants the life-germ of the new man, whom it contains in all his completeness, and from which it will proceed as surely as the wheat contained in the seed proceeds from it.

In order to assist us in our representation of this mystery, the greatest theologian of the Reformed churches has presented the divine plan in regeneration in the following stages:

(1) In His own mind God conceives the new man; whom (2) He modifies according to a particular person, thus creating the new man; (3) He brings the germ of this new man into the center of our being; (4) in which center He effects the union between our ego and this germinating life; (5) in that vital germ God supports the formative power, which at His appointed time He will cause to come forth, by which our ego will manifest itself as a new man.

23

Regeneration and Faith

Being born again, not of corruptible seed, but of incorruptible, by the Word of God, which liveth and abideth forever— 1 Peter 1:23.

There is a possible objection to what has been said above concerning regeneration. It is evident that God's Word, and therefore our symbols of faith, offers a modified representation of these things which, superficially considered, *seems* to condemn our representation. This representation, which does not consider *children,* but *adults,* may thus be stated: Among a circle of unconverted persons God causes the Word to be preached by His ambassadors of the cross. By this preaching the *call* reaches them. If there are elect persons among them, for whom it is now the *time of love,* God accompanies the *outward* call with the *inward.* Consequently they turn from their ways of sin to the way of life. And so they are begotten of God.

Thus St. Peter presents the matter, saying: "Being born again, not of corruptible seed, but of incorruptible, by the Word of God, which liveth and abideth forever." And also St. Paul when he declares, "That faith is by the hearing, and the hearing by the Word of God" (Rom. 10:17). It fully harmonizes with what St. Paul writes concerning holy Baptism, which he calls the washing of *"regeneration,"* for in those days Jew and Gentile were baptized in the name of the Lord Jesus, immediately after their conversion, by the preaching of the apostles.

For this reason our fathers confessed in their Confession (article 24): "We believe that this true faith, being wrought in man by the hearing of the word of God, and the operation of the Holy Ghost, doth regenerate and make him a new man." And likewise teaches the Heidelberg Catechism (see question 65): "Such faith proceedeth from the Holy Ghost, who works faith in our hearts by the preaching of the Gospel, and confirms it by the use of the sacraments." And also the canons of Dort, Third and Fourth Heads of doctrine, section 17: "As the almighty operation of God, whereby He prolongs and supports this our natural life, does not exclude, but requires the use of means by which God of His infinite mercy and goodness hath chosen to exert His influence; so also the before-mentioned supernatural operation of God, by which we are regenerated, in no wise excludes or subverts the use of the Gospel, which the most wise God hath ordained to be the seed of regeneration and food of the soul. Wherefore, as the apostles and the teachers who succeeded them piously instructed the people concerning this grace of God, to His glory and the abasement of all pride, and in the mean time, however, neglected not to keep them by the sacred precepts of the Gospel in the exercise of the Word, the sacraments, and discipline; so even to this day, be it far from either instructors or instructed to presume to tempt God in the Church, by separating what He of His good pleasure hath most intimately joined together. For grace is conferred by means of admonitions; and the more readily we perform our duty, the more eminent usually is this blessing of God working in us, and the more directly is His work advanced."

And now, in order to eradicate every suspicion that we contend against this representation, we declare openly and definitely that we give it our most hearty assent.

We only beg it be considered that in this presentation both Scripture and the symbols of faith always point to the mysterious *background,* to a wonderful work of God hiding back of it, to an inscrutable mystery without which all this comes to naught.

The canons of Dort describe this mysterious, inscrutable, and wonderful background most elaborately and most beautifully in article 12, Third and Fourth Heads of Doctrine: "And this is the regeneration so highly celebrated in Scripture and denominated a new creation; a resurrection from the dead, a making alive, which God works in us without our aid. But this is in no wise effected merely by the external preaching of the Gospel, by moral persuasion, or such a mode of operation that, after God has performed His part, it still remains in the power of man to be regenerated or not, to be converted or to continue unconverted, but it is evidently a supernatural work, most powerful and at the same time most delightful, astonishing, mysterious, and ineffable; not inferior in efficacy to creation or the resurrection from the dead, as the Scripture inspired by the Author of this work declares; so that all in whose hearts God works in this marvelous manner are certainly, infallibly, and effectually regenerated, and do actually believe. Whereupon the will thus renewed is not only actuated and influenced by God, but in consequence of this influence becomes itself active. Wherefore, also, man is himself rightly said to believe and repent, by virtue of that grace received." And also in article 2: "But when God accomplishes His good pleasure in the elect, or works in them true conversion, He not only causes the Gospel to be externally preached to them, and powerfully illuminates their minds by His Holy Spirit, that they may rightly understand and discern the things of the *Spirit of God, but by the efficacy of the same* regenerating Spirit, He *pervades the inmost recesses of the man;* He opens the closed and softens the hardened heart, and circumcises that which was uncircumcised; infuses new qualities into the will, which, though heretofore dead, He quickens; from being evil, disobedient, and refractory, He renders it good, obedient and pliable; actuates and strengthens it, that like a good tree it may bring forth the fruits of good actions." The Heidelberg Catechism points to this, in question 8: "Except we are regenerated by the Spirit of God." And also the Confession, article 22: "We believe that to attain the true knowledge of this great mystery, the Holy Spirit kindleth in our hearts an upright faith, which embraces Jesus Christ with all His merits."

This mysterious background, which our fathers at Dort called "His pervading the inmost recesses of man by the efficacy of the regenerating Spirit," is evidently the same as what we call "the divine operation which penetrates the center of our being to implant the germ of the new life."

And what is this mysterious working? According to the universal testimony based upon Scripture, it is an operation of the Holy Spirit in man's innermost being.

Hence the question, whether this regenerating act *precedes, accompanies,* or *follows* the hearing of the Word. And this question should be well understood, for it involves the solution of this seeming disagreement.

We answer: The Holy Spirit may perform this work in the sinner's heart *before, during,* or *after* the preaching of the Word. The inward call may be associated with the outward call, or it may follow it. But that which precedes the inward call, viz., the opening of the *deaf ear,* so that it may be heard, is not dependent upon the preaching of the Word; and therefore may *precede* the preaching.

Correct discrimination in this respect is of greatest importance.

If I designate the whole *conscious* work of grace from conversion until death, "regeneration," without any regard to its mysterious background, then I *may* and *must* say with the Confession (article 24): "That this faith, being wrought in man by the hearing of the Word, and the operation of the Holy Spirit, doth regenerate him and make him a new man."

But if I distinguish in this work of grace, according to the claims of the sacraments, between the *origin* of the new life, for which God gave us the sacrament of holy Baptism, and its *support,* for which He gave the sacrament of the holy Supper, then regeneration ceases immediately after man is born again, and that which follows is called "sanctification."

And discriminating again between that which the Holy Spirit wrought in us *consciously* and *unconsciously,* then regeneration designates that which was wrought in us unconsciously, while conversion is the term we apply to the awakening of this implanted life in our consciousness.

Hence God's work of grace runs through these three successive stages:

1st. Regeneration in its *first* stage, when the Lord plants the new life in the dead heart.

2d. Regeneration in its *second* stage, when the new-born man comes to conversion.

3d. Regeneration in its *third* stage, when conversion merges into sanctification.

In each of these three God performs a wonderful and mysterious work in man's inward being. From God proceed quickening, conversion, and sanctification, and in each God is the Worker: only with this difference, that in the quickening He works *alone,* finding and leaving man *inactive;* that in conversion He *finds* us *inactive,* but *makes* us active; that in sanctification He works in us in such a manner that we work *ourselves* through Him.

Describing it still more closely, we say that in the first stage of regeneration, that of quickening, God works *without means;* in the second stage, that of conversion, He *employs means,* viz., the preaching of the Word; and in the third stage, that of sanctification, He uses means in addition to ourselves, whom He uses as means.

Condensing the foregoing, there is one great act of God which recreates the corrupt sinner into a new man, viz., the comprehensive act of regeneration, which contains three parts—quickening, conversion, and sanctification.

For the ministry of the Word it is preferable to consider only the last two, conversion and sanctification, since this is the appointed means to effect them. The first, regeneration, is preferably a subject of private meditation, since in it man is passive and God only active; and also because in it the majesty of the divine operation is most apparent.

Hence there is no conflict or opposition. Referring, according to the Confession, article 17, only to conversion and sanctification, the unstopping of the deaf ear as preceding the hearing of the Word is not denied. And penetrating into the work which antedates conversion, "in which God works in us without our aid" (article 12 of the canons of Dort), it is not denied, but confessed, that conversion and sanctification follow the unstopping of the deaf ear, and that, in the proper sense, regeneration is completed only at the death of the sinner.

Do not suppose that we make these two to conflict. In writing a biography of Napoleon it would be sufficient simply to mention his *birth,* but one might also mention, more in particular, the things that took place *before* his birth. Just so in this respect: I may refer either to the parts of regeneration, conversion and sanctification, or I may include also that which *precedes* conversion, and speak also of the quickening. This implies no antagonism, but a mere difference of exactness. It is more exhaustive, with reference to regeneration, to speak of *three* stages—quickening, conversion, and sanctification; although it is customary and more practical to speak only of the last two.

Our purpose, however, calls for greater completeness. The aim of this work is not to preach the Word, but to uncover the foundations of the truth, so as to stop the building of crooked walls upon the foundation-stone, after the manner of Ethicals, Rationalists, and Supernaturalists.

Exhaustiveness in treatment requires to ask not only, "How and what does the quickened sinner hear?" but also, "Who has given him hearing ears?"

And this is all the more to be insisted upon because our children must not be ignored in this respect. At Dort, in 1618, our children were taken into account, and we may not deny ourselves this pleasant obligation.

And herein lies a real danger. For to speak of the little ones without considering the first stage of regeneration—that is, the quickening—causes confusion and perplexity from which there is no escape.

Salvation depends upon faith, and faith upon the hearing of the Word; hence our deceased infants must be lost, for they cannot hear the Word. To escape this fearful thought it is often said that the children are saved by virtue of the parents' faith—a misunderstanding which greatly confused our entire conception of Baptism, and made our baptismal form very perplexing. But as soon as we distinguish *quickening,* as a stage of regeneration, from *conversion* and *sanctification,* the light enters. For since quickening is an unaided act of God in us, independent of the Word, and frequently separated from the second stage, *conversion,* by an interval of many days, there is nothing to prevent God from performing His work even in the babe, and the apparent conflict dissolves into beautiful harmony. Moreover, as soon as I regard my still unconverted children as not yet regenerate, their training must run in the direction of a questionable Methodism.* What is the use of the call so long as I suppose and know: "This ear cannot yet hear"?

Touching the question concerning "faith," we are fully prepared to apply the same distinction to this matter. You have only to discriminate between the *organ* or the *faculty of faith,* the *power to exercise faith,* and *the working of faith.* The first of these three, viz., the *faculty* of faith, is

---

* See the author's explanation of Methodism in section 5 of the Preface.

implanted in the first stage of regeneration—that is, in quickening; the *power* of faith is imparted in the second stage of regeneration—that is, in conversion; and the *working* of faith is wrought in the third stage—that is, in sanctification. Hence if faith is wrought only by the hearing of the Word, the preaching of the Word does not create the *faculty* of faith.

Look only at what our fathers confessed at Dort: "He who works in man both to will and to do produces both the *will to believe* and *the act of believing* also" (Third and Fourth Heads of Doctrine, article 14).

Or to express it still more strongly: when the Word is preached, I know it; and when I hear it and believe it, I know whence this *working* of faith comes. But the implanting of the faith-faculty is an entirely different thing; for of this the Lord Jesus says: "Thou hearest the sound thereof, but canst not tell whence it cometh, and whither it goeth"; and as the wind, so is also the regeneration of man.

24

Implanting in Christ

Having become one plant with Him—Romans 6:5.

Having discussed regeneration as God's act wrought in a lost, wicked, and guilty sinner, we now examine the more sacred and delicate question: How does this divine act affect our relation to Christ?

We consider this point more important than the first, since every view of regeneration that does not do full justice to the "mystical union with Christ" is anti-Scriptural, eradicates brotherly love, and begets spiritual pride.

The holy apostle declares: "I live, *yet not I,* but Christ liveth in me, and the life which I now live in the flesh, I live by the faith of the Son of God."* The idea that a saint can have life outside of the mystical union with Immanuel is but a fiction of the imagination. The regenerate can live no life but such as consists in union with Christ. Let this be firmly and strongly maintained.

The Scriptural expressions, "one plant with Him"† and "branches of the Vine," which must be taken in their fullest significance, are

---

* St. Paul does not declare in these words that he received another ego; on the contrary, he says emphatically that in his ego, which continued to be his, it is no more I that live, but Christ.

† At least if the words "with Him" are original.

metaphors entirely different from those which we use. We are confined to metaphors which express our meaning by analogy, but they cannot be fully applied nor express the being of the thing; hence the so-called third term of the comparison. But the figures used by the Holy Spirit express a *real* conformity, a unity of thought divinely expressed in the spiritual and visible world. Hence Jesus could say: "I am the *true* Vine," that is, "every other vine is but a figure. The true, the real Vine am I, and I alone."

Being exceedingly sober and choice in His metaphorical speech, the Lord Jesus does not say that a branch is *grafted* into the vine, simply because this is not done in nature, that is, in the creation of God. In John 15, Jesus does not even touch upon the question of how one becomes a branch. That is the work of the Father. My Father is the Husbandman. In John 15:3 he speaks only of a person who not *abiding* in Him whithers and will be burned.

Even Romans 6:5 does not speak of coming to Jesus, and Romans 11:17–25 only partly. The former calls it to become one plant with Him, but does not tell "how"; and "grafting" is not even mentioned. And the latter, speaking of broken olive-branches, and of wild olive-branches grafted upon a good olive, and lastly of broken branches restored to the original olive, makes no reference whatever to the implanting of individuals in Christ, as we will soon prove.

And yet the figure is only partly applicable. Indeed, in Romans 11, St. Paul, with his characteristic boldness of speech and style, for comparison's sake reverses God's work in nature; for while in reality the cultivated bud is grafted on the wild trunk, he makes in this instance the wild bud to be grafted upon the good trunk. A bold stroke indeed and very profitable to us, for by it he makes us see clearly and distinctly the *general implanting in Christ.* But that is all.

For, notice it well, the figure is not to be pressed too far. It is a mistake to make it refer to the regeneration of the individual sinner. For a person once implanted in Christ cannot be severed from Him: "No man can pluck them out of My hand"; "Whom He has justified, them He also glorified."

And yet, reference is made here to branches which are broken off and which were grafted in again. If this referred to particular individuals, then the Jews, who during the life of St. Paul denied the Lord, must have been regenerate persons who fell away and returned again before they died.

If this had been St. Paul's meaning, subsequent events would have belied his words, and he would have revoked the whole tenor of his other teachings. But he plainly means that the *tribes of Israel,* who were in the Covenant of Grace, had lost their position therein by their own fault; yet that even outside of the Covenant they should be preserved throughout the coming ages, and that in the course of history the way would be opened even for them to be reintroduced into the Covenant of Grace. And this shows that Romans 11:17–25 does not teach the regeneration of individual persons, and that the good olive does not signify Christ, for he that is implanted in Christ can never be severed from Him, and he that is severed from Him never belonged to Him. Do we not believe in the perseverance of saints?

It may be objected that in John 15 reference is made to branches that are cast forth from the vine; to which we answer: first, that this does not remove the difficulty that the apostate Jews of St. Paul's time were never grafted in again; and second, that with Calvin we hold that Jesus, speaking of the branches cast forth, had reference to persons who, like Judas, *seemed* to be implanted; otherwise His own words, "No man can pluck them out of My hand," cannot stand for a moment.

We arrive, therefore, at this conclusion, that neither John 15 nor Romans 11 has any reference to personal regeneration in its limited sense; while Romans 6, which speaks of becoming one plant, does not introduce the idea of engrafting, nor make the slightest allusion to the manner in which this "becoming one plant" had been accomplished.

It is unnecessary to say that not a few exegetes judge the translation, "One plant *with Him,"* incorrect, omitting the words italicized. We do not express here an opinion regarding this rendering, but it shows clearly that Romans 6 has nothing to say concerning the manner in which our union with Christ is effected.

In fact, Scripture never applies the figure of grafting to regeneration. Romans 11 treats of the restoration of a people and nation to the covenant of grace; Romans 6 speaks only of a most intimate union; and John 15 never alludes to a wild branch which became good by being planted in Christ. These figures set forth the union with Christ, but teach nothing concerning the manner in which this union is effected.

Scripture is utterly silent concerning it; and since there is no other source of information, mere human inventions are utterly useless. Even Christian experience does not throw any light upon it, for it cannot teach anything which Scripture has not taught already; and again, we can easily perceive the union with Christ where it exists, but we cannot see it where it does not exist, or where it is just forming.

And yet this union with Christ must be strongly emphasized. The theologians who represent divine truth most purely lay most stress upon this matter. And although Calvin may have been the most rigid among the reformers, yet not one of them has presented this *unio mystica,* this spiritual union with Christ, so incessantly, so tenderly, and with such holy fire as he. And as Calvin, so did all the Reformed theologians, from Beza to Comrie, and from Zanchius to Kohlbrugge. "Without Christ nothing, by this mystical union with Christ all," was their motto. And even now a preacher's value is to be strictly measured by the degree of prominence accorded to the mystical union with Immanuel, in his presentation of the truth. The strong utterance of Kohlbrugge, "One may be born again, one may be a child of God, one may be a sincere believer, yet *without this mystical union with Christ* he is nothing in himself, nothing but a lost and wicked sinner," was always the glorious confession of our churches. In fact, it is what our form for the administration of the Lord's Supper so well expresses: "Considering that we seek our life outside of ourselves in Jesus Christ, we acknowledge that we lie in the midst of death."

But it is wrong on this ground to teach—as some of our younger ministers are reported to teach—and derogatory to the work of the Holy Spirit, that regeneration *accomplishes nothing in us,* and that the whole work is performed completely *outside* of us, as some have said, "That we need not even be converted, for even that has been done for us vicariously by the Lord Jesus Christ." To say that there is no difference between a regenerate person and an unregenerate is to contradict Scripture and to deny the work of the Holy Spirit. Wherefore we strongly oppose this notion. There is indeed a difference. The former has entered into the union with Christ, and the latter has not. And upon this union *everything* depends; it makes a difference in men as between heaven and hell.

Nor may it be said, on the contrary, "That a regenerate person, even without the union with Christ, is other or better than an unbeliever"; for this puts asunder what God has joined together. Outside of Christ there is in man born of a woman nothing but darkness, corruption, and death.

Hence we firmly maintain the indissoluble oneness of these two: "There is no regeneration without establishing the mystical union with Christ"; and again: "There is no mystical union with Immanuel but in the regenerate." These two may never be separated; and on the long way between the first act of regeneration and completed sanctification, the *unio mystica* may not for a moment be lost sight of.

The Ethical theologians will probably assent to all that we have said on this subject; and yet, according to our deepest conviction, they have wholly bastardized and misapprehended this precious article of faith. Assuredly they strongly emphasize the union with Christ; they even tell us that they do this more than we, maintaining that it is immaterial whether a man is sound in the Scripture or not so long as he is united with Christ. In that case there is no more need of any formula, confession, articles of faith, or even faith in the Scripture. A prominent Ethical professor at the University of Utrecht has openly declared: "Although I should lose the entire Scripture, yea, though the truth of not one of the Gospel narratives could be verified, I would not be in the least affected, for I would still possess union with Christ; and having that, what more can a man desire?" And this has such a pious ring, and taken in the abstract is so true, that many a conscience must agree with it, not having the faintest suspicion of the apostasy from the faith of the fathers contained in it.

If one should ask us whether we do not believe that the soul united with Jesus possesses all that can be desired, we would almost refuse an answer, for he knows better. No, indeed, favored soul, having *that* you need no more; depart in peace, thrice blessed of God.

But because the mystical union with the Son of God is so weighty and precious an article of faith, we desire that every man should treat it most seriously, and examine whether the union which he says he possesses is actually the same mystical union with the Lord Jesus Christ which the Scripture promises to the children of God, and which they have enjoyed throughout the ages.

25

Not a Divine-Human Nature

I in them, and they in Me—John 17:23.

The union of believers with the Mediator, of all matters of faith is the most tender, is invisible, imperceptible to the senses, and unfathomable; it escapes all inward vision; it refuses to be dissected or to be made objective by any representation; in the fullest sense of the word it is mystical—*unio mystica,* as Calvin, after the example of the early Church, called it.

And yet, however mysterious, no man is at liberty to interpret it according to his own notions; in fact, there is need of great vigilance lest under the pious appearance of this mystic love injurious contraband be smuggled into the divine sanctuary. We have therefore raised our voice against the false representations of former mystical sects, and of the Ethical theorists of the present time.

Let us first explain the Ethical teaching on this point.

Their belief starts from the antithesis existing between *God* and *man.* God is the Creator, man is a creature. God is infinite, man finite. God dwells in the eternal, and man lives in the temporal. God is holy, and man is unholy; etc. So long as these contrasts exist, so they teach, there can be no unity, no reconciliation, no harmony. And as the pantheistic philosophy used to talk about three stages through which life must run its course—first, that of proposition (thesis), then that of contrast (antithesis), and lastly that of reconciliation, combination (synthesis)—so the Ethicals teach that between God and man there exist these three: *thesis, antithesis,* and *synthesis.*

In the first place, there is God. This is the thesis, the proposition. Opposed to this thesis in God, the antithesis, contrast, appears in man. And this thesis and antithesis find their reconciliation, synthesis, in the Mediator, who is at once finite and infinite, burdened with our guilt and holy, temporal, and eternal.

It is only recently that we quoted the following sentence from Professor Gunning's little book, *The Mediator between God and Man* (page 28): "Jesus Christ is the Mediator equally between the Jews and the Gentiles; and also between all things that need reconciliation and mediation; as between God and man, spirit and body, heaven and earth, time and eternity."

This representation contains the fundamental error of the Ethical theology. It interferes with the boundaries which God has set. It effaces them. It causes all contrasts finally to disappear. And by this very thing, without intending it, it becomes the instrument of spreading the pantheism of the philosophic school. Not understanding this system, one may be deeply in love with it. This pantheistic ferment is deeply seated in our sinful hearts. The waters of pantheism are sweet, their religious flavor is peculiarly pleasant. There is spiritual intoxication in this cup, and once inebriated the soul has lost its desire for the sober clearness of the divine Word. To escape from the witchery of these pantheistic charms, one needs to be aroused by bitter experience. And once awakened, the soul is alarmed at the fearful danger to which this siren had exposed it.

No; the contrast between God and man must *not* cease; the contrast between heaven and earth may *not* be placed upon the same line with that of Jew and Gentile; the contrast between the infinite and finite must *not* be effaced by the Mediator; time and eternity must *not* be made identical. There must be brought about a *reconciliation* for the *sinner.* That is all, and no more. "To bring about reconciliation" is the work assigned to the Mediator, and that alone. And this reconciliation is not between time and eternity, the finite and the infinite, but exclusively between a *sinful* creature and a *holy* Creator. It is a reconciliation that could not have occurred if man had not fallen, necessitated only by his fall; a reconciliation not *essential* to the being of Christ, but His *per accidens,* that is, by something independent of His being.

And since the essence of true godliness is based not in the *removal* of the divinely appointed boundaries and contrasts, but in a *deep* reverence for the same; and on this ground the creature as distinguished from the Creator may not feel himself *one with,* but absolutely *distinct* from Him, it is clear that this error of the Ethicals affects the essence of godliness.

The early Church discovered this same principle in Origen, and subsequently in Eutychus, and our fathers of the last century found it in the Hernhutters and sharply opposed it. And only because we lack knowledge and penetration have these Ethical doctrines been able to spread so rapidly here, in Germany, in Switzerland, and even in Scotland, their pantheistic tendencies undetected.

And now does this evil affect their Christology? It affects it to such extent that it is entirely different from that of the Reformed churches. Though they tell us, "We disagree in our views on the Scriptures, but agree in our confession of Christ," yet this is absolutely untrue. Their Christ is not the Christ of the Reformed churches. Christ, as the Reformed Church according to the Scripture and the orthodox Church of all ages confesses Him, is the Son of God, eternal Partaker of the divine nature, who in time, in addition to the divine nature, adopted the human nature, uniting these two natures in the unity of one *person.* He unites them in such a way, however, that these natures continue each by itself, do not blend, and do not communicate the attributes of the one to the other. Hence two natures are united most intimately in the unity of one person, but continuing to the end, and even now in heaven, to be *two natures* each with its own peculiar properties. "He is one not by *conversion* of the Godhead into flesh, but by *taking* of the manhood into God" (Confession of Athanasius, article 35). And again: "He is one not by mixture of substance, but by unity of person" (article 36).

In like manner do we confess in article 19 of our Confession: "We believe that by this conception the person of the Son is inseparably united and connected with the human nature; so that there are not two Sons of God, nor two persons, but two natures united in one single person; *yet each nature retains its own distinct properties.* As then the divine nature has always remained uncreated, without beginning of days or end of life, filling heaven and earth; so also hath the human nature not lost its properties, *but remained a creature,* having beginning of days, being a *finite* nature, and retaining all the properties of a real body. And though He hath by His Resurrection given immortality to the same, nevertheless He hath not changed the reality of His human nature; forasmuch as our salvation and resurrection also depend on the reality of His body. But these two natures were so closely united in one person that they were not separated even by His death."

This clear confession, which the orthodox Church has always defended against the Eutychians and Monothelites, and which our Reformed churches in particular have maintained in opposition to the Lutherans and Mystics, is opposed by the Ethical view all along the line. The late Professor Chantepie de la Saussaye said distinctly in his Inaugural that it was impossible to maintain the old representation on this point, which was also upheld by our Confession, and that his confession of the Mediator was another. Hence the Ethical wing deviates from the old paths not only in the matter of the Scripture, but also in the confession of the person of the Redeemer. It *teaches* what the Reformed churches have always *denied,* and denies what the Reformed churches have always maintained in opposition to churches less correct in their views.

Under the influence which Schleiermacher's training among the Moravian brethren, and his pantheistic development and Lutheran dogmatics, have exerted upon the Ethicals, a Christ is preached by them who is not *the* Christ to whom the orthodox Church of all ages has bowed the knee; and whose confession has always been preserved incorrupt by the Reformed, and especially by our national, theologians. For their conclusions are as follows:

1st. That the Incarnation of the Son of God would have taken place even if Adam had not sinned.

2d. That He is Mediator not only between the sinner and the holy God, but also between the finite and the infinite.

3d. That the two natures mix together, and communicate their attributes to each other in such a measure that from Him, who is both God and man, there proceeds that which is *divine-human.*

4th. That this divine-human nature is communicated to believers also.

This error is immediately recognized by the use of the word *divine-human.* Not that we condemn its use in every instance. On the contrary, when it refers not to the *natures,* but to the *person,* its use is legitimate, for in the one person the two natures are inseparably united. Still it is better in our days to be chary of the word. Divine-human has in the present time a *pantheistic* meaning, denoting that the contrast existing between God and man did not exist in Jesus, but that in Him the antithesis of the divine and the human was not found.

And this is wholly anti-Scriptural, and results in its final consequences in a pure theosophy. For the actual result is a blending of the two natures: a divine nature in God, a human nature in man, and a divine-human nature in the Mediator. So that if man had not fallen, the Mediator would nevertheless have appeared in a divine-human nature.

This is a truly abhorrent doctrine. It puts in the place of the Savior from our sins another and entirely different person; the contrasts between the Creator and the creature disappear, the divine-human nature of the Christ is actually placed above the divine nature itself. For the Mediator in the divine-human nature possesses something that is lacking in the divine nature, viz., its reconciliation with the human.

This shows how much further the Ethicals have departed from the pure confession of the Lord Jesus Christ than is generally believed. According to them there is in the Person of the Mediator a kind of *new* nature, a kind of *third* nature, a kind of *higher* nature, which is called "human-divine." And the union with Christ is found (not subjectively, but objectively) in the fact that the Lord Jesus Christ pours into us that new, third, higher kind, viz., the divine-human nature. Hence the regenerate are the persons who have received this new, third, higher kind of nature. This has no connection with sin, but would have appeared even in the absence of sin. The reconciliation of sinners is something additional, and does not touch the root of the matter.

The real and principal thing is, that the Mediator between the *"finite* and the *infinite"* (to use the very words of Professor Gunning) imparts unto us, who have the lower, human nature, this new third, higher, *divine-human* nature.

Not that the human nature is to be removed and the divine-human nature take its place. No, indeed, but, according to the Ethical theologians, the human nature is originally intended and destined to be thus ennobled, refined, and exalted. As the slip of a plant, under the influence of the sun, develops and produces by and by choice flowers, so does the human nature develop and unfold itself under the influence of the Sun of Righteousness into this higher nature.

That this must be accomplished by means of *regeneration* is *on account of sin.* If there had been no fall in Paradise, and no sin after the fall, there would have been no regeneration, and our nature's lower degree would have passed over spontaneously into that higher, divine-human nature. And this is, in the circles of the Ethicals, the basis of that much-lauded *unio mystica* with the Christ.

The invisible church is, according to their view, that circle of men into whom this higher and nobler tincture of life has been instilled, and others not so favored still stand without. Hence their lack of appreciation of the visible churches; for does not the divine-human tincture of life determine this circle of itself? Hence their preference for the *"unconscious";* conscious confession and expression of thought is immaterial; the principal thing is to be endowed with this new, higher, more refined, divine-human nature. This explains their generally lofty bearing toward men not sharing their opinions. They belong to a sort of spiritual aristocracy; they are of nobler descent, acquainted with more refined forms, living a higher life, from which with pitying eyes they look down upon those who do not dream their dreams of the higher life-tincture.

Let it suffice here only to say that the Reformed churches cannot endorse this representation of the *unio mystica,* but must positively reject it.

26

The Mystical Union with Immanuel

Christ in you the hope of glory—Colossians 1:27.

The union of believers with Christ their Head is not effected by instilling a divine-human life-tincture into the soul. There is no *divine-human life.* There is a most holy Person, who unites in Himself the divine *and* the human life, but both natures continue unmixed, unblended, each retaining its own properties. And since there is no divine-human life in Jesus, He cannot instill it into us.

We do heartily acknowledge that there is a certain conformity and similarity between the divine nature and the human, for man was created after the image of God; wherefore St. Peter could say, "That we become partakers of the divine nature" (2 Peter 1:4), but, according to all sound expositors, this means only that unto the sinner are imparted the attributes of goodness and holiness, which he originally possessed in his own nature in common with the divine nature, but which he lost by sin.

Compared with the nature of material things, and with that of animals and of devils, there is indeed a feature of conformity and similarity between the divine and human natures. But this may not be understood as obliterating the boundary between the divine nature and the human. And, therefore, let this glorious word of St. Peter no longer be abused in order to justify a philosophic system which has nothing in common with the soberness and simplicity of Holy Scripture.

What St. Peter calls "to become partaker of the divine nature" is called in another place, to become *the children of God.* But although Christ is the *Son* of God, and we are called the *children* of God, this does not make the Sonship of Christ and our sonship to stand on the same plane and to be of the same nature. We are but the *adopted* children, although we have another descent, while He *is* the *actual* and eternal Son. While He is essentially the eternal Son, partaker of the divine nature, which in the unity of His Person He unites with the human nature, we are merely *restored* to the *likeness* of the divine nature which we had lost by sin.

Hence as *"to be adopted as a child,"* and *"to be the Son forever"* are contrasts, so are also the following: *"to have the divine nature in Himself,"* and *"to be only partakers of the divine nature."*

The friend who shares a bereaved mother's mourning is not bereaved himself, but through love and pity he has become partaker of that mourning. In like manner, accepting these great and precious promises, believers become partakers of the divine nature, although in themselves wholly devoid of that nature. Partaker does not denote what one possesses in himself, as his own, but a partial communication of what does not belong to him, but to another.

Hence this glorious, apostolic word should no longer be used in pantheistic sense. As it is unlawful to say that we are the *essential* children of God, but must humbly confess, through Christ, to be His *adopted* children, so it is not lawful to say that by faith we become in ourselves bearers of the divine nature, but we must be satisfied with the confession that through the fellowship of love, God makes us partakers of the vital emotions of the divine nature, so far as our human capacities are able to experience them.

This brings us back to the *unio mystica* with Christ, which, although a great and impenetrable mystery, ought to be sufficiently defined to keep us from falling into error. We mention, therefore, its vital points and thus embody our confession concerning it:

The *first* point is that the Lord Jesus does not require us to be purified and sanctified in order to be united to His Person.

Jesus is a Savior not of the righteous, but of sinners. And for this reason He has adopted the human nature; not as the Baptist teaches, by receiving from heaven a newly created body, like the Paradise body of Adam, but by becoming partaker, as the little children, of our flesh and blood. And the same is true of His union with believers. He does not wait until they are pure and holy, then to be spiritually betrothed unto them, but He betroths Himself unto them that they may become pure and holy. He is the rich Bridegroom, and the soul the poverty-stricken bride. In the shining robes of His righteousness He comes and, finding her black, unsightly, and in her native defilement, He says not, "Get thyself clean, wise, and rich, and as a rich bride I will betroth thee unto Me," but, "I take thee just as thou art. I say unto thee, in thy blood, Live. Though thou art poor, betrothing thee, I will make thee partaker of Myself and of My treasure. But a treasure of thine own thou shalt never possess."

This point should be firmly established. The Lord Jesus unites unto Himself not the righteous, but sinners. He marries not the pure and the spotless, but the polluted and the unclean.

When the holy apostle Paul speaks of a bride whom he will present without spot or wrinkle, he has reference to something entirely different; not to His betrothal with the individual, but to the marriage of the Lord Jesus with His Church as a whole. So long as the Church continues in the earth, separated from Him, she is His bride, until in the fullness of time, the separation ended, He will introduce her to the rich and full communion of the united life in glory.

The *second* point to which we call attention is the time when this union begins.

To say that this *unio mystica* is the result of faith alone is only partly correct. For Scripture teaches very distinctly that we were already in the Lord Jesus when He died on Calvary, and when He arose from the dead; that we ascended with Him unto heaven; and that for eighteen centuries we have been seated with Him at the right hand of God. Hence we must carefully distinguish between the five stages in which the union with Immanuel unfolds itself:

The *first* of these five stages lies in the decree of God. From the very moment that the Father gave us to the Son, we were really His own, and a relation was established between Him and us, not weak and feeble, but so deep and extensive that all subsequent relations with Immanuel spring from this fundamental root-relation alone.

The *second* stage is in the Incarnation, when, adopting our flesh, entering into our nature, He made that preexisting, essential relation actual; when the bond of union passed from the divine will, that is, from the decree, into actual existence. Christ in the flesh carries all believers in the loins of His grace, as Adam carried all the children of men in the loins of his flesh. Hence, not figuratively nor metaphorically, but in the proper sense, Scripture teaches that when Jesus died and arose we died and arose with Him and in Him.

The *third* stage begins when we ourselves appear not in our birth, but in our regeneration; when the Lord God begins to work supernaturally in our souls; when in love's hour Eternal Love conceives in us the child of God. Until then the mystic union was hid in the decree and in the Mediator, but in and by regeneration the person appears with whom the Lord Jesus will establish it. However, not regeneration first and then something new, viz., union with Christ, but in the very moment of completed regeneration that union becomes an internally accomplished fact.

This third stage must be carefully distinguished from the *fourth,* which begins not with the quickening, but with the first *conscious exercise of faith.* For, although in regeneration the faculty of faith was implanted, it may for a long time remain inactive; and only when the Holy Spirit causes it to act, producing genuine faith and conversion in us, is the union with Christ established *subjectively.*

This union is *not* the subsequent fruit of a higher degree of holiness, but coincides with the *first exercise* of faith. Faith which does not live in Christ is no faith, but its counterfeit. Genuine faith is wrought in us by the Holy Ghost, and all that He imparts to us He draws from Christ. Hence there may be an apparent or pretended faith without the union with Christ, but not a real faith. Wherefore it is an assured fact that the first sigh of the soul, in its first exercise of faith, is the result of the wonderful union of the soul with its Surety.

We do not deny, however, that there is a gradual increase of the conscious realization, of the lively feeling, and of the free enjoyment of this union. A child possesses its mother from the first moment of its existence, but the sensible enjoyment of its mother's love gradually awakens and increases with the years, until he fully knows what a treasure God has given him in his mother. And thus the consciousness and enjoyment of what we have in our Savior becomes *gradually* clearer and deeper, until there comes a moment when we fully realize how rich God has made us in Jesus. And by this many are led to think that their union with Christ dates from that moment. This is only apparently so. Although then they became *fully conscious* of their *treasure* in Christ, the union itself existed (even subjectively) from the moment of their first cry of faith.

This leads to the *fifth* and *last* stage, viz., death. Rejoicing in Him with joy unspeakable and full of glory, although not seeing Him, much more remains to be desired. Hence our union with Him does not attain its fullest unfolding until every lack be supplied and we see Him as He is; and in that blissful vision we shall be like Him, for then He will give us all that He has. Therefore faith makes us partakers first of *Himself* and then of all His *gifts,* as the Heidelberg Catechism clearly teaches.

The *third* point to which we call attention is the nature of this union with Immanuel.

It has a nature *peculiar* to itself; it may be *compared* to other unions, but it can never be *fully* explained by them. Wonderful is the bond between body and soul; more wonderful still the sacramental bond of holy Baptism and the Lord's Supper; equally wonderful the vital union between mother and child in her blood, like that of the vine and its growing branches; wonderful the bond of wedlock; and much more wonderful the union with the Holy Spirit, established by His indwelling. But the union with Immanuel is distinct from all these.

It is a union invisible and intangible; the ear fails to perceive it, and it eludes all investigation; yet it is very real union and communion, by which the life of the Lord Jesus directly affects and controls us. As the unborn babe lives on the mother-blood, which has its heart-beat *outside* of him, so we also live on the Christ-life, which has its heart-beat *not* in our soul, but *outside* of us, in heaven above, in Christ Jesus.

In the *fourth* place, although the union with Christ coincides with our *covenant*-relation to Him as the Head, yet it is not *identical* with it.

Our relations of fellowship to Christ are many. There is a fellowship of feeling and inclination, of love and attachment; we are disciples of the Prophet; we are His blood-bought possession; the subjects of the King; and members of the Covenant of Grace of which He is the Head. But instead of absorbing the *"unio mystica,"* they are all *based* upon it. Without this real bond all the others are only imaginary. Hence, while we know, feel, and confess that it is glorious to be safely hid in our Covenant-Head, it is sweeter, more precious and delightful to live in the mystical fellowship of Love.

Fifth Chapter
Calling and Repentance

27

The Calling of the Regenerate

Whom He did predestinate, them He also called—Romans 8:30.

In order to hear, the sinner, deaf by nature, must receive hearing ears. "He that hath ears let him hear what the Spirit saith unto the churches."

But by nature the sinner does not belong to these favored ones. This is a daily experience. Of two clerks in the same office, one obeys the call and the other rejects it; not because he despises it, but because he does not hear God's call in it. Hence God's quickening act antedates the sinner's hearing, and thus he becomes able to hear the Word.

The quickening, the implanting of the faith-faculty, and the uniting of the soul to Christ, apparently three acts, are in reality but one act, together constituting (objectively) the so-called *first grace.* In the operation of this grace the sinner is *perfectly passive* and indifferent; the subject of an action which does not involve the slightest operation, yielding, or even non-resistance on his part.

In fact, the sinner, being dead in trespasses and sins, is under this first grace like a *soulless, motionless* body, with all the passive properties belonging to a corpse. This fact cannot be stated with sufficient force and emphasis. It is an *absolute* passivity. And every effort or inclination to claim for the sinner the minutest cooperation in this first grace destroys the Gospel, severs the artery of the Christian confession, and is not only heretical, but anti-Scriptural in the highest sense.

This is the point where the sign-post is erected, where the roads divide, where the men of the purified, that is, the Reformed Confession, part company with their opponents.

Having stated this fact forcibly and definitely, it is of the utmost importance to state with equal emphasis that, in all the subsequent operations of grace (so-called *second grace)*, this absolute passivity is made to cease by the wonderful act of the first grace. Hence in all subsequent grace the sinner to some extent cooperates.

In the first grace the sinner is absolutely like a corpse. But the sinner's first passivity and his subsequent cooperation must not be confounded. There is a passivity, after the Scripture, which cannot be exaggerated, which must be left intact, but there is also a passivity which is pretended, anti-Scriptural, and sinful. The difference between the two is not that the former is partially cooperating, and the latter without any cooperation whatever. Surely by such temporizing the churches and the souls in them are not inspired with energy and enthusiasm. No; the difference between the sound and the sickly passivity consists herein, that the former, which is absolute and unlimited, belongs to the *first grace, to which it is indispensable;* while the latter clings to the *second grace, where it does not belong.*

Let there be clear insight into this truth, which is after all very simple. The elect but unregenerate sinner can do nothing, and the work that is to be wrought in him must be wrought by another. This is the first grace. But after this is accomplished he is no longer passive, for something was brought into him which in the second work of grace will cooperate with God.

But it is not implied that the elect and regenerate sinner is now able to do anything without God; or that if God should cease working in him, conversion and sanctification would follow of themselves. Both these representations are thoroughly untrue, un-Reformed, and unchristian, because they detract from the work of the Holy Spirit in the elect. No; all spiritual good is of grace to the end; grace not only in regeneration, but at every step of the way of life. From the beginning to the end and throughout eternity the Holy Spirit is the Worker, of regeneration and conversion, of justification and every part of sanctification, of glorification, and of all the bliss of the redeemed. Nothing may be subtracted from this.

But while the Holy Spirit is the only Worker in the first grace, in all subsequent operations of grace the regenerate *always* cooperates with Him. Hence it is not true, as some say, that the regenerate is just as passive as the unregenerate; this only detracts from the work of the Holy Spirit in the *first grace.* Neither is it true that henceforth the regenerate is the principal worker, only *assisted* by the Holy Spirit; for this is equally derogatory to the Spirit's work in the *second grace.*

Both these errors should be opposed and rejected. For although, on the one hand, it is said that the regenerate, considered out of Christ, still lies in the midst of death; yet, though he be *considered* a thousand times out of Christ, he remains in Him, for once in His hand no one can pluck him out of it. And although, on the other hand, the regenerate is constantly admonished to be active and diligent, yet, though the horse does the pulling, it is not the horse but the driver *who drives the carriage.*

Reserving this last point until we consider sanctification, we now consider the *calling,* for this sheds more light upon the confession of the Reformed churches concerning the *second grace* than any other part of the work of grace.

After the elect sinner is born again, that is, quickened, endowed with the faculty of faith, and united with Jesus, the next work of grace in him is *calling,* of which Scripture speaks with such emphasis and so often. "But as He which has *called* you is holy, so be ye holy in all manner of conversation"; "Who hath *called* you out of darkness into His marvelous light"; "The God of all grace who hath *called* us unto His eternal glory"; "Whereunto He *called* you by our Gospel, to the obtaining of the glory of our Lord Jesus Christ"; "Who hath *called* you unto His Kingdom and Glory"; "I beseech you to walk worthy of the calling wherewith ye were called"; and not to mention more: "Give diligence to make your *calling* and election sure; for if ye do these things ye shall never fall."

In the Sacred Scripture *calling* has, like *regeneration,* a wider sense and a more limited.

In the former sense, it means to be called to the *eternal glory;* hence this includes all that *precedes,* that is, calling to repentance, to faith, to sanctification, to the performance of duty, to glory, to the eternal kingdom, etc.

Of this, however, we do not speak now. It is now our intention to consider the calling in its limited sense, which signifies exclusively the calling whereby we are called from darkness into light, that is, the call unto *repentance.*

This call unto *repentance* is by many placed upon the same level with the "drawing," of which, for example, Jesus speaks: "No man can come unto Me except the Father *draw* him." This we find also in some of St. Paul's words: "Who hath *delivered* [Dutch translation, *drawn]* us from the power of darkness"; "That He might deliver *[draw]* us from this present evil world according to the will of God and our Father." However, this seems to me less correct. He that must be *drawn* seems to be *unwilling.* He that is *called* must be *able* to come. The first implies that the sinner is still passive, and therefore refers to the operation of the *first grace;* the second addresses the sinner himself, and counts him able to come, and hence belongs to the *second grace.*

This "calling" is a summons. It is not merely the calling of one to tell him something, but a call implying the command to come; or a beseeching call, as when St. Paul prays: "As though God did beseech you, be ye reconciled to God"; or as in the Proverbs: "My son, give Me thine heart."

God sends this call forth by the preachers of the Word: not by the independent preaching of irresponsible men, but by those whom He Himself sends forth; men especially endowed, hence whose calling is not their own, but His. They are the ministers of the Word, royal ambassadors, in the name of the King of Kings demanding our heart, life, and person; yet whose value and honor depend exclusively upon their divine mission and commission. As the value of an echo depends upon the correct returning of the word received, so does their value, honor, and significance depend solely upon the correctness wherewith they call, as an echo of the Word of God. He who calls correctly fills the highest conceivable office on earth; for he calls kings and emperors, standing above them. But he who calls incorrectly or not at all is like a sounding brass; as a minister of the Word he is worthless and without honor. True to the pure Word, he is *all;* without it, he is *nothing.* Such is the responsibility of the preacher.

This should be noticed lest Arminianism creep into the holy office. The preacher must be but instrument of the Holy Spirit; even the sermon must be the product of the Holy Ghost. To suppose that a preacher can have the least authority, honor, or official significance outside of the Word, is to make the office Arminian; not the Holy Spirit, but the dominie, is the worker; he works with all his might, and the Holy Spirit may be the minister's *assistant.* To avoid such mistake, our Reformed churches have always purged themselves of the leaven of clericalism.

And through this office the call goes forth from the pulpit, in the catechetical class, in the family, in writing, and by personal exhortation. However, not always to every sinner directly through the office. On a ship at sea God may use a godly commander to call sinners to repentance. In a hospital without spiritual supervision the Lord may use a pious man or woman, both to nurse the sick and call their souls to repentance. In a village where the quasi-minister neglects his duty, the Lord God may be pleased to draw souls to life by printed sermons and books, by a newspaper even, or by individual exhortation.

And yet in all these the authority to call reposes in the divine embassy of the ministry of the Word. For the instruments of the call, whether they were persons or printed books, proceeded from the office. The persons were themselves called through the office, and they only transmitted the divine message; and the printed books offered on paper what otherwise is heard in the sanctuary.

This calling of the Holy Spirit proceeds in and through the preaching of the Word, and calls upon the *regenerated* sinner to arise from death, and to let Christ give him light. It is not a calling of persons still *un*regenerate, simply because such have *no hearing ear.*

It is true that the preaching of missionary or minister of the Word addresses itself also to others, but this is not at all in conflict with what we have just said. In the first place, because there is also an outward call to the unregenerate, in order to deprive them of an excuse, and to show that they have *no hearing ears.* And second, because the minister of the Word does not know whether a man is born again or not, wherefore he *may make no difference.*

As a rule, every baptized person should be reckoned as belonging to the regenerated (but not always converted); wherefore the preacher must call every baptized person to repentance, as though he were born again. But let no one commit the mistake of applying this rule, which applies only to the *Church as a whole,* to *every person* in the Church. This would be either the climax of thoughtlessness or a complete misunderstanding of the reality of the grace of God.

28

The Coming of the Called

That the purpose of God according to election might stand, not of works, but of Him that calleth—Romans 9:2.

The question is, whether the elect cooperate in the call. We say, Yes; for the call is no call, in the fullest sense of the word, unless the called one can hear and hears so distinctly that it impresses him, causes him to rise and to obey God. For this reason our fathers, for the sake of clearness, used to distinguish between the *ordinary* call and the *effectual* call.

God's call does not go forth to the elect alone. The Lord Jesus said: "Many are called, few are chosen." And the issue shows that masses of men die unconverted, although called by the outward, ordinary call.

Nor should this outward call be slighted or esteemed unimportant; for by it the judgment of many shall be made the heavier in the day of judgment: "If the mighty works which have been done in you had been done in Tyre and Sidon, they would have repented long ago in sackcloth and ashes. Therefore it shall be more tolerable for Tyre and Sidon than for you"; "And the servant which knew the Lord's will and did not according to His will shall be beaten with many stripes." Moreover, the effect of this outward call reaches sometimes much deeper than is generally supposed, and brings one sometimes to the very point of real conversion.

The unregenerate are not so insensible to the truth as never to be touched by it. The decisive words of Hebrews 6, concerning the apparently converted who have even tasted of the heavenly gift, prove the contrary. St. Peter speaks of sows which were washed and then returned to the wallowing in the mire. One can be persuaded to be *almost* a Christian. But for the selling of his goods the rich young ruler would have been won for Christ. Wherefore the effect of the ordinary call is by no means as weak and meager as is commonly believed. In the parable of the sower the fourth class of hearers alone belong to the elect, for they alone bear fruit. Still there is among two of the remaining classes a considerable amount of growth. One of them even produces high stalks and ears; only there is *no fruit.*

And for this reason the men that company with the people of God should earnestly examine their own hearts, whether their following of the Word is the result of having the seed sown in "good ground." Oh, there is so much of illumination and of delight even; and yet only to be choked, because it does not contain the *genuine* germ of life.

All these unregenerate persons lack *saving grace.* They hear only with the carnal understanding. They receive the Word, but only in the field of their unsanctified imagination. They let it work upon their natural conscience. It plays merely upon the waves of their natural emotions. Thus they may be moved to tears, and they ardently love whatever so affects them. Yea, they often perform many good works which are truly praiseworthy; they may even give their goods to the poor, and their bodies to be burned. Their salvation is therefore considered to be a matter of fact. But the holy apostle completely destroys their hope, saying: "Though you speak with the tongues of men and of angels, though you understand all mystery, though you give all your goods to feed the poor, and though you give your body to be burned, and have not *love,* it profiteth you nothing."

Hence to be God's child and not a sounding brass, deep insight into the divine mysteries, an excited imagination, a troubled conscience, and waves of feeling are not required, for all these may be experienced without any real covenant grace, but what is needed is true, deep love operating in the heart, illuminating and vitalizing all these things.

Adam's sin consisted in this, that he banished all the love of God from his heart. Now it is impossible to be neutral or indifferent toward

God. When Adam ceased to love God, he began *to hate* Him. And it is this hatred of God which now lies at the bottom of the heart of every child of Adam. Hence conversion means this, that a man get rid of that *hatred* and receive *love* in its place. He who says from the heart, "I love the Lord," is all right. What more can he desire!

But as long as there is no love for God, there is *nothing.* For mere willingness to do something for God, even to bear great sacrifices, and to be very pious and benevolent, except it spring from the right motive, is in its deepest ground nothing but a despising of God. However beautiful the veneering, all these apparently good works are inwardly cankered, sin-eaten, and decayed. Love alone imparts the real flavor to the sacrifice. Wherefore the holy apostle declares so sternly and sharply: "Though you give your body to be burned, and have not *love,* it profiteth you *nothing.*"

To perform good works in order to be saved, or to oblige God, or to make one's own piety lofty and conspicuous, is a growth from the old root and at the most but a *semblance* of love. To cherish true love for God is to be constrained by love to yield one's ego with all that it is and has, and to let God be God again. And the ordinary, the general, the outward call never has such effect; it is incapable of producing it.

Wherefore we leave the ordinary call and return to the call which is particular, wonderful, inward, and effectual; which addresses itself *not to all,* but exclusively to the *elect.*

This call, which is spoken of as *"heavenly"* (Heb. 3:1), as *"holy"* (2 Tim. 1:9), as *"being without repentance"* (Rom. 11:29), is *"according to God's purpose"* (Rom. 8:28), is *"from above in Christ Jesus our Lord"* (Phil. 3:14), and does not have its starting-point in the preaching. He that calls by it is *God,* not the minister. And this call goes forth by the means of two agencies, one coming to man from without and the other from within. Both these agencies are effectual, and the call has accomplished its purpose and the sinner has come to repentance as soon as their workings meet and unite in the center of his being.

Hence we deny that the regenerate, hearing the preached Word, will come of *himself.* We do not thus understand their cooperation. If the inward call is sufficient, how is it that the regenerate can sometimes hear the preaching without arising, unrepentant, refusing to let Christ give him light? But we confess that the call of the regenerate is twofold:

from without by the preached Word, and from within by the exhortation and conviction of the Holy Spirit.

Hence the work of the Holy Spirit in the calling is *twofold:*

The *first work* is, as He comes with the Word: the Word which is inspired, prepared, committed to writing, and preserved by Himself, who is God the Holy Ghost. And He brings that Word to the sinners by preachers whom He Himself has endowed with talents, animation, and spiritual insight. And so wonderful does He conduct that preaching through the channel of the office and of the historical development of the confession, that at last it comes to him in the form and character required to affect and win him.

We see in this a very mysterious leading of the Holy Spirit. Afterward a preacher will learn that, under his preaching in such a church and at such an hour, a regenerate person was converted. And yet he had not specially prepared himself for it. Frequently he did not even know that person; much less his spiritual condition. And yet, without knowing it, his thoughts were guided and his word was prepared in such a way by the Holy Ghost; perhaps he looked at the man in such a manner that his word, in connection with the Spirit's inward operation, became to him the real and concrete Word of God. We hear it often said: "That was directly preached at me." And so it was. It should be understood, however, that it was not the minister who preached at you, for he did not even think of you, but it was the Holy Spirit Himself. It was He who thought of you. It was He who had it all prepared for you. It was He Himself who wrought in you.

The ministers of the Word should therefore be exceedingly careful not in the least to boast of the conversions that occur under their ministry. When after days of failure the fisherman draws his net full of fishes, is this cause for the net to boast itself? Did it not come up empty again and again; and then was it not nearly torn asunder by the multitude of fishes?

To say that this proves the efficiency of the preacher is against the Scripture. There may be two ministers, the one well grounded in doctrine, the other but lightly furnished; and yet the former has no conversions in his church, while the latter is being richly blessed. In this the Lord God is and remains the Sovereign Lord. He passes by the heavily armed champions in Saul's army, and David, with scarcely any weapons at all, slays the giant Goliath. All that a preacher has to do is to consider how, in obedience to his Lord, he may minister the Word, leaving results with the Lord. And when the Lord God gives him conversions, and Satan whispers, "What an excellent preacher you are, that it was given you to convert so many men!" then he is to say, "Get thee behind me, Satan," giving the glory to the *Holy Spirit alone.*

However, it is not the Holy Spirit's only care in such a way and focus of life to cause the Word to come to a regenerate person, but He adds also a *second work,* viz., that by which the preached Word effectively enters the very center of his heart and life.

By this *second* care He so illuminates his natural understanding and strengthens his natural ability and imagination that he receives the general tenor of the preached Word and thoroughly understands its contents.

But this is not all, for even pretended believers may have this. The seed of the Word attains this growth also in those who have received the seed into a rocky ground and among thorns. Hence to this is added the *illumination* of his understanding, which wonderful gift enables him not only to apprehend the general sense of the preached Word, but also to perceive and realize that this Word comes to him directly *from God;* that it affects and condemns his very *being,* thus causing him to penetrate into its hidden essence and feel the sharp sting which effects *conviction.*

Lastly, the Holy Spirit plies this conviction—which otherwise would quickly vanish—so long and so severely, that finally the sting, like the keen edge of a lancet, pierces the thick skin and lays open the festering sore. This is in the called a very wonderful operation. The general *understanding* puts the matter before him; the *illumination* reveals to him what it contains; and the *conviction* puts the sharp two-edged sword directly upon his heart. Then, however, he is inclined to shrink from that sword; not to let it pierce through, but to let it glance harmlessly from the soul. But then the Holy Spirit, in full activity, continues to press that sword of conviction, driving it so forcibly into the soul that at last it cuts through and takes effect.

But this does not end the *calling.* For after the Holy Spirit has done all this, He begins to operate upon the *will;* not by forcibly bending it, as an iron rod in the strong hand of the blacksmith, but by making it, though stiff and unyielding, pliant and tender *from within.* He could not do this in the unregenerate. But having laid in regeneration the foundation of all these subsequent operations in the soul, He proceeds to build upon it; or, to take another figure, He draws the sprouts from the germ planted in the ground. They do not start of themselves, but He draws them out of the germ. A grain of wheat deposited in a desk remains what it is, but warmed by the sun in the soil, the heat causes it to sprout. And so it is here. The vital germ can do nothing of itself; it remains what it is. But when the Holy Spirit causes the fostering rays of the Sun of Righteousness to play upon it, then it germinates, and thus He draws from it the blade and the ear and the corn in the ear.

Hence the yielding of the will is the result of a tenderness and emotion and affection which sprang from the implanted germ of life, by which the will, which was at first inflexible, became pliant; by which that which was inclined to the left was drawn to the right. And so, by this last act, conviction, with all that it contains, was brought into the will; and this resulted in the yielding of self, giving glory to God.

And in this way love entered the soul—love tender, genuine, and mysterious, the ecstasy of which vibrates in our hearts during all our after-life.

And this finishes the exposition of the divine work of calling. It belongs to the elect alone. It is irresistible, and no man can hinder it. Without it no sinner ever passed from the bitterness of *hatred* to the sweetness of *love.* When the call and regeneration coincide, they seem to be one; and so they are to our consciousness, but actually they are distinct. They differ in this respect, that *regeneration* takes place independently of the *will* and *understanding;* that it is wrought in us without our aid or cooperation; while in *calling,* the will and understanding begin to act, so that we *hear* with both the outward and inward ear, and with the inclined will are *willing* to go out to the light.

29

Conversion of All That Come

Turn Thou me and I shall be turned—Jeremiah 31:18.

The elect, born again and effectually called, *converts himself.* To remain unconverted is impossible, but he inclines his ear, he turns his face to the blessed God, he is converted in the fullest sense of the word.

In conversion the fact of cooperation on the part of the saved sinner assumes a clearly defined and perceptible character. In regeneration there was none; in the calling there was a beginning of it; in conversion proper it became a fact. When the Holy Spirit *regenerates* a man, it is an "Effatha," that is, He opens the ear. When He effectually *calls* him, He speaks into that opened ear, which cooperates by receiving the sound, that is, by harkening. But when the Holy Spirit actually *converts* the man, then the act of man coalesces with the act of the Holy Spirit, and it is said: "Let the wicked forsake his way, *and let him return* unto the Lord, and He will have mercy upon him"; and in another place: "The law of the Lord is perfect, converting the soul."

It is a remarkable fact that the Sacred Scripture refers to conversion almost *one hundred and forty times* as being an act of man, and only *six times* as an act of the Holy Ghost. It is repeated again and again: "Repent and turn to the Lord your God"; "Turn, O backsliding children, saith the Lord" (Jer. 3:22); "Sinners shall return unto Thee" (Ps. 51:13, Dutch Version); "Repent and do thy first works" (Rev. 2:5).

But conversion as an act of the Holy Spirit is spoken of only in Psalm 19:8, "The law of the Lord is perfect, converting the soul"; in Jeremiah 31:18, "Turn Thou me and I shall be turned"; in Acts 11:18, "That God also to the Gentiles *granted* repentance unto life"; Romans 2:4, "That the goodness of God *leadeth* thee to repentance"; in 2 Timothy 2:25, "If God peradventure will *give* them repentance"; in Hebrews 6:6, "That it is impossible to *renew* such (as fall away) to repentance."

This fact should be carefully considered. When Scripture presents conversion as the Spirit's act but six times, and as man's act one hundred and forty times, in preaching the same proportion should be observed. And, therefore, the preachers who, when preaching on conversion, treat it almost invariably in its passive aspect and in the abstract; who apparently lack the courage and boldness to declare to their hearers that it is *their* duty to convert *themselves* unto God, seriously err. It has a very pious look, but it is against the Scripture. And yet it is perfectly natural that one should hesitate to say, *"You* must convert *yourself,"* so long as regeneration and conversion are still confounded. For then the declaration, *"You* must convert yourself," ignores the sovereignty of God, and implies that a dead sinner is still able to do something of himself. And this is the reason why the preachers who will not surrender the sovereignty of God, and who will not deduct anything from the deadness of the sinner, are afraid "to speak to deaf ears." Hence they *pray* for the conversion of the hearers, but dare not in the Name of the Lord *demand* it of them.

And nothing may be deducted either from the divine sovereignty or from the sinner's deadness. Every demand for conversion which has such tendency is Pelagianism, and must be rejected. But if the teaching of the Reformed Church in this respect be thoroughly understood, the whole difficulty disappears.

It should be noticed, however, that Scripture, speaking of conversion, does not always imply that it is *saving* conversion. The real work of salvation is always accompanied on its way by a phantom. Alongside of saving faith goes *temporal* faith; alongside of the effectual call, the *ordinary* call; and alongside of saving conversion, *ordinary* conversion.

Conversion in its saving sense occurs but once in a man's life, and this act can never be repeated. Once having passed from death unto life, he is alive and will never return unto death. Perdition is not a stream spanned by many bridges; nor does the saint, tossed between endless hopes and fears, cross the bridge leading to life, by and by to return by another to the shores of death. No; there is but one bridge, which can be crossed but once; and he that has crossed it is kept by the power of God from going back. Though all powers should combine to draw him back, God is stronger than all, and no one shall pluck him out of His hand.

We state this as distinctly and forcibly as possible, for at this point souls are often led astray. It is heard repeatedly these days, "Your conversion is not a momentary act, but an act of life which repeats itself constantly; and woe to the man who fails for a single day to be converted anew." And this is altogether wrong. Language should not be so confounded. Though the child *grows* for twenty years after he is *born,* and before he attains maturity, yet he is born but once, and neither *conception* nor *pregnancy* before it, nor *growth* after it, is called *"birth."*

The fixed boundary should be respected also in this instance. It is true that conversion is preceded by something else, but that is called not "conversion," but "regeneration" and "calling"; and so there is something following "conversion," but that is called "sanctification." No doubt the word "conversion" may also be applied to the return of the converted but backslidden child of God, after the example of Scripture, but then it refers not to the saving act of conversion, but to the continuance of the work once begun, or to a return not from death, but from a temporary going astray.

In order to discriminate correctly in this matter, it is necessary to notice the *fourfold use* of the word conversion in the Scripture.

1. "Conversion," in its *widest* scope, signifies a forsaking of wickedness and a disposition to morality. In this sense it is said of the Ninevites that God saw their works, that they turned from their evil works. This does not imply, however, that all these Ninevites belonged to the elect, and that every one of them was saved.

2. "Conversion," in its *limited* sense, signifies saving conversion, as in Isaiah 55:7: "Let the wicked forsake his way, and the unrighteous man his thoughts, and let him return unto the Lord, and He will have mercy upon him, and to our God, for He will abundantly pardon."

3. And *again,* "conversion" signifies that, even after it has become a

fact in our hearts, its principles must be applied to every relation of our life. A converted person may for a long time continue to indulge in bad habits and ungodly practices, but gradually his eyes are opened for the evil, and then he repents and forsakes the one after the other. So we read in Ezekiel 18:30: "Repent and turn yourselves from *all* your transgressions."

4. *Lastly,* "conversion" signifies the return of converted persons to their first love, after a season of coldness and weakness in the faith, for example, "Remember, therefore, from whence thou art fallen, and repent and do thy first works" (Rev. 2:5).

But in this connection we speak of *saving* conversion, of which we make the following remarks:

First—It is not the spontaneous act of the regenerate. Without the Holy Spirit conversion would not follow regeneration. Even though called, he could not come of himself. Hence it is of primary importance to acknowledge the Holy Spirit, and to honor His work as the first cause of conversion as well as of regeneration and calling. As no one can pray as he ought unless the Holy Spirit prays in him with groans that cannot be uttered, so no regenerate and called person can convert himself as he ought unless the Holy Spirit begin and continue the work in him. The redemptive work is not like the growing plant, increasing of itself. Nay, if the saint is a temple of God, the Holy Spirit dwells in him. And this indwelling indicates that everything accomplished by the saint is wrought in him in communion with, by the incitement and through the animation of the Holy Spirit. The implanted life is not an isolated germ left to root in the soul without the Holy Spirit and the Mediator, but it is carried, kept, bedewed, and fostered from moment to moment out of Christ by the Holy Spirit. As men cannot speak without air and the operation of Providence vitalizing the organs of respiration and articulation, so it is impossible that the regenerated man can live and speak and act from the new life without being supported, incited, and animated by the Holy Spirit.

Hence when the Holy Spirit calls that man and he turns himself, then there is not the slightest part in this act of the will which is not supported, incited, and animated by the Holy Spirit.

Second—This saving conversion is also the conscious and voluntary choice and act of the person born again and called. While the air and impulse to speak must come from without, and my organs of speech must be supported by the providence of God, *yet it is I who speak.* And in much stronger sense does the Holy Spirit in conversion work upon the wheels and springs of man's regenerated personality, so that all His operations must pass through man's ego.

Many of His operations do not affect the ego, as in Balaam's case. But not so in conversion. Then the Holy Spirit works only *through* us. Whatever He wills He brings into *our will;* He causes all His actions to be effected through the organism of *our being.*

Hence man must be commanded, "Convert thyself." The teacher bids the pupil speak, although he knows that the child cannot do so unaided by Providence. In the new life the ego depends upon the Holy Spirit who dwells and works in him. But in conversion he knows nothing of this indwelling, nor that he is born again; and it would be useless to speak to him about it. He must be told, "Convert thyself." If the Spirit's action accompanies that word, the man will convert himself; if not, he will continue unconverted. But though he convert himself, he will not boast, I have *done this myself,* but bow down in thankfulness and glorify that divine work *by which he was converted.*

In these two we find the evidence of genuine conversion: first, the man bidden, converts himself, and then he gratefully gives glory to the Holy Spirit *alone.* Not that we fear a man's conversion will be hindered by someone's neglect. In all the work of God's grace His Almightiness sweeps away everything that resists, so that all opposition melts away like wax, and every mountain of pride flees from His presence. Neither slothfulness nor neglect can ever hinder an elect person from passing from death into life at the appointed time.

But there is a *responsibility* for the preacher, for the pastor, for parents and guardians. To be free from a man's blood, we must tell every man that conversion is his *urgent duty;* and *to be without excuse before God,* after his conversion, we must give thanks to God, who alone has accomplished it in and through His creature.

Sixth Chapter
Justification

30

Justification

Being justified freely by His grace, through the redemption that is in Christ Jesus—Romans 3:24.

The Heidelberg Catechism teaches that true conversion consists of these two parts: the *dying* of the old man, and the *rising again* of the new. This last should be noticed. The Catechism says not that the new life *originates* in conversion, but that it *arises* in conversion. That which arises must exist before. Else how could it arise? This agrees with our statement that regeneration precedes conversion, and that by the effectual calling the newborn child of God is brought to conversion.

We now proceed to consider a matter which, though belonging to the same subject and running parallel with it, yet moves along an entirely different line, viz., *Justification.*

In the Sacred Scripture, justification occupies the most conspicuous place, and is presented as of greatest importance for the sinner: "For all have sinned, and come short of the glory of God being justified freely by His grace, through the redemption that is in Christ Jesus" (Rom. 3:24). "Therefore, being *justified* by faith, we have peace with God through our Lord Jesus Christ" (Rom. 5:1); "Who was delivered for our offenses and raised again for our *justification*" (Rom. 4:25);

"Who of God is made unto us from God, wisdom and *righteousness* and sanctification and redemption" (1 Cor. 1:30).

And not only is this so strongly emphasized by *Scripture,* but it was also the very kernel of the *Reformation,* which puts this doctrine of "justification by faith" boldly and clearly in opposition to the "meritorious works of Rome." "Justification by faith" was in those days the shibboleth of the heroes of faith, Martin Luther in the van.

And when, in the present century, a self-wrought sanctification presented itself again, as the actual power of redemption, it was the not insignificant merit of Köhlbrugge, that he, though less comprehensively than the reformers, fastened this matter of justification, with penetrating earnestness, upon the conscience of Christendom. It may have been superfluous for the churches still truly Reformed, but it was exceedingly opportune for the circles where the garland of truth was less closely woven, and the sense of justice had been allowed to become weak, as partially in our own country, but especially beyond our borders. There are in Switzerland and in Bohemia groups of men who have heard, for the first time, of the necessity of justification by faith, through the labors of Köhlbrugge.

Through the grace of God, our people did not go so far astray; and where the Ethicals, largely from principle, surrendered this point of doctrine, the Reformed did and do oppose them, admonishing them with all energy, and as often as possible, not to merge justification in sanctification.

Regarding the question, how *justification* differs, on the one hand, from "regeneration," and, on the other, from "calling and conversion," we answer that justification emphasizes the idea of *right.*

Right regulates the relations between two persons. Where there is but one there is no right, simply because there are no relations to regulate. Hence by *right* we understand either the right of man in relation to man, or the claim of God upon man. It is in this last sense that we use the word right.

The Lord is our Lawgiver, our Judge, our King. Hence He is absolutely Sovereign: as Lawgiver determining what is right; as Judge judging our being and doing; as King dispensing rewards and punishments. This sheds light upon the difference between justification and regeneration.

The new birth and the call and conversion have to do with our *being* as sinners or as regenerate men, but justification with the *relation* which we sustain to God, either as sinners or as those born again.

Apart from the question of right, the sinner may be considered as a sick person, who is infected and inoculated with disease. After being born again he improves, the infection disappears, the corruption ceases, and he prospers again. But this concerns his *person* alone, how he is, and what his prospects are; it does not touch the question of right.

The question of right arises when I see in the sinner a creature not his own, but *belonging* to another.

Herein is all the difference. If man is to me the principal factor, so that I have nothing else in view but his improvement and deliverance from misery, then the Almighty God is in this whole matter a mere Physician, called in and affording assistance, who receives His fee, and is discharged with many thanks. The question of right does not enter here at all. So long as the sinner is made more holy, all is well. Of course, if he is made perfect, all the better. Clearly understanding, however, that man belongs not to himself, but to another, the matter assumes an entirely different aspect. For then he cannot *be* or *do* as he pleases, but another has determined what he must be and what he must do. And if he does or is otherwise, he is guilty as a transgressor: guilty because he rebelled, guilty because he transgressed.

Hence when I believe in the divine sovereignty, the sinner appears to me in an entirely different aspect. As infected and mortally ill, he is to be pitied and kindly treated, but considered as belonging to God, standing under God, and as having robbed God, that same sinner becomes a guilty transgressor.

This is true to some extent of animals. When I lasso a wild horse on the American prairies for training, it never enters my mind to punish him for his wildness. But the runaway in the city streets must be punished. He is vicious; he threw his rider; he refused to be led and chose his own way. Hence he needs to be punished.

And man much more so. When I meet him in his wild career of sin, I know that he is a rebel, that he broke the reins, threw his rider, and now dashes on in mad revolt. Hence such sinner must be not only healed, but *punished.* He does not need *medical* treatment alone, but before all things he needs *juridical* treatment.

Apart from his disease a sinner has done evil; there is no virtue in him; he has violated the right; he deserves punishment. Suppose, for a moment, that sin had not touched his person, had not corrupted him, had left him intact as a man, then there would have been no need of regeneration, of healing, of a rising again, of sanctification; nevertheless he would have been subject to the vengeance of justice.

Hence man's case in relation to his God must be considered *juridically.* Be not afraid of that word, brother. Rather insist that it be pronounced with as strong an emphasis as possible. It must be emphasized, and all the more strongly, because for so many years it has been scorned, and the churches have been made to believe that this *"juridical"* aspect of the case was of no importance; that it was a representation really unworthy of God; that the principal thing was to bring forth fruit meet for repentance.

Beautiful teaching, gradually pushed into the world from the closet of philosophy: teaching that declares that morality included the right and stood far above the right; that "right" was chiefly a notion of the life of less civilized ages and of crude persons, but of no importance to our ideal age and to the ideal development of humanity and of individuals; yea, that in some respects it is even objectionable, and should never be allowed to enter into that holy and high and tender relation that exists between God and man.

The fruit of this pestilential philosophy is, that now in Europe *the sense of right* is gradually dying of slow consumption. Among the Asiatic nations this sense of right has greater vitality than among us. Might is again greater than right. Right is again the right of the strongest. And the luxurious circles, who in their atony of spirit at first protested against the *"juridical"* in *theology,* discover now with terror that certain classes in society are losing more and more respect for the "juridical" in the *question of property.* Even in regard to the possession of land and house, and treasure and fields, this new conception of life considers the "juridical" a less noble idea. Bitter satire! You who, in your wantonness, started the mockery of the "juridical" in connection with God, find your punishment now in the fact that the lower classes start the mockery of this "juridical" in connection with your money and your goods. Yea, more than this. When recently in Paris a woman was tried for having shot and killed a man in court, not only did the jury acquit her, but she was made the heroine of an ovation. Here also other motives were deemed more precious, and the "juridical" aspect had nothing to do with it.

And, therefore, in the name of God and of the right which He has ordained, we urgently request that every minister of the Word, and every man in his place, help and labor, with clear consciousness and energy, to stop this dissolution of the right, with all the means at their disposal; and especially solemnly and effectually to restore to its own conspicuous place the juridical feature of the sinner's relation to his God. When this is done, we shall feel again the stimulus that will cause the soul's relaxed muscles to contract, rousing us from our semi-unconsciousness. Every man, and especially every member of the Church, must again realize his juridical relation to God now and forever; that he is not merely man or woman, but a creature belonging to God, absolutely controlled by God; and guilty and punishable when not acting according to the will of God.

This being clearly understood, it is evident that regeneration and calling and conversion, yea, even complete reformation and sanctification, cannot be sufficient; for, although these are very glorious, and deliver you from sin's stain and pollution, and help you not to violate the law so frequently, yet they do not touch your juridical relation to God.

When a mutinous battalion gets into serious straits, and the general, hearing of it, delivers them at the cost of ten killed and twenty wounded, who had not mutinied, and brings them back and feeds them, do you think that that will be all? Do you not see that such battalion is still liable to punishment with decimation? And when man mutinied against his God, and got himself into trouble and nearly perished with misery, and the Lord God sent him help to save him, and called him back, and he returned, can that be the end of it? Do you not clearly see that he is still liable to severe punishment? In case of a burglar who robs and kills, but in making his escape breaks his leg, and is sent to the hospital where he is treated, and then goes out a cripple unable to repeat his crime, do you think that the judge would give him his liberty, saying: "He is healed now and will never do it again"? No; he will be tried, convicted, and incarcerated. Even so here. Because by our sins and transgressions we have wounded ourselves, and made ourselves wretched, and are in need of medical help, is our guilt forgotten for this reason?

Why, then, are such undermining ideas brought among the people? Why is it that under the appearance of love a sentimental Christianity is introduced about the "dear Jesus," and "that we are so sick," and "the Physician is passing by," and that "it is, oh, so glorious to be in fellowship with that holy Mediator"?

Are our people really ignorant of the fact that this whole representation stands diametrically opposed to Sacred Scripture—opposed to all that ever animated the Church of Christ and made it strong? Do they not feel that such a feeble and spongy Christianity is a clay too soft for the making of heroes in the Kingdom of God? And do they not see that the number of men who are drawn to the "dear Jesus" is much smaller now than that of the men who formerly were drawn to the *Mediator of the right,* who with His precious blood hath fully *satisfied* for all our sins?

And when it is answered, "That is just what we teach; reconciliation in His blood, redemption through His death! It is all paid for us! Only come and hear our preaching and sing our hymns!" Then we beseech the brethren who thus speak to be serious for a moment. For, behold, our objection is not that you deny the reconciliation through His blood, but that, by being silent on the question of God's right, and of our state of condemnation, and by being satisfied when the people "only come to Jesus," you allow the *consciousness of guilt* to wear out, you make genuine *repentance* impossible, you substitute a certain discontent with oneself for *brokenness of heart;* and thus you weaken the faculty to feel, to understand, and to realize what the meaning is of reconciliation through the blood of the cross.

It is quite possible to bring about reconciliation without touching the question of the right at all. By some misunderstanding two friends have become estranged, separated from, and hostile to each other. But they may be reconciled. Not necessarily by making one to see that he violated the rights of the other; this was perhaps never intended. And even if there was some right violated, it would not be expedient to speak of the past, but to cover it with the mantle of love and to look only to the future. And such reconciliation, if successful, is very delightful, and may have cost both the reconciled and the reconciler much of conflict and sacrifice, yea, prayers and tears. And yet, with all this, such reconciliation does not touch the question of right.

In this way it appears to us these brethren preach reconciliation. It is true that they preach it with much warmth and animation even, but—and this is our complaint—they consider and present it as an enmity caused by whispering, misunderstanding, and wrong inclination, rather than *by violation of the right.* And, in consequence, their preaching of reconciliation through the blood of the cross no longer causes the deep chord of the right to vibrate in men's souls, but it resembles the reconciliation of two friends, who at an evil hour became estranged from each other.

31

Our Status

And he believed in the Lord: and he counted it to him for righteousness—Genesis 15:6.

The right touches a man's status. So long as the law has not proven him guilty, has not convicted and sentenced him, his legal status is that of a free and law-abiding citizen. But as soon as his guilt is proven in court and the jury has convicted him, he passes from that into the status of the bound and law-breaking citizen.

The same applies to our relation to God. Our status before God is that either of the just or of the unjust. In the former, we are not condemned or we are released from condemnation. He that is still under condemnation occupies the status of the unjust.

Hence, and this is noteworthy, a man's status depends not upon what he *is,* but upon what he *is,* but upon the decision of the proper authorities regarding him; not upon what he *is actually,* but upon what he is *counted* to be.

A clerk in an office is innocently suspected of embezzlement, and accused before a court of law. He pleads not guilty, but the suspicions against him carry conviction, and the judge condemns him. Now, though he did not embezzle, is actually innocent, he is *counted* guilty. And since a man does not determine his own status, but his sovereign or judge determines it for him, the status of this clerk, although innocent, is from the moment of his conviction, that of a law-breaker. And the contrary may occur just as well. In the absence of convicting evidence the judge may acquit a dishonest clerk, who, although guilty and a law-breaker, still retains his status of a law-abiding and honest citizen. In this case he is dishonorable, but he is *counted* honorable. Hence a man's status depends not upon what he actually is, but what he is *counted* to be.

The reason is, that man's status has no reference to his inward *being*, but only to the *manner* in which he is to be treated. It would be useless to determine this himself, for his fellow citizens would not receive it. Though he asserted a hundred times, "I am an honorable citizen," they would pay no attention to it. But if the judge declares him honorable, and then they should dare to call him dishonorable, there would be a power to maintain his status against those who attack him. Hence a man's own declaration cannot obtain him a legal status. He may fancy or assume a status of righteousness, but it has no stability, it is no *status*.

This explains why, in our own good land, a man's legal status as a citizen is determined not by himself, but solely by the king, either as sovereign or as judge. The king is judge, for all judgment is pronounced in his name; and, although the judiciary cannot be denied a certain authority independent of the executive, yet in every sentence it is the king's judicature which pronounces judgment. Hence a man's status depends solely upon the king's decision. Now the king has decided, once for all, that every citizen never convicted of crime is counted honorable. Not because all are honorable, but that they shall be *counted* as such. Hence so long as a man was never sentenced, he passes for honorable, even though he is not. And as soon as he is sentenced, he is considered dishonorable, though he is perfectly honorable. *And thus his status is determined by his king;* and in it he is accounted not according to what he is, but what his *king* counts him to be. Even without the judiciary, it is the king who determines a man's state in society, not according to what he is, but what the king counts him to be.

A person's sex is determined not by his condition, but by what the registrar of vital statistics in his register has *declared* him to be. If by some mistake a girl were registered as a boy, and therefore counted as a boy, then at the proper time she would be summoned to serve in the militia, unless the mistake were corrected, and she be counted to be what she is. It may be a *pretended,* and not the *real,* child of the rich nobleman in whose name it is registered. And yet it makes no difference whose child it really is, for the state will support it in all its rights of inheritance, because it passes for the child of that nobleman, and is *counted* to be his legitimate child.

Hence it is the rule in society that a man's status is determined *not* by his actual condition, nor by his own declaration, but by the sovereign under whom he stands. And this sovereign has the power, by his decision, to assign to a man the status to which, according to his condition, he belongs, or to put him in a status where he does not belong, but to which he is accounted to belong.

This is the case even in matters where mistakes are out of the question. At the time of the king's death and of the pregnancy of his widow, a prince or princess is counted to exist, even before he or she is born. And, accordingly, while the child is still a nursing baby, it is counted to be the *owner* of large possessions, even though these possessions may be entirely lost, before the child can hear of them. And so there are a number of cases where *standing* and *condition,* without anybody's fault or mistake, are entirely different; simply because it is possible that a man be in a state into which he has not yet grown.

The king alone can determine his own status; if it pleases him to register tomorrow *incognito,* as a count or a baron, he will be relieved from the usual royal honors.

We have elaborated this point more largely, because the Ethicals and the Mystics have got our poor people so bitterly out of the habit of reckoning with this *counting of God.* The word of Scripture, "Abraham believed, and it was *counted* to him for righteousness," is no longer understood; or it is made to refer to the *merit* of faith, which is Arminian doctrine.

The Holy Spirit often speaks of this *counting* of God: "I am *counted* with them that go down into the pit"; "The Lord shall *count* them when He writeth up the peoples"; "And it was *counted* unto Phineas for righteousness unto all generations, forevermore." So it is said of Jesus, that "He was *counted* [numbered] with the transgressors"; of Judas that "he was *counted* with the eleven"; of the *un*circumcision which keeps the law, that "it shall be *counted* unto him for circumcision"; of Abraham that "his faith was *counted* unto him for righteousness"; of him "that worketh not, believeth on Him that justifieth the ungodly," that "his faith is *counted* unto him for righteousness"; and of the children of the promise that "they are *counted* for the seed."

It is this very counting that appears to the children of this present age so incomprehensible and problematic. They will not hear of it. And, as Rome at one time severed the tendon of the Gospel, by merging justification in sanctification, mixing and identifying the two, so do people now refuse to listen to anything but an Ethical justification, which is actually only a species of sanctification. Hence God's *counting* counts for nothing. It is not heeded. It has no worth nor significance attached to it. The only question is what a man *is*. The measure of worth is nothing else but the worth of our *personality*.

And this we oppose most emphatically. It is a denial of justification *in toto;* and such denial is essentially mutiny and rebellion against God, a withdrawing of oneself from the authority of one's legal sovereign.

All those who consider themselves saved because they have holy emotions, or because they think themselves less sinful, and profess to make progress in sanctification—all these, however dissimilar they may be in all other things, have this in common, that they insist on being counted according to their own declaration, and not according to what God counts them to be. Instead of leaving, as dependent creatures, the honor of determining their status to their sovereign King, whose they are, they sit as judges to determine it themselves, by their own progress in good works.

And not only this, but they also detract from the redemption which is in Christ Jesus, and from the reality of the guilt for which He satisfied. He who maintains that God must count a man according to what he is, and not according to what God wills to count him, can never understand how the Lord Jesus could bear our sins, and be a "curse" and "sin" for us. He must interpret this sin-bearing in the sense of a physical or Ethical fellowship, and seek for reconciliation not in the cross of Jesus, but in His manger, as many actually do in these days.

And as they thus make the actual bearing of our guilt by the Mediator unthinkable, so they make inherited guilt impossible. Assuredly, they say, there is inherited stain, taken in a Manichean sense, but no original guilt. For how could the guilt of a dead man be counted unto us? It is evident, therefore, that by this thoughtless and bold denial of the right of God, not only is justification disjointed, but the whole structure of salvation is robbed of its foundation.

And why is this? Is it because the human consciousness cannot conceive the idea of being counted according to what we are not? Our illustrations from the social life show that men readily understand and daily accept such a relation in common affairs. The deep cause of this unbelief lies in the fact that man will not rest in *God's* judgment concerning him, but that he seeks for rest in his *own* estimate of himself; that this estimate is considered a safer shield than God's judgment concerning him; and that, instead of living with the reformers by faith, he tries to live by the things found in himself.

And from this men must return. This leads us back to Rome; this is to forsake justification by faith; this is to sever the artery of grace. Much more than in the political realm must the sacred principle be applied to the Kingdom of heaven, that to our Sovereign King and Judge alone belongs the prerogative, by His decision, absolutely to determine our state of righteousness or of unrighteousness.

The sovereignty which reposes in an earthly king is only borrowed, derived, and laid upon him, but the sovereignty of the Lord our God is the source and fountainhead of all authority and of all binding force.

If it belongs to the very essence of sovereignty, that by the ruler's decision alone the status of his subjects is determined, then it must be clear, and it cannot be otherwise than that this very authority belongs originally, absolutely, and supremely to our God. Whom He judges guilty is guilty, and must be treated as guilty; and whom He declares just is just, and must be treated as just. Before He entered Gethsemane, Jesus our King declared to His disciples: "Now are ye *clean* through the word which I have spoken unto you." And this is His declaration even now, and it shall forever remain so. Our state, our place, our lot for eternity depends not upon what we are, nor upon what others see in us, nor upon what we imagine or presume ourselves to be, but only upon what God *thinks* of us, what He *counts* us to be, what He, the Almighty and Just Judge, *declares* us to be.

When He declares us just, when He thinks us just, when He counts us just, then we are by this very thing His children who *shall not lie,* and ours is the inheritance of the just, although we lie in the midst of sin. And in like manner, when He pronounces us guilty in Adam, when in Adam He counts us subject to condemnation, then we are guilty, fallen, and condemned, even though we discover in our hearts nothing but sweet and childlike innocence.

In this way alone it must be understood and interpreted that the Lord Jesus was *numbered* with the *transgressors,* although He was holy; that He was made *sin,* although He was the living Righteousness; and that He was declared a *curse* in our place, although He was Immanuel. In the days of His flesh He was numbered with transgressors and sinners, He was put in their *state,* and He was treated accordingly; as such the burden of God's wrath came upon Him, and as such His Father forsook Him, and gave Him over to bitterest death. In the Resurrection alone He was restored to the status of the righteous, and thus He was raised for our justification.

Oh, this matter goes so deep! When to the Lord God is again ascribed His sovereign prerogative to determine a man's status, then every mystery of Scripture assumes its rightful place, but when it is not, then the entire way of salvation must be falsified.

Finally, if one should say: "An earthly sovereign may be mistaken, but God cannot be; hence God must assign to every man a status which accords with his work"; then we answer: "This would be so, if the omnipotent grace of God were not irresistible." But since it *is,* you are not esteemed by God according to what you are, but you are what God esteems you to be.

32

Justification from Eternity

The righteousness which is of God by faith—Philippians 3:9.

It has become evident that the question which most closely concerns us is, not whether we are more or less holy, but whether our *status* is that of the just or of the unjust, and that this is determined not by what we are at any given moment, but by God as our Sovereign and Judge.

In Adam's creation God put us, without any preceding merits on our part, in the state of original righteousness. After the fall, according to the same sovereign prerogative, He put us, as Adam's descendants, in the state of unrighteousness, imputing Adam's guilt to each personally. And in exactly the same manner He now justifies the ungodly, that is, He places him, without any previous merit on his part, in the state of righteousness according to His own holy and inviolable prerogative.

In the creation He did not first wait to see whether man would develop holiness in himself, so as to declare him righteous on the ground of this holiness, but He declared him originally righteous, even before there was a possibility on his part of evincing a desire for holiness. And after the fall He did not wait to see whether sin would manifest itself in us, so as to assign us to the state of the unrighteous on the ground of this sin, but before our birth, before there was a possibility of personal sin, He declared us guilty. And in the same manner God does not wait to see whether a sinner shows signs of conversion in order to restore him to honor as a righteous person, but He declares the ungodly just before he has had the least possibility of doing any good work.

Hence there is a sharp line between our *sanctification* and our *justification.* The former has to do with the quality of our being, depends upon our faith, and cannot be effected outside of us. But justification is effected outside of us, irrespective of what we are, dependent only upon the decision of God, our Judge and Sovereign; in such a way that justification *precedes* sanctification, the latter proceeding from the former as a necessary result. God does not justify us because we are becoming more holy, but when he has justified us we grow in holiness: "Being now justified by His blood, we shall be saved from wrath through Him."

There should never be the least doubt regarding this matter. Every effort to reverse this established order of Scripture must earnestly be resisted. This glorious confession, declared with so much power to the souls of men in the days of the Reformation, must continue the precious jewel, to be transmitted intact by us to our posterity as a sacred inheritance. So long as we ourselves have not yet entered the New Jerusalem, our comfort should never be founded upon our sanctification, but exclusively upon our justification. Though our sanctification were ever so far advanced, so long as we are not justified we remain in our sin and are lost. And if a justified sinner die immediately after his justification is sealed to his soul, he may shout with joy, for, in spite of hell and of Satan, he is sure of his salvation.

The deep significance of this confession is faintly discernible in our earthly relations. In order to do business on the floor of the exchange, a trader must be an honorable citizen. If convicted of crime, justly or unjustly, he will be expelled from exchange, though he be ten times more honest than others whose fraudulent transactions have never been discovered. And how will this dishonored man be restored to his former position? On the ground of future honest business transactions? That is out of the question; for as long as he is counted dishonorable, he is not allowed to do business on the floor. Hence he cannot prove his honesty by any dealings on exchange or in the market. So in order to start again, he must *first* be declared an honorable man. Then, and not before, can he set up in business once more.

Call this doing of business *sanctification,* and this declaration of being a man of honor *justification,* and the matter will be illustrated. For as this merchant, being declared dishonorable, cannot do business so long as he continues in that state, and must be declared honorable before he can begin anew, so a sinner cannot do any good work so long as he is counted lost. And so he must first be declared just by his God, in order to transact the honorable business of sanctification.

To prove that this is effected absolutely without our own merit, doing or not doing, and entirely without our actual condition, we refer to the royal prerogative for granting pardon and reinstatement. Although, among us, decisions of the judiciary are rendered in the name of the king, and yet not by the king himself, a certain opposition between the king and the judiciary is thinkable. It might occur that the judiciary declared a man guilty and dishonorable, whom the king wished not to be so declared. To keep the majesty of the crown inviolate in such cases, the prerogative of granting pardon and reinstatement is retained by almost every crowned head, a prerogative which in the present day is narrowly circumscribed, but which nevertheless represents still the exalted idea that the decision of the king, and not our actual condition, determines our lot. Hence a king can either grant pardon, that is, remit the penalty and release the guilty person from all the consequences of his crime, or, stronger still, he can grant reinstatement, that is, he can restore the accused and condemned to the condition of one who had never been declared guilty.

And this exalted royal prerogative, of which on account of sin there remains in earthly kings but a faint shadow, is the inviolable right in which God rejoices, Himself being the Source and all-comprehending Idea of all majesty. Not you, but He determines what His creature shall be; hence He sovereignly disposes, by the word of His mouth, the status wherein you will be set, whether it be of righteousness or of unrighteousness.

It is also evident that the sinner's justification need not wait until he is converted, nor until he has become conscious, nor even until he is born. This could not be so if justification depended upon something within him. Then he could not be justified before he existed and had done something. But if justification is not bound to anything in him, then this whole limitation must disappear, and the Lord our God be sovereignly free to render this justification at any moment that He pleases. Hence the Sacred Scripture reveals justification as an *eternal* act of God, that is, an act which is not limited by any moment in the human existence. It is for this reason that the child of God, seeking to penetrate into that glorious and delightful reality of his justification, does not feel himself limited to the moment of his conversion, but feels that this blessedness flows to him from the eternal depths of the hidden life of God.

It should therefore openly be confessed, and without any abbreviation, that justification does not occur when we become conscious of it, but that, on the contrary, our justification was decided from eternity in the holy judgment-seat of our God.

There is undoubtedly a moment in our life when for the first time justification is *published* to our consciousness, but let us be careful to distinguish justification itself from its publication. Our Christian name was selected for and applied to us long before we, with clear consciousness, knew it as our name; and although there was a moment in which it became a living reality to us and was called out for the first time in the ear of our consciousness, yet no man will be so foolish as to imagine that it was then that he actually received that name.

And so it is here. There is a certain moment wherein that justification becomes to our consciousness a living fact, but in order to become a living fact, it must have existed before. It does not spring *from* our consciousness, but it is mirrored *in* it, and hence must have being and stature in itself. Even an elect infant which dies in the cradle is declared just, though the knowledge or consciousness of its justification never penetrated its soul. And elect persons, converted, like the thief on the cross, with their last breath, can scarcely be sensible of their justification, and yet enter eternal life exclusively on the ground of their justification. Taking an analogy from daily life, a man condemned during his absence in foreign lands was granted pardon through the intercession of his friends, wholly without his knowledge. Does this pardon take effect when long afterward the good news reaches him, or when the king signs his pardon? Of course the latter. Even so does the justification of God's children take effect, not on the day when for the first time it is *published to their consciousness,* but at the moment that God in His holy judgment-seat declares them just.

But—and this should not be overlooked—this publishing in the consciousness of the person himself *must necessarily follow,* and this brings us back again to the special work of the Holy Spirit. For if in God's judiciary it is more particularly the *Father* who justifies the ungodly, and in the preparing of salvation more particularly the *Son* who in His Incarnation and Resurrection brings about justification, so it is, in a more limited sense, the *Holy Spirit* particularly who reveals this justification to the persons of the elect and causes them to appropriate it to themselves. It is by this act of the Holy Spirit that the elect obtain the *blessed knowledge* of their justification, which only then begins to be a living reality *to them.*

For this reason Scripture reveals these two positive, but apparently contradictory truths, with equally positive emphasis: (1) that, *on the one hand,* He has justified us in His own judgment-seat *from eternity;* and (2) that, *on the other,* only in conversion are we justified *by faith.*

And for this reason faith itself is fruit and effect of our justification; while it is also true that, for us, justification begins to exist only as a result of our faith.

33

Certainty of Our Justification

Being justified freely by His grace, through the redemption that is in Christ Jesus—Romans 3:24.

The foregoing illustrations shed unexpected light upon the fact that God justifies the *ungodly,* and not him who is actually just in himself; and upon the word of Christ: "Now are ye clean through the word which I have spoken unto you." They illustrate the significant fact that God does not determine our status according to what we *are,* but by the status to which He assigns us He determines what we shall be. The Reformed Confession, which in all things starts from the workings of God and not of man, became again clear, eloquent, and transparent. So the divine Word, ordinarily lowered to a mere *announcement* of what God finds in us, becomes once more the *fiat* of His creative power. He found an ungodly man and said, "Be righteous," and behold he became righteous. "I said to thee in thy blood, Live."

In this way the various parts of the redemptive work are arranged chronologically each in its own place.

So long as the false and narrow idea prevailed that a man was justified *after* conversion on the ground of his apparent holiness, justification could not *precede* sanctification, but must *follow* it. Then man becomes first holy, and as a reward or as a recognition of his holiness, he is declared righteous. Hence sanctification is *first,* and justification *second;* a justification, therefore, without any value, for what is the use of declaring that *a ball is round?*

The Scripture refuses to acknowledge a *posterior* justification. In Scripture, justification is always the *starting-point.* All other things spring from it and follow it. "Christ was made unto us wisdom and righteousness," and only then "sanctification and redemption." "Therefore *being justified by faith,* we have peace with God through our Lord Jesus Christ, by whom we also have access." "Being justified freely by His grace, through the redemption that is in Christ Jesus." and, "Whom He called, them He also justified; and whom He justified, them He also glorified."

For this reason the Reformation made justification by faith the starting-point for the conscience, and by this confession bravely and energetically opposed Rome's justification by good works; for in this justification by good works that priority of sanctification found its root.

The Church of Christ cannot deviate from this straight line of the Reformation without estranging itself and separating itself from its Head and Fountain of Life, vitally injuring itself. Sects which, like the Ethicals and the Methodists,* detract from this truth sever the faith from its root. If our churches desire once more to be strong in the doctrine and bold in witness-bearing, they must not repose in lethargy on the mere form of the doctrine, but must heartily embrace the doctrine; for it presents this cardinal point in a superior and excellent manner. He only who heroically dares accept *justification of the ungodly* becomes actual partaker of salvation. He only can confess heartily and unreservedly redemption which is sovereign, unmerited, and free in all its parts and workings.

The *last question* that remains to be discussed is: How can the justification of the ungodly be reconciled with the divine Omniscience and Holiness? It must be acknowledged that, in one respect, this whole representation seems to fail. It *must* be objected:

"Your argument is wittily thought out, but it does not stand the test. When an earthly sovereign decided that a man's state shall be oth-

---

* See section 5 of the author's Preface.

erwise than it actually is, he acts from *ignorance, mistake,* or *arbitrariness.* And since these things cannot be ascribed to God, these illustrations cannot be applied to Him."

And again: "That an earthly judge sometimes condemns the innocent and acquits the guilty, and makes the former to occupy the status of the latter, and *vice versa,* is possible only because the judge is a fallible creature. If he had been infallible, if he could have weighed guilt and innocence with perfect accuracy, the wrong could not have been committed. Hence if sin had not come in, that judge could not have acted arbitrarily, but he would have acted according to the right, and decided for the right because it is right. And, since the Lord God is a Judge who trieth the reins and who is acquainted with all our ways, in whom there can be no failure or mistake or ignorance, it is not thinkable, it is impossible, it is inconsistent with God's Being, that as the just Judge He ever could pronounce a judgment that is not perfectly in accordance with the conditions actually existing in man."

Without the slightest hesitation we submit to this criticism. It is well taken. The mistake whereby a boy can be registered as a girl; the peasant's child for that of a nobleman; whereby a law-abiding citizen can be judged as a law-breaker, and *vice versa,* is out of the question with God. And, therefore, when He justifies the ungodly, as the earthly judge declares the dishonorable to be honorable, then these two acts, which are apparently similar, are utterly dissimilar and may not be interpreted in the same way.

And yet the correctness of the objection does not in itself invalidate the comparison. Scripture itself often compares men's acts, which are necessarily sinful, to the acts of God. When the unjust judge, weary of the widow's tears and importunity, finally said, "I will avenge her, lest she come at last and break my head" (Dutch Translation), the Lord Jesus does not for a moment hesitate to apply this action, though it sprang from an unholy motive, to the Lord God, saying: "And shall not God avenge His own elect, who cry night and day unto Him?"

It cannot be otherwise. For since all acts of men, even the very best of the most holy among them, are always defiled with sin, either it would be impossible to compare any deed of man with the doings of God, or one must necessarily consider such deeds of men apart from the sinful motive, and apply to God only *the third of the comparison.*

And as Jesus could not mean that at last God must answer His elect, "lest they come and break His head," but without speaking of the motive, simply pointed to the fact that the inopportune prayer is finally heard, so did we compare the *wrong* decision of the judge, declaring the guilty innocent, to the *infallible* decision of God, justifying the ungodly, since, in spite of the difference of motive, it coincides with a third of the comparison.

Moreover, human mistakes are out of the question with reference to the granting of pardon and reinstatement. Hence this expression of royal sovereignty is indeed a direct type of the sovereignty of the Lord our God.

But this does not settle the question. Although we concede that the unholy motive of mistake cannot be attributed to God, yet we must inquire: What is God's motive, and how can the justification of the ungodly be consistent with His divine nature?

We reply by pointing to the beautiful answer of the Catechism, question 60: "How art thou righteous before God? Only by a true faith in Jesus Christ; so that, though my conscience accuse me, that I have grossly transgressed all the commandments of God, and kept none of them, and am still inclined to all evil; notwithstanding, God, without any merit of mine, but only of mere grace, grants and imputes to me the perfect satisfaction, righteousness, and holiness of Christ; even so as if I never had had, nor committed any sin: yea, as if I had fully accomplished all that obedience which Christ hath accomplished for me; inasmuch as I embrace such benefit with a believing heart."

That the Lord God justifies the ungodly is not because He enjoys fiction, or delights by a terrible paradox *to call* one righteous who in reality *is* wicked, but this fact runs parallel with the other fact, that such an ungodly one is really righteous. And that this ungodly one, who in himself is and remains wicked, at the same time is and continues *righteous,* finds its reason and ground in the fact that God puts this poor and miserable and lost sinner into partnership with an infinitely rich Mediator, whose treasures are inexhaustible. By this partnership all his debts are discharged, and all those treasures flow down to him. So though he continues, in himself, poverty-stricken, he is at the same time immensely rich in his Partner.

This is the reason why all depends upon faith in the Lord Jesus Christ; for that faith is the bond of partnership. If there is *no* such faith, there can be no partnership with the wealthy Jesus; and you are still in your sin. But if there is faith, then the partnership is established, then it exists, and you engage in business no longer on your own account, but in partnership with Him who blots out all your indebtedness, while He makes you the recipient of all His treasure.

How is this to be understood? Is it the Person of the Christ who takes us into partnership? And, since God has no longer to reckon with our poverty, but can now depend upon the riches of Christ, does He therefore count us good and righteous? No, brethren, and again, no! It is not so, and it may not so be presented; for then there would be no justification on God's part. You have a bill to collect from a man who failed in business, but who was accepted as the partner of a rich banker, who discharged all his debts. Is there now the slightest mercy or goodness on your part, when you endorse that man's check? Doing otherwise, would you not flatly contradict solid and tangible facts?

No, the Lord God does not act that way. Christ does not blot out the debt, and obtain us treasure *outside* of God; nor does the ungodly enter, through faith, into partnership with the wealthy Jesus *independently* of the Father; neither does God, being informed of these transactions, justify the ungodly, who already had become a believer. For then there would be no honor for God, nor praise for His grace; it would be not the ungodly, but, on the contrary, a believer that was justified.

The matter is not transacted that way. It was the Lord God, first of all, who, without respect of person, and hence without respect to faith in the person, according to His sovereign power, chose a portion of the ungodly to eternal life; not as Judge, but as Sovereign. But being Judge as well as Sovereign, and therefore incapable of violating the right, He who has chosen, that is, the Triune God, has also created and given all that is necessary and required for salvation; so that these elect persons, at the proper time and by appropriate means, may receive and undergo the things by which in the end it will appear that all God's doing was majesty and all His decision just.

And, therefore, this whole ordering of the Covenant of Grace; and in this Covenant of Grace the ordering of the Mediator; and in the Mediator that of all satisfaction, righteousness, and holiness; and of that satisfaction, righteousness, and holiness, first the *imputation,* and after that the *gift.*

Wherefore God does indeed declare the ungodly just *before* he believes, *that* he may believe, and not *after* he believes. This justifying act is the creative act of God, in which is also deposited the satisfaction, righteousness, and holiness of Christ, and from which flow also the imputation and granting of all these to the ungodly. Wherefore there is in this act of justification not the slightest mistake or untruth. He alone is declared just who, being ungodly in himself, by this declaration is and becomes righteous in Christ.

In this way alone it is possible fully to understand the doctrine of justification in all its wealth and glory. Without this deep conception of it, justification is merely the pardon of sin, after which, being relieved of the burden, we start out with newly animated zeal to work for God. And this is nothing else than genuine, fatal Arminianism.

But, with this deeper insight, man acknowledges and confesses: "Such pardon of sin does not avail me. For I know:

"1st. That I shall be again daily defiled with sin;

"2d. That I shall have a sinful heart within me until the day of my death;

"3d. That until then, I shall never be able to accomplish the keeping of the whole law;

"4th. That, since I am already condemned and sentenced, I cannot do business in the Kingdom of God as an honorable man."

The answer of justification, such as Scripture reveals and our Church confesses it, covers these four points most satisfactorily. It accepts you not as a saint, with a self-assumed holiness, but as one who confesses: "My conscience accuses me that I have grossly transgressed all the commandments of God, and have kept none of them, and that I am still inclined to all evil"; and yet, you are not cast out. It tells you that you cannot depend upon any merit of your own, but must rely on grace alone. Wherefore it begins with putting you in the ranks of the law-abiding, of them that are declared good and righteous, "even so as if you never had had nor committed any sin." As the ground of godliness it does not require of you the keeping of the law, but it imputes and imparts to you Christ's fulfillment of the law; esteeming you as if you had fully accomplished all that obedience which Christ has accomplished for you. And effacing hereby the difference of your past and future sin, it imputes and grants unto you not only Christ's satisfaction and holiness, but even His original righteousness, in such a manner that you stand before God once more righteous and honorable, and as though the whole history of your sin had been a dream only.

But the closing sentence of the Catechism should be noticed: "Inasmuch as I embrace such benefit with a believing heart." And that "believing heart," and that "embracing"—behold, that is the very work of the Holy Spirit.

Seventh Chapter
Faith

34

Faith in General

Through faith; and that not of yourselves, it is the gift of God—Ephesians 2:8.

When the judicial act of the Triune God, justification, is announced to the conscience, faith begins to be active and expresses itself in works. This leads us to call the attention of our readers to the work of the Holy Spirit, which consists in the *imparting of faith.*

We are saved through faith; and that faith is not of ourselves, it is the gift of God. It is very specially a gift of the Triune God, by a peculiar operation of the Holy Ghost: "No man can say that Jesus is the Lord but by the Holy Ghost" (1 Cor. 12:3). St. Paul calls the Holy Spirit the Spirit of faith (2 Cor. 4:13). And in Galatians 5:22 he mentions faith as the fruit of the Holy Spirit.

In salvation nearly everything depends upon faith; hence a correct conception of faith is essential. It has always been the aim of error to poison faith's being, and thus to destroy weak souls as well as the Church itself. It is therefore the urgent duty of ministers to instruct the churches concerning faith's being and nature; by correct definitions to detect prevailing error, and thus to restore the joy of a clear and well-founded consciousness of faith.

For years the people have listened to the poorest and vaguest theories of faith. Every minister has had his own theory and definition, or worse, no definition at all. In a general way they have felt what faith is, and presented it eloquently, but these brilliant, metaphorical, often flowery descriptions have frequently been more obscuring than illuminating; they have failed to instruct. The definition of faith being left to the inspiration of the moment, it often occurred that the minister unconsciously offered to his people one Sunday the very opposite of what he had eloquently proclaimed the week before. This should not be so. The Church must increase in knowledge also; and what sufficed for the apostolic Church is not sufficient now. The ideas of faith were confused then; and the earliest writings show that the various problems regarding faith had not been solved.

But not so in the apostolic writings, whose inspiration is proven from the fact that they contain a clear and definite answer to nearly all these questions. But after the apostles had passed away, the depth of their word not yet understood, there was a childlike confusion of ideas in the Church of the first centuries; until the Lord allowed various heretical forms of faith to appear, which the Church was compelled to oppose by the real forms of faith. To do this successfully it had to emerge from that confusion and to arrive at clearer distinctions and conceptions.

Hence the many differences, questions, and distinctions which subsequently arose regarding faith's being and exercise. Owing to the earnest debates, the real being of faith became gradually more defined and clearly distinguished from its false forms and imitations. That in the present time every path, good and bad, has its own distinctive signpost, so that no one can turn in the wrong direction ignorantly, is the fruit of the long conflict waged with so much patience and talent.

Undoubtedly ignorance has caused much misunderstanding. But we maintain that a guide who neglects to examine the roads before he undertakes to guide travelers is unworthy of his title. And a minister of the Word is a spiritual guide, appointed by the Lord Jesus to conduct pilgrims traveling to the heavenly Jerusalem through the high Alps of faith, where the ordinary communications of the earthly life have ceased, from one mountain-plateau to another. Hence he is inexcusable when, merely guessing at the location of the heavenly city, he advises his pilgrims to try the path which *seems* to lead in that direction. By virtue of his office he should make it his chief business to know which is the shortest, safest, and most certain way, and then tell them that this and none other is the way. Formerly, when the various paths had not yet been examined, it was to some extent praiseworthy to try them all, but now, since their misleading character is so well known, it is unpardonable to try them again.

And when the easy-going people say, "Above all things let us retain our simplicity; what is the use in our Christian faith of all those wearisome distinctions," we would ask of them whether in the case of a surgical operation they would prefer a surgeon who in his simplicity only cuts no matter where or how; or in case of sickness, an apothecary who simply puts a mixture together from his various jars and bottles, regardless of the names of the drugs; or, to take another example, in case of a sea-voyage, would they embark in a vessel whose captain, chary of the use of charts and instruments, in sweet simplicity steers his ship, merely trusting in his luck?

And when they answer, as they must, that in such cases they demand professionals thoroughly acquainted with the smallest details of their professions, then we ask them in the name of the Lord and of their accountability unto Him, how they can go to work so simply, that is, so carelessly and thoughtlessly, when it concerns spiritual disease, or the voyage across the unfathomable waters of life, as though in these matters thoughtful discrimination were immaterial.

We refuse, therefore, to be influenced by that sickly talk about simplicity regarding faith, or by the impious cry against a so-called dogmatism, but shall diligently seek to give an exposition of the *being of faith,* which eradicating error, will point out the only safe and reliable path.

As a starting-point, let it be plainly understood that there is a sharp distinction between saving faith and the faith which in the various spheres of life is called *"faith in general."*

When Columbus is incited, by internal compulsion, to direct his restless eye across the western ocean to the world which he there expects with almost absolute certainty, we call this faith; and yet, with this instinctive inclination in the mind of Columbus *saving faith* has nothing to do. And the preacher, using this and similar examples otherwise than as a faint analogy, does not explain but obscures the matter, and leads the Church in the wrong direction.

Sometimes we have among our children one whose mind is constantly occupied by an unconscious aim or idea, that leaves him no rest. In after years it may appear to be his life's aim and purpose. This is the compulsion of an inward law belonging to his nature; the mysterious, constraining activity of a ruling idea governing his life and person. People thus constrained conquer every obstacle; however opposed, they come ever nearer to that unconscious purpose, and at last, owing to this irresistible impulse, they attain what they have been so long aiming at. And this is also frequently called *faith, but* it has little more than the name in common with the faith of which we are about to speak. For while such faith excites human energy, and exalts and glorifies it, saving faith, on the contrary, casts down all human greatness.

The same is true of the so-called *faith in one's ideas.* One is young and enthusiastic; he dreams beautiful dreams of a golden age of happiness and sees delightful ideals of righteousness and glory. That beautiful world of his fancy seems to comfort him for the disappointments of this matter-of-fact world. If that were the real world, and if it were always to remain so, it would have broken his youthful heart and prematurely quenched its enthusiasm; and, grown old when still young, he would have joined the pessimists who perish in despair, or the conservatives who find relief in the silencing of the higher dictates of the conscience. But fortunately their number is small. In this painful experience many discover a world of ideals, that is, they have the courage to condemn this sinful world, full of misery, and to prophesy of the coming of a better and happier world.

Alas! Youthful presumption, chasing after its ideals, often fancies that the cause of all evils lies in the fathers. "If my fathers had only seen and planned things as I do now, our progress would have been much greater." But those fathers did not see it so. They went wrong; hence our ideals are not yet real. But there is hope; a young generation, clearly understanding these things, will soon be heard; then great changes will occur: much of the existing misery will disappear, and our ideal world will become real. And cruel is the answer of unvarnished experience. For the son acts as foolishly as the father did before him. Consequently the ideal world is not realized. He cries aloud, but men will not hear; they refuse to be delivered from their misery, and the old sadness goes on forever.

At this point the company of idealistic men is divided. Some abandon the effort; call their dreams delusive, and, accepting the inevitable, increase the broad stream of souls trampled down to the same level. But a few nobler souls refuse to submit to this debased and ignoble wretchedness; and preferring to run their heads against the granite wall, with the cry, *"Advienne qui pourra,"* cling to their ideals. And these men who cannot be sufficiently loved and appreciated are said to *believe.* But even this faith has nothing in common with saving faith; to speak of this as the same is but confusion of tongues and a joining together of things dissimilar.

Finally, the same is true of a much lower form, ordinarily called faith, which is the light-hearted expression of cheerfulness; or the lucky guessing at something which accidentally comes to pass. There are cheery, mirthful souls, who in spite of adversity never seem to be cast down or harmed, who, however much suppressed, have always enough of elasticity in their happy spirits to let the mainspring of their inward life rebound into full activity. Such people have always an encouraging and hopeful eye for all their surroundings. They are strangers to gloomy forebodings, and unacquainted with melancholy fears. Care does not rob them of sleep, and nervous restlessness does not send the blood to the heart at quickened pace. However, they are not indifferent, only not easily affected. Things may go against them, the clouds may overcast their sky, but behind the clouds they see the sun still shining, and they prophesy, with cheerful smile, that light will soon break through the darkness. Therefore it is said that they have faith in persons and in things.

And this faith, if it be not too superficial, should be appreciated. With millions of melancholy souls, life in this country would be unbearable; and it is cause for gratitude that our national character, otherwise so phlegmatic, cultivates sons and daughters in whose hearts the faith of the cheerful burns brightly. And sometimes their prophecies are really fulfilled; everybody thought that the little craft would perish, and, behold, it safely reached and entered the harbor; and it appeared that their cheerful faith was actually one of the causes of its happy arrival. And then these prophets ask you: Did we not tell you so? Were you not altogether too gloomy? Do you not see that it came out all right?

But even this faith has nothing but the name in common with saving faith. We must note this especially because, in Christian institutions and enterprises, we frequently meet with men and women who are upheld by this spirit of cheerfulness and unquestioning confidence, and who by this hopeful spirit pilot many Christian craft, which otherwise might perish, into a safe harbor. But this spiritual cheerfulness which, in the Christian, is perhaps *fruit* of the genuine faith, is by no means the genuine *faith itself.* And when it is said, "Do you now see what faith can do?" the saving faith is again confounded with this general faith which is found sometimes even among the heathen.

35

Faith and Knowledge

He that believeth in the Son hath everlasting life; and he that believeth not the Son shall not see life—John 3:36.

In the discussion of saving faith, faith in general cannot afford us the least assistance. To understand what "faith" is, we must turn in an entirely different direction, and answer the question: "What is, among the nations, the universal root-idea and original significance of faith?"

And then we meet this singular phenomenon, that among all nations and at all times faith is an expression denoting at one time something *uncertain,* and at another something *very certain.*

It may be said: "I believe that the clock struck three, but I am not certain"; or, "I believe that his initials are H. T., but I am not certain"; or, "I believe that you can take a ticket directly for St. Petersburg, but it would be well first to inquire." In every one of these sentences, which can be translated literally in every cultivated language, "to believe" signifies a mere guess, something less than actual knowledge, a confession of *uncertainty.*

But when I say, "I believe in the forgiveness of sin"; or, "I believe in the immortality of the soul"; or lastly, "I believe in the unquestionable integrity of that statesman"; "to believe" does not imply doubt or uncertainty about these things, but signifies *strongest conviction* concerning them.

From which it follows, that every definition of the being of faith must be wrong which does not explain how, from one and the same root-idea, there can be derived a twofold, diametrically opposed use of the same word.

Of this difficulty there can be but one solution, viz., the difference in the *nature of the things* in regard to which certainty is desired; so that, with reference to one class of things, highest certainty is obtained by faith, and, with reference to another, it is not.

This difference arises from the fact that there are things *visible* and *invisible,* and that certainty regarding things visible is obtained by *knowledge* and not by faith; while certainty in regard to things *invisible* is obtained exclusively by *faith.* When a man says regarding visible things, "I believe," and not, "I know," he impresses us as being *uncertain, but* in saying regarding invisible things, "I believe," he gives us the idea of *certainty.*

It should be observed here that the expressions "visible" and "invisible" must not be taken in too narrow a sense; by things visible must be understood all things that can be perceived by the senses, as in Scripture; and by things invisible, the things that cannot be so perceived. Wherefore the things that pertain to the hidden life of a *person* must ultimately rest on faith. His deeds alone belong to the visible things. Certainty in regard to these can be obtained by the perception of the senses. But certainty regarding his inward personality, his thoughts, his affections and their sincerity, his character and its trustworthiness, and anything pertaining to his inward life, certainty regarding all these can be reached *by faith* only.

If we were to enter more deeply into this matter, we should maintain that all *certainty,* even regarding things *visible,* rests always and only upon faith; and we should lay down the following propositions: When you say that you saw a man in the water and heard him cry for help, your knowledge rests, *first,* upon your belief that you did not dream but were wide awake, and that you did not imagine but actually saw it; *second,* upon your firm belief that since you saw and heard something there must be a corresponding reality which occasions that seeing and hearing; *third,* upon your conviction that in seeing something, for example, the form of a man, your senses enable you to obtain a correct impression of that form.

And, proceeding in this way, we could demonstrate that in the end, all certainty in regard to things visible, as well as to things invisible, rests ultimately not upon perception, but upon faith. It is impossible for my ego to obtain any knowledge of things outside of myself without a certain bond of faith, which unites me to these things. I must always believe either in my own identity, that is, that I am myself; or in the clearness of my consciousness; or in the perception of my senses; or in the actuality of the things outside of myself; or in the axiomata from which I proceed.

Hence it can be stated, without the slightest exaggeration, that no man can ever say, *"I know this or that,"* without its being possible to prove to him that his knowledge, in a deeper sense and upon closer analysis, depends so far as its certainty is concerned, upon *faith* alone.

But we prefer not to consider this deeper conception of the matter, because it confuses rather than explains the being of faith; for it should be remembered that in Sacred Scripture the Holy Spirit always uses words as they occur in the ordinary speech of daily life, simply because otherwise the children of the Kingdom could not understand them. And, in the daily life, people do not make that closer distinction, but say, in the case above referred to: "I *know* that there is a man in the water, for I saw his head and I heard him cry." While, on the other hand, it is said, in the ordinary speech of daily life: "If you do not *believe* me, I cannot talk with you"; indicating the fact that, in regard to a *person,* faith is the only means by which certainty can be obtained.

And, keeping this in view, we shall, for the sake of clearness, present the matter in this way: that the Lord God has created man in such a way that he can obtain knowledge of *two* worlds, of the world of visible things, and of that of invisible things, but so that he obtains such knowledge concerning each in a special and peculiar manner. He obtains knowledge of the world of *visible things* by means of the senses, which are instruments designed to bring his mind into contact with the outside world. But the senses teach him nothing concerning the world of invisible things, for which he needs altogether different organs.

We have no names for these other organs, as we have for the five senses; yet we know that from that invisible world we receive impressions, sensations, emotions; we know perfectly well that these mutually differ in duration, depth, and power, and we also know that some of these affect us as real and others as unreal. In fact the invisible world, as well as the visible world, exerts influences upon us; not through the five senses, but by means of unnamable organs. This influence from the invisible world affects the soul, the consciousness, the innermost ego. This working makes impressions upon the soul, excites sensations in the consciousness, and causes emotions in the inner ego.

This is done, however, in such a way that there is always room for the question: "Are these impressions real? Can I trust these sensations? Is there a reality corresponding to these sensations, impressions, emotions?" And to this last question faith alone can answer "yes," in precisely the same manner as the question, whether I obtain certainty from my own consciousness and from my senses and from the axiomata, receives its *"yes"* exclusively and only by faith.

To obtain certainty regarding the things invisible, such as love, faithfulness, righteousness, and holiness, the mystic body of the Lord—in a word, regarding all things that pertain to the mystery of the *personal life* in my fellow men, in Immanuel, in the Lord our God, *faith* is the proper and only divinely ordained way; not as something *inferior* to knowledge, but equal to it, only much more certain, and from which all knowledge derives its certainty.

As regards the objection, that the Sacred Scripture declares that faith shall be turned into sight, we say that this "sight" has nothing in common with the sight by means of the senses. God sees and knows all things, and yet He does not possess any of the senses. His sight is an immediate act of penetration, with His Spirit, into the essence and consistence of all things. To Adam in Paradise something of this immediate wisdom and knowledge was imparted, but by sin he lost that glorious feature of the image of God. And Scripture promises that this glorious feature shall be restored to God's children, in the Kingdom of Glory, in much more glorious measure than in Paradise.

But, while we still sojourn as pilgrims, not yet possessing the glorified body any more than the glory of our inward status, our contact with the invisible world does not yet consist in sight; our mind still lacks the power to penetrate immediately into the things invisible; and we still depend upon the impressions and sensations produced by them. Wherefore we can have no certainty regarding these impressions and sensations, except by direct faith. Still, existing and living as pilgrims together, we believe in each other's love, good faith, and honesty of character; we believe in God the Father, in our Savior, and in the Holy Spirit; we believe in the Holy Catholic Church; we believe in the forgiveness of sin, the resurrection of the body, and the life everlasting. And we do not believe in all these with the secret after-thought that we would really prefer to *know* them, instead of *believing* them; for that would be just as absurd as to say, of an organ concert: "Really I would prefer to *see* this." Music cannot be seen any more than one can become conscious of things invisible by means of the senses. And as the *sense of hearing* is the only proper means of hearing and enjoying music, so *faith* is the peculiar and only means whereby certainty can be obtained regarding our contact with the world unseen and invisible.

This being thoroughly understood, it cannot be difficult to see that this faith in reference to things visible is far inferior to knowledge; for the visible things are intended to be ascertained, carefully and accurately, by means of the senses. Imperfect observation renders our knowledge uncertain. Hence, in regard to the visible things, no other knowledge than that obtained by the senses ought to be considered reliable.

But in a number of unimportant cases accurate knowledge is needless; for example, in the difference concerning the respective heights of two steeples. In such cases we use the word "believe," as, "I believe that this steeple is higher than the other." And again, visible things impress their image upon the memory, which in the course of years becomes dim. Meeting a gentleman I have seen before, and fully recognizing him, I say, "This is Mr. B.," but being uncertain, I say, "I *believe* that this is Mr. B." In this case we seem to be dealing with visible things, for a gentleman stands before us; yet the image which recalls him belongs to the inward contents of the memory. Hence the difference of speech.

We reach, therefore, this conclusion: First, that all certainty regarding things visible as well as invisible depends in the deepest sense upon *faith*. Second, that in ordinary speech certainty regarding things visible is obtained by means of the *senses*, and regarding things invisible, especially things that pertain to personality, by *believing*.

For this reason Brakel's effort to interpret the verb *to believe,* according to the Hebrew and Greek idioms, as meaning *to trust,* and not as *a means to obtain certainty,* was a failure. Such meanings are the same in all languages, and there is no difference, because they are the direct result of the organism of the human mind, which, in its fundamental features, is the same among all nations. Confidence is the direct result of faith, but is not faith itself.

"To believe" refers, in the first place, to the certainty or uncertainty of the consciousness concerning something. If there is no such certainty, I do not believe; being consciously certain, I believe. When a person introduces himself to me as a man of integrity, the first question is, whether I believe him. If I am not certain that he is a man of integrity, I do not believe him. But if I believe him, confidence is the immediate result. Then it is impossible not to trust him. To believe that he is what he claims to be, and not trust him, is simply impossible.

Hence "to believe" always retains the primary meaning of *"assuring the consciousness"*; and saving faith requires me *"to be certain* that Christ is to me such as *He reveals and offers Himself* in Sacred Scripture."

36

Brakel and Comrie*

If in anything ye be otherwise minded, God shall reveal even this unto you—Philippians 3:15.

We call the attention of our readers to the lines which in the last century were most correctly drawn by Brakel and Comrie respectively; and we do not deny that of the two, Comrie was the more correct.

This is not intended to hurt the friends of Brakel, for then we should wound ourselves. However, although the name of "Father Brakel" is still precious to us; although we appreciate his courageous protesting against church tyranny, and heartily acknowledge our indebtedness to his excellent writings; yet this does not render him infallible, neither does it alter the fact that in the matter of faith Comrie judged more correctly than he.

To do justice to both men, we will cite their respective arguments, and then show that Comrie, who did not always see correctly either, was more strictly Scriptural, and therefore more strictly Reformed, than Brakel.

In the chapter on Faith ("Rational Religion," 2, 776, ed. 1757), Brakel writes:

---

* Brakel and Comrie were celebrated Dutch theologians in the eighteenth century—Trans.

The question is: What is the essential, fundamental act of faith? *Is it the assent of the mind to the Gospel and its promises, or is it the trusting of the heart in Christ for justification, sanctification, and redemption?* Before we answer this question we wish to say:

First, that by 'trusting' we do not understand a Christian's assurance and confidence that he is in Christ and a partaker of Christ and of all His promises; nor his peace and rest in Christ, for that is a fruit of faith which some have more than others, but by trusting we understand the act of the soul, whereby a man yields himself to Christ and accepts Him, entrusting Him with body and soul, as, for example, one man entrusts his money to another, or as one entrusts himself to and leans on the strong shoulders of the man that carries him across a stream.

Second, that such trust necessarily requires a previous knowledge of evangelical truth and assent to its credibility; and that, after that, faith exercises itself on and by its promises.

We now answer the question already stated as follows: True, saving faith is not the act of the mind assenting to evangelical truth, but the trusting of the heart to be saved by Christ on the ground of His voluntary offering of Himself to sinners and of the promises to them that trust in Him. And we say also that *faith has its seat, not in the understanding, but in the will;* not being the assent to the truth it cannot be in the understanding, and since it is trust it must have its seat in the will.

The truth of what we have said is evident:

First, from the name itself. What we call "to believe" Scripture calls "to trust," "to confide," "to entrust." Speaking of divine things revealed to us in the Word alone, we must not be confined to our own language, for this would cause many to fall into error, but we should adapt our speech and understanding to the nature and character of the original Hebrew and Greek. For in our language 'to believe' means to accept promises and the narrative of events on the strength of another man's word, but according to the force of the original languages the words, πιστεύω, הֶאֱמִין, כָּסַל, בָּטַח, סָמַךְ are translated not only 'to believe,' but 'to trust,' 'to entrust,' 'to lean upon.' They are used, not to denote the nature of trust, but by trusting yielding oneself to Christ, relying on Him.

Secondly, the Scripture ascribes the act of faith to the heart: "With the heart man believeth unto righteousness" (Rom. 10:10); "If thou believest with all thine heart, thou mayest. And he said, I believe that Jesus Christ is the Son of God" (Acts 8:37). Trusting and believing are both acts of the heart, the will. If it be said that the heart refers also to the understanding, we answer, very rarely, and even then it refers not to the understanding alone, but also to the will, or to the soul with all its workings.

Thirdly, if the act of faith did consist in the assent of the mind to the truth, it would be possible to have saving faith without accepting Christ, without trusting Him; and you may know and acknowledge Christ as the

Savior as long as you please, but what union and communion with Christ does that afford? To accept Christ and to trust and lean on Him would be only an effect of faith, but an effect does not complete the being of a thing which is complete before the effect; and saving faith would not differ from historic faith, but be the same in its nature. For historic faith is also the assent of the mind to the truth of the Gospel, and even the devils and the unconverted have this faith. If it be said that the knowledge of the one is spiritual and that of the other is not, we answer: (1) While it is true that the knowledge of the converted is different from that of the unconverted, yet the matter remains the same. Their historical knowledge, if assented to, is historic faith in the one as well as in the other. (2) The Scripture never makes the spirituality of historic knowledge the distinctive feature of saving faith. (3) This is certain that the knowledge of faith of an unconverted person is not spiritual. And from faith itself one can never ascertain whether he truly believes; this he can learn only from the fruits, and that would be altogether wrong.

Fourthly, saving faith believes in God, in Christ, and does not stop at the Word, but through the Word reaches the Person of Christ and trusts in Him. "Neither do I pray for these alone, but for them also *who shall believe on Me, through their word"* (John 17:20). This alone gives faith its point, nature, and perfection; wherefore Scripture says that saving faith is to believe in God, in Christ: "Believe on the Lord Jesus Christ and thou shalt be saved" (Acts 16:31). To believe in Christ is faith itself and not the fruit of faith, which it must be if faith be mere knowledge and assent.

Fifthly, it is faith itself that unites the soul to Christ, appropriates the promises, satisfies the conscience, gives access to the throne of grace and boldness to call Him Father (Eph. 3:17; John 3:36; Rom. 5:1; Eph. 3:12). But mere assent to the truth cannot do any of these things. You may assent as long as you please, but that will never make a single promise your own; it will not unite the soul to Christ, nor will it give boldness to call "Abba, Father." Hence mere assent is not saving faith. It may be said that it is the work of the assenting mind to accept Christ and to trust in Him, and so the above-mentioned results flow from the assent of the truth. But I answer: (1) That mere assent as such cannot have such results, but that they are its fruits; that the assent must first work acceptance and trust in Christ; hence it is the *form* of faith, and not its nature. Moreover, Scripture ascribes all these things to faith itself, not to its fruits. (2) The same may be said of the knowledge of the mysteries of the Gospel, that it has the same effect, that this also unites to Christ, appropriates the promises, etc., but since this would be absurd, it is also absurd to say that mere assent works these things. And therefore it is certain that saving faith is not assent, but trust.

> Sixthly, the opposite of saving faith is not the rejection of the truth of the Gospel, but failure to trust in Christ. "He that believeth on the Son"; "He that obeyeth not the Son" (John 3:36, Dutch Translation); "Let not your heart be troubled—believe also in me" (John 14:1); "Where is thy faith?" (Luke 8:25). In the last text faith is contrasted with fear. Hence true faith is not assent, but trust.

Brakel's characteristic is that he considers faith, not as an inherent habit, but as an outgoing act of the heart; and, in connection with this, that the organ of faith and its seat are not in the understanding, but chiefly in the will.

Comrie, on the other hand, taught that faith is the increated and inherent habit, the principal moment of which is to be *persuaded.*

In his "Explanation of the Heidelberg Catechism" (2, 312), we read:

> The question, "What is true faith?" is very important, deserving most careful consideration; for they only that have true faith can be saved. For although in faith itself there is no inherent saving power, God has established such a connection between salvation and the imparted faith, that without the latter no person young or old can be saved. Children as well as adults must hereby be incorporated into Christ, for there is no salvation in any other.
>
> This question is terribly wrested and distorted by those that always speak of faith as an *act* or *acts.* Reading the definition of faith (Heidelberg Catechism, question 21), they say that this describes, not the *nature* and *character* of faith, but its *perfection* and *highest degree.* We will see how the Reformers have defined faith as an instrument according to the true foundation of the divine Word, in harmony with the doctrine of free grace and in its relation to justification, and not according to the principle of works of the semi-Pelagians, as many now do; who also say that the authors of the twenty-first question did not describe the *true faith* of which the preceding answer had shortly spoken, showing that they only can be saved that are engrafted into Christ and receive all His benefits by a *true faith, but* that they described the works of faith. But how is it possible that the authors of the Catechism could forget what they had just stated as the essential condition of salvation for every man, and speak of a high and perfect degree of faith, which is not attained by every one of the redeemed, if we take the words of the Catechism in their actual sense? No, beloved, the question refers to the same faith of which we have been speaking, the faith essential to all, children as well as adults; that is, the imparted faith, which we have defined as an *imparted faculty and habit, wrought in the elect by the Holy Ghost with re-creating and irresistible power, when they are incorporated into*

Christ; by which they receive all the impressions which God the Holy Ghost imparts unto them through the Word (regarding children in a manner unknown to us), and by which they are active according to the nature and the contents of the Word, the objects of which are revealed to their souls. Hence the reality or sincerity of the imparted faith does not depend upon the acts of faith, but the sincerity of these acts depends upon the reality and sincerity of the faculty or habit from which they spring; so that, although no acts spring from it, as in deceased elect children, yet they possess the *true faith,* from which acts would have sprung if they had been able to employ their rational faculties.

Moreover, the imparted faith develops all its powers, not in an instant, but gradually; and although one act does not appear as strongly pronounced as another, this is no sign of insincerity, but it is the sign that such act or acts are not apparent. For example, the sense of taste can be perfect although one never tasted sweetness, and to form an idea of sweetness is then impossible; yet when sweetness is tasted the idea is not produced by a new faculty to taste sweetness, but by a new object, which excites the faculty and produces the idea which was not possessed before.

The same is true of the inwrought faith; with reference to the habit of faith it is imparted and perfected by the supernatural operation of the Holy Spirit in a moment, but it does not act until the soul becomes conscious of it. And this is why some men, who by reason of the bondage of fear of death all their lifetime were never assured of their state in Christ, could still be saved. However, we do not dwell upon this point; we wish only to say that the answer describes the real nature and character of imparted *faith* as a faculty, whereby we receive the knowledge of all that God has revealed to us in His Word, and as a confidence that Christ and His grace are freely given us of God.

Hence it is evident: first, that faith consists in a conviction or persuasion. This is the *genus* of faith. Faith, whether human or divine, is impossible without a conviction of the mind of the reality of the matter which is believed. When this is lacking there is no faith, but only a guess, a fancy, or a supposition.

Secondly, that this conviction or persuasion is the product or act, not of faith as such, but of the testimony which is so convincing and persuading that its truth cannot be doubted. This is the nature of all persuasion; the soul in order to be persuaded does not act, but merely receives the proofs of the matter in question, and becomes so deeply convinced that it is no longer at liberty either to reject or accept that conviction, but must yield itself with greatest willingness to the truth.

Thirdly, *that according to the degree of clearness wherewith the divine testimony, as with an argument, impresses the imparted faith concerning the matters of our lost estate and the way of salvation, the conviction of the truth or of the contents of the testimony shall be more or less firm and persuasive.*

Lastly, that as faith is *wrought* by a testimony, so it is also *made active by a testimony of God's Word, rendered by an operation of the Holy Spirit.* Being therefore in the adult, the daughter of the Word (*Bathkol, filia vocis)*, it is also from beginning to end subject to the Word, obeying and in all things following it. For among the Reformed this is an established rule, that through the operation of the Holy Spirit we first receive a faculty, from which subsequent activities proceed; and that this imparted faculty does not work of its own energy except it be wrought upon *(acti a gimus:* being enabled we act) by the Word and the omnipotent power of the Holy Spirit accompanying that Word, in which and by which it enters and penetrates the soul as its instrument and organ, to excite the soul to activity and to flow into that activity.

Concerning faith itself it should be remembered—

First, that nearly all the old and private confessions of various martyrs, since the year 1527, have thus understood the imparted faith, as our Heidelberg theologians describe it, in the answer of the twentieth question in *general,* and in that of the twenty-first more particularly.

Secondly, we must call your Christian attention to the acts which flow from the imparted faith. Theologians entertain different opinions regarding the number of these acts of faith, and which is the proper act of faith. Just a word regarding both. In regard to the number, the celebrated Witzius mentions *nine:* three preceding, three proper, and three that follow. We do not object; every man is free to express himself as he pleases. Yet we prefer the ancient method which holds that faith consists of *three* things: *knowledge, assent,* and *confidence.* We have no doubt that all that God's Word teaches regarding faith can easily be arranged under each of these three acts. Concerning the proper act of faith, which is called the *actus formalis fidei,* that is, the formal act of faith, the following opinions are held: (1) that it is the *assent;* (2) that it is the *coming to Christ;* (3) the *accepting of Christ;* (4) a *certain confidence in Christ;* and lastly, that it is *love.* The discussions of the theologians on this point are violent, and many tracts are written by the various parties either to establish their own opinions or to refute those of others.

Beloved, we judge that we could let this matter pass without noticing it, were it not for the fact that this definition may favor the semi-Pelagians in this respect, who hold that faith is an act, and that it receives its formal being by an act: *"Forma dat esse rei"* (the form gives existence to the matter). And seeing that some begin to deviate, we say: *That no act or acts can give faith its form or being.* For this would imply that the imparted faith which the Holy Spirit works in the elect is an *unformed* faith, lacking that which is essential to its being. And this is absurd, since by this implied *"actus formalis"* there is ascribed to us more than to the Holy Spirit; yea, a great deal more, inasmuch as the form is more excellent than the material. According to this supposition He imparts to us only the material of faith, without its form, and by our act or acts we give form to that formless faith.

Our principal aim in citing was that the student might receive the contrast from the very lips of these two men, and so discover that the slight deviation of Amesius from Calvin and Beza in Brakel already inclines too much to the subjective; and that the *objective* character of saving grace is sufficiently covered only by the line of Augustine, Thomas, Calvin, Zanchius, Voetius, Comrie. Brakel was right in opposing the petrified dogmatism of his day. But when he systematized his opposition he went too far in that direction. In exactly the same manner as Köhlbrugge was right when, in opposition to his contemporaries, he maintained the objective as rigidly as possible, while his followers go wrong when they systematize his then necessary opposition.

Following the line of Augustine, Calvin, Voetius, Comrie, one goes safest.

37

Faith in the Sacred Scriptures

With the heart man believeth unto righteousness, and with the mouth confession is made unto salvation—Romans 10:10.

Calvin says beautifully and comprehensively that the object of saving faith is none other than the *Mediator,* and invariably in the garments of the Sacred Scriptures. This should be accepted unconditionally. Saving faith is possible, therefore, only in sinful men and so long as they remain sinful.

To suppose that saving faith existed already in Paradise is to destroy the order of things. In a sense there was no need of salvation in Paradise, because there was pure and undisturbed felicity; and for the development of this felicity into still greater glory, not faith, but works, was the appointed instrument. Faith belongs to the *"Covenant of Grace,"* and to that covenant alone.

Hence it may not be said that Jesus had saving faith. For Jesus was no sinner, and therefore could not have "that assured confidence that not only to others, but to Him also, was given the righteousness of the Mediator." We have only to connect the name of Jesus with the clear and transparent description of saving faith by the Heidelberg Catechism to show how foolish it is for the Ethical theologians to explain the words, "Jesus, the Author and Finisher of our faith," as though He had *saving* faith like every child of God.

Hence saving faith is unthinkable in heaven. Faith is *saving;* and he that is saved has obtained the end of faith. He no longer walks by faith, but by sight. It should therefore be thoroughly understood that saving faith refers only *to the sinner,* and that Christ in the garments of the Sacred Scripture is its only object.

Two things must, therefore, be carefully distinguished: faith in the *testimony* concerning a person, and faith in that *person* himself.

Let us illustrate. A ship is ready to sail, but lacks a captain. Two men present themselves to the shipowner; both are provided with excellent testimonials signed by creditable and trustworthy persons. Of the absolute truth of these testimonials the shipowner is thoroughly convinced. And yet in spite of this testimony one is engaged and the other dismissed. Conversing with both, the owner has found the first a very reasonable fellow, readily allowing him, as the owner of the ship, to issue orders; in fact, as captain he would have nothing to say. But the other, a real sailor, demanded absolute control of the ship, otherwise he would not take the responsibility. And, since the shipowner enjoyed issuing orders, he preferred the meek and tractable captain and dismissed the rough sailor. Consequently the tame commander, obeying orders, lost the ship the first voyage, while the rival ship commanded by that Jack-tar returned home laden with a rich cargo.

We distinguish here two kinds of faith. First, faith or no faith in testimony presented; second, faith or no faith in the persons to whom this testimony refers. In the illustration, faith of the first kind was perfect. Those testimonies were accepted as genuine; the shipowner had perfect faith in the signatures. And yet it did not follow that he was immediately ready to entrust his property to either one of these captains. This required another faith; not only faith in the contents of those papers, but faith also that these contents would prove true regarding the command of *his* ship. Hence he carefully considered both men, and discovering that the one left no room for his self-assertion, it was natural that he engaged the other, who flattered his egotism. And, influenced by this egotism, he did not place that second faith in the right person. His neighbor, not so egotistically inclined, kept the end in view, had faith in the bold seaman, and his profits were almost fabulous. Hence both men had unconditional faith in the testimonies, but the one, denying himself, had also faith in the excellent captain, and the other, refusing to deny himself, had not.

Applying this to our relation to Christ. That vessel is our soul. It is tossing upon the waves and needs a pilot. The voyage is long, and we ask: "Who will safely pilot it?" Then a testimony is laid before us concerning One wonderfully skilled in the art of safely guiding souls into the desired haven. That testimony is Sacred Scripture, which throughout all its pages offers but one, ever-continued, divine testimony concerning the unique excellence of the Christ as leading souls to the safe haven. With this testimony before us, it is for us to decide whether we will accept it or not. Its rejection ends the matter, and Jesus will never be the Guide of our soul. But, accepting it, saying, "We believe all that is written," we can proceed. This confession implies: (1) faith in the genuineness of the testimony; (2) faith in God who gave it; and (3) faith in the truth of its contents.

But this is not *saving faith,* only faith in the *testimony.* To believe that it will prove true in our case, in our own persons, is quite different. This depends, not upon the testimony, but upon whether we will *submit ourselves to Him of whom it speaks.* Although this Captain pilots souls safely across very deep waters, He does not pilot all souls. They must be *able* and *willing* to submit themselves to Him according to His demands. The unwilling are left behind, and, trying to pilot themselves, they miserably perish. Hence we must submit. And this requires the laying aside of all our self-conceit, the utter casting out of self. So long as self stands in the way, we refuse Him as our spiritual Guide; nor do we believe in His power. But as soon as self is cast out, the ego silenced, and the soul abandons itself to Him, the second faith awakens, and, upon bended knee, we cry: "My Lord and my God!"

It is exactly as our Catechism beautifully and comprehensively expresses it: "That true faith consists of two things, *first,* a certain knowledge whereby I hold for truth all that God has revealed to us in His Word, but *also* an assured confidence, which is a firm and steadfast confidence, which the Holy Ghost works by the Gospel in my heart; that not only to others, but to me also, remission of sin, everlasting righteousness, and salvation are freely given of God; merely of grace, only for the sake of Christ's merits."

Examining more closely what these two points have in common, we find, not that the one is *knowledge* and the other *confidence,* but that both consist in *being persuaded.*

With the testimony laid before him, the natural man is inclined to reject it. He has many objections. "Is it genuine?" "Was it not affected by various alterations? Can I rely on the truth of its contents?" For a long time he continues his resistance. He says: "No man can ever convince me; I believe a great deal, but not that impossible Scripture." But the Holy Spirit continues His work. He shows him that he is wrong; and, although still resisting, it becomes like a fire in his bones until opposition is made impossible, and he confesses that God is true and His testimony genuine.

However, this is not all. He still lacks the second faith: whether this applies to him personally. He begins with denying it. "It does not mean me," he says; "Jesus does not save a man like myself." But here the Holy Spirit meets him again. He brings him back to the Word. He holds the image of the saved sinner before him until he recognizes himself in that image. And though he still objects, "It cannot be so; I only deceive myself," yet the Holy Spirit persists in persuading him until, wholly convinced, he appropriates Christ to himself and acknowledges: "Blessed be God, that saved sinner *am I.*" Wherefore it is not first *knowledge* and then *confidence,* but both are an inward persuasion by the Holy Ghost. And the man thus *persuaded believes.* He that is persuaded of the truth of the divine testimony concerning the Guide of souls believes all that is revealed in the Scripture. And being also persuaded that the saved sinner described in Scripture is himself, he believes in Christ as his Surety.

Hence the peculiar feature of faith in both its stages is to be *persuaded.* Saving faith is a persuasion, wrought by the Holy Spirit, that the Scripture is a true testimony concerning the salvation of souls, and that this salvation includes my soul.

Is the Heidelberg Catechism wrong, then, in speaking of knowledge and of confidence? No, but it should be noticed that it speaks, not of faith's *origin,* but of its fruit and exercise, it being already established. Being persuaded that the Scripture is true, and believing the divine testimony concerning Christ, we at once possess certain and undoubted knowledge regarding these things. And being persuaded that that salvation includes my soul, I possess by virtue of this persuasion a firm and assured confidence that the treasure of Christ's redemption is also my own.

Hence faith has three stages: (1) *knowledge of the testimony; (2) certainty of the things revealed;* and (3) *persuasion that this concerns me personally.* These used to be called *knowledge, assent,* and *confidence;* and we are willing to adopt them, but they must be used carefully. By the *first* must be understood nothing more than the obtaining of knowledge independently of faith. Hence the Heidelberg Catechism omits this as not belonging to faith proper, and mentions only *assent* and *confidence.* For that certain knowledge of which it speaks is not what the scholastics put in the foreground as knowledge, but what they call *assent. Knowledge* is not the emphatic word, but *certainty.** It is not the knowledge, but the *certainty* of the knowledge that belongs to the true faith.

Wherefore some used to distinguish knowledge and assent, and treated them separately. For it should be remembered that the unconverted do not understand the Scripture, nor can they read its testimony. Not being born of water and of the Spirit, they cannot see the Kingdom of God. The natural man does not understand spiritual things. Hence we say emphatically, that the knowledge preceding faith and to which faith must assent implies the *illumination* of the Holy Spirit. Only in that light can one see the glory of Scripture and apprehend its beauty; without this it is but a stumblingblock to him. Yet it is no part of faith, but only part of the Spirit's work making faith possible.

A truth or a person is not faith, but the object of faith; faith itself is to be persuaded when, all opposition ended, the soul has obtained undoubted *assurance.* Hence the absolute absurdity of speaking of faith cut loose from Scripture, or directed upon anything but Christ; or of calling faith a universal inclination of the soul, crying after salvation, to quench its thirst. All this robs faith of its character. When I say, "I believe," I mean thereby that this or that is to me an undoubted fact. In order to believe one must be *assured, convinced, persuaded*—otherwise there can be no faith; and the fruit of this being persuaded is rich knowledge, glorious confidence, and access to the Lord.

However, it should be noticed that we have spoken of faith only as it shows itself *above the ground.* But that is not sufficient. We must still examine the root, the fibers of faith in the soul. We must examine the faculty that *enables* the soul to believe. Of this in the next article.

---

* "Certa fudicia." Not *a* certain knowledge, but *certain* knowledge.

38

The Faculty of Faith

As many as are led by the Spirit of God, they are the sons of God—Romans 8:14.

Saving faith should always be understood as a disposition of man's spiritual being by which he can become assured that the Christ after the Scripture, the *only* Savior, is *his* Savior.

We write purposely a *"disposition"* by which he *can become assured.* As water is in the pipes, although not running just now, or as gas in the tubes, although not burning, so by virtue of regeneration is faith present as a disposition in man's spiritual being, even though he believes not yet, or believes no more. If the house is connected with the city's water-works the water can run, but for this reason it does not always run; nor does the gas always burn. That in your house the water *can* flow, and gas *can* burn, is the difference between your dwelling and your neighbor's which is not so connected.

There is a similar difference between the regenerate and the unregenerate; that is, between him who is united to Jesus and him *not* so united. The difference is not that the former believes and always believes, but only this, that he *can* believe. For the unregenerate cannot believe; he has purposely destroyed the precious and divine gift whereby he could have joined himself to the life of God. God gave him eyes to see, but he has purposely blinded himself. Hence he does not see Jesus. The living Christ does not exist for him. Not so the regenerate child of

God. True, he also is a sinner; he also has purposely blinded himself, but an operation is performed upon him, restoring his eyesight, so that now he can see. And this is the implanted *faculty of faith.* This faculty touches the consciousness. As soon as the fact that Christ is the *only* Savior and *my* Savior, as an undoubted, firmly established, and fundamental truth, is introduced to my consciousness—which is the clear representation of my whole being, and is perfectly adapted and joined to it—*I believe.*

But this truth does not suit the consciousness of the natural man. He may insert it now and then by means of a temporary or historical faith, but only as a foreign element, and his nature immediately reacts against it, in precisely the same manner as the blood and tissue react against a sliver in one's finger. For this reason a temporary faith can never save a man, but, on the contrary, it injures him; for it causes his soul to fester.

The human consciousness as it is by nature, and the Christ after the Scripture, are in principle diametrically opposed. The one excludes the other. That which suits and fits the consciousness of the natural man is the persistent *denial* of Christ. This natural consciousness is the representation of his sinful existence; and since an unconverted sinner always asserts himself and thinks himself savable, and proposes to save *himself,* he cannot tolerate Christ. Christ is unthinkable to him; therefore he cannot acknowledge Him. No, there is no need of Him; he can save, too, with Jesus, or just as well as Jesus, or after the example of Jesus; wherefore this Jesus is by no means the *only* Savior.

But if the Christ after the Scripture fits his consciousness, that consciousness must have been changed from what it was by nature; and being the *reflection* and *representation* of his being and all that it contains, it follows that to make room for Christ, not to oblige Him, but from his own absolute necessity, his *being* must first be changed. Hence a *twofold change:*

First, the *new birth,* changing the position of his inward being.

Second, the change affecting his consciousness, by introducing the disposition to accept Christ. And this disposition, being the organ of his consciousness whereby he can do this, is the *faculty of faith.*

The fathers have correctly observed that this disposition imparts itself also *to the will.* And it cannot be otherwise. The will is like a wheel moving the arms of a windmill. In sinless Adam this wheel stood squarely upon its shaft, turning with equal ease to the right and to the left—that is, it moved as freely toward God as toward Satan. But in the sinner this wheel is partly moved from the shaft, so that it can turn only to the left. When he wants to sin, he can do so. In this direction the shaft is clear; he has the power to sin. But the wheel cannot turn the other way; a little perhaps, with much difficulty and much squeaking, but never sufficiently to grind corn. The working of his will can never produce any saving good. He cannot make the wheel of his life run with the energy of the will toward God.

Even after he is inwardly changed, and the faith faculty has entered his consciousness, it is useless so long as the powerless will enters the consciousness to expel his Christian assurance. Therefore the will must be divinely wrought upon to serve the changed consciousness. Hence the disposition of faith is imparted not only to the consciousness, but also to the will, to adapt itself to the Christ of the Scripture. The will of the saint is made to move again freely toward God. When the ego is turned and the will changed, then only can the new disposition enter the consciousness, to be assured that Christ after the Scripture is the only Christ and his Christ.

The faculty of faith is therefore something complex. It cannot be independent from the consciousness and knowledge; for it implies a change of man's being and the will's liberty to move toward God. Hence this faculty is not a spontaneous growth from the implanted life, neither is it independent of it, but as a disposition it can enter us only after regeneration, and even then it must be given us by the grace of God.

Of course, the man in whom the faculty of faith begins to work believes in Scripture, in Christ, and in his own salvation, but without it he continues to the end to object against Scripture, Christ, and his own salvation. He may be almost convinced; wholly convinced he will never be. This is temporary faith, historical faith, faith in ideals, but never saving faith.

But if a man has received this disposition, is it possible for him immediately and always to believe? Surely not, no more than a normal infant can read, write, or think logically. And when at sixteen he can do these things, it is owing not to new faculties received since his birth, but to the development of those born in him. A new-born child of God possesses the faculty to believe, but there is no immediate and actual believing. This requires something more. As a child cannot learn and develop without teachers and in connection with his own environment, so the faculty of faith cannot be exercised without the guidance of the Holy Spirit in connection with the contents of Scripture.

How this was effected in deceased infants we cannot tell; not because the Holy Spirit cannot work in them as well as in adults, but because they do not know the Scripture. However, since the Scriptures testify only of Christ, He may have a way to bring the not-thinking child into connection with Christ, as He provided Scripture for thinking men.

In either case, the faith faculty cannot produce anything of itself, but must be stimulated and developed by the Holy Spirit's training and exercise, gradually learning to believe—a training continued to the end; for until we die the working of faith increases in strength, development, and glory.

But this is not all. A man may have the faculty of faith fully developed and exercised, but it does not follow that therefore he *always believes.* On the contrary, faith may be interrupted for a season. Hence faith should not be called *the breath of the soul;* for when a man ceases to breathe he dies. No; the faculty of faith is more like the power of a tree to blossom and bear fruit: apparently dead one season, and beautiful with blossoms the next. That I possess the faculty to think is evident, not from my uninterrupted thinking, for when asleep I do not think, but it is evident from my thinking when I *must* think. Even so with the faculty of faith, which occupies the same position as the faculties of thinking, speaking, etc.

Regarding these faculties, we distinguish three things: (1) the faculty itself; (2) its necessary development; (3) and its exercise when sufficiently stimulated. Hence we notice not only the Spirit's first operation, *implanting* the faith faculty; nor only the second, *qualifying* that faculty for exercise, but also the third, *stimulating* and calling out the act of believing whenever it pleases Him.

There is no man possessed of the faith faculty but the Holy Spirit has thus *endowed* him. There is no man enabled by this faculty to believe but the Holy Spirit has also *qualified* that faculty. Nor is there a man using this qualification, actually believing, unless the Holy Spirit has *wrought* this in him.

Life has its ups and downs. We see it in our love. You have a child whom you love tenderly. But in the daily life you do not always feel that love, and sometimes you charge yourself with being cold without warm attachment for the child. But let somebody injure him, or let him be taken ill—or worse, let his life be in danger—and your slumbering love will at once be aroused. That love did not come to you from without, but it dwelt in the depths of your soul, slumbering until fully awakened by the sharp sting of sorrow. The same applies to faith. For days and weeks we may have to reproach ourselves for the faithless condition of our own heart, when the soul seems dry and dead, as though there were no bond of love between us and our Savior. But lo! The Lord reveals Himself to us, or distress overwhelms us, or the earnestness of life suddenly lays hold of us, and at once that apparently dead faith is aroused and the bond of Jesus' love is strongly felt.

And more than this: inspired by love, you are constantly doing something for your darling without saying: "I do this or that for him because I love him so much." So also regarding faith: saving faith is a disposition whose activity we do not always notice, but like other faculties it works continually, its functions unnoticed. Hence we frequently exercise faith without being specially conscious of it. We prepare ourselves *especially* to think or speak when *special* occasion calls for it; and so we act from faith with conscious purpose when, peculiarly circumstanced, we must boldly stand up as witnesses or make some important decision.

But our comfort is this, that faith's saving power depends, not upon some special believing act; nor upon acts less conscious; nor even upon the acquired ability of faith, but solely upon the fact that the germ of faith has been planted in the soul. Hence a child can have saving faith, even though it never performed a single act of faith. And so we continue saved, even though the act of faith slumbers for a season. The man, once endowed with saving faith is saved and blessed. And when by and by the act of faith appears, he is not saved in *higher degree,* but it is only the evidence that, through the infinite mercy of God, the germ of faith has been planted in him.

39

Defective Learning

He that believeth on Him shall not be confounded—1 Peter 2:6.

St. Paul declares that faith is the gift of God (Eph. 2:8). His words, "And that not of yourselves, it is the gift of God," refer to the word "faith."

A new generation of youthful expositors confidently assert that these words refer to "by grace are ye saved." The majority of them are evidently ignorant of the history of the exegesis of the text. They only know that the pronoun "that" in the clause "and that not of yourselves" is a Greek neuter. And without further examination they consider it settled that the neuter pronoun cannot refer to "faith," which is a Greek feminine.

Allow us to put our readers on their guard against the thoughtless prattle of shallow school-learning. It should be remembered that while our exegesis is and always had been the one accepted almost without exception, the opposite opinion is shared by only a few expositors of later times. Nearly all the church fathers and almost all the theologians eminent for Greek scholarship judged that the words "it is the gift of God" refer to *faith.*

1. This was the exegesis, according to the ancient tradition, of the churches in which St. Paul had labored.

2. Of those that spoke the Greek language and were familiar with the peculiar Greek construction.

3. Of the Latin church fathers, who maintained close contact with the Greek world.

4. Of such scholars as Erasmus, Grotius, and others, who as philologists were without peers; and in them all the more remarkable, since personally they favored the exposition that faith is the work of man.

5. Of Beza, Zanchius, Piscator, Voetius, Heidegger, and even of Wolf, Bengel, Estius, Michaelis, Rosenmüller, Flatt, Meier, Baumgarten-Crusius, etc., who to the present day maintain the original tradition.

And lastly, Calvin, although he is said to have favored the other exegesis. But if he had surrendered the original interpretation, he would have given some reason for it; for he was thoroughly acquainted with it. And this makes it probable that he never intended to discuss the question. That he adhered to the traditional exegesis is proven from his own words, in his "Antidote Against the Decrees of the Concilium of Trente" (p. 190, edition 1547): "Faith is not of man, but of God."

Even our educated Reformed laymen are acquainted with the fact, if it were only from the study of the magnificent commentary on the Ephesians by Petrus Dinant, minister at Rotterdam, who flourished in the latter part of the seventeenth century. He published it in 1710, and the book had such a large sale that it was reissued in 1726; even now it is in great demand. We quote from it the following (vol. 1, p. 451): " 'And that not of yourselves, it is the gift.' The word 'that,' τοῦτο, refers either to the preceding 'being saved,' or to 'faith.' To the former it cannot refer, St. Paul having stated already that salvation is a gift of God. Hence it must refer to faith. It is true the Greek τοῦτο, is a neuter, while πίστεως, faith, is a feminine. But Greek scholars know that the relative pronoun may refer just as well to the following δῶρον, gift, which is neuter, as to the preceding πίστεως, which is feminine, according to the rule in Greek grammar governing this point. Hence 'that,' viz., '*faith, is not of yourselves, it is the gift of God.*' "

But recent discoveries may have upset this ancient exegesis. If the modern expositors of Utrecht, Gröningen, and Leyden, who make a hobby of this modern exegesis, will therefore show us this recent discovery, we will give them an attentive hearing. But they fail to do this. On the contrary, they say: "The matter is settled, and so plain that even a tyro in Greek can see it." And by saying this, they judge themselves.

For brains incomparably superior such as Erasmus and Hugo Grotius, knew so much of Greek that they were at least acquainted with the Greek rudiments. And we may venture to say that all the Greek scholarship now lodged in the brains of our exegetes at the universities just named would not half fill the cup which Erasmus and Grotius together filled to the brim. Wherefore we confidently maintain the traditional exegesis.

The positive assurance wherewith these young expositors make their assertions need not surprise us. The explanation is easily found. They were nearly all prepared at universities whose professors of New-Testament exegesis seek to estrange their students from the traditional interpretation of the Scripture by making surprising observations; for example, the students had learned at home that "the gift of God," in Ephesians 2:8, refers to faith, but they had never consulted the original text. Then the professor observed, with perfect correctness, that it does not read ἁυτη, but τοῦτο, adding: "The gentlemen can see for themselves that this cannot refer to faith." And, unacquainted with the subject, his inexperienced hearers suppose that nothing more remains to be said. If their Greek scholarship had been more thorough and extensive, they would have been able to judge more independently.

With this conviction they enter the church; and when a simple layman repeats the old exegesis, they delight, at least on such occasions, to parade the fruit of their academic training; and the simple layman is made to understand that he knows nothing of Greek, and that the Greek text plainly reads the other way, and that therefore he may not support the antiquated exegesis.

When sometimes the *Heraut** dares to repeat the old, well-tried opinion, these youthful savants cannot help but think: "The *Heraut* does not act in good faith; the editor knows perfectly well that it reads, τοῦτο, and that πίστεως is feminine." Of course, the *Heraut* knows this very well—just as well as Erasmus and Grotius knew it—and, knowing a little more of Greek than these child-like rudiments, has taken the liberty, supported by the goodly company of the scholars just named, to entertain an opinion different from that of the Utrecht graduates.

---

* A religious weekly publication edited by the author—Trans.

Undoubtedly every man has a right to his own opinion and to reject the traditional exegesis. Moreover, in Philippians 1:23, it is distinctly stated that faith is a gift of God. But we protest against the shallowness and artlessness of men who in their ignorance pose as scholars, and make it appear as though even a tyro in Greek, if he be only an *honest* man, could not support the opposite opinion for a moment. For this is inexcusable in one who presumes to pronounce judgment upon another who knows what he is talking about, as will appear from the postscript of this article.

The reader will kindly bear with us for treating this matter somewhat extensively, for it touches a principle. Our universities deny our confession of faith. They may still concede that God is the Author of salvation, but faith (such as they interpret it) is taken in the sense of a medium which originates from the union of the breath of the soul and the inworking of the Holy Spirit. Hence their manifest preference for such novel exegesis, apparent also from the energetic and persistent effort to popularize it.

And this tendency is manifest in many other directions. For individual, original research there is little opportunity. Hence the instruction received at Utrecht is the only source of information. And this is so thoroughly rooted in heart and mind that the student cannot conceive that it can be otherwise. Moreover, the arguments have been presented so concisely and incessantly that convincing arguments for opposite views seem utterly impossible.

This being the case, our young theologians, honest in and loyal to their convictions, declare from the pulpit and in private conversation that uncertainty regarding various doctrinal points is out of the question; so that it must be conceded and acknowledged that the ancient expositors were decidedly wrong. And this is the cause of the strong opposition against many established opinions, even among our best ministers; not from love of opposition, but because sincere convictions forbid them to follow any other line of conduct, at least as long as they are not better informed.

And this may not remain so. There is no earnestness in that position. It is unworthy of the man scientifically trained; it is unworthy of the minister. There is need of *individual* research and investigation. These Utrecht novelties should be received with a considerable grain of salt. It may even be freely surmised that the learning of the Utrecht faculty, when they oppose the learning of the whole Church, must be discredited.

And thus our young men will be compelled to return to original research. Not only that, but they will be compelled to buy books. The libraries of nearly all our young theologians contain scarcely anything but German works, products of the mediation theology; hence exceedingly one-sided, not nation, foreign to our Church, in conflict with our history. This lack ought first to be supplied. And then we hope that the time soon will come when every minister in our Reformed churches shall be in the possession of at least a few solid and better works. And when thus the opportunity is born for more impartial and more correct study, the rising generation of ministers should once more *resume their studies,* and obtain the conviction by their own experience, even as others have done, that the work of study and research, which will bear good fruit for the Church of God, is not yet finished, but really only just begun. Then a generation of more earnest and better-trained men will treat the opinions which we have advanced with a little more appreciation, and, what is of much higher importance, they will treat the being of faith with more thoughtfulness.

It is of vital interest that the *exercise* of faith and the *faculty* of faith be no longer confounded, and that it be acknowledged the latter may be present without the former. Otherwise there will be a complete deviation from the line of the Scripture, which is also that of the Reformed churches. It will make salvation dependent upon the *exercise* of faith, that is, upon the act of accepting Christ and all His benefits; and since this act is an act, not of God, but of man, we imperceptibly lose our way in the waters of Arminianism.

Hence everything depends upon the correct understanding of Ephesians 2:8. For faith is not the act of believing, but the mere possession of faith, even of faith in the germ. He that possesses that germ or faculty of faith, and who at God's time will also exercise faith, is saved, saved by grace, for to him was imparted the gift of God.

Formerly theologians were used to speaking of faith's being and well-being, but this had reference to another distinction, which must not be confounded with the one thus far treated. Sometimes the plant of faith seems more vigorous in one than in another, and its development riper and fuller, bearing branch, twig, leaf, blossom, and fruit—which is evidence of the well-being of faith. It may also be that, in the same person, faith seems to pass through the four seasons of the year: there is first a spring-tide, in which it grows, followed by a summer, when it blossoms, but there is also an autumn when it languishes, and a winter when it slumbers. And this is the transition from the *well*-being of faith to its mere being. But as a tree remains a tree in winter, and will possess the *being* of a tree even though it has lost its well-being, so faith may remain still living faith in us, though temporarily without leaf and blossom.

For the comfort of souls, our fathers always pointed to the fact, and so do we, that salvation does not depend upon the *well*-being of faith, so long as the soul possesses the *being* of faith. Although, after the example of our fathers, we add, that the tree does not live in winter, except it hastens on toward spring, when it shall bud again; and that the *being* of faith gives evidence of its presence in the soul only by hastening on toward its *well*-being.

Postscript

It is necessary to point out two things regarding the shallowness of which we complain.

First, that the construction of a *neuter* pronoun with a *feminine* noun as its antecedent is not a mistake, but *excellent Greek.*

Second, that the Church had reasons why until now she made the words "and that not of yourselves" refer to faith.

In regard to the *first point,* we refer not to a Hellenistic exception, but to the ordinary rule, which is found in every good Greek syntax, and which every exegete ought to know.

A rule which, among others, was formulated by Kühner, in his "Ausführliche Grammatik der Griech. Sprache," vol. 2, 1, p. 54 (Han., 1870), and which is as follows: *"Besonders häufig steht das* Neutrum *eines demonstrativen Pronomens in Beziehung auf ein männliches oder* weibliches *Substantiv, indem der Begriff desselben ganz allgemein als blosses Ding oder Wesen, oder auch als ein ganzer Gedanke aufgefasst wird."* Which is in English: A *neutral* demonstrative pronoun is frequently used to refer to a preceding masculine or *feminine* noun, when the meaning expressed by this word is taken in a general sense, etc.

The examples cited by Kühner deal a death-blow to the Utrecht exegesis. Take, for instance, these from Plato and Xenophon:

Plato, "Protagoras," 357, C.:

῾Ομολογοῦμεν ἐπιστήμης μηδὲν εἶναι κρεῖττον, ἀλλὰ τοῦτο ἀεὶ κρατεῖν, ὅπου ἄν ἐνῇ, καὶ ἡδονῆς καὶ τῶν ἀλλῶν ἁπάντων.

Plato, "Menon," 73, C.:

῾Επειδὴ τοίνυν ἡ αὐτή ἀρετὴ πάντων ἐστί, πειρῶ εἰπεῖν καὶ ἀναμνησθῆναι, τί αὐτό φησι Γοργίας εἶναι.

Xenophon, "Hiero," ix:9.

Εἰ ἐμπορία ὠφελεῖ τι πόλιν, τιμώμενος ἄν ὁ πλεῖστα τοῦτο ποιῶν καὶ ἐμπόρους ἄν πλείους ἀγείροι.

To which we add three more from Plato, and a fourth from Demosthenes: Plato, "Protag.," 352, B.:

Πῶς ἔχεις πρὸς ἐπιστήμην; πότερον καὶ τοῦτό σοι δοκεῖ ὥσπερ τοῖς πολλοῖς ἀνθρώποις, ἢ ἄλλως.

Plato, "Phaedo," 61, A.:

῾Υπελάμβανον; . . . καὶ ἐμοὶ οὕτω ἐνύπνιον, ὅπερ ἔπραττον, τοῦτο ἐπικελεύειν, μουσικὴν ποιεῖν, ὡς φιλοσοφίας μὲν οὔσης μεγίστης μουσικῆς, ἐμοῦ δὲ τοῦτο πράττοντος.

Plato, "Theaetetus," 145, D.:

Σοφία δὲ γ᾽ οἶμαι σοφοί;—ναί—τοῦτο δὲ νῦν διαφέρει τι ἐπιστήμης.

Demosthenes, "Contra Aphob.," 2:

᾽Εγὼ γὰρ, ὦ ἄνδρες δικασταὶ, περὶ τῆς μαρτυρίας τῆς ἐν τῷ γραμματείῳ γεγραμμένης εἰδὼς ὄντα μοι τὸν ἀγῶνα, καὶ περὶ τούτου τὴν ψῆφον ὑμᾶς οἴσοντας ἐπιστάμενος ᾠήθην δεῖν κ. τ. λ.

For the present we postpone the discussion of the *second point* to another time. But it is evident that these citations upset all the quasi-learning of this defective scholarship; and that the words, "And that not of —yourselves, it is the gift of God," just with the neutral pronoun, in purest Greek, can refer to *faith;* hence that all this fuss about the difference of gender, not only is without any foundation, but also leaves a very poor impression regarding the scholarship of the men who raised the objection.

Moreover, we must also show not only that the ancient rendering of Ephesians 2:8 *may* be correct, but also that it cannot be anything else but correct.

It reads: "For by *grace* are ye saved through *faith,* and that *not* of yourselves, it is the *gift of God;* not of *works,* lest any man should boast. For we are *His workmanship."* The principal thought is the mighty fact that the causative worker of our salvation is *God.* St. Paul expresses this in the most forcible and most positive terms by saying: "You are saved *from* grace, *through* grace, and *by* grace." If then it should follow, "And that not of yourselves, it is the gift of God," we would have a dragging sentence of superfluous clauses, thrice repeating the same thing: "You have received it by grace, not of yourselves, it is the gift of God." And this might do, if it read, "You are saved by grace, and *therefore* not of yourselves," but it does not read so. It is simply, *"and* that not of yourselves." The conjunction *"and"* stands in the way.

Or, if it read, "Ye are saved by grace, not of yourselves, it is God's work," it would sound better. But first to say, "Ye are saved by grace," and then without adding anything new to repeat, "and that not of yourselves," is harsh and halting. And all the more so, since in the ninth verse it is repeated for the fourth and fifth time, *"not of works;* we are *His workmanship."* And while all this is stiff and forced, labored and superfluous, by adopting the exegesis of the ancient expositors of the Christian Church it becomes all at once smooth and vigorous. For then it reads: "You are saved by mere grace, by means of faith. (Not as though by this means of faith the grace of your salvation would be partly *not* of grace; no indeed not, for even that faith is *not of yourselves,* it is the *gift of God.)* And, therefore, saved through faith, not of works, lest any man should boast, for we are His workmanship."

But then this creates a parenthesis, which is perfectly true, but even this is truly Pauline. St. Paul hears the objection, and refutes it again and again, even where he does not formulate the contrast.

40

Faith in the Saved Sinner Alone

And they believed in the Scripture—John 2:22.

Faith is not the working of a faculty inherent in the natural man; nor a new sense added to the five; nor a new soul-function; nor a faculty first dormant now active, but a disposition, mode of action, implanted by the Holy Spirit in the consciousness and will of the regenerate person, whereby he is enabled to accept Christ.

From this it follows that this disposition cannot be implanted in sinless man, and that it disappears as soon as the sinner ceases to be a sinner. The saint believes until he dies, but no longer. Or more correctly: faith disappears as soon as he enters heaven, for then he lives no more by faith, but by sight.

The importance of this distinction is obvious. The Ethical theologians, denying that faith is a specially implanted disposition, but rather a sense or its organ, first dormant then awakened, cannot admit this, but repeat that faith is perpetual, basing their opinion upon 1 Corinthians 13:13. According to their theory, there is no absolute difference between the sinner and the sinless; they do not believe that to save the sinner the Holy Spirit introduces an extraordinary expedient into his spiritual person. Hence their persistent effort to make us understand that Adam believed before the fall, and that even Jesus, the Captain and Finisher of our faith, walked by faith.

But this whole presentation is opposed by the apostolic words: "We walk by faith, and not *by sight*" (2 Cor. 5:7). And again, "Now I know in part, but then shall I know even as also I am known" (1 Cor. 13:12), in connection with the preceding: "When that which is perfect is come, then that which is in part shall *be done away*" (vs. 10). And not less by the word of our Lord, that we shall see God as soon as we are pure in heart (Matt. 5:8).

And starting from this point, we know positively that faith in the sense of saving faith is not perpetual; that it did not exist in Paradise, but can only be found in a lost sinner. To be endowed with saving faith, he must be a sinner, just as much as relief from pain can be given only to one suffering pain.

"Very well," say the Ethicals, "we accept this. But when the physician tries to improve the breathing of the asthmatic by making him inhale fresh air, it does not follow that a healthy person does not inhale. On the contrary, a healthy man inhales strongly and deeply, and it is the physician's purpose to *assist* the *normal* function of breathing. And the same applies to faith. True the Holy Spirit can give faith only to the *sinner,* but a healthy saint, like Adam before the fall and Christ, did most assuredly believe; for faith is but the breath of the soul. In Adam and Christ this breathing was spontaneous; in sinners like ourselves it is disturbed. Hence we need help to be healed. But when our souls once more freely inhale the breath of faith, we have received only what Adam and Jesus had before us."

And this we oppose. Saving faith is not the ordinary breath of the soul, first disturbed, then restored. No; it is the specific remedy for one lost in sin; an expedient extended to him because he *became* a sinner; retained as long as he *continues* a sinner; withdrawn as soon as he *ceases* from sin. When the expedient is no longer needed, and the soul redeemed from sin can breathe freely toward God without the expedient of faith, wholly restored, entirely redeemed, then only he receives once more that natural, spontaneous communion with the Eternal which needs no intervening aid, but which is like that of holy Adam and Jesus.

Faith is like a pair of glasses, not only useless, but hurtful to good eyes; very helpful for diseased or weak eyes. So long as eyes are abnormal, glasses are indispensable; before they became abnormal, glasses were useless (Adam before the fall). Eyes never abnormal never needed them (Jesus). As soon as wholly restored, they are laid aside (the redeemed in heaven).

Next in order is faith in connection with Sacred Scripture; and here the error of the Ethicals becomes very apparent. Their theory that sinless Adam and Christ exercised faith, and that the redeemed in heaven still believe, leads away from Scripture. In Paradise sinless Adam had no Scripture; neither has Christ on the throne; and in death the redeemed forever lose their Bible. Hence it is the logical consequence of this error that the faith of the Ethicals is possible *without Scripture,* and is not necessarily intended for Scripture. According to their theory, to believe is the soul's breathing, but little more than another name for prayer. Indeed, there should have been no Scripture, and in the absence of sin there would have been none; hence faith, which is only the restoration of a soul-function disturbed by sin, is possible with Scripture.

This theory is far-reaching. They believe that even among the heathen the Lord had His elect, though they never had heard of the Scripture. The heathen of classic times were a sort of unbaptized Christians, entering the Kingdom of heaven under the leadership of their patriarch Plato. Though modern rationalists reject Scripture, yet they are such lovely and devoted people that faith cannot be denied them. Reasoning in this way, they arrive at the following conclusions:

1. Not the Confession, but the *motive* of the heart is the main thing; and

2. Though men claim to have discovered intentional frauds in Scripture, and therefore reject it, they are still "brethren beloved."

The consistency is evident. Wherefore ministers loyal to the Word should be careful how they speak of the being of faith, lest they feed the evil which they seek to restrain. All that vague and flowery talk about faith as the breath of the soul, as the soul's sweet trust of love, etc., has a direct tendency toward Ethical error. For the line is a dividing-line. Do you acknowledge or deny it?

The Ethicals deny it. There is no settled boundary between God and man, but a certain transition between the finite and infinite in the God-man; no absolute separation between the elect and the lost, but a sort of gradual transition in the presentation of a universal redemption; no absolute separation between sin and holiness, but a certain conciliation in the sanctification of the saints; no absolute separation between life before and after death, but a bridge across the chasm in the state of believing. Nor is there between the Bible and the books of men, but a kind of affinity in the legends of Scripture; and, finally, not between the condition with or without faith, but a transfer from the one into the other in the preparatory workings.

The practical result of this false standpoint is the belief in a *medium* between believers and unbelievers, viz., a *third* state for troubled souls. Or we may call it philosophy, but then it is earth-born, in its pantheistic obstinacy refusing to admit the absolute contrast between the Creator and the creature, and boldly interpreting Scripture's ministry of reconciliation in the sense of an essential system, that is, the blending of one being with another.

Scripture is diametrically opposed to this: "And God divided the light from the darkness"; "And God divided the waters from the dry land"; "And God divided the day from the night." Hence all who acknowledge the absolute separation between faith and unbelief must array themselves in direct opposition to the Ethicals. This explains the cause of our ecclesiastical conflict.

They that deny the contrasts and efface the divinely ordained boundaries *must* be irenical; that is, they must contend that a breach in the Church cannot be allowed. The fatal inference of their pantheistic tendency is "No *breaches,* but *bridges.*" Hence our position antagonizes this standpoint along the whole line of our ecclesiastical and theological life, with definite, stern, and absolute consistency: particular grace, or Christ *pro omnibus;* only two states, or three; direct regeneration, or universal, preparatory operations; no divided Church, or a Church loyal to the Word of God; a God-man, or a Mediator between God and man; a Scripture absolutely inspired, or full of enlightened human opinions; and regarding faith, a disposition expressly brought into the sinner, or the restoration of a soul-function. Hence there is opposition all along the line.

From this the relation between Scripture and faith is easily ascertained. Both exist for the sake of the sinner by virtue of sin, and to remove sin; the one not without the other, both belonging together. Without Scripture faith is an aimless gazing. Without faith Scripture is a closed book.

Experience proves it. Persons endowed with the faculty of faith, but ignorant of Scripture or wrongly instructed, make no progress; once instructed, they live and gain strength. On the contrary, to persons familiar with Scripture from their youth, but without faith, the Bible is a closed book; the Word cannot enter them. But when both Scripture and saving faith bless the soul, then the glory of the Holy Spirit appears; for it was He who first granted the particular grace of Scripture, and then also that of faith.

This is the reason why the arguments for the truth of the Scripture never avail anything. A person endowed with faith gradually will accept Scripture; if not so endowed he will never accept it, though he should be flooded with apologetics. Surely it is our duty to assist seeking souls, to explain or remove difficulties, sometimes even to silence a mocker, but to make an unbeliever have faith in Scripture is utterly beyond man's power.

Faith and Scripture belong together; the Holy Spirit intended the one for the other. The latter is so arranged as to be accepted by the sinner endowed with faith. And faith is a disposition, completely reconciling the consciousness and the Scripture. Hence the *testimonium Spiritus Sancti* should be taken, not in the rationalistic or Ethical sense of being the operation upon a certain universal disposition, but as a real testimony of the Holy Spirit, who dwells in the consciousness, and gives us to experience the adaptation—like that of the eye to color—of Scripture to faith.

41

Testimonies

Without faith it is impossible to please God—Hebrews 11:6.

In order to prevent the possibility of being led into paths of error, faith is directed, not to a Christ of the imagination, but to "the Christ in the garments of the Sacred Scripture," as Calvin expresses it.

And therefore we must discriminate between (1) faith as a *faculty* implanted in the soul without our knowledge; (2) faith as a *power* whereby this implanted faculty begins to act; and (3) faith as a *result,* since with this faith (1) we hold the Sacred Scripture for truth, (2) take refuge in Christ, and (3) are firmly assured of our salvation in insepa-rable love for Immanuel.

To which must finally be added that this is the work of the Holy Spirit alone, who (1) gave us the Holy Scriptures; (2) implanted the faculty of faith; (3) caused this faculty to act; (4) made this faith to manifest itself in the act; (5) thereby witnessed to our souls concerning the Sacred Scriptures; (6) enabled us to accept Immanuel with all His treasures; and, lastly, made us find in the love of Immanuel the pledge of our salvation.

Wholly different from this is the *historical* faith, which Brakel briefly describes as follows: "Historical faith is thus called because it knows the history, the narrative, the description of the matters of faith in the Word, acknowledges them to be the truth, and then leaves them alone as matters that concern it no more than the histories of the world; for one cannot use them in his business, neither does it create any emotion in the soul, not even sufficiently to cause man to make a confession: 'Thou believest that there is one God; thou doest well, the devils also believe and tremble' (James 2:19). 'King Agrippa, believest thou the prophets? I know that thou believest' (Acts 26:27)."

Next comes *temporary* faith, of which Brakel gives the following description:

> *Temporary faith* is a knowledge of and a consent to the truths of the Gospel, acknowledging them as the truth; which causes some natural flutterings in the affections and passions of the soul, a confession of these truths in the Church, and an external walk in conformity with that confession, but without a real union with Christ, to justification, sanctification, and redemption: "But he that received the seed into stony places, the same is he that heareth the Word, and anon with joy receiveth it; yet, hat he not root in himself, but dureth for a while; for when tribulation or persecution ariseth because of the Word, by and by he is offended" (Matt. 13:20, 21). "For it is impossible for those who were once enlightened, and have tasted of the heavenly gift, and were made partakers of the Holy Ghost, and have tasted the good Word of God, and the powers of the world to come, if they shall fall away, to renew them again unto repentance" (Heb. 6:4, 5). "For if, after they have escaped the pollution of the world through the knowledge of the Lord Jesus Christ, they are again entangled therein, and overcome, the latter end is worse with them than the beginning" (2 Pet. 2:20).

There is also a *faith of miracles,* which Brakel describes in these words:

> The faith of miracles is a being inwardly persuaded, by an inward working of God, that this or that work shall be wrought, in a supernatural manner, upon our word or command, in ourselves or in others. But the ability to perform miracles is not of man, but of God, by His almighty power, in answer to faith: "If ye have faith as a grain of mustard-seed, ye shall say unto this mountain, Remove hence to yonder place, and it shall remove; and nothing shall be impossible unto you" (Matt. 17:20). "And though I have all faith, so that I could remove mountains" (1 Cor. 13:2). "The same heard Paul speak: who steadfastly beholding him, and perceiving that he had faith to be healed, said with a loud voice, Stand upright on thy feet. And he leaped and walked" (Acts 14:9, 10). This faith was found especially in the days of Christ and of the apostles, for the confirmation of the truth of the Gospel.

These three kinds of faith do in some respects resemble saving faith, but they lack its *being.* Least of all is the faith to perform miracles, which was found also in Judas. Faith which removes mountains is not justifying faith. *Historical* faith comes a little nearer, unless, by reason of a slothfulness and indifference, it merely echoes the words of others without accepting their truth, and thus opens the way to Pharisaism. *Temporary faith* comes nearest, which is indeed wrought by the Holy Spirit, and affords a taste of the heavenly gifts, but which has not root in itself. It is a bouquet of flowers, that for a day adorns the breast of the person who wears it, but which, being cut from its root, is not a plant in him.

Finally, we might speak of faith in its *most general sense,* which is the absence of all hesitation, doubt, or obstacle to receiving in ourselves the immediate and direct inworking of the holy majesty of God, and of the majesty of His truth, in such a penetrating manner that spontaneously we believe that the Word and Being of God are the ground and foundation of all things. In this general sense St. Paul says that, "Without faith it is impossible to please God"; and in a most general sense faith also belonged to the Lord Jesus Christ. But this is not a saving faith, for it has nothing to do with salvation.

Saving faith embraces Christ. How could such Christ-embracing faith dwell in Immanuel?

Rather than to spend our strength in proving this clear fact, we lay before our readers Comrie's beautiful exposition of the saving knowledge of faith, in which he speaks in the following penetrating manner.

> We will shortly enumerate the objects of this knowledge of faith:
>
> First, this knowledge *is a divine light of the Holy Ghost, through the Word, by which I become acquainted, to some extent, with the contents of the Gospel of salvation,* which hitherto was to me a sealed book; which, although I understood it after the letter and in its connections, I could not apply to myself, to direct and support my soul in the great distress, conflict, and anguish which the knowledge of God and of myself had brought upon me. But now it became plain and knowable to me. Now I learn by the inshining of the Holy Ghost the contents of the Gospel, so that I can deal and commune with it. And so I suck from these breasts of consolation the pure, rational, and unadulterated milk of the everlasting Word of God. Truly, the souls that are really humbled by the imparted faith do not derive any benefit from their own notions and opinions of the truth of the

Gospel; on the contrary, they tend to fill them with dismay, because their knowledge which is so great is of no use to them whatever. I have known men of excellent letter-knowledge who, by reason of their natural understanding of the truth, in their legal fear almost cried out in the words of devils: "Thou comest to torment us before our time." Only remember Spira and others. I believe that the letter-knowledge of the Gospel, which was despised here, shall be a hell in hell. For it often occurs that this understanding of the letter, which is only an assent to the truth by itself, when neglected causes the soul to think: "This is not for me, but for others." God knows how many a poor soul sinks away in this depth, and is kept there by others who speak boastingly. However, when the Holy Spirit causes the divine Gospel to shine into the dark prison of the soul, to illuminate the eyes of the inwrought faith with a heavenly and divine light, the soul receives the Gospel as good news, and as a word of instruction, encouragement, and direction; and is led by it, step by step, as a child, which from its A B C learns to spell and read. Now it is: "Behold, I see a way appear!" And then: "Great sinners have been saved, surely there must be hope for me!" In the distance the gates of the City of Refuge are seen wide open, and Jesus is waiting behind those walls—yea, His glory is seen shining through the gates. And in this way, by means of the heavenly light, which pours in upon the inwrought faith, the soul obtains knowledge of the secret of the Lord in Christ, who is revealed to her. How often this knowledge causes the soul to go out in holy desires, we need not tell. Many seem to attain with one step or bound the highest degree, but, like noble exotics, the true faith grows slowly, step by step, from preceding depths of humiliation, until it is perfected in actual work and exercise.

Second, this knowledge *is a divine light of the Holy Spirit in, from, and through the Gospel, by which I know Christ, who is its Alpha and Omega, as the glorious, precious, excellent, and soul-rejoicing Pearl and Treasure hid in this field.* Although I knew all things, and I did not know Jesus by the light of the Spirit, my soul would be a shop full of miseries; a sepulcher appearing beautiful without, but within full of dead men's bones. And this knowledge of Christ, imparted to the soul by the inshining of divine light, through the Gospel, can never from itself give any light to the soul so long as it is not accompanied by the immediate inworking and illumination of the Holy Spirit. For it is not the letter which is effectually working in the soul, but the direct working of the Holy Spirit by means of the letter.

And now you may ask, In what respect must I know Jesus? We will confine ourselves to the following matters: This knowledge of faith, the object of which is Christ in the Gospel, is a knowledge by which I know, through the divine light of the Holy Spirit, my absolute need of Christ. I see that I owe ten thousand talents, and that I have not a farthing to pay; and that I must have a surety to pay my debts. I see that I am a lost sinner, who is in need of Savior. I see that I am dead and impotent in myself and that I need Him who is able to quicken me and to save me. I see that I go astray, and that He must seek after me. Oh! The more this necessity of Christ presses upon me, from this true knowledge of faith, the more earnest, intense, heart-melting, and persevering the outgoings of my soul are from the inwrought faith, and attended with greater conflict. Many do not appreciate them because they do not have them, but, being the effects of the Holy Spirit and the results of the inwrought faith, and attended with greater conflict. Many do not appreciate them because they do not have them, but, being the effects of the Holy Spirit and the results of the inwrought faith, they are pleasing to God, to whom they are directed. For "*He will regard the prayer of the destitute,* and will not despise their prayer"—Psalm 102:17.

Third, it is through this knowledge *that I, by the light of the Spirit, know Jesus in the Gospel, as adapted in every respect to my need.* It is the very conviction of the fitness of a thing which persuades the affections to choose that thing above every other; which makes one resolute and persevering in spite of every obstacle, never to abandon the determination to secure to himself the thing or person chosen for this fitness to his need. You can see it in the matter of marriage.

A young man may judge it absolutely necessary for him to marry. And yet, although convinced of this necessity, he is groping in the dark. Now he is fully determined, and tomorrow he is not. Now he wants this woman, and the next day another. But as soon as he meets a person whom he considers adapted to him in every respect, he is fully resolved. This fitness is the arrow that penetrates his soul, and that causes the scale of his unsettled affections to turn in favor of the congenial object. Hence nothing can draw him away from her so long as he considers her adapted to himself; if need be he will work for her as a slave twice seven years, which time will seem to him but as so many days by reason of the hope to call her his own in the end.

And this can easily be applied to the spiritual. It shows that although one may be convinced of his need of Christ as his Savior, yet so long as he does not see and know Him by faith as wonderfully adapted to his person in particular, the affections are not drawn to Him. From which it follows that many, in ordinary soul-trouble, act so undecidedly: today they desire Christ, and tomorrow they do not. This moment they wish to be converted, and the next they do not. This is the reason that many who once were touched by Christ's fitness to their need, and therefore were seekers after Him for a season, go back again and no more ask for Him, simply because they do not think Him so much adapted to their need as to be able for His sake to bear the heat of the day and the cold of the night, or sacrifice all things, to possess Him. And this proves that they never have known His real fitness, that they never have seen it with the eye of faith; otherwise the seed of God would have remained in them. But when the divine light of the Holy Spirit, in the Gospel, illuminates my soul, and I receive this knowledge of faith from Jesus, oh! Then I see in Him such fitness as a Surety, a Mediator, a Prophet, Priest, and King that my soul is touched in such measure that I judge it impossible to live another happy hour, except this Jesus becomes my Jesus. My affections are inclined, taken up, directed, and settled upon this object, and my resolution is so great, so determined, so immovable, that if it required the loss of life and property, of father and mother, sister, brother, wife and child, right eye or right hand—yea, though I were condemned to die at the stake, I would lightly esteem all this, and would suffer it with joy, to have this wonderfully fit Savior to be my Savior and my Jesus. Oh! My friends, examine your hearts, for, from the very nature of the case, anything less than this will not suffice. If you possess this you will joyfully part with all your sins, you will bid an eternal and joyful adieu to your most cherished lusts and bosom passions; it will make you count all your righteousness, which you esteemed a gain, nothing but loss, rejecting them as unprofitable refuse, for the excellency of the knowledge of Christ; it will make you take joyfully the spoiling of your goods; it will make you count it an honor, with the apostle, to be scourged for Christ's sake; it will make you say: 'Though I have not yet found Him, and am only seeking after Him, whom my soul loveth, and although I dare not say, My Beloved is mine and I am His, yet if I were to labor for Him twice seven years, and spend them in groaning and weeping, in tears and supplications, I would count them but as so many days, if only at last I might find Him to be my own.' God Himself must fix your mind upon these things; these results are the infallible signs of the inward root of the matter.

Fourth, this knowledge of faith *is a divine light of the Holy Spirit by which I know Christ in the Gospel in all His sufficient fullness.* By this I see not only that He is well disposed toward poor sinners such as myself—for a man might be favorably disposed toward another to assist him in his misery, but he might lack the power and the means to do so, and the best that he could do might be to pity the wretch and say, 'I pity your misery, but I cannot help you'—but this divine light teaches me that Christ can save to the uttermost; that though my sins are as scarlet and crimson, heavier than the mountains, greater in number than the hairs of my head and the sands of the seashore, there is such abundance of satisfaction and merits in the satisfaction, by virtue of His Person, that, though I had the sins of the human race, they would be, compared to the satisfaction of Christ, which has by virtue of His Person an infinite value, as a drop to a bucket and as a small dust in the balance. And this convinces my soul that my sin, instead of being an obstacle, much rather adds to the glory of the redemption, that sovereign grace was pleased to make me an everlasting monument of infinite compassion. Formerly, I always confessed my sin reluctantly; it was wrung from my lips against my will only because I was driven to it by my anguish, for I always thought, The more I confess my sin, the farther I will be from salvation and the nearer my approach to eternal condemnation; and, fool that I was, I disguised my guilt. But, since I know that Jesus is so all-sufficient, now I cry out, much more with my heart than with my lips, "Though I were a blasphemer and a persecutor and all that is wicked, *this is a faithful saying, and worthy of all acceptation, that Jesus Christ has come into the world to save sinners, of whom I am chief.*" And, if need be, I am ready to sign this with my blood, to the glory of sovereign grace. In this way every believer, if he stands in this attitude, will feel inclined to testify with me.

Fifth, it is this knowledge by which I know, *in the light of the Holy Spirit shining into my soul through the Gospel Jesus Christ, as the most willing and most ready Savior, who not only has the power to save and to reconcile my soul to God, but who is also exceedingly willing to save me* "My God, what is it that has brought about such a change in my soul? I am dumb and ashamed, Lord Jesus, to stand before Thee, by reason of the wrong I have done Thee, and of the hard thoughts which I entertained concerning Thee, O precious Jesus! I thought that Thou wast unwilling and I willing; I thought that the fault lay with Thee and not with me; I thought that I was a willing sinner and that Thou hadst to be entreated with much crying and praying and tears to make of Thee, *un*willing Jesus, a *willing* Christ; and I could not believe the fault lay with me."

This opposition or controversy often lasts a long time between the sincere soul and Christ, and never ends until by the divine light one sees the willingness of Jesus. However, it must not be supposed that there has been no faith in the soul during that time. But it may be said that, although there has been faith, there has been no exercise of faith in relation to this matter. And when this appears, the soul says: "With great shame and confusion of soul I now see Thy willingness. Thou hast given me the evidence of Thy willingness by Thy coming into the world; by Thy suffering of the penalty; by Thy invitation to me, and by the perseverance of Thy work upon my heart." I recall my former unbelieving words, spoken from the deep unbelief of my heart, and I cry out: "Thou art a willing Christ and I was an unwilling sinner. My God, now I feel that Thou art too mighty for me, Thou hast persuaded me; and now in this day of Thy power I will not and cannot hesitate any longer, but with my hand I write it down that I will be the Lord's."

The believing knowledge of the willingness of Jesus, in the light of the Holy Spirit through the Gospel, makes me see my former unwillingness. But as soon as this light arises in the soul the will is immediately bent over and submissive. They who say that Jesus is willing, but that I remain unwilling, speak from mere theory, but they lack the knowledge of faith, and have not discovered this truth. For as the shadow follows the body, and the effect the cause, so is the believing knowledge of the willingness of Christ toward me immediately followed by my willingness toward Him, with perfect abandonment of myself to Him. "Thy people shall be willing in the day of Thy power" (Ps. 110:3).

"Lastly, by this knowledge *through the promise of the Gospel, and by the light of the Holy Spirit, I learn to know the Person of the Mediator in His personal glory, being so near to Him that I can deal with Him.* I say, 'in the promise of the Gospel,' to show the difference between a vision of ecstasy like that of Stephen and the conceited knowledge of which heretics speak outside of and against the Word. The Word is the only mirror in which Christ can be seen and known by saving faith. And herein I see Him in His personal glory with the eye of faith, so near as I ever have seen any object with the bodily eye. For this inwrought faith and the light of the Holy Spirit shining thereon brings the Person Himself in substantial form to the soul, so that she falls in love with Him, and is so enchanted with Him that she exclaims: "My Beloved is white and ruddy, the chiefest among ten thousand. . . . For His love is stronger than death; jealousy is more cruel than the grave; the coals thereof are coals of fire, flames of the Lord. Many waters cannot quench that love, if a man would give all the substance of his house for love, it would be utterly contemned" (Song 5:10; 8:6, 7).

My beloved, faith embraces not only the words and letters of the Gospel, but Christ Himself in them. Faith converses, not with the letter alone, but with Christ in the letter. Faith has two foundations, *the Word* and *the Substance.* It does not build upon the *Word* alone, which is the letter of the Gospel, but also upon the Substance in the Word, viz., Jesus Christ—1 Corinthians 3:2. The Gospel is a mirror, but if Christ does not appear before the mirror, He cannot be seen. And when He presents Himself, it is not the mirror which is the end of faith, but the Image seen in the mirror. It is wisdom rightly to discern this.

Is this not beautifully said? The Lord our God grant to many of us this rich and pure delight.

Volume Three

The Work of the Holy Spirit in the Individual (Continued)

First Chapter
Sanctification

1

Sanctification

Of Him ye are in Christ Jesus, who of God is made unto us wisdom, and righteousness, and sanctification, and redemption— 1 Corinthians 1:30.

Sanctification is one of the most glorious gifts which, by the Covenant of Grace, the Mediator bestows upon the saint. It covers his entire mental, spiritual, and physical nature. We should, therefore, thoroughly understand it, and learn how to obtain it, and every believer, whatever the measure of his faith, should be fully aware of his attitude toward it; for erroneous views concerning this will surely lead us astray from the living Christ.

It is foolish to think that, although present-day heresies have affected the doctrines of Christ, Sin, and Regeneration, Sanctification is so simple as not to be affected. Yet even ministers fall into this sad delusion. Men of spiritual fervor, they strictly oppose heresies concerning these others, in their catechetical and pulpit instructions, and in their writings, regarding such as fundamental error, but somehow they never realize that the doctrine of sanctification can be imperiled, and they fail to put the Church on guard.

Such imperiling was impossible; and so, indeed, they hardly care to have sanctification distinguished as a dogma at all. "On the contrary," they say, "it is the beauty of sanctification that it is *life;* hence utterly independent of the mysteries of a *dogma.* In the life of sanctification believers may be charged with neglect, careless living, slow progress—in brief, with faulty *doing* and *working;* for what is sanctification but betterment of self and daily growth in holiness? But never with faulty *confessing,* with faulty views of the doctrine; for sanctification is not doctrine, but life." In this way they have come to deny it the value and dignity of a dogma or doctrine; to make it almost synonymous with bettering of life; hence to make it the common property of all that try to lead earnest and pious lives.

Then the idea naturally grew that many persons of unsound doctrine might lead more spiritual lives. This supposed fact was even fortified with the word of Jesus, that publicans and harlots go into the Kingdom of God before us; and the congregations often received the impression that rationalism itself might lead to better results than sometimes flow from an orthodox belief. And the result was that this so-called sanctification led to a weakening of the faith, to a considering of purity of doctrine as immaterial; until finally it assumed a hostile attitude toward the mysteries of the truth. This was the natural effort of confounding self-betterment with sanctification, and of opposing life to doctrine as gold to tinsel.

The spread of these false ideas of sanctification has not benefited Christianity in these provinces, but, as in pre-Reformation days, it has led the people astray from its pure doctrine.

Rome once suffered and suffers still from the same evil. Not as though it surrendered or even slighted its doctrine, but, even in the flourishing days of its hierarchy, the necessity of reformation of life was so strongly felt that it resulted in a one-sided urging of sanctification. Its favorite motto was: "Good works." They were of greatest importance: not words, but power; not the confession, but the earnestness and willingness to do good, not merely in secret, but openly so that men could see it! This was carried so far that finally Rome ceased to be satisfied with good works as fruit of conversion, and even began to look upon them as a primary and meritorious cause of salvation; and thus it broke down the mystery of faith by a false preaching of sanctification. As now, unintentionally, by the cry, "Not doctrine, but life," men are driven, as by iron necessity, first to underestimate the value of doctrine, then to disapprove of it, and lastly to pronounce it injurious, yea, even dangerous; so did the cry for good works induce Rome gradually to divorce the mystery of the forgiveness of sin from the cross of Calvary, not in the confession, but in the conscience of its members.

For the sake of clearer insight and safer procedure, we must return to the definite teaching that sanctification is a *doctrine*, an integral part of the *confession*, a *mystery*, just as much as the doctrine of reconciliation, and therefore a *dogma*. In fact, in the treatment of sanctification we penetrate the very *heart* of the confession, the dogma which scintillates in the doctrine of sanctification.

Of course we are not to divorce sanctification from life. No child of God denies that the doctrine has its application in life; there is no truth whose operation is not felt in his life. To him every doctrine is instinct with life, a live coal, a radiating fire, a lamp always burning, a well of living water springing up to eternal life. The content of every doctrine, of every mystery, is something in the living God or in His creature; the confession of a condition, a power, a working, a person who actually exists, who lives, who works. The blood of atonement means, not those particular drops which flowed from the cross, and were lost in the inhospitable ground of Calvary, but a treasure in the living Christ, unceasingly at work in heaven, by which He enriches His children on earth, the glorious power of which they know and experience.

And this is true of every mystery, as our confession of the Holy Trinity shows, which says of this deepest and most incomprehensible dogma: "That God's children know this as well from the testimonies of Holy Writ as from the operations of the divine Persons, and chiefly by those we feel in ourselves" (art. 9).

And this applies to the doctrine of sanctification as well as to all other doctrines; for it is not, any more than the other dogmas, the confession of a lifeless matter, but the confession of an awful power, which lives and works effectually in us. Hence sanctification must be preached once again as a *doctrine;* it must be confessed, examined, and studied as a doctrine; to be followed by an appropriate application like the preaching of any other doctrine; and godliness, spiritual life, and good works will be the result. But to obtain this result a clear exposition of the cause and animating power of sanctification is necessary.

When on a cold morning the fire does not burn, and the family suffers, it is foolish to say: "Since the fire does not burn remove it, and get warm without it." To keep from freezing requires *more fire;* not the fire, but the cause of its failure, must be removed. And this applies to sanctification. There is a general and bitter complaint of the coldness that has fallen upon the Church; and it requires the powerful working of sanctification to save the Church.

But the means employed frequently show poor judgment. Formerly the Church confessed a pure doctrine by which it kept close to the source of vital heat which is given us in God's Word; and the powers and workings deposited in the Mediator for the Church radiated in glorious activity. Then the Church flourished and faith celebrated its greatest triumphs. It was severely cold without, but, while the world lay perishing in its cerements, truth filled the Church with light and heat, and the sacred fire of a pure doctrine glowed and sparkled. But the light grew dim, and the fire went out; and the Church of God became dark and cold. And the saints, half frozen and stiff, became deeply conscious of the loss they had suffered, and of the need of light and heat. And now, instead of advising them to light the lamp of truth and rekindle the fire of the confession, that their souls may be revived and comforted, many say: "Dear brethren, there is no salvation in dogma or confession; they are utterly unprofitable; nothing remains but to kindle light and heat in your souls without them." And thus the Church is threatened with death and destruction.

In quiet assurance of the blessing of God, we proceed in the opposite direction, and advise the brethren to fill the lamp of the divine mysteries with oil, to put more fuel upon the fire of the confession; then there shall be light, and heat, and the Church shall be saved. This shall be so, provided—and this needs no emphasis—that the doctrine be really *confessed. To confess* is not merely to say, "There is a comfortable fire in the house," and then to stay out in the cold, but to accept its comfort and benefit for others as well as for ourselves.

The cry, "Not dogma, but life," is folly and unbelief. Let us rather oppose the shallow and unsound teaching of the day. The doctrine should be a faithful expression of the mystery; the mystery should stand clearly before the spiritual eye and illuminate the soul, as it radiates from the living Christ, according to the design of salvation. Instead of turning the people away from the doctrine, we should make them see how little they understand it; how they have trifled with it, and not confessed it; that their soul's welfare requires its earnest study, that so the act of confessing may deepen and enrich their spiritual life. And then let us imagine, not that the fruit of life must still be imported from elsewhere, but that the doctrine, rightly confessed, becomes its own instrument to manifest its power in us.

Thus sanctification should be treated.

2

Sanctification Is a Mystery

Let us cleanse ourselves from all filthiness of flesh and spirit, perfecting holiness in the fear of God— 2 Corinthians 7:1.

Sanctification belongs to the mysteries of faith; hence it cannot be confessed but as a dogma.

By this statement we intend to cut off at once every representation which makes "sanctification" to consist of the human effort to make oneself holy or holier.

To become more holy is undoubtedly the duty which rests upon every man. God has condemned all unholiness as an accursed thing. Inferior holiness cannot exist before Him. Every man more or less holy is bound to forsake all unholiness, to resign all lesser holiness, and let perfect holiness dwell and be manifest in him instantly. The commandment, "Be ye holy as I am holy," may not be weakened. The laxity of the current morale requires that God's absolute right to demand absolute holiness of every man be incessantly presented to the conscience, bound as a memorial upon the heart, and proclaimed to all with no uncertain sound.

In the innumerable territories of heaven where God gathers His redeemed, all unholiness is excluded and absolute holiness is the never-failing characteristic. And as it is in heaven, so it ought to be on earth. God, the sovereign Ruler of all the kingdoms of this world, has strictly forbidden the least unholiness in heart or home or any other place on earth under the penalty of death. In fact, there is on earth no unholiness, of whatever name or form, that does not exist in defiance of His express will.

It must be conceded, therefore, that it is His revealed will and commandment that all this unholiness must cease immediately, and be replaced directly by what is holy and good. He is of purer eyes than to behold iniquity.

It must be equally conceded that it is every man's duty to remove unholiness, and to advance the things that are holy. He that caused the hurt must also heal it. He that destroyed must also restore the things destroyed. He that desecrated the holy must also reconsecrate it. Men still alive to a sense of justice will not contradict us.

The obligation to resanctify this world's life rests in its deepest sense upon Satan. He instilled into our veins the poison which generates the diseases of our souls. The spark that caused the fire of sinful passions to break out in human nature was kindled by him. That Satan is hopelessly lost and condemned, does not annul God's eternal right. Even Satan himself, according to this right, ought immediately to repent and stand before God holy as in the beginning. And this world of men, which he corrupted, was not his, but belonged to God. He should never have touched it. Hence the obligation continues to rest upon him not only to stop his unholy working in it, but also to reconsecrate perfectly what he has so bitterly and maliciously profaned.

That Satan neither will nor can do this justifies his fearful judgment, but it does not annul God's right and never will. If in Paradise man had *unwillingly* fallen a victim to Satan, the obligation to resanctify the life of this world would have rested upon Satan, but not upon him. But man fell *willingly;* sin owes its existence not only to the fatherhood of Satan, but also to the motherhood of man's soul; hence man himself is involved in the guilt and included under the judgment of death, and therefore obliged to restore what he has ruined.

God created man holy, with the power to continue holy; holy also by virtue of the increasing development of the implanted germ. But man ruined God's work in his heart. He soiled the undefiled raiment of holiness. And doing this he violated the right. If he had belonged to himself, if God had allowed him to do with himself as he pleased, the right would not have been violated. But He did not give man to himself; He retained him for Himself as His own property. The hand that ruined and desecrated man destroyed *God's* property, encroached upon the divine right of sovereignty—yea, upon His very right of ownership, and thus became liable (1) to the penalty for this encroachment, and (2) to the obligation of restoring the ruined property to its original state.

Hence the undeniable and positive obligation of man's self-sanctification. This obligation rests, not upon God, nor upon the Mediator, but upon man and Satan. The prayer, "Lord, sanctify me," upon the lips of the unconverted, not under the Covenant of Grace, is most unbecoming. First willfully to destroy God's property, and then to take the ruined thing to Him demanding that He heal and restore it, antagonizes the right and reverses the ordinances. Nay, outside of the mysteries of the Covenant of Grace, under the obligations of simple justice, we are not to ask: "Lord, sanctify Thou us," but God is to enforce His righteous claim: "Sanctify thyself."

Sanctify thyself does not mean that man should *fulfill the law.* The keeping of the law and sanctification are two entirely different things. Let the sinner first be sanctified, and then he shall also fulfill the law. First *sanctification,* then *fulfillment of the law.*

It is like a harp with broken strings. The harp was made to produce music by harmonious vibration of the strings. But the production of music is not the mending of the harp. The broken strings must be replaced, the new strings must be tuned, and then is it possible to strike the melodious chords. The human heart is like the harp: God created it pure that we might keep the law; which an impure heart cannot do. Hence being profaned and unholy, it must be sanctified; then it will be able to fulfill the law.

For the sake of clearness, two acknowledged facts should be noticed:

First, if man had never been profaned by sin, it would never have entered his mind to sanctify himself; and yet the law would have been fulfilled without disturbance. This shows that sanctification and fulfillment of the law are two entirely different things.

Second, sanctification continues until a man dies and enters heaven. Then he is holy. Hence there is no sanctification in heaven. Yet the only occupation of the saints in heaven is the doing of that which is good. Hence sanctification is a matter by itself; it does not consist in the doing of good works, but must be an accomplished fact before a single good work can be done.

Since man profaned himself, he is called of God to resanctify himself. Hence the *claim* of sanctification contains not even the shadow of a mystery. It has nothing to do with the mysteries, therefore is no dogma. It is the simplest and most natural verdict of God's right in the conscience. That we speak of unholiness implies that we are convinced that we ought to be holy.

Is there contradiction, then, when we say, first, that sanctification itself is a mystery, and can be confessed only in the dogma; second that the *demand* of sanctification has nothing to do with the dogma?

Not in the least. Sinners of whom God demands that they sanctify themselves are, individually and collectively, totally unable to satisfy that demand. To a certain extent they can withdraw from sin and worldliness, and often have done so. Many unconverted men have done many praiseworthy works. In many cases lives have been reformed, the whole tone of existence has been improved from mere impulse, without a trace of real conversion. And, conceiving sanctification to consist in the doing of less evil and of more good, and that from an improved motive, it was thought that unholy man, though unable to satisfy this divine claim *perfectly,* might satisfy it to some extent. But all this has nothing in common with sanctification, and can be accomplished wholly without it. With all his self-betterment he cannot effect the least part of it; though told a thousand times to sanctify himself, he is both unwilling and unable.

Hence the question: *How, then, is sanctification to be accomplished?* And since the question never received an answer from any of the sages, but only from God in His Word, therefore not the *demand,* but the *means,* of sanctification is for us incomprehensible and mysterious. Hence the *character* of sanctification must be emphasized as a mystery.

And what is the reason for denying that sanctification is a mystery, that is, the content of a dogma? The supposition that it is of human origin, that man is not totally unable, and that sanctification is betterment of character and life. Hence it is tantamount to (1) a lowering of holiness to the human standpoint; (2) an opposing sanctification as a work of God. And this is a very serious matter. We should again become clearly conscious of the fact that the holiness without which no man shall see God is not attained by the departing from some evil and the habitual doing of some good.

The *demand* of sanctification belongs to the Covenant of Works; sanctification *itself* to the Covenant of Grace. This makes the difference very obvious. Not as though the Covenant of Works commanded man to sanctify himself; given to holy men, it excluded sanctification. But God gave the Covenant of Grace to unholy men. And the only connection between the demand for sanctification and the Covenant of Works is, that the latter ever pursues fallen man with this demand, and with the terror of Horeb. Unholiness destroys the foundation of the Covenant of Works and renders compliance with its conditions impossible. Hence the absolute contradiction between it and the sinner's personal life. The one must make room for the other; they cannot stand together.

In this painful conflict we are often tempted to ask whether God is not unjust in His law to demand of us the impossible, and to lay the blame on Him; for did He not make us so? And from this difficulty the Arminian in our own heart seeks to escape, either by denying that there ever was a Covenant of Works, or by substituting the fulfillment of the law for sanctification.

Wherefore it is our aim, especially regarding this doctrine, to escape from this harmful confusion of ideas, and to arrive at a correct understanding and purity of expression. The preaching must not add to the chaos, but lead us to clear insight and understanding.

Instead of sweetly cradling ourselves upon the Word, we must earnestly endeavor to *understand* it. In city and country church the Word must be preached persistently, and with ever-increasing purity, until, convicted of personal unholiness, men begin to see that by absolute sanctification, not mere self-betterment, they must restore unto God His right; until, feeling their inability, with broken hearts they turn to God to receive the *Mystery of Sanctification* from the treasures of the Covenant of Grace.

3

Sanctification and Justification

Yield your members servants to righteousness unto sanctification—Romans 6:19.

Sanctification must remain sanctification. It may not arbitrarily be robbed of its significance, nor be exchanged for something else. It must always signify the making holy of what is unholy or less holy.

Care must be taken not to confound sanctification with justification; a common mistake, frequently made by thoughtless Scripture readers. Hence the importance of a thorough understanding of this difference. Being left unnoticed, it may lead to confused preaching, which causes one-sidedness; and active and thoughtful men invariably systematize their one-sidedness.

What, then, is the difference? According to our ancient theologians it is fourfold:

1. Justification works *for* man; sanctification *in* man.
2. Justification removes the *guilt;* sanctification the *stain.*
3. Justification imputes to us an *extraneous* righteousness; sanctification works a righteousness *inherent* as our own.
4. Justification is at once *completed;* sanctification increases gradually; hence remains *imperfect.*

In the main the answer is correct, but insufficient to meet present error. It is shallow, external, and incomplete; makes too much of righteous-*making* and holy-*making,* while it does not consider righteous*ness* and holi*ness,* a correct idea of which is absolutely necessary for the clear understanding of justification and sanctification.

Let us examine these fundamental ideas, first, in God Himself. It becomes evident at once that the words, "Our God is righteous," impress us otherwise than, "Holy, holy, holy is the Lord!"

The latter impresses us with the feeling that the name of Jehovah is infinitely exalted above the low level of this impure and sinful life; we discover a distance between Him and ourselves which, as it widens in more transcendent holiness, casts us back into ourselves as impure creatures, while it causes His Being to be resplendent in the light unapproachable. If the angels exalting His holiness cover their faces with their wings, how much more ought we sinful men consider it with covered face and in godly fear! "The Lord is of purer eyes than to behold evil," impresses us with the deep sense of God's unspeakable sensitiveness, which is so keen that even the faintest suggestion of sin or impurity arouses in Him such antipathy that He cannot bear the sight of it.

But *guilt* is out of the question. In the presence of the divine holiness we do not feel guilty, but are overwhelmed by the consciousness of our utter uncleanness and wickedness. Even among men we do not always feel quite satisfied with ourselves. Our brother's warmer zeal and love often make us feel ashamed. Yet the feeling does not amount to loathing of self. But in the presence of the holiness of God we feel at once with Isaiah our spiritual impurity, and are inclined to cry for a live coal from the altar to sanctify our lips; and the word "loathing of self" is not too strong to express our feeling as we prostrate ourselves before the holiness of the Lord Jehovah.

This establishes the antithesis at once. The divine holiness in its most exalted aspect affects us, not with fear of punishment, or with anguish, because we owe a debt that we cannot pay, but with *dissatisfaction* with ourselves, with abhorrence of our uncleanness, and contempt for our righteousnesses which are as filthy rags. It makes us feel, not our *guilt,* but our *sin;* not our *condemnation,* but our hopeless *wickedness;* it does not crush us under the penalty of the law, but it causes us to be consumed by our impurity; it does not overwhelm us by righteousness, but it uncovers our unholiness and inward corruption.

But the divine righteousness affects us altogether differently. It does not impress me with the transcendence of His exalted Covenant name as the divine holiness, but in God's hand it oppresses me, pursues me, leaves me no rest, seizes me, and breaks me to pieces under its weight. His holiness makes the soul thirst after holiness, and with sorrow we see His majesty depart. But His righteousness antagonizes the soul, which does not *desire* it, but struggles to *escape* from it.

Sometimes it seems different, but only seemingly so. Godly men in the Old and New Covenants frequently invoke the divine righteousness. "Shall not the Judge of all the earth do right?" This divine upholding of the right is the strength, the prospect, and the consolation of His oppressed people. This is why in the closing article of their Confession our fathers cry for the day of judgment, when as the righteous Judge He shall destroy all His enemies and ours. Yet the difference is only seeming. In this case the divine right is directed against others, not ourselves, but the effect is the same. It is His people's prayer and hope that the divine right pursue those enemies, and deal with them according to their deserts.

Hence God's righteousness impresses us, first, with the fact of His authority over us; that not *we,* but *He* must determine what is right, and how we ought to be; that all our opposition is vain, for His power will enforce the right; hence that we must suffer the effects of that righteousness.

But it is not merely the *power* of the right that impresses us, neither the consciousness that we are taken and judged, but much more, that we are taken and judged *righteously.* And not this arbitrarily; on the contrary, we feel inwardly that the divine might is right, and therefore may and must overpower us.

Hence the divine righteousness includes the creature's acknowledgment: "The prerogative to determine the right is not mine, but His." And not only this, but our souls are deeply conscious that God's decisions are not only right and good, but *absolutely* righteous and *superlatively* good.

The divine righteousness brings us face to face with a direct working of the divine *sovereignty.* All earthly sovereignty is but a feeble reflection of the divine, but sufficiently clear to show us its fundamental features. A sovereign is deemed sufficiently *wise* to see how things ought to be; and *qualified* to determine that so they shall be; and *powerful* to resist him who dares be otherwise. This applies also to the King of kings; or rather, it applies, not to Him *also,* but to Him *alone.* He alone is the *Wisdom* with absolute certainty to choose, and according to this choice to see how everything must be to be its best. He alone is the holy *Qualified One,* according to this to determine how everything must be. And He is the alone-*Mighty* to condemn and destroy what dares to be otherwise.

And this reveals the deepest features of the contrast. The holiness of God relates to His *Being;* the righteousness of God to His *Sovereignty.* Or, His righteousness touches His *relation* and *position* to the creature; His holiness points to His own inward *Being.*

4

Sanctification and Justification (Continued)

He that is holy, let him be holy still—Revelation 22:2.

The divine Righteousness, having reference to the divine Sovereignty in one sense does not manifest itself until God enters into relationship with the creatures. He was glorious in holiness from all eternity, for man's creation did not modify His Being, but His righteousness could not be displayed before creation, because right presupposes two beings sustaining the jural relation.

An exile on an uninhabited island cannot be righteous nor do righteously; he cannot even conceive of the jural relation so long as there is no man present whose rights he must respect, or who can deny his rights. The arrival of other men will necessarily create the jural relation between him and them. But so long as he remains alone, he may be holy or unholy, but he cannot be said to be righteous or unrighteous. In like manner it may be said of God that before creation He was holy, but could not display His righteousness simply because there were no creatures sustaining toward Him the jural relation. But immediately after the creation the display of righteousness became possible.

Still the illustration can be applied to God only to a certain extent. Essentially God is not alone, but Triune in persons; hence there is between the Father and the Son and the Holy Spirit a mutual relation.

This relation, being the highest, tenderest, and most intimate, contains from eternity the completest expression of righteousness. And even with reference to the creature, the divine righteousness did not originate until after the creation, but finds perfect expression in the eternal counsel. That counsel not only determines every possible jural relation between the creatures and the Creator, and the creatures themselves, but indicates also the means whereby this relation must be restored when broken or disturbed.

Hence His righteousness is as eternal as His Being; yet, in order to express clearly the difference between holiness and righteousness, we may say that as His holiness was glorious from eternity, so is His righteousness displayed and exercised only *in time,* that is, since the creature began to exist. It did not originate then, but became perceptible then. Whatever may be said on the subject, the fundamental difference remains that God is holy even though considered alone by Himself; while His *righteousness* begins to radiate when He is considered in relation to His creatures.

God is holy essentially; before the least impurity existed, there was in Him vital pressure to repel all foreign mingling with His Being. But only *as Sovereign* could He determine the right, maintain the violated right, and execute righteousness upon the violator.

In its fundamental features this applies to us as men. Even in us righteousness is entirely different from holiness; the former has exclusive reference to our relation to and position before God, man, and angel; while holiness refers, not to any *relation,* but to the quality of our inner being. We speak of righteousness only when it concerns our relation to God or man. Noah is said to have been a righteous man "in his generation," which indicates not his essential *quality,* but his relation to others.

Righteousness implies right, which is unthinkable but as existing between two persons in connection with the qualification of either one or of a third to determine that right. Hence man's righteousness with reference to God has a twofold aspect: *First,* it implies the acknowledgment of God's sovereign qualifications to determine man's relation to God and man. *Second,* it implies reverence for the divine laws and ordinances enacted with regard to man's service of God.

A man may keep strictly some of these ordinances, not from the motive of reverence, but because he is compelled to approve them. In some respects he gives God His due, but His position is wrong. He fails to honor God as his sovereign Ruler, to acknowledge God as God, and to bow before His majesty.

Or he may reverence the divine authority in the abstract, but in practice constantly rob God of His right.

Therefore *original* righteousness, which has reference to man's status before God as a creature, and *derived* righteousness, which refers to the act of honoring the divine ordinances, are two different things. Both are righteousness—*i.e.,* the act of occupying the position divinely ordained. But the first refers to our personal standing in the position determined by God; the second to the act of conforming our thoughts, words, and deeds to His divine requirements.

It is unnecessary to speak particularly of righteousness with reference to men. Whatever we do in relation to them is righteous or unrighteous according to its conformity or non-conformity to the divine ordinance, and every transgression against the neighbor becomes sin only because it is in non-conformity to the righteousness of God.

Briefly, man's righteousness consists of two parts: *First,* that his status be what God has determined. *Second,* that his *thoughts, words,* and *deeds* be conformed to the divine ordinances. Hence our righteousness *need not be the product of our own soul's labor.* The original righteousness of Adam and Eve lacked nothing, although they had not done anything to it personally. They simply stood in the right position before God—a position not self-assumed, but divinely determined. And so may the right, after it is disturbed, be restored independently of the violator, by a third person. The question is not *how* the right relation was restored, but whether it agrees again with God's sovereign will.

He that delivers a debtor from imprisonment by paying his debts restores him to his right relation to his former creditors, even though the prisoner himself did not pay a farthing of the debt. Because righteousness has reference to mutual relations, the right is satisfied as soon as the disturbed relation is restored and the lost position recovered. *How* it was accomplished is immaterial.

This gives us a deeper insight into the profound significance of the cross, and why it is that our righteousness cannot be increased nor decreased, although it does not affect our essential character.

Entirely different is the soul's holiness, which touches directly the quality of person and character; as our ancient theologians correctly expressed it: "Justification acts *for* man; sanctification *inheres in man.*"

The ungodly is justified, that is, the very moment that he believes; before sanctification has begun to operate in him, he knows that he stands before God perfectly right. He is not merely beginning to be right; partly right, to be a little more right tomorrow, and perfectly right when he enters heaven, but perfectly right now, henceforth, and forevermore. He is righted not only for the present and for all eternity, but also for the past. He is assured of standing before God in flawless right, as though he had never been wrong, nor ever could be wrong again.

Hence the consciousness of being justified is instantaneous and at once complete, and cannot be increased nor decreased. And this is possible because this righteousness has nothing to do with his being, but has exclusive reference to the relation in which he sees himself placed. This relation was miserable and wholly unrighteous, but another, outside of himself, has restored that relation and made it what it ought to be. Hence he stands right, without any reference whatever to his personal being. This is the deep significance of the confession that he who is justified is always *an ungodly person.*

But this is not the case in regard to man's holiness; that touches his person and cannot be effected outside of his inward being.

5

Holy Raiment of One's Own Weaving

I dwell in the high and holy places—Isaiah 57:15.

Holiness inheres in man's *being.* There is *external* holiness, that is, that of the Levitical order, effected by washing or sprinkling with sacrificial blood; or *official* holiness, denoting separation for divine service, in which sense the prophets and apostles are called holy, and church-members are called holy and beloved. But these have nothing to do with the sanctification now under discussion.

Sanctification as a gift of grace refers to a man's *personal holiness.* As the divine holiness is God's exaltation above, and angry recoil from all impurity and defilement, so is human holiness man's essential disposition by which spontaneously he loves purity and hates the unclean. Victory over temptation after a long and painful conflict, in which our feet had well-nigh slipped, is not holiness.

Holiness signifies a disposition, an inherent quality, or, by another manner of speaking, a tint or shade adopted by the soul, so that the heart's evil manifestations and Satan's wicked whisperings fill us with positive horror. As the musically trained ear is painfully affected by a dissonance as it vibrates along the shuddering auditory nerve, while the unmusical ear never perceives the offense against the purity of tone, so is the difference between the sanctified and the unsanctified. Whatever the world's moral dissonances may be, they fail to affect the ungodly, who even praise the music, but they distress the saint whose soul delights in the harmony of holy concord.

This holy or unholy disposition includes our entire inward being; it inheres in mind, conscience, understanding, will, feelings, and inclinations. Evil and impure speech affords pleasure or pain to all these.

Yet this is not the final token of being holy or unholy. Something more is required. Do not many of the unregenerate shudder at much that is evil, and delight in much that is good? Sympathy for the good may be called holiness only when it possesses this essential feature, that it wills the good *for God's sake alone.*

God alone is holy. There is no holiness but that which descends from Him, the Fountain of all good, hence of all holiness. Mere human holiness is a counterfeit, an attack upon God's honor of being the sole and only Fountain of all good. It is the creature's effort to be equal with God, and as such essential sin. Nay man's holiness must be the divinely implanted disposition, stirring his entire being to love what God loves, not from his own taste, but for His Name's sake.

Being planned after the divine image, Adam and Eve possessed this holiness; hence discord between them and their Maker was impossible. Their holiness was not in *germ* merely, but *complete,* for everything in them was in perfect accord with God. And the redeemed in heaven are holy; in death they are severed completely from the internal source of sin; they are essentially in full and warm sympathy with the divine holiness, whose every feature attracts them.

But the sinner has lost this holiness. It is his misery that every expression of his being is naturally in collision with the will of God, whose holiness does not attract, but repels him. And mere regeneration does not sanctify his inclination and disposition; nor is it able of itself to germinate the holy disposition. But it requires the Holy Spirit's *additional* and very *peculiar* act, whereby the *disposition* of the regenerated and converted sinner is brought gradually into harmony with the divine will; and this is the gracious gift of *sanctification.*

But this does not imply that a man who dies immediately after conversion enters heaven without sanctification. This would be a very comfortless doctrine, and would unintentionally encourage Antinomianism. God's child entering heaven is completely sanctified; not *in* this life, but *after* it.

According to Scripture there is in heaven a difference between the spirits of the redeemed; they do not resemble each other as do two drops of water. In the parable of the talents Christ teaches clearly that in heaven there is a difference in the distribution of talents. He who denies this robs himself of the positive promise that "the Father who seeth in secret shall *reward* openly." The heavenly state which we preach is not based upon the principles of the French Revolution; on the contrary, in the assembly of just men made perfect we shall never ascend to the rank of apostle or prophet, probably not even to that of martyr. Nevertheless there is in heaven no saint whose sanctification is incomplete. In this respect all are alike.

But there will be room for development. The complete sanctification of my personality, body and soul, does not imply that my holy disposition is now in actual contact with *all* the fullness of the divine holiness. On the contrary, as I ascend from glory to glory, I shall find in the infinite depths of the divine Being the eternal object of richest delight in ever-increasing measure. In this respect the redeemed in heaven are like Adam and Eve in Paradise, who, though perfectly holy, were destined to enter more fully into the life of the divine love by endless development.

It should therefore be thoroughly understood that at the moment of their entering heaven the sanctification of the redeemed *lacks nothing.* Nevertheless their sanctification will receive fullest completion when, risen from the grave, in the glory of the resurrection-body, they enter the Kingdom of Glory after the day of judgment. Until that hour they are in a state of separation from the body, resting in peace, awaiting the coming of the Lord.

Since sanctification includes body and soul, exhaustive treatment requires that we call attention to this point. Not as though this intermediate state were sinful, a sort of purgatory; for the Scripture teaches clearly that in death we are *separated* from the body. The fact that the body remains impure until the day of glorification does not affect the holy state of the departed saint. Being freed from the body, he is no more affected by it. And when, in the notable day of the Lord, the body shall be restored to him, it shall be perfectly holy, pure, and glorified.

That which belongs to Jesus enters heaven perfectly holy. The slightest lack would indicate something internally sinful; would annihilate the glorious confession that death is a dying to all sin, as well as the positive declaration of Scripture, that nothing that defiles shall enter the gates of the city. Hence it is the unalterable rule of sanctification that every redeemed soul entering heaven is perfectly sanctified.

This applies to the infant who being regenerated in the cradle is carried thence to the grave, in whom, therefore, conscious exercise of holiness is out of the question; and to every converted person who dies suddenly; and to the man who, hardened all his life, in his dying hour repents before God, and departs one of the redeemed of the Lord.

The supporters of the ordinary Arminian doctrine consider this representation impossible. They believe that sanctification is an effect of the saint's own exertion, exercise, and conflict. It is like a beautiful garment of fine linen, very desirable, but it must be of one's own weaving. This labor is begun immediately after the saint's conversion. The loom is set up, and he begins to weave. He continues his spiritual labor with but few interruptions. The piece of linen gradually increases under his hand, and assumes form and shape. If not cut down in early life, he expects to finish it even before the hour of his departure.

The pulpit must oppose this theory, which comes, not from Arminius's books, but from man's wicked heart. For it is not only very *comfortless,* but also *wicked.*

It is *comfortless:* for, if true, then all our precious little ones who died in the cradle are lost, for they could not put one stitch in this raiment of their glory; comfortless: for if the saint should happen to be behindhand with his weaving, or be taken away in the midst of his days before he could half finish it, he would surely be lost. Nor is it less comfortless for him whose death-bed conversion is utterly useless, for it came too late for the weaving of this garment of sanctification.

And it is also *wicked:* for then Christ is no sufficient Savior. He may effect our justification and open the gates of Paradise, but the weaving of our own wedding-garments He lays upon *us,* without insuring us sufficient time to finish them. Yea, wicked indeed is it; for this makes the weaving of the fine linen *our* work, sanctification *man's* achievement, and God is no longer the only Author of our salvation. Then it is not grace, and man's own work is again on its feet.

In thus subverting the very foundation of holy things, thoughtless Ethical theologians ought to consider the destruction they bring upon Christ's Church. Our fathers never believed this doctrine, and always opposed it. "There is no Gospel in it," they said. It is the concision of the Covenant of Grace; laying upon God's saints the fear and distress of the Covenant of Works.

6

Christ Our Sanctification

Christ Jesus who of God is made unto us . . . sanctification—
1 Corinthians 1:30.

The redeemed soul possesses *all things* in Christ. He is a complete Savior. He lacks nothing. Having Him we are saved to the uttermost; without Him we are utterly lost and undone.

We must earnestly maintain this point, especially with reference to sanctification; and repeat with increasing clearness that Christ is given us of God not only for wisdom and righteousness, but also for *sanctification.*

It reads distinctly that Christ is our righteous*ness* and sanctifi*cation.* This translation is perfectly correct. The Greek does not read, *"dikaiōsis,"* which is *justification,* but *"dikaiosúnē,"* which never refers to the act of *making* righteous, but to the condition of being righteous, therefore righteous*ness.* So it does not read, *"hágios"* or *"hagiosúnē,"* which might refer to holiness, but it reads distinctly, *"hagiosmós,"* which points to the act of *making* holy.

What the apostle distinguished so clearly should not be confounded.

St. Paul and the Church of Corinth are believers. They are justified in Christ already, once for all; for Christ was made righteousness unto them. But this is not the case with sanctification. "Even the holiest men have only small beginnings of this obedience, which constrain them to live not only according to some, but according to all the commandments of God" (Heidelberg Catechism, q. 114). But the work is only just begun. Compared to former times, there is a holier love and spirit in them, but they are by no means *wholly* sanctified. They are under the treatment of the Spirit, their Sanctifier. They become more and more conformable to the image of God (q. 15). Hence there are degrees of progress in holiness. In those but recently converted, sanctification has progressed but little, in others it has made glorious progress. So there are in the Church holy, holier, and holiest persons (q. 114).

Since the justification of the ungodly is at once finished, and the sanctification of the regenerate proceeds but slowly and gradually, St. Paul writes to the Corinthians with perfect precision that Christ is to him and them no more righteous-*making,* but righteous*ness;* on the contrary, He had not yet become to them holi*ness,* but only holy-*making.*

This being well-understood, it is impossible to be mistaken. If the apostle had intended to enumerate in the *abstract* all that a lost sinner possesses in Christ, he would have said: "Wise-*making,* righteous-*making,* and holy-*making";* for a lost sinner walks still in his foolishness, is not yet made righteous, etc. But he describes his own experience, saying, that like a star the wisdom of God had arisen in his dark soul; that for Christ's sake he has obtained pardon and satisfaction, wherefore he stands perfectly righteous before God; and that now he is being *made holy* and *being redeemed.* He is not yet redeemed entirely; the Greek *"apolútrosis"* denotes also here a *continued* action of being made free from inward and outward misery.

The Heidelberg Catechism (q. 60) describes the righteous standing of the soul before God in the following striking manner:

> Q. How art thou righteous before God?
>
> A. Only by a true faith in Jesus Christ: so that, though my conscience accuse me that I have grossly transgressed all the commands of God, and kept none of them, and am still inclined to all evil; notwithstanding, God, without any merit of mine, but only of mere grace, grants and imputes to me the perfect satisfaction, righteousness, and *holiness* of Christ; even so as if I never had had, nor committed any sin: yes, as if I had fully accomplished all that obedience which Christ hath accomplished for me; inasmuch as I embrace such benefit with a believing heart.

The fact that this answer makes righteousness to include holiness has led less thoughtful men to infer that sanctification and justification are the same thing. Discussed at the Synod of Dort, this question was settled by inserting into article 22 of the Confession the following clause: "Jesus Christ imputing to us all His merits, and so many holy works, which He has done for us and in our stead, is our Righteousness."

What does justification then include? Not the sanctification of *our persons,* but the sum-total of the holy works which we owe God according to the law. Question 60 calls this *"our holiness."*

The difference between the two is clearly seen in Adam and Eve in Paradise. They were created *personally* holy; there was nothing unholy about them. But they had not yet fulfilled the law. They did not possess holy works. They had not acquired a treasure of holiness. Personally, one can be holy without having a single grain of accomplished or acquired holiness; and, on the other hand, one may have a perfectly fulfilled law without having the slightest function of personal holiness. Christ in the manger was perfectly holy, but He had not yet fulfilled the law, hence He had not an acquired holiness to present to us in our place. But in the hour of his justification the child of God receives (1) the complete remission of his punishment on the ground of Christ's *atonement;* (2) the complete remission of his indebtedness on the ground of Christ's *satisfaction.* And this satisfaction is but a perfect fulfillment of the law; a complete presentation of all good works; hence a perfect manifestation of holiness. Between questions 114 and 115 there is, therefore, not the slightest conflict.

Sanctifi*cation* and holi*ness* are two different things. Holiness, in the 60th question, has reference, not to personal dispositions and desires, but *to the sum-total of all the holy works required by the law.* Sanctification, on the contrary, refers not to any work of the law, but exclusively to the work of *creating holy dispositions in the heart.*

If one asks, Is Christ your holiness as much as He is your *righteousness* and in the same sense? we answer: Yes, indeed, bless the Lord; He is my complete holiness before God, just as much as my perfect righteousness. The one is just as absolute and certain as the other. The performance of all the holy works required by the law of every man, according to the Covenant of Works, is a vicarious act of Christ in the fullest sense of the word. Wherefore we confess that the holy works which Christ has done for us are just as positively an *imputed* holiness, as we stand right before God by an *imputed* righteousness. Nothing can be added to it. It is whole, perfect, and complete in every respect.

And that which is done for us in our stead is not again required of us. This would be morally absurd. According to the Covenant of Works, neither the law nor the lawgiver has anything more to demand of us. It is a finished work. The penalty is suffered, and the holiness required by the law is presented. We are perfectly righteous before God and our own consciousness, inasmuch as we receive this unspeakable benefit with a believing heart.

But all that has nothing to do with our *sanctification.* In addition to the imputed righteousness and holy works, our sanctification comes next in order.

From sin proceed guilt, penalty, and stain. From these three we must be delivered. From the penalty by Christ's *atonement;* from guilt by His *satisfaction;* and from the stain by *sanctification.* After God has redeemed us from the everlasting doom, we are still unholy, downtrodden in our unclean blood. Adam's inherent, holy disposition and desire are not yet restored to us. On the contrary, the stain of sin is there still. We delight in the law of God after the inward man, but we also find sin present always and everywhere in the sin-stain of body and soul. And God wills that this shall not continue. For the stain of sin He will substitute a holy disposition. He resolves to reform us inwardly, to renew us after the image of His dear Son, that is, to sanctify us.

It is only now that He begins to make us *personally* holy. As His children, we are dear to Him as the apple of His eye; He has engraven our names in the palms of His hands. We neglect things indifferent, but we polish the precious jewel. An old garment is cast aside, but we remove the stain from the costly silken gown. The housewife adorns the beloved homestead, and the gardener pulls the weeds from his garden-beds. In like manner, compelled by His love, God wills that His child, body and soul, be made bright until sin's stain be wholly removed.

This is the work of sanctification, aiming exclusively at our personal sanctification, to restore unto us the holiness of Adam before he had performed any holy work.

In Adam, *personal* holiness came first, then holiness consisting in the fulfillment of the law, but to God's child, the *latter,* imputed to him for Christ's sake, is imparted first, and his personal holiness follows. As Adam was *created* holy, so the regenerated is *made* holy.

The personal sanctification of the regenerated and converted sinner begins after the quickening of faith; continues with more or less interruption all the days of his life; is finished, so far as the soul is concerned, in death, and, regarding the body, at the coming of the Lord. And since this is wrought by Christ, through the Holy Spirit, the Scripture confesses that Christ is not only our Righteousness, but also our Sanctification.

7

Application of Sanctification

Whom He did foreknow, He also did predestinate to be conformed to the image of His Son, that He might be the firstborn among many brethren—Romans 8:29.

At His own time, and with irresistible grace, God translates His elect from death unto life. He gives them faith and the consciousness of being justified in Christ; and by conversion He puts their feet in the way of life. Thus they are free from guilt. There is for them no condemnation. Neither hell nor devil can prevail against them. Hence the apostle's shout of victory: "Who shall lay anything to the charge of God's elect? It is God that justifieth. Who is he that condemneth? It is Christ that died, yea, rather that is risen again, who is even at the right hand of God, who also maketh intercession for us."

God's child has formal proof of his justification not only in the Word, but also in Christ Himself, who continually presents His sacrifice before the Throne. Whether he has conscious enjoyment of this is immaterial. In his sleep, in fever's delirium, bereft of reason by physical causes, he continues as God's child. Independent of sensations, experiences, and frames of mind, yea, though he has never wept a tear of repentance, he possesses his treasure under all circumstances. Idiots even may possess it. Why should God have no children among them? Of course, under normal conditions *conscious faith* is the rule, but salvation does not depend upon the soul's actual experience. When you walk in the sun your shadow is visible, but your existence does not depend upon your shadow.

It should be emphasized that sanctification does not imply human efforts and exertions to supplement Christ's work, but it is the additional grace of creating in the saint supernaturally *a holy disposition.*

Sin imparts pollution, that is, there can be no sin without begetting sin. Sin generates sin, imparts sin, is always the mother of sin. If this sin-begetting process were not stopped in our hearts, sin's chain would remain unbroken, link upon link, and only sin would be the result.

But this is not the divine purpose. God wills that men should see our good works and glorify the Father which is in heaven. Therefore God has prepared good works that we should walk in them. But if the stain of sin were to work in us without any interruption, we could not walk in them. Not one of us could ever do a single good work. Light would never shine in the children of light, and there would be no occasion to glorify the Father in heaven. Good works wrought in us by the Holy Spirit *independently of us cannot* offer such occasion. His works are always *holy;* there is nothing surprising in that. But when He causes holy works to proceed *from us* in such a way that they are truly *our own,* then there is occasion for praise—Matthew 5:16. Then men will ask in surprise, Who wrought this in them? And looking up will glorify the Father. And then the fearful continuity of sin called "stain" is broken; then the law that sin must beget sin, that is, cultivate the sinful disposition, is replaced by another law which gradually introduces the holy disposition.

This holy disposition cannot spring from man, not even from regeneration. A starving child cannot grow, neither can the child of God proceed to sanctification if left to himself. Although sanctification is organically connected with the implanted life, yet it does not germinate without the constant showers of grace. Wherefore it is the free gift of the Father of Lights.

The indwelling Spirit is the actual Worker. He performs it in all the saints, not partly, but wholly, both in life and in death, or in the hour of death alone. The latter applies to elect children, to idiots and insane persons, and to persons converted on their death-bed. In all others He performs it during their lifetime and in the hour of their departure.

But there is a difference in different persons. In some the Holy Spirit begins sanctification in their childhood; in others at maturity. In some it proceeds almost without any interruption; in others it is hindered by conflict or apostasy. But in all He acts according to His pleasure. Sanctification is an artistic embroidery wrought in the soul, and He insures that it shall be finished at the moment appointed for our entrance into the New Jerusalem, but the manner and measure of progress depend solely upon His pleasure and purpose.

First, sanctification is closely related to Christ, and is part of the Covenant grace which He insures to us as our Surety. It is not merely His work, but a grace inherent in His Person, and so identified with Him that the apostle exclaims: "Who of God is made unto us wisdom, righteousness, and sanctification?" It is related to the *unio mystica:* He vitally in us, and we vitally in Him; He the Vine, and we the branches: "It is not I that live, but Christ liveth in me"; He the Head, and we the members. All these indicate the vital union between the believer and the Mediator. The unborn child may be said to breathe through the mother's breath, and the mother to breathe in the child. The same is true here, although the comparison illustrates, but does not exhaust the matter.

Hence God's child can never be but in Christ. Not that he is always conscious of it. He often feels as though Christ were far from him, and, deceived by this, he often strays so far that the bond of union seems to be utterly dissolved. This is really not so, for Christ never loses His hold, but to him it seems so. And this is the cause of the difficulty. In this condition his sinful nature alone is left him; all his treasure of grace is left with Jesus. For this reason the liturgy says: "Outside of Christ we lie in the midst of death." When with Dinah we leave the patriarchal tent to take the road to Shechem, we do so at our own risk and charges, having but Adam's inheritance, viz., a dead soul and a corrupt nature. Then to imagine that we have anything in ourselves acceptable to God is tantamount to a denial of Immanuel. With Köhlbrugge we say: "Considered outside of Christ, the converted and the unconverted are exactly alike."

But, although we forsake Him, He never forsakes us; there is between the converted in his deepest fall and the unconverted this immeasurable difference, that the soul of the former is inseparably bound to Jesus and the soul of the latter is not.

Second, the sanctification of the saint is unthinkable without Christ, because the implanting of the holy disposition by the Divine Spirit is: "That we become more and more conformable to the image of God until we arrive at the perfection proposed to us in a life to come" (Heidelberg Catechism, q. 115). And is this not Christ's image?

To be sanctified, then, means *to have Christ obtain stature in us.* It is not a few confused signs of holiness, but an *organic whole* of pure desire and inclination stamped upon the soul, embracing all the powers of the human spirit and disposition. Hence its progress cannot be measured or numbered, ten degrees now and fifteen next year. It is the reflection of Christ's form upon the mirror-surface of the soul; first in dim outlines, gradually more distinct, until the experienced eye recognized in it the form of Jesus. But even in the most advanced it is never more than a *daguerreotype;* Immanuel's *perfect image* will be revealed in us only in and through death.

The holy disposition is a "perfect man," that is, a form embracing the saint's *whole personality;* an expression of Christ's *complete* image, and therefore covering our entire human being.

How foolish, then, to speak of sanctification as a result of human effort. When the person disappears, does not his shadow go with him? How, then, could Christ's image, form, or shadow remain in us when in our wanderings the soul is separated from Him? The brightness disappears with the light. A shadow cannot be retained. This is why Immanuel is our sanctification in the fullest sense of the word. *His form reflecting itself in the soul* and *the soul retaining that reflection* is the whole work of sanctification.

Finally, to the question, How can sanctification implant a holy disposition, if it depends upon the reflection of Jesus' form in the soul, since a denial or temporal apostasy separates us from Him? we answer: Can an inherent disposition not exist and continue without being exercised? One may have acquired the disposition (habit) of speaking fluent English, but not speak it for a whole year. So may the disposition or habit of holy desire cleave to the soul, even though the stream of unholiness cover it for a season. And the soul is fully aware of this by the inward struggle of the conscience. If Jesus could lose His hold upon us, yea, then the holy disposition could not remain. But, since amid the deepest fall, the soul remains unconsciously in His hand, the objection has no weight.

8

Sanctification in Fellowship with Immanuel

But now have ye your fruit unto sanctification, and the end everlasting life—Romans 6:22.

The *third* reason why our sanctification is in Christ is: that He has *obtained* it, that it flows *from Him,* and that He *guarantees* it. Having your mind thoroughly divested from the false idea that sanctification is your own embroidery, holding fast the clear doctrine that it is a gift of grace, this third reason will *appeal* to you. If sanctification is a gift, a favor, the question arises: What for? Is it a reward for the labor of your soul? Fruit of your prayer? Encouragement on the way? Is it on account of your loveliness, piety, goodness? Is it for anything *in you?* For there must be a *motive.* That God should bestow the precious and enduring gift of sanctification on persons who with both hands oppose it, and with rough fingers mar its beauty, is inconceivable. What was it, then that moved the Lord God to favor you? You say: "His unfathomable pleasure, which is the deepest ground of all our salvation." Very well, but the divine counsel does not work as by magic. All that proceeds from that counsel runs its course, and shows its links that give it consistency.

Hence the question must be asked: "Who is it that obtained for you the gracious gift of sanctification?" And the answer is: "Our Redeemer;

sanctification is the fruit of the Cross." There is no division of labor in the redemptive work. Christ did not obtain on the cross our righteousness only, leaving it for us by conflict and self-denial to obtain our sanctification, but there is One who labors, the others enter into His rest; He has trodden the wine-press alone, and of the people there was none with Him.

God has ordered our sanctification to flow from Christ directly. The Holy Spirit is the Worker, yet whatever He imparts to us He takes from Christ. "He shall receive of Mine; and He shall glorify Me." This is no empty phrase, but sober reality.

What a redeemed soul needs is a *human* holiness. A *man* must be sanctified, not an angel. The latter cannot be sanctified. Once fallen, he is lost forever. Created and fallen like Adam, he cannot be restored like Adam. Knowing nothing of redemption, angels desire to look into it. Hence when, despite sin, God brings an innumerable company of men and angels to eternal life, He effects this by sanctifying the elect among unholy men; while the elect angels need no sanctification, for they have never become unholy. Sanctification refers, therefore, exclusively to *men;* imparts a holiness made possible and ordained only for men; creates a disposition bearing a human form and character, calculated for the peculiar needs of the human heart.

The Holy Spirit finds this holy disposition in its required form, not in the Father, nor in Himself, but in Immanuel, who as the Son of God and the Son of *man* possesses holiness in that peculiar *human* form.

Christ also *guarantees* to us this gracious gift. Justification being *at once* an accomplished fact does not require this, but sanctification is *gradual.*

The lack of such guaranty would fill us with doubt and uncertainty concerning our own sanctification, seeing that its beginning is small and progress slow; and concerning that of deceased infants and persons converted late in life. Such doubts would cause us fear and rob us of the comfort of the finished work.

Christ says: "Come unto Me, all ye that labor and are heavy-laden, and I will give you rest"; yet experience teaches that to many believers the inherent unholiness causes constant unrest. They know that in

Christ they are righteous, yet they are not comforted; for God says in His Word: "Be ye holy as I am holy." If it only read, "*Act* holily," Christ's merits might suffice, but it reads, "*Be* holy," and that means *inherent,* holy dispositions. Or if it spire them with hope. But it reads inexorably, "*Be* holy," and that causes their wounded souls to fear.

Not as though *every* believer is troubled on this account. Alas! Many scarcely ever, and the large majority never, give the matter any thought. So long as they have reconciliation and satisfaction, including *finished* good works, preached to them, they are at rest. Their fleshly nature is quite well satisfied with this. But there are others, more thoughtful and of tenderer conscience, who do not accept the "wide gate and the broad way" thus opened to their souls, but who believe the word: "Strait is the gate and narrow the way." To them it reads, "*Be* holy"; and there can be no rest or comfort for the conscience until they are reconciled with that word.

Hence we say that it is not enough that Christ has *obtained* sanctification, that the Holy Spirit *imparts* it, but also that Christ *guarantees* it to us, not once, but forever; so that whenever we appear before the Holy One we may be actually holy in Christ.

And this is the blessed comfort of the Word, that Christ *Himself is our sanctification.* As in fallen Adam his descendants have the fearful certainty that their nature is wholly unclean, so in the risen Christ, His redeemed have the glorious guaranty that in Him they shall be completely holy.

This is the mystery of the Vine and the branches, and of the profound word: "Now are ye clean through the word which I have spoken unto you." As our Surety He assures us hereby: (1) that the holy disposition once created in us, although temporarily overwhelmed by sin, can never be lost; (2) that Christ's form, of which there is but a small beginning in us, shall attain full perfection before we enter the New Jerusalem; (3) that as our Surety He appears before the Father in our behalf, having deposited in the treasury of His merits all that we still lack, *in our name.* In this knowledge the troubled soul finds rest.

Let us be careful that the precious vessel in which God presents to us this grace remains *intact,* for the sinner can suffice with nothing less.

But we should also be careful to avoid the other extreme, which, under the plea that Christ is our sanctification, denies the work of the Holy Spirit in the soul. The supporters of this view concede that Christ is our sanctification, that the Holy Spirit works in us and that good works are the result, but in such a way that our own person as such remains just as wicked and unprofitable as before. To be regenerate or not, believing or unbelieving, is all the same. The only difference between the two is, that independent of our own person, and against our will, the Holy Spirit makes us walk unconsciously in the way of life.

This pernicious teaching opposes Romans 7 and the Confession of the Reformed churches. The apostle does not say that his desires and inclinations are still wicked, and that the Holy Spirit performs good works independently of him and yet by him, but he grieves that, while his desire is in sympathy with the divine will and wills the good, evil is still present. In similar sense the Catechism teaches that man is inclined to all evil so long as he is not born again, but *no longer.* For the quickening of the new man consists in a "sincere joy of heart in God, through Christ, and with love and delight to live according to the will of God" (q. 90).

And the soul of the unconverted is not so disposed. Hence the difference between the two is so great that the gulf of heaven and hell yawns between them.

It may therefore be profitable to our readers to lay before them once more the Confession of the Reformed theologians of the churches of Switzerland, Germany, England, and the Netherlands on this point (1619).

They confessed: "That the Holy Spirit pervades the inmost recesses of the man; He opens the closed and softens the hardened heart, and circumcises that which was uncircumcised; infuses new qualities into the will, which, though heretofore dead, He quickens; from being evil, disobedient, and refractory, He renders it good, obedient, and pliable; actuates and strengthens it, that, like a good tree, it may bring forth the fruits of good actions" (third section, fourth Head of Doctrine, art. 2).

And this glorious work is, according to the unanimous Confession of the Reformed churches, performed in the following manner: "That the Lord does not take away the will and its properties, neither does violence thereto, but spiritually quickens, heals, corrects, and at the same time sweetly and powerfully bends it; that where carnal rebellion and resistance formerly prevailed, a ready and sincere spiritual obedience begins to reign; in which the true and spiritual restoration and freedom of our will consist" (third section, fourth Head of Doctrine, art. 16).

9

Implanted Dispositions

Perfecting holiness in the fear of the Lord— 2 Corinthians 7:1.

To deny that the Holy Spirit creates new *dispositions* in the will is equivalent to a return to Romish error; even though Rome argues the matter in a different way.

Rome denies the total corruption of the will by sin; that its disposition is wholly *evil.* Hence, the will of the sinner not being wholly useless, it follows: (1) that the regenerate does not need the implanting of a new disposition; (2) that in this respect there is no difference between the regenerate and unregenerate. They who introduce into the Reformed churches this and similar teachings ought to consider that they impair one of the foundations of the Reformation, and, however unintentionally, lead us back to Rome.

The principal question in this controversy is: whether man is *something* or *nothing.*

If man is absolutely *nothing,* as some fondly proclaim, then God cannot work in him; for He cannot work in nothing. In nothing one can make nothing. In nothing nothing can be implanted. To nothing nothing can cleave. Nothing cannot be a channel for anything. If man is nothing, there can be neither sin nor justification, for the sin of nothing is nothing, and nothing is no sin. Nothing cannot be born again, or be converted, or share the glory of the children of God. And if there is no sin, there is no need of a Savior to atone for sin; for to atone for nothing is no atonement. Then there is no need of discussing sanctification at all. This shows that the idea that man is nothing cannot be taken in the absolute sense. Since man is a *being,* he must be something; and they who maintain that he is nothing show by their actions that they consider themselves far from nothing.

But if we put it, "Man is nothing *before God,"* it becomes at once intelligible. Then every good Christian subscribes to it unconditionally; he mourns only that it is so hard to become nothing before God; and with all the saints he prays that he may more sincerely deny himself, die to himself, and know himself as nothing before God. Measured by God, man has no value. All his endeavor to be something before God is ridiculous folly. Every pulpit ought to cast down, as with trumpet-tones, every mountain of pride, and humble man before God, so that, feeling himself a mere drop in the bucket—yea, less than nothing—he may find rest in the adoration of the divine Majesty.

Before God man is not anything, not even the regenerate man, but in His hand, by His ordinance, and in His estimation, he is so great that "God crowns him with glory and honor," loves him as His child, makes him an heir of the heavenly bliss, and invites him to spend eternity with Him.

These two may never be confounded; man's absolute nothingness *before God* may never be applied to man as an instrument *in God's hand.* And man's mighty significance as *God's instrument* may never tend to make him the merest something before God *as a being.*

So we oppose pantheistic *Mysticism* and deadly *Pelagianism.* The essential mistake of the latter is, that it gives man as such a certain standing before God, and refuses to acknowledge that even the most learned and most excellent, whose breath is in his nostrils, "Yea, wherein is he to be esteemed?" is less than nothing before God. And false *Mysticism* is that injurious tendency of the human mind which, in all ages and among all nations, for the sake of being nothing before God, denies man's significance even as God's instrument. In its writings it is reiterated that before God man is nothing, that in God he disappears and loses himself, that God absorbs him. And this being absorbed is pushed so far that nothing remains to which sin or guilt can be ascribed. And thus the consciousness of responsibility and the conception of *imputability* were lost. Christian men, carried away by the fascination of being nothing, have sung hymns and preached sermons very acceptable to the Buddhists of India, but entirely outside of the pale of Christianity.

Man as God's instrument is significant indeed. In creating him from nothing He created, not nothing, but something; and that something was so important that all creatures made before him pointed to him; in Paradise he alone was the bearer of the divine image. Dominion over all the earth was given to him; he is even to judge the angels. "The Son assumed the nature, not of angels, but of man."

To say that this means that man is only a *mirror* reflecting the divine nature is the vain effort of this sickly mysticism to reconcile man's significance with its own pantheistic theories. The Scripture teaches, not that God *reflects* something in us, but that He *imparts* it to us. The love of God by the Holy Spirit is *shed abroad* in our hearts. The Lord makes us His temple and *enters* therein. A divine *seed* is placed in the soul. Pure water is *sprinkled* upon us. The Scripture uses many other images to warn us against the false theory that denies the inherent disposition in the soul and reduces man to a mere looking-glass. The *branch* is not a reflection of the *vine*, but grows from the trunk bearing leaf and cluster. A *child* is not a mere mirror of the father, but a being possessed of life and quality. An *enemy* is not one who merely fails to reflect correctly, but a being endowed with real existence.

To make man, even as God's instrument, a mere mirror in principle denies sin, destroys the sense of responsibility, and changes actual life into the fancies of a dream.

The Scripture teaches on this point that before God man is nothing; that only through God man is something; and that all inherent and acquired goodness comes only from the Fountain of all good. And, following in the steps of the Reformed fathers, we must maintain this doctrine. But to deny man's real and peculiar being is inconsistent with Scripture and with the Confession.

Thus escaping from the chaos of a false mysticism, and returning to the purified and ordained truth, we find no more difficulty in sanctification. Of course, if God's child is but a polished mirror, then they who deny the inherent, holy disposition are right, and such disposition is out of the question. As a mirror, man is dead, and all that can be seen in him is but a faint and passing reflection of the image of God. But if man, as God's instrument, has being of his own kind, it is natural that besides *being,* God gave him also *qualities.* A being without qualities is unthinkable. There are qualities in every sphere: in the material world, for man eats, drinks, walks, and sleeps; in the intellectual world, for he thinks, judges, and decides; in matters of taste, for he judges things to be beautiful, ugly, or indifferent; and in the moral world, for his desires are righteous or unrighteous, noble or base, good or evil.

And these qualities differ in different men. One loves food which another abhors. The judgment of one is blunt, and of another sharp. One calls handsome what another calls unsightly; good, what another deems evil. Hence there must be a difference in men's essential conditions, which may spring from their respective tempers, education, occupations, etc. Some men have these differences in common. Men of one group do not consider cursing sinful, but rather seem to enjoy it; those of another abhor it and protest against it. This proves that between these two there must be a difference of something; for without a different cause there can be no different effect. And this difference which causes some men to enjoy cursing and others to abhor it is called the *disposition* of a man's personality.

It may be *holy* or *unholy,* but never indifferent. Being corrupt and unholy in unregenerate human nature, it cannot be holy in the regenerate unless God create it in them. That which is born of the flesh is flesh. All our running and racing, toiling and slaving, cannot create in us a holy disposition. God alone can do that. As He has the power by regeneration to change the *root* of life, so can He also by sanctification change the *disposition* of the affections. And He could have done this *at once,* just as in regeneration, by making our nature at once perfect in all its dispositions, but He that giveth no account of any of His matters has not been pleased to do so.

Of course, He delivers His child at once from the bondage of sin, but as a rule the sanctification of his dispositions is gradual—except in deceased infants elect, and men converted on their death-bed. In all others the implanting of holy dispositions goes step by step, sometimes even with temporal relapse. *Without* this increase in Christ there can be no sanctification; and the soul that falls short of sanctification, what ground has it to glory in its election?

10

Perfect in Parts, Imperfect in Degrees

And the very God of peace sanctify you wholly; and I pray God your whole spirit and soul and body be preserved blameless unto the coming of our Lord Jesus Christ—1 Thessalonians 5:23.

The Scriptural doctrine that sanctification is a gradual process perfected only in death must be maintained clearly and soberly: *first,* in opposition to the Perfectionist, who says that saints may be "wholly sanctified" in this life; *secondly,* to those who deny the implanting of inherent holy dispositions in God's children.

It should be noticed, therefore, that Sacred Scripture distinguishes sanctification imperfect in *degrees,* and sanctification perfect in *parts.* A normal infant, though small, is a perfect human being. Of course it must grow, but it has all the parts of the human body. The mental faculties cannot be examined. but the bodily members are obviously *perfect* and complete. The head may not be covered with hair, various members may be still incomplete, but that does not impair its perfection; in a small beginning the constituent parts and members are all present. Hence the child is called perfect *in parts.*

Yet it is not perfect in degrees, that is, it has not attained its full growth. It must grow and increase in every respect. And this is a slow and imperceptible progress. A garment fitting perfectly at night is never too small in the morning. One night's growth is imperceptible. Yet we grow and increase, and until death's hour the body changes constantly. And this increase and the subsequent decrease of old age affect all the parts *equally.* It never happens that a child's arm grows, but not his leg, that his neck expands, while the head remains small. This gradual increase is the expanding force of an inherent vital principle, pervading all the members and every part.

This applies to the children of God in the second birth even more forcibly, for in the divine kingdom are no deformities; all proceed from the hand of their Creator a perfect creation. This perfection is in the *parts,* that is, they have what essentially belongs to them. And every member is internally animated and wrought upon from one vital principle, by the Holy Spirit, in such a way that all the parts are affected by it spontaneously. Hence in sanctification holy desires and inclinations must spring from that internal, vital principle in the parts and pervade every member.

In this sense sanctification is a *perfect* work; not externally, but on God's part, in that He causes the sanctifying principle to affect every member. He does not first sanctify the will, then the understanding, or first the soul and then the body, but His work embraces the entire new man at once.

But sanctification is *imperfect* in the degree of its development. When for ten years God has wrought in us, the holy desire must be much stronger than in the beginning. This is the result of growth, of gradual increase, despite many ups and downs, almost imperceptible. Hence there are steps, *ascending* from less to more with reference to the new man; and *descending* from more to less in the dying of the old, but in both a gradual change, ever farther from Satan and nearer to God.

"Perfect in parts, imperfect in degrees," as our godly fathers used to say, by which they illustrated the second birth by comparing it with the first; and in this they simply followed Scripture, which places the perfection of God's gift alongside the imperfection of our gradual increase. The Cathechism expresses it as follows: "Even the holiest men, while in this life, have only small beginnings of this obedience; yet so that with a sincere resolution they begin to live not only according to *some,* but to *all,* the commandments of God" (q. 114). St. Paul says that "Christ has given some pastors and some teachers, for the perfecting of saints, for the work of the ministry, for the edifying of the body of Christ; till we all come in the unity of the faith and of the knowledge of the Son of God, unto a perfect man, unto the measure of the stature of the fullness of Christ" (Eph. 4:12). In 2 Corinthians 10:15 he hopes to be enlarged among them when their faith shall be *increased.* To the Colossians he writes: "That ye might walk worthy of the Lord, unto all pleasing, being fruitful in every good work, and increasing in the knowledge of God" (Col. 1:10). To the Thessalonians: "Your faith groweth exceedingly, and the charity of every one of you all toward each other aboundeth" (2 Thess. 1:3). The psalmist sings that "the righteous shall flourish as a palm-tree"; and St. Paul says to Timothy, his son in Christ: "Give thyself wholly to these things, that thy perfecting may appear to all" (1 Tim. 4:15). From his own experience the apostle testifies: "Not as though I had already attained, but I follow after if that I may apprehend." And writing to the Corinthians, he draws a picture of the fruit of sanctification, saying: "But we all are changed unto the same image from glory to glory, even as by the Spirit of the Lord."

But we should not fall in the common error of applying to sanctification what Scripture teaches concerning the "children" and the "perfect." This causes confusion. Speaking of different classes of believers, Scripture recognizes the fact that there are different *degrees.* This appears most clearly from St. John's first epistle (2:12–14), where he addresses believers as "young men" and as "fathers," evidently with reference to their age, for he places the latter as more mature in spiritual experience above the former. In Hebrews 5:13, 14, St. Paul distinguishes the "perfect" who use strong meat, and the "babes" who depend upon milk. To the Corinthians: "Brethren, I could not speak unto you as unto spiritual, but as unto carnal," that is, to those who cannot bear meat, but who must still be fed with milk (1 Cor. 3:2ff.). That these words relate to sanctification is evident from what follows: "For ye are yet carnal, whereas there is among you envying and strife (v. 3). Of himself he testifies: "When I was a child I understood as a child, but when I became a man I put away childish things" (1 Cor. 13:2).

He exhorts the Ephesians (4:14): "Be no more children tossed to and fro with every wind of doctrine"; and among the Philippians he distinguishes the perfect and the not perfect, saying: "Let us, therefore, as many as be perfect, be thus minded" (3:15).

Hence the apostle evidently distinguished two classes of believers: those whose condition is normal, and those who are still in a preliminary condition. Scripture designates the former as "perfect," "adults," "men and fathers" to whom belongs the strong meat; the latter as "babes," "young men" who still use the milk.

Now the question arises whether the transition from the former unto the latter is the same as the gradual increase of sanctification. Generally the answer is affirmative, but Scripture answers it negatively, for reasons as clear as daylight. Convincing proof we find in Philippians 3:12–15. In verse 12 St. Paul says, "I am *not yet* perfect"; and directly after that (v. 15), and in the same connection, he puts himself just as distinctly among the perfect; yea, he offers himself even as their example.

It is evident that when St. Paul, under the direct leading of the Holy Spirit, declares in the same moment that he is not yet perfect, and that he is perfect, yea, the example of the perfect, the word "perfect" may not be taken in the same sense in both cases; in the one it must have a different meaning from that in the other.

They who believe in *gradual* sanctification should not appeal to this and similar passages to support their doctrine. Such misapplication of Scripture is grist for the mill of the Perfectionists, who with good reason reply: "The apostles were evidently acquainted with saints *'wholly sanctified'* like ourselves."

And what is the difference?

A child and a man are not the same; the latter is physically full grown, the former is not. The latter having attained manhood enters upon the new process of becoming nobler, more refined, *inwardly stronger.* The oak continues to grow until it has attained its full height, which process covers many years. But this is not the end of its development. On the contrary, it does not begin to acquire its iron qualities until it is full grown. The child is sent to school for the exercise of its powers. Having passed through successive institutions, and being graduated from the highest, he receives his diploma which declares that his education is finished and that he is ready to enter upon his life's career; that is, his education is finished so far as the *school* is concerned. But this does not imply that he has nothing more to learn. On the contrary, only now are his eyes opened to see the reality and actual condition of things. His education is finished, and yet he only begins to learn.

And the same applies to those whom Scripture calls "perfect." A new convert should first go to school, and not, after the practice of Methodism,* be directly put to work to convert others as a perfect believer. He is only a babe, says the apostle, a partaker of milk; and a babe cannot be expected to assist a midwife or nurse in the spiritual birth of other babes.

It is the great mistake of many Sunday-schools to make sucking lambs do the work of ewes; of neglecting to feed the new-born babes with spiritual knowledge and discipline. And the insane notion, which is gaining ground more and more, that a young man who has evinced but a slight stir of spiritual life must be promoted at once to the state of the mature Christian, brings destruction upon the Church. This is why so few inquire after the truth, or seek to enrich themselves with spiritual knowledge; why the spiritual life seems to consist only of running and racing until, spiritually exhausted and impoverished, men sit down bitterly disappointed. This makes unhealthy Christians, spiritually consumptive, tall and thin, with glittering eye and hectic cheek, but without manly strength and vigorous pulse. Of course, such cannot resist the whirlwind of strange teachings without being carried about with every wind of doctrine.

Wherefore we repeat that a new-born babe must first be fed with milk; then be sent to school, not to teach, but to learn. And the ministers of the Word in the pulpit, parents at home, and teachers in our Christian schools should examine themselves whether they understand the art of feeding the babes with milk, whether in the teaching the bread is not too heavy, whether they have not forgotten that there are sucking lambs in the flock.

---

* For the author's sense in which he takes Methodism, see section 5 of the Preface—Trans.

Of course, the time will come when the suckling will be able to digest solid food. Knowledge will accumulate, and by and by his education be finished. And then it would be exceedingly foolish not to go on to perfection, but to withhold solid food, and to continue to feed all the members of the church alike on milk. Such a course would soon empty the church. Men provided with spiritual teeth cannot live on such diet. The preaching which is always laying the first foundations kills both preacher and people.

Hence there is a time in the life of the saint when this first process of growth is finished; when believers, having become men, take their place among the mature and perfect. And in this sense we hear the apostle say: "I do not belong to the babes in their mother's lap, nor to the children at school, but to the adults and the perfect whose education is finished. But, O brethren, do not think that I am perfect inwardly, for I have not yet attained, but I follow after, if that I may apprehend that for which also I am apprehended of Christ Jesus."

We see the same difference in plant and animal, in the natural and spiritual birth. There is first a growth to attain the *full stature,* then only the real development begins which in the children of God is the unfolding of the holy disposition in their own person.

11

The Pietist and the Perfectionist

He chastens us for our profit, that we might be partakers of His holiness—Hebrews 12:10.

Sanctification is a gracious work of God, whereby in a supernatural way He gradually divests from sin the inclinations and dispositions of the regenerate and clothes them with holiness.

Here we meet a serious objection which deserves our careful attention. To the superficial observer, the spiritual experience of God's children seems diametrically opposed to this professed gift of sanctification. One says: "Can it be that for more than ten years I have been the subject of a divine operation whereby my desires and inclinations were divested of sin and clothed with holiness? If this is the Gospel, then I belong not to the Lord's redeemed; for in myself I perceive scarcely any progress; I only know that my first love has become cold and that the inward corruption is appalling. Some dream of progress, but I discover in myself scarcely anything but backsliding. No gain but loss, is the sad footing-up of the account. My only hope is Immanuel my Surety."

While the experience of a broken heart vents its grief in this way, others exhort us not to encourage spiritual pride. They say: "We should not foster spiritual pride in God's children, for by nature they are already thus inclined. What is more conducive to spiritual pride than the conceit of an ever-advancing holiness? Is not holiness the highest and most glorious attainment? Is it not our comprehensive prayer to be made partakers of His holiness? And would you have these souls imagine that, since they were converted a number of years ago, they have attained already a considerable degree of this divine perfection? Would you give license to older Christians to feel themselves above their younger brethren? Holiness wants to be noticed; hence you incite them to a display of their good works. What is this but to cultivate a spirit of Pharisaism?"

We may not rest until this objection of the sensitive conscience is entirely removed.

Not as though we could escape all dangers of Pharisaism. This would silence every exhortation to holy living. Light without shadows is impossible; the shadows disappear only in absolute darkness. In the days of the ancient Pharisee, Jerusalem, compared with Rome and Athens, was a God-fearing city. Pharisaism was never more bold than in the days of Jesus. And history shows that the danger of Pharisaism has always been least in the Romish and greatest in the Reformed churches; and among the latter, it is strongest where the name of God is most exalted. Godliness is impossible without the shadow of Pharisaism. The brighter the light and glory of the former, the darker the shadow of the latter. To escape Pharisaism altogether one must descend into the lowest pest-holes of society, where nothing bridles the passions of men.

And this is natural. Pharisaism is not a common corruption, but the mildew of the noblest fruit the earth ever saw—viz., godliness. The circles that are free from Pharisaism also lack the *highest* good; how, then, could it decay there? And the circles in which this danger is greatest are the very circles in which the highest good is known and exalted.

But, apart from this aimless skirmishing with the Pharisaic phantom, the scruple mentioned above has our heartiest sympathy. If it were true that sanctification so impressed the soul as to incite it to pride, it could not be the real article; for of all unholiness pride is the most abominable. It is David's sweet and sincere supplication: "Keep back thy servant also from presumptuous sins; let them not have dominion over me; then shall I be upright and shall be innocent from the great transgressions." The fundamental conception of grace is so intimately connected with the idea of becoming *a little child,* and its gift is so strongly conditioned upon a humble disposition, that the gift which encourages spiritual pride cannot be a gift of grace.

But we are confident that the doctrine of sanctification, as presented in these pages according to the Holy Scripture, has nothing in common with this caricature. Since in Paradise sin sprang from the first satanic incitement to pride, and all spiritual and carnal unholiness still grows from that poisonous root, it is evident that the first effect of the implanted, holy disposition must be the humbling of this pride, the pulling down of this stronghold; and at the same time the quickening of a humble, meek, and childlike spirit.

The idea that sanctification consists in inspiring the saint with horror for gross and outward sins, without a previous breaking down of self-conceit, is unscriptural and opposed by the Reformed churches. The Scripture teaches that the Holy Spirit never applies sanctification to the believer without attacking *all his sins at once.* "A sincere resolution to live not only according to *some,* but to *all* the commandments of God" (Heidelberg Catechism).

Of all sins pride is the most accursed, for in all its manifestations it is the transgression of the first commandment. Hence real and divinely wrought sanctification is inconceivable without, first of all, destroying pride, and creating a humble, quiet, self-distrusting, and childlike disposition.

And this solves the whole difficulty. He who fears that gradual sanctification will lead to pride and self-conceit confounds its human counterfeit with the real work divinely wrought. Wherefore, with this objection, he must attack the hypocrite, and not us.

However, a wrong interpretation of what the Scripture calls "flesh" might suggest it. If "flesh" signifies sensual inclinations and bodily appetites, and sanctification consisted almost entirely in warring against these sins, sanctification thus understood might be accompanied by an increase of spiritual pride. But by sinful "flesh" the Scripture denotes the entire man, body and soul, including sins which are spiritual as well as sensual; hence sanctification aims at once at the change of man's spiritual and sensual inclinations, and first of all at his tendency to pride.

In the preceding article we said that sanctification included a *descent* as well as an *ascent.* When the Lord raises us, we also descend. There is no rising of the new man without a death of the old; and every attempt to teach sanctification without doing full justice to both is unscriptural.

We oppose, therefore, the attempts of the Pietist and of the Perfectionist, who say that they have nothing more to do with the old man, that nothing remains in them to be mortified, and that all that is required of them is to hurry the growth of the new man. And we equally oppose the opposite, which admits the dying of the old man, but denies the rising of the new, and that the soul receives all that it lacks.

Every true and lasting conversion, according to our Catechism, must manifest itself in these two parts, viz., a *mortification* of the old man, and a *rising* of the new, in equal proportions.

And in answer to the question, "What is the mortification of the old man?" the Heidelberg Catechism answers, "*A gradual decrease,"* for it says: "It is a sincere sorrow of heart that we have provoked God by our sins; and more and more to hate and flee from them." While the quickening of the new man is expressed just as positively: "It is a sincere joy of heart in God through Christ, and with love and delight to live according to the will of God in *all* good works"—a declaration that is repeated in the answer of the 115th question, which thus describes this mortification: "That all our lifetime we may learn more and more to know our sinful nature"; and which speaks of the quickening of the new man as "becoming *more* and *more* conformable to the image of God."

Hence there are two parts, or rather two aspects of the same thing: (1) the breaking down of the old man; (2) a growing conformity to the divine image.

To *mortify* and to *quicken,* to kill and to make alive, *more and more*—this is, according to the Confession of the fathers, the work of the Triune God in sanctification.

Sin is not merely the "lack of righteousness." As soon as righteousness, goodness, and wisdom disappear, unrighteousness, evil, and folly take their place. As God implanted in man the first three named, so does sin not merely rob him of them, but it puts the last three in their place. Sin did not only kill in Adam the man of God, but also quickened in him the man of sin; hence sanctification must effect in us the very opposite. It must mortify that which sin has quickened, and quicken that which sin has mortified.

If this rule is thoroughly understood, there can be no confusion. Our idea of sanctification necessarily corresponds to our idea of sin. They who consider sin as a mere poison, and deny the loss of original righteousness, are Pietists, they ignore the mortification of the old man, and always busy themselves adorning the new. And they who say that sin is the loss of original righteousness, and deny its positive, evil effects, are inclined to Antinomianism, and reduce sanctification to a fancied emancipation from the old man, rejecting the rising of the new.

Of course, this touches the doctrine of *the old man and the new.*

The representation that the soul of the converted is an arena where the two are engaged in a hand-to-hand fight is incorrect, and has not a single satisfactory text for its support. We reject the two following representations: that of the Antinomian, who says: "The believing ego is the new man in Christ Jesus; I am not responsible for the old man, the personal, sinful ego; he may sin as much as he please"; and the representation of the Pietist, who considers him still the old man, partly renewed, and who is always busy to remodel him. These two do not belong to Christ's Church.

The Scripture teaches, not that the old man is sanctified by being changed into the new, but that the old man must be mortified until nothing of him remains. Neither does it teach that in regeneration a small part only of the old man is renewed—the remainder to be patched up gradually—but that *an entirely new man* is implanted.

This is of greatest importance for the right understanding of these holy things. Sin wrought in us an old man, the body of sin; not merely a part, but the whole, with all that belongs to him, body and soul. Hence that old man must die, and the Pietist with all his works of piety can never galvanize a single muscle in his body. He is altogether unprofitable, and must perish under his just condemnation.

In like manner God graciously regenerates in us a new creature, which is also a *complete* man. Therefore we may not take the new man as the gradual restoration of the old. The two have nothing in common but the mutual basis of the same personality. The new does not spring from the old, but supersedes him. Being only in the germ, he may be buried in the newly regenerate, but he will arise and then God's work appears gloriously. God is his Author, Creator, and Father. Not the old man, but the new man cries out: "Abba, Father!"

However, our ego is related to the dying old man and the rising new. The ego of a non-elect person is identified with the *old* man; they are the same. But in the consummation of the heavenly glory, the ego of God's children is identified with the *new* man.

But during the days of our earthly life this is not so. The new man of an unregenerate, but elect person *exists apart* from him, but hid in Christ. He is still wedded to his old man. But in regeneration and conversion God dissolves this unholy marriage, and He unites his ego to the new man. Yet, despite all this, he is not yet rid of the old man. Before God and the law, from the viewpoint of eternity, he may be so considered, but not actually and really.

And this is the cause of the conflict within and without. All evil ties are not dissolved at once, and all holy ties are not united at once. By the mystic union with Christ the child of God actually possesses the entire new man, even though he should die tomorrow, but he has not yet the enjoyment of it. Being wedded to the new man before God, he is, by a painful process, yet to die to the old man, and by divine grace the new man is to be raised in him. And this is his sanctification: the dying of the old and the rising of the new, by which God increases and we decrease. Blessed manifestation of faith!

12

The Old Man and the New

That we being dead unto sin should live unto righteousness—1 Peter 4:24.

The Psalmist sings: "They go from strength to strength, every one of them in Zion appeareth before God." We must maintain this glorious testimony, although our own experience often seems to contradict it. Not experience, but the Scripture, teaches us divine truth; nor is it as though the procedure of the divine operation in our own heart could differ from the testimony of the Sacred Scripture, but that our experience often interprets our real spiritual condition *incorrectly.*

Our knowledge of self is very small. The plummet of our self-consciousness scarcely reaches below the surface, while God's holy eye penetrates the waters of the soul to the very bottom. We are ignorant of much that takes place in the soul, and what we perceive of it often presents itself to our consciousness as different from what it is in reality. If our self-knowledge were perfect, the testimony of our spiritual experience would be as reliable as that of Scripture. But this not being so, not even among God's children, spiritual experience, though helpful, may never weaken the Word of God. Hence, though we discover in ourselves an ever-growing weakness, the Scripture testimony is still sure: "They go from strength to strength."

But who goes from strength to strength? Surely not the *old* man. It may not be said that regeneration effected a change in him which is constantly increasing, which enables him to make such commendable progress that by divine help he will probably succeed in the end. This is not so. Scripture teaches that the old man is dead, condemned to die forever; that he is incorrigible and cannot be restored, saved or reconciled. He is hopelessly lost. And instead of gradually becoming himself again he must be crucified, slain, and buried. Instead of expecting anything good of him, it should be our glory to die to him and be rid of him.

Neither does the *new* man go from strength to strength. He is not being put together little by little until he can stand on his own legs, but, since we are to live forever in the new creature, it must be a real man *born* in us. And as such he cannot increase nor decrease; he only slumbers in the germ and must arise.

But *my person,* as by faith I stand in Christ, must go from strength to strength. That person was once born in the old man, and therefore was born in trespasses and sin, and is a child of wrath by nature. And he would never have come out and escaped from the old man of himself. That he could not do. He was identified with the old man so completely that the latter was his very ego. He had no other life or existence. But in regeneration a change took place. By this divine act our person is in principle *detached* from his former ego in the old man. The root was notched and, by the constant action of storm and gravitation, the severed parts separated more and more. Our person is no longer identified with the old man, but opposes him. Even though he succeeds in enticing us again to sin, even in the yielding we do not what we *will,* but what we *hate.* Only hear what St. Paul says: "The good which I would I do not, but the evil which I would not that I do. Now, if I do that I would not, it is no more I that do it, but sin that dwelleth in me."

Wherefore the child of God must not be identified with the old man after regeneration, for this opposes the plain teaching of the Word. He is the old man no more, but wars against him. As God's child he is become the new man—not in part, but wholly. "Old things are passed away, behold all things are become new." In this, and nothing less, is cause of his glorying. His person is passed from death into life. He is translated from the kingdom of darkness into the kingdom of God's dear Son. He is so fully identified with the new man that, while still living in this world, he is already set with Christ in heaven, where his citizenship is, and where his life is hid with Christ in God.

If the word of the Psalmist does not refer to the *old* man nor to the *new,* to whom, then, does it refer? The Scripture answers: to *believers,* their *persons,* their *ego,* which, being detached from the old man and opposing him, is identified with the new. *They go* from strength to strength. It is true the use of "ego" in both senses is apt to confuse one; yet St. Paul does the same thing. He says "I" and "not I": "I live, yet not I, but Christ liveth in me." The same person who fell in Adam and out of Adam received the old man with whom for a time he was identified, is now changed, translated, and risen with Christ; out of Christ he received a new man, and with that new man he is being more and more identified. Hence he goes from strength to strength.

This identification of our person with the new man is, immediately after regeneration, still very slight; while we are so thoroughly bound to the old man, with almost all the fibers of our being, that it seems as though he were still our very self. But by the operation of the Holy Spirit we gradually die to the old man, and at the same time the new man is quickened in us more and more. And, since both the dying of the old and the gradual rising of the new man are profitable to our person, the Holy Spirit testifies concerning His own work that we, God's children, go from strength to strength until every one of us in Zion appeareth before God. It refers not only to our growing *into the new man,* but just as much to our gradual deliverance *from the dying old man.* In both it is the same working; hence both afford us *increase* of strength.

We consider first the *dying of the old man* as far as it relates to sanctification.

This dying has no reference to our *own activity,* alluded to by the office of baptism, "That we manfully fight and overcome sin and the devil and all his dominion"; on the contrary, it refers to the fruit of the cross of Christ. The question, "What further benefit do we receive from the sacrifice and death of Christ on the cross?" the Reformed

Church answers: "That by virtue thereof our old man is crucified, and buried with Him; that so the corrupt inclinations of the flesh may no more reign in us" (Heidelberg Catechism, q. 43). Hence the dying of the old man is not the fruit of *our* labor, BUT Christ accomplishes it in us by virtue of His cross through the Holy Spirit.

In order to effect this in us the Holy Spirit diverts our personal affections, inclinations, and dispositions from the old man, to whom hitherto they have been ardently attached, so that now we begin to hate him.

It is possible for friendship to die. We may have been intimate with a person whom we afterward discovered to be a bad character. Then not only is the friendship broken, but our affection ceases. We regret our former intimacy, and we despise him all the more cordially as he proves to be more deceitful and malicious. And this applies to our relation with the old man. Formerly we were most intimate with him. We shared his will, his sympathies, and his affections. We lived one life with him. We felt ourselves bound to him by the tenderest ties. We could not be happy but in his company. But there came a change. We acquired a different taste. We became acquainted with another and better man—viz., the new man in Christ Jesus—and we became very intimate with him. And this noble intercourse discovered to us the thorough baseness and corruption of the old man. Then our love ceased and we began cordially to hate him.

It is true that our former connection brings us in frequent contact with him. On such occasions he often entices us by his cunning, but *not to our delight;* and being only half willing, our souls protest; and as soon as the sin is committed we are filled with self-loathing and contrition.

And this reversal of our affections is not our work, but that of the Holy Spirit. Not that we deny that He often uses us as instruments, or prompts us to exert ourselves, but the changing of our inclinations is not our work, but the direct operation of God the Holy Spirit.

How it is performed we can understand but partly. Essentially it is a mystery, just as much as regeneration. Being God, the Holy Spirit has access to our heart, He discovers our personality, the nature of our affections, and in what way their action may be reversed. But our inability to fathom this mystery does not in the least affect our faith in the matter.

Since the dying of the old man is effected, not by our good works, but by the implanting of a disposition and inclination repugnant to the old man, our own work is entirely out of the question; for our own heart is inaccessible to us. We have no power over our *inward* person; we lack the means to create another inclination; and when we deny this we are self-deceived. God the Creator alone can do this, and in doing it He is *irresistible.* Hatred against the old man, once having entered the soul, is a power that simply overwhelms us. Even when enticed by him, we cannot but hate him.

The seventh chapter of Romans is very instructive in this respect. St. Paul says, "I delight in the law of God after the inward man," that is, after my inward affections. There is indeed another law in his members, which brings him into captivity to the law of sin, but he has not the least love or sympathy for that law, but with the *law of his mind* wars against it.

Any other representation contradicts this positive testimony, uttered by the mouth of the most excellent of the apostles, under the seal of the Holy Spirit. He that believes embraces the Son, and cannot but receive impressions and be swayed by influences that cause his affections and inclinations to become radically changed. A believer is internally wrought upon. All his former dealing with the old man—pride, hardness of heart, deceit, and thirst for revenge—now fill him with horror; what was formerly to him the pride of life and the lust of the eyes is now vexation of spirit, as he realizes how shameful and abominable it is.

So he gradually dies to the old man, until, in the hour of death, he is fully delivered. *God's child remains the old man's grave-digger until the hour of his own departure.*

Nevertheless he dies to him so completely that at last he loses all confidence in him, thoroughly convinced that he is without excuse, an abominable wretch, a reprobate, and a deceiver, capable of all evil. And when occasionally he indulges in scornful mirth at the old man's pride and practices, it is not in boastfulness of his own work or of his fellow men, but glorying only in the gracious work of his God.

13

The Work of God in Our Work

And the very God of peace sanctify you wholly; and I pray God your whole spirit and soul and body be preserved blameless unto the coming of the Lord Jesus Christ—1 Thessalonians 5:23.

The difference between *sanctification* and *good works* should be well understood.

Many confound the two, and believe that sanctification means to lead an honorable and virtuous life; and, since this is equal to good works, sanctification, without which no man shall see God, is made to consist in the earnest and diligent effort to do good works.

But this reasoning is false. The grape should not be confounded with the vine, lightning with thunder, the birth with the conception, any more than sanctification with good works. Sanctification is the kernel from which the blade and full ear of good works shall spring, but this does not identify the kernel with the blade. The former lies in the ground and by its fibers attaches itself to the furrow *internally.* The latter shoots from the ground *externally* and visibly. So is sanctification the implanting of the germ, of the disposition, and inclination which shall produce the blossom and fruit of a good work.

Sanctification is *God's* work in us, whereby He imparts to our members a holy disposition, inwardly filling us with delight in His law and with repugnance to sin. But good works are acts of *man,* which spring from this holy disposition. Hence sanctification is the source of good works, the lamp that shall shine with their light, the capital of which they are the interest.

Allow us to repeat it: "sanctification" is a work of God; "good works" are of men. "Sanctification" works internally; "good works" are external. "Sanctification" imparts something to man; "good works" take something out of him. "Sanctification" forces the root into the ground; to do "good works" forces the fruit out of the fruitful tree. To confound these two leads the people astray.

The Pietist says: "Sanctification is man's work; it cannot be insisted upon with sufficient emphasis. It is our best effort to be godly." And the Mystic maintains: "We cannot do good works, and may not insist upon them; for man is unable; God alone works them in him independently of him."

Of course, both are equally wrong and unscriptural. The former is reducing sanctification to good works, takes it out of God's hand and lays it upon man, who never can perform it; and the latter, in making good works take the place of sanctification, releases man from the task laid on him and claims that God will perform it. Both errors must be opposed.

Both sanctification and good works should receive recognition. Ministers of the Word, and through them the people of God, should understand that sanctification is an *act of God* that He performs in man; and that God has commanded *man* to do good works to the glory of His name. And this will have twofold effect: (1) God's people will acknowledge their complete inability to receive a holy disposition otherwise than as a gift of free grace, and then they will earnestly pray for this grace. (2) They will pray that His elect, in whom this work is already wrought, may show it forth in God-glorifying works: "Chosen in Christ Jesus, that we should be holy and without blame before Him in love" (Eph. 1:4).

Though this distinction is very clear, two things may cause confusion:

First, the fact that holiness may be attributed to the good works themselves. One may *be* holy, but also *do* holy works. The Confession speaks of the "many holy works which Christ has done for us and in our stead" (art. 22). Hence holiness may be *external* and *internal.*

The following passages refer, not to *sanctification,* but to *good works:* "Seeing that all these things shall be dissolved, what manner of persons ought ye to be in all holy conversation?" (2 Peter 3:2). "As He which hath called you is holy, so be you holy in all manner of conversation" (1 Peter 1:15). "That we being delivered out of the hands of our enemies, may serve Him without fear, in holiness and righteousness all the days of our life" (Luke 1:75).

We find that the word "holy" is used of both our *inward disposition and of its result,* the *outward life.* It may be said of the spring as well as of the water, that it contains iron, of the tree as well as of the fruit, that it is good; of the candle as well as of the light, that it is bright. And, since holiness may be attributed to both the inward disposition and the outward life, sanctification may be understood as referring to the sanctification *of our life.* This may lead to the supposition that an outwardly blameless life is the same thing as sanctification. And if this is so, then sanctification is but a *duty imposed,* and not a *gift imparted.* It should therefore be carefully noticed that the sanctification of the mind, affections, and dispositions is not our work, but *God's;* and that the holy life which springs from it is *ours.*

Second, the other cause of confusion is the many Scripture passages that exhort and encourage us to sanctify, purify, and perfect our lives, yea, even "to perfect our holiness" (2 Cor. 7:1); to "yield ourselves as servants to holiness" (Rom. 6:19); and to be "unblamable in holiness" (1 Thess. 3:13), etc.

And we should not weaken these passages, as the Mystics do, who say that these texts mean, not that *we* should yield our members, but that God Himself will take special care that they be so yielded. These are tricks that lead men to trifle with the Word. It is an abuse of the Scripture for the sake of introducing one's own theories under the cover of divine authority. The preachers who for fear of imposing responsibilities upon men abstain from exhortation, and dull the edge of the divine *commandments* by representing them as *promises,* take a heavy responsibility upon themselves.

For although we know that no man has ever performed a single good work without God, who wrought in him both to will and to do; although we heartily agree with the Confession, "That we are beholden to God for our good works and not God to us" (art. 24); and rejoice with the holy apostle in the fact, "That God has before ordained the good works that we should walk therein"; yet this does not absolve us from the duty of exhorting the brethren.

It is a fact that God is pleased to use man as an instrument, and by the spur of his own ability and responsibility to incite him to *activity.* A cavalryman on the battle-field is fully aware how much he depends upon the good services of his horse; and also that the animal cannot run unless God enabled it. Being a godly man, he prays before mounting that the Lord enable his horse to bring him victory, but after he is mounted, with spur and knee, rein and voice, he uses all his strength to make the horse do what it should do. And the same is true of sanctification. Unless the breath of the Lord blow through the garden of the soul, not a leaf can stir. The Lord alone performs the work from the beginning to the end. But He performs it partly by the aid of means; and the instrument chosen is often *man himself,* who cooperates with God. And to this human instrumentality the Scripture refers when, in connection with sanctification, it admonishes us to good works.

As in nature God gives the seed and the forces in the soil and rain and sunshine to mature the fruit of the earth, while at the same time He uses the farmer to perfect His work, so it is also in sanctification: God causes it to work effectually, but He employs the human instrument to cooperate with Him, as the saw works together with him that handles it.

However, this should not be understood as though in sanctification God had made Himself absolutely dependent upon the human instrument. This is impossible; by nature man can indeed *mar* sanctification, but never *further* it. By nature he hates and opposes it. Moreover, he is absolutely unable to produce from his own corrupt nature anything for his growth in sanctification. His instrumental cooperation should therefore not be abused either by ascribing to man a power for good, or to obscure the work of God.

Careful discrimination is necessary. He that implants the holy disposition is the Lord. The combined exertions of all these instruments could not implant one single feature of the holy mind, any more than all the carpenter's tools together could draw the molding of one panel. The artist paints upon the canvas, but with all their exertions his palette, brush, and paint-box could never draw a single figure. The sculptor molds the image, but of themselves his chisel, mallet, and stool cannot detach a single chip from the rough marble. To engrave the features of holiness in the sinner is a work in the highest sense artistic, unspeakably divine. And the Artist who executes it is the Lord, as St. Paul calls Him, the *Artist* and *Architect* of the City which has foundations. The fact that the Lord is pleased to use instruments for some parts of the work does not impart to them any value, much less any ability to accomplish anything of themselves without the Artist. He is the only Worker.

But as Artist He uses three different instruments, viz., the *Word, His providential dealings,* and *the regenerate person himself.*

1. The Word is a vital power in the Church which pierces even to the dividing asunder of the joints and the marrow, and as such it is a divinely ordained instrument to create impressions in a man; and these impressions are the means by which holy inclinations are implanted in his heart.

2. *Life's experiences* also make impressions in us more or less lasting; and these God uses also to create holy dispositions.

3. The third instrument refers to the effect of *habit.* Repeated sinful acts make the sinner bold and create sinful habits; in this way he cooperates to make himself a greater sinner. In a similar sense the saint cooperates in his own salvation by allowing the holy disposition to radiate in good works. The frequent act of doing good creates the habit. The habit gradually becomes a second nature. And it is this mighty influence of habit which God uses to teach us holiness. In this way God can make one saint instrumental in the sanctification of another.

An architect builds a palace which makes him famous as an artist. It is true the contractor, an important person in his place, erects the structure, but his name is scarcely mentioned, it is the architect alone from whom all the praise is reserved. In sanctification it is not the Word by itself that is effectual, but that Word handled by the *Holy Spirit.* Neither is it the experience of life alone, but that experience employed by the *Holy Artist.* Neither is it the regenerate person who serves as foreman, but the glorious Triune God, in whose service he labors.

14

The Person Sanctified

The putting off of the body of the sins of the flesh—Colossians 2:2.

Sanctification embraces the whole man, body and soul, with all the parts, members, and functions that belong to each respectively. It embraces his *person* and *all* of his person. This is why sanctification progresses from the hour of regeneration all through life, and can be completed only in and through death.

St. Paul prays for the church of Thessalonica: "The God of peace sanctify you *wholly*, and may your whole spirit and soul and body be preserved blameless unto the coming of our Lord Jesus Christ." Sanctification is essentially a work of one piece, simply because our person is not pieced together, but is organically *one* in all its parts.

The sinner's holiness or unholiness embraces his whole being. He is a sinner not only in his *body*, but in his soul, and even more so; and in his *soul* not only because his will is unholy, but also because his understanding is unholy, and even more so. The memory, the imagination, and all that belongs to him as a man are radically defiled, desecrated, and corrupted by sin. He lies in the midst of death. Even in a small child, every part is affected. Without the least exertion he learns a street-song, while it seems almost impossible to commit one stanza of a psalm.

If sanctification has reference to the inherited stain, as justification to the inherited guilt, it follows that sanctification must extend as far as the inherited stain. If man's entire person is covered with the poison of the stain, it must be covered much more abundantly by sanctification.

Sin is disturbance, derangement, discord, and warfare in home and heart, and is not overcome completely until superseded by holy peace. This is the reason why St. Paul calls the God of sanctification the God of peace; and so he prays for the Church that the God of peace sanctify them *wholly*, or literally, *"unto the full end,"* so that the end of sanctification may be accomplished in them perfectly.*

However, the starting-point of this grace lies not in the body, but in the soul. Sin started in the soul, not in the body; hence the mortification of sin must also begin in the soul.

It is directed, first of all, to the *consciousness* and to its faculties of cognition, contemplation, reflection, and judgment. Sanctification proceeds, not from the will, but from the consciousness. Sanctification is to make conformable to the will of God, and this requires, *in the first place,* that His good and perfect and acceptable will become a living reality to the consciousness, conviction, and conscience. The things of which one is ignorant do not affect him, but ignorance of the divine will is sin, and this must be overcome first of all.

But how? By committing to memory? By learning the Catechism? By no means. The sanctification of the consciousness consists in God's act of writing His law in our hearts. True, there are still a few traces of that law written in the sinner's heart, as the apostle writes that the Gentiles who are without the law are a law unto themselves, but this is at the most but the fermentation of a higher principle in a *sinful* person which cannot maintain itself. The Nihilist and Communist of the day

* This is not the place to discuss the opinion held by many, that 1 Thessalonians 5:23 teaches trichotomy, that is, the threefold division of man's being. Let this only be observed, that it does not read, ὁλόμορους, "in all your parts," followed by the summing up of those parts, *spirit, soul,* and *body, but* it reads ὁλοτελεῖς, which refers, not to the parts, but to the final end, τέλος. Moreover, it should be noticed that in those passages which oppose the *spiritual* man to the *natural*—that is, the pneumatical to the psychical, as in 1 Corinthians 2:14, 15—the word πνεῦμα indicates the new life-principle, of which it never can be said that it be preserved blameless. For this πνεῦμα is sinless *by nature.* Calvin explains "spirit" and "soul" by making them to refer to our rational and moral existence as beings endowed with reason and volition, both modes of the soul's existence.

show to what extent the heart may lose the sense of the first principles of right and righteousness. But when the Scripture promises that the Lord shall write the law in their hearts, and that they shall teach no more every man his neighbor, saying, "Know the Lord, for all shall know him from the least unto the greatest," it offers us something entirely different and far more glorious. And this is accomplished, not by outward study, but by inward apprehension; not by an exercise of the memory, but by a renewing of the mind, as St. Paul writes: "Be not conformed to this world, but be ye transformed by the renewing of your mind, that ye may prove what is that good and acceptable and perfect will of God."

Ezekiel prophesied of this renewing of the mind when he said: "A new heart also will I give you, and *a new spirit will I put within you.*" Instruction formerly received may be used as a means to that end, but the instruction which the human spirit receives in sanctification is not human, but divine. Hence it is said: "They are taught of the Lord"; "Every man, therefore, that hath heard and learned of the Father cometh unto Me"; "I will put My law into their minds, and will write it in their hearts."

Since the books of Moses emphasize the fact that the tables of the law were written, not by Moses, Aholiab, nor Bezaliel, but directly by God's own finger, it follows from the nature of the case that the Scripture intends to present this writing upon the tables of the heart, not as the work of man, but as the direct work of God. The sanctification of the human consciousness is wrought in us by God in a divine, unfathomable, and irresistible way, but not independently of the Word, for that Word itself is divine, and the preaching of the Word is divinely ordained and instituted. But, since the Word and the preaching can only present the matter to the consciousness, it is the Holy Ghost who makes the heart to understand it, declares it to the consciousness, works conviction, and causes the consciousness to assent to it, and thus enables it to feel the pressure which proceeds from that which is written on the heart.

Hence the sanctification of the consciousness consists, not only in receiving new knowledge, and in being impressed with quickened conceptions, but also in having the reason qualified for the exercise of entirely different *functions.* For the natural man does not understand the things of the Spirit of God, but the spiritual man, that is, he whose consciousness is regenerated, sanctified, and enlightened *discerns* all things; for such a man, says St. Paul, has the mind of Christ.

However, the sanctification of our consciousness does not complete the sanctification of our person. On the contrary, for although the *will* is absolutely dependent upon the consciousness, yet even the will itself is corrupted by sin. It did not lose its functional operation, but, as in the sinner the judgment still judges and the feeling still feels, so is the will still able *to will.* But its ability to reach out in every direction is lost; and the calamity has befallen us that by nature we cannot will what God wills.

And that stiffness and hardness which prevent the will's free action in this respect must be removed. The Scripture calls this the taking away of the stony heart and the giving of a heart of flesh which is no longer hard and insensible. Where sin had bound the will by inclining it to evil, thereby depriving it of the power of bending in the opposite direction, that is, toward God, the gracious gift of sanctification now comes to relieve that bending over to hell, and to give it power to incline to God.

Formerly our knowledge and conviction of the oughtness of things did not avail; for they left our will powerless as a chained wheel, unable to turn in the right direction. But not only had the consciousness a better idea of and clearer insight into the oughtness of things, and we had assented to it, but the will was also inclined by correct volition to choose the good; then the work of God had attained its end, had accomplished its purpose, and had changed the whole man.

And thus man regains also control over his *passions.* Every man has passions and propensities which sin has made unruly and uncontrollable. In fact, man is their toy; they can use him as they please. It is true the unconverted sometimes succeed in curbing and muzzling one passion, but always by becoming more hopelessly the slaves of another. Dissipation is conquered only by the excitement of avarice; sensuality by cherishing inward pride; anger by nursing the thirst for revenge. Kamosh is cast out only to make room for Molech; the north wind conjured away only to be followed by a blast from the east.

But the passions of the saint are controlled in a different way. Sanctification gives them another direction. He feels their whip and spur, but they are to him the violence of a foreign power. Wherefore St. Paul declares: "It is no more I that do it, but sin that dwelleth in me." And no passion can overtake him which in the power of God he cannot master and control.

Sanctification embraces, *in the second place,* the body. Both sin and holiness affect the body not as though it were the seat of sin, which is Manichean heresy, but in the sense in which Scripture disapproves the act of touching a corpse. The body is the instrument of the soul; hence the members may be used for holy or unholy purposes, and offer either their cooperation or resistance for such purposes. Who does not know that an excess of blood inflames the ugly temper and excites to anger; that irritable nerves make one impatient; and great muscular energy tempts to recklessness? Many are the connections between the operations of body and soul; and, inasmuch as the Holy Spirit brings the bodily members into subjection to the reign of the new life, sanctification does indeed affect the life of the body. This appears from the fact that the body is called the temple of the Holy Spirit. St. Paul calls it "the putting off of the body of sin of the flesh" (Col. 2:2); and again he saith: "Let not sin reign in your mortal body, that ye should obey the lusts thereof" (Rom. 6:12).

Hence the old man is just as bad and becomes even worse, but there is at the same time a gradual weakening—and thus dies to his evil lusts, while the new man continues not only holy and intact, but gradually masters us and enables us to present our bodies a living sacrifice, holy and well-pleasing to God, which is our reasonable service (Rom. 12:1).

All this is wrought by the Holy Spirit who dwells in our hearts, the Comforter, Guide, and Teacher of the desolate. Christ is far from us in heaven sitting at the right hand of God. But the Holy Spirit is poured forth. He dwells in the Church on earth. He abides with us as our Comforter.

Hence we should not imagine that we are a full-rigged, well-provisioned craft which, at its own risk and without a pilot, swiftly carries us to the haven of rest; for without wind and tide we cannot move our craft at all. The heart of the saint is a Bethel; when he rises from blessed dreams he is ever surprised to find that God is in this place and he knew it not. When we are called to speak, act, or fight, we do so as though we were doing it all ourselves, not perceiving that it is Another who works in us both to will and to do. But as soon as we have finished the task successfully and agreeably to the will of God, as men of faith we prostrate ourselves before Him and cry, "Lord, the work was Thine."

And this goes against the old man. Before the work is undertaken he is fearful and ill at ease, but as soon as it is finished he is full of boasting, and the incense of human praise is sweet in his nostrils. But God's child works in simplicity and spontaneously; brings the sacrifice of his labor hoping against hope, with all the exertion of the talent which God gave him. But the labor finished, he wonders how he ever accomplished it, and he finds the only solution in the fact that there is One who powerfully wrought in and through him.

15

Good Works

For we are His workmanship, created in Christ Jesus unto good works, which God hath before ordained that we should walk in them—Ephesians 2:10.

Good works are the ripe fruit from the tree which God has planted in *sanctification.* In the saint there is life; from that life workings proceed; and those workings are either good or evil. Hence good works are not added to sanctification for mere effect, but belong to it. The discussion of sanctification is not complete without the discussion of Good Works.

Whatever man may be, works always proceed from him; and since works are never neutral, but either conform or do not conform to the divine law, it follows that every man's works are either good or evil, actual sins *(peccata actualia)* or good works. In fact, every life has its own energizing. Without it, it is no life. Properly speaking, life in the saint does not proceed from *sanctification,* but sanctification lends it tone, color, and character.

In a garden where the conditions are all equal, and there is the same soil, the same fertilizer, etc., different fruit-trees are planted. Evidently, the working that makes the trees grow is from the soil; for if planted in the garret, they will not grow. But the cause that produces peaches on one tree and grapes on another is not in the soil, but in the trees. Hence we must distinguish *the working itself* from the shade, the tone, the character, the peculiar property which that working assumes. The wind that produces sweetest music from the Eolian harp, by blowing through a broken window-pane produces doleful sounds. It is one operation but different effects. In the meadow next to the tender clover grows the poisonous wolf's-milk. Yet both lift their little heads from the same soil and drink in the same air, sunlight, and rain. Although the vital energy is the same, the difference in the seeds causes difference in the plants, and opposite effects.

The same applies to the garden of the soul, where the human life is in full activity. But that same human life produces a base act today and a heroic act tomorrow. There is but one working, but the colors vary, it may be white or black, dark or light.

And this we find, that in the garden of the soul all *spontaneous* growth is a growth of *weeds;* while the seed which God has planted produces precious *fruit.* The effects of sanctification are evident. It causes sweet waters to flow from a bitter fountain. It lends to every operation its own quality and property, and gives it a direction which works for good. And thus good works proceed from the man lost in himself.

Of course, in the root, this apparently identical working is *twofold.* One springs from the old nature, the other from the new; the one from the natural, the other from the supernatural. But since this distinction was discussed at large in the chapter on Regeneration, we treat it now simply from *the unity of the person.*

Although we heartily agree with the Confession, "That a regenerated person has in him a twofold life: the one *temporal* and *corporeal,* that which he has from the first birth and is common to all men; the other *spiritual* and *heavenly,* which is given him in the second birth, and which is peculiar to God's elect" (art. 35); yet this does not affect the *unity* of the person, nor does it alter the fact that the operations of both the old and the new life are *my* operations. If I divide my person, and take the natural and the supernatural each by itself, then there is no sanctification at all; for the corrupt life of my old nature is not sanctified, but crucified, dead, and buried; and my heavenly, spiritual, and regenerated life cannot be sanctified inasmuch as it never was sinful nor ever can be. Hence in sanctification we have to consider life from the viewpoint of the *unity* and *indivisibility* of the person. The man who was first wedded to the corrupt nature, and who is now wedded to the new man, was then evil and is now to become good; wherefore his life must receive the holy desire, inclination, and disposition. And then only it is possible for it to produce good works.

A work is *good* when it is conformable to the divine law.

1. The *first point* is that God alone possesses the right to determine what is good or evil.

Man also can acquire this discernment, but only by being taught of God. But as soon as he presumes himself to determine the difference between good and evil, He violates the divine majesty and God's inalienable right to be God. Not *one* man, nor *many* men, nor all men and angels together may do this. It does not belong to them. It is the eternal prerogative of the Almighty Creator of heaven and earth. He alone determines good and evil, for every creature, for time and eternity.

That which He demands of each life shall be the law of that life, of all that belongs to it, and under all circumstances; a law in which all the divine ordinances are comprehended. His law, though its principles are briefly comprehended in the Ten Commandments, rises from these ten stems in branches and boughs broad and dense, and forms in its completeness one immeasurable roof of leaves which overshadows the entire human family in all its variegations.

Hence there is not the remotest chance here to compromise. God's will and law are absolute; rule over all; are binding in every domain, and can never be repealed. And where, in the delicate works of a watch, the thousandth part of a millimeter is allowed to a wheel for variation, in the divine law such play is unthinkable. The law of God brooks not even the deviation of a hair's breadth, nor of any infinitesimal fraction thereof.

Hence a good work does not signify a work merely *not evil;* nor a work containing some good, or simply passable; nor a work whose good intention is evident. But a good work is nothing else and nothing less than a *good* work. And it is not good unless it is absolutely good, that is, in all its parts equally conformable to the divine will and law. A peach is not half a pear and half a grape, but absolutely a peach; so a good work is not merely passable, partly well intentioned, but absolutely conformable to what God has determined to be good with regard to that work.

It is readily seen that unless sanctification were adapted to enable man to perform such a work, he would never accomplish it. As it is the peculiar habit of a peach tree, through its ascending life, to impart to the fruit the flavor of the peach, and of the grapevine to give to its fruit the flavor of the grape, so it is the peculiar quality of the soul sanctified in principle to impart to its fruit the flavor of the *law.* Sanctification does not merely inspire the soul with a desire for something higher, but it imparts to it such a disposition, tone, shade, flavor, and character that it yields to the divine law. And the law puts its impress upon the soul. The soul's aspiration is no more a vague ideal, but is has a positive pleasure in and a desire and love for all the commandments of God. And, since sanctification engrafts the law upon the soul, it is possible that the working which follows should be conformable to the law.

We say "possible," for from his own sad experience God's child knows that it is possible to be *otherwise,* and that many summers come and go without reaping from *his* branches any noticeable harvest for the glory of God.

2. This brings us to the *second point. A good work must be of faith.*

Sanctification itself is not of faith. It has nothing to do with faith. It is wrought by God Himself. What could faith then accomplish in this respect?

But it is different with reference to *good works;* for they must be *our* good works. Man is and should be passive in all other respects, but not in his *work.* Work is the *end* of one's passive condition. To work and to be passive are opposites. To imagine that work can be passive or actively passive is like imagining that a circle is square, that ink is white, that water is dry. Wherefore the Heidelberg Catechism rightly asks: "Why must *we* still do good works?"

Hence there can be no good work unless it is wrought by *ourselves.* And every representation as though man did not perform good works, but that the Holy Spirit performs them in him and in his place, is to subvert the Gospel and to wrest the Scripture.

The work of Christ is vicarious, that of the Holy Spirit is not. He works *in* man, but not *in his place.* And however extensive His work may be in us, being wrought independently of us, it can never be counted as our own. Christ died and rose from the dead for us and independently of us. But the Holy Spirit cannot draw fruit from the tree except our ego executes the work.

But—and this should be emphasized—our ego cannot execute it except "the work is wrought in us with power." The inward higher life does not act like the sap in the vine, for this enters the vine *naturally.* But the working of the holy life is different. Although a holy disposition is implanted, God's child does not produce any good fruit of himself. Although well-furnished and well-equipped, if left to himself he produces nothing; not a single good work, however small.

The most skillful diamond-cutter, though supplied with the best tools, cannot furnish the smallest diamond rose except the proprietor of the establishment gives him the diamond, the steam-power in his tools, and even the gas-light upon his hands. In like manner it is impossible for the most excellent among God's children, though their souls be well equipped, to furnish a single good work, except the Proprietor of the holy-art establishment gives them the material, the power, and the light.

Hence the content and entire form of every good work is not of man, but of the Holy Ghost, so that when it is finished we owe thanks to God, and not He to us. In every man who performs a good work He works both to will and to do.

But when the Holy Spirit has furnished everything necessary, then one thing is still lacking, viz., *that the saint do it* and make the work his own. And this is the wonderful act of faith.

There is not one good work which God has not prepared before, that we should walk in it; and this is why it is not wrought until *we walk in it.* The Lord says to Ezekiel, "I will cause you to walk in my statutes," but the Lord does not cause us to walk therein until we actually walk in them. We shall neither be carried nor be wheeled into them. This would have no value before the divine Majesty; that would be no art. Even we can wheel the cripple in his carriage, but the art of making him to walk, yea, even to leap as a hart, is not human, but worthy of God alone. And we may not allow this to be taken from Him by a sickly mysticism, and thus rob God of this glory.

To say, as many do, that the Lord carries His children *imperceptibly* into good paths, and that this constitutes their *good works,* is to despise holy things. No one should touch the honor of our God; and we may not rest until the pure doctrine burns again from the candlestick: that the power of God is manifest in the fact that He causes the cripple to *walk, to run,* and *to leap as a hart.*

And this is the act of faith, that is, that wonderful act of the soul of casting itself into the deep, knowing that it shall fall into the everlasting arms of mercy, though it is utterly unable to see. Faith in this respect is to agree with the divine will; to accept the good work which God has prepared for us, as our own; to appropriate to ourselves what God gives us.

An awkward schoolboy has to make a speech before a strange audience. It is a difficult task, and he does not even know how to begin. All his own efforts are useless. Then his father calls him and says: "If you commit this little speech which I have prepared, and recite it without missing a word, it will be a success." And the boy obeys. There is nothing of himself—it is all his father's work; he merely believes that what his father has prepared for him is good. And in this confidence he goes before the strange audience, delivers his father's composition, and succeeds. However, the writing of the speech did not end the matter, and it could not be ended until the boy had done his part. When God has prepared the good work for us, the matter is not ended until we do what God has prepared for us.

Coming home the boy does not proudly ask a reward, but with gratitude he embraces his father for his love and faithfulness. Having obtained success, God's children are profoundly thankful for their Father's excellent help; and they acknowledge that they owe it all to Him. And if He is pleased to give them a reward, it is not because they have deserved it; for if it were a question of desert, the children would have to give everything to the Father! But it is merely a reward of love for the future support of their faith.

16

Self-Denial

If any man will come after Me, let him deny himself, and take up his cross, and follow Me.—Matthew 16:24.

Good works are not the saint's sanctification, any more than drops of water are the fountain, but they spring as crystal drops from the fountain of sanctification. They are good, not when the saint intends them to be good, but when they conform to the divine law and proceed from a true faith. Yet the *intention* is of great importance; the Church has always taught that a work could not be called good unless it is directed *to the glory of God.*

This is a vital point which must animate and give direction to the whole matter: *only to the glory of God.* Every other intention makes the good work evil. Even the effort to do good works is impossible without the "Soli Deo Gloria."

This is the reason why so many well-meant efforts at so-called sanctification become sinful. For the man who applies himself earnestly and diligently to good works, solely to attain a holier status and thus become a holier person, has lost his reward. His end in view is not God, but himself; and while every good work humbles a man and real sanctification leads to the breaking down and casting out of self, this wrongly planned sanctification causes self-exaltation and spiritual pride.

To think that by self-sanctification God is honored and His glory exalted is self-deception. The divine honor and majesty are so holy and exalted that His glory must be the direct end in view. To work for self-sanctification *directly*, and for His honor *indirectly*, is unworthy of His holiness.

The end and aim of all things must be the Lord God alone. Justice must dwell in the land, not only to preserve order, but to remove iniquity from before the presence of the Lord. The missionary cause must be supported not only to convert souls, but to summon the nations to appear in Zion before God. Prayer must be offered not only to obtain the good which is bestowed without prayer, but because every creature, morning and evening, must lie in the dust, crying, "Holy, holy, holy is the Lord!" making the whole earth full of His glory. And hence every creature *must* do good works, and all the children of God *can* do good works; not that they may become a little more holy, but that the glory of holiness might shine to the praise of our God.

3. This *third point* should therefore never be omitted. Though our works are according to the law and of faith, but not directed to the glory of God, they cannot please Him. It avails nothing, though the bow be strongly bent and the cord of the best material, if the arrow upon the cord be not turned in the right direction.

The doctrine of Good Works touches the most delicate and most sensitive of our internal emotions, viz., *self-denial.*

Superficial minds, poor in grace and godliness, speak of self-denial but rarely, and then without understanding its meaning. They think that it consists in making room for others; in argument to be the least; to renounce pleasure or profit for a higher purpose; to care for others, not for self. Surely this is a precious fruit; earnestly to be desired; and if it were found more abundantly among the children of God we should thank Him for it. But, alas! there is such leanness of soul even in the most earnest, so much selfishness, ambition, anger, confidence in the creature, that every manifestation of nobler impulse has a most refreshing effect.

But the question now before us is this, whether such making room for others, such self-sacrifice, deserves the name of *self-denial.* And the answer must be a most emphatic "No!" The saint's self-denial has reference, not to *man,* but to *God,* and for this reason it is superlatively high and holy, difficult and almost impossible.

Of course God's child loves his heavenly Father, but not with an unalterable love. In spite of his love he is sometimes very unlovely. Still, when the question echoes through his soul, "Simon Bar-Jonah, lovest thou Me?" and he feels tempted by self-reproach to say, "No, Lord," then the response flashes from the bottom of his soul against all contradiction: "Yes, Lord, Thou knowest that I love Thee."

Therefore nothing would seem more natural than to find pleasure in denying himself for God's sake. And this is actually the case. He spends his happiest moments in sincere self-denial; for then he is never alone, but always with Jesus, whom he follows. Then he realizes the holiness and transcendent glory of the claim: "If any man will come after Me, let him deny himself, take up his cross, and follow Me."

But while the blessedness of his *former* self-denials is still fresh in his memory, when called to a new act of the same nature he shrinks from it and finds it almost impossible. Self-denial extends so far. Its depth cannot be fathomed. When the plummet has descended the whole length of the line, there is still such a yawning depth beneath that actually the bottom is never touched. It refers, not to a few things, but to all things. It embraces our entire life and existence, with all that is in us, of us, and around us; our entire environment, reputation, position, influence, and possession; it includes all the ties of blood and affection that bind us to wife and children, parents and brothers, friends and associates; all our past, present, and future; all our gifts, talents, and endowment; all the ramifications and extensions of our outward and inward life; the rich life of the soul and the tenderest emotions of our holier impulses; our conflict and our strife; our faith, hope and love—yea, our inheritance in the Son, our place in the mansions above, and the crown which the righteous Judge shall one day give us; and as such, in that entire scope of life, we must deny ourselves before God.

We are, to use an illustration, in all our life and existence like a fruit-tree, broadly rooted, full grown, planted in fertile soil, adorned with a crown of many branches and a glorious roof of leaves; and like that tree with its roots far and wide in the earth, and its branches high and broad in the air, are we deeply rooted, possessing an existence obtained by means of money, reputation, property, and descent, faith, hope, love, and the promises of God. And to that whole tree, to that entire unit, from deepest root to highest bough, which as our ego, full of might, and majesty, stands before our consciousness and in our life—to all this the ax must be laid; of all this the self-denying soul must say: "God is all and I am nothing."

Many say, "This is correct and exactly my idea," and say it quite too often; for when these most difficult and excellent words again and again pass the lips as mere hollow sounds, they strike a discord to the earnest, sensitive soul. But when we grasp the thought as an actual fact, then we find that this denial of our entire existence and being is almost entirely beyond our grasp. Self can minify itself to such extent that we really think that it is gone and denied, while at the same time it stands behind our back, grinning with Satanic glee. Self, big and inflated, is not hard to deny. In this way the unconverted stands before God, but not the saint. That has been taken from him. Such is no more the impulse of his desire. But self shrunk, reduced, partly unclothed, hiding behind pious emotions and piles of good works, is extremely dangerous. For what more is there to be *denied?* There is scarcely anything left. He seeks no longer the world, nor his own glory; his only end in view is the glory of God. At least, so he thinks. But he is mistaken. Self is there still. It is like a spring tightly bent for a time, but only to rebound with accumulated force. And what was called self-denial is really nothing else *than self taking care of its own.* And that is the worst of it, self is so dangerously cunning. The heart of man is "deceitful above all things and desperately wicked; who can know it?"

When we are inclined to sin, self leaves its hiding-place and with all its power labors hard to make us sin. But when the Holy Spirit woos and constrains us, weaning us from sin, then, slunk in a corner, it hides itself, decoying us into the delusion that it has ceased to be. It is then that, with evident satisfaction, deluded piety asks whether the denial of *self* is not complete.

But the true saint is known by this: while the self-deluded one is satisfied with this spiritual trickery, he is not. He discovers the trick. Then he reproaches himself. He drives self from its place of concealment. He scolds and curses that evil being that always stands between him and his God. And with groans he supplicates: "Almighty, merciful, and gracious God, have mercy upon me."

Self-denial is not an outward act, but an inward turning of our being. As the steamship is turned about by the rudder, which is swung by the means of a wheel, so there is within our being a rudder, or whatever you may call it, which is turned by a small wheel, and as we turn the entire craft either leeward or windward, we deny either self or God. In its deepest sense we *always* deny either the one or the other. When we stand well we deny *self;* in all other cases we deny *God.* And the internal wheel by which we turn the entire craft of our ego is our *intention.* The rudder determines the course of the ship; not its rigging and cargo, nor the character of the crew, but its *direction,* the destination of the voyage, its final haven. Hence, when we see our craft steering away from God, we swing the rudder the other way and compel it to turn toward God.

Notice the rigging and the cargo. The former may be magnificent: excellent talent, superior mind, a rich state of grace. The latter may be very precious: a treasure of knowledge, or moral power, of consecrated love, of melting and adoring piety. And yet with that excellent rigging and that precious cargo, we can steer our craft away from God and aim at self. Then only is there *self-denial* when, without regard to rigging and lading, a man causes his craft to run directly to the glory of God.

The *intention* is everything. And it is this very intention which can so bitterly mislead us. That small wheel of our intention is so exceedingly sensitive that a mere touch of the finger can reverse its action. This is why we are such ready believers in the goodness and beauty of our intentions.

Hence the need of deep, correct, intimate *knowledge of self.* And who possesses this? And since by His light the Holy Spirit constantly refines and chastens our self-knowledge, is it not perfectly natural that, while today we imagine ourselves to be quite advanced in self-denial, only next week we discover how bitterly mistaken we are?

To seek and look for one's highest good and eternal salvation, not in every creature, but in God; to use spiritual or material gifts not for ourselves, but for His glory; to esteem all perishable things of no account compared to the eternal; unwilling to be one's own lord, but as God's servant to enter His employ; no longer to possess any precious things, as money or treasure, or even one's children, as one's own, but to know oneself the appointed steward of the Lord; to have no more care or anxious thought, but renouncing every trust in man, in capital or fixed income, or in any other creature, to trust only and solely in the faithful

God; to be at peace with one's lot and with God's will; and, finally, to direct all intentions and emotions away from oneself upon the Beloved and Glorious One—is this not far-reaching? And can our own progress in regard to it ever satisfy us?

And yet such self-denial is required to render our works *good works* indeed, in which the angels can rejoice.

Thus the things which the Holy Spirit took from Christ to give unto us return to our Surety; for it is evident that not one of our good works can ever be complete in that sense. Our self-denial is never perfect. Hence the sad complaint that "our best works are ever polluted before God"; and the prayer for the cleansing even of our good works.

And this must be so; it has been divinely ordained that God's children shall never leave Christ. If they really obtained perfection they would lose sight of their Surety, but the fact that even their best effort is defiled drives them to Christ for the atonement and cleansing in His blood. *Self-denial is a fruit of the atonement made perfect only by the atonement.* And thus, in the growing and ripening of spiritual fruit, God uses our thoughts, words, and deeds as instruments of sanctification.

For does not the exercise of frequent self-denial and the subsequent yielding of the fruit of righteousness, under the Spirit's gracious operation, create holy habits in the soul? Is not in this way the natural bent of the heart transferred from Satan to God? And when the Holy Spirit makes these holy habits, this bent of the heart toward holiness, a permanent disposition, then we have become fellow workers with God in our own sanctification. Nor is it as though He did one part and we another, but He using our work as a chisel in the sculpturing of our own soul.

And from this motive the faithful ministers of the Word should persuade, incite, and constrain believers to be always abounding in the work of the Lord. Sanctification must be preached as with the mouth of loudest trumpet. The Church of Christ imperatively needs it. The word which declares that God is a God who justifieth the ungodly may not be severed from that other word: "Be ye holy, for I am holy." The operations of the Word and of the Holy Spirit flow together. Therefore every young disciple of Christ should not only confess His name and live according to the desires of his heart, but flee from worldly lusts to walk holily and sincerely before the Lord.

Ministers of the Word should be careful not to conceal the majesty of the Lord Jehovah behind the cross of Christ. The responsibility must be fearful, if ever it should appear that our preaching of the cross of Christ, instead of having smothered sin, had quenched holy living.

Second Chapter
Love

17

Natural Love

And hope maketh not ashamed; because the love of God is shed abroad in our hearts by the Holy Ghost which is given unto us—Romans 5:5.

Sanctification does not *exhaust* the work of the Holy Spirit. It is an *extraordinary* work, necessitated by man's *fall into sin. Love,* of which we now will treat, is His deepest and most proper work, which He would have wrought even if sin had *never been heard of;* which He will continue after death; which He works now already in the angels, and which He will continue in us in the mansions of the Father's house evermore. Necessarily, across the path of quickening love falls the dark shadow of that terrible operation of *judgment* and *hardening* which the Holy Spirit works in the lost. We will close with a sketch of *the unpardonable sin* against the Holy Ghost.

Our subject is not love in general, but *Love.* The difference is evident. Love signifies the only pure, true, *divine* Love; by love in general is understood every expression of kindness, attachment, mutual affection, and devotion wherein are seen reflections of the glory of Eternal Love.

Love in its general sense is also found in the world of animals; a love so strong sometimes that it shames man, casting reproach upon his conscience. The tenderness of the mother hen is proverbial. The same hen which at other times runs away at the distant approach of dog or cat, flies at the ugliest cat or fiercest bulldog when she has chickens to defend. Every mother bird defends her eggs at the price of her life. And although neither cat nor dog has the least consideration for the mother love of hen or duck, yet both manifest the same love for their young ones. The most blood-thirsty animals, even tigers and hyenas, are never more enraged than when the hunter approaches their whelps too closely. It is unnecessary to say that love in this sense has no moral value. Yet it is not valueless. Christ made the love of the mother hen a type of His own love for His people and for Jerusalem. And when our small boys are furious when they see the male rabbit kill his young while the female fights for them, there is in their boyish hearts a pure voice of praise for the superior love of that littler mother. However, praise for this love which is merely instinctive, increated, and irresistible belongs, not to the mother hen or mother lion, but to Him who created it in them.

Turning from the love of instinct to the world of men, we are surprised to meet phenomena closely resembling it. A coquettish maiden, apparently devoid of all devotion, becomes a wife and mother, and suddenly she seems to have been initiated into the mysteries of love. Her infant is the only object of all her thoughts. She suffers for it without complaint, fondles and cherishes it; and if a cruel dog were to attack the babe, as a heroine the otherwise timid maiden would fight the monster.

And yet with all these similarities there is a difference. Love in that mother is *weaker* than in the animal. For hours she can leave her child in the care of others, while the brooding mother bird scarcely leaves the nest at all. The former has affection for other members of the family, but the latter with shrieks drives away all that dare approach the nest. In a word, the animal's maternal love is more absolute, and in this respect excels the love of the young mother. But when the chickens are half-grown, the mother forgets and forsakes them; while the love of most mothers for their tender infants gradually assumes a nobler character, rising from *instinctive* love to *spiritual* love. A mother's power lies in the fact that she *prays* for her child.

Evidently we must distinguish here two kinds of love: a lower form which springs from the blood, which the mother has in common with the bird, but which is less constant; and a superior love of another sort lacking in the hen, by which the human far surpasses the animal.

This lower form is *from the blood;* not altogether instinctive as in the dove, yet nearly so, that is, independent of the moral development of the mother. This can be seen in girls of inferior moral development, who, when they become mothers, fall almost desperately in love with their babes; while in others, who stand much higher morally, maternal love is much more moderate. And this shows that the irresistible passion of maternal love lacks a higher motive. Like the animal's love it springs from nature. And when we see and enjoy the spectacle, we realize that the glory of it belongs, not to the woman, but to Him whose work we admire in the inclinations of the creature.

Next to this instinctive love we find in the mother something superior; not only in the few, but in all. And we say this in spite of the fact that there are unnatural mothers who are almost entirely devoid of this higher love. Only, it should be remembered, that the human soul contains much that is suppressed which one was active; that in dehumanized women, when only partly reclaimed, this nobler feature often reappears; yea, that in the lives of such mothers, amid sin and shame, there are momentary sparks of a higher love which illumine their moral darkness like a flash of lightning.

This higher grade of maternal love bears an entirely different character. The sight of the sweet and lovely babe may support it, but cannot account for it, nor produce it. It has a higher origin. Its sign is: a mother carrying her child to *holy Baptism.* For although much of this is done out of custom and from love of display, yet essentially it is the declaration that a human child is greater than young bird or animal's whelp. Even when the French Revolution had temporarily abolished *holy* Baptism, it replaced it by a sort of *political* baptism. The young mother is constrained to see in her child something greater than mere *"clods of infant flesh."* And although in many mothers it has become almost imperceptible, sunk so low that many have been seen to drag their children into the paths of sin; yet in nobler natures, and under more favorable circumstances, this refreshing parental love has the power to develop the energy of the moral growth of future generation. In understanding the difference between father and mother one will be able to distinguish this lower and higher mother love, even in their finer variations. Of course, the instinctive love is not so strong in the father as in the mother; hence the love which bears the moral character of duty and vocation is more conspicuous in the former.

But even where this wonderful mingling of *instinctive* and *moral* love in the mutual love of husband and wife manifests itself most beautifully, in *parental* love and by counter-action in *filial* love, and as a connecting link in *fraternal* love, it is still a form of love that can exist in total independence of the conscious love of God. Often it strongly expresses itself among pronounced unbelievers.

And the same is true of that freer expression of love which, independently of the ties of blood, often develops itself in beautiful forms between friends, between congenial minds, between comrades in the same struggle, between the leaders and the led; yea, which from the things visible can rise to embrace the things invisible, and unfold itself in fairest forms of love for art and science, for king and country, for the nation and its history, for inherited rights and privileges—in brief, for all that inspires the breast with the noble feelings of consecration and sacrifice. For, whatever its wealth and scintillating beauty may be, in itself it is apart from the Love of the Eternal. In order not to betray their accomplices, hardened criminals have endured cruel tortures upon the rack with marvelous constancy. Communists, dying upon the barricades of Paris in defense of the most blasphemous barbarism, have displayed a heroism similar to that of our heroes at Waterloo and Dogger-Bank. Profane and wanton soldiers have cast themselves upon the enemy with rare contempt of death. But in all these manifestations of love, blood heated by passion on the one hand, and impure motives on the other, may play their part and rob it almost entirely of its divine character.

Yea, even in its highest manifestations among men, such as pity for the suffering and mercy toward the fallen and perishing, it may still be devoid of the spark of *holy* Love. There are natural men who cannot bear the sight of suffering; who are so deeply affected by the heart-breaking spectacles of sorrow and mourning that they *must* show pity; to whom the offering of sympathy is a natural necessity; who count the soothing of other men's sorrow a joy rather than a sacrifice.

But even in this highest form, most closely approaching the divine mercies, it is frequently without any connection with the Eternal Love. It may be an impulse from instinct, an inclination from temperament, the effect of a noble example, or for the sake of fame almost everywhere obtainable by works of mercy, but the love of Christ is lacking. It is not the throbbing of the Love of God that vibrates in these manifestations. There is love that is to be appreciated, but the Love of which St. John declares that God is Love, is found only when the Holy Spirit enters the soul and teaches it to glory "in the love of God which is shed abroad in our hearts by the Holy Spirit which is given us."

18

Love in the Triune Being of God

God is Love—1 John 4:8.

Between *natural* love even in its highest forms and *Holy Love* there is a wide chasm. This had to be emphasized so that our readers might not mistake the *nature* of Love. Many say that God is Love, but measure His Love by the love of men. They study love's being and manifestations in others and in themselves, and then think themselves competent to judge that this human love, in a more perfect form, is the *Love of God.* Of course they are wrong. Essential Love must be studied as it is in God Himself; as He has manifested it in His Word. And the scintillations of the creature's feeble love must be looked upon only as sparks from the fire of the divine Love.

Our God is the very liberal Fountain of all good. Love being the highest good, God must be the very liberal Fountain of all Love. And from that Fountain flows every earthly love of whatever name, however faint or feeble. The Creator alone can create in His creature the irresistible love of *instinct,* in which we see a display of His glory. For the same end He created a strong creaturely attachment, *not wholly* instinctive, yet to some extent *unconsciously* active; to this belong the mother's love for her babe, love at first sight, brotherly love, etc. Higher than this is the love of *moral kinship,* whereby He has disposed spirit to spirit for congenial fellowship and mutual love. These are three forms in which is found something of the Love of God, but still belonging to

Creation and Providence, in no wise partaking of the treasure of the divine Life.

Love on earth adopts this higher character only when it becomes self-consecrating, self-denying, self-sacrificing; when the object of love does not attract, but only repels. The devoted nurse caring for the pest-stricken stranger finds nothing in him to attract her; rather the reverse. And still she stays, she perseveres, not only from a sense of duty, but attracted by the misery and desolation of the sufferer. This is indeed the effect of a higher love, which flows from the Fountain of Eternal Love. That nurse exhibits devotion to the invisible, apprehension of the spiritual.

And although God has so constituted our nervous system that suffering causes us discomfort, that the sight of pain affects us painfully, so that from a mere fellow feeling we are instantly ready to bear relief to the sufferer, yet that higher form of love usually rises from the lower nervous life to a higher expression which is impossible without an inward operation of grace.

It thus prepares the way for the highest love, that directs itself not only to the invisible *things,* but to the Invisible *One,* attracting the soul toward Him with irresistible drawings. And only then is Love itself reached.

The Word declares that God is Love, and the Spirit's testimony says in every heart: "Amen, not in us, but in Thee, O Eternal One. Thou art Love. There is no love that does not spring from Thee!" And this is a mystery that men and angels fail to fathom. Who ever expressed its perfection in words? Who does not realize that it is a harmony marvelously beautiful, blessed, and divine which the confused ear of the creature cannot fully appreciate? Men confess it, drink in its sweetness and loveliness; the heart is blessed and cherished by it, but after the bliss is tasted and the cup taken from the lips, we know no more of the nature of Love than the babe that has enjoyed love at his mother's breast. We cannot describe or analyze it; we cannot fathom or penetrate its hidden essence. It takes possession of us, pervades us, refreshes us, but as the wind, of which we know not whence it cometh and whither it goeth, so in our best moments are the wonderful drawings of the Love of our God. It is not created nor conceived. It is eternal as God Himself. Love was never outside of Him, so as to come to Him from elsewhere; nor for a single moment throughout eternity was He without it. Without bearing in Himself deep eternal Love, without being Love, He cannot be our God.

Superficial minds, however, conceive of the Love of God only as forgiving sin; as too good to tolerate suffering; too peaceable to allow war. But the Word teaches that the Love of God is a *holy* Love, intolerant of evil, for its own sake causing the sinner to suffer that he may turn from his false joys. It was this very Love that said in Paradise, immediately after the breach of sin: "*I* will put enmity!"

God's children have derived from the Word deeper and richer conceptions of the divine Love, for they confess a Triune God, Father, Son, and Holy Ghost, one God in three Persons: the Father, who generates; the Son, who is generated; and the Holy Spirit, who proceeds from both Father and Son. And the Love-life whereby these Three mutually love each other is the Eternal Being Himself. This alone is the true and real life of Love. The entire Scripture teaches that nothing is more precious and glorious than the Love of the Father for the Son, and of the Son for the Father, and of the Holy Spirit for both.

This Love is nameless: human tongue has no words to express it; no creature may *inquisitively* look into its eternal depths. It is the great and impenetrable mystery. We listen to its music and adore it, but when its glory has passed through the soul the lips are still unable adequately to describe any of its features. God may loose the tongue so that it can shout and sing to the praise of eternal Love, but the intellect remains powerless.

Before God created heaven and earth with all their inhabitants, the eternal Love of Father, Son, and Holy Spirit shone with unseen splendor in the divine Being. Love exists, not for the sake of the world, but for God's sake; and when the world came into existence, Love remained unchanged; and if every creature were to disappear, it would remain just as rich and glorious as ever. Love exists and works in the Eternal Being apart from the creature; and its radiation upon the creature is but a feeble reflection of its being.

Love is not God, but God is Love; and He is sufficient to Himself to love absolutely and forever. He has no need of the creature, and the exercise of His Love did not begin with the creature whom He could love, but it flows and springs eternally in the Love-life of the Triune God. God is Love; its perfection, divine beauty, real dimensions, and holiness are not found in men, not even in the best of God's children, but scintillate only around the Throne of God.

The unity of Love with the Confession of the Trinity is the starting-point from which we proceed to base Love independently in God, absolutely independent of the creature or anything creaturely. This is not to make the divine Trinity a philosophic deduction from essential love. That is unlawful; if God had not revealed this mystery in His Word we should be totally ignorant of it. But since the Scripture puts the Triune Being before us as the Object of our adoration, and upon almost every page most highly exalts the mutual Love of Father, Son, and Holy Spirit, and delineates it as an *Eternal* Love, we know and plainly see that this holy Love may never be represented but as springing from the mutual love of the divine Persons.

Hence through the mystery of the Trinity, the Love which is in God and is God obtains its independent existence, apart from the creature, independent of the emotions of mind and heart; and it rises as a sun, with its own fire and rays, outside of man, in God, in whom it rests and from whom it radiates.

In this way we eradicate every comparison of the Love of God with our love. In this way the false mingling ceases. In principle we resist the reversing of positions whereby arrogant man had succeeded in copying from himself a so-called God of Love, and into silencing all adoration. In this way the soul returns to the blessed confession that God is Love; and the way of divine mercy and pity is opened whereby the brightness of that Sun can radiate in a human way, that is, in a finite and imperfect manner to and in the human heart, to the praise of God.

19

The Manifestation of Holy Love

And we have known and believed the love that God hath to us—1 John 4:16.

The question which now presents itself is: In what way is the divine, majestic act of making man a partaker of true love accomplished? We answer that this is—

1. Prepared by the Father in Creation.
2. Made possible by the Son in Redemption.
3. Effectually accomplished by the Holy Spirit in Sanctification.

There is in this respect, *first* a work of the *Father,* which the Heidelberg Catechism designates, "Of God the Father and our Creation," following the example of St. Paul, who wrote: "But to us there is but one God the Father, of whom are all things" (1 Cor. 8:6). By this we do not mean to deny that God the Father works also in redemption and in sanctification, for all the outgoing works of God belong to the three Persons. We only wish to indicate that seeking for the *origin* of things, one cannot stop at the Holy Spirit, for He proceedeth from the Son and the Father; nor at the Son, for He is generated by the Father, but at the Father, for He neither proceedeth from anyone, nor is He generated.

In this Scriptural sense we say, that the work of making man a partaker of Love is prepared by the Father in creation.

For every exercise of love, both in man and animal, finds its ground in *creation.* In the animal God created instinctive love directly; in the man He created love by making all men of one blood, by ordaining husband and wife to be each other's helpmeets, and by creating in the blood itself that wonderful attraction of the one to the other.

Moreover, He also implanted in man's consciousness the *sense* of love. The animal loves, but without knowing it. On the contrary, not only does man feel the *impulse* of love, but this impulse is also reflected in the mirror of his soul wherein he beholds the *beauty* of love; thus he learns to cherish love and to rise to the act of loving with full consciousness.

Finally, by His providence, which is but an effect of creation, the Father ordains that man should meet man, come into contact with man, that in this way the sense of love may become *active* in him. For whether it be a poor sufferer whose distress arouses my love, or a bold character that appeals to my sympathy, or lastly a pure and beautiful figure that attracts me irresistibly, it is always God the Father who allots me these meetings, who by His providential leadings makes the kindling of love possible.

This is followed, *in the second place,* by the work of the *Son,* who became flesh to reveal to us the fullness of divine Love in the flesh. Hence the manifestation of Love in the *redemptive* work.

This is entirely different from what the Father did in creation; for, although in creation divine love was foreshadowed, its conception implanted, and its imperfect exercise made possible, yet the divine Love itself was not revealed. But it is revealed in the advent of the Son: "For God so loved the world that He gave His only-begotten Son, that whosoever believeth on Him might not perish, but have everlasting life"; "Herein is love, not that we loved God, but that He loved us, and gave us His son to be a propitiation for our sins." This is the "Peace on earth, good will toward men" of which the angels sang in the fields of Bethlehem; this is the mystery that the angels desire to look into.

Here we notice again two things:

First, the Love wherewith God loved the world proven by the fact that he spares not His own Son, but delivers Him up for us all.

Second, the love of Christ for the *Father,* whose work He finished, and *for us,* whom He saved.

The *second* is of greatest importance to us. In Christ, whom we honor as God manifest in the flesh, the divine Love is seen; in Him it appeared and scintillated with all-surpassing brightness. The reality of the divine Love appeared to men for the first time and once for all in Him: "That which we have heard, which we have seen with our eyes, which we have looked upon and our hands have handled, declare we unto you"; and that was always the glory of the eternal Love which had captivated and pervaded their whole soul.

Until now men had walked in Love's shadow, but in Immanuel Love itself appeared in the flesh and after the manner of men. It was not merely a radiation of Love, its reflection, an increated feature, sense, or inclination, but the fresh, irresistible waves of Love's own constraining power issuing from the depths of His divine heart. It was this Love which, in the heart of Immanuel, brought heaven down to earth, and which by His ascension to heaven uplifted our world to the halls of eternal light. Even though Europe had felt nothing of it, and America had never thought of a Savior, though Africa had not heard the tidings, and it was but a small spot in Asia where His feet pressed the ground, yet it was the heart of Immanuel that bound every continent and the world—yea, the very universe around it, to the divine Mercy.

That Love shone forth as a love for an *enemy*. Man had become the enemy of God: "There is none that doeth good, no not one." The creature hated God. The enmity was absolute and terrible. There was nothing in man to attract God; rather everything to repel Him. And when all was enmity and repulsion, then the Love of God was made manifest in that Christ died for us when we were enemies.

Love among men and animals rests upon mutual attraction, sympathy, and inclination; even the love that relieves the sufferer feels the power of it. But here is a love that finds no attraction anywhere, but repulsion everywhere. And in this fact sparkles the sovereign liberty of divine Love: it loves because it will love, and by loving saves the object of its love.

Since this Love attained its severest tension on Calvary, its symbol is and ever shall be the Cross. For the Cross is the most fearful manifestation of man's enmity; and by the very contrast the beauty and adorableness of divine Love shine most gloriously: Love that suffers and bears everything, Love that can die voluntarily, and in that death heralds the dawn of a still more glorious future.

But even the work of the Son does not finish the work of putting the impress of God's Love upon the human heart. Wherefore, as the Creation is followed by the Incarnation, so does Pentecost follow the Incarnation; and it is God the *Holy Spirit* who accomplishes this *third work* by His descent into the heart of man.

"It is expedient for you that I go away; for if I go not away, the Comforter will not come unto you." This implies that the Holy Ghost would give the disciples still a higher good than the Son could give them. This is not independently of the Son; for the Scripture teaches emphatically that He neither will nor can do anything without the Son, and that He receives of the Son only to give unto us. However, the difference remains that, although Jesus suffers and dies and rises again for us, nevertheless the actual work in the souls of men awaits the gracious operation of the Holy Spirit. It is, as St. Paul writes to the Romans, that "the Love of God is shed abroad in our hearts by the Holy Ghost."

And this is the proper work of the Holy Spirit, that shall remain His forevermore. When there remains no more sin to be atoned for, nor any unholiness to be sanctified, when all the elect shall jubilate before the throne, even then the Holy Spirit shall perform this divine work of keeping the Love of God actively dwelling in their hearts. *How,* we cannot tell, but this we understand, that it is the Holy Spirit who, being the *same in all, unites* all souls in blessed union. When at the same moment spiritual life is wrought in your soul and mine and in the souls of others, the mutual bond of Love must be the result. For, although men and things are grounded in the Father, and the souls of the redeemed are united in the Son, yet personally to enter into every soul, making it His temple and dwelling-place, is the work of the Holy Spirit.

Hence it is the same Spirit who as God enters the heart of every one of the redeemed, and as God performs and perfects His work in every heart irresistibly. And, though different circumstances and manifold sins have caused differences of opinion among the persons in whom the same Holy Spirit has been at work, so that at times they have held strongly opposite views, yet the fact of their inward union remains, which by the working and indwelling of the Holy Spirit in their hearts is made a real and even indissoluble union.

This may not always come to the surface, but inwardly the matter is all the more real and glorious. Moreover, the Holy Spirit is always actively at work to remove every outward obstacle. And if this is not altogether a success before we die, there is no need of fear so long as in death the scales shall, as it were, fall from our eyes, and Love shall conquer. Compared to eternity, life on earth is but a moment. Hence it may not be denied that the bond of union, the intertwining and interlacing that must bind the children of God together in the divine fire of Love, is, by the working and indwelling of the selfsame Spirit, a real fact. It is the selfsame Holy Spirit who, dwelling in every heart, directs them altogether to one end, who, consecrating every soul to be His tabernacle, in that He is God and therefore Love, brings it about that, in and through and with Himself, the Love of God is shed abroad in every heart. Think of Him as banished from their souls, and the Love of God has fled from their hearts, but let every grace be concealed and slumbering, let the outward appearance deny the inward grace, so long as we are assured that the Holy Spirit dwells in our hearts we may rest assured that even the Love of God dwells in us.

Moreover, the Holy Spirit is not a *Stranger* in our hearts, but penetrates our deepest selfhood and brings to each of us a gift, a word, a consolation peculiarly adapted to our individual need. Of course this is a much-varied work, but, despite its multiformity, it is not a *pieced* work without inward connection, but an executing of the plan of the Father in accordance with the eternal counsel. Wherefore, however delicate its nature may be, it is always aiming at that pure and perfect harmony which in God's counsel is prepared not only for every one of the redeemed, but for the whole house of God, and the body of Christ in all its proportions.

As the selfsame Spirit, He not only works in all, uniting all, but, since He proceeds from Father and Son, He also arranges and directs His work in one soul with regard to that in another, so that the interlacing and welding together of the souls of the saints *must* be the result. When according to the same glorious plan one Worker works in all, then every wall of separation must fall; Love must prevail, and all its sweet and blessed influence be felt: not as something that proceeds from ourselves and belongs to us, but as a Love even foreign to us, which coming from God penetrates and refreshes the soul; not the mere ideal of enthusiasts, but a divine power that masters and overcomes us; not an abstract conception merely charming us, but the Holy Spirit whom we feel and discover in the soul as Love; a warm, full, blessed outpouring of Love that is stronger than death and that many waters cannot quench.

20

The Love Which Dwells in the Heart

It is like the precious ointment upon the head, that ran down upon the beard, even Aaron's beard; that went down to the skirts of his garments—Psalm 133:2.

The fact that love can radiate within man does not insure him the possession of true and real Love, unless, according to His eternal counsel, God is pleased to enter into *personal* fellowship with him. So long as man knows Him only from afar and not near, God is a stranger to him. He may admire His Love, have a faint sense of it, be pleasantly affected by it, and even rejoice to see others drink from its Fountain, yet never come a step nearer to it. In God's hand he may be the means of showing others the way to it, without knowing it by personal experience.

The true Love is one with and inseparable from God. It may radiate its brightness even in the animal, but Love itself cannot enter the heart except God come first. And God's elect have the royal privilege of calling this gift their own. All their wealth and treasure consist in the fact that from the hand of their Lord they have received this gold tried in the fire.

Not, however, as though this love, wholly possessing them, shall henceforth be of all their actions the only impulse. From St. Paul we learn that, while the Love of God is shed abroad in our hearts by the Holy Ghost, much evil may be found among us; wherefore we are admonished to exercise patience and self-denial. But though, like faith, Love may be in the germ and nothing be visible on the surface, in the warm soil, germ-like, it may swell, sprout, and strike out its roots in the ground. Hence, however defective and incomplete its form, Love itself dwells in our hearts; and by our own experience we are conscious of it. Who of God's children does not recall the blessed moments when this Love fell upon the soul as mild dew drops upon the thirsty leaf, filling him with a felicity unknown heretofore? This blessed experience was heavenly and supernatural. The soul actually felt the everlasting arms underneath, and acknowledged that God is good and essentially Love. It is true the divine Majesty as it were consumed the soul, but at the same time it uplifted and glorified it. The soul realized that it was surrounded by Love, uplifted above the low plain of vanity, and, more blessed still, that it had received power to embrace God with the arms of its own love. It is true this does not last. The evening star of hope is followed again and again by the dawn of the common, everyday life, but by that experience we have seen the heavens opened, the sign of Eternal Love descending, and heard the music of its voice saying: *"Behold your God."*

Hence these *two* must always go together: (1) Love shed abroad in our hearts by the Holy Ghost, and (2) the glad tidings that our God has come to us. And these are one and the same, for, as we have seen before, when the Eternal One comes to dwell with man, it is not the Father, nor the Son, but the *Holy Spirit* whose office is to enter into man's spirit and to establish the most intimate relation between him and God. The Father and the Son will also come to dwell with him; the Son is even said to stand at the door and knock waiting to be admitted, but both Father and Son do this through the Holy Spirit. These three are One: the Holy Spirit is in the creation, but only through His essential union with the Father and the Son. He is also in the redemptive work, for He is bound to the pleasure of the Father and the Incarnation of the Son. In like manner both the Father and the Son dwell in the saints, but only through the Holy Spirit.

If witnessing of the Holy Spirit were only momentary, if He came to tarry only for a night, the blessed work of Love could not be wrought.

And if He had to leave the saints in one part of the world to visit others in other parts, it would be altogether out of the question. But He is God, unlimited: in my closet He abides with me just as really as with thousands in all parts of the earth at the same time; and not only with the saints below, but in a higher sense in all the redeemed already arrived in the heavenly Jerusalem. As the sun shines brightly into your chamber, while it radiates light and heat upon millions in distant lands, so is the operation of the Holy Spirit not local and limited, but divinely omnipresent in you and me, though neither knows the other's face nor yet has heard his name.

For the Holy Spirit does not dwell in our hearts as we dwell in our house, independent of it, walking through it, shortly to leave it, but He so inheres in and cleaves to us that, though we were thrown into the hottest crucible, He and we could not be separated. The fiercest fire could not dissolve the union. Even the body is called the temple of the Holy Spirit; and though at death He may leave it at least in part, to bring it again in greater glory in the resurrection, yet as far as our inward man is concerned, He never departs from us. In that sense He abides with us forever.

Distressed and overwhelmed by the sense of guilt and shame, we may cry with David: "Take not Thy Holy Spirit from me!" but His indwelling in our souls cannot be destroyed. An ancient temple was remarkable for the fact that, although visitors came and went, and successive generations brought their sacrifices to the altar, yet the same idol remained for ages standing behind that altar immovable and steadfast. St. Paul wrote about the temple of the Holy Spirit, not to the people of Jerusalem, but to the Corinthians; wherefore it is evident that he borrowed his image from the idol-temple in their city, and not from that of Jerusalem. He meant to say that, as the image of Diana dwelt in the temple of Corinth permanently and without being removed, so does the Holy Spirit dwell permanently and steadfastly in the souls of the called of God.

David says of Love: "It is like the precious ointment upon the head, that ran down upon the beard, that went down to the skirts of his garments" (Ps. 133:2)—a figure not very attractive for us who are unfamiliar with perfumed oils. But when you remember that the oil used for the anointing of the high priest was fragrant and volatile, so that when the precious bottle was opened it filled the whole house with its fragrance, you will appreciate the beauty of the figure; for when the golden oil is poured out upon the head and runs down the flowing robe of the high priest, its all-pervading fragrance is found the next morning in the trailing hem of the garment. The high priest, in his robes of office, is the image of the Church of the living God, and his head the image of Christ. The anointing oil represents the Holy Spirit, who, being poured out upon the head of Christ, flows down from Him upon all who belong to His glorious, mystical body; reaching down so far that even the least esteemed, who are but as the hem of His garment, are pervaded by the selfsame precious ointment.

This beautiful figure illustrates the unity which, as the fruit of Love, is wrought by the selfsame Holy Spirit who in all ages, among all nations, in all tongues and languages, enters into the hearts of God's elect, abiding with them, planting Himself in them, never to leave them; who dwelling and working in all not according to His own choice, but according to the disposition of the members in the body of Christ, under Him as their glorious Head, has established the most blessed fellowship between that Head and the members; has entered every heart and penetrated to its deepest stratum; has united the whole assembly of the elect into one glorious, concordant whole, in perfect Love, now and forever.

And this mighty fact, that the selfsame Holy Spirit dwells and works in all, is not only the prophecy of Love, but the demonstration of the fact that Love exists, and that every disturbing element is but the dust that still covers the diamond, and the dross that prevents the glittering of the gold. God the Holy Spirit lives, is, and feels Himself One in all God's children; and although each experiences this in his own way, and expresses it in his own tongue, it is One and the Same who comforts and works in them all.

Hence the Holy Spirit who dwells in us, loves His own work which He works in others. The Holy Spirit in one, cannot deny Himself in another. From this it follows that the indwelling of the same Holy Spirit in all not only guarantees a real and substantial unity for the future and for the present, whether visible or invisible, but the very fact itself causes the Love of God to be shed abroad in the hearts of the saints, since the Holy Spirit *must* always love *Himself.*

If He merely hovered over the *surface* of the soul's life, this would not mean much, but there can be no stratum in the soul so low that He does not penetrate it. The fountain that He has opened in us pours forth from the spot where the first pulsations, the deepest motives and workings of the new man, originate. On the surface we may therefore cherish another love, but when, deceived and disappointed by that love, with contrite hearts we feel that the creature cannot be trusted, then we find on the bottom of our own soul the same old, faithful, blessed, and divine Love by which the Holy Spirit comforts us and teaches us to comfort others. Even though at times of indifference all may seem lost, we need not fear, for as soon as the foundations of the soul are uncovered the presence of that eternal Love manifests itself. Underneath, in the hidden, mystic life, lies the foundation of all love in the presence of the Holy Spirit.

God is Love, and through the Holy Spirit Love dwells in all God's children; and these children united under their glorious Head in one body are one—one by the same new birth, by the same life, and the same Love; and, if it were possible at once to remove all earthly rubbish and pollution, we would *see* the sparkle of that Love in all and among all, beautiful and glorious.

21

The Love of the Holy Spirit in Us

O Jerusalem, Jerusalem, . . . how often would I have gathered thy children together, even as a hen gathereth her chickens under her wings, and ye would not—*Matthew 27:37.*

The Scripture teaches not only that the Holy Spirit dwells in us, and with Him Love, but also that He *sheds abroad that Love in our hearts.*

This *shedding abroad* does not refer to the coming of the Holy Spirit's Person, for a *person cannot* be shed abroad. He comes, takes possession, and dwells in us, but that which is shed abroad must consist of numberless particles. The verb "to pour out" (to shed abroad) is used primarily of water, grain, or fruit; that is, of liquids or solids composed of parts or particles of one kind, passing from one vessel into another. In Scripture the verb is used metaphorically. Hannah said: "I have poured out my soul before the Lord"; the Psalmist: "Pour out your heart before Him"; Isaiah: "They poured out a prayer before Him." "To pour out" always signifies that the heart is filled to overflowing with so many complaints, cares, griefs, or distresses that it can no longer contain them, but pours them out before God or men in groans and prayers.

With reference to God, we read that He poured out the fierceness of His anger upon His enemies; and again, "that He shall pour out the Spirit of prayer and supplication." In the *first* passage, the metaphor is borrowed from the hail-storm which overtakes the traveler and prostrates him. So shall the blows of divine wrath descend like hail upon the heads of its enemies and prostrate them. And in the *second* it is signified that with overwhelming power His people shall be constrained to prayer.

In this latter sense, the Scripture frequently applies it to the advent of the Holy Spirit. Both prophets and apostles declare that the Lord shall pour out His Spirit upon all. Finally, we read that the Holy Spirit was poured out. But even here the *primary* meaning of the word must be retained, for by the outpouring of the Holy Spirit we understand the flowing down into our hearts, or into the Church, of a multitude of powers of the same kind that fill the emptiness of the soul.

It may be objected—and this deserves careful consideration—that in this thought we contradict our former statement, that it is the Holy Spirit, the Third Person in the Trinity, who takes possession of the heart and dwells therein; for we now say that it is, not the *Person* who *comes in,* but a *working,* an *element,* a *power* which is *poured out.* But, instead of being contradictory, these two are the same; only, by their mutual connection, they give us a more correct insight—and that is just what we need. When I carry a lighted lamp into a dark room, *I enter* as the light-bearer, while at the same moment the light is *poured out* in the room. These two should not be confounded. I am not poured out, but the light. I enter the room, but the light is carried into it. And this is exactly what the Holy Spirit does. When He enters the heart the brightness of His Person is poured out therein.

It is true that in these cases the Holy Spirit is mentioned in a somewhat *modified* sense, but when we speak of the light the same is true. Of an approaching light we say, "There comes the light," although we know that someone carries the light. At sunrise we say, "The sun is rising," although it would be more correct to say: "The light of the sun is rising." In like manner the name of the Holy Spirit is used in Scripture in a twofold way: *first,* with reference to the Third Person in the Trinity; *secondly,* with reference to the heavenly brightness and blessed activity which He carries with Himself. And instead of being more or less incorrect, this twofold use of the name is much more correct with reference to the Holy Spirit than when it refers to artificial light or to the sun. We should remember that there is a difference between the lamp and its radiating light; and that the immense body of the sun and its light are also two different things. But this is not so with reference to the Holy Spirit. There is no difference between Himself and His operations. We make the distinction to assist our representation, but in reality it has no existence. Where the Holy Spirit is, there He works; and where He works, there is the Holy Spirit. They are the same. The one is even unthinkable without the other.

There is an advantage in the use of the metaphor "to pour out." It teaches that the dwelling of the Holy Spirit in the congregation of the elect is neither inactive, nor from compulsion keeping himself aloof from their persons, but that He cannot come among them with *pouring Himself out* in them. And, dwelling in the elect, He does not slumber, nor does He keep an eternal Sabbath, in idleness shutting Himself up in their hearts, but as the divine Worker He seeks from within to fill their individual persons, pouring the stream of His divine brightness through every space.

But we should not imagine that every believer is instantly filled and permeated with that brightness. On the contrary, the Holy Spirit finds him filled with all manner of evil and treachery. Iniquities are piled up on every side. Horrible sins rise from underneath. The consciousness of his bitter, spiritual misery harasses him. Moreover, his heart is divided by many walls and partitions. Even the brightest light cannot penetrate the whole at once; and by far the greater part remains for the present at least in deepest darkness.

From this it follows that, when the Holy Spirit has entered man's heart, His task is not ended, but only just begun—a task so difficult that the power of the Holy Spirit alone can perform it. His method of procedure is not with divine power to *force* a man as though he were a stock or block, but by the power of love and compassion so to influence and energize the impulses of the feeble will that it feels the effect, is inclined, and finally consents to be the temple of the Holy Spirit.

Being once firmly established, He gradually subjects the most hidden impulses and intentions of the saint's personality to the power of His Love, in order thus to prevail. For this end He uses at once the *external* means of the preached Word which penetrates the consciousness and takes hold of the person, and the *internal* operation of blessing the

Word and making it effectual. This operation is different in each person. In one it proceeds with marvelous rapidity; in another, progress is exceedingly slow, being checked by serious reaction which in some rare cases is overcome only with the last breath. There are scarcely two men in whom this gracious operation is completely the same.

It may not be denied that the Holy Spirit often meets serious opposition on the part of the saint: not from enmity, for he is an enemy no more, but because he is commanded to depart from sin, to renounce his idols, his sinful affections, the many things that seem indispensable to his joy and life, and especially when, pointing to the cross, the Holy Spirit imposes sacrifices, pursues him with afflictions, covers him with ignominy. Then that opposition can become so strong and grievous that one would almost say: "He is no more a child of God."

And the Holy Spirit bears all this resistance with infinite pity, and overcomes it and casts it out with eternal mercy. Who that is not a stranger to his own heart does not remember how many years it took before he would yield a certain point of resistance; how he always avoided facing it, restlessly opposed it, at last thought to end the matter by arranging for a sort of *modus vivendi* between himself and the Holy Spirit? But the Holy Spirit did not cease, gave him no rest; again and again that familiar voice. And after years of resistance he could not but yield in the end; it became like fire in his bones, and he cried out: *"Thou, Lord art stronger than I; Thou hast prevailed."*

In this way the Holy Spirit breaks down every wall of partition, pouring out His light in all the heart's empty spaces, gradually opening every door, gaining access to the soul's most secret chambers, even to the vaults underneath the structure of our being, until finally, either *before* or *in* death, the outpouring of His brightness is complete in all our personality, and the whole heart has become His temple.

This task is executed only by means of Love. The Holy Spirit allows Himself to be grieved, provoked, and insulted, but He never yields. He is never weary of repeating the same thing to the ear that once was deaf. In our past or present there can be no sin, however base, of which He does not comfort us, which He does not pardon. He gives healing balm for every inner wound. He always has a word in good season for all that are weary. It is Love always filling us with shame, but at the same time ever uplifting, never despairing, unceasing in its devotion.

It is not merely a Love for men in general, but in the most exclusive sense a personal Love for the individual; not only Love for the redeemed taken as a multitude, but a Love individual, peculiarly tinted to meet the special peculiarity of our being. It is not only a pity for all who suffer, like that of the nurse for the patients of her ward, but Love that cannot meet the need of anyone else, but is for me personally just what it must and cannot otherwise be.

Hence the divine patience in winning *thee.* One might say: "There are thousands of others whom He might take and influence with much less trouble perhaps." But that is not the question. With all the depth of His divine Love He sought thee personally. It is Love in the richest, purest, tenderest sense of the word.

The Holy Spirit prevails by loving us, by proving His Love, by breathing Love, while, at the same time, His victory carries Love *into our hearts.* Allow Him to enter your soul, and He will carry Love therein, which imperceptibly imparts itself to your heart and inclination. We yield, not because we are compelled by superior power, but being drawn by Love, we are so affected that we cannot resist it.

And this is the glorious, divine, and beautiful art of which the Holy Spirit is the chief Artist. He alone understands it, and they whom He has taught. All other love is but a feeble shadow or faint imitation. Not until through Love the Holy Spirit has prevailed can Love enter our hearts, and then we, the formerly sinful and selfish, learn to appreciate Love.

22

Love and the Comforter

By the Holy Ghost, by love unfeigned—2 Corinthians 6:6.

The question is, In what sense is the *pouring out of Love* an ever-continued, never-finished work? Love is here taken in its highest, purest sense. Love which gives its goods to the poor and its body to be burned is out of the question. St. Paul declares that one may do these things and still be nothing more than a sounding brass, utterly devoid of the least spark of the true and real Love.

In 2 Corinthians 6:6 the apostle mentions the motives of his zeal for the cause of Christ; and it is remarkable that among them he mentions these three, in the following order: "By *goodness,* by the *Holy Ghost,* by *love unfeigned.*" Goodness indicates general benevolence and readiness to sacrifice; of these we find among worldly men many examples that make us ashamed. Then comes the stimulating and animating influences of the Holy Spirit; lastly, Love unfeigned which is the true, real, and divine Love.

In his hymn of eternal Love the apostle gives us an exquisite delineation of this "Love unfeigned," which shall not cease to command the admiration of the saints on earth as long as taste for heavenly melodies shall dwell in their hearts:

"Love suffereth long and is kind; Love envieth not; Love vaunted not itself, is not puffed up, doth not behave itself unseemly, seeketh not her own; is not easily provoked; thinketh no evil; rejoiceth not in iniquity, but rejoiceth in the truth; beareth all things, believeth all things, hopeth all things, endureth all things. Love never faileth. . . . For now we see in a mirror, darkly, but then face to face; now I know in part, but then I shall know even as also I am known. And now abideth faith, hope and love, these three, but the greatest of these is Love."

This teaches how the Holy Spirit performs His work of Love. And so, says the apostle, must the fruit of His work be in our hearts. Very well; if such is the glorious fruit of His work and men know the tree by its fruit, may we not conclude that this is but the description of His own work of Love?

The means employed by the Holy Spirit in the shedding abroad of the Love of God in our hearts is simply *Love.* By loving us He teaches love. By applying love to us, by expending love upon us, He inculcates love on us. It is the Love of the Holy Spirit whereby the shedding abroad of love in our hearts has become possible. As, according to 1 Corinthians 13, Love ought to manifest itself in our lives, *so* has the Holy Spirit wrought it in our hearts. With endless long-suffering and touching kindness He sought to win us. Of the love which we gave to the Father and the Son He was never envious, but rejoiced in it. His Love never made a display of us by leading us into unendurable temptations. It never impressed us as being self-seeking, but always as *ministering* love. It ever accommodated itself to the needs and conditions of our hearts. However much grieved, it was never provoked. It never misunderstood or suspected us, but ever stimulated us to new hope. Wherefore it rejoiced not in iniquity to sanctify it, but when the truth prevailed in us. And when he had strayed and done wrong, it covered the wrong whispering in our ear that it still believed and hoped all good things of us. Wherefore it endured in us all evil, all unloveliness, all contradictions. It failed us not as a lamp that goes out in the dark. The Love of the Holy Spirit *never faileth.* And while we enjoy here all its sweetness and tenderness, it prophesies that only hereafter it will manifest the fullness of its brightness and glory, for on earth it is only known in part. Its perfect bliss shall appear only when, looking no more by means of the glass at the phenomenal, we shall behold the eternal verities. For whatever may fail, being among all our spiritual blessing the highest, the richest, and therefore the *greatest,* Love shall abide forever.

In this way we begin to understand something of *Comfort.* Christ calls the Holy Spirit the "Comforter." He says: "I will send you *another* Comforter, and *He will abide with you forever."*

This does not refer to the "only comfort in life and death," for that consists in "that I am not my own, but belong unto my faithful Savior Jesus Christ" (Heid. Cat., q. 1). Christ speaks, not of comfort, but of the *Comforter.* Not a thing, an event, or a fact, such as the paying of the ransom of Calvary, but of a Person, who by His personal appearance actually comes to comfort us. Overwhelmed by distress and sorrow, we have not lost the *comfort,* for nothing can come to us without the will of our heavenly Father, but we may have lost the *Comforter.* It is one thing to be watching by the bedside of my sick child, and to remember that even this affliction may be to God's glory and a blessing to the child; and quite another when a faithful parent enters the room, and seeing my tears wipes them away; reading my sorrow seeks to drive it from my heart; with the warmth of his love cherishing me in the coldness of my desolation; and leaning my head against his breast looks me hopefully in the eye; and smoothing my brow, with holy animation, points me to heaven, inspiring me with trust in my heavenly Father.

Comfort is a deposited *treasure* from which I can borrow; it is like the sacrifice of Christ in whom is all my comfort, because on Calvary He opened to all the house of Israel a fountain for sin and uncleanness. But a comforter is a *person,* who, when I cannot go to the fountain nor even see it, goes for me and fills his pitcher and puts the refreshing drops to my burning lips. When Ishmael lay perishing with thirst, his mother's comfort was nearby in the cleft of the rock from which the water came gushing down; yet with comfort so near he might have died. But when the angel of the Lord appeared and showed her the water, then Hagar had found her *Comforter.*

And such is the Holy Spirit. So long as Jesus walked on earth He was the Comforter of His disciples. He lifted them when they stumbled; when discouraged and distressed by fear and doubt, He was their faithful Savior and Comforter. But Himself was not comforted. When in Gethsemane, being exceedingly sorrowful even unto death, He asked them for comfort, they could not give it to Him. They were powerless; they slept and could not watch with Him one hour. So He struggled alone, uncomforted and comfortless, until an angel came and did what sinners could not do comforting the Savior in His distress.

When about to depart from the earth, Jesus foreknew how desolate His disciples would be. They were weak, helpless, broken reeds. As the slender vine clings to the oak, so they cling to their Lord. And now, as the tree was to be removed and the vines would lie on the ground a tangled mass, they needed to be comforted as one whom his mother comforts. And were they now to be left as orphans, since He who had comforted them even more tenderly than a mother was to go away? And Jesus answers: "No, I will not leave you orphans, I will send you another Comforter, that He may abide with you forever."

Thus the deep meaning of Christ's word, that the Holy Spirit is our Comforter, naturally discloses itself. Of course, in order to comfort us He must personally be with us. One can comfort only by means of love. It is the lifting of the too heavy cross from the shoulders, the constant whispering of loving words, the gathering of tears, the patient listening to the complaints of our affliction, the sympathizing with our suffering, the being oppressed with our distresses, the identification with our suffering person. Surely, even a gift can afford comfort; a letter from a distant land can cast a ray of hope into the troubled soul, but to comfort us in such a way that the burden falls from the shoulder, and the soul revives and loves, in its love expecting to rejoice—such comfort we can expect only from the living person who, coming to us with the key to our heart, cherishes us with the warmth of his own soul.

And since no one else can always be with us, wholly enter into our sorrows, fully understand and comfort us with infinite love, therefore is the Holy Spirit the Comforter. He abides with us forever, enters the deep places of every soul, listens to every throb of the heart, is able to relieve us of all our cares, takes all our troubles upon Himself, and by His tender and divinely loving words and sweet communion raises us out of our comfortless condition.

This glorious work of the Holy Spirit must be studied with extreme carefulness.

You can compare it, not to that of the artist who chisels a statue out of marble, but to that of the godly mother who with sacrificing love studies the characters of her children, watches over their souls while they themselves have no thought of it, nurses them in sickness, prays with them and for them so that they might learn to pray for themselves, bends a listening ear to their trifling griefs, and who in and through all this spends the energy of her soul with warnings and admonitions, now chiding, then caressing, to draw their souls to God.

And yet, even this is no comparison; for all the sacrifices of the godliest mother, and all the comfort wherewith she comforts her children, are utterly nothing compared to the delightful and divine comfort of the Holy Spirit.

Oh, that Comforter, the Holy Ghost, who never ceases to care for God's children, who ever resumes with new animation the weaving of their soul-garments, even though their willfulness has broken the threads! On earth there is no suitable comparison for it. In the human life there may be a *type* somewhere, but a *full-sized image* to measure this divine comfort there is not. It is wholly unique, wholly divine, the measure of all other comfort. The comfort wherewith we comfort others has value and significance only when it is bright with the spark of the divine comfort.

The Song of Songs contains a description of the tender love of Immanuel for His Church: He, the Bridegroom who calls for the bride; she, the bride who pines with love for her God-given Bridegroom. This is, therefore, something entirely different: the love, not of comfort, but of the tenderest, most intimate communion and mutual belonging together; the one not happy without the other; both destined for each other; by the divine ordinance united, and by virtue of that same ordinance wretched unless the one possesses the other. Such is not the Holy Spirit's love in the comforting. The communion of Christ and the Church is for time and eternity, but the comfort of the Holy Ghost will cease—not His work of love, but that of the comforting. Comfort can be administered only so long as there is one uncomforted and comfortless. So long as Israel must pray to be delivered from iniquities; so long as tears flow; so long as there is bitter sorrow and distress—so long will the Holy Spirit be our Comforter.

But when sin is ended and misery is no more, when death is abolished and the last sorrow is endured and the last tear wiped away, then,

I ask, what remains there for the Holy Spirit to comfort? How could there still be room for a Comforter?

To the question, Why, then, did the Lord say, "I will send you another Comforter, that He may abide with you *forever*"? I answer with another question: Is it to the honor of a child that, while he cries for his mother's comfort, he forgets her as soon as the sorrow is past? This cannot be; this would be a denial of the nature of love. He that is truly comforted entertains for his comforter such intense feelings of gratitude, obligation, and attachment that he cannot be silent, but after having enjoyed the comfort craves also the sweetness of love. The same is true regarding the Holy Spirit. When He shall have comforted us from our last distress, and removed us from sorrow forever, then we cannot say, "O Holy Spirit, now Thou mayest depart in peace," but we shall be constrained to cry, "Oh, refresh and enrich us now with Thy Love forever!"

This would not be so if sin still dwelled in us; for sin makes one so unthankful and self-sufficient that after having tasted the comfort he can forget the Comforter. But among the blessed there is no ingratitude, but from deep inward compulsion we shall love and laud Him who, with captivating love, has divinely comforted us.

Hence a Comforter who is to depart after having comforted us cannot be the Comforter of God's children. Wherefore Jesus assured His disciples: "I will not leave you comfortless. I will send you another Comforter, that He may *abide with you forever.*"

23

The Greatest of These Is Love

The greatest of these is Love—1 Corinthians 13:13.

That the *shedding abroad of Love* and the glowing of its fire through the heart is the eternal work of the Holy Spirit, is stated by no one so pithily as by St. Paul in the closing verse of his hymn of Love. Faith, Hope, and Love are God's most precious gifts, but Love far surpasses the others in preciousness. Compared with all heavenly gifts, Faith, Hope, and Love stand highest, but of these three *Love is the greatest.* All spiritual gifts are precious, and with holy jealousy the apostle covets them, especially the gift of prophesying, but, among the various paths of obtaining spiritual gifts, he knows a way still more excellent, viz., the royal road of Love.

We know that some deny us the right thus to interpret the thirteenth verse, but with little effect. To assert that in the heavenly life faith and hope, like Love, will abide forever, opposes the general teaching of the Scripture, and especially of St. Paul's course of reasoning. In his Epistle to the Corinthians, he opposes faith to sight, saying, "We walk by faith, not by sight"; wherefore he cannot mean that after all faith shall continue when turned into sight. If faith is the evidence of things *not* seen, how can it continue when we shall see face to face? How is it possible to maintain that St. Paul represents faith as an eternal gift when in the twelfth verse he says, "Then we shall know even as we are known"? And he makes the same representation with reference to hope, "For we are saved by hope," adding, "Hope which is seen is no hope, for what a man seeth why doth he yet hope for?" (Rom. 8:24). Wherefore faith and hope cannot be represented as abiding and enduring elements in our spiritual treasure. Neither faith nor hope belongs to the inheritance bequeathed to us by testament. They are springs of spiritual life and joy to us now, because we do not yet possess the inheritance, but when once the inheritance is ours, why should we still care for the will? As proof and earnest that the inheritance cannot be lost, the will is very precious to us, but when the inheritance is delivered into our hands it is mere waste paper, and only the inheritance is of value.

Even Drs. Beets and Van Oosterzee, although they choose to walk in paths somewhat different from those of the fathers, fully concede this point, as their beautiful comments on the last verse of 1 Cor. 13 plainly show. Dr. Beets writes:

> Without apparent cause, at the end of a digression upon the excellency of love, the apostle mentions faith and hope before love. It is evident that, while thinking of the latter, he cannot overlook the former. May we not infer from this that faith and hope are just as essential to the Christian as love? A Christian without love! It is indeed a contradiction of terms. The apostle says: "He that hath not love is nothing." How could he be a Christian? Ah, what deception, what hypocrisy, what horrible sin to disguise a life without love, a loveless heart under the Christian name! But what do you think of a Christian without hope? Is not this just as absurd and just as offensive? What! Life and immortality brought to light by Jesus Christ; He the Resurrection and the Life, having the words of eternal life; His Evangel the glad tidings of the forgiveness of sin, of reconciliation to God, of an opened heaven of bliss; and still it is thought possible that amid present suffering and sorrow a Christian can live without the delightful prospect and expectation of such a glorious future! Without hope! Is this not a fatal feature in the apostle's sad picture of the blind heathen? Is this not the same as to be without Christ? without God? Surely without Christ no man can know this hope, and no one who knows Christ can be without it.
>
> And again, can one be a Christian without faith in God, who "so loved the world that He gave His only-begotten Son, that whosoever believeth on Him should not perish, but have everlasting life"? without faith in Christ who has said, "Let not your heart be troubled; ye believe in God, believe also in Me"? without faith in that faithful and true word of the divine promise which centers in the fact that Jesus Christ has come into the world to save sinners? A Christian without faith—I do not say power of faith by which he can remove mountains, but without faith which is the

evidence of things not seen? Reader, if perhaps you are such a Christian, what is your Christianity? What profit is it to you? With what right, with what conscience, with what purpose do you persist in claiming the name of a Christian? A Christian without faith is one without hope; and as such he is a mortal, a sinner without comfort in life and death.

Perhaps someone will answer: "Even as such my Christianity may be a great deal to me, and serve me the highest and best purpose, if it only cause me to go on to love. Even though I had faith so that I could move mountains, and had not love, I would be nothing. Only through love one is something, is much, is all. Having love, I have enough; and having love, I cannot be altogether without hope." These three being equally indispensable, they are equally inseparable from the Christian. No Christian without faith, without hope, without love. No Christian hope nor Christian love without Christian faith. And, on the other hand, no Christian faith without Christian hope; nor Christian faith without Christian love. Faith, Hope, Love, these three originate the one in the other; sustain each other; these three are one. They become one more and more; they strengthen, purify, regenerate each other. Love is not first, nor hope, but faith. However, faith is impossible, even for a moment, without hope and love.

But among these three, that are indispensable to the Christian and absolutely so to each other, love is the greatest and most excellent of all:

First, because of its importance to the *Christian.* Faith is the inward salvation, and hope the new-born happiness of a fallen man, but love is the growing perfection of restored man.

Second, because of its *relation to God.* Of faith and hope God is the Object and Example. To believe in God is to cast oneself in the arms of God; to hope is to rest upon His heart, but to love is to bear His image. His own Being is Love. To love is divine. God is Love, and he that abideth in love abideth in Him and He in him.

Third, love is greatest by *its working.* Of the deeply rooted tree of faith, it is the fruit which glorifies God and the shadow which diffuses a blessing. By love all that believe are one; by it they strengthen, serve, and bear each other. "Love edifieth." It builds up the Body of the Lord; it spreads His Church among a sinful race, and carries on the labor of His love. For love's sake His Church, His Cross, His Person find grace and honor in the sight of unbelievers. It shames unbelief and silences mockery.

Fourth, love is greatest by reason of *its endurance.* Love never faileth. When time is merged in eternity, prophecy shall be silent. When the redeemed of all nations shall join in the song of the Lamb, tongues shall cease; and knowledge which is in part shall vanish away when that which is perfect is come. And when all is sight there shall be no more room for faith; and where shall hope be when all shall be fulfilled?

Lastly, love *never faileth.* When this corruptible shall have put on incorruption, and this mortal shall have put on immortality; when it shall be revealed to us what we shall be; when bowed down in adoration we shall see Him as He is, in whom, though not seeing Him, yet believing, we rejoice with joy unspeakable and full of glory, then shall our whole being, all our faith and hope, be only love. Then love, purified of her last stain and having attained to her highest truth, shall forever be in us the inexhaustible source of happiness and inexhaustible power of God glorifying activity. Only then shall we realize perfectly, that is forever, what it means to love, and also how little they have known of love who, denying the love of God in Christ, counted the exercise of holy love consistent with the persevering in blasphemous unbelief.

And Dr. Van Oosterzee has written with no less animation:

They are noble companions even when we consider each by herself: Faith, not merely a certain confidence of the soul in the reality of things invisible, and in the certainty of the revelation of God in Christ Jesus, but that saving faith which builds upon the Person and work of the Redeemer; which enters into closest communion with Him; Hope of the perfect fulfillment of all the promises of God which are yea and amen in Christ Jesus; and Love which unites the believer, not only with God and Christ, but with all his brethren and sisters in the Lord, and with the whole race which in heaven and earth is named after God.

Lovely picture: at the right, Faith embracing the saving Cross; at the left, Hope leaning upon the infallible anchor; and in the midst, Love holding in her hand the burning heart, her daily sacrifice consecrated to the God of Love. And yet, although in representation they may be separated, in reality they cannot be, being companions inseparable, not only from every Christian, but also from one another. For what is faith without hope and love? A cold conviction of the understanding, but without quickening power in heart, and without ripened fruit in life. Without hope, faith could not once see heaven, but even if it could enter heaven without love, it would lose its highest felicity. And what is hope without faith and love? At the most a vain delusion, followed by a painful awakening; a fragrant blossom soon to wither without once bearing fruit. And finally, what is love without hope and faith? Perhaps the welling up of the natural feeling, but by no means a spiritual, vital principle. If love does not believe, it must die; and if it does not hope as well as love, it must be a source of measureless suffering.

To separate one of these three sisters from the others is to write the death-sentence of the one, and to destroy the beauty of the others. Inseparably united, however, they deserve to be called companions in the fullest sense of the word. Faith is much, hope is more, and love is most. Faith unites us with God; hope lifts us up to God, but love makes us conformable to God, for God is Love. Faith is the child of humility, hope is

> the offspring of persecution, but love the fruit of faith and hope together. By faith and hope we do in a certain sense seek ourselves; love alone makes us forget ourselves, working for the salvation of others. Faith kneels down in the closet, and hope, in holy ecstasy, sees the heavens opened, but love sends us thence back into the world to impart the treasure of comfort there received to others. Yea, of love, not of faith and hope, can it be said, that it never faileth. Faith is turned into sight and hope into enjoyment, for what a man seeth why doth he yet hope for? But even before the throne of God, love remains as young as when for the first time it was born in the heart. Even there the bond of perfection is at once the condition and the pledge of an infinite increase in holiness and blessedness; and, therefore, it is the greatest forever, both here and there, even though its name has merely third place. To the Christian here these three are constant companions; whatever may change and vanish away, they can abide, for they are the unchangeable mark of every believer. They must abide, or our entire Christianity becomes a form without life. They will abide, for they are so sublimely divine and so truly human. Faith may have to wrestle with darkness, hope with doubt, love with resistance, but where Christ truly lives in the heart, they must abide forever.

There are, of course, expressions in these passages for which these two divines alone are responsible; we mean to show only that these two men have strongly felt that Love's superiority of place and quality is principally conspicuous from the fact that, while faith and hope will finally cease, Love abides forever.

Surely, faith and hope do not cease in the sense that other spiritual gifts cease. The word "temporal" has a twofold meaning. Temporal is the worm that die and from which nothing remains. Temporal is the caterpillar that must dies as a worm, but that rises beautiful again as a butterfly. The same is true of faith and hope, as compared with the spiritual gifts of speaking with tongues and healing the sick. The latter will fail altogether. They will completely disappear. They will vanish away, as St. Paul says in 1 Corinthians 13:8. But the failing of faith and hope may not be taken in that sense. They fail only to rise again in the fuller, richer, and more beautiful form of sight and enjoyment.

But Love does not know this metamorphosis. It not only abides forever, but it ever abides *unchanged.* In the fact that all other gifts perish or change, and that Love alone is eternal, we see the never-ending work of the Holy Spirit scintillating in the hearts of believers; in our meditation on Love we apprehend His proper work in all its depths, even to the root.

24

Love in the Blessed Ones

That God may be all in all—1 Corinthians 15:28.

Sanctification and the shedding abroad of love are not the same. Before the fall Adam could not have been the subject of a single act of sanctification, for he was holy, but Love could have been shed abroad in his heart ever more richly, fully, and abundantly. And this would have been the work of the Holy Spirit.

The unholy alone need sanctification, but to suppose that Love is exhausted in the victory over selfishness is a great mistake. Of course, selfishness is utterly inconsistent with Love, but Love is not the mere *absence* of selfishness, as in Adam; nor its *rebuke* and blood-bought *victory* in the saint; in fact, Love begins to unfold and develop only after the last traces of selfishness are wholly effaced.

The same is true of health, which is not merely the throwing off of disease and its subtle poison; for then convalescents alone could be called healthy, and real healthful life and the life of health would be out of the question. On the contrary, health exists independent of sickness, antedates it, and drives it out when it invades the system; for this is one of its essential operations. And after its fight with sickness it goes on more richly and exuberantly, as though there had been no sickness at all, developing powers and offering enjoyments that are ever new and glorious. So does Love antedate selfishness. And when selfishness appeared, Love immediately prepared to drive it out. And having succeeded, its work was not ended, but as though nothing had happened it continued its life of Love.

Victory over an invading enemy does not end the national existence, but the nation's development and prosperity quietly and gratefully continue. Satan invaded Paradise, Love's dwelling-place, and with all his evil powers of selfishness opposed Love. Then Love had to fight, not because it was in its nature, but in self-defense. Indeed, it may not cease to fight until all selfishness is under perfect control. And when Love's rule is safe, Love does not recline in everlasting slumber, but with strong impulse and holy animation continues the unfolding of its holy and restful life.

This fight is not fought in every heart separately. The fact that Satan is the author and inspirer of all selfishness proves the mutual relation of selfishness in every heart. To some extent even selfishness is organized. Hence victory over individual selfishness does not avail so long as selfishness continues in others. The selfishness of one will necessarily affect the other, and Love cannot celebrate its triumph.

It is true, in death God cuts off all sin from our hearts; and so far as we are concerned selfishness is cast out. He who awakes in eternity with selfishness in his heart is on the way to hell. But although God in death graciously draws the last threads of selfishness from the hearts of His elect, yet their warfare against selfishness is not ended. For even from heaven Christ wages war, until the hour when, as the true Michael, with all His angels He shall deliver the last blow upon Satan and his unholy demons. And if immediately after death the elect will enjoy with Immanuel the communion of Love, then of course they will engage with Him in the conflict against Satan and fight with Him day and night. No saint can see his Savior fight and remain neutral. Nay, the Love of God is so deep, stirring, and captivating that he cannot but enter the conflict.

How in heaven the redeemed partake of the conflict we do not know. When in times of war husbands, fathers, and sons go out to meet the foe, wives, mothers, and daughters stay at home and never see the battle-field, but nevertheless they are partakers of the conflict: in their hearts and prayers; by their letters of love inspiring the men in the field; with their own hands providing for their necessities; by nursing the wounded and dying; by honoring the returning heroes and those fallen in battle. Even on earth one can be engaged in the fight without moving a foot, wielding no weapon other than Love. This answers in some measure the question how in heaven the redeemed partake of the warfare with Michael against Satan: *through the great Love in their hearts;* and by anticipation they enjoy the fulfillment of the promise that with Immanuel they shall sit upon His throne.

However, this condition is only provisional and will end with the dawn of that notable day when from heaven the cry will be heard, "It is done," as once it was heard from Calvary: "It is finished!" Then, the last enemy destroyed, all shall be subject to Christ. Then all selfishness, all unholiness ended, and all opposition to Love being vanquished, God's children shall enjoy an eternal and undisturbed existence in which Love shall reach its zenith; and this is, as the Scripture expresses it: *"That God shall be all in all."*

"God all in all," considered in connection with the Spirit's work of shedding abroad the Love of God in the hearts of the saints, sheds new light upon the subject. If by His indwelling the Holy Spirit sheds abroad the Love of God in the hearts of the saints, and causes that Love like rivers of water to flow over the fields of their spiritual life; if this cultivating of Love is His most proper work, then this "God all in all" is at once flooded with light. For then it means no more nor less than that the Holy Ghost, having entered the last of the elect, shall dwell in the hearts of *all the saints;* shall have pervaded the whole body of Christ in such completeness that selfishness shall not only be cast out, and even the conflict with selfishness be ended, but it shall not even be remembered, nor its possible return be feared.

Although "God all in all" has undoubtedly reference to Satan and the lost, for they shall forever abide under the anger of the Almighty and be consumed by His wrath; yet in its proper and full significance it refers only to the elect. In them alone He takes up His abode personally; in them alone He became *something;* in them alone He became gradually *more and more;* in them alone He became *all.* "In all," referring to the *number of the elect,* signifies that in them, not individually, but collectively as the body of Christ, Love's triumph shall be complete.

But even then the work of the Holy Spirit is not finished, but thenceforth shall continue forevermore. Then the heavenly felicity will only *begin* to unfold itself in a way wholly divine, and without the slightest impediment the Rose of Love will disclose its brilliant beauty. When, as a bridegroom coming forth from his chamber, the sun rises from the womb of the morning and causes his golden rays to wrestle with the dark clouds of the parting night, till, having scattered all, he stands forth magnificent conqueror in the deep azure of a cloudless sky, his splendor does not then decline with the last vanishing vapors, but only begins to shine out in greater brightness and power. And the same is true of the Sun of Love. He first fights and wrestles to vanquish the resistance of the darkened clouds and vapors of selfishness; and only gradually, after what has seemed an endless conflict, He succeeds in scattering and in driving them away before the splendor of His brightness. But when the victory is His, and the Sun of Love stands at last in dazzling glory in the cloudless sky, then, and only then, does He begin to show His perfect beauty and to radiate His blessed, cherishing rays.

After the day of judgment the Holy Spirit cannot cease to feed, cultivate, and strengthen the Love of God in the elect; for, if but for a moment He should withdraw from them, they would cease to be His children, and the body of Christ would lose the bond which binds it to its sacred Head.

God's elect do not exist without the indwelling of the Holy Spirit. We derive all that we are not from ourselves, but from that rich Dweller in our hearts. We, His poor host, have nothing, and from our own treasury can produce not even a grain of love, but our rich Guest works in us with all His wealth. Or rather, not with His own, but with the riches of Christ's cross-merits; and with lavish hands He spends these cross-merits upon the poor owner of the house, making him unspeakably rich. But He does this, not in such a way as to make the saint the possessor of an independent capital, to be spent without the Holy Spirit. Nay, it is the Holy Spirit who from moment to moment holds the lamp that radiates Love's brightness in the heart in His own hand. Hence, if after the judgment, the Holy Spirit should cease to work in, or depart from, the hearts of the saints, all their life, light, and love would at once be quenched. They are what they are by His indwelling, and Love can celebrate its triumph only by pervading their whole personality with His influences. And what is this but that "God is all in all"; for by the Holy Spirit even the Father and the Son come to dwell in them.

Owing to the many obstacles that now prevent Love's light and brightness from pervading them, this indwelling is very imperfect. Even in heaven it is more or less hindered, owing to the conflict of Christ and His people against Satan. But after the judgment, these internal hindrances and external conflicts being ended forever, the Holy Spirit's working shall penetrate from center to circumference and gloriously unfold the inner beauty of the body of Christ.

25

The Communion of Saints

There is one body and one Spirit; even as ye are called in one hope of your calling—Ephesians 4:4.

To classify Love among the works of the Holy Spirit is not a new invention. In this connection, to assign Love such a conspicuous place may be new, but the doctrine itself is as old as the Apostolic Creed, which confesses: "I believe in the *Holy Ghost;* in the Holy, Apostolic, Christian Church, *in the communion of saints.*"

For what is the communion of saints otherwise than Love in its noblest and richest manifestation? And how is it here presented but as the very fruit of the Holy Spirit? The work of the Father is confessed *first;* that of the Son in the Incarnation *second;* and coming to the work of the Holy Spirit, the Church confesses that this is not in the creation, nor in the Incarnation, but in the communion of saints, which, among men, is Love's tenderest and most glorious expression.

"Communion of saints," that is, the rule of Love, not among the selfish, the half-hearted, or still untried, new beginners, but among the initiated children of God, whose life is from God; a communion the foretaste of which is enjoyed on earth, the full enjoyment of which can be found only in heaven; a communion sweet and blessed, because it is unalloyed, and proceeds only from holy impressions; not springing from man's heart, but shed abroad in him from above when from a sinner he became a saint, and developing in him more warmly and tenderly as in his person the new man becomes more pronounced; a communion found among saints, not by chance, but because it is born from the fact that they are saints, rooted in their being saints, and derived from Him who sanctified them to be saints. Hence it is a love which death cannot destroy; which, stronger than death, shall continue as long as there are saints, unquenched, forevermore.

From which it is evident that the fathers had a thorough grasp of the magnificent thought that the Spirit's real, characteristic, and perpetual work is the *shedding abroad of love;* and they have expressed it in a beautiful and artistic form. The Holy Spirit was to them not a mystic Person in the Godhead, to whom they looked up in holy wonder, but God the Holy Ghost working with omnipotent power within and around them. Hence they followed the confession of the Holy Spirit by that of His creation, that is, the Holy, Catholic, Christian Church, which is the body of Christ; and that by the confession of the communion of saints, wrought by the Holy Spirit in the Church.

The *Church* and the *communion of saints* are two things. The former originated and existed before there was the slightest sign of the latter. The Church exists and continues, though in unfavorable times the communion of saints suffers loss. The newborn child is unconscious of his relation to the family. He lives, but without any attachment, inclination, love, or bond of union for the family. Love does indeed exert its influence upon him, and cares for him, but does not yet live in and through him. Hence there is no communion between him and the other members of the family. And the same is true of the Church. She can exist, live, and increase before there is any conscious communion of saints. For which reason the communion of saints may languish, apparently disappear, yea, even be turned into bitterness.

Hence the *Church* and the *communion of saints* are two things. First the Church which is the body, then the communion of saints, which is its support and nourishment.

Wherefore it reads, not, I *see* or *taste,* but I *believe* the communion of saints. Communion of saints belongs to the things invisible and unknown, which on earth are part of the tenor of the faith, and which in the New Jerusalem shall be turned into a rich and blessed experience. For this article of faith speaks, not of a communion of a *few* saints, members of the same small circle, but of "the communion of *saints*";

and this rich and comprehensive confession may not be belittled by a narrow conception of it. Communion of a few saints is not a thing unknown on earth; there is scarcely a spot where some of God's dear children do not live together in sweet fellowship. But such a little circle is by no means *the* body of Christ; and such sweet fellowship would be injurious if the fact were overlooked, that it must be a communion of *all* God's saints on earth—of the present, the past, and the future.

To one living in an obscure hamlet faith in the communion of saints is the consciousness that he belongs to an exceedingly wealthy, numerous, holy, and elect family; and that instead of ever getting estranged from it, he shall ever be more closely united to it. It is the sacred knowledge that all the saints of the Old and New Covenants, all the heroes and heroines, the whole cloud of witnesses, together with apostles, prophets, and martyrs, and the redeemed in heaven, are not aliens to him, but with him belong to the same body; not only in name, but in reality, as shall once be gloriously manifested. It is the precious comfort for the lonely heart that, in all the ends of the earth, among all nations and peoples, in every city and village, God has His own whom He has called out and gathered unto life eternal; and that I share with them the same life, possess the same hope and calling, and sustain to them, however imperceptibly, the tenderest and holiest communion; yea, the firm and positive assurance that if the earth came suddenly to an end, and they only were to be saved who, being possessed of an eternal principle, had the power to bloom forever, that then all God's saints would come out as one holy family, in which holy circle the least of His servants would glitter as precious gems.

And therefore this glorious communion should no longer be belittled by confining it to one's own small, often shallow environment. Of course there is no objection, when friends living in the same place, meeting together in the Lord, understanding one another, and edifying one another through the Word, speak of their small circle, in connection with the communion of saints. For, wherever in love and worship saints dwell together, there indeed the communion of saints breaks through the clouds, and vouchsafes unto them a glimpse of its brightness and glory. But, although such dwelling together in unity stands in connection with the communion of saints, and is a result of it, and affords a foretaste of what it some time shall be, it is only a very small part and faint reflection of reality. In such a circle, however good, devout, and holy, the hearts become exclusive. Compared to the great and wide world-circle, they cannot be otherwise than a small company. And this necessarily imparts to it something private and exclusive; while the communion of saints is the very *opposite;* not *ex*clusive, but *in*clusive. It is not an idea which closes the door and shuts the windows, but, throwing doors and windows wide open, it walks through the four corners of the earth, searches the ages of the past, and looks forward into the ages to come.

Communion of saints opens its arms as wide as possible. O my God! How can I encompass and embrace all the dear children whom Thou throughout the ages hast regenerated and still dost regenerate, the redeemed both in heaven and earth! There are a few of former generations whose books lie open upon our table, so that with Calvin we can pray, or with Augustine glory in a sin-pardoning God, or with Owen lose ourselves in the contemplation of the excellencies of Christ, or with Comrie walk in the paths of righteousness divine. But what are these few that speak compared to the thousands who are silent; who were each in his own way divinely endowed and adorned with spiritual gifts; who in heaven will once appear bright with crowns, our brethren and sisters now and forevermore? The communion of saints cries out: "Lengthen thy cords and strengthen thy stakes." For it is a communion not with hundreds, but with thousands; not with ten thousand, but with millions; a multitude that no man can number, as drops of water in the crystal sea which is before the throne of God.

And this communion of saints will be real: not limited as in this earthly life, where living together in the same city we meet each other at the utmost ten times a year, but an actual living together the same life, eating together at the same board, drinking from the same cup, thinking the same thought, exhilarated by the same felicity, adoring the same unfathomable mercies of our God.

In Europe our fellowship with thousands is now much fuller and richer than our fathers ever knew it. The means of communication are wonderfully improved and multiplied. Telegraph and telephone afford men communication not confined to place nor distance. They were never dreamt of before. It never entered the mind of man that in fifteen minutes a saint in America could exchange thoughts with a brother in

Europe. This communion of saints was therefore to them an unsolved riddle. But to us the veil is partly lifted. Actually we see something of it: intercommunication of thought in minutest detail, not confined by distance, crossing the oceans, uniting continents. And yet, what are telegraph and telephone compared to the powers of the age to come? And thus we grope in the dark and wonder how it shall be when distance shall be no more, when material aids shall be superfluous, when God's children, active in whatever part of heaven, shall enjoy full, rich, and intimate communion, one in Immanuel, all partakers of the same Love.

Why is the communion of saints an article of the creed of the Church on earth? (1) Because *in the invisible world it is even now a reality;* (2) because it is *implied in the nature of the case;* and (3) because it is *already active in the germ.*

First, it exists already *in the invisible world;* for there is a triumphant Church above. Millions upon millions are fallen asleep in their Lord, and have entered the halls of the eternal Light. And although to them the full glory of the Kingdom is not revealed, tarrying as it does until after the Judgment Day, and the absence of the glorified body still detracts from the full communion of saints, yet even now the departed saints and martyrs live in such heavenly felicity that the word of the Psalmist, "Behold, how good and how pleasant it is for brethren to dwell together in unity," can be applied only to that heavenly company.

Second, and although in that sense it is not found on the earth, yet it is implied and does exist *in the nature of the case;* and as such it must be the object of faith. We profess to believe in the Holy Spirit, who does not live apart from the Church, but has descended in the Church and in all the members of Christ, in whom He dwells and works; which fact He seeks to bring to their individual consciousness. And since it is the essence of self-denial on the part of the saint to let the Holy Spirit work in him more and more, being only a co-laborer himself, it is evident that the activity of faith must have this one result: that there is in all God's saints but one Worker, working in you and me and in all who love the appearing of the Lord Jesus Christ. This is a fact of which all are conscious, the effect of which must be the most intimate harmony of life, one growth from the same root, and a strong mutual attraction between all the members. In the one Holy Spirit the work in the souls of all must concentrate. It may not appear on the surface, but underneath the surface all these waters must flow together in the communion of saints.

Third, and this is verified by experience; for we clearly discover the *germ* of it in the earth. To some extent it is evident in our own intimate circle: in the reading of old books, and in the singing of old hymns; it is evident when we hear how God's work prospers or suffers in other places, in other countries, and among other nations. For, whatever the differences, this we notice, that it is the same language of love spoken at the ends of the earth; that among all men it is the same casting down and raising up of the sinner; one blessed, divine communion of which men testify in every human tongue. Yea, more, there are but few of God's children who have not at some time in their lives seen their spiritual horizon enlarged, and heard, as it were, the Song of the Lamb ascending from the ends of the earth, and unnumbered multitudes crying: "We also glory in the Love that is eternal, merciful, and divine; we also are pilgrims to Zion, the City of the Living God." This is the activity of faith which, escaping from the present limitations, glories in the unbounded communion of God's saints, who still bear the cross, or who already wear the crown.

26

The Communion of Goods

If we walk in the light, we have fellowship one with another—1 John 1:7.

The communion of saints is in the Light. In heaven alone, in the halls of the eternal Light, it shall shine with undimmed brightness. Even on earth its delights are known only inasmuch as the saints walk in the light.

This communion of saints is a holy confederacy; a bond of shareholders in the same holy enterprise; a partnership of all God's children; an essential union for the enjoyment of a common good; a firm not of earth, but of heaven, in which the members have each an equal share, which is not taken from their own wealth, but bequeathed in their behalf by Another.

Do not think that this savors too much of secularism. Even the Lord Jesus compared the kingdom of heaven to a merchant, and to one who had found a treasure in the field. And our Catechism also explains the communion of saints as the possession of a *common good,* saying that it includes two things:

First, to be partakers of Christ and of all His riches and gifts.

Second, the obligation to employ these gifts for the advantage and salvation of other members.

Originally communion of saints was taken in the absolute sense of including *communion of earthly possessions.* Hence the peculiar phenomenon in Jerusalem of having all things common. They sold their possessions and they put the proceeds in the common treasury, which was in the hands of the apostles. And from this the poor and they who were formerly rich were supported. Hence there were no poor nor rich, but there was equality.

With reference to this communion of goods, opposite opinions are held. Some have taken it as an indication that all Christians ought to renounce their private possessions, and live after the manner of monks, as members of one family; while others have disapproved of it as an extravagance of Christian fanaticism. Both extremes are untenable.

It appears from Scripture that this generous and enthusiastic effort to escape from the plague of poverty was not only unprofitable to the few, but that it caused terrible suffering which extended over the whole Church. At least, in his epistles, St. Paul speaks again and again of the poverty-stricken saints of Jerusalem, who were always in need of a collection and in danger of starvation. In other places that did not have a communion of goods there was a surplus; and in Jerusalem, where on a large scale possessions had been divided, the people suffered lack. This shows convincingly that division of property, or communion of goods, is not the way ordained of God to overcome poverty or to attain a state of higher mutual prosperity. The subsequent efforts of various sects at Rome to realize a similar ideal on a smaller and more careful scale met with similar failures. And the secular enterprises of Proudhon and others led to similar miserable results.

But it is equally erroneous to suppose that this failure justifies us in condemning the early church of Jerusalem for this act. This would be inconsistent with the upholding of the apostolic authority. The apostles had a part in this matter; they assisted the church in receiving the money for distribution. Hence to tear the apostles' seal from this heroic act of the church of Jerusalem is simply impossible. We should be careful not to condemn what the apostles have stamped with their own sign-manual.

Judging from the results, this communion of goods and subsequent misery produced precious fruit; partly in the fact that the church of Jerusalem was thus kept from *relapsing* into worldliness and attachment to houses and lands; and more strongly in the other fact that this very impoverishing of the church became the powerful means by which the breach was prevented between the churches of Palestine and those of the Gentile world. The distress at Jerusalem quenched the rising pride of the Jewish heart; and the delight of imparting to others softened the hearts at Corinth and in Macedonia. St. Paul, traveling to Jerusalem, carrying with him European treasure, holds in his hand the silver cord that keeps together and shortly unites the troubled churches.

But, apart from these good results, this division of property embodies something of still greater and more sacred importance, which essentially belongs to the first Christian congregation. International intercommunication was to be developed gradually; the translation of the Word of God into the languages of the world for the universal preaching of the Gospel would occupy many centuries. Even now it is not universal; and only in heaven, after the judgment, the anthem shall rise to the Blessed Trinity from all peoples and tongues. And yet, while this was tarrying, and the Church of the New Testament was just beginning to manifest itself, it pleased God on Pentecost, by the miracle of tongues, to make men listen to the glorious message which came from the lips of the apostles, to everyone in his own language. And the same is true with reference to the communion of goods. Even this shall one day be a reality. Heaven's outward, visible goods shall be for the mutual enjoyment of all the redeemed. But, by reason of sin and present limitations, this is now impossible. In Paradise private possession was out of the question. Neither Adam nor Eve had anything that did not belong to the other. The whole garden was theirs and its possession mutual. Division took place only after the breach had come, and will continue so long as the breach shall last. But as on Pentecost the miracle of tongues was the prophecy, manifestation, and incipient realization of what before the Throne of the Lamb shall be a glorious, universal reality, so was the communion of goods the prophecy, manifestation, and incipient realization of what shall be the communion of external gifts in the heavenly glory.

There is not only an immortality of the soul, but also a resurrection of the body. Wherefore the glory of the New Jerusalem may not be presented as consisting only in the spiritual and invisible. Heaven exists, and in that heaven Christ sits upon the throne in the body which the Father has prepared for Him. The Father's house is not a fiction, but a real city with many mansions; and when the glory shall have come, after the great and notable day of the Lord, the felicity of God's children shall be not only a spiritual delight, but also the enjoyment of outward and visible glory and beauty. As there were in Eden, so there will be in heaven, external goods in relation to man's external bodily appearance, when he shall walk in his glorified body. And, since body and soul in perfect and indissoluble union shall work upon each other in a harmonious manner, the communion of saints must have two sides: a communion of spiritual good, and a communion of the outward and visible glory. And inasmuch as this twofold nature of the communion of saints must be illustrated to the church of Jerusalem in its perfect unity, therefore the communion in the breaking of bread had to be accompanied by a communion equally intimate in the possession of temporal goods. The division of property contained the prophecy of this future communion, a glorious prophecy which contains a *threefold exhortation* for the Christian Church of all ages.

The *first exhortation* is what St. Paul calls *"to possess as not possessing";* to be loose from the world; the consistent carrying out of the idea that we are but stewards of the Lord Jesus Christ, who is the only Proprietor of all men's personal property and real estate. It is always the choice between Jehovah and Mammon.

Not Baal, nor Kamosh, nor Molech, but Mammon, is the idolatrous power in which Satan appears against the glory of Jehovah, especially among mercantile nations. Many men, otherwise not unspiritual, can scarcely separate from the altar of Mammon—visible things have such strong attraction, and entrench themselves so firmly in the impressionable heart.

Compared to the treasures on earth, those of heaven seem to us something accidental and of uncertain value. To possess as not possessing is to our flesh such a bitter cross. And for this reason the early church of Jerusalem appears in the beginning of the dispensation of the New Covenant glorious in her communion of goods, in order to illustrate against the dark background of the half-heartedness of Ananias and Sapphira the power of the Holy Ghost to make the children of God at Jerusalem at once loose from their earthly possessions. Of course it did not last, for the spiritual forces of Paradise were lacking to make it lasting, but it shows the majestic act of the Holy Spirit, and the majestic preaching which proceeded from it: "Do not lay up for yourselves treasures on earth, . . . but let your treasure be in heaven."

And the *second exhortation* is, *that the poor be remembered.* They did not merely sell their possessions, but they divided them among the poor; and from this divine manifestation of love sprang the fair flower of mercy, as indigenous to the Church of Christ. It may be said that it was the effect of excitement, but remember that, unless the impressions on our sinful hearts are produced in a very powerful manner, they will soon be effaced; and with this in view it must be acknowledged that no other event could have stamped upon the Church the impress of mercy, which was to last throughout the ages, so long as the Church was to last, than this general division of goods, which was wrought by the powerful pressure of the waves of love and the wonderful manifestation of the work of the Holy Spirit.

And thus, by this communion of goods, it became the indestructible character of the Church of Christ to exercise mercy, to impart to the poor, to abound in the works of benevolence, and to interpret to men the mercy of God. But not as though the Church might be reduced to a benevolent society; he that proposes such a thing cuts off her life at the root. The exercise of mercy in the Church of Christ is the fruit of the Cross. Where this is lacking, mercy languishes. But it is the Holy Spirit's pleasure to work love, to show love, to cultivate love, and to cause love to be glorified. And since the life of man and of the Church has a spiritual and a material side, the Holy Spirit perseveres with His work so long and so mightily that even the gold and silver of the earth become subject to Him and serve Him. Hence the communion of goods in Jerusalem is the impressive inauguration of the work of mercy for the whole Church of Christ, and as such it is nothing else than the power of the Holy Spirit penetrating to the circle of the material life.

Finally, the *third exhortation* is contained in the never-ceasing cry: *"Behold, He cometh."* The men in Jerusalem nineteen centuries ago would not have sold and divided their possessions so freely and readily if the expectation of the Lord's return to judgment had not taken hold of them with overwhelming power. They did undoubtedly expect that return during their own lifetime; not after many days, but shortly. And since this *expectation* depreciated the value of their possessions, they resolved to sell and distribute them much more readily than otherwise would have been possible for their covetous hearts. And although there was in their expectation something overstrained, which the succeeding ages have corrected, yet there is in this "Maranatha" of the apostolic Church an inestimable testimony, which exhorts the Church of all ages to look upon Him who shall come upon the clouds. With bread and cup we remember His death *until He comes.* All the apostles direct us to the future; and when, in the Revelation of St. John, the Book of Testaments closes, it leaves us upon the mountain-top, from which there is no other perspective than the glory of Christ's return.

Putting that return far from our thoughts, or altogether ignoring it, we cannot possibly unite our life with the life of Immanuel. The Holy Spirit works the eternal work of Love, but this work is never severed from the Love of the Son. The treasure which the Holy Spirit distributes is in Immanuel. Christ is the Blessed Head of this holy communion in which he gathers together all God's elect. And, therefore, the eye may never be taken from Christ; it must always look unto Him; it may not cease to wait for Him.

This Love wrought by the Holy Spirit is the Bride's love for her Bridegroom; and thus the communion of saints finds its completion in the heart's most intimate communion with the Redeemer of souls.

27

The Communion of Gifts

Now the end of the commandment is charity out of a pure heart, and of a good conscience, and of faith unfeigned—1 Timothy 1:5.

Communion of goods in Jerusalem was a symbol. It typified the communion of the spiritual goods which constituted the real treasure of Jerusalem's saints. The other inhabitants of that city possessed houses, fields, furniture, gold, and silver just as well as the saints, and perhaps in greater abundance. But the latter were to receive riches which neither Jew, Roman, nor Greek possessed, viz., a treasure in heaven. The saints were holy, not in themselves, but through Him who had said, "Now are ye clean through the words which I have spoken unto you." The Lord had indeed ascended unto heaven, but only "to receive *gifts for men;* yea, for the rebellious also, that the Lord God might dwell among them." And this treasure was *Christ Himself.*

Speaking of the contribution which was being collected in Macedonia, Achaia, and Corinth for the saints in Jerusalem, the apostle admonishes the Corinthian church to render thanks to God for a gift infinitely greater than the gold which was to be sent to Jerusalem; and it is in this connection that he uses that captivating expression—*"unspeakable gift"*—which we received in the surrender of God's dear Son.

It is, therefore, a mutual possession. Jesus has us, and we have Him. He possesses the saints, and they possess Him. That He possesses them is their only comfort in life and death. But that they also possess Him, as their own heart's treasure, is to them the source of all their wealth and luxury. The Catechism confesses, therefore, very correctly that the communion of saints consists first of all in the fact that they are partakers of *Him,* and then of *His gifts.*

The gift is not without the Person, nor outside of the Person, nor even before the Person. The saint partakes first of Christ, and from this sacred partnership flows every other blessing. Even as the Head possesses the Body, and the Body possesses the Head, so is this also a mutual possession. Head and Body belong to each other, even though the Head has this advantage over the Body, that it commands it at will, while the Body must follow the Head wherever it leads. "To follow the Lamb wherever He goeth" is the peculiar mark of this mutual relation.

But, with the reservation of this essential mark, the possession is absolute. The saints belong to Jesus, just as much because the Father has given and brought them to Him, as that He has bought them, not with gold or silver, but with His own precious blood. And, on the contrary, He belongs to His saints, not because by their own labor they have obtained Him, but as a gift of free grace. The Triune God has ordained the Mediator for His people, to whom He has given and brought Him; and the Mediator having come in the flesh, has given Himself to His people.

Every child of God knows from his own experience that Christ is all his treasure. When Mary Magdalen cries out, "They have taken away my Lord," she has lost all the wealth of her soul. The saints stand in the faith and have peace only when, insofar, and as long as they possess Immanuel. He is their One and All. As soon as they find Him, all their poverty is turned into wealth. Without Him they are blind and naked; with Him want and misery make place for riches and abundance. With Him they are set in heaven. And when they depart from this life their hope and lot for eternity depend upon this, whether they possess Him as their souls' Savior, glorious and altogether lovely.

Hence this is the most important: *the great treasure of the saints in Jerusalem was their Lord.* This comprehended all. Every other treasure was theirs only through Him. To possess Him was to possess all that He had obtained for them, even justification and sanctification; all the power given Him of the Father for their assistance and protection; all the wisdom and light, and all the charismata, gifts of grace, received of the Father for distribution among His people.

However, they could not make this partnership available, for their treasure lay beyond their reach; was not in earth, but in heaven. Actually they remained poor and perplexed; rich for the future, but now needy and helpless.

The following illustration will make this clear. An English millionaire, well supplied with bank-notes, in an African village finds himself reduced to beggary. The natives, ignorant of his wealth and not understanding the value of bank-notes, refuse to sell him anything but for their own currency. Hence with all his treasure he is in that distant place poor and destitute. In like manner, being pilgrims and sojourners in the earth, the saints would be spiritually poor and needy if there were no Comforter, no Go-between, who out of His heavenly treasure could supply all their need during all the days of their pilgrimage. And this Go-between is the Holy Spirit. Of Himself He has nothing. By Himself He could never save a sinner. He never adopted the flesh and blood of children and dwelled among us; never suffered, died, and rose again in their behalf. All that He can do is to pray for them with groans that cannot be uttered, and in divine love come and dwell with them. But what the Holy Spirit does not possess Christ possesses, who, in our flesh, rich in His cross-merits, lives with the Father in our behalf.

And from that treasure in Christ the Holy Spirit takes and imparts to the saints, as the money exchanger supplies the English traveler with the native currency. Not only does He give them the spiritual gold and silver as it lies in Christ's treasury, but He converts it into such forms as their present needs and conflicts require. And this is the peculiarly comforting feature of the Holy Spirit's work. He does not scatter this treasure from heaven promiscuously, but brings it home to each of us in a form adapted to meet our every condition and capacity. He does not give strong meat to babes nor milk to adults, but to every spiritual patient according to the nature of his complaint. Better than the patient himself does He understand the nature of his infirmity, to which as the divine Physician He adapts the remedy.

To the saints of Jerusalem and to those of the present time Christ *must* be a common possession. As the former had their material property in common—and this the latter should have also, in higher sense, through the works of mercy—so had they and so have we our *spiritual* treasure as a common possession, in the same Immanuel, who enriches all. But the saints being unable rightly to divide their treasure, the Holy Spirit divides it for them. He takes every member's portion as it lies in Christ, marked with His name, especially adapted for *his* particular need, and distributes it carefully and without mistakes, so that every saint receives his own. And while thus everyone partakes of Christ and of His gifts, the one Christ with His treasure is common to all.

In the child we can see something of the Love cultivated by a mutual possession. Love between the parents may have grown cold, but so long as both can say of their little one, She is mine, and "mine" may become "ours," there is hope that the former love may return. In spite of their differences both possess the one child, who with all her love and sweetness belongs to both. And this applies in higher sense to the Christ. In the Church are many saints, and everyone says: "Immanuel is *my* Bridegroom." And this individual testimony is turned at last into the general anthem of praise: "Immanuel is *our* Lord." Surely every saint finds in Christ something especially adapted to himself, yet all possess the one Lord and all His treasure. And this is the very power of love which in blessing watches over all. Love may grow cold and in an evil hour be turned into bitterness, but this is only temporarily; love must return. As in the wealth of the mutual possession husband and wife felt their union, so do the saints, considering their mutual possession of Immanuel, feel themselves bound together by Love's overwhelming impression.

"One baptism, one faith, one Lord, one Jesus for every heart;" "one Immanuel whom all call precious," and herein alone lies Love's power to keep in unity, and, after temporary separation, to reunite all the saints of God.

And as the communion of goods in Jerusalem was a symbol of the saints' mutual possession in Immanuel, so it was also the symbolic indication of their individual obligation, to have the gifts in common possession, by willingly and diligently using them for the highest advantage of the other members.

The Lord imparts "gifts," "ministrations," and "operations" as St. Paul calls them (1 Cor. 12:4, 5, 6); adding that all these gifts are of the same Spirit, and these ministrations of the same Lord, and these operations of the God who worketh all in all. And then he shows that it is the duty of the saints to use these gifts, ministrations, and operations not selfishly for one's own glory, but for the Body of the Lord, which is His Church.

And by this God's true children are best known; and they know themselves best in the gracious operation of which they are the subjects. For when the Holy Spirit imparts talents and gifts, the tempter whispers in the ear that it will be for their best advantage to use these gifts for each one's own glory, with their brightness to shine and to make himself a name among men, and in that way the blessing will crown the labor as a matter of course. And alas! Many listen to these whisperings and thus defraud the household of faith of their individual gifts, not understanding the meaning of the beehive, which teaches that one can purify honey without eating of it.

And we should not judge too severely; this temptation is much harder than many are willing to acknowledge, especially for the ministers of the Word. The people greatly admire your sermon, praise you for it, talk about it, and carry you upon their shoulders. And by this miserable burning of incense one is intoxicated before he knows it. It is no more the question whether Jesus is satisfied, whether there is a spiritual gain for the glory of His name, but almost exclusively: Did the people like it? How did it affect them? And after a ten-years' ministry under the influence of such evil whisperings, the result can scarcely be anything but the talent buried out of sight, the sacred office desecrated, all spiritual operation suspended, and the minister of the Word little more than a minister to his own glory. And the same evil appears among the laymen. There is a lack of tenderness, of love, of consecration, frequently an abuse of spiritual gifts for the gratifying of the ambitious heart. Oh, we are so fearfully weak and sinful! Surely, every talent would be buried and every good gift spoiled were there no Holy Spirit, who with divine and superior power watches against this evil.

For when in the Church the conscience awakes, and talents and gifts are once more emancipated from the yoke of selfish ambition, we see in it not our work, but the Holy Spirit's. Then we do our duty. Then the communion of saints revives. Then the saints are once more ready with gift and talent to serve the Lord and their brethren. But the power which wrought the miracle of Love was not ours, but of the Holy Spirit.

28

The Suffering of Love

Greater love hath no man than this, that a man lay down his life for his friend—John 15:13.

Love suffers because the spirit of the world antagonizes the Spirit of God. The former is unholy, the Latter is holy, not in the sense of mere opposition to the world's spirit, but because He is the absolute Author of all holiness, being God Himself. Hence the conflict.

There is no point along the whole line of the world's life which does not antagonize the Holy Spirit whenever He touches it. Whenever we are tempted by the world and inwardly animated by the Holy Spirit, there is a clash in the conscience. As soon as one member breathes a worldly spirit and another testifies against it in the Spirit of holiness, there is trouble and strife in the family. When in state, school, church, or society a worldly tendency appears and a current from the divine Spirit, there is trouble and strife in one or all. These two oppose each other and cannot be reconciled. Compromise is impossible. Either one, the worldly spirit, at last closes our hearts against the Holy Spirit, and then we are lost; or after long conflict the Holy Spirit vanquishes the world's spirit; then the prince of this world finds nothing in us, and our names are written in the gate of the New Jerusalem.

And this causes *love* to *suffer.* When love increases in our hearts, owing to the Holy Spirit's increasing activity, it must come into conflict with all that pertains to the world's spirit and seeks to maintain itself in the soul.

This is evident more or less in little children. Indulgence is the easiest, but not the best, method of education. The indulgent mother does not love her children, but sacrifices them to her weakness. She finds it easier not to oppose their wrongdoing; thus avoiding tears, contradiction, and ill-will. When they call her "darling mother" it is sweet music to her ear; hence she never looks displeased, and rather than deny them anything she anticipates their desires. So she loves, not them, but herself. Her aim is not their good, or the doing of God's will concerning them and herself, but to save unpleasantness and to insure to *herself* the children's affection. But not so she who loves her children with the Love shed abroad by the Holy Ghost. Actuated by His Love, looking upon them in His light, she seeks their eternal good. To her each child is a patient in need of bitter medicine, which she may not withhold. Her aim is not the gratification of the child's wish, but his highest advantage in the way of life. And this causes conflict; for while the indulgent mother is ever pleased with her children and ever ready to hear men praise them, the other is often tossed between hope and fear, saying, "What will the end be?" Moreover, the time will come when her child, not understanding her love, will resist her, when he will think her lovely only when she indulges him, when he will reward her devotion with angry look and voice and willful disobedience, when his conversation becomes constraint, when, regarding her as jealous of his pleasures, with a rebellious heart he will turn away from her love, while before God she is conscious that she seeks only his highest and holiest interests.

There is another picture of suffering love. There never arose among men one that had greater love than Christ. In the human heart love never shone with brighter light, never glowed with brighter flame. Without measure He had received the Holy Spirit, who abode upon Him, who filled Him with tenderest love that pervaded the soul and softened the heart. His love understood the secret of embracing in truest intimacy all that was *human,* and at the same time of breathing love that came like a benediction to every *individual.* He gave Himself to the whole race, and He opens His heart for an old, blind Jew in the gate of Jericho. Such is the infinite, rich, and almost omnipotent power of His love. It encompasses eternity, yet there is no outcast, however degraded, too low for its compassions.

And what reception did the world prepare for Him? Did it offer Him love, honor, and admiration? Did it appreciate His holy love and kindle its own heart by its flame? On the contrary, the world was offended by it, could not bear it, counted it as mortal hatred; for He denied it its joys and sinful pleasures. He did not even smile when it was full of laughter, but when it begged for His applause He had only rebuke. He prevented the Jerusalem aristocrat from being a Pharisee, and the worldling from being a Sadducee. His whole appearance was a living protest against the world's regime. Hence the world opposed Him, treated His Love as hatred, and returned it with contempt. Of course, if He had only lamented when it mourned, or danced when it piped unto Him in the marketplace, it would have built Him a throne. But since He loved it with a holy love and yielded not to its entreaty, therefore it beat Him, embittered His life, and covered Him with shame and mockery. And when He persisted to love and admonish, it pronounced its "Anathema," and the planting of the cross on Calvary was only a question of time.

And what it did to Jesus it has done to all His followers. He that yields is tolerated. He that makes room for the world's spirit receives burning of incense. He that makes compromise with it may be assured of honor and glory, but he that refuses to compromise, loving the world with holy love, must sooner or later experience its wrath. God's people in every place and nation have ever sung: "Many are the afflictions of the righteous." Every age has its martyr-history. And the best ages of our race, in which the Holy Spirit exerted His mightiest power, are but the times when the noblest and godliest saints suffered cruelest tortures and endured greatest wrongs.

Cause for love's suffering lies in its *origin.* Since it is the Holy Spirit who radiates its heat in the heart, and keeps its fire burning from moment to moment, the unholy hate and reject it.

Love can bear, but not *tolerate,* all things. It bears sufferings, because it does not tolerate the worldly spirit, but the cry of "mildness" and "moderation" never tempts it to quench the *hatred* with which it has entered the conflict with unholiness. For real *love* is also real *hatred.*

He that loves feebly or falsely cannot hate energetically. But if ardent, animating love reigns in your heart, than hatred reigns with it. He that loves the beautiful hates the ugly. He that loves harmony hates discord. In like manner, he that has fallen in love with holiness has conceived by the Holy Spirit an equally strong hatred for all unholiness. Love for Jesus cannot exist but with *hatred* for Satan. And the best measure for the love of God in our hearts is the depth of contempt for sin.

He that loves the world hates God, and has made God his enemy; as the Catechism correctly remarks: "By nature we are prone to hate God and our neighbor." "The carnal mind is enmity against God." But the man whose soul overflows with the love of God hates the unholy spirit of the world in and around him, and fights against it until the hour of his death. David's testimony—"Do I not hate them, O Lord, that hate Thee? I hate them with perfect hatred" (Ps. 139:21)—is only the reverse of the stamp of love. And if among those born of the will of man there never was one who could truly say, "Lord, I hate them with perfect hatred"; yet there was One in whose heart this hatred was deep and true, who alone could say "that He love God with *all* His heart and soul and mind and strength."

This mutual position is therefore very clear. There are degrees both in love and in hatred. In proportion as the heart beats strongly or feebly, that is, in proportion as the spirit of this world or the Holy Spirit dwells in us and animates us to stronger expression, in that proportion that love or that hatred shall rise in us in higher degree. And according to that degree shall the proportion of our present conflict, sorrow, and suffering be.

"Through suffering to glory" is true especially with reference to love. *Being love,* it cannot be neutral or insensible. And while its contact with men causes it much suffering, this suffering is increased by the conflict *in its own bosom.*

For this pure, holy love loves itself, but only in a holy sense. Although it cannot purge its heart all at once from all unholiness and impurity, yet it constantly wars against them and separates itself from them. And since in that conflict it is often convinced of its own lack of love and faithfulness, and of having grieved the divine Love, it sorrows much. Frequently it feels so humbled in the presence of Jesus that it scarcely dares look up to Him; humbled in the presence of His cross;

conscious of its inability to self-sacrifice; humbled before its own loved ones whom it ought to bless, whom it frequently injures; and especially in the presence of the Holy Spirit, who tenderly sought to animate it, and whom it often silenced by this lack of courage and will power.

And this grieves the soul of the saint, who seeks in vain for the evidence of his sonship in the love of his own fickle heart. And if this love were of man, it would perish at last. But it is not. It is of the Holy Spirit, shed abroad and fanned by Him continually. Hence it is never quenched, but however near perishing, it is reanimated, and, burning anew with a bright flame, it re-enters the conflict.

History offers the evidence. There were times when the early Church was nearly exterminated; when the Waldensians were nearly blotted out from the face of the earth; when our fathers consecrated and sacrificed their lives on this blood-drenched soil, in order not to deny the Lord their God. For among these martyrs there were men and women to whom it seemed impossible to give their lives for Christ; who often thought: "When it comes to me, I will surely fail." And yet when it did come, the Holy Spirit so graciously and extraordinarily *steeled* these souls that the cripple at once leaped like a hart, and they who did not think it possible to yield their *goods,* sacrificed their *lives* for His Name's sake. Then it was shown that in God's child the love of Christ is an eternal love, which, being born of *His* sacrifice, is stronger than death—yea, fearless in the presence of torture and martyrdom.

29

Love in the Old Covenant

A new commandment I give unto you, that ye love one another—John 13:34.

In connection with the Holy Spirit's work of shedding abroad the love of God in our hearts, the question arises: What is the meaning of Christ's word, "A new commandment I give unto you"? How can He designate this natural injunction, "To love one another," a *new* commandment?

This offers no difficulty to those who entertain the erroneous view that during His ministry on earth Christ established a new and higher religion, to supersede the antiquated religion of Israel.

They assert that the ancient religious ideas of the Jews were crude, defective, and primitive, even far below pagan morality. Among Israel themselves it was an eye for an eye, a tooth for a tooth. For their enemies they nursed vindictive hatred. They sang imprecatory psalms. And to crown all, they indulged the bloodthirsty desire of dashing the enemy's innocent babes against the stones. Among this rude and barbarous people Jesus arose to proclaim a higher and nobler religion. He said: "Ye have heard it was said of old time, 'An eye for an eye, a tooth for a tooth!' but I say: 'Resist him not that is evil.' Ye have heard that it was said, 'Thou shalt hate thine enemy', but I say unto you: 'Love your enemies.' And whatever shortsighted Moses may have taught ancient Israel, I, Jesus, give you a new commandment, that ye love one another."

In this sense the words *"new commandment"* offer no difficulty. *"New,"* representing the Christian religion, is opposed to the *"old,"* which stands for the Mosaic law. But however plausible, this representation is thoroughly false and contradicted by obvious facts.

In Matthew 5:17–20, Christ introduces the subject by showing that He does not oppose His Gospel as a superior code of morals to the antiquated and inferior Mosaic code, but that it is His aim, by opposing the *false interpretations* of Moses by the liberal, rabbinical schools, to restore the Mosaic law to its *legitimate position.* He says: "Think not that I am come to destroy the law, but to fulfill; not merely in a general sense, as though the valuable germ which it may contain needed, for its development, only to be divested from its outward covering, but to fulfill it to its *very jot or tittle.* For whosoever shall do and teach them shall be called great in the Kingdom of heaven." From verse 20 it is clear that He opposes, not the *righteousness of Moses,* but the *false interpretation* of it by the liberal rabbis.

And after this introduction He continues: "Ye have heard that it was said to them of old time, Thou shalt love thy neighbor and hate thy enemy." Did you ever find this in the Old Testament? Indeed not; on the contrary, in Proverbs 25:21 it reads: "If thine enemy be hungry, give him bread to eat; and if he be thirsty, give him water to drink"; and in Exodus 23:3, 4, Israel was taught: "If thou meet thine enemy's ox or ass going astray, thou shalt surely bring it back to him again. If thou see the ass of him that hateth thee lying under his burden, and wouldest forbear to help him, thou shalt surely help with him."

Hence it is unfair to say that the Old Testament teaches a low and unholy morality, for it inculcates the very opposite. The words disapproved by Jesus are found not in the Old Testament, but in the writings of the liberal rabbis. "Liberal," we say, for many of the rabbis did not support this interpretation. This shows that a man actually lowers himself when he lays upon the lips of Jesus a charge against the Old Testament which can be preferred only against the liberal rabbis.

Without going into the details of Matthew 5:21ff., there is another reason why *"new commandment" cannot* be interpreted by making it to oppose the law of Christian love to the Mosaic commandment of hatred. If Matthew 5:43, "Ye have heard that it has been said, Thou shalt love thy neighbor and hate thine enemy," had been the old commandment of Moses, Jesus could have opposed it by this new commandment: "But I say unto you, Love thy neighbor *and thine enemy.*" That would have had sense. But of the "new commandment" He speaks, *not in this passage,* but in John 13:34, where He treats, not of love for the *enemy,* but of *neighborly* and *brotherly* love. He has just washed the disciples' feet; no enemy is present, He is among friends. And then He says, not, "Moses gave you the old commandment to love one another, but I say, Love even your enemy, and this is My new commandment," but, "A new commandment I give unto you, that [in your own circle] you love one another."

Hence it is evident that this whole representation, as though the new commandment of love opposed the Mosaic commandment of hatred, cannot for a moment be maintained. And apart from this, the divine law of Sinai cannot be anything but a perfect law; and Jesus, Himself being its Author, cannot contradict Himself.

In order to prevent the drawing of such pernicious inference from the words "a new commandment," St. John declares emphatically: "And now I beseech thee, lady, not as though I wrote a new commandment unto thee, but that which we have had from the beginning, that we love one another" (2 John 5). And to make it still more impossible, he calls the same commandment *old* and *new,* according to the viewpoint from which it is considered: "Brethren, I write no new commandment unto you, but an old commandment, which ye had from the beginning. The old commandment is the word which ye have heard from the beginning. Again a new commandment I write unto you, which thing is true in Him and in you; because the darkness is past and the true light now shineth."

The way is now open to arrive at the right understanding of this new commandment, especially with reference to the subject under treatment.

Jesus and the disciples have entered the inner sanctuary of His passion. Golgotha discloses itself. The painful strife of the feetwashing and of the expulsion of the traitor is ended. And during these solemn moments Jesus speaks of His departure, of the coming of the Holy Spirit, and of the new relation which henceforth God's people shall sustain to the Messiah. From Paradise to the Lord's return there is but one salvation for all the elect, but one way in which all walk, but one gate through which all must pass. The whole redemptive work flows from one unchangeable counsel. And herein lies the unity of the Old and New Covenants.

But, although we fully acknowledge this unity, we may not overlook the fact that, in different dispensations and circumstances, the saints sustain different relations to their Lord. To see the atonement typified in the promises of the ceremonial sacrifice is one thing, to look at it as finished on Calvary is quite another; and the difference creates a modified relation. The same is true of living before or after the Incarnation. To walk with Jesus on earth, or to know Him in heaven, puts the saints in a different position. Our departed friends and those who shall live at the return of the Lord are in different relations; for the latter shall not die, but be changed in a moment when this mortal shall be swallowed up of life.

The subject of Christ's conversation before He entered Gethsemane was *this change of the mutual position and relation.* He strongly emphasizes the new fact of the coming of the Holy Spirit to be their Comforter. He Himself will depart, but their treasure will be even richer and more glorious. Hence they need not fear. They will receive the Holy Spirit whom He will send them from the Father. Not as though the Holy Spirit had not wrought already for and in Israel's saints; for then faith and salvation would have been impossible. In fact, His work in the souls of men is as old as the generation of the elect, and originates in Paradise. But to the saints under the Old Covenant this operation came from *without;* while now, being freed from the fetters of Israel, the body of the Church itself becomes the bearer of the Holy Spirit, who descends upon it, dwells within it, and thus works upon its members from *within.*

This is the *new* thing. This is Pentecost. This is all the difference between the dispensation before and after Christ's Resurrection. This is His promise to and for His disciples and for all His saints.

And in this connection Christ speaks of the new commandment, that they should love one another. The same love commanded them by Moses was now to affect them in a different way, since by His departure they were to enter into a different relation. It is not a rare occurrence when the children of the same family, suddenly orphaned, feel as it were a more intimate relation to each other than they ever felt before, and at their parents' grave pledge one another a new love. As they stand at the open sepulcher and look at each other, they suddenly feel a sensation in their hearts hitherto unknown; it is the realization of a new relation. It is the old, and yet a new love, with a new conception, a new motive, a new consecration. So it is here. So long as they were with Jesus, the disciples loved one another; yet they never understood the close and unique character of the relation. But when Jesus suddenly left them, they realized the truth of His new commandment, and their love became consciously deeper, more intimate, really *new* love.

And this new love is the fruit of the Holy Spirit dwelling in the Church. It is like the difference between carrying water with great exertion from a distant fountain, and having a stream from that fountain flow by one's own door, from which he can drink copiously, by whose invigorating scent he feels his spirits revived, into which he can throw himself for a refreshing bath. The Holy Spirit comes with glorious blessings to the children of God under the New Covenant. They drink, not with scant measure, but from a full and overflowing cup. They revel in the fullness of eternal Love. And He that creates this blessedness is the Holy Spirit, the Comforter, whom Jesus has sent from the Father.

30

Organically One

From whom the whole body, fitly joined together and compacted, maketh increase unto the edifying of itself in love — Ephesians 4:16.

The *newness* of holy Love lies *in the Church.* As we look at the withered state of the Church in almost every period, we almost hesitate to make this statement; yet in principle we maintain it to its fullest extent and power.

The Church of Christ on earth is like an "incluse." The "inclusi" were honorable men and women who in the Middle Ages immured themselves in little cells of stone, built under the street, just high enough to allow a man to stand erect. After the incluse had descended into his cell, it was closed over him with a grating and thus he spent his lonely, comfortless life in voluntary isolation. Passers-by could see but little of him. Through the grating the faint outline of a dark form was dimly visible, but it did not seem to possess the least attraction; did not once suggest what manly and noble stature might be concealed in that cell; much less what extraordinary power might be embodied in that incluse, and what hours and days were spent in inward conflict. And such is the image of the Church of Christ on earth. It is enclosed and cannot reveal itself. Of its real form only a faint outline appears, almost always unfavorable and unprepossessing. Unless its spiritual wealth and nobility are discovered in some other way, no one will surmise that this is the Church which shall one day decide the destiny of heaven and earth.

Still this is the fact. The Father loves the Son. The body of the Son is the Church. Hence no one can be saved but he who is incorporated into His body the Church.

Surely it requires a great stretch of the imagination to believe that this muddy shell of the visible Church contains such a precious pearl, but the initiated believe it. They know that in this respect the Church resembles its glorious Head, in the days of His flesh; of whom it was said: "When we shall see Him there is no beauty that we should desire Him. He is despised and rejected of men; we hid, as it were, our faces from Him; He was despised and we esteemed Him not." And when Herod's soldiers mocked and shamefully entreated Him, when stripped and dying He moaned upon the cross, "I thirst," no one but those who looked beneath the surface could surmise that this man was the Lord of Glory. And yet so He proved to be. "He received beauty for ashes, the oil of joy for mourning, the garment of praise for the spirit of heaviness." And so it may be said of the Church while on earth. When we see her, there is no beauty that we should desire her; she is despised and rejected. Everyone is, as it were, hiding his face from her. Still, she is the Lamb's Bride-elect; and the holy Church, which without spot or wrinkle shall one day be presented to the heavenly Bridegroom, is concealed within her. And therefore holy Love must celebrate its triumph in the Church.

The *newness* of the commandment, "Love one another," consists in the fact that, being freed from the bonds of the Jewish national character, love can effectually operate in the Church. And though it be objected a thousand times that love is nowhere a greater stranger than in the Church, and that rather strife and division, backbiting and devouring one another, always have seemed to be the order of the day, yet this lamentable fact does not alter the foregoing positive statement.

It should be remembered, in the *first* place, that strife and division assume the fiercest aspect among those that are most closely related; between brothers and sisters they are more serious than between strangers. Cain and Abel were too intimately connected. This is why differences between husband and wife leave such deep and painful impressions. Their mutual love cannot treat the matter lightly. It is the very intimacy of the relation that gives the difference such a serious character.

Secondly, we should not forget that even in the Church strife and division make the loudest noise, while love unseen quietly pursues its way. Among the initiated in the Church there ever has been a communion of soul which has nowhere its equal—an attachment and opening of hearts impossible but in the Christian life; a brotherly love so sweet as to surpass every other love.

And *finally,* for the present time these discords must continue, that in the last day the beauty and symmetry of the structure may appear to highest advantage. During the construction of a palace one looks in vain for symmetry; the eye meets but disproportions and jarring contrasts. It cannot be otherwise. Confusion there must be until the work is completed. Then the pure and perfect symmetry of the whole will be seen and admired. To call for it during the time of the building would make the final beauty impossible. It would be no profit, but loss. It would spoil the work. Perfect agreement of the parts, finished and unfinished, is out of the question so long as the whole work is not completed. Until then perfect harmony is a matter of faith, not of sight. This is why the saint can say, not, I see, but, "I believe in, the Holy, Catholic, Christian Church."

This is caused by another separating element in the Church antagonizing love, viz., *the truth.* This is evident from the apostolic word warning us against sentimental love, saying: "That we be no more children, but, *doing the truth** in love, we grow up in all things unto Him who is the Head, even Christ" (Eph. 4:15).

What are we to understand by truth opposing love? Are not both from the same source?

Love is union; it joins and binds together severed parts that belong together. And this may be done in two ways. The easiest way to match two non-fitting cogwheels is to *remove* the teeth; then their faces will cover each other. A much more difficult way is *to file each tooth to the required size.* Let us apply this to love. To make the wheels fit each other by removing the teeth is undoubtedly a work of love; for now the wheels are perfectly matched; they seem to be of one piece. But the truth is lost; the wheels are no longer cogwheels. The teeth which made them so are missing. It is true, to fit them by filing each tooth to the

* Dutch Translation.

right size requires inexhaustible patience, but it retains the truth; the wheels remain cogwheels; even though love, which is the matching of the wheels, comes slowly, that is, not until the last tooth is filed to its proper size.

The love which ought to reign among God's people is not the excitement of a dreamy, mystic feeling, destroying individuality, but such uniting and knitting together of the elect that each can attain the full measure of his individual growth ordained for him in the divine counsel; so that in this completion the glory of their membership in the same body may appear and be tasted in the blessed consciousness of the most tender and intimate union.

This is contained in Ephesians 4:16: "From which the whole body fitly framed together, and compacted by that which every joint supplieth, according to the effectual working in the measure of *every* part, maketh increase of the body unto the edifying of itself in love." In the first place, the apostle does full justice to the divine ordinance and honors the divine disposition in the "joining together" and "compacting" and "joints of supply"; and then, by this clearly defined path, he returns with the words, "To the edifying of itself in love," to the deep mystery of this holy intimacy.

It is easy to cultivate love without regarding the truth. It requires neither conflict nor exertion. We simply file down every rough place and rub away ever wrinkle; and at last nothing remains to oppose love. But in that way the Lord's disposition is simply set aside, His ordinance made of no effect, and His truth stumbles in the street. But if you acknowledge the truth and the divine counsel and disposition; if you do not cavil at the divine ordinance and arrangement; if you do not plane, file, and level, but seek the union of spirits in such a way that together they form a whole, so that the teeth of the wheels always clasp each other—then the cultivation of love meets many more obstacles and requires infinitely more care and labor. But finally it will be crowned with the glorious success of obtaining love *without sacrificing divine truth.*

Or to express it more comprehensively: God Himself is the greatest obstacle in the way of that quickly grown and immature love. If God did not exist, two seriously-minded men could be made to agree much more easily. Then they would be at liberty to dispose and arrange matters to suit themselves, according to their *own choice.* But God exists;

hence the disposition of things must be according to *His choice.* In the covenant of love between two persons He is always the Third, and claims that He and His name be not sacrificed to their mutual love. Hence all the conflict, difficulty, and vexation of spirit. Among God's people love in whatever form is ever subject to the first and greatest commandment: God first and last. This is why it is not lawful to cherish and cultivate an affection which excludes His love. In their mutual affection they may not ignore God; act as though God did not exist; be indifferent to His name and truth as though they were of little account and their mutual love the principal thing.

Nay, the wisdom which is from above is first *pure,* then peaceable. Mutual love among the saints cannot flourish unless the saint acknowledge God, confess His name, exalt His truth as their shield and buckler; praise His virtues and reverence His counsel, especially regarding their own person and destiny. Christian love, new and unfailing, born here to live forever, can scintillate only where the name of the Lord shines forth in His truth, where that truth, bearing and animating souls, is experienced and confessed. And this exists, not in sentimentalism, wheedling tones, or sinful indulgence, but in being united and knit together by the Holy Spirit according to the divine foreordination.

At this point the work of the Holy Spirit returns to the eternal counsel of the Lord Jehovah. From that counsel it flows; in that counsel every life has its starting-point, and to that counsel every completed development must return, impelled from its own internal pressure. Every development, though adorning itself with fairest names, which opposes that counsel, proceeds in a wrong direction, and must change its course or run into eternal death. That which is to receive consistency, endurance, and eternal, inexhaustible fullness must spring from that counsel, and in the end, with reference to itself, correctly reflect its fullness.

And since in that counsel the parts do not lie loose, side by side, but are destined to form one rich, spiritual whole, it is the Holy Spirit who, by fitly joining together these parts—that is, the elect children of God—unites and knits them together according to that counsel. Only when this is accomplished, love's perfect beauty shall appear. Then the Church of Christ shall shine as the bearer of that love in the presence of the Lord. And then only the Holy Spirit, even the Spirit of *Truth,* shall have finished His greatest work—that of the *cultivation of Love.*

31

The Hardening Operation of Love

Being grieved for the hardness of their heart—Mark 3:5.

Love may also be reversed. Failing to cherish, to uplift, and to enrich, it *consumes* and *destroys.* This is a mystery which man cannot fathom. It belongs to the unsearchable depths of the divine Being, of which we do not wish to know more than has been revealed. But this does not alter the fact.

No creature can exclude itself from the divine control. No man can say that he has nothing to do with God; that he or any other creature exists independent of God; for God upholds, bears, and carries him from moment to moment, giving him life and power and all his faculties. Even Satan is not self-existing. If it pleased God to discontinue his existence, he would cease from being. Satan and all his demons and all flesh live and move and have their being in God. This apostolic word does not signify an intimate acquaintance with the secret of the Lord, but is merely the clear and sober statement of every creature's essential relation to the Creator. Whether sinner or saint, angel in heaven or demon in hell, even plant or animal, each lives, moves, and exists in God.

Hence to withdraw oneself from God is utterly impossible. Psalm 139 is not merely a sketch of the divine omnipresence, but much more, in holy sense, a testimony and confession from the very root of man's being, of the creature's absolute inability to withdraw himself from

God's active control. The misery of the lost in hell consists in the fact that in their unholy and wicked hearts they are subject to the active, divine control. The cry which once escaped from moaning lips, *"Let me alone* before I go hence" (Job 20:21), is the presentment of the unavoidable control of God, which overwhelms the ungodly as a calamitous flood. If God would let them alone, there would be no hell and no misery. The unquenchable fire would be quenched, and the worm would die. But He does *not* let them alone. He continues His hold upon them. And this causes the eternal pain, and overwhelms them with destruction and condemnation forever.

It is represented sometimes as though God's *material* dealings were to be continued with every man, whether good or evil, while His *spiritual* dealings are confined to the elect. But this is a mistake. It is true His sun rises upon the good and the evil, and His rain comes down upon the just and the unjust, but the same is true spiritually. There is this difference, however, that while the just and the unjust are both profited by the rain and sunshine, the radiation of the Sun of Righteousness and the rain of grace result in blessing for the elect and in destruction for the lost.

This is clearly illustrated by the effects of the rays of the sun in nature. In March they melt the snow and warm and fertilize the soil, while in August they harden the field and scorch its fruit. This is caused by the field's too close proximity to the sun in summer, while in spring it occupies the right position in relation to the sun. And this applies to the Sun of Righteousness. Standing in the proper position regarding that Sun, one feels its fostering and fertilizing effects, but forsaking that position through self-exaltation, aspiring to loftier heights, he discovers immediately that the Sun of Righteousness no longer can bless him, but must consume him with divine fire.

The Scripture teaches this fearful truth in various ways and under various images. St. Paul says that the same Gospel is to one a savor of life unto *life,* and to another a savor of death unto *death.* Concerning the holy Infant, Simeon prophesies that He is set for the *fall* and *rising again* of many in Israel; and the prophet declares that to the saints Messiah shall be a rock of *de*fense, and to those who forsake their God He shall be an *of*fense and a stone of stumbling. There are branches apparently on the same vine; yet some are cast into the fire, and others blossom and bear much fruit. It is one clay and the same potter; yet from the same lump are formed a vessel of honor and a vessel of dishonor, but in both cases it is the same power.

The Scripture introduces this operation unto death and destruction with the somber word, *"hardening of heart"*; especially when the hardening is the result of resisting eternal Love.

Not every effect, however, of the divine operation, destructive to the sinner, is in itself a hardening of heart. There is also a mere *"giving up,"* or *"letting alone."* This is followed by the more gloomy *"darkening."* And only then comes the deadly operation in its proper and limited sense, "hardening of heart," in its worst and most fearful degree.

The mildest and yet awful form of this destruction consists in the fact that, according to the testimony of the apostle, the Lord gives the impenitent sinner over to a reprobate mind: "Wherefore God *gave them up* to uncleanness; who changed the truth of God into a lie, and worshiped and served the creature more than the Creator" (Rom. 1:24, 25). Again he declares in verse 26: "For this cause God *gave them up* unto vile affections." And for the third time in verse 28: "And as they did not like to retain God in their knowledge, God *gave them over* to a reprobate mind, to do things that are not convenient, being filled with all unrighteousness."

This *"giving up"* is related to the *"darkening,"* of which St. Paul speaks in the same connection (v. 21): "They became vain in their imaginations, and their foolish heart was darkened." In Romans 11:8, he describes the same thing in the words of Isaiah: "God hath given them the spirit of slumber, eyes that they should not see, ears that they should not hear." Thus the *"darkening"* and *"the spirit of slumber"* are the gradual transitions between the *"being given over to a reprobate mind"* and the *"hardening of heart"* in its proper sense.

When a sinner is given over to a reprobate mind, the Lord allows him the desire of his heart. He had opened for him another way, but the sinful heart's desires and inclinations bend in a different direction. At first, divine Love, watching over him, prevents him from gratifying these desires. And for this he would thank God, if his heart were right. But he murmurs at this loving interference of his heavenly Father, and seeks the means to obtain what God so far denies him. A painful tension is the result: on the one hand, the sinner bent upon the execution of his evil intentions; and on the other, God, who temporarily prevents this by withholding the opportunity. But when the sinner persists in his evil course and sears his conscience, then God finally withdraws His loving care; the tension ceases; He lets the sinner have his desire; and the latter, given over to a reprobate mind, revels in the gratification of his unholy passions; and, instead of mourning in repentance before the holy God, enjoys his victory.

However, even from this awful condition return is possible. For the first joy of victory is followed by a positive and painful feeling of *disappointment.* Surely he has conquered, but his conquest is unsatisfactory: first, because every sinful gratification alarms the conscience, and this is misery to the soul; secondly, because unholy pleasure is always exhausting and disappointing, never yields what it promised, never proves to be what first it seemed. In such moments salvation is still possible. Better feelings may be aroused, and may lead the sinner to realize that God is right and loves him better than he loves himself. And, acknowledging that God is right, he may cease to justify himself. Then salvation's gates are open, and he may not be far from the heavenly kingdom.

But, overcoming the feeling of disappointment, he falls immediately into a deeper depth. Then he explains his feelings in the opposite way: disappointed not because he has already drank too deeply from the cup of sin, but not deeply enough. He acknowledges his disappointment, but he fancies that greater boldness in sin will remedy this. And so comes the turning-point. When the fearful thought is once conceived and admitted, and the heart's demon-like desire has sprung up deeply and systematically to revel in sin's pleasures, then he is lost. Then "the vain imagination and *darkening* of a foolish heart" is added to being "given over to a reprobate mind." Then the spirit of slumber takes possession of him. He can no longer discern the real cause of his dissatisfaction and disappointment. Sin intoxicates him more and more. And the more he indulges the greater his blindness for the consequences. Things lose their forms. The phenomenal take the place of the real. He has eyes, but not for the real and the true; ears, but not for the voice of the eternal Speaker. And so he rushes on from one sin to another; dissatisfied with sin, yet thirsting after more. As St. Paul says, even anxious to see others sin.

In the way of salvation it is "grace for grace," but in the way of sin, it is sin for sin. To stand still is impossible. The path inclines.

Thus God lets the sinner go. He intoxicates him so that he does not see the precipice that yawns before him. And this opens the way for the hardening. Every effort to make such a one the subject of saving grace is like casting pearls before swine; then Immanuel must hide His love, that seeing he see not, and hearing he understands not.

32

The Love Which Withers

Therefore hath He mercy on whom He will have mercy, and whom He will He hardeneth—Romans 9:18.

The idea of hardening is so awful that, with all its unsanctified pity and natural religion, the human heart rejects it as a horrible thought. Natural compassion cannot bear the idea that a fellow man, instigated to evil by it, should forever ruin himself. And natural religion cannot conceive of a God who, instead of persuading His creature to virtue, should give him up and incite him to sin. This entire representation of hardening is in such open and irreconcilable conflict with all the feelings of the human heart that it is impossible to suppose that it originated in the human mind.

When as children we heard of this hardening of heart for the first time, we could not receive it. Our whole nature rose up against it. And later on, when, in connection with this doctrine, we heard of the mysterious imprecatory psalms and of an unavoidable, eternal doom, then our human nature rebelled against these fearful things with such irrepressible force that we preferred temporarily to forsake our confession rather than to be forced to accept such a horrible idea. Wherefore skeptics are right when they say that, to prove the inconsistency of the Scripture, its miracles need not be attacked, for that its doctrine of hardening and cursing antagonizes the claims of the heart even more than the doctrine of miracles opposes the claims of the reason.

Hence the opposition against the Sacred Scripture always proceeds from two sides at once: on the one hand, from coldly intellectual minds that are always shocked at the Scripture's so-called absurdities and impossibilities; and on the other hand, from the emotional folk, whose feelings are ever hurt by Holy Writ. The effort to compromise can never satisfy anyone. To say, "To me the Scripture is God's own precious Word, but when I come to the 'imprecatory Psalms' and the 'hardening of heart,' then I simply close my eyes and hold my tongue," is no position at all, but mere self-contradiction.

And yet it should be remembered that the vast majority of Christians lose themselves in this unfortunate half-heartedness. The Arminian-tinted do this consciously; willfully they erect their Dagon of the free will as often as the testimony of the Ark of the Covenant has cast them down. They are a singular people. When a doubter refuses to believe the Godhead of Christ, they are immediately ready with their Bible to prove from this text, that passage, and these recorded facts that Christ must be the Son of God and therefore God Himself. But when, with reference to the doctrine of salvation, one proves to them from the same Bible, with similar texts, passages, and facts, that there is indeed a hardening of heart wrought at times by God Himself, then there is no end to their contradiction and they refuse to submit themselves to the Word. They do not seem to notice the unreasonableness and dishonesty of this course. It only shows that, when people propose to decide arbitrarily which portion of the Scripture is true and which is spurious, they betray inward disloyalty and a culpable lack of conviction.

For it is either the Scripture which decides what is true, or I decide. If it is the Scripture, then I must accept its statements concerning the Godhead of the Lord Jesus and of the hardening of the heart. But if I decide according to my own ideas, then I presume to make myself a judge of the Scripture, and, in the very nature of the case, its authority as being a divine and absolute testimony fails to affect me.

We do not stop to consider those who deny the hardening *willfully*. They have departed from the Scripture and from the divine truth. But we notice those who *practically* deny this doctrine, partly by ignoring it, partly by refusing to acknowledge it as part of their confession relating to the divine Being. They rehearse the Scriptural statements regarding this doctrine faithfully and correctly; if need be they are ready to defend, rather than for the sake of human sensitiveness to deny it. On the contrary, their orthodoxy even on this point is above reproach. What the Scripture teaches they teach, the doctrine of the hardening included. But they only *rehearse* it. They know not how to use it. It leaves them cold; they are not in touch with it. While they never neglect to give it a place in their inventory, they do not work with it. And this is the serious part of their position, for it is *inconsistent.* He who treats holy things honestly and sincerely must consider that the acceptance or rejection of this doctrine necessarily affects his representation of the divine Being. The representation of our own heart naturally excludes the hardening. From this it follows that the God of Scripture who effects the hardening, and from whom it cannot be separated, does not agree with our heart's representation of Himself, and therefore requires that we adopt another.

And this is the difficulty with these practical doubters. While they record the doctrine as a memorial in their books, they never apply it: partly because they never consider the fearfulness of the thought, and therefore speak of it unfeelingly; partly—and this deserves special attention—because they never consider how the earnest confession of the doctrine necessarily affects their representation of the divine Being.

This last point if of greatest importance. According to the representation of our natural heart, it is immaterial who or what God is really and essentially if He only loves us, whatever we are, and to such extent as to ever to restore what we destroy. Hence God Himself is of no account. Man is the principal thing; and the highest aim of divine love is to bring man sooner or later to the highest enjoyment of bliss, whatever his conduct, even though to his last breath he should kick against the pricks. Such a God would exactly suit us: a God without a character; who in matters great and small counts for nothing; who by reason of His ill-proportioned love is insensible to any insult that we may offer Him. Hence, however wicked a man may be, however insolent his treatment of the Holy One, the good and benevolent Father will find a way eventually to lead him to eternal bliss; if not in this life, then in the life to come. From that follows that in proportion as God *decreases,* in that proportion His love *increases.* His love will be perfect and all-excelling only when He Himself becomes nothing and utterly discounts Himself.

Such representation of God is the result of a natural process. To man, love means self-denial and self-sacrifice. He is egotistic; and love cannot have full sway within and around him unless he first deny himself, count himself nothing, mindful only of the neighbor's needs. His human love requires that he more and more ignore himself, and make the salvation of others the only object of his existence. And since love so works in *him,* he imagines that it must so work in *God.* Unconsciously he applies to God the same human conception of love; and finally he fancies that the love of God rises higher and higher as His grace becomes more universal.

When one may say that there can be no sinner so wicked and dishonorable but divine Love will eventually receive him in perfect felicity, and another, "You are right, although I would make Judas and those like him an exception," then the former appears the more plausible. He alone who includes even Judas among the blessed has the most worthy idea of the Love of God. The least doubt about it disparages that Love. And the measure of that disparagement is determined by his estimate both of the numbers of the blessed and of the lost.

The point at issue is the *Being of God.* If the human conception of love is applied to God, then all men must be saved, and God has no right to be anything in relation to the creature. But if we confess that of all beings God is the Source, to whom therefore the conception of creaturely love cannot be applied, for then He would cease from being the Supreme Being, then the whole objection becomes invalid. For then we *ignore* our own ideas concerning this mystery, and acknowledge that they cannot but lead us astray. We also distrust the teachings of others, knowing that no more their heart than our own can teach us anything in this respect. And, from the nature of the case, we are made to see that on this subject God alone can enlighten us.

Hence either we must deny that there is a revelation concerning divine Love, so that therefore we can neither deny nor confirm anything concerning it; or we must confess that the Scripture offers us such revelation, and then must also acknowledge as true all that Scripture teaches regarding it.

We do not deny that we ourselves feel the antagonizing influence of the doctrine, and we confess that it does not at all agree with our creaturely conception of love. Neither skeptic nor Arminian need remind us of it. We are much too human and free and untrammeled to deny it. But we absolutely deny our own heart and feelings the right to decide this matter, or even to have any voice in it, and claim that we and our opponents should unreservedly submit to all that God in His Word has revealed in this respect.

While the human heart contends that God cannot harden any man's heart, Scripture meets us, whether we like it or not, with the awful testimony: "And whom He will He hardens." And let us reverently believe it, though it be with inward trembling of soul.

33

The Hardening in the Sacred Scripture

He hath hardened their heart—John 12:40.

The Scripture teaches positively that the hardening and "darkening of their foolish heart" is a divine, intentional act.

This is plainly evident from God's charge to Moses concerning the king of Egypt: "Thou shalt speak all that I command thee; and I will harden Pharaoh's heart, and multiply My signs and wonders in the land of Egypt. But Pharaoh shall not harken unto you, and I will lay My hand upon Egypt, and the Egyptians shall know that I am the Lord" (Ex. 7:3–5). Before this the Lord had said to Moses: "When thou goest to return unto Egypt, see that thou do all those wonders before Pharaoh, which I have put in thine hand, but I will make his heart stubborn, that he shall not let the people go" (Ex. 4:21).

The principal person in the Scripture in whom this awful truth obtains its clearest revelation is Pharaoh. Why in him we cannot tell. And, instead of looking down on him from the heights of our own imagined piety, we should rather remember the word of the apostle: "And whom He will He hardens."

However, the subject of this terrible judgment of hardening is not the individual Pharaoh in his private life, but the king, the mighty prince and sovereign, the ruler and despot, who in the majesty of his crown and scepter represented the supremacy of the first great world-empire over the nations of the earth.

In those days Egypt occupied the position subsequently attained by Nineveh, Babylon, Macedonia, and Rome; it was the embodiment of all the luster and glory which the natural, sinful, and God-rejecting world could create. In the cities of Upper and Lower Egypt men reveled in the refined pleasures of life. From all the surrounding countries gold came pouring into Egypt. The rulers built themselves great cities and strong fortresses, sphinxes and mountain-like pyramids. Cities of the dead were hewn out of the rocks. Magnificent sarcophagi were chiseled out of exquisitely beautiful marble. In a word, the world's proud and majestic creations of those days were found on the shores of the Nile. The Pharaoh of Egypt was the mightiest man of the earth.

And as such he is the subject of the hardening. That St. Paul views the conflict between Jehovah and Pharaoh in this light is evident from his quotation of Exodus 9:16, where it is expressed in strongest and plainest language: "For I will at this time send all My plagues upon thine heart, and upon thy servants, and upon thy people; that thou mayest know that there is none like Me in all the earth. And *in very deed for this cause have I raised thee up, for to show in thee* My power; and that My name may be declared throughout all the earth" (Rom. 9:2).

These words are meaningless if they are made to refer to the private life of the individual Pharaoh. No private individual ever possessed such power. But if they are understood as referring to Pharaoh the great world-ruler, they assume an entirely different aspect. For he was not the creator of that power, neither was that power the creation of a day, but the result of a gradual development under God's own direction. Four centuries before Moses, God had already spoken to Abraham of this mighty Egypt and predicted the conflict which His power would bring upon it. Many dynasties of absolute monarchs had succeeded one another. And when Pharaoh's dynasty ascended the throne, the centralized government of the empire was thoroughly vested in his person.

In His unfathomable counsel the Lord had evidently led the godless world of that day to concentrate all its wisdom, power, intellect, and refinement in Egypt's limited territory. He had *raised up* Egypt, He had *raised up* its great dynasties, and lastly *raised up* Pharaoh, who, wholly absorbed into Egypt's luxury, power, and world-majesty, was the embodiment of what the world could oppose in one man, and he therefore *a man of sin,* against the majesty of God.

And this haughty monarch enclosed *Israel* in the bonds of death, and with them the *Hope of the fathers,* the preparation of *Messiah* after the flesh, and the Church of God in its patriarchal state. He should have honored and blessed this people, but he treated it cruelly. The sciences of those days flourished in Egypt. Historical events were chiseled in hieroglyphs upon stone, and published upon obelisks and sarcophagi for the information of the public. Hence Egypt could not plead ignorance as an excuse; at the royal court Joseph was still remembered as the benefactor of Egypt, who saved it from famine; and the Egyptians could not have forgotten their solemn promises to the Hebrews. And yet Pharaoh tyrannized over the people, and even sought to prevent their increase by ordering the destruction of all male infants.

Hence Pharaoh, enslaving Israel, represents the evil world-power which kept the Christ in bondage. Wherefore God said: "I have called My Son out of Egypt." With Israel He called the Messiah out of Egypt. The fearful conflict was *for* Messiah *against* Pharaoh.

This sheds some light upon the puzzling words: "For this cause have I raised thee up." Having lost its prop by its departure from God, the world could not manifest its sinful power but in a world-empire, and in individual monarchs. And such manifestation was not fortuitous, but a logical necessity, divinely intended, that the divine power might triumph over it. For this reason it is repeatedly stated: *"But the Lord hardened Pharaoh's heart"* (Ex. 10:20); *"And I will harden Pharaoh's heart,* that he shall follow after them, and I will be honored upon Pharaoh and upon his host, that the Egyptians may know that I am the Lord" (Ex. 14:4); *"And the Lord hardened the heart of Pharaoh,* and he pursued after the children of Israel" (Ex. 14:8). Later on the hardening came upon all Egypt: *"And I, behold, I will make stubborn the hearts of the Egyptians,* and I will get Me honor upon Pharaoh and upon all his host" (Ex. 14:17).

Throughout this whole terrible history the prospective hardening is first announced, then carried into effect, and finally recorded as accomplished in Pharaoh. For—and this deserves special notice—every announcement of the divine hardening is followed by the announcement from the subjective standpoint that Pharaoh himself hardened his heart: *"And Pharaoh's heart was stubborn"** (Ex. 7:13); and again: "And the magicians of Egypt did so with their enchantments, *and Pharaoh's heart was hardened"** (Ex. 7:22); and again: *"And Pharaoh's heart was stubborn,* neither would he let the children of Israel go" (Ex. 9:35). And for this reason St. Paul writes: "Is there unrighteousness with God? God forbid. For He saith to Moses, I will have compassion on whom I will have compassion. So then it is not of him that willeth, nor of him that runneth, but of God that showeth mercy. For the Scripture saith unto Pharaoh, Even *for this same purpose have I raised thee up,* that I might show My power in thee" (Rom. 9:14–17).

Although Pharaoh is the most conspicuous figure in this respect, yet the hardening is not confined to him alone. Of Sihon, the feared despot of Hesbon, it is written: "The Lord thy God *hardened his spirit and made his heart obstinate,* that He might deliver him into thine hand, as appeareth this day." Of the allied kings of North Palestine, who under Jabin, king of Hazor, declared war against Joshua, it is written: "For it was of the Lord to harden their hearts, that they should come against Israel in battle" (Joshua 11:20).

Satan said that he tempted David to number the people (1 Chr. 21:1), but, from 2 Samuel 24:1, it is evident that he did not act without divine direction and obeyed only reluctantly.

The prophet mournfully asks: "O Lord, why hast Thou made us to err from Thy ways and hardened our hearts from Thy fear?" (Is. 63:17); a touching complaint which echoes the awful prophecy of his installation: "Go and tell this people, Hear ye indeed but understand not, and see ye indeed but perceive not. Make the heart of this people fat and make their heart heavy, and shut their eyes; lest they see with their eyes and hear with their ears, and understand with their hearts, and convert and be healed" (Is. 6:9, 10).

To the objection that this is Old Testament theology, but that such harshness is foreign to the Christian Church in which Christ has instituted the reign of Love, we reply that that Church is as old as Paradise, that in both covenants it is the same divine Speaker, and that Christ and His apostles reveal the same hardening. In Matthew 13:14, Mark

* "And Pharaoh's heart *hardened itself"* (Dutch Translation).

4:12, 14, Luke 8:10, Christ largely dwells upon the fact, and states it, even for the direction of conduct, in the very words of Isaiah's inauguration prophecy, that sometimes God causes the Word to come to a man in such a way that hearing he hears not, but hardens his heart. And St. Paul addressed the same words to the Romans (Acts 10:8; 28:26). We have already noticed his words, "To give over to a reprobate mind," and to the darkening of heart, which have the same effect as the hardening.

It is remarkable that the New Testament especially presents the idea of hardening in a passive form, not as an act of the subjects themselves, but as a calamity which has come upon them as a terrible consequence of their sins. In Romans 11:25 it reads: "For I would not, brethren, that ye should be ignorant of this mystery, that a *hardening in part is happened to Israel";* in 2 Corinthians 3:14: "But their minds *were* hardened"; in Romans 11:7, "And the rest *were* hardened." So also in Mark 6:52: "Their heart *was* hardened"; in Acts 19:9: "But diverse *were* hardened"; and lastly in Hebrews 3:13: "But exhort one another while it is called today; lest any of you be hardened through the deceitfulness of sin."

With these passages before us, it is impossible to deny that the Scripture reveals God as the Author of the hardening. And he who says that the God whom he worships cannot harden any man's heart, ought to see that he does not worship the God of the Scripture.

The objection that, if hardening is a divine operation, then warning and admonition are vain and useless, points to another extreme. The same Scripture which says, "And whom He will He hardeneth," says also, "But exhort one another while it is called today, lest any of you be hardened." To both these passages we submit, bringing into captivity every thought to the obedience of the Word.

34

Temporary Hardening

Lord, why hast Thou hardened our heart?—Isaiah 63:17.

That there is a hardening of heart which culminates in the sin against the Holy Spirit cannot be denied. When dealing with spiritual things we must take account of it; for it is one of the most fearful instruments of the divine wrath. For, whether we say that Satan or David or the Lord tempted the king, it amounts to the same thing. The cause is always in man's sin; and in each of these three cases the destructive fatality whereby sin poisons and destroys the soul cannot be severed from the government of God.

However, in studying this matter, we should remember for our comfort that the hardening is not essentially and invariably absolute and irreparable. We should distinguish between a *temporary* and a *permanent* hardening. The latter is absolute; the former passes away and dissolves into saving faith.

Crying, "Lord, why hast Thou hardened our heart?" Isaiah represents persons who are now in glory before the throne; moreover, the question itself, the sorrow expressed, and the longing after God of which it speaks, suffice to assure us that Isaiah was no Pharaoh. That Israel is exhorted, "Harden not your hearts as in the provocation" (Ps. 95:8), proves that the hardening spoken of had not been intended forever. And the hardening that, according to St. Paul, had come *"in part"* to Israel was not absolute, as appears from the words "in part."

The *temporal* and the *permanent* hardening should not be confounded. This would drive the guilty sinner into spiritual despair, and raise the Cain-thought in his heart—a danger that requires the most earnest and watchful care. Satan, the enemy of souls, thoroughly understands all the weaknesses of the human heart. In this respect he knows more than the best informed among men. He knows whether to attack a man in the front or from behind, to ruin him with threats or with flattery, to frighten him with despair or to ensnare him with the prospects of peace. This is why he delights again and again in making a man either trifle with the deadly danger of his soul, or to believe that he is hopelessly lost and beyond the power of redemption.

How many souls has not Satan terrified with the sin against the Holy Spirit! Souls who never thought of such a thing; who, on the contrary, had a tender regard for the Holy Spirit's honor in the hope of their salvation, but whom nevertheless he decoyed into the fearful belief of being utterly cast away, of having committed the unpardonable sin. Of course, if such souls had lived nearer the Word, more earnestly searched it, and adhered more closely to the guidance of the Church's interpretation of this dark mystery, they would not have fallen into this snare. But as it was, Satan whispered it into their ear, and, almost smothering their spiritual life, kept them, sometimes for years, languishing in the mortal fear of being lost forever. And so dark was the spiritual night that it seemed that no ray of light would ever pierce it.

And the same is true of the hardening. Even with this awful spiritual operation Satan plays his horrible game of robbing God's children of their spiritual peace. Of course, this is never without their own fault. All the spiritual distress of the saints is the necessary result of their transgressions, whether public or private. But he that sowed the hurtful seed, in the field fertilized by sin, was no other than the tempter of souls, who stealthily came to their side and suggested that their grievous state was worse than being merely *"forsaken";* that there must be signs of *hardening* which would steadily increase; wherefore the flower of hope was withered and all expectation cut off.

And for this danger the soul must be prepared by the clear and definite distinction between the *temporary* and the *permanent* hardening. The former comes to every one of God's children. There is not one, among those grown old in the way, who cannot recall the time when he felt the love of God drawing him to separate him from some sin or unbelief, but this seemed only to incite him all the more to resist that love, to close his ears to it and with greater energy to embrace the evil. It was not with the intention to persist in it, but merely to gain time wherein to enjoy the sinful delights a little longer, while the divine love is resisted. We say: "Once more, and then we will stop our resistance." In reality, while we thus trifle with the love of God, we believe that it is quite strong enough to endure this little opposition. And this may result in a temporary hardening, which is sometimes very serious, and which is marked by and consists in the fact that the saint who intended the next time to break with his sin, then discovers, to his dismay, that by his temporary indulgence the power to resist has been lost.

And this is God's righteous reward. The love that the disobedient saint resisted for the sake of sin is insulted and refuses to be trifled with. Although he did not expect it, yet by his obstinate resistance of that first love the power of sin was strengthened, the soul's tender sensitiveness was dulled, and the heart was made callous. What was first a mere sliver in the flesh became a malignant boil. An evil power developed itself imperceptibly and unexpectedly. He fights against it, but in vain. After repeated falls, he ceases the fight, and gradually lapses into a condition of hardening so grievous that he cannot discover in his heart the least trace of the divine love.

However, this hardening is only partial, for it has reference only to some special matter; and this is the difference between it and the permanent hardening. Apart from this matter, he can still burn with love and zeal for his God; he can still open his heart for the operation of the gracious powers of eternal life, and even have blessed communion with the Lord. But these slowly disappear. The malignant abscess gradually imparts its fever-heat from one part to another. The blood in the veins of the soul is kept in restless tension, and to this partial hardening is added a sense of general forsakenness that causes his communion to become more rare and less refreshing. There may be an occasional drop of oil, but there is never a full, fresh anointing. As a result, he feels himself poor, dry, and dead; he goes about with the sentence of condemnation in his conscience, but in the midst of his anguish his soul groans unto God.

And the Lord hears that groan. There may be no prayer, and the Holy Spirit may be too far gone to enable his soul to pour itself out in supplications; yet so long as there is a smoking flax and a broken reed that vainly tries to lift itself, so long as there is a sense of shame and an inward groan to God for deliverance, the Lord inclines His ear, full of compassion, and the hour approaches when the Sun of Righteousness shall dispel the clouds and melt the hardness of his heart. The love first resisted now returns with irresistible power to gladden his soul. The crust of ice begins to melt. A blessed emotion unknown for years makes itself felt. The dry eye becomes dim and the inflexible knee and stiff neck bend in prayer. And the mercy and long-suffering of God cause the fresh oil to flow, and, with a self-abasement hitherto unknown, the soul believes and praises and adores once more the grace of the Lord Jesus Christ and the rich mercy of His God.

Although a real hardening, yet it is like that which falls upon the streams and fields in winter, when the yellow leaves fall from the trees, the sun-rays slant, and the waters congeal. But that winter does not last forever. Spring is coming soon. And when the grass is green again and the birds sing in the woods, it seems as though, after its winter sleep, nature is quickened into a richer and more glorious life. Such is the temporal hardening of the called of God: a winter followed by spring, until the dawn of the eternal morning in the realms of the everlasting light.

But the permanent, the eternal hardening is not so. This causes us to think of the world of eternal snow and ice in the polar regions, where it freezes never to thaw, and where nature is covered with somber cerements, to be uncovered only when the Lord shall come upon the clouds, and the whole world shall melt with fervent heat.

It is true, even amid that eternal snow and ice, a single ray may for a while pierce the darkness, the icicles may drop, and the ice-fields may separate, but the heart of that ice-world remains unaffected and its eternal foundations unmoved. One iceberg may get loose from the rest, but it remains an iceberg. It cannot thaw out; eternally hardened, even in nature!

And that world of ice is the awful image of the Sihons and Pharaohs, and of everyone who is permanently hardened and given over to the judgment of God. The Love of God has been sinned against forever, and every expression of life only adds to the callousness of the heart, until all feeling, conception, and sensibility with reference to spiritual things are utterly gone. And if there be any life and growth left, they are the life and growth of the mildew which poisons, of the parasite which destroys. So fearful is the hardening that the subject himself is utterly insensible of it. In his temporal hardening the child of God shall weep at last, but the other moves on with boisterous laughter to meet his doom.

The Lord God have mercy on us! God's judgment of hardening is such an awful thing!

35

The Hardening of Nations

The election hath obtained it, and the rest were hardened—
Romans 11:7.

Saint Paul's word, at the head of this article, is strikingly impressive, and its content exceedingly rich and instructive. It clearly announces the fact that the hardening is not exceptional or occasional, but *universal,* affecting all, who, being in contact with the divine Love, are not saved by it.

The last limitation is necessary, for of the heathen it cannot be said that they are hardened. Only they can be hardened who live under the Covenant of Grace. It is true that the heathen develop a reprobate mind. Their heart is darkened. Walking in their own ways they are impelled irresistibly, for the process of sin cannot be stopped, but this is not the proper conception of the hardening as the Scripture presents it.

Heathen nations and individuals may come in direct contact with the Lord and His Anointed, as Pharaoh and Sihon through their relations with Israel; and as the Turks and the peoples of India and China who now are in touch with Christian nations and missionaries. Of course, we do not mean to say that mere casual contact with a Christian nation or missionary makes a Mohammedan or heathen nation responsible. This is impossible. When in Epirus the Turks meet hordes who call themselves Christians, but are utterly devoid of the Spirit of Christ and in savagery rather surpass the bashi-bazouks, then no ray from the cross falls upon the crescent by this meeting. The fact that a missionary settles in an obscure corner of a heathen nation, opens a little school, and talks about the Scripture with a few individuals, in a manner which betrays his ignorance of human nature, does not make that nation responsible. They know nothing about it; it leaves the national life wholly untouched.

The Christian nations, their governments, their churches, and their missionaries, may well ask themselves whether by such playing at missions they do not increase their own responsibilities rather than those of the heathen nations. How serious these responsibilities, especially regarding the heathen and Mohammedan nations! Owing to the divine pleasure the Christian nations possess a moral and material superiority. England alone is perfectly able to control China, Japan, the whole of India and Turkey besides. There is not the slightest prospect that the heathen nations will, for a long time to come, be able to cope successfully with the nations of Christendom. In their own native jungles they may be able to maintain themselves, but as soon as they come in the open field they are vanquished. We may harass the Achinese, but it never enters our minds that they will effect a landing upon our shores.

Whether this will continue is another question. As the Christian nations return more and more to Judaism, and thence to heathenism, it is very possible that they will lose also their material superiority. There are already signs showing that China may some time seriously vex the Christian nations; and in India our possession is not as undisturbed as once it was. The ancient moral greatness and world-supremacy of the heathen nations should not be forgotten; it is only fifteen centuries ago that that state of things was reversed. All the more reason why the Christian nations should consider that they owe their power and glory only to the name of Christ; and that they are responsible unto God for the performance of their duty toward these nations. God demands that we bring them in contact with Christ; and they themselves are entitled to it.

This contact should be comprehensive. It should be noticeable in the European and American settlers in those countries; in the laws and institutions which we impose upon them; in the writings and information which we bring them; especially in our preaching of Christ among them. And comparing these moderate claims with the reported shameful manner in which men calling themselves Christians act in those countries, their immoralities, their cruelties, their grasping, their corrupting of the nations by their unjust laws and iniquitous practices—for example, the opium traffic—it is obvious that, instead of our being the cause of the hardening of the heathen nations, our own debt and responsibilities with regard to them are largely increased.

It is true that some nations have labored among the heathen with great success; there are even some small heathen nations which, owing to their contact with excellent Christian men, governors and missionaries, may be said to have come into contact with Christ; and, if they did not receive Him, such contact must be the cause of their hardening. But these are exceptions, and we members of the Reformed churches cannot boast that our share in revolutionizing the heathen world will be very great.

But with these exceptions we limit the hardening to men who, living in Christian countries, have long been under the influence of the Gospel. This applies also to Israel under the Old Covenant. The Church now spread among the nations was hid in Israel. The hardening seldom occurred among the heathen, and as a rule was confined to the Jews. In saying that the elect have obtained it, while the rest were hardened (Rom. 11:7), St. Paul evidently refers to Israel exclusively, as appears from the context: "*Israel* hath not obtained that which he seeketh for, but the election hath obtained it, and the rest were hardened." And then follows a description of this hardening, borrowed from Isaiah 29:10: "The Lord hath poured out upon them a spirit of deep sleep; eyes that they should not see, and ears that they should not hear." Hence the hardening which now manifests itself as a *new* working is confined to the Christian Church. The hardening still upon Israel is an *after*-effect of the *ancient* judgment; it is not new. By their Christ-rejection before Gabbatha, on Calvary, and on Pentecost, they brought it upon themselves, and cannot be delivered from it except through the gift of new grace. Hence in the discussion of *present* hardening it does not come into consideration.

As a rule, the hardening which in our days and in our own circles manifests itself is confined to the Christian Church, and follows in the track of holy Baptism.

And here we distinguish a *personal* and a *collective* hardening. With reference to the latter, a sad but well-known fact will explain our meaning. In many districts, here and elsewhere, the correct ideas of holy wedlock are falsified; not only recently, but for ages. This is evident from the fact that the marital relation is entered upon through sin before the marriage is confirmed, making it *"obligatory,"* as it is said. This is a collective hardening against the divine blessing of holy wedlock. It is a popular sin which affects not only the individual, but his entire generation and whole environment. In like manner there is sin in every trade and business, without which it is said one cannot be a business man. "Every man is a thief in his own store"; and with such-like sinful jests the matter is dismissed. Every new clerk is properly initiated. He that does not know the tricks is deemed incompetent, and the unwilling are said to spoil the game.

In this sense there is a collective hardening in many countries and churches which has fallen upon the multitudes as a spirit of slumber. One has only to compare the churches of Scotland and of Spain to be convinced of the fact. The churches of both countries confess the name of the same Lord Jesus Christ; they read the same Gospel; partly sing the same psalms; there is scarcely one mystery of faith confessed in Scotland that is not confessed in Spain. But with all this similarity, what immeasurable difference! In both nations one is baptized with the same Baptism and nourished with the same Lord's Supper, but how vastly different the manifestation of the ecclesiastical life! We do not deny that in the churches of Scotland there may be many a lack and defect. We even allow that in the Church of Spain there may be an occasional tender glow of love, while in the north of Great Britain we find something cold and chilling. But apart from this, what clear and positive consciousness in Scotland, and how heavy the veil which covers the face of Christ's Church in Spain! It is true Spain still possesses the confession of saving truth, but deeply buried under numberless human institutions. The luster of holy things divine is dim and feeble. We deny not the working of divine grace in the Spanish Church, and we gladly admit that Christ is preached even under the veil, and that His elect are being gathered unto eternal life. But for the rest, what dullness of soul, what hardening of spirit! It is evident that in that grandly beautiful country an evil power oppresses the spirits, against which they wrestle in vain.

Although less conspicuously and on a smaller scale, the same collective hardening is found everywhere. In the Scottish Highlands the Church is much purer than in the Lowlands. In the Lutheran Church in Norway spiritual life is much more tender than in Saxony. In the Canton du Vaud it is much more energetic than in Berne. And in our own land, who does not mourn for Drente as compared to Zeeland? Who does not know that the rural districts of South Holland are spiritually much more susceptible than those of North Holland? And who can fail to notice the difference between sand and clay in Friesland and in Gelderland? But if we possess deeper insight and larger life, owing to the more favorable circumstances of environment and education, we should not boast ourselves. If we had been planted in such dry ground, we should probably have grown up just as thin and ill-favored.

To measure every man's guilt with reference to this collective hardening is not our business, but the Lord is the Judge of all the earth. But it is our business to oppose this hardening, wherever we meet it, with the leaven of the Word, and to pray without ceasing for deliverance from this spiritual plague. Again and again the hardening, which had been upon villages and cities and whole countries, has been lifted by the boldness of a single preacher of righteousness. It may be incurable as in Sodom and Gomorrah, which were to be destroyed, while Nineveh could still repent. But this is exceptional. Ordinarily we see the most hardened nations awake from their spiritual slumber as soon as the preacher of repentance summons them to return to God.

Altogether different is the personal hardening which, in greater or smaller measure, comes upon all who live under the influence of the Gospel without being quickened by it—who were baptized with water and not with the Holy Spirit; and of this personal hardening the apostle testifies: "The election hath obtained it, but the rest were hardened."

36

The Apostolic Love

He hath blinded their eyes and hardened their hearts—John 12:40.

It is singular that the hardening, in its most awful manifestation, finds its exponent not in Jeremiah, the stern preacher of repentance, nor in St. Paul, the logic confessor and witness of the divine sovereignty, but in St. John, the *apostle of love.* St. John knows men whom he designates as "children of the devil," who as such are the opposite of the children of God.

Jesus had entered the holy city amid the hosannas of the enthusiastic multitudes. All Jerusalem apparently came out to hail Him. Even the resident Greeks asked for Him. It was the hour of triumph and glory. And yet, in the midst of this popular applause, Jesus knows that He is the "Man of Sorrows," and declares to His disciples that He is like the grain of wheat which, "except it fall into the ground and die, abideth alone, but if it die it bringeth forth much fruit." Then He cried out: "Now is My soul troubled. And what shall I say? Father, save Me from this hour, but for this cause came I unto this hour. Father, glorify Thy name." And immediately there came a voice from heaven, saying: "I have both glorified it and will glorify it again." The people that surrounded Him "thought that it had thundered, and others said that an angel had spoken to Him." It was one of the most solemn and impressive signs that ever have attended the preaching of the Word—an event like that of Carmel; a direct answer from heaven.

Still under its impression, Jesus continues His words to the multitude, saying: "While ye have the light believe in the light, that ye may be the children of the light." And what was the answer? Another hosanna like that when Jesus had raised Lazarus from the dead, and which was honestly meant by some? Indeed not. When, instead of promising them that He would raise up the kingdom and deliver it from Roman bondage, Jesus presented to them the claims of faith, then they resisted Him, and the evil in their eyes betrayed the opposite of peace in their hearts. The same Nazarene whom a moment ago they had hailed with the waving of palms, they now are ready to bury under showers of stones. Jesus, seeing this, departed and hid Himself from them. And thus, on that public square of Jerusalem, the multitude was left alone. They had rejected the King whom they should have adored. A voice had spoken from heaven, but they had stopped their ears.

Deluded people! You know not whom ye have rejected, and that your rejection of today must lead to His crucifixion tomorrow. You rejected Him, and, with Him, yourselves forever. For this is what St. John, the witness of peace and love, under the direct inspiration of the Holy Spirit, writes concerning them: "Though He had done so many miracles before them, yet they believed not on Him, that the saying of Esaias the prophet might be fulfilled, which he spake, Lord, who hath believed our report? And to whom is the arm of the Lord revealed? Therefore they *could not believe,* because Esaias said again, He hath blinded their eyes and hardened their hearts; that they should not see with their eyes, nor understand with their heart, and be converted, and I should heal them."

"They *could not* believe." No judgment could be keener, more direct, more fearful! Who can hear these words without an aching heart? Who trembles not when the holy apostle declares that such are the ordinances of the Kingdom? Who does not bow the head in the presence of such blinding mysteries? Oh, that we might erase these words from the Gospel! But we may not. Though they most painfully affect us, though we cannot sufficiently admonish one another never to speak of these fearful mysteries but with a loving and sorrowing heart, yet they may not be taken from the Gospel. Without them even St. John's Evangel would not be intact, rich, and complete. The Scripture may not be emasculated.

It was Jesus who discovered that these wretchedly sinful men of Jerusalem were hardened and stiff-necked. This comes, not to men in Rome or Athens, but to men in the Jewish capital. It is remarkable that when the Greeks came to Philip naively asking for Jesus, these children of Abraham should be manifested as hardened in their hearts. There had been such men in Jericho, Bethany, and Jerusalem twenty years ago, but the apostle declares that this somber prophecy of the completed hardening was fulfilled to its fullest extent only in the men who were then the leaders of public opinion in Jerusalem, who were hardened by their contact, not with John the Baptist, but *with Jesus.*

The effect of contact with Jesus is so decisive that it determines the whole subsequent course of a man's life and being forever. There is no one greater and more glorious than Jesus. Whom Jesus does not save cannot be saved. He who sees no light in Jesus must forever wander in darkness. He is *the* touchstone. Tested by Him, the soul stands revealed.

From this narrative, and from all that the Scripture reveals on this subject, it is therefore piteously evident that our greatest glory, viz., our Christian assurance and the most awful misery which the soul can conceive, *the hardening of a human being,* stand side by side, belong together in causal connection. Rock of offense; fall and rising again for many in Israel; a sign that shall be spoken against; savor of life, but also savor of death—we wonder how it is possible that He who is the Savior of the soul can also cause its deadly corruption to become manifest!

And yet it is a fact; the Word of God leaves no room for doubt. And what is still more wonderful, this fearful operation of being a savor of death proceeds from Christ in one of the most glorious moments of His life: in the moment when He shines in all the greatness of His majesty. The hour had come when, like a grain of mustard seed, He should fall into the ground. The Galileans saw their Lord. The Greeks asked after Him. The voice from heaven was still vibrating in their ears. With touching entreaty He called them to repentance. And it is in that moment that the enmity of the human heart shows Him its deadly hatred, and in its base resistance compels Him to hide Himself. And then their hardening of heart becomes manifest.

There is no escape from this critical moment. Every man *must* be drawn to Christ. And he that has come to Him must see more and more of His greatness and holiness, and become more intimately acquainted with Him. And by this very entrance into the inner sanctuary the lost soul discovers its own true inwardness, and whether it will ever come to a rending of the veil.

But from this we should never draw the wrong inference, that it is then the safest course never to bring our children to Jesus. This is not left to our decision. The Lord of Hosts is He who commands us: "Suffer the little children to come unto Me." But what this deep mystery ought to teach us is not to throw holy things to the dogs, nor to make an ostentatious display of divine truth. Although we do not judge others, but rather let their zeal in spreading the Gospel rebuke our lukewarmness, yet we must remind them of the fact that *they deal with fire.* Surely no other than the sharp two-edged sword of the Spirit can reach the inward seat of corruption, but remember, carelessly handled, it may wound some vital part. And therefore, in the spirit of love, we must ever admonish the brethren never to preach the awful Gospel in a thoughtless and careless manner, but always with greatest caution and holy earnestness. For the work of preaching the Gospel is exceedingly delicate.

As to the question, How does the hardening occur? we simply say that every effort to be wise above that which is written must be opposed; being conscious of our own limitations, we prefer to watch lest our own soul fall under this terrible judgment, rather than to lose ourselves in the vain effort to analyze what we cannot conceive of but in the unity of the holy mystery.

But this we may say: that in nature God offers us many illustrations of the fact that in its highest activity the same power can have opposite effects. Without rain the field parches and vegetation burns, but the same rain that elsewhere makes the grain to grow, in the ill-drained field causes the crop to decay. The same sun that warms the ground and matures the grain in one acre, will harden the ground and scorch the crop in another. The same food that nourishes and strengthens the healthful, burdens the weak and endangers the life of the sick. Knowledge is glorious, and at its fountain man loves to quench his thirst, but how appalling the corruption caused, either by its one-sided application or by an ill-proportioned estimate of its value! Holy and tender is the bond between husband and wife, mother and child, but is there any passion that has added more to the pollution and desecration of human life than this very desire for the married state and this longing to become a mother?

The law is universal that the highest excellency, failing to accomplish its purpose, reverses its action and causes destruction, pollution, and often hopeless ruin, in much greater measure than if it were less excellent. And knowing this, is it strange that the same law prevails in the highest domain, viz., the Love of God?

Hardening is but the effect of the divine Love turned in the opposite direction. It cherishes or it consumes. It draws to heaven or it blights in hell.

37

The Sin against the Holy Ghost

The blasphemy against the Holy Ghost shall not be forgiven unto men—Matthew 12:31.

Although the love of God, failing of its purpose, always causes hardening of heart, yet at times it has a still more terrible effect, for it may lead to *the sin against the Holy Ghost.*

The results of this sin are especially crushing and terrible. Christ's words concerning it are startling and penetrating, casting the guilty soul into everlasting despair:

"He that is not with Me is against Me; and he that gathereth not with Me scattereth abroad. Wherefore I say unto you, All manner of sin and blasphemy shall be forgiven unto men, but the blasphemy against the Holy Ghost shall not be forgiven unto men. And whosoever speaketh a word against the Son of man, it shall be forgiven him, but whosoever speaketh against the Holy Ghost, it shall not be forgiven him, neither in this world, neither in the world to come" (Matt. 12:30–32).

St. Mark puts it still more harshly: "Verily I say unto you, All sins shall be forgiven unto the sons of men, and blasphemies wherewith soever they shall blaspheme. But he that shall blaspheme against the Holy Ghost hath never forgiveness, but is guilty of an eternal sin" (Mark 3:28, 29, R.V.).

St. John writes concerning it: "If any man see his brother sin a sin which is not unto death, he shall ask, and He shall give him life for him that sins not unto death. There is a sin unto death; I do not say that he shall pray for it. All unrighteousness is sin, and there is a sin not unto death. We know that whosoever is born of God sinneth not, but he that is begotten of God keepeth himself, and that wicked one toucheth him not" (1 John 5:16–18).

And St. Paul writes: "For it is impossible for those who were once enlightened, and have tasted of the heavenly gift, and were made partakers of the Holy Ghost, and have tasted the good Word of God, and the powers of the age to come, if they shall fall away, to renew them again unto repentance; seeing they crucify unto themselves the Son of God afresh, and put Him to an open shame. For the earth which drinketh in the rain that cometh oft upon it, and bringeth forth herbs meet for them by whom it is dressed, receiveth blessing from God, but that which beareth thorns and briers is rejected, and is nigh unto cursing; whose end is to be burned" (Heb. 6:4–8). Such cutting words would perplex the soul, if he had not added: "But, beloved, we are persuaded better things of you, and things that accompany salvation, though we thus speak. For God is not unrighteous to forget your work and labor of love, which ye have showed toward His name" (vv. 9, 10).

They are words of comfort, which, however, do not detract from the dead earnestness with which he speaks in the tenth chapter: "For if we sin willfully after that we have received the knowledge of the truth, there remaineth no more sacrifice for sins, but a certain fearful looking for of judgment and fiery indignation, which shall devour the adversaries. He that despised Moses' law died without mercy under two or three witnesses. Of how much sorer punishment, suppose ye, shall he be thought worthy who hath trodden under foot the Son of God, and hath counted the blood of the covenant, wherewith he was sanctified, an unclean thing, and hath done despite unto the Spirit of grace? For we know Him that saith, Vengeance belongeth unto Me, I will recompense, saith the Lord. And again, The Lord shall judge His people. It is a fearful thing to fall into the hands of the living God" (Heb. 10:26–31).

Much more might be added. It is written of Esau that he could find no place of repentance. St. Peter and St. Jude, full of indignation, write of persons who "have gone the way of Cain," who "ran greedily after the error of Balaam," and who "perished in the gainsaying of Korah."

But these words have no direct reference to the sin against the Holy Spirit. Enough has been said to convince our readers that we treat this fearful sin, not upon our own authority, but upon the authority of the Holy Spirit.

We open the discussion by emphasizing that no child of God could or ever can commit this sin. It is necessary to say this to prevent many souls from being troubled. There is such unutterable distress in these words of Jesus: "All manner of sin shall be forgiven unto men, but the blasphemy against the Holy Spirit shall not be forgiven; neither in the present world, neither in the world to come." For that sin there is no intercession either in heaven or on earth. Such prayer is even denounced and forbidden as unholy. Indeed, we realize how afflicted souls, tossed with tempest and not comforted, especially when suffering from a weak brain and unsound nerves, can become so morbid as to ask: Have I committed that sin? And if so, what is the use of prayers and tears? For then I am lost, hopelessly and forever.

And such cruel spiritual distress may not be allowed. It is the result of a defective religious training, and, still more, of the preaching which, culpably ignorant of the deep ways of the soul, prates about many things, but scarcely ever treats the solemn things that pertain to eternity. It must be reiterated to these afflicted souls referred to, clearly and distinctly, that no child of God ever *can* commit this sin. It does not belong to the broken and contrite heart, but cankers only in the proud spirit that opposes the Lord and His holy ordinances.

It is true the apostle declares that the men guilty of this sin *"were once enlightened,"* and *"have tasted of the heavenly gift,"* and *"were made partakers of the Holy Ghost,"* and *"have tasted the good Word of God and the powers of the age to come," but* they are never said to have had *a broken and a contrite heart.* On the contrary, they mind high things; they rely upon their exalted experiences; boast of a certain partiality which the Lord has lately shown them, but give no evidence that they ever smote the breast, or fell down as dead before the divine Majesty, or ever found it a consuming fire.

It is a singular fact that the very persons who make us think of the word of Scripture, "Let him that thinketh he standeth take heed lest he fall," are never afraid of eternal perdition; while those who are the least likely to sin against the Holy Ghost are frequently in fear and trembling lest they fall into it. Physicians of insane asylums are familiar with the facts.

And there is but one remedy for these afflicted souls, viz., to feed them with Scripture before they are afflicted. Of course, he that broods and mutters about his sin outside of the Word cannot escape being haunted by the Cain-thought of a sin too great to be forgiven, and in the end the loss of his mind. But he who lives near the Word is safe and cannot be so afflicted.

The Scripture gives a clear and transparent exposition of the sin against the Holy Spirit. The scribes who had come down from Jerusalem were seeing glorious things and were hearing heavenly words, for Jesus was standing in their midst. And while with eye and ear they were tasting of these heavenly gifts, they dared say: "He hath Beelzebub, the prince of the devils." And to this blasphemous statement Jesus answered immediately that these persons had committed the sin against the Holy Ghost, *"because they said He had an unclean spirit."* Wherefore, among well-disposed persons, there can be no difference of opinion in this matter. The sin against the Holy Spirit can be committed only by persons who, beholding the beauty and majesty of the Lord, turn the light into darkness and deem the highest glory of the Son of God's love to belong to Satan and his demons. And, since the afflicted souls already referred to are conscious of their inability to grasp holy things, and are acquainted with the sinful suggestions of their own heart, yet, despite these suggestions, earnestly desire to be persuaded of their Savior's love, therefore it is impossible that they can ever become the *guilty* victims of despair.

It may not be denied, however, that in the hearts of the saints awful thoughts sometimes arise against the Holy One. The pool of iniquity underneath our hearts, with its poisonous gases, continues until death. While we are engaged in the reading of the Word, in prayer, or in holy meditation, suggestions sometimes flash through the mind which startle us as the poisoned sting of a wasp, which we would like to tear from head and heart, from which we shrink with the cry as though struck by lightning: O God, deliver me! But these suggestions have nothing to do with the sin against the Holy Spirit; for we do not identify ourselves with them, do not cherish them, but cast them aside as we would an adder. They come *through* us, but are not *of* us. Or, rather, they spring from our sinful nature, but are unwedded to our will—in fact, repugnant to our will.

We should take heed, therefore, lest, by departing from the Scripture, we estrange our souls from the love of God. This would please Satan only too well. He loves to use that sin against the Holy Spirit to vex weak souls, and their anguish delights his heart. Therefore they must not be allowed to brood upon this fearful word of Scripture. It is true the Gospel is terribly in earnest, but at the same time it is the Gospel of *all consolation,* and no man may ever rob it of that character.

In close adherence to the Word, we add that ordinary wanderers from God do not commit the sin against the Holy Spirit; for they have seen naught of the powers and glories of the age to come (Heb. 6). To commit this sin two things are required, which absolutely belong together:

First, close contact with the glory which is manifest in Christ or in His people.

Second, not mere contempt of that glory, but the declaration that the Spirit which manifests itself in that glory, which is the Holy Spirit, is a manifestation of Satan.

One may sin against the Son and not be lost forever. There is hope of pardon in the day of judgment for the men who crucified Him. But he who desecrates, despises, and slanders the Spirit, who speaks in Christ, in His Word, and in His work, as though He were the spirit of Satan, is lost in eternal darkness. This is a willful sin, intentionally malicious. It betrays *systematic* opposition to God. That sinner cannot be saved, for he has done despite unto the Spirit of all grace. He has lost the last remnant in the sinner, the taste for grace, and with it the *possibility* of receiving grace.

Hence this word of Jesus is divinely intended to put souls on their guard; the souls of the *saints,* lest they treat the Word of God coldly, carelessly, indifferently; the souls of *false* shepherds and *deceivers* of the people who, ministering in the holy mysteries of the cross, contemptuously speak of the "blood theology"—blaspheming the supremest manifestation of divine love as an unrighteous abomination; the souls of *all* who have forsaken the way, who once knew the truth and now reject it, and who in their self-conceit decry their still-believing brethren as ignorant fanatics. Their judgment shall be heavy indeed. Nineveh did not resist the prophet, and was exalted above Capernaum and Bethsaida!

From this, Christian love deduces a twofold exhortation:

First, to professed believers, by ignorance and presumption not to tempt others to fall into this sin.

Second, to erring brethren, not to say that *skepticism* is the way leading to the truth. For this very skepticism is the fatal gate by which the sinner enters upon the awful sin against the Holy Spirit.

38

Christ or Satan

But the greatest of these is Love—1 Corinthians 13:13.

However fearful the Scripture's revelation of the hardening of heart, yet it is the only price at which the Almighty offers man the blessed promise of Love's infinite wealth.

Light without shadow is inconceivable; and the purer and the more brilliant the light, the darker and the more distinctly delineated the shadows must be. In like manner, faith is inconceivable without the opposite of *doubt;* hope with the distressful tension of *despair;* the highest enjoyment of love without the keenest incision of *hatred.* If this is so among men, how much more strongly must it appear when God sheds abroad His love by the Holy Spirit?

Even among men love always loses in depth what it gains in breadth. Hence there are multitudes of men of whom all speak well and no one speaks ill; who, though not pursued by hatred, are neither loved with passionate love. And there are men whom no one can treat with indifference; who inspire some with ardent love and others with violent hatred. How devoted the love of Timothy and Philemon for St. Paul, and with what hatred did the Jewish teachers persecute him! How affectionate the attachment of the circle of German Reformers for Martin Luther, and how bitter the violence of the Romish hierarchy against him! How deep and tender the love of our Christian people for Groen van Prinsteren, the noble champion of our Christian interests, and how fierce the hatred and bitterness wherewith the men of neutrality have pursued him all the days of his life! The court circles of St. Petersburg almost worship the Russian Czar, while every nihilist abhors him as an incarnate devil.

And this is true in every country and every age. As soon as love has taken root in the *soil of principles,* it separates the best friends and finds its opposite pole in the most fearful hatred. Love which is inspired only by amiable traits, which has no other ground than mutual good will, which is the daughter of a complaint disposition, which is supported by mutual service, burning of incense or self-interest, never arouses such hatred. But as soon as love adopts a nobler and holier character; when it loves the friend not for his appearance, disposition, winning ways, and pleasing forms, but in spite of his unyielding nature, stern claims, and disagreeable traits, simply because he is the bearer of a conviction, the interpreter of a principle, the mighty pleader of an ideal, then hatred cannot tarry a year, but follows love in its wake, and rages as bitterly and violently as love's attachment is tender and animating.

This was never more obvious than in the Person of Christ. His contemporaries are entitled to fair treatment. With the exception of those to whom it had been specially revealed, not one saw in the Rabbi of Nazareth the Son of God, the Hope of the Fathers, and the Promised Messiah. The great mass of the people hailed Him merely as the Hero of His conviction, the Preacher of Righteousness, One who was filled with zeal for high and holy principles.

And what does the history of His life reveal? That at the first meeting, enchanted by His holy eye, touched by His eloquent word, overcome by His word of love, men offer Him homage and join the hosannas of the multitudes. But also that this superficial acquaintance is soon followed by a change of inclination and disposition, in some developing into positive faith and entire surrender to His Person, and in others into hatred which becomes more violent day by day.

Jesus troubled no one. No bitter word ever escaped His lips. There were thousands whom He blessed and not one whom He harmed. Even the little children He drew to Himself and kissed their smiling lips. And yet, already at His first appearance in Nazareth, evil passions begin to rage against Him. What the wrong was that He had done no one could tell, but they could not bear Him; He annoyed them; He was to them an eyesore; He must go. So long as He remains in the land of the living, there can be no rest in Palestine, so they thought.

This accounts for the frequent efforts of the mob to stone and kill Him; for the foul epithets they applied to Him, saying "that He was beside Himself," "that He had a devil and was mad," "that He stirred up the people," that He was a "glutton" and "wine-bibber." And when all this was of no avail, and Jesus continued to inspire the few with still greater love, and the number of the Johns and Marys increased, then they judged that severer measures should be taken; then the hatred became persecution; then the honest women of Jerusalem cried, "His blood be upon us and upon our children"; and, thirsting after His blood, the mob cried, "Crucify Him!" and the tempest of unholy passion abated not until they saw Him dying upon the cross. Hence by the cross stood John and Mary, whose love for Jesus was never surpassed, side by side with the leaders of Jerusalem, who dare mock and defy Him even in His dying moments, while they almost suffocate with their own rage.

If Jesus had not come and openly testified of the Father, Jerusalem's grave gentlemen would never have been guilty of such base and dishonorable passions. In fact, His public appearance in Jerusalem and in Judea was the spark which ignited these passions. Without Him the rabbis would never have committed such heinous sin; if Jesus had not come from heaven, the earth would never have looked upon a hatred so base, bitter, and violent.

Why, then, did He not rather stay away? Why did He come on the earth? For He knew what hatred His coming would arouse. He knew that—indirectly—He would cause Iscariot to become a Judas, a child of the devil. He knew that He would become a fall and a rising again of many; a stone of stumbling; a sign that should be spoken against. He knew that by contact with Him thousands would become transgressors, and some even would commit the sin against the Holy Ghost. He knew all this, for He suffered all by the determinate counsel and foreknowledge of God. And yet He came. He spoke. He executed His awful task upon the earth, to be a Savior to thousands of souls, but also a rock of offense to thousands of others.

And why was He not prevented from coming, that all this terrible evil might be avoided? For *the sake of Love,* O children of the Kingdom!

For Love is *greatest;* Love is the highest *right;* and Love, full, rich, and divine, could *not* be shed abroad in the hearts of men but at this price. Love less great would have stirred up hatred less violent. If this Love had not come at all, hatred would have been wholly quenched. This Love alone aroused that hatred. Inflamed by the perfection of this Love, it broke forth into such demoniac maliciousness. No sooner does Love show its shining countenance than hatred belches forth its lurid flames. Without this fearful outbreak of unholiness, holiness cannot exist in this sinful world.

This brings us back to the Holy Spirit. The character and power of any form of love are determined by the holy or unholy nature of the spirit which dwells in it. Of course, earthly love cannot realize its highest power unless the Holy Spirit dwell in it and kindle its holy spark in the human heart. And since He animates all created life, He animates also the life of love; and then it begins to live, receives a soul, is truly animated, and the promise of the Father is fulfilled in the Church and in our hearts, and love is shed abroad by the Holy Ghost.

So the full and penetrating operation of love came only on Pentecost. Then the walls that separated Israel were broken down, and the river of its life disclosed its bed broad and deep for every people and nation. There were tongues as of fire, and there was a speaking with the tongues of all nations. They had all things in common. They were embraced in the union of one purpose. The melody of the psalm of praise pervaded every circle which called upon the name of the Lord.

But, alas! With the light of love came also the fearful shadow of hatred, which works obstinacy, ends in hardening, and adds unto itself the death by the sin against the Holy Ghost.

And this is a fearful thing. Yet if you could prevail upon the Father of Lights to quench the pure light of love, would you say: "Lord, quench it"? Would you dare pray that the shedding abroad of that love should cease from the earth?

And thus, amid the difference, wranglings, and discords, amid the tumult of hatred and the din of profanity and blasphemy, the work of redemption goes on, and the operation of the Holy Spirit continues to fulfill the counsel of God. Thus the King reigns royally; souls are converted; the rebellious are comforted; acts of self-denial and noble consecration are multiplied; pity shines and mercy scintillates; and, hid from the eyes of men, perfect love cherishes the soul that was chilled by its own guilt, and imparts to the earth something of the sweetness and blessedness of its own holy being.

And all this will continue until the Church militant has finished its last fight. Then shall the end come, the token of the Son of Man shall be seen in the clouds, and then only the consummation of glory shall appear, wherein every work of the profane spirit shall be destroyed and the work of the Holy Spirit shall be completed—completed in the manifestation of glory, in the wiping away of many tears, in the removing of every hindrance, in the beholding of what eyes have never seen and the hearing of what ears have never heard, in the ecstasy of what never has entered the human heart, but, more than all this, in the perfect revelation of love in its holiest and purest manifestation, in the undisturbed communion with the Lord our God.

Third Chapter
Prayer

39

The Essence of Prayer

Praying always with all prayer and supplication in the Spirit, and watching thereunto with all perseverance and supplication for all saints—Ephesians 6:18.

In the last place we consider the work of the Holy Spirit in *prayer.* It appears from Scripture, more than has been emphasized, that in the holy act of prayer there is a manifestation of the Holy Spirit working both *in* us and *with* us. And yet this appears clearly from the apostolic word: "Likewise the *Spirit* helpeth also our infirmities: for we know not what we should pray for as we ought, but the *Spirit Himself* maketh intercession for us with groanings which cannot be uttered. And He that knoweth the heart, knoweth what is the mind of the Spirit, because *He maketh intercession for the saints* according to the will of God" (Rom. 8:26, 27). Christ expresses this with equal clearness when He teaches the woman of Samaria that "God is a Spirit, and the true worshipers worship the Father in spirit and in truth"; for so He adds, "the Father seeketh such to worship Him." In almost similar sense St. Paul writes to the Ephesians: "Praying always with all prayer and supplication in the Spirit, and watching thereunto with all perseverance and supplication for all saints."

They already possess the ancient promise to Zacharias: "And I will pour upon the house of David, and upon the inhabitants of Jerusalem, the Spirit of grace and of *supplication*" (Zech. 12:10). And this promise was fulfilled when the apostle could testify concerning Christ: "For through Him we both have access by *one Spirit* unto the Father" (Eph. 2:18). In the "Abba, Father" of our prayers the Holy Spirit beareth witness with our spirits that we are the children of God (Rom. 8:15). And in her longing for the coming of the Bridegroom, not only the Bride, but the *Spirit* and the Bride pray: "Come, Lord Jesus, come quickly." Upon closer examination, it appears that prayer cannot be separated from the spiritual rule that we must pray: "Not as though we had received the spirit of the world, but the *Spirit of God,* that we might know the things that are freely given us of God"; a prayer which we then offer, "Not with the words which man's wisdom teacheth, but which the *Holy Ghost teacheth,* comparing spiritual things with spiritual" (1 Cor. 2:12, 13).

Hence there can be no doubt that even in our prayers we must acknowledge and honor a work of the Holy Spirit; and the special treatment of this tender subject may bear fruit in the exercise of our own prayers. We do not propose, however, to treat here the entire subject of prayer, which belongs to the explanation of the Heidelberg Catechism on this point, but we wish simply to emphasize the significance of the Holy Spirit's work for the prayers of the saint.

In the first place, we must discover the silver thread that, in the nature of the case, connects the essence of our prayer with the work of the Holy Spirit.

For all prayer is not equal. There is a great difference between the high-priestly prayer of the Lord Jesus and the prayer of the Holy Spirit with groans that cannot be uttered. The supplications of the saints on *earth* differ from those of the saints in *heaven,* those who rejoice *before* the throne and those who cry from *under* the altar. Even the prayers of the saints of earth are not the same in the various spiritual conditions from which they pray. There are prayers of the *Bride,* that is, from *all the saints* on earth as a whole; and prayers of the *local assemblies* of believers, supplications from the circles of *brethren* when two or three are gathered in the name of Jesus; and supplications of *individual believers* poured out in the *solitude* of the closet. And distinguished in the root from these prayers of the saints are the prayers of the *still unconverted,* whether regenerate or not, who cry unto God whom they do not know and whom they oppose.

The question is whether the Holy Spirit is active, either in one or in all these prayers. Does He affect our prayers only when, in the rare moments of exalted spiritual life, we have intimate communion with God? Or does He affect only the prayers of the *saint,* excluding those of the *unconverted?* Or does He affect all prayer and supplication, whether from saint or sinner?

Before we answer this question, it is necessary accurately to define prayer. For prayer may be taken in a limited sense, as a religious act requesting something of God, in which case it is merely the expression of a desire springing from a conscious want, void, or need which we ask God to supply; an application to the divine power and providence, in poverty to be enriched, in danger to be protected, in temptation to be kept standing. Or it may be taken in a *wider* sense and include *thanksgiving.* In the Reformed Church the Service of Prayer always includes the Service of Thanksgiving. In this sense the Heidelberg Catechism treats it, calling prayer the chief part of thankfulness (q. 116). In fact, we can scarcely conceive of prayer, in the higher sense, ascending to the Throne of Grace *without* thanksgiving.

Moreover, prayer also includes *praise* and every *outpouring* of the soul. Prayer without praise and thanksgiving is no prayer. In the supplication of saints, *prayer* and *adoration* go together. Oppressed with the multitude of thoughts, the soul may have no definite supplication, or thanksgiving, or hymn of praise, yet frequently feels constrained to pour out those thoughts before the Lord. When, in Psalm 90, Moses pours out his prayer, there is: (1) a supplication, "Lord, how long! And let it repent Thee concerning Thy servants"; (2) thanksgiving, "Lord, Thou hast been our dwelling-place in all generations"; (3) praise, "Before the mountains were brought forth, or ever Thou hadst formed the earth and the world, even from everlasting to everlasting Thou art God." And besides these there is (4) an outpouring of the thoughts that fill his soul, "We are consumed by Thine anger, and by Thy wrath are we troubled"; and stronger still, "The days of our years are threescore years, yet is their strength labor and sorrow, for it is soon cut off and we fly away."

And so we find in the high-priestly prayer of Christ: (1) a supplication, "And now, O Father, glorify Thou *Me* with Thine own self, with the glory which I had with Thee before the world was"; or, "Holy Father, keep through Thine own name those whom Thou hast given *Me,* that they may be one as We are"; (2) thanksgiving, "Thou hast given Me power over all flesh, that I should give eternal life to as many as Thou hast given Me"; (3) praise, "O righteous Father, the world hath not known Thee, but I have known Thee, and these have known that Thou hast sent Me"; (4) and besides these a manifold outpouring of the soul, which is neither prayer, praise, nor thanksgiving, "All Mine are Thine, and Thine are Mine"; "I have glorified Thee on the earth; I have finished the work which Thou gavest Me to do"; "For their sakes I sanctify Myself, that they also might be sanctified through the truth."

We did not assign a special place to the confession of guilt and sin, because this is included in supplication, to which it leads and of which it is the moving cause; while the confession of the soul's lost condition and natural liability to condemnation necessarily must lead to the pouring out of the soul.

Therefore, speaking comprehensively, we understand by prayer: *every religious act by which we take upon ourselves directly to speak to the Eternal Being.*

The only difficulty is in the Hymn of Praise. For it cannot be denied that in a number of psalms there is a direct speaking to God in hymns of praise; and thus the distinction between the Prayer and the Hymn of Praise might be lost sight of.

There are four steps in the Hymn of Praise: it may be a singing of the praise of God *before one's own soul;* or *before the ear of the brethren;* or *before the world and the demons;* or lastly, *before the Lord God Himself.*

When the flame of holy joy burns freely in the heart of the saint, although he be alone or in chains in the dungeon, he feels constrained, for his own satisfaction as it were, with a loud voice to sing a psalm to the praise of God. Thus it was that David sang: "I love the Lord because He hath heard my voice and my supplication." Different is the Hymn of Praise when, with and for the brethren, the saint sings in their company; for then they sing, "Blessed is the people that know the joyful sound; they shall walk in the light of Thy countenance"; or directly addressing the people of God: "O ye seed of Abraham, His servant, ye children of Jacob His chosen, He is the Lord our God, His judgments are in all the earth." And another is the Hymn of Triumph, which the Church sings as it were before the world and the demons; then the saints sing: "Thou art the glory of our strength; and in Thy favor our horn shall be exalted; for the Lord is our defense; the Holy One of Israel is our King."

But the Hymn of Praise rises highest when it addresses the Eternal One directly; when the saint thinks not of himself, nor of his brethren, nor of the demons, but of the Lord God alone. This is praise in its most solemn aspect. In the singing of the opening sentences of Psalm 51 or Psalm 130 the difference is immediately felt:

> After Thy loving-kindness, Lord, have mercy upon me,
> For Thy compassion great blot out all my iniquity;

or:

> Lord, from the depths to Thee I cried,
>   My voice, Lord, do Thou hear;
> Unto my supplication's voice
>   Give an attentive ear.

Then praying and singing are actually become one. In order to pray aloud, the Church must sing, although more for the sake of the supplication than of the singing.

40

Prayer and the Consciousness

Call upon Me in the day of trouble; I will deliver thee, and thou shalt glorify Me—Psalm 50:15.

The *form* of prayer does not affect its character. It may be a mere groaning in thought, or a sigh in which the oppressed soul finds relief; it may consist of a single cry, a flow of words, or an elaborate invocation of the Eternal. It may even turn into speaking or singing. But so long as the soul, in the consciousness that God lives and hears its cry, addresses itself directly to Him as though it stood in His immediate presence, the character of prayer remains intact. However, discrimination between these various forms of prayer is necessary in order to discover, in the *root* of prayer itself, the work of the Holy Spirit.

The suppliant is you; your ego; neither your body nor your soul, but your *person.* It is true, both body and soul are engaged in prayer, but yet in such a way that your person, your ego, your self, pours out the soul; in the soul becomes conscious of your prayer, and through the body gives it utterance.

This will become clear when we consider the part which the body takes in prayer; for no one will deny that the body has something to do with prayer. Mutual prayer is simply impossible without the aid of the body, for that requires a voice to utter prayer in one, and hearing ears in the others. Moreover, prayer without words rarely satisfies the soul.

Mere mental prayer is necessarily imperfect; earnest, fervent prayer constrains us to express it in words. There may be a depth of prayer that cannot be expressed, but then we are conscious of the lack; and the fact that the Holy Spirit prays for us with groans that cannot be uttered is to us source of very great comfort.

When the soul is perfectly composed, mere mental meditation may be very sweet and blessed, but no sooner do the waters of the soul heave with broader swell than we feel irresistibly constrained to utter prayer in words; and although in the solitude of the closet, yet the silent prayer becomes an audible and sometimes a loud invocation of the mercies of our God. Even Christ in Gethsemane prayed, not in silent meditation nor in unuttered groans, but with strong words which still seem to sound in our ears.

And not only in this, but in other ways, the body largely affects our prayer. There is, in the *first* place, a natural desire to make the whole body partake of it. For this reason we kneel when we humble ourselves before the majesty of God. We close the eyes not to be distracted by the world. We lift up the hands as invoking His grace. The agonized wrestler in prayer prostrates himself on the ground. We uncover the head in token of reverence. In the assembly of the saints the men stand on their feet, as they would if the King of Glory should come in.

In the *second* place, the effect of the body upon prayer is evident from the influence which bodily conditions frequently exert upon it. Depressing headache, muscular or nervous pains, congestive disorders causing undue excitement, often prevent not the sigh, but the full outpouring of prayer. Everyone knows what effect drowsiness has upon the exercise of warm and earnest prayer. While, on the other hand, a vigorous constitution, clear head, and tranquil mind are peculiarly conducive to prayer. For this reason the Scripture and the example of the fathers speak of fasting as means to assist the saints in this exercise.

Lastly, bodily distress prior to distress of the soul has often opened mute lips in prayer before God. Families that were strangers to prayer have learned to pray in times of serious illness. In threatening dangers of fire or water, lips that were used to cursing have frequently cried aloud in supplication. Compelled by war, famine, and pestilence, godless cities have frequently appointed days of prayer with the same zeal wherewith formerly they appointed days of rejoicing.

Hence the significance of the body in this respect is very great—in fact, so great that when abnormal conditions cause the bond between body and soul to become inactive, prayer ceases at the same time. However, mere bodily exercise is not prayer, but lip-service. Mere imitation of the form, mere sounds of prayer rolling from the lips, mere words addressed to the Eternal One without conscious purpose in the soul, are the form of prayer, but not the power thereof.

And this is not all. To trace the work of the Holy Spirit in prayer we must enter more deeply into this matter. According to the ordinary representation, which is partly correct, prayer is impossible without an act of the *memory,* by which we recall our sins and the mercies of God; without an act of the *mind,* choosing the words to express our adoration of the divine virtues; without an act of the *consciousness,* to represent our needs in prayer; without an act of *love,* enabling us to enter into the needs of our country, church, and place of habitation, of our relatives, children, and friends; and lastly, without meditating upon the fundamentals of prayer, recalling the promises of God, the experiences of the fathers, and the conditions of the Kingdom.

All these are activities of the brain, which is the seat of the thinking mind; as soon as this is disturbed by abnormal conditions, the consciousness is obscured and the thinking ceases or becomes confused. Without the brain, therefore, there can be no thinking; with thinking there can be no thoughts; without thoughts there can be no accumulation of thoughts in the memory; and without meditation, which is the result of the former two; there can be no prayer in the proper sense of the word. From which it is evident that prayer depends upon the exercise of bodily functions much more largely than is generally supposed.

And yet, let us be on our guard not to push this too far, and imagine that the root of prayer is in the *brain,* that is, in a member of the body; for it is not. Our own experience in prayer teaches us, agreeably to the Scripture, that it is in the *heart.* As from the heart are the issues of life, so are also the issues of prayer. Unless the heart compels us to pray, all our cries are in vain. Men with magnificent brains but cold hearts have never been men of prayer; and, on the contrary, among the men of poor mental development, but with large, warm hearts are found a number of souls mighty in prayer.

And even this is not all; for the heart itself is a bodily organ. In proportion as the blood circulates through the heart with strong or feeble pulsation, in that proportion is the soul's vital expression strong and overwhelming, or weak and weary; and, dependent upon this, prayer is warm and animated, or cold and formal. When the heart is weak and suffering, the life of prayer generally loses something of its freshness and power.

We are men, and not spirits; and, unlike angels, we cannot exist without the body. God created us body and soul. The former belongs to our being essentially and forever. Hence an utterance of our life like prayer must necessarily be dependent upon soul and body, and that in much stronger sense than we usually suppose.

However, the fact must be emphasized that prayer's dependence upon the body is not absolute. Otherwise there could be no prayer among the angels, nor in the Holy Spirit. Our prayer depends upon the *consciousness;* when that is lost, prayer ceases. And, since we are men, consisting of body and soul, the human consciousness is, in the ordinary sense, related also to the body. But that this dependence is not absolute is evident from the fact that the Eternal Being, whose divine consciousness is but dimly reflected in that of man, has no body. "God is Spirit." And the same is true of the world of spirits, who, although incorporeal, yet possess a consciousness; and of the three Persons of the Trinity, especially of the Holy Spirit.

Hence the question arises whether man separated by death from the body loses consciousness. To this we reply in the affirmative. Our human consciousness, as we possess it in our present earthly existence, is lost in death, to be restored to us in the resurrection, in a *form* stronger, purer, and holier. St. Paul says: "We," that is, our human consciousness, "now know in part, but then we," the same human consciousness, "shall know face to face, even as we are known."

But from this it does not follow that in the intermediate state the soul must be denied all self-consciousness. The Scripture teaches the very contrary. Of course, for this knowledge we depend upon the Scripture alone. The dead cannot tell us anything of their state after death. No one but God, who ordained the conditions of life in the intermediate state, can reveal to us what those conditions are. And He has revealed to us that immediately after death the redeemed are *with Jesus.* St. Paul says: "I have a desire to depart and to be with Christ." And, since a friend's presence does not afford us pleasure except we are conscious of it, it follows that the souls of the saints, in the intermediate state, must possess some sort of consciousness different from that which we now possess, but sufficient to realize and enjoy the presence of Christ. For which reasons the fathers rejected every representation of death as a sleep; as though our persons from the moment of death to that of the resurrection should sleep in perfect forgetfulness of the glorious things of God; although they denied not the intermediate state in which the soul is separated from the body.

Wherefore it seems possible for the soul to be conscious in a higher sense, *without the aid of the body,* independently of the heart and the brains—a consciousness which enables us to realize the glorious things of God and the presence of the Lord Jesus Christ.

How this higher consciousness operates is a deep mystery; nor is the nature of its operation revealed. And since we can have no representations than those formed by means of the brain, it is impossible for us to have the slightest idea of this higher consciousness. Its existence is revealed, but no more.

The following may be considered as settled, and this is the principal thing in our present inquiry: In that temporary consciousness in which we will work in the intermediate state, the same person will become self-conscious who now is conscious by means of heart and brain. Even after death it shall be our own person that shall be bearer of that consciousness, and by it I shall be conscious of myself. It cannot be otherwise; or else consciousness after death is impossible, for the simple reason that consciousness alone cannot exist without a person. And another person it cannot be. Hence my own person shall be bearer of that consciousness; and thus shall I be enabled to enjoy the presence of Jesus.

From this we draw the following important conclusion: that so far as the *form* of the ordinary consciousness is concerned, it is dependent upon the body; while essentially it is not so dependent. Essentially it continues to exist, even when sleep obscures the thought, or insanity estranges me from myself, or a swoon makes me lose consciousness; essentially it continues to exist even when death temporarily separates me from the body. From which it follows that the root and seat of the consciousness must be looked for in the *soul,* and that heart and brain are but the *vehicles, conductors,* which our person uses to manifest that consciousness in ideas and representations.

And since prayer is a speaking to the Eternal, that is, a conscious standing before Him, it follows that the root of prayer has its seat in our *person* and in our *spiritual being;* and, although bound also to the body, so far as the *germ* is concerned rests in our personal ego, insofar as the ego, conscious of the existence of the divine Persons and of the bond that unites it to them, allows that bond to operate.

And thus we come to this final conclusion: that the possibility of prayer finds its deepest ground in the fact of our *being created after the image of God.* Not only is our self-consciousness a result of that fact, for God is eternally self-conscious, but from it also springs that other mighty fact that I, as a man, can be conscious of the existence of the Eternal, and of the intimate bond which unites me to Him. The consciousness of this bond and relation manifests itself in prayer as soon as we address ourselves to God. Hence the work of the Holy Spirit in prayer must be looked for in His work of the creation of man. And since, in our former study on this point, we discovered that it is God the Holy Spirit who in man's creation caused this consciousness to awake, carrying into it and maintaining by it the consciousness of the existence of God and of the bond which unites man to Him, it is evident that prayer, as a phenomenon in man's spiritual life, finds its basis directly in the work of the Holy Spirit in *man's creation.*

41

Prayer in the Unconverted

When Thou saidst, Seek ye My face, my heart said unto Thee, Thy face, Lord, will I seek—Psalm 27:8.

The faculty of *prayer* is not an acquisition of later years, but is *created in us,* inherent in the root of our being, inseparable from our nature.

And yet consistent with this fact is the fact that the great majority of men do not pray. It is possible to possess a faculty dormant in us for a whole lifetime. The Malay possesses the faculty for studying modern languages as well as we, but he never uses it. In sleep we retain our faculties of seeing and hearing, but then they are inactive. Although possessed of great power, the big fellow did not lift a finger against the little scamp who tormented him. Hence a faculty may remain in us wholly undeveloped and dormant for a lifetime, or partly developed but suppressed. And the same is true of the faculty of prayer. Among the fourteen hundred millions of the earth's population, there are scarcely two hundred million who do not appear to be acquainted with prayer, although their form of prayer is very defective. Of the non-praying masses, who almost exclusively occupy Europe, one half remember the time when, in some way or other, they used to pray. Many of those who have lost even that, still breathe an occasional prayer. And the number of them who wish that they could pray is very large; and among the non-praying people they represent undoubtedly the noblest.

Hence we maintain our starting-point, that we owe the faculty of prayer to our creation. God created man as a being disposed to prayer. If this were not so, the faculty of prayer could not be among his endowments. We are created for prayer, otherwise we could never have tasted of its sweetness.

To the question, Why in our creation is this a peculiar work of the Holy Spirit? we answer: Prayer is the drawing and pressing of the *impressed image* toward its *Original,* which is the Triune God. To be the bearers of that impressed image is the marvelous honor bestowed upon men. Although marred by sin—God grant by regeneration restored in you—yet the original features of that image are still the original features of our human being. Without that image we would cease to be men.

And, owing its origin to the impress of that original Image, our inward being draws toward It, naturally, urgently, and persistently. It cannot live without it, and the fact that, on the other hand, the original Image of the Eternal One draws the impressed image in man to Himself, is the ultimate and constraining power of all prayer. However, to be exalted to the dignity of prayer, this drawing to God must not be like the involuntary suction of water to the deep, or the turning of the opening rose-bud toward the light. For the water knows not whither it is going, and the rose-bud is unconscious of the sunshine which governs it. That almost irresistible drawing can be called prayer only when *we know* that it is prayer, when we *perceive* it, and, knowing to whom it draws us, make it our own conscious, cooperating act.

Hence prayer does not spring from the will. The Triune God is He who rouses the soul to prayer, who draws us, and not we ourselves. Wherefore the Psalmist says: "When Thou saidst, Seek ye My face, my heart said unto Thee, Thy face, Lord, will I seek." And how does this first impulse from God reach us? Not externally as the wind, but internally in the heart. And knowing that it does not *proceed from* me, but *comes to* me, it must be from the Holy Spirit who works in me. Are not all the internal impulses that proceed from the Eternal One *the proper work of the Holy Spirit?* We can have no fellowship with the Son but through the Holy Spirit; none with the Father but through the Son to whom the Holy Spirit has introduced us.

However, we do not speak now of the state of regeneration. In our treatment of prayer thus far, we have reference to man in his original state, and independent of the restoration; and in that state we say, prayer is not the cry of an independent being for a God to him unknown, with whom he hopes thus to become acquainted, but, on the contrary, that all prayer presupposes, on man's part, an inward sense of the Eternal Being of God, and of the fact that, being created after His image, he belongs to Him and *consciously* draws to his original Image. Wherefore we may call it a spiritual magnetism, which operates unceasingly upon him, and originated in his creation. However, it is different from magnetism in a twofold aspect: (1) in that man is *conscious* of it; (2) in that it is a *mutual* attraction.

The *second point* needs special emphasis. In magnetic attraction the magnet is active and the iron passive, but in prayer it is not so. Prayer rests upon the foundation of *mutual* attraction. So long as it proceeds from God's side alone, there is no prayer, but there is, when our being begins to draw to God, when we feel the impulse if possible to draw God to us: "Come, Lord, how long! Lord, delay not! Come quickly!"

This is the power of love which finds in prayer its most glorious manifestation. Prayer is the fairest flower that grows upon the stem of holy love. Then love works in God *for man,* on account of the image in which He created him. And in man love works *for God,* because of the Image after which he was created. In fact, every distress from which we cry to be delivered is to the soul but the conscious need of the power and faithfulness of God. So love labors to meet love, that in tranquil whisperings it may pray not for deliverance from trouble, but to possess Him for whose love alone the heart is yearning.

Upon a lower level prayer certainly assumes a lower form, which by sin has become so low and selfish that prayer, which should be love's breath, has become an egoistic cry. But we discuss prayer as it was originally, before sin had affected it. And as the true heir of heaven yearns for his heavenly home not for the sake of crown and palm and golden harp, but for his God alone; so is prayer, pure and undefiled, a longing, not for God's gifts, but for God Himself. As the Shulamite calls for her bridegroom, so does the praying soul, from the consuming desire of love, pray and thirst for the possession of its Maker and to be possessed of Him.

Since it is the Third Person in the Godhead who makes this communion between God and the soul possible, working and maintaining it in the soul, it is evident that prayer belongs to the proper domain of the Holy Spirit; only when thus considered can prayer be understood in its deepest significance.

The other question now arises, regarding the work of the Holy Spirit in *our* prayer, *after that we became sinners.*

For even sinners pray. This is evident from the heathen world, which, however low its forms of prayer, yet offers up supplications and petitions. It is evident from the ease with which a little child, taught by its mother, learns to pray; and from the many who, estranged from prayer, in sudden calamities bend the knees, and, although they cannot pray, still assume the attitude of prayer, willing to give half their kingdom if they only could pray. And lastly, it is evident from the thousands and tens of thousands who, convinced of the impossibility of praying for themselves, cry to others: "Pray for us!"

Prayer in higher, holier sense the sinner cannot offer. Everything in him is sinful, even his prayer. In his sin he has reversed the established order of things: not he existing for God, but God existing for him. Confirmed in his selfishness, the God of heaven and earth is to him little more than a Physician in every sickness and a Provider in every need; a wonderful Being, ever ready at his first cry to supply out of His fullness his every necessity.

This is the egoism that inseparably belongs to every sinner's prayer. The prayer of the redeemed saint is: "Our Father, who art in heaven, hallowed be Thy name, Thy Kingdom come, Thy will be done on earth as it is in heaven. For Thine is the Kingdom, and the Power, and the Glory forever. Amen." The *converted sinner* offers first the petitions for *His* name, *His* Kingdom, and *His* will; then he adds the petitions for bread, for forgiveness, for protection from sin. But the *unconverted sinner* has no conception of a prayer for God's name, Kingdom, and will. He prays for bread only; for forgiveness also, but only from the motive that bread and luxury and deliverance from trouble may not be denied him.

Wherefore it is impossible to have *too low* an estimate of the sinner's prayer. The depth of our fall is in nothing so apparent as in the sin of this degenerate, bastardized prayer. All such prayer may be designated as a defying and vexing of God and His eternal love. In this sense the prayer of the sinner contains nothing of the work of the Holy Spirit. All this prayer springs from the egoism of the sinful heart, and has not the least value, rather the opposite.

But—and this is the principal thing—although our hands have unstrung the harp so that it produces nothing but discord, yet the artist is just as great, for he had so planned and constructed and tuned the instrument that it could produce the purest tones and fairest music. And such is man's heart. Sin did not remove the strings, for then it could not produce even discord, but sin has put it out of tune, and now its tones are harsh and grating upon the ear. And yet these very strings testify of the work of the original Master, for by *His* original work they are still sound-producing. So long as the strings are only loose upon the harp, it may be repaired, but when they are altogether broken and gone, it is no longer a harp, but a useless piece of wood. Every prayer of the sinner is a discord which jars against the beautiful harmony of the eternal love of God; nevertheless the very discords of that prayer are the evidences that the Holy Spirit had originally placed the strings upon the heart.

If the Holy Spirit had never performed such a work upon the heart, there would be no harp at all; the heart could not produce even the discord. The fact that it does, shows that there are strings which originally were perfectly attuned. Hence prayer in the sinner is unthinkable without the work of the Holy Spirit.

But this is not all. Not only the possibility of such discordant prayer, but the discord itself is but the reversed working of a power created, supported, and actuated by the Holy Spirit's work. To put this in the strongest light, we add: that all cursing and blasphemy is the reversed action of a power of the Holy Spirit. Blasphemers and men given to profanity indulge in their terrible sin, because they realize that the Almighty God lives, and that His power is something terrible. Cursing and blasphemy are hellish tones and vibrations from the same harp of prayer, which the Holy Spirit created in the soul. An animal cannot curse; and if the Holy Spirit had not strung the soul with these strings of prayer, no curse could ever have passed the lips of man. Cursing is a malignant boil, but it springs directly from the artery of prayer. Consider it well, even Satan has not a single power directly from himself; and all the power with which, in his blasphemous and insane rage, he wars against God is a power from God reversed by Satan.

Even the sinner's prayer is a manifestation of *power.* There must be an impulse and incitement, however weak, which causes him to pray. And this requires strength of consciousness and an expression of the will. And these powers he does not create himself, but the Holy Ghost; he only abuses or corrupts them.

When an unpracticed hand touches the harp-strings and produces discords, it does not *create* those discords, but they are formed from the sounds and tones which are in the vibrating strings of the harp. The same is true of the sinner's prayer. He could not offer his sinful prayer if there were no tone of prayer in the strings of his heart. That he can pray at all, he owes to the fact that the Holy Spirit created the tones of prayer in his heart; which he brings forth, alas! only to make them discords.

However, in this respect, ordinary grace in its sometimes preparatory character ought not to be overlooked. The sinner is on earth, and not yet in hell. Between the two is, first, this difference, that on the former there is preventive grace, which bridles the power of sin and prevents it from breaking out in all its violence. Sin on earth is like a chained bulldog or a muzzled hyena. Secondly, God loves this world. He has thoughts of peace concerning it. He does not forsake the work of His creation, and by His sovereign grace He provides a redemption which saves the organism of the world and of the race; so that the tree is saved, while the useless shoots and dry leaves are gathered to be cast into hell. Having this is in view, ordinary or general grace aims at the preservation of the powers of the original creation, to develop them to some extent, and thus to prepare the field in which by and by the seed of eternal life will be planted. And, although this ordinary grace is not effectual to salvation, any more than the mere plowing of the field can ever germinate the wheat which is not sown in the furrows, yet this plowing of ordinary grace has real significance for the future growth of the seed of eternal life.

And in this general grace, the grace of prayer occupies an important place. If there were no general grace, muzzling sin and plowing the field, the sinner could no more pray than Satan, but like him would curse God without ceasing. But now he still prays, he has prayed for ages, and by his prayer, even though it is the fruit of tradition, he has sometimes risen above the sinful egoism of his heart. But this prayer never sprang from the root of sin, nor from something good which he had kept along with sin in the holy closet of his heart; it was but the gracious work of the Holy Spirit.

Evidence of the deep inworking of this grace is found in the exalted devotions that still sound in our ears from the most ancient traditional prayers of Indian, Egyptian, and Greek antiquity; and in the ministry of prayer from the pulpit by unconverted ministers whose supplications often move and touch the soul.

However, the glory of this does not belong to the sinner; nor does it in the least affect the absolute character of man's depravity by sin. But it shows that the Lord God did not leave the sinner to his sin, but even in the absence of regeneration, and to the glory of His name, caused general grace to intervene, which frequently illuminated the life of prayer.

And when such a people, still acquainted with these holy traditions and gracious operations, received the knowledge of Christ crucified and of His power to save, it became evident afterward that the prayers which, independently of himself, were laid upon the sinner's lips had prepared a way and opened a gate through which the King of Glory could come into such a people. And taking it in individual cases, it appears from the experience of many that, long before the soul became conscious of saving grace, the grace of God not only kept him from violent outbreaks of sin, but, through the *tradition of prayer,* wrought a work in him the blessed effects of which were understood only long afterward.

And all these operations of *general grace* are, as soon as they touch the life of prayer, the work of the Holy Spirit. He who in creation strung the harp of prayer in the soul is the same who causes not only the tone of prayer to vibrate even in our egoistic petitions, but who, in a more glorious way, sometimes even as though the soul were an Aeolian harp, touches the strings with the breath of His mouth, and draws from it the beautiful and entrancing tones of prayers and supplications.

42

The Prayer of the Regenerated

Likewise the Spirit helpeth our infirmities; for we know not what we should pray for as we ought: but the Spirit itself maketh intercession for us with groanings which cannot be uttered—Romans 8:26.

Next in order comes the question: What is the work of the Holy Spirit in the *prayer of the regenerated?* Here we distinguish (1) the prayer of the saint, and (2) that of the Holy Spirit for him.

The last we consider first, because, through the Apostle Paul, we receive clearest revelation concerning it: "Likewise the Spirit helpeth our infirmities; for we know not what we should pray for as we ought, but the Spirit itself maketh intercession for us with groanings that cannot be uttered" (Rom. 8:26). For the better understanding of this passage, observe:

In the *first* place, that the apostle refers to the prayer or groan arising not from the regenerated person himself, but from another in his behalf. It is not a prayer, but an intercession from the Holy Spirit for him.*

* Expositors of an earlier period judged with Calvin that the intercession of the Holy Spirit signified a working upon us, by virtue of which *we ourselves groaned in ourselves.* But this view is incorrect; for verse 23 states what Calvin supposed to be stated in verse 26. In the former, the apostle speaks of groanings that proceed [*continued*]

In the *second* place, it is necessary to distinguish between the intercession of the Holy Spirit and of Jesus Christ the Righteous.

Christ intercedes for us in *heaven,* and the Holy Spirit on *earth.* Christ our Holy Head, being *absent* from us, intercedes *outside* of us; the Holy Spirit our Comforter intercedes *in our own heart* which He has chosen as His temple.

There is a difference, not only of place, but also in the *nature* of this twofold intercession. The glorified Christ intercedes in heaven for His elect and redeemed, *to obtain for them the fruit of His sacrifice:* "If any man sin, we have an Advocate with the Father, Jesus Christ the Righteous" (1 John 2:1). But the object of the Holy Spirit's petitions is the laying bare of all the deep and hidden *needs* of the saints before the eye of the Triune God.

In Christ there is a union of God and man, since, being in the form of God, He took upon Himself the human nature. Hence His prayer is that of the Son of God, but in union with the nature of man. He prays as the Head of the new race, as King of His people, as the one that seals the covenant of the New Testament in His blood. In like manner, there is to some extent a union between God and man, when the Holy Spirit prays for the saints. For, by His indwelling in the hearts of the saints, He has established a lasting and most intimate union, and by virtue of that union putting Himself in their place, He prays for them and in their stead.

In each instance there is intercession, but in each in a *different manner.* In his priestly capacity, as head of the family, the father prays for

---

from us, wrought in us by the Holy Spirit. Verse 26 cannot be a mere repetition; for the word "likewise" introduces a new thing, although it is similar to the preceding. Moreover, the word here applied to the Holy Spirit is the same as the one used in verse 34, *"entunchánein,"* which signifies the intercession of the Holy Spirit. And again, the *word "sunantilambánesthai,"* which is translated "to help," requires that the person rendering assistance be not only *in* us, but also works *with* us and *for* us. Verse 27 leads to the same conclusion, first, because it speaks of the mind of the *Spirit,* and not of man's mind; secondly, because the intercession is said to be according to God, *"katá Theón," not "eís Theón," i.e.,* according to the will of God, and this can be said of the Holy Spirit alone. We do not, however, deny that, in one respect, this groaning makes instrumental use of the vocal organs, as in the matter of the *"glóssais lalein,"* the speaking with tongues. We maintain only that the unutterable groaning does not imply the use of those organs; rather the opposite.

his family not because the members could not offer similar prayer, but on account of his calling as their head to represent them before God. All pray, but he as their head prays for them all. And thus, as the Head of the Body, it is the calling of Christ to pray for the Body. Though their prayer were perfect, His prayer would still be needed. All the members must pray, but He must pray for them all. Entirely different, however, is the prayer of the mother for her dying child. Being only five or six years old, the little one can scarcely pray for himself. He has not the slightest conception of what is happening to him, nor of his own needs. Then his mother kneels by his side and prays for him, "helping his infirmities, for he knoweth not what to pray for as he ought." If he were twenty years older, there would be no need of it; he himself could understand his condition and pray for himself. And this applies to the intercession of the Holy Ghost. If the saint were what he ought to be, and could pray as he ought, there would be no need of this intercession. But, being imperfect and beset by weaknesses, not knowing what to pray for, the Holy Spirit helpeth his infirmities, and prays for him.

Christ intercedes for the body because He is the Head; even though the prayers of the members were perfect and mature, He would still intercede with the Father in their behalf. But the Holy Spirit prays because the prayers of the saints are *imperfect, immature,* and *insufficient.* His prayer is *complementary* and necessary, inasmuch as the saint cannot yet pray as he ought; hence *decreasing* as the saint learns to pray more and more correctly.

The intercession of the Holy Spirit is according to the saint's *condition,* which is described in the seventh chapter of Romans. Surely, the Lord God might have been pleased to regenerate the sinner in such a way as to deliver him at once and completely from sin, and from all the after-effects of his old nature, but He has ordained it otherwise. Regeneration does not effect such a sudden change. It does indeed change his *state* before God at once and completely, but it does not place him at once in a *condition* of perfect holiness. On the contrary, after regeneration it remains, on the one hand, "I delight in the law of God after the inward man," but also, on the other, "I see another law in my members, warring against the law of my mind." Hence the cry: "O wretched man that I am, who shall deliver me from the body of this death?"

And the intercession of the Holy Spirit fully meets this condition. If in regeneration we became perfectly holy, without any infirmity, with perfect knowledge what we should pray for, there would be no need of this intercession. But, this not being so, the Holy Spirit comes to help our infirmities, *in* us to pray *for* us, as though *it were our own prayer.*

This *last point* must be emphasized. The Holy Spirit prays for men called *saints;* and it must be maintained that every regenerated person is a saint, his infirmities notwithstanding: a saint, not for what he is in himself, but because of the word of Christ: *"Thou art Mine."* And these two conditions, (1) of being a saint, and (2) still unholy in himself, cannot remain unreconciled. Wherefore the Sacred Scripture teaches that, although we lie in the midst of death, yet in Christ we are holy; hence we have a holiness, yet not *in* us, but *outside* of us in Christ Jesus. "Our Life is hid with Christ in God." And the same applies to our *prayers.* We *are* saints not only in name, but in deed. And therefore the prayers that ascend to the mercy-seat from our hearts *must be holy prayers.* It is the sweet incense of the prayers of the saints. But being unable of ourselves to kindle the incense, the Holy Spirit helps our infirmities, and from our hearts prays to God in our behalf. We are not conscious of it; He prays for and in us with groans that cannot be uttered; which does not mean that He makes *us* utter groans for which we cannot account, but that He groans in us with affections and emotions which may comfort us, but which have nothing in common with the sighing of our respiratory organs. This is clear from verse 27, where St. Paul declares, that He that searcheth the hearts, knoweth what is the mind of the Spirit.

Apart from the intercession of the Holy Spirit in our behalf there is also a work of His Person *in our own prayers.*

The proportion between these two operations is different according to our different conditions. The child, regenerated in the cradle and deceased before conversion was possible, could not pray for himself; the Holy Spirit prayed therefore for and in him with groans that cannot be uttered. But if the child had lived and was converted at a later age, it would first have been the prayer of the Holy Spirit alone; and after his conversion his own prayers would have been added. And, even after his conversion, he may become indifferent and fall into a temporary apostasy, so that his own prayer fails altogether; yet the prayer of the Holy Spirit in him never fails.

Finally, according to the measure of his spiritual growth, his progress in prayer will be either slow or rapid. The Holy Spirit prays in us as long and in as much as we cannot pray for ourselves, but at the same time He teaches *us* to pray, that gradually His prayer may become superfluous. This includes that when temptations threaten us of which we are ignorant, we are in the midst of assaults and conflicts which we fail to understand, the Holy Spirit immediately renews His prayer, and cries unto God in our behalf.

But this should not be understood as though the Holy Spirit teaches us to pray, that He may withdraw Himself altogether from our prayers. On the contrary, every prayer of the saint must be *in communion with the Holy Spirit.* In order to be more earnest in prayer we must sustain a more intimate communion. The more we pray alone and of ourselves, the more our prayer degenerates into a *sinful* prayer, and ceases to be the prayer of a *child of God.* Wherefore St. Jude admonishes us to pray *in the Spirit.*

There is only this difference: when the Holy Spirit prays *for* us, He prays *independently of us,* although in our own heart, but when we have learned to pray, although the Holy Spirit continues to be the real Petitioner, ye He prays *with* us and *through* us, and cries unto God from our lips. As a mother first prays *for* her child without his knowledge, and then teaches him to pray that by and by she may pray *with* him, so also is the work of the Holy Spirit. He begins with praying for us; then He teaches us to pray; and when we have made some progress in the school of prayer, then He begins to pray with us not only *in* us, but *through* us. This is the Spirit of adoption, by whom we cry "Abba, Father," but in such a way that at the same moment He testifies with our spirits that we are the children of God.

For this reason the Lord said to the woman of Samaria: "The hour cometh and now is when the true worshipers shall worship the Father in Spirit and in truth." The addition "in truth" had reference to the symbolic service of ceremonies in Israel. The land of Canaan was the type of heaven, Jerusalem of the inner sanctuary, and Zion was the throne of

God; the bloody sacrifices of ram and heifer signified the remission of sin; the altar of incense was a symbol of the prayers of the saints. All this was truly typical, but it was not the truth itself. Jerusalem was not the sanctuary of the Lord Jehovah, and Zion was not the mercy-seat. The truth of all this was and is in the heaven of heavens, and thus truth and grace came by Jesus Christ, even as its symbol and shadow had come by the law of Moses. After the coming of Christ, the prayers of the saints were to be separated from Jerusalem; wherefore Jesus said to the woman: "Jerusalem and Gerizim are out of the question; they belong to the dispensation of shadows; and that dispensation ceased with My coming into the world. Henceforth there will be no more worship in shadows, but a worship of the Father in actuality and in truth." And this gives us the true interpretation of the addition: "in Spirit." So long as the people depended upon the service of shadows, they looked upon *external* things as supports of their prayers. But, since it was to be a worship in *truth,* it needed the *inward* support which the *Comforter,* the Holy Spirit, offered them.

The saint is a saint because he received the Holy Spirit, who took up His abode with him and inwardly married Himself to the soul. Every vital utterance proceeding from him, apart from the Holy Spirit in him, is foreign to his sonship and is sin. Only insofar as he is moved and operated upon by the indwelling Spirit are his thoughts, words, and deeds the utterances of the child of God in him. And if this is true of the whole domain of his life, how much more of his *life of prayer?* After his conversion he often prays of himself apart from the Holy Spirit, but that is the prayer, not of God's child, but of the old sinner. But when the communion of the Holy Spirit is active in his heart, and works in him both the impulse and the animation of his prayer, then it is truly the prayer of the child of God because it is wrought in him by the Holy Spirit.

Wherefore Zacharias combines the Spirit of grace and of supplication. It is the same Spirit who, entering our hearts, unlocks unto us the grace of God, enriches us with that grace, teaches us to realize that grace, and at the same time causes our *thirst* for that grace to utter itself *in prayer.* Prayer is the cry for grace, and cannot be uttered until the Holy Spirit presents to the spiritual eye the riches of grace which are in Christ Jesus. And, on the other hand, the Holy Spirit cannot cause these riches of grace to scintillate before the eye of the soul without creating in us thirst and longing desire for this grace; thus compelling us to pray.

Or, to put it more comprehensively, the prayer of the saint requires three things:

First, an insight into the riches of eternal redemption.

Second, vivid impressions of his spiritual deadness and distress.

Lastly, the earnest desire for lively fellowship with the unsearchable treasures of divine grace.

And how can the holy presence of the Lord Jehovah be revealed to him in peace but by the Holy Spirit entering into his heart? And how can he have a *vivid* realization of his spiritual distress except the Holy Spirit reveal it to him? And how shall he be so bold, out of that distress, to cry unto God in the fellowship of love except the Holy Spirit create boldness and confidence in his soul?

43

Prayer for and with Each Other

Confess your faults one to another and pray one for another, that ye may be healed. The effectual, fervent prayer of a righteous man availeth much—James 5:16.

Let our last article touch once more the key of love wherein the article preceding that of prayer was set. To speak of the Spirit's work in our prayers, omitting *the intercession of the saints,* betrays a lack of understanding concerning the Spirit of all grace.

Prayer for others is quite different from prayer for ourselves. The latter is indeed lawful; God even commands us "in everything by prayer and supplication with thanksgiving to make our requests known unto God." Yet it may contain refined egoism even though it be followed by thanksgiving; hence to prayer is added *intercession,* that in prayer the breath of love may quench gently, yet effectually, remaining egoism, and leads us to the still holier prayer for the heavenly King and His Kingdom.

Christ prays for us, but the Bride must also pray for her heavenly Bridegroom. David's prayer for Solomon points beyond Solomon to the Messiah: "Give the King Thy judgments, O God" (Ps. 72:1). In the twentieth and sixty-first Psalms the same thought is expressed. However, this is not a prayer for His Person (for as such He is glorified already), but for the coming of His Kingdom, for the extending of His Name to the ends of the earth, for the gathering in of the souls of His elect.

In the Lord's Prayer, this most holy petition stands even in the foreground; for when we pray, "Hallowed be Thy name, Thy Kingdom come, Thy will be done," we are inspired, not by love for self or for others, but by love for Him who is in heaven. It is true, we realize that the fulfilling of that prayer is most desirable for others and ourselves; still it is the *love for God* that stands here in the foreground. It is the summary of *prayer* eminently fitting the summary of the *law:* "Thou shalt love the Lord thy God." This is the first and great *commandment.* Then, "Thou shalt love thy neighbor as thyself." And so in our prayer: first, for the cause of God, this is the first and great *petition;* then, prayer for the neighbor as for ourselves. Our *prayer* is the test of our relation to the first and great *commandment.*

And what is the work of the Holy Spirit in the prayer of intercession?

It is necessary here, for a clear understanding, to distinguish between *a twofold intercession:* (1) there is a prayer for the things that pertain to the body of Christ; and (2) another for the things that do not belong to that body, according to our impression and conception of the matter.

Prayer for kings, and for all that are in authority, does not concern the things that pertain to the body of Christ; neither does the prayer for our enemies, nor that for the place of our habitation, for country, army, and navy, for a bountiful harvest, for deliverance from pestilence, for trade and commerce, etc. All these pertain to the *natural* life, and to persons, whether saints or sinners, in their relation to the life of creation, and not to the Kingdom of Grace. But our prayer does concern the body of Christ, when we pray for the coming of the Lord, for a fresh anointing of the priests of God, for their being clothed upon with salvation, for success in the work of missions, for a baptism of the Holy Spirit, for strength in conflict, for forgiveness of sin, for the salvation of our loved ones, for the effectual conversion of the baptized seed of the Church. The first intercession has reference to the realm of nature, the second to the Kingdom of Grace. Hence in each of these two we must look for the bond of fellowship from which springs our prayer of intercession.

For every prayer of intercession presupposes *fellowship* with them for whom we pray; a fellowship which casts us into the same distress, and from which we look for deliverance, and that in such a way that the sorrow of one burdens us, and the joy of another causes us to give thanks. Where such vital fellowship does not exist, nor the love which springs from it, or where these are temporarily inactive, there may be a formal intercession of words, but real intercession from the heart there cannot be.

With reference to the intercession in the realm of nature, the ground of this fellowship is naturally found in the fact that we are created *of one blood.* Humanity is one. The nations form an organic whole. It is a mighty trunk with leafy crown; the nations and peoples are the branches thereof, successive generations the boughs, and each of us is a fluttering leaf. Belonging together, living together upon the same root of our human nature, it is one flesh and one blood, which from Adam to the last-born child covers every skeleton and runs through every man's veins. Hence the desire for universal philanthropy; the claim that nothing be alien to us that is human; the necessity of loving our enemy and of praying for him, for he also is of our flesh and of our bones.

If we were like grains in a heap of sand, each grain might possibly send forth a sigh, but the mutual prayer of intercession would be out of the question. Being leaves, however, of the same tree of life, there is, apart from the groaning of every leaf, also a prayer for one another, a mutual prayer of the entire human life; "the whole creation groaneth."

But in the Kingdom of *Grace* the fellowship of love is much stronger, firmer, and more intimate. There is here also an organic whole, even the body of Christ under Him the Head. It is not one converted person independent of another, and the two united by a mere outward tie of sympathy; nay, but a multitude of branches all springing from the same root of Jesse; growing from the one vine; all organically one; saved and redeemed by the same ransom of His blood; proceeding from the one act of election; born again by the self-same regeneration; brought nigh by the same faith; breaking one bread and drinking from one cup.

And let us notice it well, this unity is doubly strong; for it is not independent of the fellowship of nature, but added to it. They who become members of the body of Christ are with us created from the one blood of Adam, and with us they are redeemed by the one blood of Christ. Hence there is here *double* root of fellowship. Flesh of our flesh, bones of our bones. Moreover, born from one decree; sealed by one baptism; joined together in one body; included in one promise; by and by sharers with us of the same inheritance.

In this double fellowship of life is rooted the *love* which mutually unites the children of God, especially in their prayers of intercession, a union which appears sometimes in their mutual prayer. Vital fellowship does not spring from our love for the people of God, but that love springs from the fellowship of the life of grace, common to all His saints. That which grows not from one root, and, therefore, shares not the same life, cannot attain to love in higher sense. Prayer for one another is born of the love to one another; and the love which unites us ascends from the one root of life upon which we all are grafted through grace, upon which by virtue of our creation from Adam we all were set. And thus the work of the Holy Spirit in the prayer of intercession will appear in clearest light.

In the realm of nature, our vital *power* is from the *Father,* our *human kinship* through the *Son,* and the conception of that kinship from the Holy Ghost. Hence in the ordinary manifestations of benevolence, such as helpfulness in distress, friendliness in daily life, and the desire for social intercourse, it is the work of the Holy Spirit to keep alive in us the conception of our human kinship. It is true that sin has terribly disturbed this conception. Yet the Holy Spirit has not forsaken His work, but, when a man seeing a strange child drowning, and, without considering his own life, jumps into the water and saves him, then it is the constraining power of the Holy Spirit that must be honored in this heroic act of philanthropy.

But much more apparent is the work of the Holy Spirit in the prayer of intercession which belongs to the domain of grace. For with reference to the fellowship of the body of Christ, it is again the *Father* from whom *proceeds* our redemption, the *Son* in whom we are *united,* and the *Holy Spirit* who imparts to us the conception and consciousness of this unity and holy fellowship. The mere fact of being chosen by the Father and redeemed by the Son does not constrain us to love; it is the act of the Holy Spirit, who, revealing to our conception and consciousness this wonderful gift of grace, opening our eyes for the beauty of being joined to the body of Christ, kindles in us the spark of the love for Christ and for His people. And when this double work of the Holy Spirit effectually operates in us, causing our hearts to be drawn to all that belong to us by virtue of our human kinship, and much more strongly to the people of God by virtue of our kinship in the Son, then there awakes in us the love of which the apostle says that it is shed abroad in our hearts by the Holy Ghost.

And yet this is not all of the Holy Spirit's work, Love can be tender without compelling one to prayer. This is evident from the universal love of benevolence. A man may rush into a burning building to save another from perishing by fire, while he is a perfect stranger to prayer for others. And, on the contrary, there are people who always talk of praying for others, who constantly enlarge the phylacteries of their own prayer of intercession, who ever say to others, "Pray for me," and who would yet, in the hour of danger, quietly allow us to drown or perish in the flames; who carefully guard their pockets lest mercy call upon them to assist us with their money.

From which it is evident that there must be a connecting link between *love* and *the prayer born of love.* As soon as *love* begins to pray it is joined to *faith;* and by this union prayer becomes active. Love alone is not yet prayer. And the mere prayer of intercession is not the evidence of love. Then alone is there real intercession, when love, being joined to faith, constrains us to carry the object of love before the throne of grace.

Let us, therefore, be careful in our prayers of intercession; especially when the person for whom we pray is *present.* For then there is danger lest our prayer in his behalf have the tendency to show him how much we think of him and love him, rather than constrain us to ask something for him of God. Methodism* has often sinned in this respect, and many a prayer has been desecrated by this insincere intercession.

This shows clearly what is the additional work of the Holy Spirit in this respect: not merely that He quicken in us general faith, nor that He fan in us the flames of brotherly love, but that He also cause faith to join love in holy wedlock, directing them thus united to the brother for whom we are to pray. This is the object of St. Paul, when he desires that there shall be a fellowship of saints, not only in the gift of God, but also in the prayer of thanksgiving; not only for our sakes, but "That the abounding grace might through the thanksgiving of many rebound to the glory of God" (1 Cor. 4:15).

---

* See section 5 in the Preface for the author's explanation of Methodism.

Just as in a drawing-room whose walls are lined with crystal mirrors, the light of the chandelier is reflected not only by every mirror, but also from mirror to mirror, so that there is an endless reflection of the light, so also is it with reference to the prayer of intercession and thanksgiving in the body of Christ. In this chamber of glory Christ is the Light which is reflected in the mirror of the soul. But it is not sufficient that every soul-mirror receive the light, and reflect it in thanksgiving, but from mirror to mirror this glory of the Son must be reflected here or there until there is a never-ending scintillation of increasing brightness, and everything is baptized in the overflowing luster in which the Son glorifies Himself.

And this leads us to speak of *mutual prayer.*

Mutual prayer is intercession of the richest sort; for its value is enhanced by the consciousness of its being *mutual.* In ordinary intercession, one prays for another not knowing whether the other also prays for him, but in the mutual prayer, "I" is turned into "we," as in the Lord's Prayer. It is no longer *one* wrestling before the throne of grace, but *all together,* thus giving expression to the unity and fellowship of the body of Christ. They cry from one distress; they bless Him for the same grace; they plead the same promise; they look forward to the same glory; they come to the same Father in the name of the one Mediator, leaning upon the same atoning blood. Then it is that the work of the Holy Spirit attains its highest glory. Then He joins faith and love, not in one heart, but in many; then He opens the hearts and unites the souls of the saints; then He causes them to meet together in the audience-chamber of the Lord God, one people, a multitude of believers, who in their spiritual kinship reflect the unity of the body of Christ.

Hence there is nothing so difficult as mutual prayer. Prayer in the closet is easy; to pray for others is not hard, but to pray with each other requires such exalted spiritual tone, such pure love, such clear perception of the unity of the body, as, alas! in the midst of this sinful life is rarely attained by large bodies of believers. And the leader, if he be indeed the mouthpiece of the people, has a very difficult task, and must himself be in a thoroughly spiritual frame of mind.

Surely if the Holy Spirit left us to ourselves, every activity of faith, love, and prayer would soon be paralyzed. But, blessed be God! He knows our infirmity, and with divine pity He looks upon our painful helplessness. He is and remains the Comforter; His work is never ended. When we slept, having no oil in our lamps, He watched over our souls. When our love failed, He loved us just the same. When our faith became dull and faint, and prayer became dumb upon our lips, He prayed for us with groanings that cannot be uttered.

And this is His work continually. It is He that is the divine Bearer of every higher conception and holier consciousness in the children of men; He, the Spirit of the Father and of the Son, that exhibits all the riches of the Mediator to the Bride, making her eager to possess them; He that quickens the treasures of the Word by the spark of His holy fire, bringing them to the consciousness of the inward man.

Blessed is the man to whom has been given a taste of the work of the Holy Spirit in his own experience. Blessed is the Church which in its service has proved the inworking of the Spirit of grace and of supplication. Blessed is he who, constrained to love by the love of the Holy Spirit, has opened his heart in thanks, praise, and adoration, not only to the Father who from eternity has chosen and called him, and to the Son who has bought and redeemed him, but also to the Third Person in the Holy Trinity, who has kindled in him the light and keeps it burning in the inward darkness; to whom, therefore, with the Father and the Son, belongs forever the sacrifice of love and devotion of all the Church of God.

Subject Index